HISTORY (GENERAL) AND HISTORY OF EUROPE

Library of Congress Classification

2001 EDITION

Prepared by the
Cataloging Policy
and Support Office,
Library Services

Library of Congress, Cataloging Distribution Service, Washington, D.C.

The additions and changes in Class D-DR adopted while this work was in press will be cumulated and printed in List 283 of *LC Classification — Additions and Changes*

Library of Congress Cataloging-in-Publication Data

Library of Congress.
Library of Congress classification. Class D-DR. History (General) and History of Europe / prepared by the Cataloging Policy and Support Office, Library Services. — 2000 OR 2001? ed.
p. cm.
Rev. ed. of: Classification. Class D-DR. History (General) and History of Europe / Subject Cataloging Division. Processing Services, Library of Congress. 1982.
Includes index.
1. Classification, Library of Congress. 2. Classification—Books—Law. 3. Classification—Books—Germany. 4. Law—Germany—Classification. I. Title: Law of Germany. II. Library of Congress. Cataloging Policy and Support Office. III. Library of Congress. Subject Cataloging Division. Classification. Class KK-KKC. Law of Germany. IV. Title.

Z696.U5K7 2001
025.4'634943—dc21 2001027703
CIP

ISBN 0-8444-1050-0

For sale by the Library of Congress,
Cataloging Distribution Service,
Washington, DC 20541-5012

PREFACE

Class D, History, was first drafted in 1901 and, after undergoing revision, was published in 1916. Two supplements were published: European War (first edition, 1921; second edition, 1933; reprinted in 1954 with additions and changes) and Second World War (1947). The second edition of class D was published in 1959, containing additions and changes through June 1957. A reprint edition was published in 1966, containing a supplementary section of additions and changes through July 1965. The third edition was published in five parts between 1987 and 1990: D-DJ, DJK-DK, DL-DR, DS, and DT-DX. In 1998, a new edition of subclasses DS-DX (History of Asia, Africa, Australia, New Zealand, etc.) was published. This 2001 edition of subclasses D-DR (History (General) and History of Europe) complements the 1998 edition of DS-DX. It has been produced using a new automated system developed at the Library of Congress for this purpose. The system will allow for the production of new editions on a regular and frequent basis.

In 1992, Rebecca Guenther, Network Development and MARC Standards Office, began overseeing the conversion of Library of Congress Classification data to machine-readable form using the provisionally approved USMARC format for classification data. In 1993-1994, the Cataloging Distribution Service developed programs for producing printed classification schedules from the MARC records in cooperation with Lawrence Buzard, editor of classification schedules, Paul Weiss, senior cataloging policy specialist, and Rebecca Guenther. The Cataloging Distribution Service also coordinated the layout and design of the new schedules.

The classification data for class D were originally converted to the MARC format without editing or revision. Mary K. D. Pietris, senior cataloging policy specialist, proofread the converted data and made many changes, both substantive and editorial.

As in previous editions, the extent of detail provided for local history and description varies widely, each country having been developed at a different time and according to different principles. For example, at one extreme the counties and regions of England have been provided with only one number, with occasional provision for serials separate from monographs, while at the other extreme detailed tables or printed subarrangements were provided for provinces in France and the Netherlands. For most countries where detail has been provided, the subarrangements under cities include provision for separate designation of city sections, streets, buildings, parks, etc. However, for some countries, such as Germany, the tables for cities are the same as those for states, provinces, regions,etc.. Inconsistencies such as these are a reflection of the historical development of the D subclasses over the last century. In order to avoid adverse impact on existing classified collections, no attempt has been made to standardize for all countries the level or type of detail provided.

Because of the difficulty of interpreting the six tables that had formerly been provided for use with DC611+ (Local history of France), the full range of numbers for many regions, provinces and departments of France has been provided in the text of the schedule itself, based on information in the Library of Congress shelflist. The number of tables has been reduced to two; these are used only where specified in the text of the schedule. Additional information has been provided to clarify the alphabetical order for provinces and cities whose names begin with **St.**

Several specific regions, provinces, and cities in DD801+ (Local history of Germany) that had not been included in previous editions are listed in this new edition, many with subarrangements provided in the schedule, and a smaller number where tables are applied.

It is intended that there will be no further development of subtopics under local history and description in D-DR, except to provide for current time periods, as needed.

In some cases, especially in subclass DD (Germany), new filing rules adopted in 1981 have caused confusion as to proper filing order. For example, whereas umlauts are now ignored in filing, under earlier rules they were regarded as significant for filing order. In order to clarify the filing order that has been used, the spelling of some captions has been changed to remove the umlaut and substitute a conventional spelling. For example **Düsseldorf** has been changed to **Duesseldorf** under DD901.

Some changes have been made to standardize captions, such as the substitution of the caption **Pictorial works** for **Views**. Some information was moved from captions to "Including" notes. The beginning or ending numbers of some spans that are printed in the schedule have been changed from the previous edition.

Other editorial changes in this edition include deleting some unneeded or outdated examples and confer notes, updating some notes and captions, such as those for geographic names, creating new tables or expanded text in lieu of some "divide like" notes, and deleting many superfluous "General special" captions that had served to group the captions for military history, political history, and foreign and general relations.

The list of countries and regions in one alphabet that had been included in earlier editions does not appear in this edition. That list is maintained in the *Subject Cataloging Manual: Shelflisting* (G 300). Tables for subarrangement of biography are no longer included as part of the D schedules. The policies for classifying and shelflisting biographies are described in the *Subject Cataloging Manual: Classification* (F 275) and in the *Subject Cataloging Manual: Shelflisting* (G 320).

New or revised numbers and captions are added to the L.C. Classification schedules as a result of development proposals made by the cataloging staff of the Library of Congress and cooperating institutions. Upon approval of these proposals by the weekly editorial meeting of the Cataloging Policy and Support Office, new classification records are created in the master database or existing records revised. The Classification Editorial Team, consisting of Lawrence Buzard, editor, and Barry Bellinger, Kent Griffiths, Nancy Jones, and Dorothy Thomas, assistant editors, is responsible for creating new classification records, maintaining the master database, and creating index terms for the captions.

Thompson A. Yee, Acting Chief
Cataloging Policy and Support Office

May 2001

OUTLINE

D	1-2009	History (General)
	1-24.5	General
	25-27	Military and naval history
	31-34	Political and diplomatic history
	51-90	Ancient history
	101-110.5	Medieval and modern history, 476-
	111-203	Medieval history
	135-149	Migrations
	151-173	Crusades
	175-195	Latin Kingdom of Jerusalem. Latin Orient, 1099-1291
	200-203	Later medieval. 11th-15th centuries
	(204)-(475)	Modern history, 1453-
	219-234	1453-1648
	242-283.5	1601-1715. 17th century
	251-271	Thirty Years' War, 1618-1648
	274.5-6	Anglo-French War, 1666-1667
	275-276	War of Devolution, 1667-1668
	277-278.5	Dutch War, 1672-1678
	279-280.5	War of the Grand Alliance, 1688-1697
	281-283.5	War of Spanish Succession, 1701-1714
	284-297	1715-1789. 18th century
	291-294	War of Austrian Succession, 1740-1748
	297	Seven Years' War, 1756-1763
	299-(475)	1789-
	301-309	Period of the French Revolution
	351-400	19th century. 1801-1914/1920
	371-(379)	Eastern question
	383	1815-1830. Congress of Vienna
	385-393	1830-1870
	394-400	1871- . Later 19th century
	410-(475)	20th century
	461-(475)	Eastern question
	501-680	World War I (1914-1918)
	720-728	Period between World Wars (1919-1939)
	731-838	World War II (1939-1945)
	839-860	Post-war history (1945-)
	880-888	Developing countries
	890-893	Eastern Hemisphere
	900-2009	Europe (General)
	901-980	Description and travel
	1050-2009	History
DA	1-995	History of Great Britain
	10-18.2	British Empire. Commonwealth of Nations. The Commonwealth
	20-690	England
	20-27.5	General

OUTLINE

DA	History of Great Britain
	England - Continued
28-592	History
28-35	General
40-89.6	Political, military, naval, and Air Force history. Foreign relations
90-125	Antiquities. Social life and customs. Ethnography
129-592	By period
129-260	Early and medieval to 1485
140-199	Celts. Romans. Saxons. Danes. Normans
200-260	1154-1485. Angevins. Plantagenets. Lancaster-York
300-592	Modern, 1485-
310-360	Tudors, 1485-1603
350-360	Elizabeth I, 1558-1603. Elizabethan age
385-398	Early Stuarts, 1603-1642
400-429	Civil War and Commonwealth, 1642-1660
430-463	Later Stuarts
498-503	1714-1760
505-522	George III, 1760-1820
550-565	Victorian era, 1837-1901
566-592	29th century
600-667	Description and travel. Guidebooks
670-690	Local history and description
670	Counties, regions, etc., A-Z
675-689	London
690	Other cities, towns, etc., A-Z
700-745	Wales
700-713	General
714-722.1	History
725-738	Description and travel
740-745	Local history and description
750-890	Scotland
750-757.7	General
757.9-826	History
757.9-763	General
765-774.5	Political and military history. Antiquities, etc.
774.8-826	By period
777-790	Early and medieval to 1603
783.2-783.45	War of Independence, 1285-1371
783.5-790	Stuarts, 1371-1603
800-814.5	1603-1707/1745
807	The Union, 1707
813-814.5	1707-1745. Jacobite movements
815-826	19th-20th centuries
850-878	Description and travel

OUTLINE

DA — History of Great Britain
Scotland - Continued
880-890 Local history and description
900-995 Ireland
900-908.7 General
909-965 History
909-916.8 General
920-927 Antiquities. Social life and customs. Ethnography
930-965 By period
930-937.5 Early and medieval to 1603
933.3 English conquest, 1154-1189
938-965 Modern, 1603-
949.5 The Union, 1800
949.7-965 19th-20th centuries. Irish question
963 1922- . Republic of Ireland. Irish Free State
969-988 Description and travel
990-995 Local history and description
990.U45-U46 Northern Ireland (Ulster)

DAW 1001-1051 History of Central Europe
1001-1028 General
1031-1051 History

DB 1-3150 History of Austria. Liechtenstein. Hungary. Czechoslovakia
1-879 Austria. Austro-Hungarian Empire
1-20.5 General
21-27.5 Description and travel
29-34.5 Antiquities. Social life and customs. Ethnography
35-99.2 History
35-40.5 General
42-49 Military, naval, and political history. Foreign relations
51-99.2 By period
51-64 Early and medieval to 1521
60-64 Wars with the Turks
65-99.2 1521-
65.2-65.9 1521-1648
66-69.5 1648-1740
69.7-77 1740-1815
80-99.2 19th-20th centuries
83 Revolution, 1848
96-99.2 Republic, 1918-
99-99.1 1938-1955. German annexation. Allied occupation
99.2 1955-

OUTLINE

DB — History of Austria. Liechtenstein. Hungary. Czechoslovakia

Austria. Austro-Hungarian Empire - Continued

- 101-879 — Local history and description
  - 101-785 — Provinces, regions, etc.
  - 841-860 — Vienna
  - 879 — Other cities, towns, etc., A-Z
- 881-898 — Liechtenstein
- 901-999 — Hungary
  - 901-906.7 — General
  - 906.9-920.5 — Description and travel. Antiquities. Ethnography
  - 921-958.6 — History
    - 927-958.6 — By period
      - 927-932.9 — Early to 1792
        - 929-929.8 — Árpád dynasty, 896-1301
        - 929.95-931.9 — Elective kings, 1301-1526
      - 932.95-945 — 1792-1918. 19th century
        - 934.5-939.5 — Revolution of 1848-1849
        - 940-945 — 1349-1918
      - 946-958.6 — 20th century
        - 955-955.8 — 1918-1945. Revolution of 1919-1920
        - 955.9-957.5 — 1945-1989. Revolution of 1956
        - 957.9-958.6 — 1989-
  - 974.9-999 — Local history and description
    - 974.9-975 — Counties, regions, etc.
    - 981-997 — Budapest
- 2000-3150 — Czechoslovakia
  - 2000-2035 — General. Description and travel. Antiquities. Social life and customs
  - 2040-2043 — Ethnography
  - 2044-2247 — History
    - 2080-2247 — By period
      - 2080-2133 — Early and medieval to 1526
      - 2135-2182 — Hapsburg rule, 1526-1918
      - 2185-2241 — Czechoslovak Republic, 1918-1992
      - 2242-2247 — 1993- . Independent Czech Republic
  - 2300-2650 — Local history and description of Czech lands
    - 2300-2421 — Moravia
    - 2600-2649 — Prague (Praha)
  - 2700-3150 — Slovakia
    - 3100-3139 — Bratislava (Pressburg)

DC 1-947 — History of France

- 1-20.5 — General
- 21-29.3 — Description and travel
- 30-34.5 — Antiquities. Social life and customs. Ethnography

OUTLINE

DC History of France - Continued

35-424 History
- 35-41 General
- 44-59.8 Military, naval, and political history. Foreign relations
- 60-424 By period
  - 60-109 Early and medieval to 1515
    - 62-64 Gauls. Celts. Franks
    - 64.7-94 476-1328. Merovingians. Carlovingians. Capetians
    - 95-109 1328-1515
      - 96-101.7 Hundred Years' War, 1339-1453
      - 101.9-109 15th century. Jeanne d'Arc, Saint
  - 110-424 Modern, 1515-
    - 111-120 1515-1589. 16th century
      - 118 Massacre of St. Bartholomew, 1572
    - 120.8-130 1589-1715. Henri IV, Louis XIII, Louis XIV
    - 131-138 1715-1789. 18th century. Louis XV, Louis XVI
    - 139-249 Revolutionary and Napoleonic period, 1789-1815
    - 251-354.9 19th century
      - 256-260 Restoration, 1815-1830
      - 261-269 July Revolution of 1830. July Monarchy, 1830-1848
      - 270-274.5 February Revolution and Second Republic
      - 275-280.5 Second Empire, 1852-1870
      - 281-326.5 Franco-German or Franco-Prussian War, 1870-1871
      - 330-354.9 Later 19th century
    - 361-424 20th century
      - 397 1940-1946
      - 398-409 Fourth Republic, 1947-1958
      - 411-424 Fifth Republic, 1958-

600-801 Local history and description
- 601.1-609.83 North, East, etc. France
- 611 Regions, provinces, departments, etc., A-Z
- 701-790 Paris
- 801 Other cities, towns, etc., A-Z

921-930 Andorra

941-947 Monaco

DD 1-(905) History of Germany
- 1-21 General
- 21.5-43 Description and travel
- 51-78 Antiquities. Social life and customs. Ethnography
- 84-257.4 History
  - 84-96 General

OUTLINE

Class	Numbers	Topic
DD		History of Germany
		History - Continued
	99-120	Military, naval, and political history. Foreign relations
	121-257.4	By period
	121-124	Earliest to 481
	125-174.6	Early and medieval to 1519
	126-155	Medieval Empire, 481-1273
	127-135	481-918. Merovingians. Carolingians
	136-144	919-1125. Houses of Saxony and Franconia
	145-155	1125-1273. Hohenstaufen period
	156-174.6	1273-1519. Houses of Habsburg and Luxemburg
	175-257.4	Modern, 1519-
	176-189	1519-1648. Reformation and Counter-reformation
	181-183	Peasants' War, 1524-1525
	184-184.7	Schmalkaldic League and War, 1530-1547
	189	Period of Thirty Years' War, 1618-1648
	190-199	1648-1815. 18th century. French Revolutionary and Napoleonic period
	201-257.4	19th-20th centuries
	206-216	1815-1871
	217-231	New Empire, 1871-1918
	228.8	Period of World War I, 1914-1918
	233-257.4	Revolution and Republic, 1918-
	253-256.8	Hitler, 1933-1945. National socialism
	(256)	Period of World War II, 1939-1945
	257-257.4	Period of Allied occupation, 1945-
	258-262	West Germany
	280-289.5	East Germany
	301-454	Prussia
	301-312	General
	314-320	Description and travel
	325-339	Antiquities. Social life and customs. Ethnography
	341-454	History
	701-901	Local history and description
	701-788	North and Central, Northeast, etc. Germany
	801	States, provinces, regions, etc., A-Z
	851-900	Berlin
	900.2-900.76	Bonn
	901	Other cities, towns, etc., A-Z
DE	1-100	History of the Greco-Roman world
	1-15.5	General
	23-31	Geography
	46-73.2	Antiquities. Civilization. Culture. Ethnography
	80-100	History

OUTLINE

DF	10-951	History of Greece
	10-289	Ancient Greece
	10-16	General
	27-41	Geography. Travel
	75-136	Antiquities. Civilization. Culture. Ethnography
	207-241	History
	207-218	General
	220-241	By period
	220-221	Bronze Age, Minoan, and Mycenaean ages
	221.2-224	ca. 1125-500 B.C. Age of Tyrants
	225-226	Persian wars, 499-479 B.C.
	227-228	Athenian supremacy. Age of Pericles. 479-431 B.C.
	229-230	Peloponnesian War, 431-404 B.C.
	230.9-231.9	Spartan and Theban supremacies, 404-362 B.C.
	232.5-233.8	Macedonian epoch. Age of Philip. 359-336 B.C.
	234-234.9	Alexander the Great, 336-323 B.C.
	235-238.9	Hellenistic period, 323-146.B.C.
	239-241	Roman epoch, 140 B.C.-323/476 A.D.
	251-289	Local history and description
	501-649	Medieval Greece. Byzantine Empire, 323-1453
	501-518	General
	520-542.4	Antiquities. Social life and customs. Ethnography
	545-548	Military history. Political history. Empire and papacy
	550-649	History
	550-552.8	General
	553-599.5	Eastern Empire, 323/476-1057. Constantine the Great
	599.8-649	1057-1453
	610-629	1204-1261. Latin Empire
	630-649	1261-1453. Palaeologi
	645-649	1453. Fall of Constantinople
	701-951	Modern Greece
	701-720	General
	720.5-728	Description and travel
	741-748	Social life and customs. Ethnography
	750-854.32	History
	750-760	General
	765-787	Military, naval, and political history. Foreign relations
	801-854.32	By period
	801-801.9	Turkish rule, 1453-1821
	802-832	1821-1913
	804-815	War of Independence, 1821-1829
	816-818	Kapodistrias, 1827-1831
	833-854.32	20th century
	848	Republic, 1924-1935

OUTLINE

OUTLINE

DG		History of Italy
		Medieval and modern Italy, 476- - Continued
	461-583.8	History
	461-473	General
	480-499	Military, naval, and political history. Foreign relations
	500-583.8	By period
	500-537.8	Medieval, 476-1492
	503-529	476-1268
	506-514.7	489-774. Gothic and Lombard kingdoms. Byzantine exarchate, 553-568
	515-529	774-1268. Frankish and German emperors
	530-537.8	1268-1492
	532-537.8	Renaissance
	538-583.8	Modern, 1492-
	539-545.8	16th-18th centuries
	546-549	1792-1815. Napoleonic period
	548-549	Kingdom of Italy
	550.5-564	19th century
	552-554.5	1848-1871. Risorgimento
	553-553.5	1848-1849. Austro-Sardinian War
	555-575	1871-1947. United Italy (Monarchy)
	571-572	1919-1945. Fascism
	576-583.8	1948- . Republic
	600-684.72	Northern Italy
	600-609	General
	610-618.78	Piedmont. Savoy
	631-645	Genoa
	651-664.5	Milan. Lombardy
	670-684.72	Venice
	691-817.3	Central Italy
	691-694	General
	731-759.3	Tuscany. Florence
	791-800	Papal States (States of the Church). Holy See. Vatican City
	803-817.3	Rome (Modern city)
	819-875	Southern Italy
	819-829	General
	831	Sicily and Malta
	840-857.5	Naples. Kingdom of the Two Sicilies
	861-875	Sicily
	975	Other cities (non-metropolitan), provinces, etc., A-Z
	987-999	Malta. Maltese Islands
DH	1-925	History of Low Countries. Benelux Countries
	1-23	General
	31-40	Description and travel

OUTLINE

DH		History of Low Countries. Benelux Countries - Continued
	51-92	Antiquities. Social life and customs. Ethnography
	95-207	History
	95-109	General
	113-137	Military, naval, and political history. Foreign relations
	141-207	By period
	141-162	Early and medieval to 1384
	171-184	1384-1555. House of Burgundy
	185-207	Wars of Independence, 1555-1648
	401-811	Belgium
	401-430	General
	431-435	Description and travel
	451-492	Antiquities. Social life and customs. Ethnography
	503-694	History
	503-527	General
	540-569	Military, naval, and political history. Foreign relations
	571-694	By period
	571-584	Early and medieval to 1555
	585-619	1555-1794. Spanish and Austrian rule
	611-619	1714-1794. Austrian Netherlands
	620-676	1794-1909
	631	French rule, 1794-1813
	650-652	Revolution of 1830
	677-694	20th century
	801-811	Local history and description
	801	Provinces, regions, etc., A-Z
	802-809.95	Brussels
	811	Other cities, towns, etc., A-Z
	901-925	Luxembourg
DJ	1-(500)	History of Netherlands (Holland)
	1-30	General
	33-41	Description and travel
	51-92	Antiquities. Social life and customs. Ethnography
	95-292	History
	95-116	General
	124-150	Military, naval, and political history, etc. Foreign relations
	151-292	By period
	151-152	Early and medieval to 1555
	154-210	1555-1795. United provinces
	180-182	Anglo-Dutch wars, 1652-1667
	190-191	War with France, 1672-1678
	193	Anglo-Dutch War, 1672-1674
	196-199.2	Stadtholders, 1702-1747
	205-206	Anglo-Dutch War, 1780-1784
	208-209	War with France, 1793-1795

OUTLINE

DJ		History of Netherlands (Holland)
		History
		By period - Continued
	211	1795-1806. Batavian Republic
	215-292	19th-20th centuries
	401-411	Local history and description
	411.A5-A59	Amsterdam
DJK	1-77	History of Eastern Europe (General)
	26-28	Ethnography
	27	Slavic peoples (General)
	30-51	History
	61-77	Local history and description
	61-66	Black Sea region
	71-76	Carpathian Mountain region
	76.2-76.8	Danube River Valley
	77	Pannonia
DK	1-949.5	History of Russia. Soviet Union. Former Soviet Republics
	33-35.5	Ethnography
	36-293	History
	70-112.42	Early to 1613
	70-99.7	Rus'
	99.8-112.42	Muscovy
	112.8-264.8	House of Romanov, 1613-1917
	265-265.95	Revolution, 1917-1921
	266-292	Soviet regime, 1918-1991
	293	1991-
	500	Regions not limited to one Republic, A-Z
	501-949.5	Local history and description
	502.3-502.75	Baltic States
	503-503.95	Estonia
	503.92-503.939	Tallinn
	504-504.95	Latvia
	504.92-504.939	Riga
	505-505.95	Lithuania
	505.92-505.939	Vilnius
	507-507.95	Belarus. Byelorussian S.S.R. White Russia
	507.92-507.939	Minsk
	508-508.95	Ukraine
	508.92-508.939	Kiev
	509	Southern Soviet Union
	509.1-509.95	Moldova. Moldovian S.S.R. Bessarabia
	509.92-509.939	Chisinau. Kishinev
	510-651	Russia (Federation). Russian S.F.S.R.
	541-579	Saint Petersburg. Leningrad. Petrograd
	588-609	Moscow

OUTLINE

DK		History of Russia. Soviet Union. Former Soviet Republics
		Local history and description - Continued
	670-679.5	Georgia (Republic). Georgian S.S.R. Georgian Sakartvelo
	679.2-679.39	Tbilisi. Tiflis
	680-689.5	Armenia (Republic). Armenian S.S.R.
	689.2-689.39	Yerevan. Erevan
	690-699.5	Azerbaijan. Azerbaijan S.S.R.
	699.2-699.39	Baku
	751-781	Siberia
	845-860	Soviet Central Asia. West Turkestan
	901-909.5	Kazakhstan. Kazakh S.S.R.
	909.2-909.39	Alma Ata
	911-919.5	Kyrgyzstan. Kirghiz S.S.R. Kirghizia
	919.2-919.39	Frunze
	921-929.5	Tajikistan. Tajik S.S.R. Tadzhikistan
	929.2-929.39	Dushanbe
	931-939.5	Turkmenistan. Turkmen S.S.R. Turkmenia
	939.2-939.39	Ashkhabad
	941-949.5	Uzbekistan. Uzbek S.S.R.
	949.2-949.39	Tashkent
	4010-4800	History of Poland
	4120-4122	Ethnography
	4123-4452	History
	4186-4348	To 1795
	4348.5-4395	1795-1918. 19th century (General)
	4397-4420	1918-1945
	4429-4442	1945-1989. People's Republic
	4445-4452	1989-
	4600-4800	Local history and description
	4610-4645	Warsaw (Warszawa)
	4650-4685	Gdansk (Danzig)
	4700-4735	Krakow (Cracow)
DL	1-1180	History of Northern Europe. Scandinavia
	1-6.8	General
	7-11.5	Description and travel
	20-42.5	Antiquities. Social life and customs. Ethnography
	43-87	History
	43-49	General
	52-59	Military, naval, and political history. Foreign relations
	61-87	By period
	61-65	Earliest to 1387. Scandinavian Empire. Northmen. Vikings
	75-81	1387-1900
	83-87	1900- . Period of World War I, 1914-1918

OUTLINE

DL

History of Northern Europe. Scandinavia - Continued

101-291	Denmark
101-114.5	General
115-120	Description and travel
121-142.5	Antiquities. Social life and customs. Ethnography
143-263.3	History
143-151	General
154-159.5	Military, naval, and political history. Foreign relations
160-263.3	By period
160-183.9	Early and medieval to 1523
162-173.8	750-1241. Norwegian rule, 1042-1047
174-183.9	1241-1523. Union of Kalmar, 1397
184-263.3	Modern, 1523-
185-192.8	1523-1670
190	War with Sweden, 1643-1645
192	War with Sweden, 1657-1660
193-199.8	1670-1808
196.3	Period of Northern War, 1700-1721
201-249	1808-1906. 19th century
217-223	Schleswig-Holstein War, 1848-1850
236-239.6	Schleswig-Holstein War, 1864
250-263.3	20th century
269-291	Local history and description
271	Counties, regions, islands, etc., A-Z
276	Copenhagen
291	Other cities, towns, etc., A-Z
301-398	Iceland
301-334	General. Description and travel, etc.
335-380	History
396-398	Local history and description
401-596	Norway
401-414	General
415-419.2	Description and travel
420-442.5	Antiquities. Social life and customs. Ethnography
443-537	History
443-451.5	General
453-459	Military, naval, and political history. Foreign relations
460-537	By period
460-478	Early and medieval to 1387
480-502	1387-1814. Union of Kalmar, 1397
499	War of 1807-1814
500-502	Union with Sweden, 1814
503-526	1814-1905. 19th century
525	Dissolution of the Swedish-Norwegian union, 1905
527-537	20th century. Period of World War II, 1939-1945

OUTLINE

DL

History of Northern Europe. Scandinavia

Norway - Continued

576-596	Local history and description
576	Counties, regions, etc., A-Z
581	Oslo (Christiania)
596	Other cities, towns, etc., A-Z
601-991	Sweden
601-614.5	General
614.55-619.5	Description and travel
621-642	Antiquities. Social life and customs. Ethnography
643-879	History
643-651	General
654-659	Military, naval, and political history. Foreign relations
660-879	By period
660-700.9	Early and medieval to 1523. Union of Kalmar, 1397
701-879	Modern, 1523-
701-719.9	Vasa dynasty, 1523-1654. Gustaf II Adolf, 1611-1632
710-712	Wars with Denmark, Russia, Poland
721-743	Zweibrücken dynasty, 1654-1718
733-743	Northern War, 1700-1721
747-805	1718-1818
790	Revolution and loss of Finland, 1809
805	Union with Norway, 1814
807-859	1814-1907. 19th century
860-879	20th century
971-991	Local history and description
971	Provinces, regions, etc., A-Z
976	Stockholm
991	Other cities, towns, etc., A-Z
1002-1180	Finland
1002-1014.5	General
1015-1015.4	Description and travel
1016-1022	Antiquities. Social life and customs. Ethnography
1024-1141.6	History
1024-1033	General
1036-1048	Military, naval, and political history. Foreign relations
1050-1141.6	By period
1050-1052.9	Early to 1523
1055-1141.6	Modern, 1523-
1070-1078	Revolution, 1917-1918. Civil War
1090-1105	1939-1945
1095-1105	Russo-Finnish War, 1939-1940

OUTLINE

DL		History of Northern Europe. Scandinavian
		Finland - Continued
	1170-1180	Local history and description
	1170	Regions, provinces, historical regions, etc., A-Z
	1175-1175.95	Helsinki (Helsingfors)
	1180	Other cities, towns, etc., A-Z
DP	1-402	History of Spain
	1-27	General
	27.5-43.2	Description and travel
	44-53	Antiquities. Social life and customs. Ethnography
	56-272.4	History
	56-75	General
	76-86	Military, naval, and political history. Foreign relations
	91-272.4	By period
	91-96	Earliest to 711
	92-96	Pre-Roman, Roman, and Gothic periods
	97.3-160.8	711-1516. Moorish domination and the Reconquest
	100-123	Moors in Spain. Córdoba. Kingdom of Granada
	124-133.7	Aragon (Catalonia)
	134-143.8	Castile and Leon
	145-152.8	León (Asturias)
	153-160.8	Navarre
	161-272.4	Modern Spain, 1479/1516-
	161.5-166	1479-1516. Fernando V and Isabel I
	170-189	1516-1700. Habsburgs
	192-200.8	1700-1808. Bourbons
	201-232.6	1808-1886. 19th century
	204-208	1808-1814. Napoleonic period
	212-220	1814-1868. Bourbon restoration
	219-219.2	Carlist War, 1833-1840
	222-232.6	1868-1886
	224-226	Revolution, 1868-1870
	230-231.5	First Republic, 1873-1875
	233-272.4	20th century. 1886-
	250-269.9	Second Republic, 1931-1939
	269-269.9	Civil War, 1936-1939
	269.97-271	1939-1975
	272-272.4	1975-
	285-402	Local history and description
	285-295	Northern, Northwestern, Southern Spain
	302	Provinces, regions, ets., A-Z
	350-374	Madrid
	402	Other cities, towns, etc., A-Z

OUTLINE

DP	501-(900.22)	History of Portugal
	501-520	General
	521-526.5	Description and travel
	528-534.5	Antiquities. Social life and customs. Ethnography
	535-682.2	History
	535-546	General
	547-557	Military, naval, and political history. Foreign relations
	558-682.2	By period
	558-618	Early and medieval to 1580
	568-578	House of Burgundy, 1095-1383
	580	Interregnum, 1383-1385
	582-618	House of Aviz, 1385-1580
	620-682.2	1580-
	622-629	1580-1640. Spanish dynasty (Sixty years' captivity)
	632-644.9	1640-1816. House of Braganza
	645-669	1816-1908
	650	Revolution of 1820
	657	Wars of succession, 1826-1840
	670-682.2	20th century
	674	Revolution of October 1910
	675-682.2	Republic, 1910- . Revolution of 1919
	702-802	Local history and description
	702	Provinces, regions, etc., A-Z
	752-776	Lisbon
	802	Other cities, towns, etc., A-Z
DQ	1-851	History of Switzerland
	1-20	General
	20.5-26	Description and travel
	30-49.5	Antiquities. Social life and customs. Ethnography
	51-210	History
	51-57	General
	59-76	Military and political history. Foreign relations
	78-210	By period
	78-110	Early and medieval to 1516
	79-84	Early to 687. Celts and Romans. Teutonic tribes
	85-87	687-1291. Carolingian and German rule
	88-110	1291-1516. Federation and independence
	111-123	1516-1798
	124-191	19th century
	131-151	1789/1798-1815. Helvetic Republic, 1798-1803
	154-161	1815-1848. Sonderbund, 1845-1847
	171-191	1848-1900
	201-210	20th century

OUTLINE

DQ — History of Switzerland - Continued

- 301-851 Local history and description
  - 301-800.35 Cantons (and cantonal capitals)
  - 820-829 Alps
  - 841 Regions, peaks, etc., A-Z
  - 851 Cities, towns, etc., A-Z

DR 1-2285 — History of Balkan Peninsula

- 1-11 General
- 11.5-16 Description and travel
- 20-27 Antiquities. Social life and customs. Ethnography
- 32-48.5 History. Balkan War, 1912-1913
- 50-50.84 Thrace
- 51-98 Bulgaria
  - 51-56.7 General
  - 57-60.2 Description and travel
  - 62-64.5 Antiquities. Social life and customs. Ethnography
  - 65-93.47 History
    - 65-69.5 General
    - 70-73 Military and political history. Foreign relations
    - 73.7-93.47 By period
      - 73.7-80.8 Early and medieval
        - 74.5-77.8 First Bulgarian Empire, 681-1018
        - 79-79.25 Greek rule, 1018-1185
        - 80-80.8 Second Bulgarian Empire, 1185-1396
      - 81-84 Turkish rule, 1396-1878
      - 84.9-89.8 1878-1944
      - 89.9-93.34 1944-1990
      - 93.4-93.47 1990-
  - 95-98 Local history and description
    - 95 Provinces, regions, etc., A-Z
    - 97 Sofia
    - 98 Other cities, towns, etc., A-Z
- 201-296 Romania
  - 201-206 General
  - 207-210 Description and travel
  - 211-214.2 Antiquities. Social life and customs. Ethnography
  - 215-269.6 History
    - 215-218 General
    - 219-229 Military, naval, and political history. Foreign relations
    - 238-269.6 By period
      - 238-240.5 Early and medieval to 1601. Roman period
      - 241-241.5 Phanariote regime, 1601-1822
      - 242-249 1822-1881. 19th century
      - 250-266.5 1866/1881-1944
      - 267-267.5 1944-1989
      - 268-269.6 1989-

OUTLINE

DR History of Balkan Peninsula

Romania - Continued

279-296	Local history and description
279-280.74	Transylvania
281	Other provinces, regions, etc., A-Z
286	Bucharest
296	Other cities, towns, etc., A-Z
401-741	Turkey
401-419	General
421-429.4	Description and travel
431-435	Antiquities. Social life and customs. Ethnography
436-605	History
436-446	General
448-479	Military, naval, and political history. Foreign relations
481-605	By period
481	Earliest to 1281/1453
485-555.7	1281/1453-1789. Fall of Constantinople, 1453
511-529	1566-1640. Period of decline
515-516	Cyprian War, 1570-1571. Holy League, 1571
531-555.7	1640-1789
534.2-534.5	War of Candia, 1644-1669
556-567	1789-1861. 19th century
568-575	1861-1909. War with Russia, 1877-1878
576-605	20th century. Constitutional movement
701-741	Local history and description (European Turkey)
701	Provinces, regions, etc., A-Z
716-739	Istanbul (Constantinople)
741	Other cities, towns, etc., A-Z
901-998	Albania
901-914.5	General
915-918	Description and travel
921-926	Antiquities. Social life and customs. Ethnography
927-978.52	History
927-946	General
947-953	Military, naval, and political history. Foreign relations
954-978.52	By period
954-960.5	To 1501
961-969	1501-1912. Turkish rule
969.8-978.52	20th century
996-998	Local history and description
996	Provinces, regions, etc., A-Z
997	Tiranë
998	Other cities, towns, etc., A-Z
1202-2285	Yugoslavia
1202-1218	General
1220-1224	Description and travel
1227-1231	Antiquities. Social life and customs. Ethnography

OUTLINE

DR		History of Balkan Peninsula
		Yugoslavia
	1232-1321	History
	1232-1249	General
	1250-1258	Military, naval, and political history. Foreign relations
	1259-1321	By period
	1259-1265	Early and medieval to 1500
	1266-1272	1500-1800
	1273-1280	1800-1918
	1281-1321	1918-
	1313-1313.8	Yugoslav War, 1991-1995
	1350-2285	Local history and description
	1352-1485	Slovenia
	1502-1645	Croatia
	1620-1630.5	Dalmatia
	1633-1636.5	Slavonia
	1652-1785	Bosnia and Hercegovina
	1802-1928	Montenegro
	1932-2125	Serbia
	2075-2087.7	Kosovo
	2090-2101.5	Vojvodina
	2106-2124.5	Belgrade
	2152-2285	Macedonia

	History (General)
	Including Europe (General)
	For individual counties, see the country
1	Periodicals. Societies. Serials
2	Yearbooks. Registers
	Congresses, conferences, etc.
	International Congress of Historical Sciences
3.A15-A19	Serials
3.A2	Reports. By date
3.A22	Works about the I.C.H.S.
3.A3A-Z	Other international, A-Z
3.A4-Z	By region or country, A-Z
5	Sources and documents
5.5	Minor. Source books
	Collected works (Monographs, essays, etc.). Festschriften
6	Several authors
7	Individual authors
8	Pamphlets, etc.
9	Dictionaries
10	Minor reference books (Anecdotes, curiosa, allusions, etc.)
11	Chronological tables, etc.
11.5	Special
	Including books of days, dates, etc., famous events throughout the calendar year, etc.
	Historical atlases
	General, see G1030+
12	Pictorial atlases
	Historiography
	For historiography of the history of individual countries, see DA-DU
13	General works
13.2	Criticism and reviews
13.5.A-Z	By region or country, A-Z
	Biography of historians
14	Collective
15.A-Z	Individual, A-Z
	e.g.
15.A25	Acton, John Emerich E.D.A., Baron
15.B8	Burckhardt, Jakob Christoph
15.R3	Ranke, Leopold von
15.R6	Roscoe, William
15.R7	Rotteck, Karl Wenzeslaus R., von
	Methodology. Relation to other sciences
	Cf. D56+, Methodology in ancient history
16	General works
	Special topics
16.115	Abstracting and indexing
16.117	Computer network resources
16.12	Data processing
16.13	Historiometry
	Indexing, see D16.115

Methodology. Relation to other sciences
Special topics -- Continued
16.14 Oral history
16.15 Periodization
16.155 Photography
16.16 Psychohistory
16.163 Public history
16.166 Social sciences and history
16.17 Statistical methods
16.18 Television
Including video tapes
Study and teaching
For study and teaching in elementary grades, see LB1581+
For study and teaching in primary grades, see LB1530
16.2 General works
16.25 General special
Including area studies
16.255.A-Z Special topics, A-Z
16.255.A8 Audiovisual aids
16.255.C65 Computer-assisted instruction
16.255.S5 Simulation methods
By region or country
16.3 United States
For United States history, see E175.8
16.4.A-Z Other regions or countries, A-Z
16.5.A-Z Schools. By name or place, A-Z
Philosophy of history
General works
16.7 Through 1800
16.8 1801-
16.9 Special topics
Including periodicity in history, historical materialism, etc.
World histories
17 Chronicles and works written before 1525
Including ancient history
18 Chronicles and works written from 1525-1800
20 General works, 1801-
21 Compends. Textbooks. Outlines. Syllabi. Questions
21.1 Pictorial works
21.3 General special
21.5 Historical geography
22 History of several countries treated together
23 General popular works
23.5 Comic and satirical works
24 Historical events not restricted to one country or period
Including disasters as historic events
For specific disasters treated as historic events in individual countries, see the country in DA-F

World histories -- Continued
24.5 Other
For folklore and history, see GR41
For great cities of the world, see G140
Military history
Including Europe
For individual countries, see DA-DU
25.A2 Dictionaries. Chronological tables, etc.
25.A3-Z General works
25.5 General special
25.9 Pamphlets, etc.
27 Naval history
Including Europe
For individual countries, see DA-DU
Political and diplomatic history
Including Europe
31 General works
Including Europe
32 General special
33 Pamphlets, etc.
34.A-Z Relations between Europe and individual countries, A-Z
For relations between Europe and individual countries limited to 1945- , see D1065.A+
Biography (Collective)
General works
see CT
Rulers, kings, see D107
Ancient history
Including Europe
For individual countries, see DA-DU
51 Periodicals. Societies. Serials
52 Sources and documents
Collected works
53.A2 Several authors
53.A3-Z Individual authors
54 Dictionaries
54.5 Chronological tables, etc.
55 Biography (Collective)
Cf. D107, Rulers, kings, etc.
Cf. DE7, Classical antiquity
Historiography. Methodology
56 General works
Biography of historians
56.5 Collective
56.52.A-Z Individual, A-Z
e.g.
56.52.H45 Herodotus
General works
Cf. DS62.2+, Ancient Orient
To 1525, see D17
57 1525-

Ancient history -- Continued
58 Works by classical historians
e.g., Diodorus, Herodotus, Polybius
At the Library of Congress the distinction in use between Classes D and PA in classifying works by ancient Greek and Roman historians, as well as criticism and commentaries on such works, is as follows: In Class D: (1) Translations with or without original text, except translations into Latin (PA) (2) Criticism and commentaries (with or without the original text), if substantive in nature, i.e., dealing primarily with the historical events discussed by the original author. In Class PA: (1) Original Greek and Latin texts (except as noted above) (2) Latin translations (3) Philological or textual criticism and commentaries (with or without the original text) (4) Commentaries specifically designed for use in conjunction with the original text
59 Compends. Textbooks. Outlines. Syllabi. Questions
60 Addresses, essays, lectures
62 General special
Earliest history. Dawn of history
Cf. DS62.2+, Ancient history
Cf. GN803+, Prehistoric antiquities in western Europe
65 General works
70 Celts. Celtic antiquities
Cf. CB206, Celtic culture
Cf. GN549.C3, Celtic race (Anthropology
For Celts in the Balkan Peninsula, see DR39.3
General classical antiquity. Ancient nations
Including manners and customs, etc.
For archaeology, see CC1+
For Greek and Roman antiquities, see DE46
78 Early works through 1700
80 1701-
85.A-Z Special topics, A-Z
85.B7 Bow and arrow
90.A-Z Ancient peoples not limited to one country, A-Z
Cf. D135+, Migrations of peoples
Dacians, see DR239.2
Illyrians, see DR39.5
Saka, see DS328.4.S35
95 Naval history
Medieval and modern history, 476-
Including Europe
For individual countries, see DA-DU
Periodicals. Societies. Serials, see D1
Yearbooks. Registers, see D2

Medieval and modern history, 476- -- Continued
101 Sources and documents
For collections of treaties of peace, alliance, and confederation, see KZ184+
For individual treaties and related legal materials of war, peace, and alliance to ca. 1900, see KZ1328+
101.2 Minor collections
101.5 Dictionaries. Albums
101.7 Chronological tables, etc.
102 General works
Early, see D17
103 Compends. Textbooks. Outlines. Syllabi. Questions
104 General special
105 Political and diplomatic history
Pamphlets, see D8
Biography and memoirs
106 Collective
107 Rulers, kings, etc.
Including works covering ancient and modern rulers
107.3 Queens. Women rulers. Women heads of state
Including female consorts
107.5 Princes and princesses
107.6 Claimants to royalty. Pretenders
107.7 Favorites
107.9 Houses, noble families, etc.
108 Public men
109 Women
110 Other special classes
110.5 Other
Medieval history
Including Europe
For individual countries, see DA-DU
111 Periodicals. Societies. Serials
113 Sources and documents. Collections. Chronicles
113.5 Minor collections
114 Dictionaries
115 Biography (Collective)
Historiography
116 General works
Biography of historians
116.5 Collective
116.7.A-Z Individual, A-Z
General works
117.A2 Early
For chronicles, see D113
117.A3-Z Modern
118 Compends. Textbooks. Outlines. Syllabi. Questions
119 Addresses, essays, lectures
By period
121-123 Early to 10th century
121 General works

Medieval history
By period
Early to 10th century -- Continued
123 9th-10th centuries
Later, see D135+
125 Antiquities
(127) Social life and customs
see GT120
Civilization, see CB351+
128 Military and naval history
Political history and institutions
Including feudalism
For theory, see JC109+
131 General works
(133) Church and state
see BV629+
134 The medieval city
Cf. HT115, Urban communities
Cf. JS61, Local government
Migrations
135 General works
137 Goths (General). Visigoths
Cf. DG506+, Gothic Kingdom in Italy, 489-553
Cf. DP96, Visigoths in Spain, 414-711
138 Ostrogoths
139 Vandals
Cf. DT171, Vandals in North Africa, 439-534
Huns. Attila
Cf. DB927+, History of Hungary to 1301
141 General works
143 Battle of Chalons, 451
145 Lombards
Cf. DG511+, Lombard Kingdom, 568-768
147 Slavs
Cf. D377.A+, Eastern question (19th century)
Cf. DK33+, Ethnography of Soviet Union
Cf. DR25, Slavs in the Balkan Peninsula
Cf. GN549.S6, Ethnological works on Slavic peoples in general
148 Normans
Cf. DA190+, Normans in England, 1066-1154
Cf. DC611.N841+, Normandy
149 Other special
Crusades
Sources and documents
151 Collections of chronicles, etc.
152 Individual chronicles
153 Statutes, registers, etc.
155 Dictionaries
156 Biography
For memoirs, see the individual crusade
156.5 Peter, the Hermit
156.58 Historiography

Medieval history
Crusades -- Continued
157 General works
158 Compends. Textbooks. Outlines. Syllabi. Questions
159 Addresses, essays, lectures
160 Other
First crusade, 1096-1099
161 Sources
161.1 Memoirs and contemporary accounts
161.2 General works
161.3 Pamphlets, etc.
161.5.A-Z Part taken by individual countries, A-Z
Second crusade, 1147-1149
162 Sources
162.1 Memoirs and contemporary accounts
162.2 General works
162.3 Pamphlets, etc.
162.5.A-Z Part taken by individual countries, A-Z
Third crusade, 1189-1193
163.A2 Sources
163.A3 Memoirs and contemporary accounts
163.A4-Z General works
163.3 Pamphlets, etc.
163.5.A-Z Part taken by individual countries, A-Z
Fourth crusade, 1196-1198; 1204-1219
Including the siege of Constantinople, 1203-1204
164.A2 Sources
164.A3 Memoirs and contemporary accounts
Class here text of Villehardouin's Conquête de Constantinople
For biography and criticism, see PQ1545.V475
164.A4-Z General works
164.3 Pamphlets, etc.
164.5.A-Z Part taken by individual countries, A-Z
165 Fifth crusade, 1217-1221
Including the siege of Damietta, 1218-1219
166 Sixth crusade, 1228-1229
167 Seventh crusade, 1248-1250
168 Eighth crusade, 1270
169 Children's crusade, 1212
Later crusades in the 13th, 14th, and 15th centuries. Crusades in the east
171 General works
172 General special
173 Crusades in the west
Latin Kingdom of Jerusalem. Latin Orient. 1099-1291
Cf. DF610+, Latin Empire, 1204-1261 (Greece)
175 Periodicals. Societies. Serials
176 Sources and documents
177 Chronicles
Collected works
178 Several authors

Medieval history
Latin Kingdom of Jerusalem. Latin Orient. 1099-1291
Collected works -- Continued
179 Individual authors
Biography, memoirs, journals
Cf. D156, Memoirs of the crusades
180 Collective
181.A-Z Individual, A-Z
e.g.
181.P5 Philippe, of Novara
General works
Chronicles, see D177
182.A2 Early through 1800
182.A3-Z 1801-
183 General special
Individual rulers
183.3 Godfrey of Bouillon, 1099
183.5 Baldwin I, 1100-1118
183.7 Baldwin II, 1118-1131
183.9 Foulque, 1131-1143
184 Baldwin III, 1143-1162
184.3 Amalric I, 1162-1174
184.4 Baldwin IV, 1174-1183
184.5 Baldwin V, 1183-1192
184.7 Guy of Lusignan, 1186-1192
184.8 Conquest of Jerusalem by Saladin, 1187
184.9 Conrad of Montferrat, 1192
185 Henry I (II of Champagne), 1192-1197
185.3 Amalric II, 1197-1205
185.5 Mary, 1205-1210
185.7 John of Brienne, 1210-1225
186 Frederick II, 1225-1250
186.3 Conrad IV, 1250-1254
186.5 Conradin, 1254-1268
187 Hugh I (III of Cyprus), 1269-1284
187.3 John, 1284-1285
187.5 Henry II, 1285-1291
Local
190 Edessa
192 Antioch
194 Tripoli
195.A-Z Other, A-Z
e.g.
195.S9 Syria
Cf. DS97+, Medieval Syria, 638-1517
(198-199.7) Arab (Islamic) Empire
see DS36.85+, DS38.14+
Later medieval. 11th-15th centuries
200 General works
11th-12th centuries
201 General works
11th century
201.3 Sources and documents. Contemporary works

Medieval history
Later medieval. 11th-15th centuries
11th-12th centuries
11th century -- Continued
201.4 General works
12th century
201.7 Sources and documents. Contemporary works
201.8 General works
13th-15th centuries
202 General works
13th century
202.3 Sources and documents. Contemporary works
202.4 General works
14th century
202.7 Sources and documents. Contemporary works
202.8 General works
203 15th century
Modern history, 1453-
Including Europe
For individual countries, see DA-DU
Periodicals. Societies. Serials, see D1
Yearbooks. Registers, see D2
Sources and documents, see D5
(204) Collected works
see D6+
205 Dictionaries
Biography, see D106
206 Historiography
208 General works
209 Compends. Textbooks. Outlines
210 General special. Addresses, essays, lectures
(211) Social life and customs
see GT129
213 Pamphlets, etc.
214 Military history
215 Naval history
217 Political and diplomatic history. European concert.
Balance of power
1453-1648
Including 16th century
Cf. BR300+, Reformation
Cf. CB361+, Renaissance
219 Periodicals. Serials
220 Sources and documents
221.A-Z Reports and communications of ambassadors, etc.
By accrediting country, A-Z
Collected works
223 Several authors
224 Individual authors
Biography and memoirs
226 Collective
226.3 Women
226.6 Military and naval

Modern history, 1453-
1453-1648
Biography and memoirs
Collective -- Continued
226.7 Rulers, kings, queens, etc.
226.8.A-Z Individual, A-Z
e.g.
226.8.C5 Christine, Consort of Francis I, Duke of Lorraine
228 General works
229 Pamphlets, etc.
231 General special
234 Political and diplomatic history
1601-1715. 17th century
242 Sources and documents
Biography and memoirs
244 Collective
244.3 Women
244.5 Public men
244.6 Military and naval
244.7 Rulers, kings, queens, etc.
244.8.A-Z Individual, A-Z
e.g.
244.8.E4 Elizabeth of England, Consort of Frederick I, King of Bohemia
244.8.F4 Feuquières family
246 General works
247 General special
Thirty Years' War, 1618-1648
Cf. DD189, Germany during the period of the war
251 Sources and documents
256.A-Z Memoirs, A-Z
Cf. D270.A2+, Biography of participants
258 General works
259 Pamphlets, etc.
260 Other
261 Causes, etc.
262 Bohemia, 1618-1623, and Palatinate
263 Denmark, 1623-1629
Including the Peace of Lübeck, 1629
Cf. KZ1330.5+, Treaty of Lübeck, 1629
264 Sweden, 1630-1635
265 1635-1648
267.A-Z Special events, battles, etc., A-Z
e.g.
267.B3 Bergen op Zoom, Siege of, 1622
267.B8 Brünn, Siege of, 1645
(267.E3) Edict of Restitution, 1629
see KZ1330.7.E3
267.F85 Freiburg i. B., Battle of, 1644
267.H2 Hameln, Siege of, 1633
267.H3 Heilbronn, Union of, 1633

Modern history, 1453-
1601-1715. 17th century
Thirty Years' War, 1618-1648
Special events, battles, etc., A-Z -- Continued
267.J3 Jankau, Battle of, 1645
267.L3 Leipzig, Battle of, 1631
267.M2 Magdeburg, Siege and sack of, 1631
267.N7 Nördlingen, Battle of, 1634
267.N8 Nördlingen, Battle of, 1645
267.O6 Oldendorf, Battle of, 1633
267.R3 Ratisbon, Electoral Assembly of, 1630
267.R6 Rocroi, Battle of, 1643
267.S8 Stralsund, Siege of, 1628
267.U6 Ulm, Truce of, 1647
For legal works, including texts of the treaty and related documents, see KZ1330.9
267.W4 Weisser Berg, Battle of, 1620
267.W6 Wittstock, Battle of, 1636
269 Peace of Westphalia, 1648
Cf. KZ1331+, Treaties of Münster and Osnabrück, 1648
Biography of participants
270.A2 Collective
270.A3-Z Individual, A-Z
270.A7 Arnim, Hans Georg von
Gustaf II, Adolf, King of Sweden, see DL706
270.M3 Mansfeld, Ernst, graf von
270.T5 Tilly, Jean t'Serclaes, comte de
270.T8 Torstenson, Lennart, greve af Ortala
270.W19 Wallenstein, Albrecht Wenzel E. von
271.A-Z Relations of individual countries, A-Z
1648-1715
273.A2 Sources and documents
273.A3-Z General works
273.5 General special
273.7 Diplomatic history
Biography and memoirs
Collective, see D244
274.A-Z Individual, A-Z
e.g.
274.E8 Eugène, Prince of Savoie-Carignan
274.5 Anglo-French War, 1666-1667
274.6 Peace of Breda, 1667
Cf. DA448, England, 1660-1685
Cf. DJ180+, Netherlands, 1652-1702
Cf. KZ1333.3, Treaty of Breda, 1667
War of Devolution, 1667-1668
275 General works
275.5 Pamphlets, etc.
276.A-Z Special events, battles, etc., A-Z
e.g.

Modern history, 1453-
1601-1715. 17th century
1648-1715
War of Devolution, 1667-1668
Special events,
battles, etc., A-Z -- Continued
276.A3 Aix-la-Chapelle, Peace of, 1668
Cf. KZ1333.32, Treaty of Aix-la-Chapelle, 1668
Dutch War, 1672-1678
Cf. DJ190+, Netherlands during war with France
277 General works
277.5 General special
278.A-Z Special events, battles, etc., A-Z
e.g.
278.E6 Enzheim (Entzheim, Ensheim), Battle of, 1674
278.S4 Seneffe, Battle of, 1674
278.S7 Solebay (Sole Bay, Southwold), Battle of, 1672
278.T4 Texel, Battle of the, 1673
278.5 Peace of Nijmegen, 1678-1679
Cf. KZ1333.4, Treaty of Nijmegen, 1678-1679
War of the Grand Alliance, 1688-1697
279 General works
279.5 General special
280.A-Z Special events, battles, etc., A-Z
e.g.
280.A8 Ath, Siege of, 1697
280.F6 Fleurus, Battle of, 1690
280.H6 Hogue, La, Battle of, 1692
280.N2 Namur, Siege of, 1692
280.5 Peace of Ryswick, 1697
Cf. KZ1333.5, Treaty of Ryswick, 1697
War of Spanish Succession, 1701-1714
281.A2 Sources and documents
281.A3-Z Memoirs and early works
281.5 General works
282 General special
282.5 Pamphlets, etc.
283.A-Z Special events, battles, etc., A-Z
e.g.
283.B3 Barcelona, Siege of, 1713-1714
283.B6 Blenheim, Battle of, 1704
283.L5 Lille, Siege of, 1707
283.T7 Toulon, Siege of, 1707
283.T8 Turin, Siege of, 1706
283.5 Congress of Utrecht, 1713
Cf. KZ1334+, Treaty of Utrecht, 1713
For the Treaty of Rastatt and Baden, 1714, see KZ1335.5
1715-1789. 18th century
284 Sources and documents

Modern history, 1453-
1715-1789. 18th century -- Continued
284.5 Historiography
Biography and memoirs
Collective
285 General works
285.1 Minor
285.3 Women
285.5 Public men
285.7 Rulers, kings, queens, etc.
285.8.A-Z Individual, A-Z
e.g.
Ahmet, Paşa, Kumbaracibaşi, 1675-1747, see D285.8.B6
285.8.B6 Bonneval, Claude Alexandre, comte de, 1675-1747
285.8.C4 Casanova, Giacomo, 1725-1798
For literary works (French), see PQ1959.C6
For literary works (Italian), see PQ4687.C274
285.8.H7 Hordt, Johann Ludwig, graf von
285.8.L5 Ligne, Charles Joseph, prince de
285.8.P7 Pöllnitz, Karl Ludwig, freiherr von
285.8.T65 Trenck, Franz
285.8.T7 Trenck, Friedrich
286 General works
Diplomatic history. Foreign relations
287 General works
287.5 Quadruple Alliance, 1718
Cf. KZ1339.Q83, Quadruple Alliance Treaty, 1718
287.7 Alliance of Hanover, 1725
Cf. KZ1339.H36, Treaty of Hanover, 1725
287.8 Negotiation of Seville, 1729
Cf. KZ1339.S48, Treaty of Seville, 1729
288 Other special
1740-1789
Cf. D295, Political and military history, 1750-1789
289 General works
289.4 Family Pact, Fontainebleau, 1743
For legal works, including texts of the treaty and related documents, see KZ1339.F66
289.5 Family Pact, Paris, 1761
For legal works, including texts of the treaty and related documents, see KZ1339.P37
290 18th century minor works. Pamphlets, etc.
War of Austrian Succession, 1740-1748
Cf. DB72, Austria during the period of the war
291 Sources and documents
292 General works
292.8 Pamphlets, etc.
293 Silesian campaigns. International relations
For military history, see DD406+

Modern history, 1453-
1715-1789. 18th century
War of Austrian
Succession, 1740-1748 -- Continued
Rhine and Danube, 1741-1744
293.2 General works
293.3.A-Z Special events, battles, etc., A-Z
Italy, 1741-1748
293.4 General works
293.5.A-Z Special events, battles, etc., A-Z
e.g.
293.5.A8 Assietta, Battle of, 1747
293.5.V4 Velletri, Battle of, 1744
293.55 Other
Netherlands, 1743-1748
293.6 General works
293.7.A-Z Special events, battles, etc., A-Z
e.g.
293.7.F6 Fontenoy, Battle of, 1745
Colonial, 1739-1748. Naval operations
293.8 General works
Cf. E198, King George's War, 1744-1748
293.9.A-Z Special events, battles, etc., A-Z
294 Peace of Aix-la-Chapelle, 1748
Cf. KZ1339.A59, Treaty of Aix-la-Chapelle, 1748
1750-1789
295 Political and military history
Including history of the armed neutrality of 1780
Cf. E208, American Revolution, 1775-1783
Cf. JZ6422+, Neutrality
For the Treaty of Versailles, 1783, see KZ1339.V47
Seven Years' War, 1756-1763
297 General international aspects, results, etc.
Peace of Paris, 1763
Cf. DS462+, French (1664-1761) and English (1761-1798) in India
Cf. KZ1336+, Treaty of Paris, 1763
For French and Indian War, 1756-1763, see E199
For the war between Friedrich II and Maria Theresia, see DD409+
1789-
Including 18th and 19th centuries together
299 General works
1789-1815. Period of the French Revolution
301 Periodicals. Sources and documents. Collections
304.A-Z Biography and memoirs, A-Z
e.g.
Cf. DC145+, Biography, memoirs, etc. of French contemporaries of the French Revolution

Modern history, 1453-
1789-
1789-1815. Period of the French Revolution
Biography and memoirs, A-Z -- Continued
304.J7 Jomini, Henri, baron
304.M15 Maistre, Joseph Marie, comte de
308 General works
309 Other
Revolutionary and Napoleonic wars, see DC220+
19th century. 1801-1914/1920
351 Sources and documents
Biography and memoirs
352 Collective
352.1 Rulers, kings, princes, etc.
352.3 Queens, princesses
352.5 Public men
352.7 Women
352.8.A-Z Individual, A-Z
e.g.
352.8.L6-L7 Lieven, Dar'i͡a Khristoforovna (Benckendorff), kni͡aginii͡a
352.8.M4 Metternich-Winneburg, Pauline Clementine M.W. (Sándor von Szlavnicza), fürst von
352.8.P3 Pückler-Muskau, Hermann, fürst von
352.8.S7 Stockmar, Ernst Alfred C., freiherr von
352.9 Historiography
Collected works
353 Several authors
354 Individual authors
355 Addresses, essays, lectures
356 Dictionaries, etc.
358 19th century (General)
358.5 Popular works
359 Europe in the 19th century, 1801-1914
For sources, biography, etc., see D351+, D359.2+
359.2 Syllabi, outlines, tables, etc.
359.7 General special
(360) Social life and customs
see GT146
Civilization, see CB415+
361 Military history
362 Naval history
363 Political and diplomatic history
Eastern question
371 General works
372 General special
373 Early history to 1800
374 19th century
Cf. DR475, Turkey, 1812-1918
For legal works on the Treaty of Paris, 1856,, see KZ1369
For the Congress of Paris, 1856,, see DK215

Modern history, 1453-
1789-
19th century. 1801-1914/1920
Eastern question
19th century -- Continued
375 General special
375.3 Conference of Berlin, 1878
Cf. DR573.7, San Stefano, 1878
For legal works on the Treaty of Berlin, 1878,, see KZ1383
20th century, see D461+
376.A-Z Relations of individual countries, A-Z
Slavs
377.A1 Periodicals. Societies. Serials
377.A2-Z General works
Panslavism
Cf. D449, Panslavism, 20th century
377.3 General works, especially political
377.5.A-Z By region or country, A-Z
Central Asian question
Cf. DK750, Soviet Asia
378 General works
378.5.A-Z By region or country, A-Z
(379) Far East
see DS515+
383 1815-1830. Congress of Vienna, 1814-1815. Holy Alliance. Quadruple Alliance, 1815
For legal works on the Holy Alliance Treaty, 1815,, see KZ1358+
1830-1848
385 General works
387 1848
1848-1859
388 Sources and documents
389 General works
1860-1870
391 Sources and documents
392 General works
393 Pamphlets, etc.
1871- . Later 19th century
394 Sources and documents
395 General works
395.2 Syllabi, outlines, tables, questions, etc.
396 Military history
397 Political and diplomatic history
Including Franco-Russian alliance, Triple Alliance, 1882
For legal works on the Triple Alliance Treaty, 1882,, see KZ1384
398 Other
Biography and memoirs
399 Collective
399.5 Women

Modern history, 1453-
1789-
19th century. 1801-1914/1920
1871- . Later 19th century
Biography and memoirs
Collective -- Continued
399.6 Public men
399.7 Rulers, kings, etc.
399.8 Queens, princesses, etc.
400.A-Z Individual, A-Z
e.g.
400.B6 Blount, Sir Edward Charles
400.B85 Bunsen, Marie von
400.P3 Paget, Walpurga Ehrengarde H. (von Hohenthal), lady
400.R33 Redesdale, Algernon Bertram Freeman-Mitford, Baron
400.R5 Rennell, James Rennell Rodd, Baron
400.R7 Rumbold, Sir Horace, bart.
400.S2 Salm-Salm, Agnes (Joy), prinzessin zu
400.Z3 Zaharoff, Sir Basil
20th century
410 Periodicals. Societies. Serials
410.5 Yearbooks of current events (nonserial)
Including pictorial works
Arrange chronologically by year; subarrange by author
411 Sources and documents
Biography and memoirs
412 Collective
412.5 Women
412.6 Public men
412.7 Rulers, kings, etc.
412.8 Queens, princesses, etc.
413.A-Z Individual, A-Z
413.5 Historiography
Collected works
414 Several authors
415 Individual authors
416 Pamphlets, etc.
419 Dictionaries
421 20th century (General)
422 Popular works
Europe in the 20th century
For periodicals, etc., see D410
For sources, etc., see D426
424 General works
Europe, 1945- , see D1050+
425 Popular works
426 Pictorial history
427 Syllabi, outlines, tables, etc.
(429) Social life and customs
see GT150

Modern history, 1453-
1789-
20th century -- Continued
Civilization, see CB425+
431 Military history
436 Naval history
437 Air warfare
Political and diplomatic history
Including world politics, Triple Entente, 1907
Cf. D397, Political and diplomatic history of the later 19th century
Cf. D511+, Causes and origins of World War I, 1914-1918
440 Annual registers
Cf. D2, Annual registers (General history)
441 Sources and documents
442 Collected works
443 General works
445 General special
e.g. Imaginary wars and future world politics
446 Anglo-Saxon supremacy
Cf. CB216, Anglo-Saxon civilization
Cf. DA118, National characteristics of the English
447 Pangermanism (International)
Cf. DD118.5+, German imperialism
Panislamism
see DR476, DS35.7
448 Panlatinism
448.5 Panceltism
449 Panslavism
Cf. D377.A+, Panslavism in the 19th century
450 Pamphlets, etc.
Diplomatic history. Foreign relations
451 Sources and documents
453 General works
455 General special
457 Pamphlets, etc.
(458) Triple Alliance, 1882
see D397, KZ1384
(459) Triple Entente, 1907-
see D443, D511, JZ1391.2
460 Little Entente, 1920-1939
Eastern question
Cf. D371+, Eastern question in the 19th century
Cf. DR475, Political and diplomatic history of Turkey
461 Sources and documents
462 Conferences, etc. By date
e.g.

Modern history, 1453-
1789-
20th century
Eastern question
Conferences, etc. By date -- Continued
462 1922 Lausanne
463 General works
465 General special
468 Pamphlets, etc.
469.A-Z By region or country, A-Z
Central Asian question
1901-1914, see D378+
471 1914-
472.A-Z By region or country, A-Z
Macedonian question, see DR2152+
(475) Moroccan question
see DT317
Far East, see DS515
World War I (1914-1918)
501 Periodicals. Serials
502 Societies
Cf. D570.A1+, American Legion, Disabled American Veterans of the World War, etc.
503 Museums. Exhibitions, etc.
Cf. CJ5780, Medals of the 20th century
Cf. N9152.A+, Art exhibitions of World War I
504 Congresses, conferences, etc.
505 Sources and documents
Biography
507 Collective
Individual
see individual countries, classes D-F
509 Collected works
510 Dictionaries
Causes. Origins. Aims
511 General works. Triple Entente, 1907
Cf. JZ1391.2, International relations
512 Austria
513 Serbia
514 Soviet Union. Panslavism
515 Germany
Cf. DD119, Pangermanism
516 France
517 Great Britain
Including colonies (General)
518 Belgium
519 Japan
520.A-Z Other regions or countries, A-Z
e.g.
520.A8 Arabia
Armenia, see DS195+
520.B6 Bohemia

World War I (1914-1918)
Causes. Origins. Aims
Other regions or countries, A-Z -- Continued
520.I65 Ireland
Cf. DA962, Ireland, 1914-1921
520.I7 Italy
Cf. D617, Neutrality of Italy
Latin America, see D520.S8
520.O8 Orient. Far East
Poland, see DK4390+
520.S8 South America. Latin America
520.T8 Turkey. Islam
521 General works
522 Pictorial works
For art and the war, see N9150+
522.22 Films, slides, etc. Catalogs
522.23 Motion pictures about the war
522.25 Posters
522.27 Collectibles
(522.3) Maps and atlases
see G1037, etc.
522.4 Study and teaching
522.42 Historiography
522.5 Outlines, syllabi, tables, etc.
522.6 Examinations, questions, etc.
522.7 Juvenile works. Elementary textbooks
523 General special
524 Ethical and religious aspects. Prophecy
Cf. D639.R4, Religion and Christianity in the war
524.5 Psychological aspects
525 Pamphlets, addresses, sermons, etc.
War poetry
see class P
526 Satire, caricature, etc.
526.2 English
526.3 French
526.5 German
526.7.A-Z Other languages, A-Z
e.g.
526.7.I8 Italian
526.7.R8 Russian
(527-527.5) Pictorial works
see D522+
527.8 Commemorative ribbons, etc.
528 Guides to the battlefields
For guides to special battlefields, see the battle
528.5 Beginnings of the war. Mobilization, etc.
Military operations
529 Collections of official reports
General works, see D521
Special arms
529.3 Infantry

World War I (1914-1918)
Military operations
Special arms -- Continued
529.4 Cavalry
529.5 Artillery
529.7 Engineers
529.9.A-Z Other special, A-Z
Cf. D600+, Aerial operations, tank operations
For individual countries, see D570+
Western
530 General works
German
Including memoirs by Falkenhayn, Hindenburg, and Ludendorff
531 General works
Prussian
532 General works
532.1 Army
532.2 Corps
532.3 Infantry
532.4 Cavalry
532.47 Uhlans
532.5 Artillery
532.6 Machine gun regiments
532.7 Gas regiments
532.8 Engineers
532.9 Other
Baden
533 General works
533.1 Army
533.2 Corps
533.3 Infantry
533.4 Cavalry
533.47 Uhlans
533.5 Artillery
533.6 Machine gun regiments
533.7 Gas regiments
533.8 Engineers
533.9 Other
Bavaria
534 General works
534.1 Army
534.2 Corps
534.3 Infantry
534.4 Cavalry
534.47 Uhlans
534.5 Artillery
534.6 Machine gun regiments
534.7 Gas regiments
534.8 Engineers
534.9 Other
Hessian

World War I (1914-1918)
Military operations
Western
German
Hessian -- Continued
535 General works
535.1 Army
535.2 Corps
535.3 Infantry
535.4 Cavalry
535.47 Uhlans
535.5 Artillery
535.6 Machine gun regiments
535.7 Gas regiments
535.8 Engineers
535.9 Other
Saxon
536 General works
536.1 Army
536.2 Corps
536.3 Infantry
536.4 Cavalry
536.47 Uhlans
536.5 Artillery
536.6 Machine gun regiments
536.7 Gas regiments
536.8 Engineers
536.9 Other
Württemberg
537 General works
537.1 Army
537.2 Corps
537.3 Infantry
537.4 Cavalry
537.47 Uhlans
537.5 Artillery
537.6 Machine gun regiments
537.7 Gas regiments
537.8 Engineers
537.9 Other
538.A-Z Other, A-Z
538.5.A-Z German local history, A-Z
Austrian. Austro-Hungarian
539 General works
539.5.A-Z Special, A-Z
539.5.C8 Czechoslovak troops
539.7.A-Z Local history, A-Z
Hungarian
540 General works
540.5.A-Z Special, A-Z
Belgian and operations in Belgium
541 General works
For the Flemish movement, see DH682

World War I (1914-1918)
Military operations
Western
Belgian and operations in Belgium -- Continued

542.A-Z Individual campaigns, sieges, battles, etc., A-Z
542.A6 Antwerp, Siege of, 1914
542.B7 Bruges
542.C4 Charleroi
542.D4 Dinant
542.D5 Dixmude
542.D8 Duffel
542.L5 Liége
542.L7 Louvain
542.L8 Lys, Battle of the, 1918
542.M3 Malines (Mechlin)
542.M4 Messines
542.M7 Mons
542.Y5 Ypres (General)
542.Y6 Ypres, 1st battle of, 1914
542.Y7 Ypres, 2d battle of, 1915
542.Y72 Ypres, 3d battle of, 1917
542.Y8 Yser, Battle of the, 1914

Anglo-French. Allies

544 General works
545.A-Z Individual campaigns, sieges, battles, etc., A-Z
e.g.
545.A5 Aisne
(545.A55) Alsace
see DC647 +
545.A6 Argonne, Battle of the, 1915
545.A63 Argonne, Battle of the, 1918
545.A7 Arras
545.B4 Belleau Wood
545.C37 Champagne
545.C4 Château-Thierry, Battle of, 1918
545.C7 Compiègne
545.L5 Lille
545.L7 Lorraine, Battle of, 1914
545.M3 Marne, Battle of the, 1914
545.N7 Noyon
545.P5 Picardy
545.R4 Reims
545.S35 Seicheprey
545.S4 Senlis
545.S7 Somme, Battle of the, 1916
545.S75 Somme, 2d battle of the, 1918
545.V25 Verdun, Battle of, 1914
545.V3 Verdun, Battle of, 1916

English

546.A1-A19 Societies
e.g.
546.A12 Comrades of the Great War
546.A2-Z General works

World War I (1914-1918)
Military operations
Western
English -- Continued

546.3 Officers Training Corps
546.5 Individual divisions, etc. By number
Cf. D547.A+, Individual divisions by region or name
546.5 5th The Fifth Army
546.52 Artillery
546.53 Infantry
546.54 Cavalry
546.55 Engineers
547.A-Z Individual. By region or name, A-Z
e.g.
547.A1 Colonies (General)
547.A4 Africa, South
547.A5 Africa, West
547.A8 Australia. The Anzacs
547.B6 Black Watch
547.C2 Canada
547.C6 Coldstream Guards
547.G5 Glasgow Highlanders
547.G6 Gordon Highlanders
547.G7 Grenadier Guards
547.G8 Guards Division
547.I5 India
547.I6 Ireland
547.J3 Jamaica
547.K4 Kent
547.K43 King's (Liverpool Regiment)
547.K45 King's Overseas Dominions Regiment
547.K47 King's Own Scottish Borderers
547.K5 King's Own Rifle Corps
547.L2 Labour Corps
547.L6 London regiments
547.M3 Manchester Regiment
547.M8 Munster
547.N4 Negroes
547.N5 New Zealand
547.N55 Newfoundland
547.N6 North Midland Division
547.N7 Northumberland Fusiliers
547.O7 Oxford University
547.Q18 Queen's Own Oxfordshire Hussars
547.Q2 Queen's Own Royal West Kent Regiment
547.Q3 Queen's Westminster and Civil Service Rifles
547.R4 Remount Service
547.R5 Royal Artillery Regiment
547.R6 Royal Fusiliers
547.R63 Royal Highlanders of Canada
547.R7 Royal Naval Division
547.R8 Royal Scots

World War I (1914-1918)
Military operations
Western
English
Individual. By region or name, A-Z -- Continued

547.S4 Scots Guard
547.S5 Sherwood Foresters
547.S6 South Staffordshire Regiment
547.T3 Tasmania
547.W4 Wales
547.W5 West Riding Territorials
547.8.A-Z English local history, A-Z
e.g.
547.8.E3 East Anglia
547.8.H6 Hornchurch
547.8.L7 London
547.8.P7 Preston

French
548 General works
Societies
548.03 General works
548.033.A-Z Special, A-Z
Special
548.1 Army corps
548.2 Divisions
548.3 Infantry
548.35 Foreign Legion
548.4 Cavalry
548.5 Chasseurs. "Blue devils." Chasseurs à pied. Chasseurs alpine
548.6 Artillery
548.7 Machine gun regiments
548.75 Gas regiments
548.8 Engineers
548.9.A-Z Other, A-Z
Including colonial
549.A-Z Other special, A-Z
e.g.
549.C5 Chinese troops
549.C7 Colored troops
549.5.A-Z Other countries, A-Z
Portugal
Including colonial history
549.5.P8 General works
549.5.P82A-Z Local history, A-Z

Eastern
550 General works. Soviet Union (General)
551 Russo-German (Austrian)
Including Poland, Volhynia, etc.
552.A-Z Individual campaigns, sieges, battles, etc., A-Z
e.g.
552.L5 Lithuania

World War I (1914-1918)
Military operations
Eastern
Russo-German (-Austrian)
Individual campaigns, sieges, battles, etc., a-Z -- Continued
552.T3 Tannenberg, Battle of, 1914
556 Russo-Austrian
Including general Austria and Galicia
557.A-Z Individual campaigns, sieges, battles, etc., A-Z
e.g.
557.L4 Lemberg
557.P7 Przemysl, Siege of, 1914
Revolution of 1917 in Finland, see DL1070+
Revolution of 1917 in Soviet Union, see DK265+
558 Siberia
559 Archangel. Northern Russia
Balkan
560 General works
Serbian
561 General works
562.A-Z Individual campaigns, sieges, battles, etc., A-Z
Bulgarian
563.A2 General works
563.A3-Z Individual campaigns, sieges, battles, etc., A-Z
Montenegrin
564.A2 General works
564.A3-Z Individual campaigns, sieges, battles, etc., A-Z
Romanian
565.A2 General works
565.A3-Z Individual campaigns, sieges, battles, etc., A-Z
Turkey and the Near East
566 General works
Turco-Russian
567.A2 General works
567.A3-Z Individual campaigns, sieges, battles, etc., A-Z
Turco-Egyptian
568.A2 General works
568.A3-Z Individual campaigns, sieges, battles, etc., A-Z
568.2 Egypt
568.3 Dardanelles. Gallipoli
568.4 Arabia
568.5 Mesopotamia. Kut-el-Amara. Assyria
568.6 Syria
568.7 Palestine
568.8 Persia. Iran
568.9 West Turkestan and Khurasan

World War I (1914-1918)
Military operations
Eastern -- Continued
Italian
569.A2 General works
569.A25 Divisions, regiments, etc. By author, A-Z
569.A3-Z Individual campaigns, sieges, battles, etc., A-Z
e.g.
569.G7 Gorizia
569.P4 Piave, 1st battle of the, 1917
569.P5 Piave, 2nd battle of the, 1918
569.V4 Venice (Italy), Defense of
569.V5 Vittorio Veneto, Battle of, 1918
Greece. Salonica (Thessalonike). Macedonian campaign
569.2 General works
569.3.A-Z Individual campaigns, sieges, battles, etc., A-Z
569.5 Albania
United States
For internal history of the United States, 1914-1918, see E780
Societies
American Legion
570.A1 General works
570.A12A-W By state, A-W
570.A13A-Z By city, A-Z
570.A135 American Legion, France
Auxiliary
570.A14A1-A14A4 Official publications
570.A14A5 Nonofficial publications
570.A14A6-A14W By state, A-W
570.A14Z9 Pamphlets, etc.
570.A15A-Z Other societies, A-Z
e.g.
570.A15D5 Disabled American Veterans of the World War
570.A15M5 Military Order of the World War
570.A2 Collections. Serials. Official bulletins, etc.
Special documents of a general nature
Prefer the special topic
(570.A3) Legislative acts
see KF5951+
570.A35 Other special
General works on participation in the war
570.A4 Official
570.A5-Z Nonofficial
570.1 General special
570.15 Pamphlets, etc.
Causes and antecedent history, see D619
Military operations
General works, see D570.A4+
570.2 General special
Individual expeditions, battles, etc , see D545.A+
Special divisions, regiments, etc.

World War I (1914-1918)
Military operations
United States
Military operations
Special divisions, regiments, etc. -- Continued

570.25 Headquarters. General Staff

570.27 Army corps
Subarrange: General works, .A1; individual units by number and author, e.g. 1st, 2nd, 51st, etc.

570.3 Divisions
Subarrange: General works, .A1; individual units by number and author, e.g. 1st, 2nd, 51st, etc.

570.309 Engineers

570.31 Special units. By number and author

570.315 Air Defense Artillery
Subarrange: General works, .A1; individual units by number and author, e.g. 1st, 2nd, 51st, etc.

570.32 Field artillery
Subarrange: General works, .A1; individual units by number and author, e.g. 1st, 2nd, 51st, etc.

570.325 Coast artillery
Subarrange: General works, .A1; individual units by number and author, e.g. 1st, 2nd, 51st, etc.

570.327 Trench artillery
Subarrange: General works, .A1; individual units by number and author, e.g. 1st, 2nd, 51st, etc.

570.33 Infantry
Subarrange: General works, .A1; individual units by number and author, e.g. 1st, 2nd, 51st, etc.

570.34 Machine gun battalions
Subarrange: General works, .A1; individual units by number and author, e.g. 1st, 2nd, 51st, etc.

570.345 Gas regiments
Subarrange: General works, .A1; individual units by number and author, e.g. 1st, 2nd, 51st, etc.

570.346 Signal Corps
Subarrange: General works, .A1; individual units by number and author, e.g. 1st, 2nd, 51st, etc.

World War I (1914-1918)
Military operations
United States
Military operations
Special divisions, regiments, etc. -- Continued

570.348 Marine Corps (Land operations only)
Subarrange: General works, .A1; individual units by number and author, e.g. 1st, 2nd, 51st, etc.
Cf. D570.45, Marine Corps

570.35 Military police
Subarrange: General works, .A1; individual units by number and author, e.g. 1st, 2nd, 51st, etc.

570.352 Ammunition trains
Subarrange: General works, .A1; individual units by number and author, e.g. 1st, 2nd, 51st, etc.

570.354 Field hospital companies
Subarrange: General works, .A1; individual units by number and author, e.g. 1st, 2nd, 51st, etc.

570.355 Ambulance companies
Subarrange: General works, .A1; individual units by number and author, e.g. 1st, 2nd, 51st, etc.

570.358 Other

570.36 Training camps
Individual camps

570.37.A-Z In Europe. A-Z
e.g.

570.37.B7 Brest

In United States, see U294.5.A+

Naval operations

(570.4) General works
See D589.U5+

570.45 General special
e.g. Defensive areas; land batteries, Marine Corps
Cf. D570.348, Marine Corps (Land operations)

(570.5.A-Z) Individual engagements, A-Z
see D589.U6+

Aerial operations

(570.6) General works
see D606

570.65 General special

570.7 Individual squadrons

570.72 Transportation service
Including transports

570.73.A-Z Special, A-Z
e.g.

World War I (1914-1918)
Military operations
United States
Transportation service
Special, A-Z -- Continued
570.73.H7 Hoboken
570.73.L4 Le Mans
570.75 Services of supply. Quartermaster Corps
570.8.A-Z Special topics, A-Z
570.8.A6 Alien enemies
Cf. KF4850+, Law
Alien property custodian, see K728+
Americanization, see JK1758
Bolshevism (Russian Revolution), see DK265+
Bolshevism (Socialism), see HX1+
(570.8.C4) Civil liberty. Freedom of speech
see KF4741+
570.8.C5 Commissions of foreign nations, A-Z
e.g.
570.8.C5F8 Haut Commissariat de la République Française
Conscientious objectors (Law), see KF7266.C6
Conscientious objectors (Military administration), see UB341+
570.8.C7 Council of National Defense
570.8.C8A-Z Councils of defense, committees of public safety. By state, A-W
Economic aspects, see D635
Economic history of the war, see HC106.2
Education and the war, see D639.E3+
Espionage, see D619.3
570.8.E8 Executions
Food control, see HD9000.9.A1+
German-Americans and the war, see D620
570.8.I6 Indian soldiers
Cf. E98.M5, Military capacity of Indians (General)
Medals, etc.
See UB433, UC533, VB333, VC345
Missions to the United States
570.8.M5 General works
570.8.M6A-Z Individual missions, A-Z
570.8.M6B3 Belgian
570.8.M6B5 British
570.8.M6F4 French
570.8.M6G8 Guatemalan
570.8.M6I8 Italian
570.8.M6J4 Japanese
570.8.M6R7 Russian
570.8.M6S4 Serbian
570.8.N3 National Research Council
570.8.P7 Political prisoners
Prisons and prisoners, see D627.A+
Red Cross and hospital service, see D629.U6+

World War I (1914-1918)
Military operations
United States
Special topics, A-Z -- Continued

570.8.R4 Registration
Relief, charities, etc , see D637+
570.8.S4 Seizure and disposition of German ships
570.8.S5 Service flags
570.85.A-Z By region or state, A-Z
Alabama
570.85.A2 General works
570.85.A21A-Z Local, A-Z
Arizona
570.85.A7 General works
570.85.A71A-Z Local, A-Z
Arkansas
570.85.A8 General works
570.85.A81A-Z Local, A-Z
California
570.85.C2 General works
570.85.C21A-Z Local, A-Z
Colorado
570.85.C6 General works
570.85.C61A-Z Local, A-Z
Connecticut
570.85.C8 General works
570.85.C81A-Z Local, A-Z
Delaware
570.85.D4 General works
570.85.D41A-Z Local, A-Z
570.85.D6 District of Columbia
Florida
570.85.F5 General works
570.85.F51A-Z Local, A-Z
Georgia
570.85.G4 General works
570.85.G41A-Z Local, A-Z
Idaho
570.85.I2 General works
570.85.I21A-Z Local, A-Z
Illinois
570.85.I3 General works
570.85.I31A-Z Local, A-Z
Indiana
570.85.I6 General works
570.85.I7A-Z Local, A-Z
Iowa
570.85.I8 General works
570.85.I9A-Z Local, A-Z
Kansas
570.85.K2 General works
570.85.K21A-Z Local, A-Z
Kentucky

World War I (1914-1918)
Military operations
United States
By region or state, A-Z
Kentucky -- Continued

570.85.K4	General works
570.85.K41A-Z	Local, A-Z
	Louisiana
570.85.L6	General works
570.85.L61A-Z	Local, A-Z
	Maine
570.85.M2	General works
570.85.M21A-Z	Local, A-Z
	Maryland
570.85.M3	General works
570.85.M31A-Z	Local, A-Z
	Massachusetts
570.85.M4	General works
570.85.M41A-Z	Local, A-Z
	Michigan
570.85.M5	General works
570.85.M51A-Z	Local, A-Z
	Minnesota
570.85.M6	General works
570.85.M61A-Z	Local, A-Z
	Mississippi
570.85.M7	General works
570.85.M71A-Z	Local, A-Z
	Missouri
570.85.M8	General works
570.85.M81A-Z	Local, A-Z
	Montana
570.85.M9	General works
570.85.M91A-Z	Local, A-Z
	Nebraska
570.85.N19	General works
570.85.N2A-Z	Local, A-Z
	Nevada
570.85.N22	General works
570.85.N23A-Z	Local, A-Z
570.85.N24	New England
	New Hampshire
570.85.N25	General works
570.85.N26A-Z	Local, A-Z
	New Jersey
570.85.N3	General works
570.85.N31A-Z	Local, A-Z
	New Mexico
570.85.N33	General works
570.85.N34A-Z	Local, A-Z
	New York
570.85.N4	General works
570.85.N5A-Z	Local, A-Z

World War I (1914-1918)
Military operations
United States
By region or state, A-Z -- Continued
North Carolina
570.85.N8 General works
570.85.N81A-Z Local, A-Z
North Dakota
570.85.N9 General works
570.85.N91A-Z Local, A-Z
Ohio
570.85.O3 General works
570.85.O31A-Z Local, A-Z
Oklahoma
570.85.O5 General works
570.85.O51A-Z Local, A-Z
Oregon
570.85.O8 General works
570.85.O81A-Z Local, A-Z
Pennsylvania
570.85.P4 General works
570.85.P41A-Z Local, A-Z
Rhode Island
570.85.R4 General works
570.85.R41A-Z Local, A-Z
South Carolina
570.85.S6 General works
570.85.S61A-Z Local, A-Z
South Dakota
570.85.S7 General works
570.85.S71A-Z Local, A-Z
Tennessee
570.85.T2 General works
570.85.T21A-Z Local, A-Z
Texas
570.85.T4 General works
570.85.T41A-Z Local, A-Z
Utah
570.85.U8 General works
570.85.U81A-Z Local, A-Z
Vermont
570.85.V5 General works
570.85.V51A-Z Local, A-Z
Virginia
570.85.V8 General works
570.85.V81A-Z Local, A-Z
Washington
570.85.W3 General works
570.85.W31A-Z Local, A-Z
West Virginia
570.85.W4 General works
570.85.W41A-Z Local, A-Z
Wisconsin

World War I (1914-1918)
Military operations
United States
By region or state, A-Z
Wisconsin -- Continued
570.85.W6 General works
570.85.W61A-Z Local, A-Z
Wyoming
570.85.W8 General works
570.85.W81A-Z Local, A-Z
570.87.A-Z Outlying states, possessions, etc., A-Z
e.g.
570.87.H3 Hawaii
570.87.P7 Puerto Rico
570.88.A-Z Individual nationalities, A-Z
e.g.
570.88.B6 Bohemians in United States Army
570.9.A-Z Personal narratives and other accounts of American expeditions after declaration of war by the United States, A-Z
Cf. D640.A+, Personal narratives (General)
For military biography, see E745
Japanese
571 General works
572.A-Z Individual campaigns, sieges, battles, etc., A-Z
572.5 Thailand
Colonial
573 General works
German
574 General works
African
575 General works
576.A-Z Individual colonies, A-Z
e.g.
576.C3 Cameroons
576.G3 German East Africa
576.G5 German Southwest Africa
576.G7 Gold Coast (Ghana)
(576.K3) Kameruns (German West Africa)
See D576.C3
576.T7 Togoland
Pacific, Asiatic, etc.
577 General works
578.A-Z Individual colonies, A-Z
e.g.
578.N4 New Guinea
578.S2 Samoa (Western)
Naval operations
580 General works. Freedom of the seas
Anglo-German
581 General works. Blockade
582.A-Z By engagement, ship, etc., A-Z
e.g.

World War I (1914-1918)
Naval operations
Anglo-German
By engagement, ship, etc., A-Z -- Continued
582.A8 Ayesha (Schooner)
582.B3 Baralong (Cruiser)
582.D8 Dresden (Cruiser)
582.E6 Emden (Cruiser)
582.F2 Falkland Islands, Battle of, 1914
582.G7 Goeben and Breslau (Cruisers)
582.J8 Jutland, Battle of, 1916
582.K3 Karlsruhe (Cruiser)
582.K6 Königsberg (Cruiser)
582.K7 Kronprinz Wilhelm (Cruiser)
582.M6 Möwe (Steamship)
Franco-Austrian. French
583 General works
584.A-Z By engagement, ship, etc., A-Z
Japanese, see D571+
585 Russian
586 Egyptian
587 Turkish
588 Italian
589.A-Z Other, A-Z
e.g.
United States
589.U5 Documents
589.U6 General works
589.U7A-Z By engagement, ship, etc., A-Z
589.U8 Awarding of medals
Submarine operations
Including operations of submarine chasers
590 General works
German
591 General works
592.A-Z By engagement, ship, etc., A-Z
e.g.
592.D4 Deutschland (Submarine)
592.L8 Lusitania (Steamship)
592.S8 Sussex (Steamship)
English
593 General works
594.A-Z By engagement, ship, etc., A-Z
e.g.
594.Z4 Zeebrugge-Ostend raids, 1918
595.A-Z Other, A-Z
Aerial operations
600 General works
602 English
603 French
604 German
605 Russian
606 United States

World War I (1914-1918)
Aerial operations -- Continued
607.A-Z Other, A-Z
607.3 Engineering operations
(607.5) Gas warfare
See UG447
608 Tank operations
Cf. UG446.5, Military engineering
Medals, badges, decorations of honor
Including lists of recipients of medals
608.5 General works
608.6.A-Z By region or country, A-Z
Including individual recipients of medals
Registers, lists of dead and wounded, etc.
609.A2 General
609.A3-Z By region or country, A-Z
e.g.
Austria-Hungary
609.A6 General
609.A7 Slavic
609.A8 Hungarian
France
609.F8 General works
609.F82 French colonies
United States
609.U6 General
609.U7 Special
Diplomatic history
610 General works
611 General special
Including neutrality, etc.
Peace efforts during the war
Cf. D642+, Peace at close of the war
613 General works
613.5 Ford Peace Expedition
(614.A-Z) Treaties
see KZ185.5-KZ186.5
Individual regions or countries
615 Belgian neutrality. Case of Belgium
616 Greece and the war
Cf. DF837+, Greece under Constantine I
617 Italy and the war. Neutrality
Cf. D520.I7, Origins of the war in Italy
618 South America and the war
For individual countries, see D621.A+
619 United States and the war. Neutrality
Including reasons for American participation
619.3 German conspiracies. Propaganda. Espionage, etc.
619.5.A-Z Individual cases, A-Z
e.g.
619.5.A7 Archibald, James Francis J.
619.5.G7 Goltz, Horst von der

World War I (1914-1918)
Diplomatic history
Individual regions or countries
United States and the war. Neutrality
German conspiracies.
Propaganda. Espionage, etc.
Individual cases, A-Z -- Continued
619.5.M3 Martens, Ludwig Christian A.K.
619.5.O4 O'Leary, Jeremiah A.
619.5.P2 Papen, Franz von
620 German-Americans and the war
621.A-Z Other regions or countries, A-Z
e.g.
621.A8 Argentina
621.S3 Scandinavia
621.S4 Denmark
621.S45 Norway
621.S5 Sweden
Special topics
622 Catholic Church and the war
Occupied territory
Including underground movements
623.A2 General works
623.A3-Z By region or country, A-Z
e.g.
623.B4 Belgium
Atrocities. War crimes
For trials, see KZ1170+
625 General works
626.A-Z By region or country committing atrocity, A-Z
Prisoners and prisons
627.A1 Periodicals and societies (General)
627.A2 General works
627.A3-Z In individual countries, A-Z
Under each country, use .A1-.A19 for Periodicals
Medical and sanitary services. Hospitals. Red Cross
628 General works
629.A-Z By region or country
629.B4 Belgium
629.G7 Great Britain
Including Voluntary Aid Detachments work
United States
629.U6 General works
629.U62A-W By state, A-W
Hospitals and rest camps
629.U7A-Z In United States, by place, A-Z
629.U8A-Z In other countries, A-Z
Subarrange alphabetically by place, e.g. .F5-9, France; .F7, Langres
630.A-Z Biography, A-Z
e.g.
630.C3 Cavell, Edith

World War I (1914-1918)
Special topics -- Continued
Press. Censorship. Publicity
631 General works
632 The American press. Committee on public information
633 Other special
635 Economic aspects. Commerce, finance, postal service, etc. (General)
For specific topics or for individual countries, see HC, HF, HJ
Alien enemies
Cf. K7205, Law
636.A2 General works
636.A3-Z By region or country, A-Z
e.g.
636.F8 France
United States, see D570.8.A6
Relief work. Charities. Protection. Refugees
637 General works
638.A-Z By region or country, A-Z
e.g.
638.A7 Armenia
638.E2 East, Near
638.U5 United States
639.A-Z Other special topics, A-Z
For topics applicable only to the United States, see D570.8.A+
Afro-Americans, see D639.N4
(639.A6) Amnesty
see class K
639.A64 Anarchism. Anarchists
639.A65 Animals, War use of
639.A7 Anthropology and ethnology. Race problems
639.A75 Astrology
639.A8 Automobiles
Blacks, see D639.N4
639.B6 Boy Scouts
Cemeteries, see D639.D4
639.C38 Chaplains
639.C39 Chemical warfare
639.C4 Children. Orphans
639.C5 Christian Science
639.C54 Church of England
639.C75 Cryptography
639.D4 Dead, Care of. Burial. Cemeteries
Cf. D675.A+, Tomb of the Unknown Soldier
639.D45 Democracy and the war
639.D5 Deportation of Belgians, French, etc.
639.D53 Desertions
639.D6 Dogs
639.D7 Dreams
Education and the war

World War I (1914-1918)
Special topics
Other special topics, A-Z
Education and the war -- Continued
639.E2 General works
United States
639.E3 General works. Student Army Training Corps
639.E35 A.E.F. University
639.E37 A.E.F. in Great Britain
639.E4A-Z By college, school, etc., A-Z
e.g.
639.E4H3 Harvard University
639.E4S3 St. Louis public schools
639.E42A-Z By fraternity, A-Z
e.g.
639.E42S5 Sigma Alpha Epsilon
639.E45 France
639.E47 Germany
Great Britain
639.E5 General works
639.E52A-Z Colonies, A-Z
e.g.
639.E52C3 Canada
639.E53A-Z By university, A-Z
639.E6A-Z Other regions or countries, A-Z
639.E8 Entertainment and recreation for soldiers
639.F3 Fashion
639.F8 Freemasons
639.F9 Friends, Society of
639.G8 Gynecology
639.H5 Historic monuments
639.I2 Idealism
639.I5 Illegitimacy. War babies
639.J4 Jews
Including the Jewish pogroms in Ukraine
For the "Protocols of the wise men of Zion", see DS145.P49+
639.L2 Labor
For the labor situation in individual countries, see HD
639.L4 Lawyers
(639.L5) Library service to military personnel
see Z675.W2
639.M37 Mennonites
Merchant marine
639.M4 General works
639.M5A-Z By region or country, A-Z
Mutinies
639.M8 General works
639.M82A-Z By region or country, A-Z
Naturalized subjects in belligerent countries
639.N2 General works

World War I (1914-1918)
Special topics
Other special topics, A-Z
Naturalized subjects in belligerent countries -- Continued

639.N3A-Z By region or country, A-Z
For alien enemies in the United States, see D570.8.A6
For German-Americans in the United States, see D620

639.N4 Negroes. Afro-Americans. Blacks
639.P39 Photography
639.P45 Pigeons
639.P5 Population and the war
Propaganda
639.P6 General works
639.P7A-Z By region or country, A-Z
e.g.
639.P7F7 France
639.P7G3 Germany
For German propaganda in the United States, see D619.3

639.P75 Prophecies
639.P77 Protest movements
639.P78 Protestant churches
639.P8 Psychic phenomena
Public opinion
639.P87 General works
639.P88A-Z By region or country, A-Z
Race problems, see D639.A7
639.R4 Religious aspects
639.S15 Salvation Army
639.S2 Science and technology
Cf. UG447+, Chemical warfare
639.S3 Sex
639.S4 Slavs
639.S5 Snowshoes and snowshoeing
639.S6 Socialism
For Bolshevism (Russian Revolution), see DK265+
For Bolshevism (Socialism), see HX1+
Spies. Secret service
639.S7 General works
639.S8A-Z Individual, A-Z
e.g.
Mata Hari, see D639.S8Z4
639.S8Z4 Zelle (Mata Hari)
639.S9 Supplies
639.T35 Telegraph. Radio
639.T4 Telephone
639.T6 Toc H
639.T8 Transportation
Cf. D570.72, Transportation service (United States)

World War I (1914-1918)
Special topics
Other special topics, A-Z -- Continued
War babies, see D639.I5
639.W7 Women
639.Y7 Young Men's Christian Association. Young Women's Christian Association
Personal narratives and other accounts
Cf. D570.9.A+, Personal narratives of United States soldiers, etc.
640.A2 Collective
640.A22-Z Individual, A-Z
641 Armistice of Compiègne, 1918
Peace
Cf. D613+, Peace efforts during the war
642 Sources and documents
For legal works on treaties and surrender documents of Allied and Associated Powers, 1914-1920, see KZ185+
644 General works
645 General special
646 Pamphlets, etc.
Peace commissions (Personnel)
647.A2 General works
647.A3-Z Special. By region or country
e.g.
647.U6 United States
Special topics
Indemnity and reparation
Class here non-official works
Cf. KK7558.R46, Reparations and demontage
For texts of treaties and related legal materials, see KZ186.2
648 General works
649.A-Z By region or country, A-Z
649.G3 Germany
Dawes plan
see KZ186+
(649.G3A4) Texts. By date
(649.G3A45) Documents of the different countries. By date
649.G3A5-G3A59 Works on the Dawes plan. Alphabetically by author
649.G3A6-G3A7 Young plan
Subarrange like .G3A5-59
649.G3A6 Text. By date
649.G3A65 Documents of the different countries. By date
649.G3A7-G3A79 Works on the Young plan. Alphabetically by author
649.G3A8-G3Z General works
650.A-Z Other special, A-Z
e.g.

World War I (1914-1918)
Peace
Special topics
Other special, A-Z -- Continued
650.B7 Bridges of the Rhine
650.D5 Disarmament (German)
Eastern question, see D461+
Fiume (Rijeka), see D651.I6+
650.I6 Inter-allied Military Commission of Control in Germany
650.J4 Jews
650.M5 Military occupation of the Rhine
650.R8 Ruhr River and Valley
Shantung, see D651.C4+
650.T4 Territorial questions
Cf. KZ186+, Peace treaties
For special, see D651.A+
651.A-Z Individual regions or countries, A-Z
Class here works on the beginnings of organization of new countries where territorial questions are concerned
For treaties of the Allied and Associated Powers with the Central Powers, 1914-1920, see KZ186+
651.A42 Africa, German Southwest
651.A5 Albania and Epirus
651.A7 Armenia
651.A95 Austria
651.A98 Azerbaijan
651.B2 Baltic provinces
651.B25 Banat
651.B3 Belgium
651.B4 Bessarabia
651.B8 Bulgaria
651.C3 Cameroons
Carinthia, see DB281+
China
651.C4 General works
651.C5 Relations of America to Shantung
651.C6 Relations of Japan to Shantung
651.C7A-Z Relations of other countries, A-Z
651.C75 Circassia
651.C78 Croatia
651.C8 Cuba
651.C9 Czechoslovakia
651.D3 Dalmatia
Dobruja, see DR281.D5
651.E3 Egypt
651.E8 Estonia
France
General works
651.F5A1-F5A29 Collections

World War I (1914-1918)
Peace
Individual regions or countries, A-Z
France
General works -- Continued
(651.F5A3) Comprehensive treaty texts
see KZ186.2-5
651.F5A4-F5Z Other
Relations of United States to France
Including Defensive alliance between France, United States, and Great Britain
(651.F6A2) Treaty texts and related legal materials
see KZ186.2-5
651.F6A6-F6Z Nonofficial works
651.F7 Relations of other countries to France
651.G18 Galicia
651.G2 Georgia (Transcaucasia)
Germany
651.G3A2 Collections
Treaty text, see KZ186.5.A+
651.G4 Görz
651.G5-G7 Great Britain
Divide like D651.F5-D651.F7
651.G8 Greece. Unredeemed Greeks
651.H7 Hungary
651.I5 Istria
651.I6-I8 Italy
Including Fiume (Rijeka)
Divide like D651.F5-D651.F7
651.J3-J5 Japan
Divide like D651.F5-D651.F7
For Relation to Shantung, see D651.C6
Kamerun, see D651.C3
651.K87 Kurdistan
651.L4 Latvia. Letts
651.L45 Lebanon
651.L5 Lithuania
651.L8 Luxemburg
651.M3 Macedonia
Cf. DR2152+, Modern of history of Macedonia
651.M4 Mesopotamia
651.M7 Montenegro
651.N3 Nauru
651.N5 Nicaragua
651.P2 Pacific Islands, German
651.P3 Palestine
651.P4 Persia
651.P7 Poland
651.P75 Portugal
651.P8 Posen
651.P89 Prussia, East
651.P9 Prussia, West
651.R6 Romania

World War I (1914-1918)
Peace
Individual regions or countries, A-Z -- Continued
651.R8 Russia
651.R9 Ruthenia
651.S13 Saar Valley
651.S3 Samoa (Western)
651.S4 Schleswig
Serbia, see D651.Y8+
651.S5 Silesia (Upper)
651.S53 Slovenia
Soviet Union, see D651.R8
Spalato, see D651.D3
651.S7 Styria
651.S9 Syria
651.T5 Thrace
651.T7 Togoland
651.T8 Transylvania
651.T85 Trieste
651.T9 Turkey
651.T95 Tyrol
651.U6 Ukraine
Cf. DK508+, History of the Ukraine
Yugoslavia
651.Y8 General works
651.Y9A-Z Relations of other countries to Yugoslavia, A-Z
Cf. D465, Eastern question
For Fiume, see D651.I6+
Reconstruction. Post-war period
652 Sources and documents
653 General works
655 Other
Individual countries
United States
657 General works
658.A-W By state, A-W
e.g.
658.C2 California
658.I6 Indiana
658.M4 Massachusetts
658.M5 Michigan
658.N6 North Carolina
659.A-Z Other regions or countries, A-Z
Celebrations. Memorials. Monuments
Including memorials to special regiments, etc., with their history
Cf. D503, Museums
Cf. NA9325+, Fine arts
663 General works
665 Other
United States
670 General works

World War I (1914-1918)
Celebrations. Memorials. Monuments
United States -- Continued
671 Veterans Day (Armistice Day) services and addresses
673.A-W States, A-W
675.A-Z Cities, A-Z
e.g.
675.W2 Washington, D.C. Tomb of the Unknown Soldier
Including addresses
680.A-Z Other regions or countries, A-Z
Period between world wars (1919-1939)
720 General works
723 General special
725 Essays, etc.
European social life and customs. Civilization
726 General works
726.5 Fascism
727 Political and diplomatic history
728 Rome-Berlin axis
World War II (1939-1945)
731 Periodicals. Serials. Collections
732 Societies
Museums, exhibitions, etc.
733.A1 General works
733.A2-Z By region or country, A-Z
Under each country:
.x *General works*
.x2A-Z *Special, by city, A-Z*
733.D39 Denmark (General works)
733.D4C65 Copenhagen, Denmark. Museet for Danmarks frihedskamp 1940-1945
Congresses, conferences, etc.
734.A1 General works
Including works on two or more conferences
734.A2-Z Individual congresses, conferences, etc.
Sources and documents
735.A1 Collection and preservation of war records
735.A7 Atlantic Declaration, August 14, 1941
Biography
736 Collective
Individual
See country of the individual, DA-DU, E-F, or other appropriate class for biography
For personal narratives, see D811+
739 Collected works
740 Dictionaries
Causes. Origins. Aims
741 General works
742.A-Z By region or country, A-Z
743 General works
743.2 Pictorial works
For art and the war, see N9160+

World War II (1939-1945) -- Continued
743.22 Films, slides, etc. Catalogs
743.23 Motion pictures about the war
743.25 Posters
743.27 Collectibles
(743.3) Maps and atlases
See G1038, etc.
743.4 Study and teaching
743.42 Historiography
Including criticism of books on the war
743.5 Outlines, syllabi, tables, etc.
Including chronology of the war
743.6 Examinations, questions, etc.
743.7 Juvenile works. Elementary textbooks
743.9 Pamphlets, addresses, sermons, etc.
744 General special
Ethical and religious aspects
Cf. D810.C5+, Churches
744.4 General works
744.5.A-Z By region or country, A-Z
744.55 Psychological aspects
Social aspects
744.6 General works
744.7.A-Z By region or country, A-Z
War poetry
See Class P
745 Satire, caricature, etc.
745.2 English
745.3 French
745.5 German
745.7.A-Z Other languages, A-Z
e.g.
745.7.I8 Italian
745.7.P6 Polish
745.7.R9 Russian
(746-746.5) Views, films, posters, etc.
see D743.2+
747 Guides to the battlefields
For guides to special battlefields, see the individual battle
Diplomatic history. General relations (towards war)
748 General works
749 General special. Neutrality
749.5.A-Z Separate treaties during the war, A-Z
749.5.A5 Anglo-Soviet treaty, May 26, 1942
749.5.A55 Anti-Comintern pact
749.5.G7 Great Britain-Poland mutual assistance treaty, August 25, 1939
Hitler-Stalin pact, see D749.5.R8
749.5.R8 Russo-German treaty, August 23, 1939
749.5.U6 United States-Iraq mutual aid treaty, July 31, 1945
By region or country

World War II (1939-1945)
Diplomatic history. General relations (towards war)
By region or country -- Continued
750 Great Britain
751 Germany
752 France
752.8 The Americas. Neutrality
United States and the war. Neutrality
For reasons for American participation, see D742.U5
753 General works
753.2.A-Z Mutual aid (Lend-lease) agreements. By region or country, A-Z
753.3 Enemy conspiracies, propaganda, espionage, etc.
753.7 Asian Americans and the war
753.8 Japanese Americans and the war
Cf. D769.8.A6, Japanese-American relocation
754.A-Z Other regions, countries, or groups of countries, A-Z
e.g.
754.A34 Africa
754.A46 Alps, Western
754.B36 Balkan Peninsula
Ireland
754.I5 General works
754.I6 Irish Free State
754.I7 Northern Ireland
Levant, see D754.N34
754.N34 Near East
754.S29 Scandinavia
754.Y9 Yugoslavia
Military operations. The war effort
General works, see D743
By period
September 1939-December 1941
755 General works
755.1 September 1939-May 1940
755.2 1940
755.3 1941
755.4 1942
755.5 1943
755.6 1944
1945
755.7 General works
755.8 VE Day to VJ Day
By region
Western
756 General works
756.3 General special
756.5.A-Z Individual campaigns, battles, etc., A-Z
e.g.
756.5.A7 Ardennes, Battle of the, 1944-1945

World War II (1939-1945)
Military operations. The war effort
By region
Western
Individual campaigns,
battles, etc., A-Z -- Continued
756.5.A78 Arras, Battle of, 1940
756.5.C2 Calais, Battle of, 1940
756.5.D5 Dieppe raid, 1942
756.5.D8 Dunkirk, France, Battle of, 1940
756.5.M4 Meuse, Battle of the, 1940-
756.5.V3 Verdun, Battle of, 1940
Germany
757 General works
757.1 Armies
757.2 Army Corps
Infantry
757.3 General works
757.32.A-Z Divisions, regiments, etc. By author, A-Z
Mountain troops
757.39 General works
757.4.A-Z Divisions, regiments, etc. By author, A-Z
757.5 Artillery
Cf. D760.A+, By region or name
757.53 Anti-aircraft artillery
Panzer troops
757.54 General works
757.55.A-Z Divisions, regiments, etc. By name, A-Z
e.g.
757.55.R6 "Die roten Teufel"
757.56 Individual divisions. By number
757.57 Individual regiments. By number
757.6 Airborne troops
757.63 Parachute troops
757.64 Motorcycle troops
757.65 Signal Corps (Nachrichten truppen)
757.8 Engineers
757.83 Nebeltruppe
757.85 Waffenschutzstaffel of the Nazi Party (Waffen SS)
757.855 Technische Truppen
757.9.A-Z Local, A-Z
e.g.
757.9.H3 Hamburg
Great Britain
759 General works
759.5 Divisions, regiments, etc. By number
e.g.
759.5 51st The Fifty-first (Highland) Division
759.52 Artillery
Cf. D760.A+, By region or name
759.523 Anti-Aircraft Command
759.527 Light Anti-Aircraft Artillery regiments

World War II (1939-1945)
Military operations. The war effort
By region
Western
Great Britain
Divisions, regiments, etc. By number -- Continued
759.528 Armored divisions, regiments, etc.
759.53 Infantry
Cf. D760.A+, By region or name
759.54 Cavalry
Cf. D760.A+, By region or name
759.55 Engineers
Airborne troops
759.6 General works
759.63 Parachute troops
760.A-Z Special, by region or name, A-Z
e.g.
760.A1 Colonies (General)
760.A8 Auxiliary territorial service
760.D4 Devonshire Regiment
760.I7 Irish Guards
760.P5 Pioneer Corps
760.R7 Royal Armoured Corps
760.8.A-Z Local history, A-Z
e.g.
760.8.B3 Bath
760.8.B4 Belfast
760.8.B7 Bristol
760.8.C6 Coventry
760.8.D6 Dover
760.8.E3 East Downing
760.8.E7 Essex
760.8.E88 Exeter
760.8.K4 Kent
760.8.L6 Liverpool
760.8.L7 London
760.8.M3 Manchester
760.8.S75 Stepney (Middlesex)
France
761 General works
761.1 Armies
761.15 Army Corps
761.2 Divisions
Infantry
761.3 General works
761.38 Zouaves
761.5 Chasseurs. Chasseurs alpins
761.6 Artillery
761.7 Parachute troops
761.9.A-Z Other, A-Z
e.g.
761.9.A1 Colonies (General)

World War II (1939-1945)
Military operations. The war effort
By region
Western
France
Other, A-Z -- Continued
761.9.F7 France combattante. French volunteer force. Free French forces
761.9.P6 Polish forces
762.A-Z Local history, A-Z
e.g.
762.P3 Paris
763.A-Z Other regions or countries, A-Z
e.g.
Belgium
763.B4 General works
Divisions, regiments, etc.
763.B41 By number
763.B415 By name
763.B42A-Z Local history, A-Z
Denmark
763.D4 General works
763.D413-D42 Divisions, regiments, etc. By author, A-Z
763.D42A-Z Local history, A-Z
763.I2 Iceland
Italy
763.I8 General works
763.I813A-Z Divisions, regiments, etc. By author, A-Z
Corpo volontari della libertà
763.I815 General works
763.I817A-Z Divisions, brigades, A-Z
763.I82A-Z Local history, A-Z
763.L9 Luxembourg
763.M3 Malta
Netherlands
763.N4 General works
763.N41 Divisions, regiments, etc. (not A-Z)
763.N42A-Z Local history, A-Z
Norway
763.N6 General works
763.N613A-Z Divisions, regiments, etc. By author, A-Z
763.N62A-Z Local history, A-Z
763.S5 Sicily
763.5 Arctic regions
Including Greenland
Eastern
764 General works. Soviet Union (General)
764.3.A-Z Individual campaigns, battles, etc., A-Z
e.g.
764.3.L4 Leningrad, Siege of, 1941-1944
Saint Petersburg, Siege of, 1941-1944, see D764.3.L4
764.3.S7 Stalingrad, Battle of, 1942-1943

World War II (1939-1945)
Military operations. The war effort
By region
Eastern
General works.
Soviet Union (General) -- Continued
764.6 Divisions, regiments, etc. (not A-Z)
764.7.A-Z Local history, A-Z
e.g.
764.7.K5 Klintsy
Poland
765 General works
765.13 Divisions, regiments, etc. (not A-Z)
765.2.A-Z Local history, A-Z
e.g.
765.2.W3 Warsaw
765.2.W7 Wrocław (Breslau)
Finland
Including Continuation War, 1941-1944
765.3 General works
765.32 Divisions, regiments, etc. (not A-Z)
765.35.A-Z Local history, A-Z
Austria
765.4 General works
765.45.A-Z Local history, A-Z
e.g.
765.45.V6 Vorarlberg
Czechoslovakia
765.5 General works
765.53 Divisions, regiments, etc. (not A-Z)
765.55.A-Z Local history, A-Z
e.g.
765.55.P7 Prague
Hungary
765.56 General works
765.562.A-Z Local, A-Z
e.g.
765.562.B8 Budapest
Balkans and the Near East. Eastern
Mediterranean
766 General works
By country
766.3 Greece
766.32.A-Z Local history, A-Z
e.g.
766.32.C4 Cephalonia
Romania
766.4.A1-A15 Societies
766.4.A2 Collections
766.4.A3-Z General works
766.413 Divisions, regiments, etc. (not A-Z)
766.42.A-Z Local history, A-Z
Yugoslavia

World War II (1939-1945)
Military operations. The war effort
By region
Eastern
Balkans and the Near East. Eastern Mediterranean
By country
Yugoslavia -- Continued

766.6.A1-A15 Societies
766.6.A2 Collections
766.6.A3-Z General works
766.613 Divisions, regiments, etc. (not A-Z)
766.62.A-Z Local history, A-Z
e.g.
766.62.Z3 Zagreb
766.7.A-Z Other regions or countries, A-Z
e.g.
766.7.A4 Albania
766.7.C7 Crete
766.7.S9 Syria

Africa
766.8 General works
766.82 North Africa
766.83 Northeast Africa
766.84 East Africa
766.9 Egypt
766.92 Ethiopia
766.93 Libya
766.95 Zaire
766.96 French Equatorial Africa
766.97 South Africa
766.99.A-Z Other regions or countries, A-Z
e.g.
766.99.A4 Algeria
766.99.M3 Madagascar
766.99.T8 Tunisia

Far East. Battle of the Pacific
Including military and naval operations
767 General works
Japan
767.2 General works
767.23 Divisions, regiments, etc.)not A-Z)
767.25.A-Z Local history, A-Z
e.g.
767.25.H6 Hiroshima
767.25.N3 Nagasaki
Okinawa Island, see D767.99.O45
Ryukyu Islands, see D767.99.O45
767.255 Korea
767.3 China
Cochin China
767.35 General works

World War II (1939-1945)
Military operations. The war effort
By region
Far East. Battle of the Pacific
Cochin China -- Continued
767.352.A-Z Local history, A-Z
e.g.
767.352.S3 Saigon
767.4 Philippines
767.45 French Indonesia
767.47 Thailand
767.5 Malay Peninsula
767.55 Singapore
India. Burma
767.6 General works
767.63 Free India (Azad Hind), 1943-1945
Including Indian National Army, 1942-1945
767.7 Indonesia
Australia
767.8 General works
767.813.A-Z Divisions, regiments, etc. By author, A-Z
767.82.A-Z Local history, A-Z
New Zealand
767.85 General works
767.851.A-Z Divisions, regiments, etc. By author, A-Z
767.852.A-Z Local history, A-Z
Pacific islands
767.9 General works
(767.913) Aleutian Islands
see D769.87.A4
767.917 Gilbert Islands
767.92 Hawaiian Islands
767.94 Midway Islands
Cf. D774.M5, Battle of Midway, 1942
767.95 New Guinea
767.98 Solomon Islands
767.99.A-Z Other islands, A-Z
e.g.
767.99.I9 Iwo Jima
767.99.M3 Marshall Islands
767.99.N4 New Britain (Island)
767.99.O45 Okinawa Island. Ryukyu Islands
767.99.P4 Pelew Islands
767.99.S3 Saipan
The Americas
General works
768.15 Canada
Latin America
768.18 General works
768.2 Mexico
768.3 Brazil

World War II (1939-1945)
Military operations. The war effort
By region
The Americas -- Continued
United States
For the internal history of the United States, see E806+

769.A1-A15 Societies
769.A2 Collections
(769.A3) Compendium of legislative acts
see KF
769.A5-Z General works on participation in the war
769.1 General special
For reasons for American participation, see D742.U5
769.15 Pamphlets, etc.
Military operations
General works, see D769.A5+
769.2 General special
Individual expeditions, battles, etc.
See D756.5, D767, etc.
Armies, divisions, regiments, etc.
769.25 Headquarters, general staff, etc.
769.26 Armies. By number
769.27 Army Corps
Divisions, regiments, etc.
769.29 General works
Individual divisions
769.295.A-Z By name, A-Z
Subarrange by author
769.295.A5 Americal
769.3 By number
Subarrange by author
Armored divisions
769.305 General works
769.3053 By number
Subarrange by author
769.3055 Armored regiments. By name
Subarrange by author
769.3058 Reconnaissance battalions. By number
Subarrange by author
769.306 Tank battalions. By number
Subarrange by author
769.307 Tank destroyer battalions. By name
Subarrange by author
769.308 First Cavalry Division
769.309 Civil Affairs Division
Infantry
769.31 Regiments, combat teams, etc. By number
Subarrange by author
Cavalry
769.32 General works

World War II (1939-1945)
Military operations. The war effort
By region
The Americas
United States
Military operations
Armies, divisions, regiments, etc.
Cavalry -- Continued
769.325 Individual groups, squadrons, etc. By number
Subarrange by author
Engineers
769.33 General works
Individual battalions, brigades, etc.
769.335 By number
Subarrange by author
769.337.A-Z By name, A-Z
Subarrange by author
Field artillery
769.34 Individual groups, battalions, etc. By number
Subarrange by author
Anti-aircraft artillery
769.342 General works
769.343 Individual battalions, etc. By number
Airborne troops
769.345 General works
769.346 Individual battalions, etc. By number
769.347 Parachute troops
Chemical Corps
769.35 General works
769.353 Individual battalions, companies, etc. By type
Subarrange by number
Signal Corps
769.36 General works
769.363 Individual battalions, etc. By number
Marine Corps
Class here land operations only
Cf. D769.45, Naval operations
Cf. D790, Naval operations
769.369 General works
769.37 Individual divisions. By number
769.372 Individual regiments. By number
769.375 Chaplain Corps
Cf. D810.C35+, Chaplain service in the war
769.39 Women's Army Corps
769.4 Other
Naval operations
General works, see D773+

World War II (1939-1945)
Military operations. The war effort
By region
The Americas
United States
Naval operations -- Continued
769.45 General special
Including defensive areas, land batteries, Marine Corps
Cf. D769.369+, Land operations of Marine Corps
Individual engagements
See D767, D774
Fleets, squadrons, etc.
769.5 Individual fleets. By number
769.52.A-Z Forces, divisions. By name, A-Z
769.53 Task forces. By number
For individual ships, see D774.A+
Service squadrons
769.535 General works
769.537 Individual squadrons. By number
Naval operating bases
769.54 General works
769.542.A-Z Individual bases. By place, A-Z
e.g.
769.542.G5 Guam
Established by Lion Six
Construction battalions
769.55 General works
769.552 Individual battalions. By number
Construction battalion maintenance units
769.554 General works
769.555 Individual units. By number
769.585 Coast Guard Reserve (Temporary Reserve)
Including U.S. Volunteer Port Security Force
769.59 Chaplain Corps
Cf. D810.C35+, Chaplains (General)
769.597 Naval Reserve. Women's Reserve (WAVES)
769.598 Coast Guard Reserve. Women's Reserve (SPARS)
769.64 Sino-American Cooperative Organization
Transportation service
(769.72) General works
See D810.T8
Transportation Corps
769.73 General works
769.733 Individual battalions, etc. By number
Ordnance
769.74 General works
769.743 Individual battalions, etc. By number
Services of supply. Army service forces
769.75 General works

World War II (1939-1945)
Military operations. The war effort
By region
The Americas
United States
Naval operations
Services of supply.
Army service forces -- Continued
769.753 Quartermaster base depots. By number
769.76 Technical intelligence service
Provost-Marshal-General's Bureau
769.77 General works
769.775 Military Police
769.8.A-Z Special topics, A-Z
769.8.A5 Alien enemies
769.8.A6 Americans of Japanese descent. Japanese Americans. Japanese
Including evacuation, relocation, and internment
Cf. D753.8, Japanese American participation in the war
Cf. KF7224.5, Legal aspects
(769.8.C4) Civil liberty. Freedom of speech
see KF4741+
Conscientious objectors, see UB342.A+
Economic aspects, see HC106.4
Espionage, see D753.3
Food control, see HD9000.9.A1+
769.8.F6 Foreign population
Including contribution to the war effort
Cf. D769.8.A5, Alien enemies
769.8.F7A-Z Special nationalities, A-Z
Cf. D753.8, Japanese Americans and the war
Indians, see D810.I5
769.8.L6 Local government and the war
Negroes, see D810.N4
769.8.P6 Political prisoners
Red Cross and hospital service, see D807.U6+
Relief, charities, etc , see D809.U5
769.8.S5 Service flags
769.8.T8 Trophies, Military
769.85.A-Z By region or state, A-Z
Alabama
769.85.A2 General works
769.85.A21A-Z Local, A-Z
Arizona
769.85.A7 General works
769.85.A71A-Z Local, A-Z
Arkansas
769.85.A8 General works
769.85.A81A-Z Local, A-Z
California

World War II (1939-1945)
Military operations. The war effort
By region
The Americas
United States
By region or state, A-Z
California -- Continued
769.85.C2 General works
769.85.C21A-Z Local, A-Z
Colorado
769.85.C6 General works
769.85.C61A-Z Local, A-Z
Connecticut
769.85.C8 General works
769.85.C81A-Z Local, A-Z
Delaware
769.85.D4 General works
769.85.D41A-Z Local, A-Z
769.85.D6 District of Columbia
Florida
769.85.F5 General works
769.85.F51A-Z Local, A-Z
Georgia
769.85.G4 General works
769.85.G41A-Z Local, A-Z
Idaho
769.85.I2 General works
769.85.I21A-Z Local, A-Z
Illinois
769.85.I3 General works
769.85.I31A-Z Local, A-Z
Indiana
769.85.I6 General works
769.85.I7A-Z Local, A-Z
Iowa
769.85.I8 General works
769.85.I9A-Z Local, A-Z
Kansas
769.85.K2 General works
769.85.K21A-Z Local, A-Z
Kentucky
769.85.K4 General works
769.85.K41A-Z Local, A-Z
Louisiana
769.85.L6 General works
769.85.L61A-Z Local, A-Z
Maine
769.85.M2 General works
769.85.M21A-Z Local, A-Z
Maryland
769.85.M3 General works
769.85.M31A-Z Local, A-Z
Massachusetts

World War II (1939-1945)
Military operations. The war effort
By region
The Americas
United States
By region or state, A-Z
Massachusetts -- Continued

769.85.M4	General works
769.85.M41A-Z	Local, A-Z
	Michigan
769.85.M5	General works
769.85.M51A-Z	Local, A-Z
	Minnesota
769.85.M6	General works
769.85.M61A-Z	Local, A-Z
	Mississippi
769.85.M7	General works
769.85.M71A-Z	Local, A-Z
	Missouri
769.85.M8	General works
769.85.M81A-Z	Local, A-Z
	Montana
769.85.M9	General works
769.85.M91A-Z	Local, A-Z
	Nebraska
769.85.N19	General works
769.85.N2A-Z	Local, A-Z
	Nevada
769.85.N22	General works
769.85.N23A-Z	Local, A-Z
	New Hampshire
769.85.N25	General works
769.85.N26A-Z	Local, A-Z
	New Jersey
769.85.N3	General works
769.85.N31A-Z	Local, A-Z
	New Mexico
769.85.N33	General works
769.85.N34A-Z	Local, A-Z
	New York
769.85.N4	General works
769.85.N5A-Z	Local, A-Z
	North Carolina
769.85.N8	General works
769.85.N81A-Z	Local, A-Z
	North Dakota
769.85.N9	General works
769.85.N91A-Z	Local, A-Z
	Ohio
769.85.O3	General works
769.85.O31A-Z	Local, A-Z
	Oklahoma
769.85.O5	General works

World War II (1939-1945)
Military operations. The war effort
By region
The Americas
United States
By region or state, A-Z
Oklahoma -- Continued

769.85.O51A-Z Local, A-Z

Oregon
769.85.O8 General works
769.85.O81A-Z Local, A-Z

Pennsylvania
769.85.P4 General works
769.85.P41A-Z Local, A-Z

Rhode Island
769.85.R4 General works
769.85.R41A-Z Local, A-Z

South Carolina
769.85.S6 General works
769.85.S61A-Z Local, A-Z

South Dakota
769.85.S7 General works
769.85.S71A-Z Local, A-Z

Tennessee
769.85.T2 General works
769.85.T21A-Z Local, A-Z

Texas
769.85.T4 General works
769.85.T41A-Z Local, A-Z

Utah
769.85.U8 General works
769.85.U81A-Z Local, A-Z

Vermont
769.85.V5 General works
769.85.V51A-Z Local, A-Z

Virginia
769.85.V8 General works
769.85.V81A-Z Local, A-Z

Washington
769.85.W3 General works
769.85.W31A-Z Local, A-Z

West Virginia
769.85.W4 General works
769.85.W41A-Z Local, A-Z

Wisconsin
769.85.W6 General works
769.85.W61A-Z Local, A-Z

Wyoming
769.85.W8 General works
769.85.W81A-Z Local, A-Z

769.87.A-Z Outlying possessions, A-Z
769.87.A4 Aleutian Islands

World War II (1939-1945)
Military operations. The war effort
By region
The Americas
United States
Outlying possessions, A-Z -- Continued
(769.87.H3) Hawaii
see D767.92
769.88.A-Z Special nationalities, A-Z
e.g.
769.88.A7 Armenian
(769.9) Personal narratives and other accounts
See D811
Naval operations
For freedom of the seas, see KZA1348+
770 General works. Battle of the Atlantic
Anglo-German
771 General works. Blockade
772.A-Z By engagement, ship, etc., A-Z
e.g.
772.A4 Altmark (Ship)
772.A5 Anglo-Saxon (Steamship)
772.A66 Ark Royal (Aircraft carrier)
772.A7 Athenia (Steamship)
772.B5 Bismarck (Battleship)
772.D7 Dragon (Cruiser)
772.F5 Firedrake (Destroyer)
772.G7 Admiral Graf Spee (Battleship)
772.H6 Hood (Battle cruiser)
772.P4 Penelope (Cruiser)
772.S25 San Demetrio (Tanker)
772.3 Russo-German
Including Arctic Ocean and Baltic Sea only
United States
773 General works. Blockade. Patrol
774.A-Z By engagement, ship, etc., A-Z
e.g.
774.A7 Arkansas (Battleship)
774.B57 Bismarck Sea, Battle of the, 1943
774.B6 Boise (Cruiser)
774.D3 Dashiell (Destroyer)
774.E5 Enterprise (Aircraft carrier)
774.E7 Essex (Aircraft carrier)
774.G3 General W.H. Gordon (Transport)
774.H3 Hancock (Aircraft carrier)
774.H4 Helena (Cruiser)
774.H6 Hornet (Aircraft carrier)
774.L4 Lexington (Aircraft carrier, 1st of the name)
774.M3 Marblehead (Cruiser)
774.M35 Maryland (Battleship)
774.M5 Midway, Battle of, 1942
774.N4 New Orleans (Cruiser)
774.O3 O'Bannon (Destroyer)

	World War II (1939-1945)
	Naval operations
	United States
	By engagement, ship, etc., A-Z -- Continued
774.P7	Princess (Aircraft carrier)
774.S3	Saratoga (Aircraft carrier)
774.S318	Savo Island, Battle of, 1942
774.S32	Savo Island (Aircraft carrier)
774.S6	South Dakota (Battleship)
	Anglo-Italian
775	General works
775.5.A-Z	By engagement, ship, etc., A-Z
	e.g.
775.5.S8	Sydney (Cruiser)
	Japan
777	General works
777.5.A-Z	By engagement, ship, etc., A-Z
	Bismarck Sea, Battle of the, 1943, see D774.B57
	Midway, Battle of, 1942, see D774.M5
	Savo Island, Battle of, 1942, see D774.S318
779.A-Z	Other regions or countries, A-Z
	Submarine operations
	Including operations of submarine chasers
780	General works
	Including operations of submarine chasers
	Germany
781	General works
782.A-Z	By engagement, ship, etc., A-Z
	e.g.
782.C6	City of Benares (Steamship)
782.M6	Montevideo (Steamship)
782.R6	Robin Moor (Steamship)
	United States
783	General works
783.5.A-Z	By engagement, ship, etc., A-Z
	e.g.
783.5.C6	Coast guard reserve boat 3070
783.5.S4	Seawolf (Submarine)
783.5.S5	Silversides (Submarine)
783.5.S8	Sturgeon (Submarine)
	Japan
783.6	General works
783.7	By engagement, ship, etc. (not A-Z)
784.A-Z	Other regions or countries, A-Z
	Aerial operations
785	General works
	U.S. Strategic Bombing Survey reports
785.U57	General works
785.U58A-Z	By industry, A-Z
785.U6	European War
785.U63	Pacific War
786	Great Britain
787	Germany

World War II (1939-1945)
Aerial operations -- Continued
788 France
790 United States
792.A-Z Other regions or countries, A-Z
793 Tank operations
Cf. UE159, Tactics
Cf. UG446.5, Military engineering
794 Cavalry operations
Cf. D769.32+, United States
794.5 Commando operations
Engineering operations
795.A2 General works
795.A3-Z By region or country, A-Z
Medals, badges, decorations of honor
Including lists of recipients and individual recipients of medals
796 General works
796.5.A-Z By region or country, A-Z
Registers, lists of dead and wounded, etc.
797.A2 General
797.A3-Z By region or country, A-Z
Under each country:
.x *General works*
.x2A-Z *Local, A-Z*
Press. Censorship. Publicity. Radio
798 General works
799.A-Z By region or country, A-Z
800 Economic aspects. Commerce, finance, postal service, etc. (General)
For special topics or individual countries, see HC, HF, HJ
Alien enemies
801.A2 General works
801.A3-Z By region or country, A-Z
e.g.
801.F8 France
United States, see D769.8.A6
Occupied territory
Including underground movements
802.A2 General works
802.A3-Z By region or country, A-Z
e.g.
Apply table at D797.A3-Z
802.C7 Croatia
802.M3 Marshall Islands
802.N7-N72 Norway
802.R95 Ruthenia
802.S55 Sicily
802.S67 Slovenia
802.T7 Tripolitania
Atrocities. War crimes.
For war crimes trials, see KZ1174+

	World War II (1939-1945)
	Atrocities. War crimes -- Continued
803	General works
804.A-Z	By region or country (committing atrocity), A-Z
	Holocaust
	Cf. BM645.H6, Holocaust in Jewish theology
	Cf. D810.J4, Jewish military participation in World War II
	For works on the Holocaust in a particular locality, see DS135.A+
804.15	Periodicals. Societies. Serials
	Museums. Exhibitions, etc.
	Cf. D805.5.A+, Individual concentration camp memorials
804.17	General works
804.175.A-Z	Individual. By city, A-Z
804.18	Congresses
804.19	Sources and documents
	Biography and memoirs (General and Jewish)
804.195	Collective
	Individual by place, see DS135.A+
804.196	Individual not limited by place, A-Z
804.25	Dictionaries. Chronological tables, outlines, etc.
804.3	General works
804.32	Pictorial works
804.33	Study and teaching
804.34	Juvenile literature
804.348	Historiography
804.35	Holocaust denial literature
804.355	Holocaust denial. Criticism of Holocaust denial literature
	Public opinion
804.44	General works
804.45.A-Z	By region or country, A-Z
	Special groups of Jewish victims
804.47	Women
804.48	Children
804.5.A-Z	Other victim groups, A-Z
	Including biography (Individual and collective)
804.5.C45	Children (General)
	Cf. D804.48, Jewish children
804.5.G38	Gays
804.5.G85	Gypsies. Romanies
	Cf. D810.G9, Gypsies. Gypsy military participation
804.5.H35	Handicapped
	Including mentally and physically handicapped
804.5.J44	Jehovah's Witnesses
	Romanies, see D804.5.G85
	Rescue efforts
804.6	General works
	Righteous Gentiles

World War II (1939-1945)
Atrocities. War crimes
Holocaust
Rescue efforts
Righteous Gentiles -- Continued
804.65 General works
804.66.A-Z Individual, A-Z
804.7.A-Z Other topics, A-Z
804.7.D43 Death marches
804.7.E26 Economic aspects
804.7.P73 Press coverage
Prisoners and prisons
Including internment camps, concentration camps, death camps, etc.
805.A1 Periodicals and societies
805.A2 General works
805.A3-Z By individual regions or countries, A-Z
Under each country:
.A1-.A19 *Periodicals*
.A2-.Z7 *General works*
(.xZ8-9) *Individual prisons, camps, etc., see D805.5*
805.5.A-Z Individual prisons, camps, etc. By name, A-Z
e. g.
Including individual concentration camp memorials
805.5.A96 Auschwitz
Medical and sanitary services. Hospitals. Red Cross
806 General works
807.A-Z By region or country, A-Z
e.g.
807.A8 Australia
807.H3 Hawaii
United States
807.U6 General works
807.U62A-W By state, A-W
Hawaii, see D807.H3
(807.U72-U74) Army hospitals
(807.U85-U87) Navy hospitals
Relief work. Charities. Protection. Refugees. Displaced persons
Cf. D804.6+, Rescue efforts in the Holocaust
808 General works
809.A-Z By region or country, A-Z
e. g.
809.B4 Belgium
809.U5 United States
Including American relief in other countries
810.A-Z Other special topics, A-Z
Adventists, see D810.C53
Afro-Americans, see D810.N4
810.A53 Aleuts
810.A6 Anarchism. Anarchists

World War II (1939-1945)
Other special topics, A-Z -- Continued

810.A65 Animals in the war
Including war use of dogs
Cf. D810.V45, Veterinary service
810.A67 Antiquities
810.A7 Art and the war
810.A75 Astrology
810.A79 Athletes
810.B3 Bacterial warfare
Baptists, see D810.C56
810.B37 Basques
Blacks, see D810.N4
810.B66 Bomb reconnaissance
810.B7 Boy Scouts
810.B83 Buddhism
Burials, see D810.D4
810.C2 Camouflage
Carrier pigeons, see D810.P53
810.C26 Cartography
810.C27 Catalans
Catholic Church, see D810.C6
Chaplains (General)
810.C35 General works
810.C36A-Z By region or country, A-Z
e.g.
810.C36U6 United States
Cf. D769.375, Army Chaplain Corps (U.S.)
Cf. D769.59, Navy Chaplain Corps (U.S.)
810.C38 Chemical warfare
810.C4 Children. Orphans
Church of Christ, Scientist, see D810.C62
Church of the Brethren, see D810.C63
Churches
810.C5 General works
By denomination
810.C53 Adventists
810.C56 Baptists
810.C6 Catholic Church
810.C62 Church of Christ, Scientist
810.C63 Church of the Brethren
810.C64 Evangelical and Reformed Church
810.C65 Friends, Society of
810.C66 Lutheran Church
810.C665 Mennonites
810.C67 Methodist Church
810.C674 Nihon Kirisuto Kyōdan
810.C6745 Orthodox Eastern Church
810.C68 Presbyterian Church
810.C69 Civil defense
For technical works, see UA926+
810.C698 Comfort women
810.C7 Communications

World War II (1939-1945)
Other special topics, A-Z -- Continued
810.C8 Confiscation
810.C82 Conscientious objectors. War resisters. Draft resisters
810.C83 Cossacks
810.C88 Cryptography
810.D4 Dead, Care of. Burial. Cemeteries
810.D5 Deportation
810.D6 Destruction and pillage
Cf. D785.U57+, United States Strategic Bombing Survey reports
Draft resisters, see D810.C82
Education and the war
810.E2 General works
United States
810.E3 General works
810.E4A-W By state, A-W
810.E45A-Z By college, school, etc., A-Z
810.E46A-Z By fraternity, A-Z
810.E5A-Z Other regions or countries, A-Z
810.E6 Elks, Benevolent and Protective Order of
810.E8 Entertainment and recreation for soldiers
Evangelical and Reformed Church, see D810.C64
Friends, Society of, see D810.C65
810.F83 Fuel supplies
810.G57 Girl Scouts
810.G6 Governments in exile
810.G9 Gypsies. Gypsy military participation
Homing pigeons, see D810.P53
810.I5 Indians
Jewish military participation, see D810.J4
810.J4 Jews. Jewish military participation
Cf. D804.15+, Holocaust
810.L4 Lawyers and the war
810.L53 Libraries
Class here works on the condition of libraries during the war, the effect of the war on libraries, etc.
For works on library service to military personnel, see Z675.W2
Logistics
810.L64 General works
810.L642A-Z By region or country, A-Z
Lutherans, see D810.C66
Mennonites, see D810.C665
Merchant marine, see D810.T8
810.M42 Meteorology
Methodists, see D810.C67
Military intelligence, see D810.S7+
810.M8 Muslims
Naturalized subjects in belligerent countries
810.N2 General works

World War II (1939-1945)
Other special topics, A-Z
Naturalized subjects
in belligerent countries -- Continued
810.N3A-Z By region or country, A-Z
For alien enemies in the United States, see D769.8.A6
For Japanese Americans in the United States, see D753.8
810.N4 Negroes. Afro-Americans. Blacks
Nihon Kirisuto Kyōdan, see D810.C674
Orthodox Eastern Church, see D810.C6745
810.P4 Photography
810.P53 Pigeons
Presbyterians, see D810.C68
Propaganda
810.P6 General works
810.P7A-Z By region or country, A-Z
Property damage, see D810.D6
810.P75 Prophecies
810.P76 Protest movements
Public opinion
810.P8 General works
810.P85A-Z By region or country, A-Z
810.R3 Race problems
810.R33 Radio, radar, etc.
810.R6 Rotary International
810.S2 Science and technology
Search and rescue operations
810.S42 General works
810.S45A-Z By region or country, A-Z
Seventh-Day Adventists, see D810.C53
810.S46 Sex
Cf. D810.C698, Comfort women
810.S47 Shinto
810.S5 Slavs
810.S6 Socialism
810.S65 Spaniards
Spies. Secret service. Military intelligence
810.S7 General works
810.S8A-Z Individual spies, A-Z
Technology, see D810.S2
810.T4 Temperance
810.T8 Transportation
Including merchant marine
810.V45 Veterinary service
War resisters, see D810.C82
Weather, see D810.M42
810.W7 Women
810.Y7 Young Men's Christian Association. Young Women's Christian Association
810.Y74 Youth

World War II (1939-1945) -- Continued
Personal narratives and other accounts
For collective military biography of World War II, see D736
For individual biography, see country of the individual in DA-F
811.A2 Collections
811.A3-Z Individual, A-Z
811.5 Narratives by noncombatants
Including collective and individual
Armistice
812 General works
813.A-Z By region or country, A-Z
Peace
814 Sources and documents
Surrender documents. By country
814.1 Germany
814.2 Italy
814.3 Japan
814.4 Council of Foreign Ministers (General)
814.413 Meeting in London, September 11-October 2, 1945
814.415 Meeting in Moscow, December 16-26, 1945
814.42 Meeting in Paris, April, 1946
814.425 Meeting in Paris, June 15-July 1946
814.43 Meeting in New York, November-December, 1946
814.44 Meeting in Moscow, March 10-April 24, 1947
814.45 Meeting in London, November 25-December 16, 1947
814.46 Meeting in Paris, May 23-June 20, 1949
814.47 Meeting in Berlin, January 25-February 18, 1954
Treaties with Axis powers
814.55 Collections
814.56 Peace conferences (General)
814.565 Paris Conference, July 29-October 15, 1946
814.6 Germany
814.7 Italy
814.8 Japan
814.9.A-Z Other countries, A-Z
815 General works
816 General special
816.5 Pamphlets, etc.
818 Indemnity and reparation
819.A-Z By region or country, A-Z
820.A-Z Other special topics, A-Z
820.D5 Disarmament
Population transfers
820.P7 General works
820.P72A-Z By nationality, A-Z
820.T4 Territorial questions
Special, see D821.A+

World War II (1939-1945)
Peace -- Continued
821.A-Z By country, groups of countries, etc., A-Z
Class here beginnings of organization of new countries where territorial questions are concerned
e.g.
For annual reports, etc., of areas under international trusteeship, see JN and JQ
821.L4 Levant
821.L5 Lithuania
821.P3 Palestine
821.T8 Transylvania
821.Y8 Yugoslavia
Including Trieste
Reconstruction
824 Sources and documents
825 General works
826 Pamphlets, etc.
By region or country
United States
827 General works
828.A-W By state, A-W
829.A-Z Other countries or groups of countries, nationalities, etc., A-Z
e.g.
829.A33 Africa, South
829.D8 Dutch East Indies
829.E2 East Asia
829.J4 Jews
Cf. D829.P3, Palestine
829.L5 Lithuania
829.P3 Palestine
Cf. D829.J4, Jews
Celebrations. Memorials. Monuments
For memorials to special divisions, etc., see the history of the division
830 General works
831 Other
By region or country
United States
833 General works
835.A-W By state, A-W
836.A-Z By city, A-Z
838.A-Z Other regions or countries, A-Z
e.g.
Great Britain
838.G6 General works
838.G7A-Z Local, A-Z
Post-war history (1945-)
For Europe, 1945- , see D1050+
839 Periodicals. Societies. Serials
839.2 Congresses. Conferences, etc.

Post-war history (1945-) -- Continued
839.3 Sources and documents
Biography
839.5 Collective
839.7.A-Z Individual, A-Z
840 General works
842 General special
Including refugees
842.2 Military history
842.3 Naval history
1945-1965
Periodicals, see D839
842.5 General works
Political and diplomatic history
843 General works
844 Pamphlets, etc.
845 North Atlantic Treaty, 1949
845.2 North Atlantic Treaty Council
847 Soviet bloc. Communist countries
847.2 Warsaw pact, 1955
1965-1989
Periodicals, see D839
848 General works
Political and diplomatic history
849 General works
849.5 Pamphlets, etc.
850 Soviet bloc. Communist countries
1989-
856 General works
857 Social life and customs. Civilization. Intellectual life
860 Political and diplomatic history
Developing countries
880 Periodicals. Societies. Serials
881 Congresses
882 Sources and documents
883 General works
Foreign and general relations
887 General works
888.A-Z Relations with individual countries, A-Z
Eastern hemisphere
890 Periodicals. Societies. Serials
891 General works
892 Description
For voyages and travels, see G490
893 History
Europe (General)
For individual countries, see DA-DR
900 Geography
Description and travel
901 Periodicals. Collections
904 Gazetteers
905 Place names (General)

Europe (General)
Description and travel -- Continued
907 General works
908 Directories
909 Guidebooks
910 Pamphlets, etc.
Including minor cruises, itineraries, etc.
910.5 Monumental and picturesque. Castles, halls, cathedrals, etc. Views
By period
911 Through 1450
913 1451-1600
915 1601-1700
917 1701-1800
919 1801-1900
921 1901-1950
922 1951-1970
923 1971-
By region
Black Sea, see DJK63
965 Northern Europe
965.5 North Sea
967 Western Europe
Central Europe, see DAW1014+
Eastern Europe, see DJK13+
Balkan Peninsula, see DR11.5+
971 Adriatic Sea
972 East-northern Mediterranean. Adriatic and Aegean
Cf. DF895+, Islands of the Aegean
Cf. DF901.C9, Cyclades
Cf. DF901.I695, Ionian Sea
Cf. DS51.A+, Turkish Islands in the Aegean Sea
973 General Mediterranean
Including modern geography
974 Southern Europe
Including general western Mediterranean
975 Old World (Europe, including Egypt and Palestine)
Eastern Mediterranean (Bible lands, Orient), see DS41+
980 Juvenile travel
Antiquities, see CC160+
Antiquities, Prehistoric, see GN803+
990 Ethnography
History
For history of Europe to 1945, see D1+
1945-
1050 Periodicals. Sources and documents. Collections
1050.5 Congresses. Conferences, etc.
Study and teaching
1050.8 General works

Europe (General)
History
1945-
Study and teaching -- Continued
1050.82.A-Z By region or country, A-Z
Under each country:
.x General works
.x2A-Z Schools. By place, A-Z
1051 General works
1053 General special
1055 Social life and customs. Civilization
Ethnography
1056 General works
1056.2.A-Z Individual elements in the population not limited to special territorial divisions, A-Z
1056.2.A43 Algerians
1056.2.A7 Arabs
1056.2.B55 Blacks
1056.2.C55 Chinese
1056.2.F75 Frisians
1056.2.G35 Galicians (Spain)
1056.2.G45 Germans
1056.2.G73 Greeks
1056.2.I73 Iranians
1056.2.M87 Muslims
1056.2.P64 Poles
1056.2.S47 Serbs
1056.2.T87 Turks
1056.2.Y83 Yugoslavs
Political and diplomatic history
1058 General works
1060 European federation
Cf. JN15, Constitutional history
1065.A-Z Relations with region and countries, A-Z
For relations with individual countries prior to 1945, see D34.A+
1065.U5 United States
Biography
Collective
1070 General works
1071 Women
1072 Public men
1073 Rulers, kings, etc.
1074 Queens, princesses, etc.
1075.A-Z Individual, A-Z
1989-
2001 Congresses
2003 General works
2009 Political history

History of Great Britain
Historiography
1 General works
Biography of historians
3.A1 Collective
3.A2-Z Individual, A-Z
e.g.
3.F9 Froude, James Anthony
3.M3 Macaulay, Thomas Babington Macaulay, baron
For collected works and works about Macaulay as a literary author, see PR4963
4 Study and teaching
British Empire. Commonwealth of Nations. The Commonwealth
Including Great Britain, the dominions, and the colonies.
For administration of the British Colonies collectively and colonial policy, see JV1000+
For individual dominions and colonies, see DS-DU, F, etc.
10 Periodicals. Societies. Collections
10.5 General works
11 Description and travel
13 Historical geography
16 History
Biography and memoirs
16.8 Collective
17.A-Z Individual, A-Z
e.g.
17.D9 Dufferin and Ava, Frederick Temple Hamilton-Temple Blackwood, 1st Marquis of
17.E4 Elgin, James Bruce, 8th Earl of
17.M2 Maitland, Sir Thomas
17.W4 Weld, Sir Frederick Aloysius
Political history. Imperial federation
Cf. JN248, Political institutions and public administration
18 General works
18.2.A-Z Relations with Commonwealth countries. By region or country, A-Z
England
20 Periodicals. Societies
Museums, exhibitions, etc.
22.A1 General works
22.A2-Z By city and museum, A-Z
Collections
25 Official records. Sources and documents
25.A2 Deputy Keeper. By date
25.B1 Record Commission. By date
25.B5 Chronicles. By number

England
Collections
Official records.
Sources and documents -- Continued

25.C1 Calendars. By date
Class here calendars and inventories of the pre-ca. 1800 official records enumerated below. Order of entry is generally based on Scargill-Birds' Guide to the documents in the Public Record Office (1908)
For calendars and inventories of post-ca. 1800 official records, see CD1040+

25.C3 Calendarium genealogicum. Genealogical abstracts of the Inquisitions post mortem, etc., Henry III and Edward I
Edited by Charles Roberts.

25.C58 Calendar of documents relating to Scotland preserved in Her Majesty's Public Record Office. 1108-1509

25.C6 Calendar of entries in the Papal Registers relating to Great Britain and Ireland 1198-1471
Edited by W.H. Bliss and J.A. Twemlow

25.C7 Registers of the Privy Council. 1542-1627
Edited by J.R. Dasent

25.C8 Charter Rolls. 11 Henry III to 28 Edward I. 1257-1516

Patent Rolls

25.C91 Henry III. 1216-1272
25.C915 Edward I. 1272-1307
25.C917 Edward II. 1307-1327
25.C919 Edward III. 1327-1377
25.C92 Richard II. 1377-1399
25.C922 Henry IV. 1399-1413
25.C924 Henry V. 1413-1422
25.C928 Henry VI. 1422-1461
25.C93 Edward IV. 1461-1477
25.C94 Edward IV, Edward V, Richard III. 1476-1485
25.C945 Henry VII. 1485-1509
25.C95 Edward VI. 1547-1553
25.C952 Philip and Mary. 1553-1558
25.C953 Elizabeth. 1558-1603

Close Rolls

25.D314 Henry III. 1227-1272
25.D315 Edward I. 1272-1307
25.D317 Edward II. 1307-1327
25.D319 Edward III. 1327-1377
25.D32 Richard II. 1377-1399
25.D322 Henry IV. 1399-1413
25.D324 Henry V. 1413-1422
25.D325 Henry VI. 1422-1477
25.D328 Edward IV. 1461-1476
25.D3285 Edward IV, Edward V, Richard III. 1476-1485

England
Collections
Official records. Sources and documents
Calendars
Close Rolls -- Continued
25.D3286 Henry VII. 1485-1500
25.D33 Calendar of the Fine rolls preserved in the Public Record Office. 1272-1509
25.D36 Calender of the liberate rolls preserved in the Public Record Office. 1226-1272
25.D37 Calender of Chancery warrants preserved in the Public Record Office. 1244-1326
25.D38 Calendar of various Chancery rolls. 1277-1326
Inquisitions Post Mortem
25.D5 Henry III, Edward I, Edward II, Edward III
25.D52 Henry III
25.D6 Calendar of inquisitions miscellaneous (Chancery) preserved in the Public Record Office. 1219-1337
25.D7 Inquisitions and assessments relating to feudal aids. 1284-1431
Calendars of State Papers, etc.
25.E1 Letters and Papers (Foreign and Domestic). Henry VIII. 1509-1546
State Papers (Domestic)
25.E3 Edward VI to James I and addenda. 1547-1625
25.E5 Charles I. 1625-1649
25.E7 Commonwealth. 1649-1660
25.E9 Committee for the advance of money. 1642-1656
25.F1 Committee for Compounding. 1643-1660
25.F3 Charles II. 1660-1685
25.F4 James II. 1685-1689
25.F5 William and Mary. 1689-1695
25.F52 William III. 1695-1702
25.F6 Anne. 1702-1714
25.F68 George I. 1714-1727
25.F7 George III. 1760-1775
25.G3 State Papers Scotland (and relating to Mary, Queen of Scots). 1509-1603
25.G4 State Papers Scotland. 1688-1782
25.G7 State Papers Ireland (and of the reigns of Henry VIII, Edward VI, Mary, Elizabeth). 1509-1603
25.G9 State Papers Ireland (and of James I). 1603-1625
25.G92 State Papers Ireland. 1625-1670
25.H3 Calendar of state papers, foreign series, of the reign of Edward VI. 1547-1553
25.H33 Calendar of state papers, foreign series, of the reign of Mary. 1553-1558

England
Collections
Official records. Sources and documents
Calendars
Calendars of State Papers, etc. -- Continued
25.H36 Calendar of state papers, foreign series, of the reign of Elizabeth. 1558-1580
25.H4 Prospectus. Calendar of state papers, Colonial series
25.H5 Calendar of state papers, Colonial series, 1574-1738
25.H55 Journal of the commissioners for trade and plantations. 1704-1782
25.H6 Acts of the Privy council of England. Colonial series. 1613-1783
25.J1 Calendar of letters, despatches, and state papers relating to the negotiations between England and Spain preserved in the archives at Simancas and elsewhere. 1485-1558
25.J3 Calendar of letters and state papers relating to English affairs ... Simancas. 1558-1603
25.J4 Calendar of state papers and manuscripts existing in the archives and collections of Milan. 1385-1618
25.J5 Calendar of state papers and manuscripts relating to English affairs preserved ... Venice. 1202-1672
25.J6 Calendar of Carew manuscripts, preserved in the archiepiscopal library at Lambeth. 1515-1624
25.J7 Calendars of Treasury books and papers. 1556-1728
25.J72 Calendars of Treasury books and papers. 1729-1745
25.J76 Treasury Board papers. 1745-1800
25.Z5 Other. By date
26 Other collections
27 Collected works of individual authors
Including addresses, essays, lectures
27.5 General works
Description and travel, see DA605+
History
Biography (Collective)
For individual biography, see the special period, reign or place
28 General works
Dictionary of National Biography
28.D4 Original. By date
Including reprints of the original edition combined with supplementary volumes as a single set
28.D52 Abridgment or condensed version. By date
28.D525 Supplementary works. By date

England
History
Biography (Collective)
General works
Dictionary of
National Biography -- Continued
28.D53 Criticism, indexes
28.1 Rulers, kings, etc.
28.2 Queens
28.3 Princes and princesses
Houses, noble families, etc.
28.35.A1 Collective
28.35.A2-Z Individual, A-Z
e.g.
28.35.C45 Churchill family
28.4 Public men
28.7 Women
28.8 Other classes
28.9 Other
30 General works
Compends
32.A1 Compilations, anthologies, etc.
32.A2-Z General
32.3 Pictorial works
32.5 Source books
32.7 Syllabi
32.8 Stories
32.9 Rhymes
33 Comic and satiric works
34 Dictionaries. Chronological tables, outlines, etc.
35 Pamphlets, etc.
General special
Political and institutional history
For political parties, see JN1111+
For specific periods, reigns, etc., see the period or reign
40 General works
41 Medieval
42 Modern
44 Special topics (not A-Z)
Diplomatic history. Foreign and general relations
For works on relations with a specific country regardless of period, see DA47+
For general works on the diplomatic history of a period, see the period
45 General works
(46) Biography and memoirs
see DA28+, and biography numbers under special periods, reigns, etc.
Relations with individual regions or countries
(47) Europe
see D34, D1065
47.1 France

England
History
General special
Diplomatic history. Foreign and general relations
Relations with individual regions or countries -- Continued

47.2 Germany
47.3 Netherlands
47.6 Rome
47.65 Russia
47.7 Scandinavia
47.8 Spain
United States, see E183.8.A+
47.9.A-Z Other regions, A-Z

Military history
49 Periodicals. Societies. Serials
50 General works
52 Dictionaries
54 Biography (Collective)
58 Roman
59 Anglo-Saxon
60 Medieval
Modern
65 General works
16th and 17th centuries
66 General works
Biography and memoirs
66.1.A1 Collective
66.1.A2-Z Individual, A-Z
e.g.
66.1.G2 Gage, Sir Henry
18th century
67 General works
Biography and memoirs
67.1.A1 Collective
67.1.A2-Z Individual, A-Z
e.g.
67.1.W8 Wolfe, James
19th century
68 General works
Biography and memoirs
1801-1825. Napoleonic period
68.12.A1 Collective
68.12.A2-Z Individual, A-Z
e.g.
68.12.M8 Moore, Sir John
68.12.N2 Napier, Sir Charles James
68.12.W4 Wellington, Arthur Wellesley, 1st Duke of
1825-1850. Mid-century
68.22.A1 Collective

England
History
General special
Military history
Modern
19th century
Biography and memoirs
1825-1850. Mid-century -- Continued

68.22.A2-Z Individual, A-Z
e.g.
68.22.C5 Clyde, Colin Campbell, Baron
Havelock, Sir Henry, see DS475.2.H2
68.22.V5 Vicars, Hedley Shafto J.

1850-1900
68.32.A1 Collective
68.32.A2-Z Individual, A-Z
e.g.
68.32.B2 Baden-Powell, Robert Stephenson S.B., Baron
French, John Denton Pinkstone, see DA68.32.Y8
68.32.G5 Gordon, Sir Charles Alexander
68.32.G6 Gordon, Charles George
68.32.K6 Kitchener, Horatio Herbert K., 1st Earl
68.32.R6 Roberts, Frederick Sleigh Roberts, 1st Earl
68.32.W7 Wolseley, Garnet Joseph W., Viscount
68.32.Y8 Ypres, John Denton P.F., 1st Earl of

20th century
Cf. DA566.5, Military and naval history (20th century)
69 General works
Biography and memoirs
69.3.A1 Collective
69.3.A2-Z Individual, A-Z
e.g.
69.3.A57 Alexander, Harold Rupert L.G. Alexander, 1st Earl
69.3.A6 Allenby, Edmund Henry H. Allenby, 1st Viscount
69.3.H3 Haig, Douglas Haig, 1st Earl
69.3.M56 Montgomery, Bernard Law Montgomery, 1st Viscount
69.3.W37 Wavell, Archibald Percival Wavell, 1st Earl of

Naval history
70 General works
72 Dictionaries
74 Biography (Collective)
77 General special
80 Medieval
Modern

England
History
General special
Naval history
Modern -- Continued

85 General works

16th-17th centuries

86 General works

Biography and memoirs

86.1.A1 Collective

86.1.B6 Blake, Robert

Elizabeth, 1558-1603

86.21 Collective

86.22.A-Z Individual, A-Z

e.g.

86.22.C8 Cumberland, George Clifford, 3d Earl of

86.22.D7 Drake, Sir Francis

86.22.H3 Hawkins, Sir John

86.22.R2 Raleigh, Sir Walter

86.62 Later Stuart, 1660-1714

86.8.A-Z Individual battles, A-Z

Subarrange by author, A-Z

18th century

87 General works

Biography and memoirs

87.1.A1 Collective

87.1.A2-Z Individual, A-Z

e.g.

87.1.A6 Anson, George Anson, Baron

87.1.B6 Bligh, William

87.1.B8 Byng, John

87.1.C7 Collingwood, Cuthbert Collingwood, Baron

87.1.N4 Nelson, Horatio Nelson, Viscount

87.1.S2 St. Vincent, John Jervis, Earl

87.1.V5 Vernon, Edward

87.5.A-Z Individual battles, A-Z

Subarrange by author, A-Z

87.7 Other special

Including mutinies of 1797

19th century

88 General works

Biography and memoirs

88.1.A1 Collective

88.1.A2-Z Individual, A-Z

e.g.

88.1.B4 Beresford, Charles William D. Beresford, Baron

88.1.D9 Dundonald, Thomas Cochrane, 10th Earl of

88.1.G2 Gambier, James Gambier, Baron

88.1.K3 Keppel, Sir Henry

88.1.N2 Napier, Sir Charles

88.1.P14 Paget, Lord Clarence Edward

England
History
General special
Naval history
Modern
19th century
Biography and memoirs
Individual, A-Z -- Continued
88.1.P6 Popham, Sir Home Riggs
88.5.A-Z Individual battles, A-Z
Subarrange by author, A-Z
20th century
Cf. DA566.5, Military and naval history (20th century)
89 General works
Biography and memoirs
89.1.A1 Collective
89.1.A2-Z Individual, A-Z
e.g.
89.1.B4 Beatty, David Beatty, 1st Earl
89.1.F5 Fisher, John Arbuthnot Fisher, Baron
89.1.J4 Jellicoe, John Rushworth Jellicoe, 1st Earl
Air Force history
Cf. UG635.A+, Military aeronautics
89.5 General works
Biography and memoirs
89.6.A1 Collective
89.6.A2-Z Individual, A-Z
e.g.
89.6.J6 Joubert de la Ferté, Sir Philip Bennet
Antiquities
For Anglo-Saxon antiquities, see DA155
For Celtic antiquities, see DA140+
For local antiquities, see DA670+
For Roman antiquities, see DA145+
90 General works
Biography of antiquarians
92 Collective
93.A-Z Individual, A-Z
e.g.
93.B7 Britton, John
93.S64 Smith, Charles Roach
100 Monumental
Social life and customs. Civilization.
Intellectual life
110 General works
111 Court life
112 Coronations, regalia, ritual, etc.
115 Other special
For witchcraft, see BF1581
118 National characteristics. Patriotism
Ethnography

England
History
General special
Ethnography -- Continued
120 General works
123 British in foreign countries (General)
For individual countries, see DB-F
Elements in the population
125.A1 General works. Minorities. Race question
125.A2-Z By element, A-Z
For individual elements in the population of a particular place, see the place
125.A6 Americans (U.S.)
125.A72 Arabs
125.A84 Asians
125.A9 Australians
Blacks, see DA125.N4
125.C4 Celts
125.C5 Chinese
125.C85 Cypriotes
125.C9 Czechs
125.D3 Danes
East Indians, see DA125.S57
125.F7 French
125.G4 Germans
125.G7 Greeks
Hindus, see DA125.S57
125.H84 Huguenots
125.I68 Iranians
125.I7 Irish
125.I85 Italians
Jews, see DS135.E5+
125.J8 Jutes
125.L58 Lithuanians
125.M38 Mauritians
125.M87 Muslims
125.N4 Negroes. Blacks
Pakistanis, see DA125.S57
125.P6 Poles
125.Q34 Quakers
125.R65 Romanians
125.R8 Russians
125.S3 Scots
Sikhs, see DA125.S57
125.S57 South Asians
Including Bengali, East Indians, and Pakistanis
125.S62 Spaniards
125.S88 Swedes
125.S9 Swiss
125.U38 Ukrainians
125.V53 Vietnamese
125.W4 West Indians

England
History
General special
Ethnography
Elements in the population
By element, A-Z -- Continued

125.Y45 Yemenis

By period
Early and medieval to 1485

129 Dictionaries
129.5 Historiography
130 General works

Earliest to 1066

134 Sources and documents
135 General works

Celts. Pre-Romans (and Romans)

140 General works
141 General special
e.g. Bladud
142 Stonehenge
Cf. GN805+, Prehistoric remains
143.A-Z Other local, A-Z

Romans

145 General works

Biography and memoirs

145.2 Collective
145.3.A-Z Individual, A-Z
e.g.
145.3.B6 Boadicea, Queen, d. 62
146 Hadrian's Wall
147.A-Z Local, A-Z
e.g.
147.L4 Leigh, North
London, see DA677.1

Saxons, 445-1066

150 Sources and documents. Chronicles
152 General works
152.2 Social life and customs. Civilization

445-871

General works, see DA152
152.3 Hengist and Horsa
152.5.A-Z Biography, A-Z
e.g.
152.5.E2 Edmund, Saint, King of East Anglia

871-1066

General works, see DA152
153 Alfred, 871-901
154 Edward the Elder, 901-925
154.1 Athelstan, 925-940
154.2 Edmund I, 940-946
154.3 Edred, 946-955
154.4 Edwy, 955-959
154.5 Edgar, 959-975

England
History
By period
Early and medieval to 1485
Earliest to 1066
Saxons, 445-1066
871-1066 -- Continued
154.6 Edward the Martyr, 975-978
154.7 Ethelred II the Unready, 978-1016
Sweyn, 1013-1014, see DA159
154.75 Edmund II Ironside, 1016
Danish rule, 1017-1042 (General works and individual rulers), see DA158+
154.8 Edward the Confessor, 1042-1066
154.85 Harold II, 1066
Biography of contemporaries
154.88 Collective
154.9.A-Z Individual, A-Z
e.g.
154.9.H4 Hereward
155 Antiquities
Danish invasions, rule, etc.
158 General works
159 Sweyn, 1013-1014
160 Canute, 1017-1035
161 Harold I, 1037-1040
162 Hardicanute, 1040-1042
Medieval, 1066-1485
170 Sources and documents. Contemporary works
175 General works
176 General special
177 Biography (Collective)
185 Social life and customs. Civilization
188 Royal forests
Normans, 1066-1154
190 Sources and documents (Domesday book, etc.)
195 General works
195.8 Battle of Stamford Bridge, 1066
196 Battle of Hastings, 1066
197 William I, 1066-1087
197.5 William II, 1087-1100
198 Henry I, 1100-1135
Stephen, 1135-1154
198.5 General works
198.6 Matilda, Princess of England, Consort of Geoffrey, Count of Anjou
Biography of contemporaries
198.9 Collective
199.A-Z Individual, A-Z
Angevins, 1154-1216
200 Sources and documents. Contemporary works
For Magna Carta, see JN147, Political science; KD3944+, Law

England
History
By period
Early and medieval to 1485
Medieval, 1066-1485
Angevins, 1154-1216 -- Continued

205 General works
206 Henry II, 1154-1189
207 Richard I, 1189-1199
208 John, 1199-1216
209.A-Z Biography of contemporaries, A-Z
e.g.
209.E6 Eleanor of Aquitaine, Consort of Henry II
209.G5 Giraldus Cambrensis
209.T4 Thomas à Becket, Saint, Abp. of Canterbury

Plantagenets, 1216-1399

220 Sources and documents. Contemporary works
225 General works
Henry III, 1216-1272
227 General works on life and reign
227.5 Barons' War, 1263-1267
228.A-Z Biography and memoirs of contemporaries, A-Z
e.g.
228.G8 Grosseteste, Robert, Bp. of London
228.L3 Langton, Stephen, Cardinal, Abp. of Canterbury
228.M7 Montfort, Simon of, Earl of Leicester
229 Edward I, 1272-1307
230 Edward II, 1307-1327
231.A-Z Biography and memoirs of contemporaries, 1272-1327, A-Z
e.g.
231.G2 Gaveston, Piers, Earl of Cornwall
233 Edward III, 1327-1377
234 Edward, Prince of Wales, called the Black Prince
235 Richard II, 1377-1399
Including Tyler's insurrection, 1381, etc.
237.A-Z Biography and memoirs of contemporaries, A-Z
e.g.
237.T9 Tyler, Wat
237.W8 Wykeham, William of, Bp. of Winchester

Lancaster-York, 1399-1485

240 Sources and documents. Contemporary works
245 General works
247.A-Z Biography and memoirs of contemporaries, A-Z
e.g.
247.G2 Gascoigne, Sir William
247.H8 Humphrey, Duke of Gloucester
247.J6 John of Gaunt, Duke of Lancaster
247.M3 Margaret of Anjou, Consort of Henry VI

England
History
By period
Early and medieval to 1485
Medieval, 1066-1485
Lancaster-York, 1399-1485
Biography and memoirs of contemporaries, A-Z -- Continued

247.R7 Rotherham, Thomas, Abp. of York
247.S4 Shore, Jane
250 Wars of the Roses, 1455-1485
255 Henry IV, 1399-1413
256 Henry V, 1413-1422
257 Henry VI, 1422-1461
258 Edward IV, 1461-1483
259 Edward V, 1483
260 Richard III, 1483-1485. Battle of Bosworth Field, 1485

Modern, 1485-
300 General works. Collections
302 Compends
Biography and memoirs (Collective)
304 General works
Houses, noble families, etc.
305 Collective
306.A-Z Special, A-Z
307 Public men
308 Women

Tudors, 1485-1603
310 Sources and documents. Contemporary works
314 Historiography
315 General works
316 Pamphlets, etc.
Biography and memoirs
Collective
317 General works
317.1 Kings, queens, etc.
317.15.A-Z Houses, noble families, etc., A-Z
317.2 Public men
317.3 Women
317.8.A-Z Individual, A-Z
e.g.
317.8.C8 Cranmer, Thomas, Abp. of Canterbury
317.8.P6 Pole, Reginald, Cardinal
320 Social life and customs. Civilization. Intellectual life
325 Early Tudors
Henry VII, 1485-1509
330 General works
330.8.A-Z Biography and memoirs of contemporaries, A-Z
e.g.
330.8.R5 Richmond, Margaret (Beaufort) Tudor, Countess of

England
History
By period
Modern, 1485-
Tudors, 1485-1603 -- Continued
Henry VIII, 1509-1547
331 Sources and documents. Contemporary works
332 General works on life and reign
Biography
Queens
333.A2 Collective
333.A6 Catharine, of Aragon
333.B6 Anne Boleyn
333.C44 Anne of Cleves
333.H7 Howard, Catharine
333.P3 Catharine Parr
Public men
334.A1 Collective
334.A2-Z Individual, A-Z
334.C9 Cromwell, Thomas, Earl of Essex
334.M8 More, Sir Thomas, Saint
Cf. B785.M8, Philosophy
Cf. HX810.5, Utopias
Cf. PA8553, Latin literature
Cf. PR2321+, English literature
334.W8 Wolsey, Thomas, cardinal
335.A-Z Other, A-Z
337 1509-1527
338 1527-1533. Divorce, etc.
339 1533-1547
1547-1558
340 General works
Edward VI, 1547-1558
345 General works on life and reign
Biography and memoirs of contemporaries
345.1.A1 Collective
345.1.A2-Z Individual, A-Z
e.g.
345.1.D9 Dudley, Lady Jane (Lady Jane Grey)
Mary I, 1553-1558
347 General works works on life and reign
347.1.A-Z Biography and memoirs of contemporaries, A-Z
Elizabeth I, 1558-1603. Elizabethan age
350 Sources and documents. Contemporary works
352 Pamphlets. By date
355 General works works on life and reign
356 General special
357 Compends
Biography and memoirs of contemporaries
Cf. DA86.21+, Elizabethan admirals
358.A1 Collective

England
History
By period
Modern, 1485-
Tudors, 1485-1603
Elizabeth I, 1558-1603. Elizabethan age
Biography and memoirs of contemporaries -- Continued

358.A2-Z Individual, A-Z
e.g.
358.B3 Bacon, Francis, Viscount St. Albans
Cf. B1197, Philosophy
358.B9 Burghley, William Cecil, Baron
358.D8 Dudley, Amy (Robsart), Lady
358.E8 Essex, Robert Devereux, Earl of
358.G5 Gilbert, Sir Humphrey
358.L5 Leicester, Robert Dudley, Earl of
358.O8 Oxford, Edward De Vere, Earl of
358.S2 Salisbury, Robert Cecil, 1st Earl of
358.S5 Sidney, Sir Philip
358.W2 Walsingham, Sir Francis
360 Armada

17th century, 1603-1702
370 Sources and documents. Contemporary works
375 General works
Biography and memoirs
Collective
377 General works
377.1 Rulers, kings, etc.
377.2.A-Z Houses, noble families, etc., A-Z
377.3 Public men
377.5 Women
378.A-Z Individual, A-Z
e.g.
378.P4 Pembroke, Anne (Clifford) Herbert, Countess of
378.P7 Prynne, William
380 Social life and customs. Civilization

Early Stuarts, 1603-1642
385 Sources and documents. Contemporary works
390 General works
390.1.A-Z Biography and memoirs, A-Z
e.g.
390.1.C7 Coke, Sir Edward
390.1.D9 Dudley, Sir Robert, styled Duke of Northumberland and Earl of Warwick

James I, 1603-1625
391 General works on life and reign
Biography and memoirs of contemporaries
391.1.A1 Collective
391.1.A2-Z Individual, A-Z
e.g.
391.1.A6 Anne of Denmark, Consort of James I

England
History
By period
Modern, 1485-
17th century, 1603-1702
Early Stuarts, 1603-1642
James I, 1603-1625
Biography and memoirs of contemporaries
Individual, A-Z -- Continued
391.1.B9 Buckingham, George Villiers, 1st Duke of
391.1.H5 Henry Frederick, Prince of Wales
391.1.S8 Southampton, Henry Wriothesley, 3d Earl of
391.1.S9 Stuart, Lady Arabella
Gunpowder plot, 1605
392 General works
392.1.A-Z Biography of participants, A-Z
e.g.
392.1.D5 Digby, Sir Everard
392.1.G3 Gerard, John
394 Pamphlets, 1603-1624. By date
Charles I, 1625-1649
395 General works on reign
Biography and memoirs
396.A1 General collective
396.A2 Charles I
396.A22 Special
396.A3 Sermons, pamphlets, etc.
396.A5 Henrietta Maria, Consort of Charles I
396.A6 Children of Charles I
396.A8-Z Contemporaries, A-Z
e.g.
396.H18 Hampden, John
396.L3 Laud, William, Abp. of Canterbury
396.P9 Pym, John
396.S8 Strafford, Thomas Wentworth, 1st Earl of
396.W6 William, John, Abp. of York
397 General special
398 Pamphlets, 1625-1641. By date
Civil War and Commonwealth, 1642-1660
400 Sources and documents. Contemporary works
403 Historiography
405 General works
406 General special
Biography and memoirs of contemporaries
407.A1 Collective
407.A2-Z Individual, A-Z
e.g.
407.A74 Albemarle, George Monk, 1st Duke of
407.F2 Fairfax, Thomas Fairfax, Baron

England
History
By period
Modern, 1485-
17th century, 1603-1702
Civil War and Commonwealth, 1642-1660
Biography and memoirs of contemporaries
Individual, A-Z -- Continued

407.P4 Peters, Hugh
407.R9 Rupert, Prince, Count Palatine
407.S5 Shaftesbury, Anthony Ashley Cooper, 1st Earl of
407.S6 Sidney, Algernon
407.V2 Vane, Sir Henry

Civil War, 1642-1649
Including local history

410 Sources and documents
411 Contemporary newspapers
412 Pamphlets, 1642-February 1649. By date
413 Historiography
415 General works
417 Battle of Marston Moor, 1644

Biography and memoirs

419.A1 Collective
419.A2-Z Individual, A-Z

e.g.

419.S6 Slingsby, Sir Henry, Bart.
419.W2 Waller, Sir William

Regicides

419.5.A1 Collective
419.5.A2-Z Individual, A-Z

e.g.

419.5.G6 Goffe, William
419.5.H3 Harrison, Thomas

Commonwealth, 1649-1660

420 Sources and documents. Contemporary works
421 Contemporary newspapers
422 Pamphlets, March 1649-1660. By original date of publication
Subarrange by author
425 General works

Cromwell, Oliver

426 General works
427 Special
427.1 Pamphlets. By date
(427.2) Fiction
see PA-PZ
428 Compends
428.1 Essays, lectures, etc.
428.5 Cromwell, Richard
429.A-Z Biography and memoirs of contemporaries, A-Z

e.g.

England
History
By period
Modern, 1485-
17th century, 1603-1702
Civil War and Commonwealth, 1642-1660
Commonwealth, 1649-1660
Biography and memoirs of contemporaries, A-Z -- Continued

429.R7 Rogers, John
429.W5 Winstanley, Gerrard

Later Stuarts, 1660-1685

430 Sources and documents. Contemporary works
431 Contemporary newspapers
432 Pamphlets. By date
435 General works

Biography and memoirs of contemporaries

437.A1 Collective
437.A2-Z Individual, A-Z

e.g.

437.D4 Devonshire, William Cavendish, 1st Duke
437.P5 Peterborough, Charles Mordaunt, 3d Earl
440 Social life and customs. Civilization

Charles II, 1660-1685

445 General works on life and reign
446 Personal special

Biography and memoirs of contemporaries

447.A3 Collective
447.A4-Z Individual, A-Z
447.A72 Arlington, Henry Bennet
447.B9 Buckingham, George Villiers, 2d Duke
447.C3 Catharine of Braganza, Consort of Charles II
447.C6 Clarendon, Edward Hyde, 1st Earl of
447.D7 Downing, Sir George, Bart.
447.E9 Evelyn, John
447.G7 Gramont, Philibert, comte de
447.G9 Gwyn, Nell
447.J4 Jeffreys, George Jeffreys, Baron
447.L4 Leeds, Thomas Osborne, 1st Duke of
447.P4 Pepys, Samuel
447.R4 Reresby, Sir John, 2d Bart.
447.R6 Rochester, John Wilmot, 2d Earl of
447.T2 Temple, Sir William, Bart.
448 General special

Anglo-Dutch War, 1672-1674, see DJ193

448.9 Monmouth and Monmouth's rebellion, 1685

James II, 1685-1688

450 General works on life and reign
452 Other

England
History
By period
Modern, 1485-
17th century, 1603-1702
Later Stuarts, 1660-1685 -- Continued
William and Mary, 1689-1702
Cf. DJ186+, Reign of William III in Holland
For biography, see DA462.A2

460 General works on reign
461 Lancaster plot, 1689-1694
461.3 Versailles conspiracy, 1695
461.5 Conspiracy of 1696
Biography and memoirs of contemporaries
462.A2 William III
462.A3 Mary II
462.A4-Z Other individual, A-Z
e.g.
462.M3 Marlborough, John Churchill, 1st Duke
462.M4 Marlborough, Sarah (Jennings) Churchill, Duchess of
462.P7 Portland, William Bentinck, 1st Earl
463 Pamphlets. By date
Subarrange by author
Late modern, 1702-
470 General works
472 Compends
18th century
Including House of Hanover (Windsor)
480 General works
Biography and memoirs
483.A1 Collective
483.A2-Z Individual, A-Z
e.g.
483.A7 Argyll, John Campbell, 2d Duke of
483.C5 Chandos, James Brydges, 1st Duke of
483.C6 Chudleigh, Elizabeth, Countess of Bristol ("Duchess of Kingston")
483.D3 Delany, Mary (Granville) Pendarves
483.H3 Hamilton, Emma, Lady
483.H8 Huntingdon, Selina (Shirley) Hastings, Countess of
483.N2 Nash, Richard
483.P6 Pitt, William, 1st Earl of Chatham
483.P6A2 Correspondence
483.P62 Pamphlets
483.W2 Walpole, Horace, 4th Earl of Orford
For his memoirs of the reign of George III, see DA506.W2
485 Social life and customs. Civilization
486 Other
Anne, 1702-1714

England
History
By period
Modern, 1485-
Late modern, 1702-
18th century
Anne, 1702-1714 -- Continued

490 Sources and documents
495 General works on life and reign
496 Pamphlets. By original date of publication
Subarrange by author
Biography and memoirs of contemporaries
497.A1 Collective
497.A3 Children of Anne. William, Duke of Gloucester
497.A4-Z Individual, A-Z
497.O8 Oxford, Robert Harley, 1st Earl of
497.S3 Sacheverall, Henry
497.S8 Stanhope, James Stanhope, 1st Earl of
1714-1760
498 General works
499 George I, 1714-1727
500 George II, 1727-1760
Biography and memoirs
501.A1 Collective
501.A2 George I
501.A3 George II
501.A33 Carolina, Consort of George II
501.A35 Frederick Louis, Prince of Wales
William Augustus, Duke of Cumberland, see DA501.C9
501.A4-Z Other, A-Z
501.A8 Atterbury, Francis, Bp. of Rochester
501.B6 Bolingbroke, Henry St. John, Viscount
501.C5 Chesterfield, Philip Dormer Stanhope, 4th Earl of
501.C9 Cumberland, William Augustus, Duke of
501.M7 Montagu, Lady Mary (Pierrepont) Wortley
501.T3 Temple, Richard Temple Grenville-Temple, Earl
501.W2 Walpole, Robert, 1st Earl of Orford
503 Pamphlets. By original date of publication
Subarrange by author
Cf. DD412, Seven Years' War, 1756-1763
George III, 1760-1820
505 General works
Biography and memoirs of contemporaries
506.A1 Collective
506.A2 George III

England
History
By period
Modern, 1485-
Late modern, 1702-
18th century
George III, 1760-1820
Biography and memoirs of contemporaries -- Continued

506.A3 Charlotte, Consort of George III
506.A6 Edward Augustus, Duke of Kent
506.A7 Frederick Augustus, Duke of York and Albany
506.A71 Henry Frederick, Duke of Cumberland
506.A72 Mary Anne (Thompson) Clarke
506.A74 Maria, Duchess of Gloucester
506.A8 Amelia, Princess of England
506.A82-Z Other, A-Z
e.g.
506.B9 Burke, Edmund
506.C8 Cornwallis, Charles Cornwallis, 1st Marquis
506.F7 Fox, Charles James
506.F8 Francis, Sir Philip
506.M5 Melville, Henry Dundas, 1st Viscount
506.N2 Napier, Lady Sarah (Lennox) Bunbury
506.N7 North, Frederick North, Baron
Pindar, Peter, see DA506.W8
506.T6 Tooke, John Horne
506.W2 Walpole, Horace, 4th Earl of Orford
Including memoirs of the reign of George III
For Walpole's biography, see DA483.W2
506.W8 Wolcot, John (pseud. Peter Pindar)

Contemporary works
506.5 Collections
507 Pamphlets. By date
Subarrange by author
Letters of Junius
508.A2 Editions. By date
508.A3 Selections, extracts, etc. By date
508.A4A-Z Translations. By language, A-Z
508.A5 Criticism, pamphlets, etc.
508.A6 Authorship in general. By author of work
508.A7-Z Authorship, particular theories
508.F8 Francis, Sir Philip
508.P3 Paine, Thomas
509 Collected works of statesmen, etc.
For Edmund Burke's work, see DA506.B9
For memoirs, journals, letters, etc., see DA506.A1+

England
History
By period
Modern, 1485-
Late modern, 1702-
18th century
George III, 1760-1820 -- Continued
1760-1789
510 General works
512.A-Z Biography and memoirs, A-Z
e.g.
512.G6 Gordon, Lord George
512.L3 Lansdowne, William Petty, 1st Marquis of
512.W6 Wilkes, John
1789-1820
520 General works
521 1811-1820. Regency
For the proposed French invasion, see DC220.3
Biography and memoirs
522.A1 Collective
522.A2-Z Individual, A-Z
e.g.
522.C2 Canning, George
522.C5 Cobbett, William
522.E7 Erskine, Thomas Erskine, Baron
522.H85 Huskisson, William
522.L7 Liverpool, Robert Banks Jenkinson, 2d Earl of
Pitt, William 1759-1806
522.P4 Letters. By date
522.P45 Speeches. By date
522.P5 Pamphlets. By date
522.P6 Biography
522.S4 Sheridan, Richard Brinsley Butler
522.W6 Wilberforce, William
Cf. HT1029.A4+, Anti-slavery
19th century
529 Dictionaries
530 General works
531 Pamphlets. By date
Biography and memoirs
Collective
531.1 General works
531.2 Public men
Individual biography
see DA536+
533 Social life and customs. Civilization. Intellectual life
1801-1837
535 General works
Biography and memoirs, 1801-1837/1850

England
History
By period
Modern, 1485-
Late modern, 1702-
19th century
1801-1837
Biography and memoirs,
1801-1837/1850 -- Continued

536.A1 Collective
536.A2-Z Individual, A-Z
e.g.
536.B66 Blessington, Marguerite, Countess of
536.B7 Brougham and Vaux, Henry Peter Brougham, Baron
536.C6 Cobden, Richard
536.G8 Greville, Charles Cavendish Fulke
536.G84 Grey, Charles Grey, 2d Earl
(536.M15) Macaulay, Thomas Babington Macaulay
See DA3.M3
536.P2 Palmerston, Henry John Temple, 3d Viscount
536.P3 Peel, Sir Robert, Bart.
536.R9 Russell, John Russell, 1st Earl
536.S8 Stanhope, Lady Hester Lucy
1789-1820, see DA520+
George IV, 1820-1830
537 General works works on reign
Cf. DA521, Regency
Biography and memoirs of contemporaries
538.A1 George IV
538.A2 Caroline Amelia Elizabeth, Consort of George IV
538.A22 Divorce
(538.A25) Fiction
see class P-PZ
538.A3 Lady Anne Hamilton
538.A31 Miss C.E. Cary
538.A35 Mary (Darby) Robinson
538.A4 Charlotte Augusta, of Wales, Consort of Prince Leopold of Saxe-Coburg-Saalfeld
538.A5-Z Other, A-Z
e.g.
538.B6 Brummell, George Bryan
538.F5 Fitzherbert, Maria Anne (Smythe)
William IV, 1830-1837
539 General works on life and reign
540 Era of reform, 1832-1837
Biography and memoirs of contemporaries
541.A1 Collective
541.A2-Z Individual, A-Z
e.g.

England
History
By period
Modern, 1485-
Late modern, 1702-
19th century
1801-1837
William IV, 1830-1837
Biography and memoirs of contemporaries
Individual, A-Z -- Continued
541.A4 Adelaide, Consort of William IV
542 Pamphlets, etc.
Victorian era, 1837-1901
550 General works
551 Pamphlets, etc.
Victoria
552 Journal, letters, etc.
553 Memoirs by contemporaries
554 Biography
555 Personal special
556 Compends
557 Juvenile works
558 Pamphlets, etc.
558.5 Jubilee pamphlets
559.A-Z Other royal biography, A-Z
e.g.
559.A1 Albert, Consort of Victoria
559.A3 Alice, Consort of Louis IV, Grand Duke of Hesse-Darmstadt
559.A7 Arthur, Duke of Connaught
559.G4 George, 2d Duke of Cambridge
559.L6 Louise, Duchess of Argyll
559.V5 Victoria Maria Louisa, Duchess of Kent
559.5 The court
559.7 1837-1850
For Chartism, see HD8396
1850-1901
560 General works
561 Pamphlets, etc.
South African War, see DT1890+
Biography and memoirs
562 Collective
Gladstone
563 Speeches, letters, etc.
563.3 Memoirs by contemporaries
563.35 Cartoons, etc.
563.4 Biography
563.5 Special works
563.6 Compends
563.8 Pamphlets, etc.
563.9 Catherine (Glynn) Gladstone

England
History
By period
Modern, 1485-
Late modern, 1702-
19th century
Victorian era, 1837-1901
Biography and memoirs -- Continued

564.A-Z Other prime ministers, A-Z
e.g.
564.B3 Beaconsfield, Benjamin Disraeli, 1st Earl of
Disraeli, Benjamin, see DA564.B3
564.R7 Rosebery, Archibald Philip Primrose, 5th Earl of
564.S2 Salisbury, Robert Arthur Talbot Gascoyne-Cecil, 3d Marquis of
565.A-Z Contemporaries, A-Z
e.g.
565.B8 Bright, John
565.B85 Bryce, James Bryce, Viscount
565.C4 Chamberlain, Joseph
565.C6 Churchill, Lord Randolph Henry Spencer
565.C95 Curzon, George Nathaniel Curzon, 1st Marquis
565.L9 Lytton, Edward George E. Lytton Bulwer-Lytton, Baron
565.M16 McCarthy, Justin
565.M78 Morley, John Morley, Viscount
565.R8 Russell, George William Erskine
565.T2 Temple, Sir Richard, Bart.

20th century
566 General works
566.2 General special
566.3 Pamphlets, etc.
566.4 Social life and customs. Civilization. Intellectual life
566.5 Military and naval history
Cf. DA69+, Military history (20th century)
Cf. DA89+, Naval history (20th century)
566.7 Political and diplomatic history
566.8 Caricature, satire, etc.
Biography and memoirs
566.9.A1 Collective
566.9.A2-Z Individual, A-Z
e.g.
Asquith, H.H. (Herbert Henry), see DA566.9.O7
566.9.B15 Baldwin, Stanley Baldwin, 1st Earl
566.9.B2 Balfour, Arthur James Balfour, 1st Earl

England
History
By period
Modern, 1485-
Late modern, 1702-
20th century
Biography and memoirs
Individual, A-Z -- Continued

566.9.B37 Beaverbrook, William Maxwell Aitken, Baron
566.9.B5 Birkenhead, Frederick Edwin Smith, 1st Earl of
566.9.C43 Chamberlain, Sir Austen
566.9.C5 Churchill, Winston, Sir, 1874-1965
566.9.E28 Eden, Anthony
566.9.G8 Grey, Edward Grey, 1st Viscount
Isaacs, Rufus, Marquess of Reading, see DA566.9.R3
566.9.L5 Lloyd George, David
566.9.M25 MacDonald, James Ramsey
566.9.N7 Northcliffe, Alfred Harmsworth, Viscount
566.9.O7 Oxford and Asquith, Herbert Henry Asquith, 1st Earl of
566.9.R3 Reading, Rufus Daniel Isaacs, 1st Marquis of

Edward VII, 1901-1910
567 Biography
Biography and memoirs of contemporaries
568.A1 Collective
568.A2 Alexandra, Consort of Edward VII
568.A3-A5 Other royal
568.A6-Z Other, A-Z
570 Reign

George V, 1910-1936
573 Biography
Biography and memoirs of contemporaries
574.A1 Collective
574.A2 Mary, Consort of George V
Other royal
574.A33 Henry, Duke of Gloucester
574.A34 Alice, Duchess of Gloucester
574.A36 George, Duke of Kent
574.A37 Marina, Duchess of Kent
574.A4 Mary, Princess of Great Britain
574.A45A-Z Other royal, A-Z
574.A5-Z Other
574.A8 Astor, Nancy Witcher (Langhorne), Viscountess
574.M6 Mosley, Sir Oswald, Bart.
576 Reign
577 Period of World War I, 1914-1919
For the war itself, see D501+

England
History
By period
Modern, 1485-
Late modern, 1702-
20th century
George V, 1910-1936 -- Continued
578 1920-1939
Edward VIII, 1936
580 Biography
581.A-Z Biography and memoirs of contemporaries, A-Z
e.g.
581.W5 Windsor, Wallis Warfield, Duchess of
583 Reign
George VI, 1937-1952
584 Biography
Biography and memoirs of contemporaries
585.A1 Collective
585.A2 Elizabeth, Consort of George VI
585.A5A-Z Other royal, A-Z
585.A5M3 Margaret, Princess of Great Britain
585.A6-Z Other, A-Z
e.g.
585.A8 Attlee, Clement Richard
585.B4 Bevin, Ernest
585.C5 Chamberlain, Neville
585.C7 Cripps, Sir Richard Stafford
586 Reign
587 Period of World War II, 1939-1945
1945-1952. Postwar period
588 General works
588.3 Pamphlets, etc.
1952-
589.3 Addresses, essays, lectures
589.4 Social life and customs. Civilization. Intellectual life
589.7 Political history
589.8 Foreign and general relations
Elizabeth II, 1952-
590 Biography
Biography and memoirs of contemporaries
591.A1 Collective
591.A2 Philip, Prince
591.A3-A45 Other royal
591.A33 Charles, Prince of Wales
591.A34 Anne, Princess of Great Britain
591.A45A-Z Other, A-Z
591.A5-Z Other contemporaries, A-Z
e.g.
591.H4 Heath, Edward
591.T47 Thatcher, Margaret
591.W5 Wilson, Harold

England
History
By period
Modern, 1485-
Late modern, 1702-
20th century
1952-
Elizabeth II, 1952- -- Continued

592 Reign
600 Historical geography
Description and travel
605 History of travel
By period
610 Through 1600
615 1601-1700
620 1701-1800
625 1801-1900
630 1901-1945
631 1946-1970
632 1971-
640 Gazetteers. Dictionaries, etc.
645 Place names
Special, see DA670+
650 Guidebooks
655 Preservation of historic monuments, etc.
Castles, halls, cathedrals, etc.
660 General works
662.A-Z By county, A-Z
664.A-Z By manor hall, etc., A-Z
For manors, halls, etc. in cities or towns, see DA690.A+
665 Watering places
667 Picturesque places, rural scenery, etc.
668 British Islands (Collectively)
Including Hebrides, Orkneys, Shetlands, Channel Islands, Isle of Man, etc.
669 Historical accounts of disasters (Collectively)
Including earthquakes, fires, floods, storms, etc.
For individual disasters, see DA670+
Local history and description
Counties, regions, etc., A-Z
e.g.
670.A1 Collective
670.A29 Airedale
670.A96 Axholme, Isle of
670.B25 Bedford Level
Bedfordshire
670.B29 Serials
670.B3 Nonserials
670.B4 Berkshire
670.B55 Black Country (District)
670.B9 Buckinghamshire
670.C2 Cambridgeshire

England
Local history and description
Counties, regions, etc., A-Z -- Continued

670.C4 Channel Islands
670.C44 Charnwood Forest
Cheshire
670.C5 Serials
670.C6 Nonserials
670.C62 Chiltern Hills (Chilterns)
670.C63 Cleveland (District)
670.C7 Coniston
Cornwall
670.C78 Serials
670.C8 Nonserials
670.C83 Cotswold Hills
670.C86 Cranborne Chase
670.C88 Craven (District)
Cumberland
670.C89 Serials
670.C9 Nonserials
670.C93 Cumbria
670.D2 Dartmoor
670.D25 Dean, Forest of
670.D31 Dee River
Derbyshire
Including Peak District
670.D42 Serials
670.D43 Nonserials
Devonshire
670.D49 Serials
670.D5 Nonserials
Dorsetshire
670.D69 Serials
670.D7 Nonserials
670.D9 Durham
East Anglia
670.E13 Serials
670.E14 Nonserials
670.E7 Essex
670.E87 Exe River
670.E9 Exmoor
670.F33 Fens (Fenland)
670.F98 Furness
Gloucestershire
670.G4 Serials
670.G5 Nonserials
Guernsey
670.G8 Serials
670.G9 Nonserials
670.H18 Hallamshire
670.H2 Hampshire
670.H3 Hayling Island
670.H4 Herefordshire

England
Local history and description
Counties, regions, etc., A-Z -- Continued

	Hertfordshire
670.H49	Serials
670.H5	Nonserials
670.H7	Holderness
670.H8	Huntingdonshire
	Isle of Wight, see DA670.W6
670.J5	Jersey
	Kent
670.K2	Serials
670.K3	Nonserials
670.L1	Lake District
	Lancashire
670.L19	Serials
670.L2	Nonserials
670.L26	Land's End (District)
	Leicestershire
670.L49	Serials
670.L5	Nonserials
	Lincolnshire
670.L69	Serials
670.L7	Nonserials
670.L77	Lizard Head
670.L96	Lundy Island
670.M07	Malvern Hills
	Man, Isle of
670.M1	Serials
670.M2	Nonserials
670.M5	Mendip Hills
670.M6	Middlesex
670.M7	Monmouthshire
670.M9	Mowbray, Vale of
670.N5	New Forest
670.N53	Nidderdale
	Norfolk
670.N59	Serials
670.N6	Nonserials
	Northamptonshire
670.N69	Serials
670.N7	Nonserials
670.N73	Northern England Including Northeast and Northwest England
	Northumberland
670.N79	Serials
670.N8	Nonserials
	Nottinghamshire
670.N89	Serials
670.N9	Nonserials
670.O9	Oxfordshire
	Peak District, see DA670.D42+
670.P4	Pennine Chain

England
  Local history and description
    Counties, regions, etc., A-Z -- Continued

670.P98 Purbeck, Isle of
670.Q2 Quantock Hills
670.R5 Richmondshire
670.R6 Rochford Hundred
670.R82 Rossendale Forest
Rutlandshire
670.R89 Serials
670.R9 Nonserials
Salop, see DA670.S39+
670.S2 Scilly Islands
670.S29 Severn River
670.S35 Sherwood Forest
Shropshire. Salop
670.S39 Serials
670.S4 Nonserials
Somersetshire
670.S49 Serials
670.S5 Nonserials
Staffordshire
670.S69 Serials
670.S7 Nonserials
Suffolk
670.S89 Serials
670.S9 Nonserials
Surrey
670.S95 Serials
670.S96 Nonserials
Sussex
670.S97 Serials
670.S98 Nonserials
670.T15 Teesdale
670.T2 Thames River
670.T3 Thanet, Isle of
670.T9 Tyne River
670.W3 Warwickshire
670.W47 Wensleydale
670.W48 Wessex
For description and travel, see DA670.D69+
670.W496 Westmoreland
670.W56 Wharfedale
670.W6 Wight, Isle of
Wiltshire
670.W69 Serials
670.W7 Nonserials
Worcestershire
670.W89 Serials
670.W9 Nonserials
670.W97 Wye River
670.W98 Wythburn
Yorkshire

England
Local history and description
Counties, regions, etc., A-Z
Yorkshire -- Continued

670.Y59 Serials
670.Y6 Nonserials

London
675 Periodicals. Societies. Serials
Museums, exhibitions, etc.
675.5.A1 General works
675.5.A2-Z By museum, A-Z
676 Sources and documents
Biography and memoirs
676.8.A1 Collective
676.8.A2-Z Individual, A-Z
676.85 Historiography
Ethnography
676.9.A1 General works
676.9.A5-Z Individual elements in the population, A-Z
676.9.A75 Armenians
676.9.A77 Assyrians
676.9.B35 Bangladeshis
676.9.B55 Blacks
676.9.C88 Cypriotes
676.9.C93 Czechs
676.9.D8 Dutch
676.9.E95 Europeans
676.9.F74 French
676.9.G47 Germans
676.9.I75 Irish
676.9.L38 Latin Americans
676.9.M3 Maltese
676.9.M38 Mauritians
Negroes, see DA676.9.B55
676.9.O23 Oceanians
676.9.P34 Pakistanis
676.9.P6 Poles
676.9.S6 South Asians
676.9.S63 Spaniards
676.9.W4 West Indians
History, antiquities, description
677 General works
677.1 Antiquities
678 Compends. Juvenile works
679 Guidebooks
679.A11-A19 Directories
Pictorial works, see DA680+
By period
680 Medieval through 1600
681 1601-1700
682 1701-1800
683 1801-1900
684 1901-1950

England
London
History, antiquities, description
By period -- Continued

684.2 1951-1980
684.25 1981-
685.A-Z Parishes, boroughs, streets, etc., A-Z
e.g.
685.A1 General
685.A3 Aldersgate
685.B65 Bloomsbury
685.C5 Chelsea
685.E1 East London. East End of London
685.F5 Fleet Street
685.G68 Greenwich
Hampstead
685.H22 Serials
685.H23 Monographs
685.H9 Hyde Park
685.K5 Kensington
685.L7 Lincoln's Inn Fields
685.M2 Marylebone
685.P5 Piccadilly
685.S6 Soho Square
685.S65 South London
685.S7 Southwark
685.T7 Tottenham
685.W5 Westminster
Institutions
686 General works
687.A-Z Individual, A-Z
e.g.
687.A45 Albany (Chambers)
687.B9 Buckingham Palace
687.C4 Charterhouse
687.C9 Crystal Palace, Sydenham
687.D7 No. 10 Downing Street
Gray's Inn, see KD504.G7
687.H7 Holland House
Inner Temple, see KD504.I5
Inns of Chancery, see KD502
Inns of Court, see KD502
Lincoln's Inn, see KD504.I5
Middle Temple, see KD504.M5
687.S14 Saint Paul's Cathedral
Staple Inn, see KD505.S7
687.T2 Temple Church
687.T7 Tower of London
687.W5 Westminster Abbey
687.W6 Westminster Palace. Houses of Parliament
687.W65 Whitehall Palace
688 Social life and customs. Culture. Intellectual life

England
London -- Continued
689.A-Z Other, A-Z
689.B8 Bridges
Including London Bridge, etc.
689.C3 Cemeteries
689.C4 Cheapside Cross
Church records and registers, see CS436.L7A1 +
689.G3 Gardens
Including Vauxhall, etc.
689.H48 Historic houses
689.H5 Historic markers
689.H8 Hotels, taverns, etc.
689.L5 Literary landmarks
689.M37 Markets
689.M7 Monuments, statutes, etc.
689.O63 Open spaces
689.P17 Palaces (General)
689.P2 Parks (General)
689.P6 Port of London
689.S7 Squares
689.U5 Underground areas
689.W2 Water
690.A-Z Other cities, towns, etc., A-Z
e.g.
690.A1 Collective
690.A14 Abingdon
690.A79 Arundel
690.B22 Banbury
690.B26 Barnstaple
690.B29 Basingstoke
690.B3 Bath
690.B6 Birmingham
690.B65 Bolton
690.B68 Boston
690.B685 Bournemouth
690.B7 Bradford (Yorkshire)
690.B78 Brighton
690.B8 Bristol
690.B84 Bristow
690.B92 Burford
690.B97 Bury Saint Edmunds
690.B98 Buxton
Cambridge
690.C19 Serials
690.C2 Nonserials
690.C3 Canterbury
690.C335 Carlisle
690.C46 Chatsworth
690.C48 Cheltenham
690.C49 Chepstow
690.C5 Chester
690.C59 Church Stretton

England
Other cities, towns, etc., A-Z -- Continued

690.C6 Cinque Ports
690.C7 Colchester
690.C75 Coventry
690.C79 Crowland Abbey
690.C8 Croydon
690.D4 Derby
690.D63 Dorchester
690.D7 Dover
690.D96 Durham
690.E4 Ely
690.E9 Exeter
690.G45 Glastonbury
690.G5 Gloucester
690.G8 Gravesend
Greenwich, see DA685.G68
690.H17 Halifax
690.H2 Hampton Court
690.H35 Hastings
690.H54 Hereford
690.H9 Hull
690.I6 Ipswich
690.K4 Kenilworth
690.L15 Lacock
Including the village and abbey
690.L2 Lancaster
690.L35 Leamington
Leeds
690.L39 Serials
690.L4 Nonserials
690.L5 Leicester
690.L67 Lincoln
690.L8 Liverpool
690.L85 Ludlow
690.M2 Maidstone
690.M3 Malvern
690.M4 Manchester
690.M42 Margate
690.M46 Marlborough
690.M48 Matlock
690.N53 Newark
690.N55 Newbury
690.N58 Newcastle-under-Lyme
690.N6 Newcastle-upon-Tyne
690.N8 Northampton
690.N87 Northowram
690.N92 Nottingham
Oxford
690.O97 Serials
690.O98 Nonserials
690.P48 Petworth
690.P7 Plymouth

England
Other cities, towns, etc., A-Z -- Continued
690.P95 Prestwich
690.R28 Reading
690.R5 Richmond
690.R6 Rochester
690.R9 Rye
690.S13 Saint Albans
690.S16 Salisbury
Including old and new Sarum
690.S28 Scarborough
690.S54 Sheffield
690.S58 Shrewsbury
Southampton
690.S69 Serials
690.S7 Nonserials
690.S75 Southport
690.S8 Stamford
690.S92 Stratford-upon-Avon
690.T36 Tewkesbury
690.T69 Torquay
690.T92 Tunbridge Wells
690.W14 Wakefield
690.W28 Warrington
690.W3 Warwick
690.W67 Winchester
690.W76 Windsor
690.W927 Worthing
690.Y2 Yarmouth
690.Y6 York
Wales
700 Periodicals. Societies. Collections
708 General works
709 Compends
710 Biography (Collective)
711 Antiquities
Cf. DA740+, Local history and description
711.5 Social life and customs. Civilization
712 Ethnography. Races
713 Pamphlets, etc.
History
713.5 Study and teaching
714 General works
By period
715 Early and medieval
Biography
716.A1 Collective
716.A2-Z Individual, A-Z
e.g.
716.G5 Glendower, Owen
Modern
720 General works

Wales
History
By period
Modern -- Continued
19th-20th centuries
Including Rebecca Riots, 1839-1844, etc.
722 General works
Biography and memoirs
722.1.A1 Collective
722.1.A2-Z Individual, A-Z
e.g.
722.1.T9 Turner, Sir Llewelyn
Description and travel
725 Through 1700
727 1701-1800
730 1801-1950
731 1951-1980
731.2 1981-
734 Gazetteers. Dictionaries, etc. Place names
735 Guidebooks
Castles, halls, etc.
737 General works
738.A-Z Special, A-Z
Local history and description
740.A-Z Counties, regions, etc., A-Z
e.g.
740.A5 Anglesey
740.B7 The Border
740.B8 Brecknockshire
740.C3 Cardiganshire
740.C34 Carmarthenshire
740.C35 Carnarvonshire (Caenarvonshire)
740.C6 Clwyd Valley
740.D3 Denbighshire
740.F6 Flintshire
740.G5 Glamorganshire
740.L7 Llandaff (Diocese)
740.M4 Merionethshire
740.M7 Montgomeryshire
740.P3 Pembrokeshire
740.P8 Powys
740.R3 Radnorshire
740.S6 Snowdonia
745.A-Z Cities, towns, etc., A-Z
e.g.
745.C2 Cardiff
745.C3 Carnarvon (Caernarvon)
745.H2 Harlech
745.L7 Llandudno
745.W9 Wrexham
Scotland
750 Periodicals. Societies. Serials
Museums, exhibitions, etc.

Scotland
Museums, exhibitions, etc. -- Continued
751 General works
751.5.A-Z Individual. By place, A-Z
(753) Yearbooks
see DA750
Sources and documents
755 Nonofficial
757 Official
757.5 General works
757.7 Historical geography
Description and travel, see DA850 +
History
757.9 Dictionaries. Chronological tables, outlines, etc.
Biography (Collective)
For individual biography, see the special period, reign, or place
758 General works
758.1 Public men
758.2 Rulers, kings, etc.
For English sovereigns, see DA385 +
For the House of Stuart, see DA758.3.S8, for early Stuarts, see DA783.5 +, for later Stuarts, see DA784 +
Houses, noble families, etc.
Including biographical memoirs
758.3.A1 Collective
758.3.A2-Z Individual houses, etc., A-Z
e.g.
758.3.M3 Mar, Earls of
758.3.S8 Stuart, House of
758.4 Women
Historiography
759 General works
Biography of historians
759.5 Collective
759.7.A-Z Individual, A-Z
760 General works
761 Popular works
762 Compends. Juvenile works
763 Pamphlets, etc.
General special
765 Political and diplomatic history. Home rule
Cf. DA775, Special periods, reigns, etc.
767 Military history
Antiquities
Cf. DA777.5 +, Roman antiquities
Cf. DA880.A +, Local history and description
770 General works
Biography of archaeologists
771.A2 Collective
771.A3-Z Individual, A-Z
e.g.

Scotland
History
General special
Antiquities
Biography of archaeologists
Individual -- Continued
771.L3 Laing, David
Social life and customs. Civilization.
Intellectual life. National characteristics
772 General works
773 Court life and coronations
Ethnography
774 General works
774.4.A-Z Individual elements in the population, A-Z
774.4.A74 Asians
774.4.C55 Chileans
774.4.I72 Irish
774.4.I732 Italians
774.5 Scots outside of Scotland (General)
For Scots in a particular country, see the country
By period
Early and medieval to 1603
774.8 Historiography
775 General works
Early to 1057
Including antiquities
777 General works
777.3 Earliest to 844
Roman period
Including antiquities
777.5 General works
777.7.A-Z Local, A-Z
e.g.
777.7.M66 Mons Graupius
844-1057
General works, see DA777+
778 Kenneth I MacAlpin, 844-860
778.1 Constantine II, 863-877
778.2 Constantine III, 900-942
778.3 Malcolm I, 942-954
778.33 Indulph, 954-962
778.35 Duff, 962-967
778.37 Culen, 967-971
778.4 Kenneth II, 971-995
778.45 Constantine IV, 995-997
778.5 Kenneth III, 997-1005
778.6 Malcolm II, 1005-1034
778.7 Duncan I, 1034-1040
778.8 Macbeth, 1040-1057
778.9.A-Z Biography of contemporaries, A-Z
1057-1603
779 General works

Scotland
  History
    By period
      Early and medieval to 1603
        1057-1603 -- Continued
          1057-1278
780 General works
781 Malcolm III Canmore, 1057-1093
781.5 Edgar, 1097-1107
781.7 Alexander I, 1107-1124
782 David I, 1124-1153
782.2 Malcolm IV, 1153-1165
782.4 William IV, the Lion, 1165-1214
782.6 Alexander II, 1214-1249
782.8 Alexander III, 1249-1286
782.9.A-Z Biography of contemporaries, A-Z
  e.g.
782.9.M3 Margaret, Consort of Malcolm III
          1278-1488
783 General works
  War of Independence, 1285-1371
783.2 General works
783.25 John Baliol, 1292-1296
  Sir William Wallace, 1296-1305
    Including Rising, 1297-1304
783.3 General works
783.35 Special events
  1306-1371. 14th century
783.38 General works
  Robert I (Robert Bruce), 1306-1329
783.4 General works
783.41 Special events
  e.g. Battle of Bannockburn, 1314
783.43 David II, 1329-1371
783.45.A-Z Biography of contemporaries, A-Z
  1371-1488. Early Stuarts
    Cf. DA758.3.S8, House of Stuart
783.5 General works
783.52 Social life and customs. Civilization. Intellectual life
783.53 Robert II, 1371-1390
  Including Battle of Otterburn, 1388, etc.
783.57 Robert III, 1390-1406
  Including Battle of Perth, 1396, etc.
783.6 James I, 1406-1437
783.7 James II, 1437-1460
783.8 James III, 1460-1488
783.9.A-Z Biography of contemporaries, A-Z
  e.g.
783.9.C7 Crawford, Alexander Lindsay, 4th Earl of
          1488-1603
784 General works

Scotland
History
By period
Early and medieval to 1603
1057-1603
1488-1603 -- Continued
784.3.A-Z Biography and memoirs of contemporaries, A-Z
e.g.
784.3.A4 Albany, John Stewart, Duke of
James IV, 1488-1513
784.5 General works
784.6 Battle of Flodden, 1513
784.7 James V, 1513-1542
1542-1603
785 General works
Mary Stuart, 1542-1567
786 General works on reign
787.A1 History and biography
787.A2 Pamphlets, etc.
787.A3 Special works
Including iconography
787.A36 Casket letters
787.A5 Compends. Juvenile works
787.A6-Z Biography of contemporaries, A-Z
e.g.
787.B7 Bothwell, James Hepburn, 4th Earl of
787.B9 Buchanan, George
787.R6 Rizzio, David
1567-1603. James VI
788 General works
789 Gowrie Conspiracy, 1600
790.A-Z Biography and memoirs of contemporaries, A-Z
e.g.
790.M3 MacGregor, Alasdair Roy
1603-1707/1745
800 General works
Biography and memoirs
802.A1 Collective
802.A2-Z Individual, A-Z
1603-1692
803 General works
803.1 Pamphlets. By date
1603-1625
803.15 General works
803.2.A-Z Biography and memoirs, A-Z
1625-1660
Including 1625-1688
803.3 General works
1637-1649
803.6 General works
803.7.A-Z Biography and memoirs, A-Z
e.g.

Scotland
History
By period
1603-1707/1745
1603-1692
1625-1660
1637-1649
Biography and memoirs, A-Z -- Continued

803.7.A3 Montrose, James Graham, 1st Marquis of
803.7.A4 Argyll, Archibald Campbell, Marquis of
803.73 1637-1643
803.8 1649-1660
1660-1692/1715
804 General works
Biography and memoirs
804.1.A1 Collective
804.1.A2-Z Individual, A-Z
e.g.
804.1.D9 Dundee, John Graham of Claverhouse, Viscount
804.1.F6 Fletcher, Andrew
804.6 Revolution, 1688
804.7 Glencoe massacre
1692-1707
805 General works
807 The Union, 1707
18th century
809 General works
Biography and memoirs
810.A1 Collective
810.A2-Z Individual, A-Z
e.g.
810.E7 Erskine, Henry
810.K3 Kames, Henry Home, Lord
810.M3 Macgregor, Robert (Rob Roy)
Rob Roy, see DA810.M3
811 Pamphlets, etc.
812 Social life and customs. Civilization. Intellectual life
1707-1745. Jacobite movements
813 General works
Biography and memoirs
814.A1 Collective
814.A3 James, Prince of Wales, the Old Pretender
814.A4 Clementina, Consort of James
814.A5 Charles Edward, the Young Pretender
814.A52 Albany, Charlotte Stuart, called Duchess of
814.A55 Albany, Louise Maximiliane C.E., Princess of Stolberg, known as Countess of
814.A6 Henry Benedict M.C. Stuart, Cardinal York
814.A8-Z Other, A-Z
e.g.

Scotland
History
By period
18th century
1707-1745. Jacobite movements
Biography and memoirs
Other, A-Z -- Continued
814.L8 Lovat, Simon Fraser, Baron
814.M14 Macdonald, Flora
814.2 1707
814.3 1714. Battle of Sheriffmuir
814.4 1719
814.5 1745-1746. Battle of Cullodon, 1746
19th century
815 General works
Biography and memoirs
816.A1 Collective
816.A2-Z Individual, A-Z
e.g.
816.C6 Cockburn, Henry Cockburn, Lord
816.M3 Marwick, Sir James David
817 Pamphlets, etc.
818 Social life and customs. Civilization
20th century
821 General works
822.A-Z Biography and memoirs, A-Z
824 Pamphlets, etc.
826 Social life and customs. Civilization. Intellectual life
Description and travel
850 History of travel
By period
855 Through 1800
865 1801-1900
866 1901-1950
867 1951-1980
867.5 1981-
869 Gazetteers. Dictionaries, etc. Place names
870 Guidebooks
873 Preservation of historic monuments, historic houses, etc.
Castles, halls, etc.
875 General works
877.A-Z Special, A-Z
e.g.
Cf. DA890.A+, Cities and towns of Scotland
877.G6 Glamis Castle
878 Islands of Scotland (Collective)
For individual islands or groups of islands, see DA880.A+
880.A-Z Counties, regions, etc., A-Z
e.g.
880.A1 Aberdeenshire

Scotland
Counties, regions, etc., A-Z -- Continued

880.A5 Angus. Forfar
880.A6 Argyleshire
880.A7 Arran
880.A9 Ayrshire
880.B2 Banffshire
880.B5 Berwickshire
880.B72 The Border
880.B76 Breadalbane
880.B8 Buchan
880.B9 Buteshire
880.C1 Caithness
880.C5 Clackmannanshire
880.C6 Clyde River. Firth of Clyde
880.D8 Dumbartonshire
880.D88 Dumfriesshire
880.E2 East Lothian. Haddington
Edinburghshire, see DA880.M6
Elginshire, see DA880.M8
880.F4 Fife
Forfarshire, see DA880.A5
880.G1 Galloway
880.G7 Grampians
Haddingtonshire, see DA880.E2
880.H4 Hebrides
Highlands. Clans
880.H6 History
880.H7 Description
880.H76 Tartans of clans
880.I6 Inverness-shire
880.I7 Iona
880.K5 Kincardineshire
880.K53 Kinross-shire
880.K56 Kintyre
880.K6 Kirkcudbrightshire
880.K75 Knoydart
880.L2 Lanarkshire
Linlithgowshire, see DA880.W4
880.L8 Lochaber
880.L9 Lorne (District)
880.M6 Midlothian. Edinburghshire
880.M8 Moray. Elginshire
880.N3 Nairnshire
Orkney Islands
880.O5 Serials
880.O6 Nonserials
880.P3 Peeblesshire
880.P4 Perthshire
880.R4 Renfrewshire
880.R7 Ross and Cromarty
880.R8 Roxburghshire
880.S2 Saint Kilda, Hebrides

	Scotland
	Counties, regions, etc., A-Z -- Continued
	Scottish Borders, see DA880.B72
880.S4	Selkirkshire
880.S5	Shetland Islands
880.S6	Skye
880.S8	Stirlingshire
880.S96	Sutherland
880.T8	Trossachs
880.T9	Tweed River and Valley
880.U48	Ulva
880.W4	West Lothian. Linlithgowshire
880.W5	Wigtownshire
880.Y2	Yarrow
890.A-Z	Cities, towns, etc., A-Z
	e.g.
890.A2	Aberdeen
890.A5	Arbroath
890.D75	Dryburgh Abbey
890.D79	Dumfries
890.D797	Dunblane
890.D9	Dunfermline
890.D92	Dunkeld
	Edinburgh
890.E2	History
890.E3A1-E3A19	Directories
890.E3A2-E3Z	Description. Guidebooks
890.E4A-Z	Special, A-Z
890.E4C3	Castle
890.E4H7	Holyrood Palace and Abbey
890.E4M27	Marchmont
890.E4S1	Saint Giles
	Glasgow
890.G49	Serials
890.G5	Nonserials
890.G8	Gretna Green
890.H2	Haddington
890.H3	Hawick
890.I6	Inverness
890.K48	Kilmarnock
890.K53	Kirkwall
890.L3	Langholm
890.L5	Leith
890.L75	Linlithgow
890.M5	Melrose
890.P1	Paisley
890.P3	Peebles
890.P4	Perth
890.S2	Saint Andrews
890.S8	Stirling
890.S85	Strathblane
890.W5	Whithorn priory
	Ireland

Ireland -- Continued
900 Periodicals. Societies. Serials
903 Minor periodicals
905 Sources and documents
906 General works
Biography (Collective), see DA916
Historiography
908 General works
Biography of historians
908.5 Collective
908.7.A-Z Individual, A-Z
History
Study and teaching
909 General works
909.2.A-Z By region or country, A-Z
909.5.A-Z Individual schools, A-Z
910 General works
Popular works
911 General
911.2 Stories from Irish history
911.5 Comic and satiric works
912 Compends
913 Addresses, essays, lectures
General special
Military history
914 General works
915.A-Z Biography and memoirs, A-Z
916 Biography (Collective)
For individual biography, see the special period, reign, or place
916.1 Rulers, kings, viceroys, etc.
916.3 Houses, noble families, etc.
916.4 Public men
916.7 Women
916.8 Other
Including Irish in other countries
920 Antiquities
Including pre-Celtic
Cf. DA990.A+, Local history and description
Social life and customs. Civilization. National characteristics
925 General works
926.A-Z Special topics, A-Z
927 Ethnography
By period
To 1172
930 General works
930.5 Social life and customs. Civilization. Intellectual life
931 Pagan Ireland, to 433
Christian Ireland, 433-1172
932 General works
932.2.A-Z Biography and memoirs, A-Z

Ireland
History
By period
To 1172
Christian Ireland, 433-1172 -- Continued
932.4 433-795
932.6 Danish wars, 795-1014
1172-1603
933 General works
933.2 Social life and customs. Civilization. Intellectual life
Biography and memoirs
933.25 Collective
933.26.A-Z Individual, A-Z
933.3 English conquest, 1154-1189
1189-1485
934 General works
934.5 Invasion by Edward Bruce, 1315
Including biography of Bruce
1485-1603. Tudors
935 General works
936.A-Z Biography and memoirs of contemporaries, A-Z
e.g.
936.K5 Kildare, Gerald Fitzgerald, 8th Earl of
1558-1603. Elizabeth
937 General works
937.3 Tyrone's Rebellion, 1597-1603
937.5.A-Z Biography and memoirs of contemporaries, A-Z
e.g.
937.5.D4 Desmond, Katherine (Fitzgerald) Fitzgerald, Countess of
937.5.O3 O'Donnell, Hugh Roe
Modern, 1603-
938 General works
17th century
940 General works
940.3 Social life and customs. Civilization. Intellectual life
940.5.A-Z Biography and memoirs, A-Z
e.g.
940.5.C7 Cork, Richard Boyle, 1st Earl of
940.5.O5 O'Neill, Owen Roe
940.5.O7 Ormonde, James Butler, 1st Duke of
941.3 1603-1625. James I
1625-1649. Charles I
941.5 General works
943 1641-1649. Irish Confederation, 1642-1648
Including the Rebellion of 1641, etc.
944.4 1649-1660. Cromwell
944.5 1660-1685. Charles II
944.7 1685-1688. James II

Ireland
History
By period
Modern, 1603-
17th century -- Continued
945 1688-1691
Including the Siege of Londonderry, 1688-1689; Battle of the Boyne, 1690; Siege of Limerick, 1690; etc.
946 1691-1700
18th century
947 General works
947.Z9 Pamphlets, etc.
947.3 Social life and customs. Civilization. Intellectual life
948.A2 General special
Biography and memoirs
948.A5 Collective
948.3.A-Z Individual, A-Z
e.g.
948.3.C9 Curran, John Philpot
948.3.F6 Flood, Henry
948.3.G7 Grattan, Henry
1782-1800
948.4 General works
1791-1800
948.5 General works
948.6.A-Z Biography and memoirs, A-Z
e.g.
948.6.E5 Emmet, Robert
948.6.F5 Fitzgerald, Lord Edward
948.6.T6 Tone, Theobald Wolfe
1798-1800
949 General works
949.5 The Union
19th century. Irish question
Cf. JN1411, Political institutions and public administration
Cf. KDK1200+, Constitutional history
949.7 Dictionaries
950 General works
950.1 Social life and customs. Civilization. Intellectual life
1800-1848
950.2 General works
Biography and memoirs
950.21 Collective
Individual
950.22 O'Connell, Daniel
950.23.A-Z Other, A-Z
e.g.
950.23.D2 Davis, Thomas Osborne
950.23.D7 Drummond, Thomas

Ireland
History
By period
Modern, 1603-
19th century. Irish question
1800-1848
Biography and memoirs
Individual
Other, A-Z -- Continued
950.23.M6 Mitchel, John
950.23.S5 Sheil, Richard Lalor
950.29 Pamphlets. By date
950.3 1800-1829. Catholic emancipation
950.4 Tithe War, 1829-1838
950.5 1838-1848
950.7 Famine, 1845-1847
1848-1900
951 General works
Biography and memoirs
952.A1 Collective
952.A2-Z Individual, A-Z
e.g.
952.O3 O'Donovan Rossa, Jeremiah
952.R3 Redmond, John Edward
953 Pamphlets. By date
954 Fenians
955 1848-1868
1868-1900
957 General works
957.5 Parnell Commission
957.9 Other
Biography and memoirs
958.A1 Collective
958.A2-Z Individual, A-Z
e.g.
958.D2 Davitt, Michael
958.H4 Healy, Timothy Michael
958.O3 O'Brien, William
958.O5 O'Connor, Thomas Power
20th century
959 General works
959.1 Social life and customs. Civilization
1901-1922
960 General works
962 1914-1921. Period of World War I, 1914-1918
963 1922-
Including Irish Free State, 1922-1937; Éire, 1937-1949; Republic of Ireland, 1949-
Diplomatic history. Foreign and special relations
964.A2 General works

Ireland
History
By period
Modern, 1603-
20th century
Diplomatic history. Foreign and special relations -- Continued
964.A3-Z Relations with individual regions or countries, A-Z
Biography and memoirs
965.A1 Collective
965.A3-Z Individual, A-Z
e.g.
965.C25 Carson, Sir Edward Henry
965.C3 Casement, Sir Roger
965.C6 Collins, Michael
965.C7 Connolly, James
965.D4 DeValera, Eamonn
965.G8 Griffith, Arthur
965.H9 Hyde, Douglas
965.P4 Pearse, Padraic
965.P6 Plunkett, Sir Horace Curzon
969 Description and travel
By period
970 Through 1700
972 1701-1800
975 1801-1900
977 1901-1950
978 1951-1980
978.2 1981-
979 Gazetteers. Dictionaries, etc. Place names
979.5 Directories
980 Guidebooks
982 Pictorial works
Castles, halls, etc.
985 General works
987.A-Z Individual, A-Z
e.g.
987.D8 Dungory Castle
988 Islands of Ireland (Collective)
990.A-Z Counties, regions, etc., A-Z
e.g.
990.A6 Antrim
990.A8 Aran Islands
990.A85 Armagh
990.B65 Blasket Islands
990.C28 Carlow
990.C59 Clare
990.C6 Connacht (Connaught) Province
990.C7 Connemara (District)
Cork
990.C78 Periodicals. Societies. Serials
990.C79 History and description

Ireland
Counties, regions, etc., A-Z -- Continued

990.D6 Donegal
990.D7 Down
990.D8 Dublin
Cf. DA995.D75+, Dublin (City)
990.G18 Galway
990.K4 Kerry
990.K45 Killarney, Lakes of
King's, see DA990.O3
990.L5 Leinstrer
Including life of Art McMurrough, King
990.L55 Leitrim
990.L6 Leix (Laoighis), Queen's
990.L7 Limerick
990.L8 Londonderry
990.M3 Mayo
990.M7 Monaghan
990.M8 Munster
Northern Ireland, see DA990.U45+
990.O3 Offaly. King's
Queen's, see DA990.L6
990.R7 Roscommon
990.S6 Sligo
990.T3 Tara
990.T5 Tipperary
990.T9 Tyrone
Northern Ireland (Ulster)
990.U45 Periodicals. Societies. Serials
Biography
990.U452A1-U452A19 Collective
990.U452A2-U452Z Individual, A-Z
990.U46 History and description
990.W3 Waterford
990.W5 Wexford
990.W6 Wicklow
995.A-Z Cities, towns, etc., A-Z
e.g.
995.A72 Armagh
995.B21 Bandon
995.B5 Belfast
995.C3 Carrickfergus
995.C4 Cashel
995.C7 Cork
Dublin
995.D75 History
995.D8 Description
995.D9A-Z Special, A-Z
995.D9C32 Cabra
995.D9D8 Dublin Castle
995.D9I53 Inchicore
995.D9K5 King's Inns
995.D9M68 Mountjoy Square

Ireland
Cities, towns, etc., A-Z
Dublin
Special, A-Z -- Continued

995.D9N44	Nelson Pillar
995.E6	Enniskillen
995.G18	Galway
995.L7	Limerick
995.L75	Londonderry
995.W32	Waterford

History of Central Europe
Cf. DJK1+, Eastern Europe
1001 Periodicals. Societies. Serials
1004 Congresses
1005 Sources and documents
1006 Gazetteers. Dictionaries, etc.
1007 Place names (General)
1008 Guidebooks
1009 General works
1010 Pictorial works
1012 Historic monuments, landmarks, scenery, etc.
For local, see individual countries, regions, etc.
1013 Historical geography
Description and travel
1014 Early through 1980
1015 1981-
1023 Antiquities
For local antiquities, see individual countries, regions, etc.
1024 Social life and customs. Civilization. Intellectual life
For specific periods, see the period
Ethnography
1026 General works
1028.A-Z Individual elements in the population, A-Z
1028.C75 Croats
1028.P64 Poles
1028.T38 Tatars
History
Periodicals, societies, serials, see DAW1001
1031 Biography (Collective)
For individual biography, see the specific period, reign or place
Historiography
1032 General works
Biography of historians, area studies specialists, archaeologists, etc.
1033 Collective
1034.A-Z Individual, A-Z
Study and teaching. Area studies
1035 General works
1036.A-Z By region or country, A-Z
1038 General works
1042 Political history
By period, see the specific period
1044 Foreign and general relations
By period, see the specific period
1045.A-Z Relations with specific countries, A-Z
By period
1046 Early and medieval to 1500
For the Holy Roman Empire, see DD125+
1047 1500-1815
For the Austro-Hungarian Empire, see DB1+

History
By period -- Continued
1048 1815-1918
1049 1918-1945
1050 1945-1989
1051 1989-

History of Austria
Including Austro-Hungarian Empire

1 Periodicals. Societies. Serials
3 Sources and documents
Collected works
4 Several authors
5 Individual authors
14 Gazetteers. Dictionaries. etc.
15 Place names (General)
16 Guidebooks
17 General works
18 General special
19 Pictorial works
Historic monuments, landmarks, scenery, etc.
19.5 General works
For local, see DB101+
19.55 Preservation
20 Historical geography
20.5 Geography
Description and travel
21 Early through 1525
22 1526-1648
23 1649-1791
24 1792-1815
25 1816-1900
26 1901-1945
27 1946-1980
27.5 1981-
29 Antiquities
Cf. DB101+, Local history and description
30 Social life and customs. Civilization. Intellectual life
Ethnography
33 General works
For politics, the race question, the problem of nationalities, see DB46+
34.A-Z Individual elements in the population, A-Z
34.A75 Armenians
34.A97 Avars
34.B43 Blacks
34.B84 Bulgarians
34.C7 Croats
34.G7 Greeks
34.I8 Italians
34.P65 Poles
34.R7 Romance-language-speaking peoples. Latins
34.R8 Romanians
34.S35 Serbs
34.S4 Slavs
34.S5 Slovaks
34.S6 Slovenes
34.S65 Southern Slavs (in general)
34.T87 Turks

Ethnography
Individual elements
in the population, A-Z -- Continued
34.U5 Ukrainians
34.5 Austrians in foreign countries
History
35 Dictionaries. Chronological tables, outlines, etc.
Biography (Collective)
For individual biography, see the period, reign, or place
36 General works
36.1 Rulers, kings, etc.
36.2 Queens, princesses, etc.
36.3.A-Z Houses, noble families, etc., A-Z
e.g.
36.3.L6 Liechtenstein, House of
36.4 Public men
36.7 Women
Historiography
36.8 General works
Biography of historians
36.9.A2 Collective
36.9.A3-Z Individual, A-Z
36.95 Study and teaching
General works
37 Through 1800. Chronicles
38 1801-
39 Compends
40 Pamphlets, etc.
40.5 Anecdotes, etc.
41 Several part of the empire treated together
Military history
For individual campaigns and engagements, see the special period
42 Periodicals. Societies. Serials
43 General works
44 Biography (Collective)
45 Naval history
Political and diplomatic history. Foreign and general relations
Including the race questions, the problem of nationalities
Cf. D377, D449; DB33+, DB919, DB945+, DB2076+
46 Sources and documents
47 General works
48 20th century. The Austrian question
49.A-Z Relations with individual regions or countries, A-Z
By period
Early and medieval to 1521
51 General works
52 Biography (Collective)
976-1246
53 General works

History
By period
Early and medieval to 1521
976-1246 -- Continued
54.A-Z Biography, A-Z
For collective biography, see DB52
1246-1526
55 General works
56 1246-1251. Interregnum
57 1251-1278. Ottokar II
58 1278-1282. Interregnum
59.A-Z Biography, A-Z
e.g.
Collective, see DB52
59.R8 Rudolf IV, Duke of Austria
60 Wars with the Turks
61 Early invasions to 1606
62 Invasions from 1606-1791
63 Special events. By date
e.g.
Siege of Vienna, 1683, see DR536
Siege of Buda, 1686, see DR536.5
63 1699 Peace of Carlowitz
64.A-Z Biography and memoirs, A-Z
e.g.
64.S73 Starhemberg, Ernest Rüdiger, graf, 1638-1701
(64.Z9) Zrinyi, Miklós, gróf, 1620-1664
See DB932.48.Z75
1521-
65 General works
1521-1648
65.2 General works
65.3 Ferdinand I, 1521-1564
65.4 Maximilian II, 1564-1576
Rudolf II, 1576-1612
65.5 General works on life and reign
Biography and memoirs of contemporaries
65.53 Collective
65.54.A-Z Individual, A-Z
65.6 Mathias, 1612-1619
65.7 1618-1648
For works on the Thirty Years' War, see D251+
65.75 Ferdinand II, 1619-1637
65.8 Ferdinand III, 1637-1657
65.9.A-Z Biography and memoirs of contemporaries not identified with special reigns, A-Z
1648-1740
66 General works
66.5 General special
66.8.A-Z Biography and memoirs, A-Z
e.g.
Cf. DB67.8, DB69.5
66.8.S8 Starhemberg, Guido, graf

History
By period
1521-
1648-1740 -- Continued
Leopold I, 1657-1705
67 General works on life and reign
67.3 General special
67.8.A-Z Biography and memoirs of contemporaries, A-Z
e.g.
67.8.C4 Charles V, Duke of Lorraine
67.8.L74 Lobkowitz, Wenzel Franz E., fürst von
Joseph I, 1705-1701
68 General works on life and reign
Karl VI, 1711-1740
69 General works on life and reign
69.3 General special
e.g. Pragmatic sanction
Cf. JN1625, Political history
69.5.A-Z Biography and memoirs of contemporaries, A-Z
1740-1792
69.7 General works
69.8 General special
69.9.A-Z Biography and memoirs, A-Z
Cf. DB73, DB74.7
Maria Theresia, 1740-1780
70 General works on reign
71 Biography of Maria Theresia
72 Austrian succession
For works on the War of the Austrian Succession, 1740-1748, see D291+
72.5 Political and diplomatic history
Biography and memoirs of contemporaries
73.A2 Collective
73.A3-Z Individual, A-Z
e.g.
73.M2 Maria Christine, Consort of Albert Casimir, Duke of Saxe-Teschen
73.S9 Swieten, Gerard, freiherr van
73.Z5 Zinzendorf, Ludwig, graf von
Joseph II, 1780-1790
74 General works on life and reign
74.3 Political and diplomatic history
74.5 Personal special
74.6 Writings of Joseph II
74.7.A-Z Biography and memoirs of contemporaries, A-Z
Leopold II, 1790-1792
74.8 General works on life and reign
1792-1815. Period of the French Revolution
For Illyrian Provinces, 1809-1814, see DR1350.I45
75 Sources and documents
76 General works
77 Other

History
By period
1521-
1792-1815 -- Continued
Congress of Vienna, see DC249
19th century
80 General works
80.2 Social life and customs. Civilization. Intellectual life
Biography and memoirs
80.7 Collective
80.8.A-Z Individual, A-Z
e.g.
80.8.G4 Gentz, Friedrich von
80.8.J4 Jelačić, Josip, grof
80.8.J57 Johann Baptist J.F.S., Archduke of Austria
80.8.K3 Karl, Archduke of Austria
80.8.M57 Metternich, Clemens Wenzel Lothar, fürst von
80.8.S29 Schwarzenberg, Felix, fürst zu
81 Franz I (II), 1792-1835
Ferdinand I, 1835-1848
82 General works on life and reign
82.5 Pamphlets, etc.
83 Revolution, 1848
Franz Joseph I, 1848-1916
85 General works on life and reign
86 General special
Austro-Sardinian War, 1848-1849, see DG553+
Schleswig-Holstein War, 1864, see DL236+
War with Italy, 1866, see DG558
War with Prussia, 1866, see DD436+
86.7 Period of World War I, 1914-1918
For the war itself, see D501+
Biography
87 Franz Joseph I
88 Elisabeth, Consort of Francis Joseph I
89.A-Z Other members of the royal family, A-Z
e.g.
89.F7 Franz Ferdinand, Archduke
89.R8 Rudolf, Crown Prince
90.A-Z Biography and memoirs of contemporaries, A-Z
e.g.
90.B6 Beust, Friedrich Ferdinand, graf von
90.C7 Conrad von Hötzendorf, Franz, graf
90.F5 Fischhof, Adolf
90.R2 Radetzky von Radetz, Johann Joseph W.A. F.K, graf
90.S3 Schönerer, Georg, ritter von
90.T4 Tegetthof, Wilhelm von
20th century
91 General works

History
By period
1521-
20th century -- Continued
91.2 Social life and customs. Civilization. Intellectual life
Karl I, 1916-1918
92 General works on life and reign
93 General special
93.5 Zita, Consort of Karl I
Republic, 1918-
96 General works
97 Other
Biography and memoirs
98.A1 Collective
98.A2-Z Individual, A-Z
e.g.
98.D6 Dollfuss, Engelbert
98.O8 Otto, Archduke
98.S3 Schuschnigg, Kurt
98.S4 Seipel, Ignaz
98.S7 Starhemberg, Ernst Rüdiger, fürst von
99 1938-1945. German annexation
99.1 1945-1955. Allied occupation
99.2 1955-
Local history and description
Provinces, regions, etc.
101-110.15 Alps
Cf. DB761+, Tyrol
Cf. DQ820+, Swiss Alps
101 Periodicals. Societies. Serials
103 Sources and documents. Collections
105 Guidebooks
106 Description and history (General)
Description and travel
107 Early and medieval
108 1601-1800
109 1801-1945
109.2 1946-
110.15 Social life and customs. Civilization. Intellectual life
110.3 Altvater Mountains
111-130 Austria, Lower (Table D-DR6)
151-170 Austria, Upper (Table D-DR6)
(191-217) Czechoslovakia
See DB2000+
Bosnia. Bosnia and Hercegovina, see DR1652+
(261-280) Bukowina
See DK508.9.B85, Ukraine; DR281.S8, Romania
281-300 Carinthia (Table D-DR6)
For Slovenian Carinthia, see DR1475.C37
Carniola, Littoral, Julian March (Yugoslavia), see DR1350.J84

Local history and description
Provinces, regions, etc. -- Continued
Carniola, Littoral, Julian March (Slovenia), see DR1352+
Trieste (City and District), see DG975.T825
Görz and Gradiska (Gorizia region (Italy)), see DG975.G67
Istria, see DR1350.I78
Görz and Gradiska (General and Slovenia), see DR1475.G67
Croatia and Slavonia, see DR1502+
Dalmatia, see DR1620+
441-450.7 Danube River
Cf. DR49+, Lower Danube Valley
For the Danube Valley (General), see DJK76.2+
441 Periodicals. Societies. Serials
443 Sources and documents. Collections
445 Guidebooks
446 Description and history (General)
Description and travel
447 Early and medieval
448 1601-1800
449 1801-1945
449.2 1946-
450 Antiquities
450.5 Social life and customs. Civilization. Intellectual life
450.7 Ethnography
Dinaric Alps, see DR1350.D55
Galicia, see DK4600.G34
Hercegovina, see DR1775.H47
Hungary, see DB901+
Illyrian Provinces, 1809-1814 and Illyria (Kingdom), see DR1350.I45
(540.5) Liechtenstein
See DB881+
(541-560) Moravia
See DB2300+
601-620 Salzburg (Table D-DR6)
621-640 Salzkammergut (Table D-DR6)
Silesia
See DB2500.S54, (Czechoslovakia); DK4600.S42+, (General, and Poland); DK4600.C54, (Cieszyn Silesia)
(661-680) Slovakia
See DB2700+
681-700 Styria (Table D-DR6)
For Lower Styria (Slovenia), see DR1475.S89
Sudetenland. Sudetes (Sudetic Mountains)
See DB2500.S94, (General, and Czechoslovakia); DK4600.S7, (Poland)
(721-740) Transylvania
See DR279+

Local history and description
Provinces, regions, etc. -- Continued
761-780 Tyrol and Vorarlberg (Table D-DR6)
Cf. DB101+, Alps
Cf. DG975.D66+, Dolomite Alps
772.A-Z Biography, A-Z
e.g.
772.H7 Hofer, Andreas
785.A-Z Other, A-Z
Bosen, Deutsch-Sudtirol, see DG975.B68
Brixen, Bressanone, see DG975.B855
785.B8 Burgenland
785.T5 Theiss River and Valley
785.W34 Weinviertel
785.W5 Wienerwald
785.Z5 Zillertal
Vienna
841 Periodicals. Societies. Serials
843 Sources and documents
Biography
844.A1 Collective
844.A2-Z Individual, A-Z
846 Directories. Dictionaries
847 History and description (General). Pictorial works
848 Compends
849 Guidebooks
850 Antiquities
851 Social life and customs. Civilization. Intellectual life
Ethnology
851.5 General works
851.57.A-Z Individual elements, A-Z
851.57.S47 Serbs
History and description
General works, see DB847
852 Early and medieval
853 17th-18th centuries
For works limited to the siege of Vienna, see DR536
854 19th century
Revolution of 1848, see DB83
855 20th century
Sections, districts, etc., A-Z
857.A2 Collective
857.A3-Z Individual, A-Z
857.B45 1. Bezirk
857.B452 2. Bezirk
857.B453 3. Bezirk
857.B454 4. Bezirk
857.B455 5. Bezirk
857.B456 6. Bezirk
857.B457 7. Bezirk
857.B458 8. Bezirk

Local history and description
Vienna
Sections, districts, etc., A-Z
Individual, A-Z -- Continued
857.B459 9. Bezirk
857.B46 10. Bezirk
857.B461 11. Bezirk
857.B462 12. Bezirk
857.B463 13. Bezirk
857.B464 14. Bezirk
857.B465 15. Bezirk
857.B466 16. Bezirk
857.B467 17. Bezirk
857.B468 18. Bezirk
857.B469 19. Bezirk
857.B47 20. Bezirk
857.B471 21. Bezirk
857.B472 22. Bezirk
857.B473 23. Bezirk
857.B474 24. Bezirk
857.B475 25. Bezirk
857.B476 26. Bezirk
857.B477 27. Bezirk
857.B478 28. Bezirk
Streets, suburbs, etc.
858.A2 Collective
858.A3-Z Individual, A-Z
Buildings. Churches, theaters, etc.
859.A2 General works
859.A3-Z Individual, A-Z
860 Other special (not A-Z)
Budapest, see DB981+
879.A-Z Other cities, towns, etc., A-Z
e.g.
879.A8 Aussee. Bad Aussee
Bad Aussee, see DB879.A8
Bad Gastein, see DB879.G2
Bolzano. Bozen, see DG975.B68
Brasov, see DR296.B74
879.B49 Braunau
879.B5 Bregenz
Brixen, Bressanone, see DG975.B855
Brno, see DB2650.B75
Brünn. Brno, see DB2650.B75
Dubrovnik, see DR1645.D8
879.G2 Gastein. Bad Gastein
Gorizia. Görz, see DG975.G67
Görz, see DG975.G67
879.G8 Graz. Gratz
879.I6 Innsbruck
Kraków, see DK4700+
879.K9 Kremsmünster

Local history and description
Other cities, towns, etc., A-Z -- Continued
(879.K93) Kronstadt. Brasov. Stalin
See DR296.B74
879.L6 Linz
Meran, see DG975.M52
Pergine, see DG975.P37
Ragusa. Dubrovnik, see DR1645.D8
879.S18 Salzburg
Trent, see DG975.T788
Trieste, see DG975.T825
Zagreb, see DR1638

History of Liechtenstein
881 Periodicals. Societies. Serials
885 Guidebooks
886 General works
887 Pictorial works
888 Description and travel
889 Antiquities
History
891 General works
Foreign and general relations
893 General works
894.A-Z Relations with individual regions or countries, A-Z
898.A-Z Local, A-Z

History of Hungary
901 Periodicals. Societies. Serials
Museums, exhibitions, etc.
902 General works
902.2.A-Z Individual. By place, A-Z
903 Sources and documents
Collected works
903.5 Several authors
903.7 Individual authors
904 Gazetteers. Dictionaries, etc.
905 Guidebooks
906 General works
906.5 Pictorial works
Historic monuments, landmarks, scenery, etc. (General)
For local, see DB975.A+
906.6 General works
906.7 Preservation
906.75 Historical geography
Description and travel
906.9 History of travel
907 Early through 1526
910 1527-1800
914 1801-1900
916 1901-1918
917 1919-1980
917.3 1981-
Ethnography. Races. Magyars
919 General works
919.15 National characteristics
919.2.A-Z Individual elements in the population, A-Z
919.2.G3 Germans
919.2.G74 Greeks
919.2.J39 Jazyge
919.2.P34 Palocs
919.2.P66 Poles
919.2.R8 Romanians
919.2.S4 Serbs
919.2.S52 Slavs
919.2.S53 Slavs, Southern
919.2.S55 Slovaks
Southern Slavs, see DB919.2.S53
919.2.S94 Szeklers
919.2.Y8 Yugoslavs
919.5 Hungarians in foreign countries (General)
For Hungarians in a particular country, see the country
920 Antiquities
Counties, regions, etc , see DB975.A+
Cities, towns, etc , see DB999.A+
920.5 Social life and customs. Civilization. Intellectual life
History
921 Dictionaries. Chronological tables, outlines, etc.

History -- Continued
Biography (Collective)
For individual biography, see the period, reign, or place
922 General works
922.1 Rulers, kings, etc.
922.3 Houses, noble families, etc.
922.4 Public men
922.7 Women
Historiography
923 General works
Biography of historians
923.5 Collective
923.7.A-Z Individual, A-Z
923.8 Study and teaching
General works
924 Through 1800. Chronicles
925 1801-
925.1 Compends
925.3 Addresses, essays, lectures
925.5 Military history
Political and diplomatic history. Foreign and general relations
For works on relations with a specific country regardless of period, see DB926.3.A+
For general works on the diplomatic history of a period, see the period
926 General works
926.3.A-Z Relations with individual regions or countries, A-Z
By period
Early to 896
927 General works
927.3 Origins
927.5 Roman period
928 Migrations
Árpád dynasty, 896-1301
929.A3 Sources and documents
929.A4-Z General works
Biography and memoirs
929.18 Collective
929.2.A-Z Individual, A-Z
929.25 Arpád, 896-907
929.28 Taksony, 952-972
Including the Battle of Lechfeld, 955
929.3 Géza, 972-977
István, Saint, 997-1038
929.35 General works
929.36 Introduction of Christianity, ca. 1000
929.4 Lázló I, 1077-1095
929.45 Kálman, 1095-1116
929.47 István II, 1116-1131
929.5 Béla III, 1173-1196
András (Endre) II, 1205-1235

History
By period
Arpád dynasty, 896-1301
András (Endre) II, 1205-1235 -- Continued
929.6 General works
929.65 Aranybulla (Golden Bull), 1222
Béla IV, 1235-1270
929.7 General works
929.75 Mongol invasion, 1241-1242
929.8 András III, 1290-1301
Elective kings, 1301-1526
929.95 Sources and documents
930 General works
930.15 Social life and customs. Civilization. Intellectual life
930.2 Károly Róbert I, 1308-1342
930.3 Lajos I, Nagy, 1342-1382
For his reign in Poland, see DK4249
930.4 Sigismund, 1387-1437
For general works on life and reign in Germany, see DD170+
The Hunyadi
930.5 General works
930.7 Hunyadi, János, 1444-1456
931 Mátyás I, Corvinus, 1458-1490
Ulászló (Vladislav) II, 1490-1516
931.4 General works
931.5 Dózsa Uprising, 1514
931.7 Lajos (Ludvik) II, 1516-1526
Biography and memoirs
931.8 Collective
931.9.A-Z Individual, A-Z
e.g.
931.9.B5 Beatrix, Queen, Consort of Mátyás I
931.9.D69 Dózsa, György
Turkish occupation, 1526-1699
931.94 Sources and documents
931.95 General works
931.96 Social life and customs. Civilization. Intellectual life
1526-1606
932 General works
932.12 Social life and customs. Civilization. Intellectual life
Biography and memoirs
932.15 Collective
932.2.A-Z Individual, A-Z
e.g.
932.2.B63 Bocskai, István, Prince of Transylvania
932.2.Z75 Zrínyi, Miklos, grof, 1508-1566
932.25 János I Zápolya, 1526-1540
932.28 Fifteen Years' War, 1591-1606
1606-1699/1711

History
By period
Turkish occupation, 1526-1699
1606-1699/1711 -- Continued
932.3 General works
932.35 Social life and customs. Civilization. Intellectual life
932.4 Ferenc II Rákóczi
Including the Rákóczi Uprising, 1703-1711
Biography and memoirs
932.47 Collective
932.48.A-Z Individual, A-Z
e.g.
932.48.E8 Esterházy, Miklós
932.48.T45 Thököly, Imre, késmárki gróf
932.48.Z75 Zrínyi, Miklös, gróf, 1620-1664
1711-1792. Age of absolutism
932.49 Sources and documents
932.5 General works
932.7 Social life and customs. Civilization. Intellectual life
Biography and memoirs
932.8 Collective
932.9.A-Z Individual, A-Z
e.g.
932.9.M3 Martinovics, Ignác József
1792-1918. 19th century
932.95 Sources and documents
933 General works
933.15 Social life and customs. Civilization. Intellectual life
Biography and memoirs
933.2 Collective
933.3.A-Z Individual, A-Z
e.g.
933.3.D2 Deák, Ferencz
933.3.E6 Eötvös, József, báró
933.3.S8 Széchenyi, István, gróf
933.3.T3 Táncsics, Mihály
933.3.W5 Wesselényi, Miklós, báró
933.5 1792-1825
934 1825-1848. Age of reform
Revolution of 1848-1849
934.5 Sources and documents
935 General works
Kossuth, Lajos
937 General biography and criticism
937.3 Visit to the United States
937.6 Addresses, essays, lectures
937.8 Other
937.82 Personal narratives
937.83.A-Z Local revolutionary history. By place, A-Z
Foreign participation and public opinion

History
By period
1792-1918. 19th century
Revolution of 1848-1849
Foreign participation and public opinion -- Continued
938 General works
939.A-Z By region or country, A-Z
939.5.A-Z Other special topics, A-Z
939.5.I53 Influence
939.5.M55 Minorities
939.5.R44 Religious aspects
1849-1918
940 General works
940.5 Social life and customs. Civilization. Intellectual life
Biography and memoirs
941.A1 Collective
941.A2-Z Individual, A-Z
e.g.
941.A6 Andrássy, Gyula, gróf
941.A8 Apponyi, Albert, gróf
941.T58 Tisza, István, gróf
943 1849-1867
945 1867-1918. Dual monarchy
20th century
946 Sources and documents
947 General works
949.2 Social life and customs. Civilization. Intellectual life
950.A1 Biography (Collective)
For individual biography, see the individual period
953 1914-1918. Period of World War I
For the war itself, see D501+
1918-1945. Revolution. Counterrevolution, and the Regency
954 Sources and documents
955 General works
955.3 Social life and customs. Civilization. Intellectual life
955.4 Foreign and general relations
Biography and memoirs
955.5 Collective
955.6.A-Z Individual, A-Z
e.g.
955.6.B47 Bethlen, István, gróf
955.6.H67 Horthy, Miklós, nagybányai
955.6.K37 Károlyi, Mihály, gróf
955.6.K83 Kun, Béla
955.7 1919-1920. Revolution and counterrevolution
955.8 1939-1945. Period of World War II
For the war itself, see D731+

History
By period
20th century -- Continued
1945-1989. People's Republic
955.9 Sources and documents
956 General works
956.3 Social life and customs. Civilization. Intellectual life
956.4 Foreign and general relations
Biography and memoirs
956.5 Collective
956.6.A-Z Individual, A-Z
e.g.
956.6.K33 Kádár, János
956.6.N33 Nagy, Imre
956.6.R34 Rákosi, Mátyás
Revolution of 1956
956.7 Sources and documents
957 General works
957.3 Personal narratives
957.4.A-Z Local revolutionary history. By place, A-Z
957.5.A-Z Special topics, A-Z
957.5.E95 Executions
957.5.F67 Foreign public opinion
957.5.F74 Press
957.5.R43 Refugees
1989-
957.9 Sources and documents
958 General works
958.2 Social life and customs. Civilization. Intellectual life
958.3 Political history
958.4 Foreign and general relations
Biography and memoirs
958.5 Collective
958.6.A-Z Individual, A-Z
Local history and description
Counties, regions, etc.
974.9 Collective
975.A-Z Individual, A-Z
975.B15 Bácska
For Bačka (General, and Serbia), see DR2105.B32
975.B2 Banat
For Banat (General, and Romania), see DR281.B25
For Serbian Banat, see DR2105.B35
975.B3 Baranya
For Baranja (Croatia), see DR1637.B37
975.B32 Baranyai Szerb-Magyar Köztársaság
975.H4 Hegyalja
975.M4 Mecsek Mountains
Military Frontier (Territory), see DR1350.M54
975.S9 Szabolcs-Szatmár
975.V4 Vertes Mountains

Local history and description -- Continued
Budapest
981 Periodicals. Societies. Serials
981.2 Museums, exhibitions, etc.
Subarrange by author
981.3 Sources and documents
Collected works (nonserial)
981.5 Several authors
981.6 Individual authors
983 Directories. Dictionaries. Gazetteers
983.5 Guidebooks
983.7 General works
Description
984 Early and medieval
984.2 17th-18th centuries
984.3 19th century
984.4 20th century
985 Monumental and picturesque. Pictorial works
987 Antiquities
988 Social life and customs. Civilization. Intellectual life
Ethnography
988.3 General works
988.5.A-Z Individual elements in the population, A-Z
History
988.7 Biography (Collective)
989 General works
By period
989.5 Early and medieval
990 17th-18th centuries
991 19th century
992 20th century
Sections, districts, suburbs, etc. Kerultetek (i.e. numbered city sections) and named city sections
993 Collective
993.2.A-Z Individual, A-Z
993.2.A01-A22 Kerulet
993.2.K57 Kispest
993.2.V37 Városliget
Statues, etc.
993.5 Collective
993.7.A-Z Individual, A-Z
Parks, squares, cemeteries, etc.
994 Collective
994.2.A-Z Individual, A-Z
Streets, bridges, etc.
995 Collective
995.2.A-Z Individual, A-Z
Buildings. Palaces, etc.
996 Collective
997.A-Z Individual, A-Z
Other cities, towns, etc.
998.9 Collective

Local history and description
Other cities, towns, etc. -- Continued
999.A-Z Individual, A-Z

History of Czechoslovakia
Class here general works on Czechoslovakia, on Bohemia, and on the Czech Republic
For Moravia, see DB2300+
For Slovakia, see DB2700+

2000	Periodicals. Societies. Serials
	Museums, exhibitions, etc.
2001	General works
2002.A-Z	Individual. By place, A-Z
2003	Congresses
2004	Sources and documents
	Collected works (nonserial)
2005	Several authors
2006	Individual authors
2007	Gazetteers. Dictionaries, etc.
2008	Place names (General)
2009	Directories
2010	Guidebooks
2011	General works
2012	General special
2013	Pictorial works
	Historic monuments, landmarks, scenery, etc. (General)
	For local, see DB2500.A+
2015	General works
2016	Preservation
2017	Historical geography
	Description and travel
2018	History of travel
2019	Early through 1900
2020	1901-1945
2021	1946-1976
2022	1977-
2030	Antiquities
	For local antiquities, see DB2500.A+
2035	Social life and customs. Civilization. Intellectual life
	For specific periods, see the period or reign
	Ethnography
2040	General works
2041	National characteristics
2042.A-Z	Individual elements in the population, A-Z
2042.A8	Austrians
2042.B85	Bulgarians
2042.C44	Celts
2042.G4	Germans
	Gypsies in the Czech Republic, see DX222
	Gypsies in Slovakia, see DX222.5
2042.H8	Hungarians
	Jews, see DS135.C95+
2042.M33	Macedonians
2042.P6	Poles
2042.R77	Russians
2042.R8	Ruthenians

Ethnography
Individual elements in the population, A-Z -- Continued
2042.S5 Slovaks
2042.S6 Sorbs
2042.U5 Ukrainians
2043 Czechoslovaks in foreign countries (General)
For Slovaks in foreign countries (General), see DB2743
For Czechoslovaks in a particular country, see the country
History
Periodicals. Societies. Serials, see DB2000
2044 Dictionaries. Chronological tables, outlines, etc.
Biography (Collective)
For individual biography, see the specific period, reign, or place
2045 General works
2046 Rulers, kings, etc.
2047 Queens. Princes and princesses
Houses, noble families, etc.
2048 Collective
2049.A-Z Individual houses, families, etc., A-Z
2050 Statesmen
2051 Women
Historiography
2055 General works
Biography of historians and area studies specialists
2056 Collective
2057.A-Z Individual, A-Z
Study and teaching
2059 General works
2060.A-Z By region or country, A-Z
Subarrange by author
General works
2061 Through 1800
2062 1801-1976
2063 1977-
2064 Pictorial works
2065 Juvenile works
2066 Addresses, essays, lectures. Anecdotes, etc.
2068 Philosophy of Czechoslovak history
Military history
For specific periods, including individual campaigns and engagements, see the period or reign
2069 Sources and documents
2070 General works
By period
2071 Early through 1620
2072 1620-1918
2073 1918-
Political history
For specific periods, see the period or reign

History
  Political history -- Continued
2074 Sources and documents
2075 General works
  Foreign and general relations
    For works on relations with a specific country regardless of period, see DB2078.A+
    For general works on the diplomatic history of a period, see the period
2076 Sources and documents
2077 General works
2078.A-Z Relations with individual regions or countries, A-Z
  By period
    Early and medieval to 1526
2080 Sources and documents
2081 General works
2082 General special
2082.4 Addresses, essays, lectures
2082.45 Social life and customs. Civilization. Intellectual life
2082.5 Political history
2083 Biography (Collective)
      Great Moravian Empire, 9th century, see DB2385+
      Přemyslid Dynasty, 9th/10th century-ca. 1310
2085 Sources and documents
2086 General works
2087 General special
2087.5 Addresses, essays, lectures
2088 Social life and customs. Civilization. Intellectual life
2088.5 Military history
2088.7 Political history
2089 Foreign and general relations
        Biography and general memoirs
2090 Collective
2091.A-Z Individual, A-Z
          e.g.
2091.P74 Přemysl II (Otakar)
      Luxemburg Dynasty, 1311-1437
2095 Sources and documents
2096 General works
2097 General special
2097.5 Addresses, essays, lectures
2098 Social life and customs. Civilization. Intellectual life
2098.5 Military history
2098.7 Political history
2099 Foreign and general relations
        Biography and memoirs
2100 Collective
2101.A-Z Individual, A-Z
2102 Jan Lucemburský, 1310-1346
2103 Karel IV, 1346-1378

History
By period
Early and medieval to 1526
Luxemburg Dynasty, 1311-1437 -- Continued
2104 Vaclav IV, 1378-1419
Hussite Wars, 1419-1436
2105 Sources and documents
2106 General works
2107 General special
2107.5 Addresses, essays, lectures
2108 Social life and customs. Civilization. Intellectual life
2108.5 Military history
2108.7 Political history
2109 Foreign and general relations
Biography and memoirs
2110 Collective
2111.A-Z Individual, A-Z
e.g.
2111.Z45 Želivský, Jan
2111.Z59 Žižka z Trocnova, Jan
1437-1526
2115 Sources and documents
2116 General works
2117 General special
2117.5 Addresses, essays, lectures
2118 Social life and customs. Civilization. Intellectual life
2118.7 Political history
2119 Foreign and general relations
Biography and memoirs
2120 Collective
2121.A-Z Individual, A-Z
Jiří z Poděbrad (The Hussite King), 1458-1471
2125 Sources and documents
2126 General works on life and reign
2127 General special
2127.5 Addresses, essays, lectures
2128 Social life and customs. Civilization. Intellectual life
2128.7 Political history
2129 Foreign and general relations
Biography and memoirs
2130 Collective
2131.A-Z Individual, A-Z
2133 1471-1526
Hapsburg rule, 1526-1918
2135 Sources and documents
2136 General works
2137 General special
2137.5 Addresses, essays, lectures
2138 Social life and customs. Civilization. Intellectual life

History
By period
Hapsburg rule, 1526-1918 -- Continued
2138.7 Political history
2139 Foreign and general relations
Biography and memoirs
2140 Collective
2141.A-Z Individual, A-Z
1526-1618
2145 Sources and documents
2146 General works
2147 General special
2147.5 Addresses, essays, lectures
2148 Social life and customs. Civilization. Intellectual life
2148.7 Political history
2149 Foreign and general relations
Biography and memoirs
2150 Collective
2151.A-Z Individual, A-Z
e.g.
2151.R83 Rudolf II
Period of Thirty Years' War. Uprising of the Czech Estates. 1618-1648
For the Thirty Years' War (General), see D251+
2155 Sources and documents
2156 General works
2157 General special
2157.5 Addresses, essays, lectures
2158 Social life and customs. Civilization. Intellectual life
2158.7 Political history
2159 Foreign and general relations
Biography and memoirs
2160 Collective
2161.A-Z Individual, A-Z
2162 Battle of Bílá Hora (Battle of White Mountain or Weisser Berg)
1648-1815
2165 Sources and documents
2166 General works
2167 General special
2167.5 Addresses, essays, lectures
2168 Social life and customs. Civilization. Intellectual life
2168.7 Political history
2169 Foreign and general relations
Biography and memoirs
2170 Collective
2171.A-Z Individual, A-Z
Period of national awakening, 1815-1918
2175 Sources and documents
2176 General works

History
By period
Hapsburg rule, 1526-1918
Period of national awakening, 1815-1918 -- Continued
2177 General special
2177.5 Addresses, essays, lectures
2178 Social life and customs. Civilization. Intellectual life
2178.7 Political history
2179 Foreign and general relations
Biography and memoirs
2180 Collective
2181.A-Z Individual, A-Z
e.g.
2181.H39 Havlíček-Borovský, Karel
2181.J85 Jungman, Josef
2181.P35 Palacký, František
For Palacký as a historian, see DB2057.A+
2182 Revolution of 1848
Czechoslovak Republic, 1918-1992
Including the Czechoslovak Socialist Republic
2185 Sources and documents
2186 General works
2187 General special
2187.5 Addresses, essays, lectures
2188 Social life and customs. Civilization. Intellectual life
2188.7 Political history
2189 Foreign and general relations
Biography and memoirs
2190 Collective
2191.A-Z Individual, A-Z
e.g.
2191.B45 Beneš, Edvard
Dubček, Alexander, see DB2221.D93
2191.F93 Fučík, Julius
2191.G67 Gottwald, Klement
2191.H67 Horáková, Milada
Husák, Gustav, see DB2221.H96
2191.M37 Masaryk, Jan
2191.M38 Masaryk, Tomáš Garrique
1918-1939
2195 Sources and documents
2196 General works
2197 General special
2197.5 Addresses, essays, lectures
2198 Social life and customs. Civilization. Intellectual life
2198.7 Political history
2199 Foreign and general relations
Biography and memoirs
2200 Collective

History
By period
Czechoslovak Republic, 1918-1992
1918-1939
Biography and memoirs -- Continued
2201.A-Z Individual, A-Z
2202 Munich four-power agreement
Cf. D727, European political history
Period of World War II. German occupation, 1939-1945
2205 Sources and documents
2206 General works
2207 General special
2207.5 Addresses, essays, lectures
2208 Social life and customs. Civilization. Intellectual life
2208.7 Political history
2209 Foreign and general relations
Biography and memoirs
2210 Collective
2211.A-Z Individual, A-Z
e.g.
2211.H33 Hácha, Emil
1945-1968
2215 Sources and documents
2216 General works
2217 General special
2217.5 Addresses, essays, lectures
2218 Social life and customs. Civilization. Intellectual life
2218.7 Political history
2219 Foreign and general relations
Biography and memoirs
2220 Collective
2221.A-Z Individual, A-Z
e.g.
2221.D93 Dubček, Alexander
2221.H96 Husák, Gustav
2222 Coup d'etat, 1948
1968-1989
2225 Sources and documents
2226 General works
2227 General special
2227.5 Addresses, essays, lectures
2228 Social life and customs. Civilization. Intellectual life
2228.7 Political history
2229 Foreign and general relations
Biography and memoirs
2230 Collective
2231.A-Z Individual, A-Z
2232 Soviet intervention, 1968. Prague spring
1989-1993

History
By period
Czechoslovak Republic, 1918-1992
1989-1992 -- Continued
2235 Sources and documents
2236 General works
2238 Social life and customs. Civilization. Intellectual life
2238.7 Political history
2239 Foreign and general relations
Biography and memoirs
2240 Collective
2241.A-Z Individual, A-Z
e.g.
2241.H38 Havel, Václav
1993- . Independent Czech Republic
2242 Sources and documents
2243 General works
2244 Social life and customs. Civilization. Intellectual life
2244.7 Political history
2245 Foreign and general relations
Biography and memoirs
2246 Collective
2247.A-Z Individual, A-Z
Local history and description of the Czech lands
For local history and description of Slovakia, see DB3000+
Moravia
2300 Periodicals. Societies. Serials
Museums, exhibitions, etc.
2301 General works
2302.A-Z Individual. By place, A-Z
2303 Congresses
2304 Sources and documents
Collected works (nonserial)
2305 Several authors
2306 Individual authors
2307 Gazetteers. Dictionaries, etc.
2308 Place names (General)
2309 Directories
2310 Guidebooks
2311 General works
2312 General special
2313 Pictorial works
2315 Historic monuments, landmarks, scenery, etc. (General)
For local, see DB2500.A+
2316 Preservation
2317 Historical geography
Description and travel
2318 History of travel
2319 Early through 1900

Local history and description of the Czech lands
Moravia
Description and travel -- Continued
2320 1901-1945
2321 1946-1976
2322 1977-
2330 Antiquities
For local antiquities, see DB2500.A+
2335 Social life and customs. Civilization.
Intellectual life
For specific periods, see the period or reign
Ethnography
2340 General works
2341 National characteristics
2342.A-Z Individual elements in the population, A-Z
2342.C76 Croats
2342.G47 Germans
History
Periodicals. Societies. Serials, see DB2300
2345 Biography (Collective)
For individual biography, see the specific period, reign, or place
Historiography
2355 General works
Biography of historians and area studies specialists
2356 Collective
2357.A-Z Individual, A-Z
Study and teaching
2359 General works
2360.A-Z By region or country, A-Z
Subarrange by author
General works
2361 Through 1800
2362 1801-1976
2363 1977-
2364 Pictorial works
2365 Juvenile works
2366 Addresses, essays, lectures. Anecdotes, etc.
2370 Military history
For specific periods, including individual campaigns and engagements, see the period or reign
2374 Political history
For specific periods, see the period or reign
2375 Foreign and general relations
For works on relations with a specific country regardless of period, see DB2376.A+
For general works on the diplomatic history of a period, see the period
2376.A-Z Relations with individual regions or countries, A-Z
By period

Local history and description of the Czech lands
Moravia
History
By period -- Continued
Early to 1000. Great Moravian Empire

2385	Sources and documents
2386	General works
2387	General special
2387.5	Addresses, essays, lectures
2388	Social life and customs. Civilization. Intellectual life
2388.7	Political history
2389	Foreign and general relations
	Biography and memoirs
2390	Collective
2391.A-Z	Individual, A-Z
	e.g.
2391.S93	Svatopluk
	1000-1800
2395	Sources and documents
2396	General works
2397	General special
2397.5	Addresses, essays, lectures
2397.7	Social life and customs. Civilization. Intellectual life
2398	Political history
	Biography and memoirs
2400	Collective
2401.A-Z	Individual, A-Z
	19th century
2405	Sources and documents
2406	General works
2407	General special
2407.5	Addresses, essays, lectures
2408	Political history
	Biography and memoirs
2410	Collective
2411.A-Z	Individual, A-Z
	20th century
2415	Sources and documents
2416	General works
2417	General special
2417.5	Addresses, essays, lectures
2418	Political history
	Biography and memoirs
2420	Collective
2421.A-Z	Individual, A-Z

Local history and description
of the Czech lands -- Continued

2500.A-Z Counties, regions, mountains, rivers, etc., A-Z
Class here geographical features of the Czech lands and those shared by the Czech lands and Slovakia, but lying principally in the Czech lands
e.g.
For areas entirely or largely in Slovakia, see DB3000+
Beskids, see DB3000.B4
For Beskids (General, and Poland), see DK4600.B4
Bohemian Forest, see DB2500.C463
2500.B75 Brno region (Brünn region)
Carpathian Mountains, see DJK71+
2500.C462 Českomoravská vysočina
2500.C463 Český les (Bohemian Forest. Böhmerwald)
2500.C464 Český ráj
2500.C465 Český Těšín region
For Cieszyn region (General, and Poland), see DK4600.C54
2500.C54 Cheb region (Egerland)
For Egerland in Germany, see DD801.A+
Eger River and Valley, see DB2500.O57
Egerland, see DB2500.C54
Elbe River and Valley, see DB2500.L33
2500.E53 Elbe Sandstone Rocks
Cf. DD801.S281, Saxon Switzerland
Isera Mountains, see DB2500.J58
2500.J47 Jeseníky Mountains (Altvatergebirge)
2500.J553 Jihočeský kraj
2500.J555 Jihomoravský kraj
2500.J58 Jizera Mountains (Isergebirge)
For Isera Mountains (General, and Poland), see DK4600.I9
2500.J582 Jizera River and Valley (Iser)
2500.K37 Karlovy Vary region (Karlsbad region)
Karpaty, see DJK71+
2500.K75 Krkonoše (Riesengebirge). Krkonoše region. Podkrkonošský kraj
For Krkonose in Poland, see DK4600.K77
2500.K758 Krušné hory (Ore Mountains. Erzgebirge)
2500.L33 Labe River and Valley
For Elbe River (General, and Germany), see DD801.E3
Lusatian Mountains, see DB2500.L98
2500.L98 Luzické hory
Northern Bohemia, see DB2500.S48
2500.O57 Ohře River and Valley (Eger)
Ore Mountains, see DB2500.K758
2500.O75 Orlické hory (Adlergebirge)
Podkarpatská Rus, see DK508.9.Z35
Podrkonošský kraj, see DB2500.K75
Ruthenia, see DK508.9.Z35

Local history and description of the Czech lands
Counties, regions, mountains, rivers, etc., A-Z -- Continued
2500.R83 Rychlesbské hory
2500.S48 Severočeský kraj. Northern Bohemia
2500.S49 Severomoravský kraj
Silesia, see DB2500.S54
2500.S54 Slezsko
For Silesia (General, and Poland), see DK4600.S42
2500.S65 Sněžka (Sniezka. Schneekoppe)
2500.S76 Stredoceský kraj
2500.S94 Sudety (Sudetenland)
For Sudetes in Poland, see DK4600.S656
For Sudetes in Poland, see DK4600.S7
2500.S96 Šumava
2500.V57 Vltava River and Valley (Moldau)
2500.V93 Východočeský kraj
2500.Z36 Západočeský kraj
Prague (Praha)
2600 Periodicals. Societies. Serials
2601 Museums, exhibitions, etc.
Subarrange by author
2603 Sources and documents
Collected works (nonserial)
2604 Several authors
2605 Individual authors
2606 Directories. Dictionaries. Gazetteers
2607 Guidebooks
2610 General works
Description
2611 Early and medieval
2612 16th-19th century
2613 1901-1976
2614 1977-
2620 Pictorial works
2621 Antiquities
2622 Social life and customs. Intellectual life
Ethnography
2623 General works
2624.A-Z Individual elements in the population, A-Z
2624.A9 Austrians
2624.G4 Germans
Jews, see DS135.C95+
2624.R87 Russians
2624.R9 Ruthenians
2624.S5 Slovaks
2624.U5 Ukrainians
History
2625 Biography (Collective)
For individual biography, see the specific period
2626 General works
By period

Local history and description of the Czech lands
Prague (Praha)
History
By period -- Continued
2627 Early and medieval
2628 16th-19th century
2629 20th century
Sections, districts, suburbs, etc.
2630 Collective
2631.A-Z Individual, A-Z
e.g.
2631.M35 Malá Strana
Monuments, statues, etc.
2632 Collective
2633.A-Z Individual, A-Z
Parks, squares, cemeteries, etc.
2634 Collective
2635.A-Z Individual, A-Z
Streets. Bridges
2636 Collective
2637.A-Z Individual, A-Z
Buildings
2648 Collective
2649.A-Z Individual, A-Z
2650.A-Z Other cities and towns, A-Z
e.g.
For castles, manors, etc. outside cities, see DB2500.A+
For cities and towns in Slovakia, see DB3150.A+
2650.B75 Brno (Brünn)
2650.C463 České Budejovice (Budweiss)
2650.C467 Český Těšín
For Cieszyn, Poland, see DK4800.C5
2650.L53 Liberec (Reichenberg)
2650.O46 Olomouc (Olmutz)
Pilsen, see DB2650.P49
2650.P49 Plzeň
Prague, see DB2600+
Praha, see DB2600+
Slovakia
2700 Periodicals. Societies. Serials
Museums, exhibitions, etc.
2701 General works
2702.A-Z Individual. By place, A-Z
2703 Congresses
2704 Sources and documents
Collected works (nonserial)
2705 Several authors
2706 Individual authors
2707 Gazetteers. Dictionaries, etc.
2708 Place names (General)
2709 Directories
2710 Guidebooks

Slovakia -- Continued
2711 General works
2712 General special
2713 Pictorial works
Historic monuments, landmarks, scenery, etc. (General)
For local, see DB3000+
2715 General works
2716 Preservation
2717 Historical geography
Description and travel
2718 History of travel
2719 Early through 1900
2720 1901-1945
2721 1946-1976
2722 1977-
2730 Antiquities
For local antiquities, see DB3000+
2735 Social life and customs. Civilization. Intellectual life
For specific periods, see the period or reign
Ethnography
2740 General works
2741 National characteristics
2742.A-Z Individual elements in the population, A-Z
2742.A8 Austrians
2742.C9 Czechs
2742.G4 Germans
Gypsies in the Czech Republic, see DX222
Gypsies in Slovakia, see DX222.5
2742.H8 Hungarians
Jews, see DS135.C95+
2742.P6 Poles
2742.R8 Ruthenians
2742.T47 Thracians
2742.U6 Ukrainians
2743 Slovaks in foreign countries (General)
For Slovaks in a particular country, see the country
History
Periodicals. Societies. Serials, see DB2700
2744 Dictionaries. Chronological tables, outlines, etc.
Biography (Collective)
For individual biography, see the specific period, reign, or place
2745 General works
2746 Rulers, kings, etc.
2747 Queens. Princes and princesses
Houses, noble families, etc.
2748 Collective
2749.A-Z Individual houses, families, etc., A-Z
2750 Statesmen
2751 Women
Historiography

Slovakia
History
Historiography -- Continued
2755 General works
Biography of historians and area studies specialists
2756 Collective
2757.A-Z Individual, A-Z
Study and teaching
2759 General works
2760.A-Z By region or country, A-Z
Subarrange by author
General works
2761 Through 1800
2762 1801-1976
2763 1977-
2764 Pictorial works
2765 Juvenile works
2766 Addresses, essays, lectures. Anecdotes, etc.
2768 Philosophy of Slovak history
Military history
For specific periods including individual campaigns and engagements, see the period or reign
2769 Sources and documents
2770 General works
By period
2771 Early through 1620
2772 1621-1918
2773 1918-
Political history
For specific periods, see the period or reign
2774 Sources and documents
2775 General works
Foreign and general relations
For works on relations with a specific country regardless of period, see DB2778.A+
For general works on the diplomatic history of a period, see the period
2776 Sources and documents
2777 General works
2778.A-Z Relations with individual regions or countries, A-Z
By period
Early and medieval to 1800
2785 Sources and documents
2786 General works
2787 General special
2787.5 Addresses, essays, lectures
2788 Social life and customs. Civilization. Intellectual life
2788.5 Military history
2788.7 Political history
2789 Foreign and general relations

Slovakia
History
By period
Early and medieval to 1800 -- Continued
Biography and memoirs
2790 Collective
2791.A-Z Individual, A-Z
1800-1918
2795 Sources and documents
2796 General works
2797 General special
2797.5 Addresses, essays, lectures
2798 Social life and customs. Civilization. Intellectual life
2798.5 Military history
2798.7 Political history
2799 Foreign and general relations
Biography and memoirs
2800 Collective
2801.A-Z Individual, A-Z
Czechoslovak Republic, 1918-1992
2805 Sources and documents
2806 General works
2807 General special
2807.5 Addresses, essays, lectures
2808 Social life and customs. Civilization. Intellectual life
2808.7 Political history
2809 Foreign and general relations
Biography and memoirs
2810 Collective
2811.A-Z Individual, A-Z
e.g.
2811.H65 Hlinka, Andrej
2813 1918-1939
Period of World War II. Slovak Independence, 1939-1945
2815 Sources and documents
2816 General works
2817 General special
2817.5 Addresses, essays, lectures
2818 Social life and customs. Civilization. Intellectual life
2818.7 Political history
2819 Foreign and general relations
Biography and memoirs
2820 Collective
2821.A-Z Individual, A-Z
e.g.
2821.T57 Tiso, Josef
2822 Uprising, 1944
1945-1968
2825 Sources and documents

Slovakia
History
By period
Czechoslovak Republic, 1918-1992
1945-1968 -- Continued
2826 General works
2827 General special
2827.5 Addresses, essays, lectures
2828 Social life and customs. Civilization.
Intellectual life
2828.7 Political history
2829 Foreign and general relations
Biography and memoirs
2830 Collective
2831.A-Z Individual, A-Z
1968-1992
2835 Sources and documents
2836 General works
2837 General special
2837.5 Addresses, essays, lectures
2838 Social life and customs. Civilization.
Intellectual life
2838.7 Political history
2839 Foreign and general relations
Biography and memoirs
2840 Collective
2841.A-Z Individual, A-Z
2842 Soviet intervention, 1968
2844 1989-1992
1993- . Independent republic
2845 Sources and documents
2846 General works
2847 Social life and customs. Civilization.
Intellectual life
2848 Political history
2849 Foreign and general relations
Biography and memoirs
2849.5 Collective
2850.A-Z Individual, A-Z
Local history and description
3000.A-Z Counties, regions, mountains, rivers, etc., A-Z
Class here the geographical features of Slovakia, as well as those shared by Slovakia and the Czech lands, but lying principally in Slovakia
e.g.
For areas entirely or largely in the Czech lands, see DB2500.A+
3000.B4 Beskids
For Beskids (General, and poland), see DK4600.B4
3000.B55 Bílé Karpaty
Carpathian Mountains, see DJK71+
Danube, see DB3000.D85

Slovakia
Local history and description
Counties, regions, mountains, rivers, etc., A-Z -- Continued

3000.D85 Danaj River and Valley
For the Danube River (General), see DJK76.2+
Little Carpathian Mountains, see DB3000.M35
3000.M35 Malé Karpaty
3000.O73 Orava River, Valley and Reservoir
Slovak Ore Mountains, see DB3000.S56
3000.S56 Slovenské Rudohorie
3000.S65 Spiš
3000.S76 Středoslovenský kraj
3000.T37 Tatra Mountains
For Tatra Mountains in Poland, see DK4600.T3
3000.V35 Váh River and Valley
3000.V93 Východoslovenský kraj
White Carpathian Mountains, see DB3000.B55
3000.Z36 Západoslovenský kraj

Bratislava (Pressburg)
3100 Periodicals. Societies. Serials
3101 Museums, exhibitions, etc.
Subarrange by author
3103 Sources and documents
Collected works (nonserial)
3104 Several authors
3105 Individual authors
3106 Directories. Dictionaries. Gazetteers
3107 Guidebooks
3110 General works
Description
3111 Early and medieval
3112 16th-19th centuries
3113 1901-1976
3114 1977-
3120 Pictorial works
3121 Antiquities
3122 Social life and customs. Intellectual life
Ethnography
3123 General works
3124.A-Z Individual elements in the population, A-Z
3124.A8 Austrians
3124.C9 Czechs
3124.G4 Germans
Gypsies in the Czech Republic, see DX222
Gypsies in Slovakia, see DX222.5
3124.H8 Hungarians
Jews, see DS135.C95+
3124.R97 Ruthenians
3124.U67 Ukrainians
History

Slovakia
Local history and description
Bratislava (Pressburg)
History -- Continued

3125 Biography (Collective)
For individual biography, see the specific period
3126 General works
By period
3127 Early and medieval
3128 16th-19th centuries
3129 20th century
Sections, districts, suburbs, etc.
3130 Collective
3131.A-Z Individual, A-Z
Monuments, statues, etc.
3132 Collective
3133.A-Z Individual, A-Z
Parks, squares, cemeteries, etc.
3134 Collective
3135.A-Z Individual, A-Z
Streets. Bridges
3136 Collective
3137.A-Z Individual, A-Z
Buildings
3138 Collective
3139.A-Z Individual, A-Z
3150.A-Z Other cities and towns, A-Z
e.g.
3150.B35 Banská Bystrica
Bratislava, see DB3100+
3150.K65 Komárno
3150.K67 Košice
Martin, see DB3150.T97
3150.N57 Nitra
3150.T74 Trenčín
3150.T97 Turčiansky Sväty Martin. Martin

History of France
1 Periodicals. Serials
2 Societies
3 Sources and documents
Collected works
4 Several authors
5 Individual authors
14 Gazetteers. Dictionaries, etc. Place names
15 Directories
16 Guidebooks
17 General works
18 Compends
19 Historical accounts of disasters caused by the elements
Including earthquakes, fires, floods, storms, etc. (General)
For individual disasters, see DC600+
20 Pictorial works
Historic monuments, landmarks, scenery, etc. (General)
For local, see DC600+
20.2 General works
20.3 Preservation
20.5 Historical geography
Description and travel
21 Earliest through 686
22 687-1514
23 1515-1588
24 1589-1714
25 1715-1788
26 1789-1815
27 1816-1870
28 1871-1945
29 1946-1974
29.3 1975-
Antiquities
Cf. DC63, Roman, Celtic, etc., antiquities
For local, see DC600+
30 Periodicals. Collections, etc.
31 General works
Social life and customs. Civilization. Intellectual life
33 General works
33.15 Regal antiquities. Ceremonials, pageants, etc. Court life
By period
33.2 Early and medieval
33.3 Renaissance period. 16th century
33.4 17th-18th centuries
For Louis XIV, see DC128
For Louis XV, see DC133.8
For Louis XVI, see DC136+

Social life and customs.
Civilization. Intellectual life
By period -- Continued
33.5 1789-1830
Cf. DC159, Social life and customs, 1789-1815
Cf. DC256.5, Social life and customs, 1815-1830
33.6 1831-1900
33.7 1901-
33.9 French culture in foreign countries (General)
Including general works on the French in foreign countries
For the French in a particular country, see the country
Ethnography
Including national characteristics
34 General works
34.5.A-Z Individual elements in the population, A-Z
For individual elements in the population of a particular place, see the place
34.5.A37 Africans
34.5.A4 Algerians, Arab
34.5.A42 French Algerians
34.5.A44 Americans
34.5.A46 Antilleans
34.5.A7 Armenians
34.5.A8 Asians
34.5.B55 Blacks
34.5.B75 British
34.5.B8 Bulgarians
34.5.C3 Cagots
34.5.C34 Cameroonians
34.5.E35 Egyptians
34.5.F6 Foreign population (General)
34.5.G3 Germans
34.5.H3 Haitians
34.5.H54 Hmong (Asian people)
34.5.H86 Hungarians
34.5.I7 Irish
34.5.I8 Italians
34.5.K3 Kabyles
34.5.K34 Kalmyks
34.5.L4 Lebanese
34.5.M34 Malians
34.5.M38 Mauritians
34.5.M7 Moroccans
34.5.M87 Muslims
Negroes, see DC34.5.B55
34.5.N67 North Africans
34.5.P6 Poles
34.5.P67 Portuguese
34.5.R45 Réunion Islanders
34.5.R6 Romanians

Ethnography
Individual elements in the population, A-Z -- Continued

34.5.R8 Russians
34.5.S45 Senegalese
34.5.S57 Slovenes
34.5.S65 Spaniards
34.5.T84 Tunisians
34.5.T87 Turks
34.5.U37 Ukrainians
34.5.V53 Vietnamese
34.5.Y84 Yugoslavs

French people in foreign countries (General), see DC33.9

History

35 Dictionaries. Chronological tables, outlines, etc.

35.5 Albums. Pictorial atlases. Collections of historical prints and portraits, etc.

36 Biography (Collective)
For individual biography, see the period, reign, or place

36.1 General special
e.g. Les batards de la Maison de France

36.2 Women
36.3 Favorites
36.4 Public men
36.6 Rulers, kings, etc.
36.7 Queens, princesses, etc.
36.8.A-Z Houses, noble families, etc., A-Z
e.g.
36.8.A6 Anjou, House of
36.8.B7 Bourbon, House of
36.8.C6 Conde family
36.8.O7 Orléans, House of
36.8.V3 Valois, House of

Historiography

36.9 General works

Biography of historians

36.95 Collective
36.98.A-Z Individual, A-Z
e.g.
36.98.F7 Froissart, Jean
36.98.H8 Houssaye, Henry
36.98.L3 Lavisse, Ernest
36.98.M5 Michelet, Jules
Peiresc, Nicolas Claude F. de, see DC121.8.P4
36.98.T4 Thierry, Augustin

Study and teaching

36.983 General works
36.985.A-Z Local, A-Z
Subarrange by author

General works

37 To 1815. Chronicles
38 1815-

History -- Continued
39 Compends
40 Pamphlets, etc.
40.5 Anecdotes, etc.
41.A-Z Special, A-Z
For elements in the population, see DC34.5.A+
41.R4 Regionalism
General special
Military history
For individual campaigns and engagements, see the special period
44 Sources and documents
Biography (Collective)
44.5 General works
44.8 Officers
45 General works
45.5 Compends
45.7 General special
45.9 Pamphlets, etc.
By period
For the military history of special periods, reigns, etc., see the period or reign
46 Early to Reformation
46.5 16th century
46.7 17th-18th centuries
47 19th-20th centuries
Naval history
For individual campaigns and engagements, see the special period
49 Sources and documents
49.5 Biography (Collective)
General works
50.A2 Early works to 1800
50.A3-Z 1801-
51 Early and medieval
51.5 15th-16th centuries
52 17th-18th centuries
Cf. DC139+, French Revolution
53 19th-20th centuries
For 20th century, see DC368
For general modern, see DC50.A2+
55 Political and diplomatic history. Foreign and general relations
For works on relations with a specific country regardless of period, see DC59.8.A+
For general works on the political and diplomatic history of a period, see the period
56 Early and medieval
57 1515-1789. Early modern
For general modern, see DC55
58 19th-20th centuries
59 Special topics
Church and state, see BR840+

History
General special
Political and diplomatic history. Foreign and general relations -- Continued
59.8.A-Z Relations with individual regions or countries, A-Z
By period
Early and medieval to 1515
60 Sources and documents
Cf. DC3, Sources and documents
60.5 Selections, extracts, etc.
60.6 Dictionaries
General works
60.8 Through 1800. Chronicles
61 1801-
Social life and customs. Civilization.
Intellectual life, see DC33.2
Gauls. Celts
62.A2 Collections
62.A3-Z General works
62.2.A-Z Individual groups, A-Z
62.2.C34 Caletes
62.2.C37 Carnutes
62.2.C67 Coriosolites
62.2.D53 Diablintes
62.2.M67 Morini
62.2.O85 Osismii
62.2.R88 Ruteni
62.2.V57 Visigoths
62.3 Armorica
Cf. DC611.B856, Brittany (Early to 877)
62.5 Cénomanie
Cf. DC611.S361+, Sarthe
Cf. DC801.L48+, Le Mans
62.8.A-Z Biography, A-Z
e.g.
62.8.V4 Vercingetorix, chief of the Arverni
63 Antiquities (Roman, Celtic, etc.)
Cf. DG59.G2, Gallia (Roman province)
63.A3 Dictionaries
64 Franks
Merovingians, 476-687
64.7 Sources and documents
65 General works
66 Childeric I, d. 481
67 Clovis, 481-511
67.4 Theodebert I, King of the Franks, ca. 500-ca. 547
68 Brunehaut (Brunhilda), 596-613
Dagobert, 628-638
69 General works
69.8.A-Z Biography of contemporaries, A-Z
e.g.

History
By period
Early and medieval to 1515
Merovingians, 476-687
Dagobert, 628-638
Biography of contemporaries, A-Z -- Continued
69.8.G7 Gregorius, Saint, Bp. of Tours
69.85 Dagobert II, 670?-679
Carolingians, 687-987
Sources and documents
70.A1 Collections
Chronicles
70.A2 9th century
70.A3 10th century
70.A4-Z General works
70.6 Pepin of Heristal, 687-714
70.8 Childebrand
Charles Martel, 715-741
71 General works on life and reign
71.5 Battle of Poitiers (Tours), 732
Pepin le Bref, 752-768
72 General works on life and reign
Cf. DD132, Reign in Germany
Charlemagne, 768-814
Cf. DD133, Reign in Germany
73.A2 Sources and documents
General works on life and reign
73.A3-Z Modern
Contemporary and medieval
Einhard
73.2 Complete works
73.3 Vita Caroli Magni
Translations
73.32 English
73.33 French
73.34 German
73.35.A-Z Other languages, A-Z
e.g.
73.35.D3 Danish
73.4 Biography and criticism
73.5 Vita Caroli Magni sec. XII
73.55 Criticisms, etc.
73.6 Other vitae
73.7 Personal special
73.8 Pamphlets, etc.
73.9 Carloman, 768-771
73.95.A-Z Biography and memoirs of contemporaries, A-Z
e.g.
73.95.R6 Roland
Louis I le Pieux, 814-840
74 General works

History
By period
Early and medieval to 1515
Carolingians, 687-987
Louis I le Pieux -- Continued
General works on life and reign in Germany, see DD134+
74.5.A-Z Biography and memoirs of contemporaries, A-Z
e.g.
74.5.J8 Judith, Empress, Consort of Louis le Pieux
75 Treaty of Verdun, 843
For legal works, including texts of the treaty and related documents, see KZ1328.2
Charles I (II) le Chauve, 840-877
76 General works on life and reign
76.3 General special
Biography and memoirs
76.4 Collective
76.42.A-Z Individual, A-Z
77 Louis II le Bègue, 877-879
77.3 Louis III, 879-882
77.5 Carloman, 882-884
Karl II (III) der Dicke, 884-887
77.8 General works on life and reign
General works on life and reign in Germany, see DD134.6
77.9 Siege of Paris, 885-886
78 Eudes, 888-898
79 Charles III le Simple, 898-922
79.5 Robert I, 922-923
79.7 Raoul (Rodolphe), 923-936
80 Louis IV (Louis d'Outremer), 936-954
81 Lothaire, 954-986
81.5 Louis V, 986-987
Capetians, 987-1328
82.A2 Sources and documents
82.A3-Z General works
83 General special
Wars with Albigenses
83.2 Sources and documents
83.3 General works
84 Hugues Capet, 987-996
85 Robert II, 996-1031
Henri I, 1031-1060
85.6 General works on life and reign
85.8.A-Z Biography and memoirs of contemporaries, A-Z
e.g.
85.8.A54 Anne, Consort of Henry I
86 Dukes of Normandy
Philippe I, 1060-1108
87 General works on life and reign
87.7.A-Z Biography and memoirs of contemporaries, A-Z
e.g.

History
By period
Early and medieval to 1515
Capetians, 987-1328
Philippe I, 1060-1108
Biography and memoirs of contemporaries, A-Z -- Continued
87.7.H8 Hugo, Abp. of Lyons
Louis VI, 1108-1137
88 General works on life and reign
88.5 Political and diplomatic history
88.7.A-Z Biography and memoirs of contemporaries, A-Z
Louis VII, 1137-1180
89 General works on life and reign
89.7.A-Z Biography and memoirs of contemporaries, A-Z
e.g.
89.7.S8 Suger, Abbot of Saint Denis
Philippe II Auguste, 1180-1223
90.A2 Sources and documents
90.A3-Z General works on life and reign
90.7.A-Z Biography and memoirs of contemporaries, A-Z
e.g.
90.7.I6 Ingeborg, Consort of Philip II
90.8 Louis VIII, 1223-1226
Louis IX, Saint, 1226-1270
91.A2 Sources and documents
91.A3-Z General works on life and reign
91.3 Peace of Paris, 1258
For legal works on the Treaty of Paris, 1258, see KZ1329.3
91.5 Personal special
e.g. Heart of St. Louis
91.6.A-Z Biography and memoirs of contemporaries, A-Z
e.g.
91.6.B5 Blanche of Castille, Consort of Louis VIII
91.6.J6 Joinville, Jean, sire de
91.7 Philippe III, 1270-1285
92 Philippe IV, 1285-1314
Louis X, 1314-1316
93 General works on life and reign
93.3 Jean I, b. 1316
93.4 Philippe V, 1316-1322
93.7 Charles IV, 1322-1328
94.A-Z Biography and memoirs, 1270-1328, A-Z
e.g.
94.A4 Accorre, Renier
94.C4 Charles, Count of Valois
1328-1515
95.A2 Sources and documents
95.A3-Z General works
95.45 Military history
95.5 Political and diplomatic history
95.6 Special topics

History
By period
Early and medieval to 1515
1328-1515 -- Continued
95.7.A-Z Biography and memoirs, A-Z
Hundred Years' War, 1339-1453
96.A2 Contemporary and early works
96.A3-Z General works
96.5 General special
97.A-Z Biography and memoirs, A-Z
Particularly of first half of the war
e.g.
97.D8 Du Guesclin, Bertrand, comte de Longueville
14th century
97.5 General works
Philippe VI, 1328-1350
98 General works on life and reign
98.3 General special
98.5.A-Z Special events, battles, etc., A-Z
e.g.
98.5.C2 Calais, Siege of, 1346
98.5.C8 Crecy, Battle of, 1346
98.7.A-Z Biography and memoirs of contemporaries, A-Z
e.g.
98.7.C4 Cayon, Jean
Jean II, 1350-1364
99 General works on life and reign
99.2 General special
99.3 La Jacquerie, 1358
99.5.A-Z Other events, battles, etc., A-Z
e.g.
99.5.B7 Bretigny, Peace of, 1360
For legal works on the Treaty of Bretigny, 1360, see KZ1329.8.B74
99.5.P6 Poitiers, Battle of, 1356
99.5.S3 Saintes, Battle of, 1351
99.7.A-Z Biography and memoirs of contemporaries, A-Z
e.g.
99.7.L4 Le Coq, Robert, Bp.
Charles V, 1364-1380
100 General works on life and reign
100.3 General special
100.5.A-Z Special events, battles, etc., A-Z
100.7.A-Z Biography and memoirs of contemporaries, A-Z
Charles VI, 1380-1422
101 General works on life and reign
101.A2 Contemporary and early
101.3 General special
101.5.A-Z Special events, battles, etc., A-Z
101.5.A2 Agincourt, Battle of, 1415
101.5.C33 Cabochien Uprising, 1413
101.5.R8 Roosebeke, Battle of, 1382

History
By period
Early and medieval to 1515
1328-1515
14th century
Charles VI, 1380-1422
Special events,
battles, etc., A-Z -- Continued

101.5.T7 Troyes, Peace of, 1420
For legal works on the Treaty of Troyes, 1420, see KZ1329.8.T76

Biography and memoirs of contemporaries
101.6 Collective
101.7.A-Z Individual, A-Z
e.g.
101.7.I7 Isabeau, of Bavaria, Consort of Charles VI
101.7.M6 Montreuil, Jean de
101.7.O6 Orgemont, Nicolas d'
101.7.O7 Orléans, Louis de France, duc d'

15th century
101.9 General works
Charles VII, 1422-1461
102 General works on life and reign
102.A2 Contemporary and early
102.A3 General special
102.5 Special events, battles, etc.
e.g.
Arrange chronologically by affixing to .5 the last two digits of the date
102.527 Siege of Montargis, 1427
102.528 Siege of Orléans, 1428-1429
102.535 Congress and Peace of Arras, 1435
For legal works on the Treaty of Arras, 1435, see KZ1329.8.A77
102.544 Siege of Metz, 1444
Biography and memoirs of contemporaries
102.8.A1 Collective
102.8.A2-Z Individual, A-Z
e.g.
102.8.F4 Flavy, Guillaume de
102.8.J43 Jeanne, Queen, consort of René I, King of Naples and Jerusalem, 1433-1498
102.8.R2 Rais, Gilles de Laval, seigneur de
102.8.R4 René I, d'Anjou, King of Naples and Jerusalem
102.8.S7 Sorel, Agnès

Jeanne d'Arc, Saint
103.A1-A29 Sources and documents
103.A3-Z General biography
103.5 Juvenile works
104 General special. Panegyrics, etc.
105 Voices. Inspiration

History
By period
Early and medieval to 1515
1328-1515
15th century
Charles VII, 1422-1461
Jeanne d'Arc, Saint -- Continued
Campaigns, see DC103+
105.6 Imprisonment. Martyrdom
For trial, see KJV130
105.7 Rehabilitation
105.8 Jeanne des Armoises controversy
105.9 Monuments. Landmarks. Jeanne d'Arc in literature and art (General)
For works on Jeanne d'Arc in literature alone, see class P; for art alone see class N
Louis XI, 1461-1483
106 General works on life and reign
106.A2 Contemporary and early
106.3 General special
106.9.A-Z Biography and memoirs of contemporaries, A-Z
e.g.
106.9.C5 Charles de France, Duke of Berry
106.9.C8 Comines, Philippe de, sieur d'Argenton
106.9.M6 Margaret of Scotland, Consort of Louis XI
Charles VIII, 1483-1498
107 General works on life and reign
Cf. DG537+, 15th century Italy
107.A2 Contemporary and early
107.2 Anne of France (Regent, 1483-1491)
(107.3) Italian expedition
See DG541
Louis XII, 1498-1515
108 General works on life and reign
108.A2 Contemporary and early
108.2 Jeanne, Consort of Louis XII
108.3 Anne de Bretagne
108.8 Letters of Louis XII
109 Other special
e.g. The Armagnacs
Cf. DC611.A7265+, Armagnac, former province
Modern, 1515-
Including works on the modern period in general
110 General works
1515-1589. 16th century
Including wars in Italy, conflict with Austria, Renaissance and Reformation, religious wars, etc.
111.A2 Sources and documents
111.A3-Z General works
111.3 General special

History
By period
Modern, 1515-
1515-1589. 16th century -- Continued
111.5 Political and diplomatic history. Foreign and general relations
Social life and customs. Civilization.
Intellectual life, see DC33.3
Biography and memoirs of contemporaries
112.A1 Collective
112.A2-Z Individual, A-Z
112.A6 Antoine de Bourbon, King of Navarre
112.A8 Aubigné, Théodore Agrippa d'
112.B6 Bourbon, Charles, duc de
112.C6 Coligny, Gaspard de, seigneur de Châtillon
Guise, Dukes and Duchesses of
112.G8 General works
112.G81 Guise, Antoinette (de Bourbon), duchesse de
112.G83 Guise, Charles de, cardinal de Lorraine
112.G85 Guise, François de Lorraine
112.G9 Guise, Henri, duc de
112.J4 Jeanne d'Albret, Queen of Navarre
112.L45 La Noue, François de
112.L6 L'Hospital, Michel de
112.L8 Louise de Savoie, Duchess of Angoulême
112.M2 Marguerite d'Angoulême, Queen of Navarre
112.M9 Mornay, Philippe de, seigneur de Plessis-Marly, called du Plessis-Mornay
112.R4 Renée, of France, Consort of Hercules II, Duke of Ferrara
112.V75 Villeroy, Nicolas de Neuf-ville, seigneur de
François I, 1515-1547
113.A2 Sources and documents
113.A3 Contemporary and early works
113.A4-Z General works on life and reign
113.3 General special
113.5 Diplomatic history. Foreign and general relations
Including Peace of Cambrai, 1529 (Ladies' Peace); Peace of Madrid, 1526
For legal works on the Treaty of Cambrai, 1529, see KZ1329.8.C36
For legal works on the Treaty of Madrid, 1526, see KZ1329.8.M33
Henri II, 1547-1559
114 General works on life and reign
Including Peace of Cateau-Cambrésia, 1559
For legal works on the Treaty of Cateau-Cambrésis, 1559, see KZ1329.8.C38
114.3 General special
114.5 Diane de Poitiers, Duchess of Valentinois

History
By period
Modern, 1515-
1515-1589. 16th century -- Continued

115 François II, 1559-1560
Charles IX, 1560-1574
116 General works on life and reign
116.5 General special
116.7 Diplomatic history. Foreign and general relations
117.A-Z Special events, A-Z
e.g.
117.L3 Siege of La Rochelle, 1573
118 Massacre of St. Bartholomew, 1572
Henri III, 1574-1589
119 General works on life and reign
119.7 Louise of Lorraine, Consort of Henry III
119.8 Catherine de Médicis, Consort of Henry II
120 Holy League, 1576-1593
1589-1715
120.8 Historiography
121 General works
121.3 General special
121.5 Diplomatic history. Foreign and general relations
121.7 Social life and customs. Civilization. Intellectual life
Biography and memoirs
121.8.A2 Collective
121.8.A3-Z Individual, A-Z
e.g.
121.8.E7 Épernon, Jean Louis de Nogaret, duc d'
121.8.F2 Fabert, Abraham de
121.8.L3 La Rochefoucauld, François de, Cardinal
121.8.L6 Louise de Coligny, Consort of William I, Prince of Orange
121.8.P3 Pasquier, Nicolas
121.8.P4 Peiresc, Nicolas Claude Fabri de
121.9.A-Z Local, A-Z
e.g.
121.9.N2 Narbonne
Henri IV, 1589-1610
122 General works on reign
122.3 General special
Edict of Nantes, see BR845
122.5 Diplomatic history. Foreign and general relations
122.8 Biography of Henri IV
Biography and memoirs of contemporaries
122.9.A2 Collective
122.9.A3-Z Individual, A-Z
e.g.
122.9.B3 Bassompierre, François de

History
By period
Modern, 1515-
1589-1715
Henri IV, 1589-1610
Biography and memoirs of contemporaries
Individual, A-Z -- Continued

122.9.C7 Condé, Charlotte Catherine (de la Trémoille), princesse de
122.9.E7 Estrées, Gabrielle d'
122.9.M2 Marguerite de Valois, Consort of Henry IV
122.9.M3 Marie de Médicis, Consort of Henry IV
122.9.O7 Ossat, Arnaud d', Cardinal
122.9.S9 Sully, Maximilien de Béthune, duc de

Louis XIII, 1610-1643

123 General works on reign
123.A2 Collections
123.2 Regency of Marie de Médicis
For biography, see DC122.9.M3
123.3 Special topics
123.5 Diplomatic history. Foreign and general relations
123.8 Biography of Louis XIII
Biography and memoirs of contemporaries, A-Z
e.g.
Anne, Consort of Louis XIII, see DC124+
123.9.C4 Chevrèuse, Marie de Rohan, duchesse de
123.9.C6 Concini, Concino maréchal d'Ancre
123.9.L5 Le Clerc du Tremblay, François
123.9.R5 Richelieu, Armand Jean du Plessis, Cardinal, duc de
123.9.R7 Rohan, Henri, duc de

Anne d'Autriche, 1643-1661

124 General works on life and regency
124.3 Biography
124.4 Fronde, 1649-1653
124.45 War with Spain. Peace of the Pyrenees, 1659

Louis XIV, 1643-1715

124.5 Sources and documents
125 General works on reign
126 General special
Including court life
For general works on the French court and society, Louis XIV-Louis XVI, see DC33.4
127.A-Z Special topics, A-Z
127.C3 Camisards, Revolt of
Revocation of Edict of Nantes, see BR845
127.3 Diplomatic history. Foreign and general relations
127.6 Military history
127.8 Naval history

History
By period
Modern, 1515-
1589-1715
Louis XIV, 1643-1715 -- Continued

128 Social life and customs. Civilization.
Intellectual life
For court life, see DC126
128.5 Public opinion formation. Internal propaganda
129 Biography and writings of Louis XIV
Biography and memoirs of contemporaries
130.A2 Collective
130.A3-Z Individual, A-Z
e.g.
130.B4 Berwick, James Fitz-James, 1st Duke of
130.B9 Bussy, Roger de Rabutin
130.C2 Caylus, Marie Marguerite
130.C6 Colbert, Jean Baptiste
130.C7 Condé, Louis II de Bourbon, prince de
130.C77 Coulanges, Philippe Emmanuel
130.F6 Forbin, Claude, comte de
130.L2 La Fayette, Marie Madeleine (Pioche de La Vergne), comtesse de
130.L4 La Vallière, Louise Françoise de La Baume Le Blanc, duchesse de
130.L5 Lenclos, Anne, called Ninon de
130.L7 Louis, Duke of Burgundy, dauphin
130.M2 Maintenon, Françoise d'Aubigné, marquise de
130.M25 Man in the iron mask
130.M37 Marie-Thérèse, Consort of Louis XIV
130.M38 Mattioli, Ercole Antonio
Mazarin, Jules, cardinal
130.M4 General works
130.M43 Mazarinades
130.M78 Montespan, Françoise-Athénaïs de Rochechouart de Mortemart, marquise de
130.M8 Montpensier, Anne Marie L. d'Orléans, duchesse de
130.O7 Orléans, Élisabeth Charlotte, duchesse d'
130.R45 Retz, Jean François P. de Gondi, cardinal de
130.S2 Saint-Simon, Louis de Rouvoy, duc de
130.S5 Sévigné, Marie de Rabutin-Chantal, marquise de
130.T2 Tallemant des Réaux, Gédéon
130.T9 Turenne, Henri de La Tour d'Auvergne, vicomte de
130.V3 Vauban, Sébastien Le Prestre de
1715-1789. 18th century
131 General works

History
By period
Modern, 1515-
1715-1789. 18th century -- Continued
131.5 Diplomatic history. Foreign and general relations
Cf. DC57, Early modern, 1515-1789
Biography
131.8 Collective
131.9.A-Z Individual, A-Z
132 Regency of Philippe, duc d'Orléans, 1715-1723
Louis XV, 1715-1774
133 General works on reign
133.3 General special
Including court life
For general works on the French court and society, Louis XIV-Louis XVI, see DC33.4
133.4 Political history
133.5 Diplomatic history. Foreign and general relations
133.6 Military history
(133.7) Naval history
See DC52
133.8 Social life and customs. Civilization. Intellectual life
For court life, see DC133.3
Biography
134 Louis XV
134.5 Marie Leszczynska
134.7 Louis, dauphin
Contemporaries
135.A1 Collective
135.A2-Z Individual, A-Z
e.g.
135.A3 Aguesseau, Henri François d'
135.C5 Choiseul Stainville, Étienne François, duc de
135.D8 Du Barry, Jeanne Bécu, comtesse
135.D85 Dubois, Guillaume, Cardinal
135.E6 Éon de Beaumont, Charles Geneviève L.A.A.T. d'
135.E7 Épinay, Louise Florence P.T. d'Esclavelles, marquise d'
135.L5 Lespinasse, Julie Jeanne E. de
135.P8 Pompadour, Jeanne Antoinette (Poisson), marquise de
135.R5 Richelieu, Louis François A. du Plessis, duc de
135.S3 Saxe, Maurice, comte de
Louis XVI, 1774-1789/1793
136.A2 Sources and documents

History
By period
Modern, 1515-
1715-1789. 18th century
Louis XVI, 1774-1789/1793 -- Continued

136.A3-Z General works on reign
For general works on the French court and society, Louis XIV-Louis XVI, see DC33.4
For works on the last years of the reign and life of Louis XVI, see DC137+

136.5 Political history

136.6 Diplomatic history. Foreign and general relations

The Court; social life and customs, see DC136+

136.9 Other

Biography and memoirs
Louis XVI

137 General biography

137.05 Flight

137.07 Imprisonment

137.08 Trial and death

137.09 Other

Marie Antoinette

137.1 General biography

137.15 Affair of the diamond necklace

137.17 Imprisonment, trial, death
For works dealing with the last year of the royal family, see DC137.07

137.18 Death

137.19 Other

137.2 Angoulême, Marie Thérèse C., duchesse d'

137.3 Louis XVII

Lost Dauphin controversy and claimants

137.36 General works

137.37 Naundorf, Karl Wilhelm

137.38.A-Z Other claimants, A-Z

137.4 Élisabeth, Princess of France

Contemporaries

137.5.A1 Collective

137.5.A2-Z Individual, A-Z
e.g.

137.5.B6 Biron, Armand-Louis de Gontaut, duc de

137.5.F4 Fersen, Hans Axel von, grefve

137.5.L2 Lamballe, Marie Thérèse L. de Savoie-Carignan, princesse de

137.5.L3 La Motte, Jeanne de Saint-Rémy de Valois, comtesse de

137.5.M3 Malesherbes, Chrétien Guillaume de Lamoignon de

137.5.S8 Suffren de Saint-Tropez, Pierre André de

History
By period
Modern, 1515-
1715-1789. 18th century
Louis XVI, 1774-1789/1793
Biography and memoirs
Louis XVI
Contemporaries
Individual, A-Z -- Continued

137.5.T9 Turgot, Anne Robert J., baron de l'Aulne

138 Antecedent history and causes of the Revolution

Revolutionary and Napoleonic period, 1789-1815

139 Periodicals. Societies. Serials

Museums, exhibitions, etc.

139.5 General works

139.7.A-Z Individual. By place, A-Z

140 Contemporary newspaper literature, journals, etc.

Almanacs

140.4 Collective

140.5.A-Z Individual, A-Z

140.8 Anecdotes

(140.9) Poems, songs, and other illustrative literature see class P

141 Sources and documents. Collections
Including special periods

Cahiers

141.3.A1-A3 General collections

141.3.A4 Digests, résumés, extracts

141.3.A5 Introductions. Guides

141.3.A6-Z Special local

Laws, decrees, etc.

141.5 Official (Promulgated by the assemblies)

141.7 Selections, etc., by individuals

141.8 Condemnations, confiscations, etc. (Persons and property)

Collected works

142 Several authors

143 Individual authors
For works of authors contemporary to the Revolution and Empire, such as Mirabeau, Robespierre, etc., see DC146.A+

Biography, memoirs, etc., of contemporaries

145 Collective

146.A-Z Individual, A-Z
e.g.

146.C45 Chimay, Jeanne Marie I.T. (de Cabarrus), princesse de

146.C69 Condorcet, Marie Jean A.N.C., marquis de

146.C8 Corday d'Armont, M.A. Charlotte de

146.D2 Danton, Georges Jacques

146.D5 Desmoulins, Camille

History
By period
Revolutionary and Napoleonic period, 1789-1815
Biography, memoirs, etc., of contemporaries
Individual, A-Z -- Continued

146.D9 Dumouriez, Charles François D
146.G3 Genlis, Stéphanie Félicité D. de Saint-Aubin, comtesse de
146.H7 Hoche, Lazare
146.L2 Lafayette, Marie Joseph P.Y.R.G. du Motier, marquis de
Cf. E207.L2, His career in America
146.M3 Marat, Jean Paul
146.M7 Mirabeau, Honoré Gabriel R., comte de
146.M8 Moreau, Jean Victor M
146.N36 Necker, Jacques
146.O7 Orléans, Louis Philippe J., duc d'
146.R6 Robespierre, Maximilien Marie I. de
146.R65 Rochambeau, Jean-Baptiste-Donatien de Vimeur, comte de
Cf. E265, Participation in American Revolution
146.R7 Roland de la Platière, Marie Jeanne (Phlipon)
146.S135 Saint-Just, Louis Antoine de
146.S37 Ségur, Louis Philippe, comte de
146.S5 Sieyès, Emmanuel Joseph, comte
146.S7 Staël-Holstein, Anne Louise G. (Necker), baronne de
147 Dictionaries
147.5 Chronological tables, etc.
147.8 Historiography
148 General works
Including works on the Revolution alone or the Revolution and Consulate treated together
149 Compends. Textbooks. Outlines
149.5 Pictorial works
150 Pamphlets, etc.
For collected essays, see DC142+
150.B8 Burke's essay
150.B9 Essays on Burke's essay
General special
Military history
151 General works
Cf. DC220+, Revolutionary and Napoleonic wars
151.3 Pictorial works
151.5 National guard
152 Imperial guard; grande armée
152.3 Armée de Condé. Other Émigré troops
152.5 Foreign troops
153 Naval history
154 Aerial operations
155 Political and administrative history

History
By period
Revolutionary and Napoleonic period, 1789-1815
General special -- Continued
Diplomatic history. Foreign relations
157 General works
158 Émigrés
158.1 General special
Indemnity
158.13 Collections
158.15 Separate documents
158.17 General works
158.2 Religious history during the Revolution
158.5 Parties. Clubs. Societies (General)
e.g. Royalist conspiracies
158.6.A-Z Individual clubs or societies. By name, A-Z
e.g.
158.6.P4 Philadelphes
158.6.S6 Société populaire de la section Le Pelletier
158.8 Other
Including aliens, foreign public opinion, the middle class, women, Blacks, prisons, sansculottes, etc., during the Revolution
159 Social life and customs
Cf. DC202.9, Social life and customs during the Empire
Celebrations. Anniversaries
160 General works
160.2 1889
160.3 1989
By period
Assemblies to Directory, 1787/1789-1795
161 General works
162 General special
163 1787-June 17, 1789
Including the year 1789
163.4 Assembly of Notables, 1787
163.7 States-General, May 1789
Constituent Assembly, June 17, 1789-September 30, 1791
165 General works
165.5 Pamphlets, etc.
166 Special. June 17-July 14, 1789
166.062 Tennis-court oath, June 20
166.0623 Séance royale, June 23
166.0627 Fusion of orders, June 27
Fall of the Bastille, July 14, 1789
167 General works
167.5 History of the Bastille
168 Special. July 17-December 31, 1789
168.0804 Abolition of feudal rights, August 4
168.0805 Cry for bread, August 5-6

History
By period
Revolutionary and Napoleonic period, 1789-1815
By period
Assemblies to Directory, 1787/1789-1795
Constituent Assembly, June 17, 1789-September 30, 1791
Special. July 17-December 31, 1789 -- Continued
168.1006 Attack on Versailles, October 5-6
169 Special. 1790
169.01 Division into departments, January
169.07 Federation, July
170 Special. 1791
170.0717 July 17
Legislative Assembly, October 1, 1791-September 21, 1792
171 General works
171.5 General special
Special events
172 October 1-December 31, 1791
173 January-September 21, 1792
173.062 Uprising of June 20, 1792
173.081 August 10, 1792
173.092 Massacres of September 1792
Convention, September 22, 1792-October 1795
175 Sources and documents
176 General works
176.5 General special
177 Committee of public safety
178 Jacobins
179 Girondists
180 Montagnards
September 22, 1792-June 2, 1793
181 General works
181.2 September 22-December 31, 1792
181.3 January-June 1, 1793
182 Temple, and other prisons during Convention
Reign of Terror, June 2, 1793-July 28, 1794
183 General works
183.5 General special
Contemporary accounts (Personal narratives, letters, etc.)
183.7 Collective
183.8.A-Z Individual, A-Z
Special events
184 1793
185 January-July 29, 1794
185.0727 9th thermidor
185.5 July 28,1794-October 1795
Special events
185.7 1794
185.9 January-October, 1795

History
By period
Revolutionary and Napoleonic period, 1789-1815
By period -- Continued
Directory, October 1795-November 9, 1799
186 General works
186.5 General special
187 Year IV (1796)
Special
187.7 13th vendémiaire
187.8 Babeuf's conspiracy
Including Francois Noël Babeuf, also known as Gracchus or Caius Gracchus Babeuf
188 Year V (1797)
188.7 18th fructidor
189 Year VI (1798)
189.7 Special
190 Year VII and VIII (1799)
190.6 30th prairial
190.8 18th brumaire
Consulate, 1799-1804
For works treating the Consulate and Empire together, see DC197+
For works treating the Consulate and Revolution together, or the Consulate, Revolution, and Empire together, see DC139+
191 General works
192 General special
192.4 Constitution of the year VIII
192.5 Royalist insurrection, 1800
192.6 Concordat, July 1801
192.8 The conspiracies of 1802
Including attempted assassination of Napoleon
193 Life consulate, August 2, 1802
193.2 Expedition to Santo Domingo, 1803
193.4 Conspiracies (Cadoudal-Pichegru, 1803-1804)
Cf. DC192.8, Conspiracies of 1802
193.5 Duc d'Enghien (Louis Antoine Henri de Bourbon-Condé)
193.8 Other
Local history, 1789-1804
Paris
Cf. DC26, Description and travel in France, 1789-1815
Cf. DC33.5, Social life and customs in France, 1789-1830
Cf. DC731, Paris, 1789-1815
194.A2 Sources and documents
194.A3-Z General works
195.A-Z Other (Departments, cities, etc.), A-Z

History
By period
Revolutionary and Napoleonic period, 1789-1815
By period -- Continued
Empire (First). Napoleon I, 1804-1815
Including works treating the Consulate and Empire together

197 Periodicals. Sources and documents. Collections
197.5 Minor collections
Memoirs and biography of contemporaries
Cf. DC145+, Biography, 1789-1815
198.A1 Collective
198.A2-Z Individual, A-Z
e.g.
Bernadotte, Jean Baptiste (Karl XIV Johan, King of Sweden and Norway), see DL820
198.C25 Cambronne, Pierre Jacques É., baron de
Coigny, Aimée de, 1769-1820, see DC198.F61
198.D2 Davout, Louis Nicolas, duc d'Auerstaedt et prince d'Eckmühl
198.F61 Fleury, Anne Françoise Aimée de Franquetot de Coigny, duchesse de, 1769-1820
198.F7 Fouché, Joseph, duc d'Otrante
198.M8 Murat, Joachim (Joachim Murat, King of Naples)
Cf. DG848.45, Murat as King of Naples
198.N6 Ney, Michel, duc d'Elchingen, Prince de la Moskowa
199 Collections of letters, etc.
201 General works
202 General special
Including prisoners of war
202.1 Military history
Cf. DC151+, Military history, 1789-1815
Cf. DC227+, Napoleonic wars
For general history and description, see DC201
202.3 Naval history
Cf. DC153, Naval history, 1789-1815
202.5 Political history
Cf. DC155, Political and administrative history, 1789-1815
202.7 Diplomatic history
Class here general works only
Cf. DC157+, Diplomatic history, 1789-1815
For special treaties and events, see DC220+

History
By period
Revolutionary and Napoleonic period, 1789-1815
By period
Empire (First). Napoleon I, 1804-1815
General special -- Continued
202.8 Colonial policy
Cf. JV1800+, History of French colonization
202.9 Social life and customs. Culture
Biography of Napoleon
203 General works
203.2 Anecdotes
203.4 Caricature and satire
203.8 Napoleon in literature and art
203.9 Other special topics
204 Napoleon's relations with women
Personal special
205 Life before 1804
206 Coronation, 1804
209 1814-1821
211 Captivity, 1815-1821. St. Helena. Elba
For the return from Elba, see DC238
212 Illness and death
212.5 Burial in France, 1840
Cf. DC782.I5, Hôtel des invalides
Writings of Napoleon
213.A1 Complete works
213.A2-Z Correspondence and decrees
213.2 Memoirs
214.A-Z Selections, sayings, opinions, etc. By editor, A-Z
For military maxims, see U19
214.3 Will
214.5 Spurious and doubtful
215 Letters to Napoleon
215.5 Criticism of writings
Bonaparte family
216 General works
216.1 Joséphine
216.2 Marie Louise
216.3 Napoleon II (François Charles J. Bonaparte, herzog von Reichstadt)
216.35 Eugène de Beauharnais
216.4 Hortense
216.5 Joseph
Cf. DG848.44, Kingdom of Naples under his administration
Cf. DP207+, As king of Spain, 1806-1808
216.6 Lucien
216.7 Louis

History
By period
Revolutionary and Napoleonic period, 1789-1815
By period
Empire (First). Napoleon I, 1804-1815
Bonaparte family -- Continued
216.8 Jérôme
Sisters
General works, see DC216+
216.83 Élisa
216.85 Caroline
216.87 Pauline
Father and mother of Napoleon
216.88 General works
216.89 Carlo Maria Bonaparte
216.9 Maria Letizia (Ramolino) Bonaparte
216.95.A-Z Other, A-Z
e.g.
216.95.L4 Léon, Charles, called Comte Léon
217 Other material
Wars in the provinces
218 Vendean wars
Including later wars
218.1 Collective biography of participants
218.2.A-Z Contemporary records, narratives, memoirs, etc., A-Z
e.g.
218.2.C4 Charette de la Contrie, François Athanase
218.2.L3 La Rochejaquelein, Henri du Vergier, comte de
218.3.A-Z Individual events, battles, etc., A-Z
218.3.M66 Montreuil-Bellay, Battle of, 1793
218.3.Q5 Quiberon Expedition, 1795
218.5 Chouans
219 Avignon and Comtat-Venaissin
Revolutionary wars, 1792-1802
220 First and Second Coalitions, 1792-1802
220.1 General special
220.15 Pamphlets, etc.
220.2 Campaign of 1792
220.3 Proposed invasion of England
220.5 Campaign of 1793
220.6 Campaign of 1794-1795
220.8 Campaign of 1796 (other than Italian)
221 Second coalition, 1799-1802
221.5 General special
222.A-Z Individual events, battles, etc., A-Z
e.g.
222.B3 Basel, Treaty of, 1795
222.C3 Campo-Formio, Peace of, 1797
222.F6 Fleurus, Battle of, 1794
222.J4 Jemappes, Battle of, 1792

History
By period
Revolutionary and Napoleonic period, 1789-1815
Revolutionary wars, 1792-1802
First and Second Coalitions, 1792-1802
Individual events,
battles, etc., A-Z -- Continued
222.L8 Lunéville, Treaty of, 1801
222.R3 Rastatt, Congress of, 1797-1799
222.S8 Switzerland, Invasion of, 1799-1801
222.T7 Toulon, Siege of, 1793
222.V15 Valenciennes, Siege of, 1793
222.V2 Valmy, Battle of, 1792
222.W37 Wattignies (France), Battle of, 1793
222.Z8 Zurich, Battle of, September 25-26, 1799
222.5 Treaty of Amiens, 1802
Wars in Italy
223 General works
223.4 First campaign, 1796-1797
223.5 Pamphlets, etc.
223.7 Second campaign, 1800. Battle of Marengo, June 14
224.A-Z Individual events, battles, etc., A-Z
e.g.
224.G4 Genoa, Siege of, 1800
Marengo, Battle of, see DC223.7
224.P3 Peschiera, Siege of, 1801
224.8 Pamphlets, etc.
Expedition to Egypt and Syria, 1798-1801
Including occupation of Egypt, 1798-1799
Cf. DT103, Egypt, 1798-1805
225 General works
226.A-Z Individual events, battles, etc., A-Z
e.g.
226.A3 Alexandria, Battle of, 1801
226.E4 El-Arish, Convention of, 1800
226.M3 Malta, 1798
226.N5 Nile, Battle of the, 1798
Napoleonic wars, 1800-1815
Cf. DC151+, Military history, 1789-1815
226.2 Sources and documents
226.3 General works
226.4 General special
226.5 Personal narratives
226.6.A-Z Special topics, A-Z
Participation, Foreign
226.6.P36 General works
226.6.P362A-Z By region or country, A-Z
226.6.P74 Prisoners and prisons
Third Coalition, 1805. German-Austrian campaign
227.A1-A2 Sources and documents
227.A5-Z General works

History
By period
Revolutionary and Napoleonic period, 1789-1815
Napoleonic wars, 1800-1815
Third Coalition, 1805.
German-Austrian campaign -- Continued
227.5.A-Z Individual events, battles, etc., A-Z
e.g.
227.5.A8 Austerlitz, Battle of, December 12
227.5.D8 Dürnstein, Battle of, November 11
227.5.E6 Elchingen, Battle of, October 14
227.5.P8 Pressburg, Treaty of, December 26
227.5.U6 Ulm, Capitulation of, October 17
Campaigns against Prussia, Poland and Russia, 1806-1807
229 General works
230.A-Z Individual events, battles, etc., A-Z
e.g.
230.A8 Auerstedt, Battle of, 1806
230.E8 Eylau (Preussisch), Battle of, 1807
230.F7 Friedland, Battle of, 1807
230.J4 Jena, Battle of, 1807
230.K6 Königsberg, Treaty of, 1807
230.L8 Lübeck, Battle of, 1806
230.P6 Pultusk, Battle of, 1807
230.T5 Tilsit, Treaty of, 1807
Campaigns against Portugal and Spain.
Peninsular War, 1807-1814
Including narratives and letters by officers, etc., other than English
231 General works
232 Special English material
Including Wellingtoniana and narratives and letters by English officers, etc.
Cf. DA68.12.W4, Biography of Wellington, Arthur Wellesley, Duke of, 1769-1852
232.5 Pamphlets, etc.
233.A-Z Individual events, battles, etc., A-Z
233.A5 Albuera, Battle of, 1811
233.B26 Badajoz, Battle of, 1812
233.B8 Bussaco, Battle of, 1810
233.C5 Cintra, Convention of, 1808
233.C55 Ciudad-Rodrigo, Siege of, 1810
233.C7 Corunna, Battle of, 1809
233.J34 Jaén, Occupation of, 1808-1813
233.M3 Madrid, Occupation of, 1808-1813
233.O7 Orthez, Battle of, 1814
233.P67 Porto, Occupation of, 1808-1809
233.S2 Salamanca, Battle of, 1812
233.S3 Saragossa, Siege of, 1808-1809
233.S57 Sitges, Occupation of, 1808-1814
233.T7 Tortosa, Siege of, 1810-1811

History
By period
Revolutionary and Napoleonic period, 1789-1815
Napoleonic wars, 1800-1815
Campaigns against Portugal and Spain. Peninsular War, 1807-1814
Individual events, battles, etc., A-Z -- Continued
233.V3 Vitoria, Battle of, 1813
233.5.A-Z Special topics, A-Z
233.5.G8 Guerrillas
233.5.U53 Underground movements
German and Austrian campaign, 1809
234 General works
Individual events, battles, etc.
234.3 Abensberg, Battle of, April 20. Eckmühl, Battle of, April 22
234.6 Aspern, Battle of, May 21-22
234.63 Sankt Michael in Obersteiermark, Battle of, May 25
234.65 Graz, Battle of, June 15-26
234.8 Wagram, Battle of, July 5-6
234.85 Znojmo, Battle of, July 10-11
234.87 Walcheren Expedition, July-Sept.
234.9 Treaty of Vienna, (Treaty of Schönbrunn), December 14
Russian campaign, 1812
235 General works
235.1 General special
e.g. Guerrillas
235.3 Preparations. "Fürstentag" in Dresden, 1812
235.5.A-Z Individual events, battles, etc., A-Z
e.g.
235.5.B7 Borodino, Battle of, September 7
235.5.M8 Burning of Moscow
235.8 Pamphlets, etc.
1813-1814. War of Liberation
236 General works
236.1 General special
Campaign in Saxony, Germany, 1813
236.3 General works
Battle of Leipzig, October 16-19
236.5 Sources and documents
236.55 Contemporary accounts. Personal narratives
236.6 General works
236.65 Pamphlets
236.68 Special topics (not A-Z)
236.7.A-Z Other battles, events, etc., A-Z
e.g.
236.7.B3 Bautzen, May 20
236.7.D8 Dresden, August 27
236.7.L8 Lützen, May 2

History
By period
Revolutionary and Napoleonic period, 1789-1815
Napoleonic wars, 1800-1815
1813-1814. War of Liberation -- Continued
Campaign in Poland, 1813
236.72 General works
236.73.A-Z Individual events, battles, etc., A-Z
236.73.T67 Toruń
236.73.Z35 Zamość
1814
236.75 General works
236.8.A-Z Individual events, battles, etc., A-Z
e.g.
236.8.B2 Bayonne, Siege of
236.8.B4 Belgium, Campaign in
236.8.C5 Châtillon-sur-Seine Congress, February 3-March 31
For legal works on the Congress of Châtillon-sur-Seine, 1814, see KZ1346.3
236.8.H2 Hamburg, Siege of, 1814
236.8.P4 Pfalzburg, Siege of
236.8.S4 Sens, Sieges of
237 Paris in 1814
238 Abdication (April 6. 1814) and Elba
238.5 Treaty of Paris, 1814
For legal works, including texts of the treaty and related documents, see KZ1348
1815. First restoration and Hundred days
Including Paris in 1815
239 General works
240 Individual events. By date
e.g.
240 June 22 Second abdication of Napoleon
240 Nov. 20 Treaty of Paris, 1815
For legal works, including texts of the treaty and related documents, see KZ1355.5
Battle of Waterloo, June 18, 1815
241 Sources and documents
241.5 Contemporary accounts. Personal narratives
242 General works
243 Pamphlets, etc.
244 Special topics
244.5 The battlefield
Including museums
244.7 Other
Including Gordon Highlanders at battles of Quatre Bras and Waterloo
245 Austria and Italy in their relation to Napoleonic history

History
By period
Revolutionary and Napoleonic Period, 1789-1815
Napoleonic wars, 1800-1815
1815 -- Continued
249 Congress of Vienna, 1814-1815
For legal works on the Congress of Vienna, 1814-1815, see KZ1355
For legal works on the Holy Alliance Treaty, 1815, including texts of the treaty and related works, see KZ1358+
For legal works on the Ionian Islands Treaty, 1815, including texts of the treaty and related works, see KZ1370.I56+
19th century
251 General works
252 General special
252.5 Pamphlets, etc.
252.7 Military history
Biography and memoirs
19th century as a whole
254.A2 Collective
254.A3-Z Individual, A-Z
e.g.
254.C7 Crémieux, Adolphe Isaac M.
Early 19th century
255.A2 Collective
255.A3-Z Individual, A-Z
e.g.
255.C4 Chateaubriand, François Auguste R., vicomte de
For literary criticism of his Mémoires d'outre-tombe, see PQ2205
255.C7 Constant de Rebecque, Henri Benjamin
255.G8 Guizot, François Pierre G.
255.L4 Lamennais, Hugues Félicité R. de
255.M3 Mathilde Bonaparte, princess
255.M7 Montalembert, Charles Forbes R. de Tryon, comte de
255.R3 Récamier, Jeanne Françoise J.A. (Bernard)
255.T3 Talleyrand-Périgord, Charles Maurice de, prince de Bénévent
Later 19th century
See DC280.5, DC342.8
Restoration, 1815-1830
Including reign of Louis XVIII
256 General works
256.5 Social life and customs. Civilization
256.8 General special
257 Biography of Louis XVIII, 1815-1824
Charles X, 1824-1830
258 General works on reign

History
By period
19th century
Restoration, 1815-1830
Charles X, 1824-1830 -- Continued
259 Biography
259.5 Personal special
260.A-Z Biography and memoirs of contemporaries, A-Z
e.g.
260.B5 Berry, Marie Caroline F.L. de Naples, duchesse de
260.F5 Feuchères, Sophie (Dawes), baronne de
260.J6 Joséphine, Consort of Louis XVIII
260.P4 Périer, Casimir Pierre
261 July Revolution, 1830
262 Pamphlets, etc.
July monarchy, 1830-1848
265 Sources and documents
266 Reign of Louis Philippe
266.5 Political and diplomatic history
267 General special
267.8 Abdication, etc.
Cf. KJV4126.A23, Constitutional law
Biography
268 Louis Philippe
269.A-Z Contemporaries, A-Z
e.g.
269.B9 Bugeaud de la Piconnerie, Thomas Robert, duc d'Isly
269.C3 Carrel, Armand
269.M3 Marie Amélie, Consort of Louis Philippe
269.O68 Orléans, Ferdinand Philippe L.C.H., duc d'
269.T3 Talleyrand-Périgord, Dorothée (von Biron), duchesse de
February Revolution and Second Republic
Revolution, 1848
270 General works. Paris
271.A-Z Other local, A-Z
Second Republic, 1848-1851
271.5 Sources and documents
272.A2 Periodicals
272.A3-Z General works
272.5 General special
272.7 Provisional government
Cf. KJV4129.P76, Constitutional law
273 Outbreaks of May and June 1848
273.6 Foreign affairs
274 Coup d'état, December 2, 1851
274.5 General special
Second Empire, 1852-1870
275 Sources and documents
275.2 Minor collections
Including works of Napoleon III

History
By period
19th century
Second Empire, 1852-1870 -- Continued
276 General works
276.5 General special
277 Political and diplomatic history
277.5 Military history
277.8 Naval history
278 Social life and customs. Civilization
279 Other
Biography and memoirs
280 Napoleon III
For his works, see DC275.2
280.2 Eugénie, Consort of Napoleon III
280.3 Louis Napoleon, prince imperial
280.4 Family (Napoleon III and his court)
Contemporaries, 1830-1870
280.45 Collective
280.5.A-Z Individual, A-Z
e.g.
280.5.A8 Aumale, Henri Eugène P.L. d'Orléans, duc d'
280.5.B3 Bazaine, Achille François
280.5.C38 Chambord, Henri Charles F.M.D. d'Artois, duc de Bordeaux, comte de ("Henri of France," "Henry V")
280.5.F3 Favre, Jules
280.5.M7 Morny, Charles Auguste L.J., duc de
280.5.T5 Thiers, Adolphe
Franco-German or Franco-Prussian War, 1870-1871
281 Periodicals. Societies. Serials
282 Sources and documents
285 Memoirs. Personal narratives
289 General works
290 Compends
291 Pamphlets, etc.
292 Causes
e.g. Spanish succession
Cf. DC300, Diplomatic history of the war
Military history
293 General works
293.05 Pamphlets, etc.
French army
293.1 General works. Causes of defeat, etc.
294 Regular army
294.A 1st 1. corps d'armée
294.B 1st 1. division
294.C 1st 1. brigade
294.D 1st 1. régiment d'infanterie
294.F 1st 1. division de cavalerie
294.H 1st 1. bataillon de chasseurs à pied
294.K 1st 1. régiment de chasseurs

History
By period
19th century
Franco-German or Franco-Prussian War, 1870-1871
Military history
French army
Regular army -- Continued

294.L 1st 1. régiment de cuirassiers
294.M 1st 1. régiment de dragons
294.N 1st 1. régiment de hussards
294.R 1st 1. régiment d'artillerie
Volunteer troops, irregulars, etc.
295.A2A-Z Garde nationale mobile. A-Z
295.B2A-Z Garde nationale mobilisée, A-Z
295.C2A-Z Garde nationale, A-Z
295.F2A-Z Francs-tireurs
295.H2A-Z Corps francs, A-Z
295.5 Other
German army
296 General works
297 Prussian army
297.1 Baden army
297.2 Bavarian army
297.4 Hessian army
297.6 Saxon army
297.8 Württemberg army
297.9 Other
298 Naval history
299 Political history
Cf. DC310, Gouvernement de la défense nationale
300 Diplomatic history
Including general relations of Second Empire with Germany
Campaigns and battles
Army of the Rhine
301 General works
301.5 Pamphlets, etc.
302 Saarbrücken, August 2, 1870
302.3 Weissenburg, August 4, 1870
302.5 Wörth, August 6, 1870
302.6 Pamphlets, etc.
302.7 Spicheren, August 12, 1870
302.9 Pont-à-Mousson, August 12, 1870
303 Colombey-Nouilly, August 14, 1870
303.2 Vionville (Rezonville), Mars-la-Tour, August 16, 1870
303.4 Gravelotte, August 18, 1870
303.6 Beaumont, August 30, 1870
303.8 Noisseville, August 31-September 1, 1870
304 Metz, 1870
304.5 Bazaine affair

History
By period
19th century
Franco-German or Franco-Prussian War, 1870-1871
Campaigns and battles -- Continued
Operations in the provinces
305 General works
305.1 Nord
305.3 Ouest
Loire (Armées de la Loire)
305.5 General works
305.6 Battle of Orléans, 1870
305.7 Vosges. Siege of Dijon, 1870-1871
305.8 German communications
Est
305.9 General works
305.92 Belfort (Siege and battle), 1870-1871
Sedan (Armée de Châlons), September 1, 1870
306 General works
306.5 Pamphlets, etc.
307 Celebrations. By date and place
e.g.
307 1895.C4 Chicago
308 Siege of Strassburg (Strasbourg), 1870
309.A-Z Other battles, sieges, etc., A-Z
e.g.
309.A5 Amiens (Villers-Bretonneux), Battle of, November 27, 1870
309.B4 Beaune-la-Rolande, Battle of, November 28, 1870
309.B5 Bitche (Bitsch), Siege of, 1870-1871
309.C4 Châteaudun, Siege of, 1870
309.C7 Coulmiers, Battle of, November 9, 1870
309.C8 Cussey, Battle of, October 22, 1870
309.D3 Dammartin-en-Goële, Occupation of, 1870-1871
309.E8 Épinal, Battle of, October 12, 1870
309.L2 Landrecies, Siege of, 1871
309.L7 Loigny-Poupry, Battle of, December 12, 1870
309.L8 Longwy, Siege of, 1871
309.M4 Mézières, Siege of, 1870-1871
309.M8 Montmédy, Siege of, 1870
309.N3 Neubreisach (Neuf-Brisach), Siege of, 1870
309.P2 Pas-de-Calais, Invasion of, 1870-1871
309.P4 Peronne, Siege of, 1870
309.R2 Rambervillers, Battle of, October 9, 1870
309.R8 Rouen, Occupation of, 1870-1871
309.S3 Sélestat (Schlettstadt), Siege of, 1870
309.V4 Verdun, Siege of, 1870
310 Gouvernement de la défense nationale
Siege of Paris (and Commune), 1870-1871
311.A2 Sources and documents

History
By period
19th century
Franco-German or Franco-Prussian War, 1870-1871
Siege of Paris (and Commune), 1870-1871 -- Continued

311.A3-Z General works
312 General special
313 Other special
e.g. Marine
314 Personal narratives
315 Pamphlets, etc.
315.5 Pictorial works
Commune, 1871
316 General works
317 General special
318 Pamphlets, etc.
319 Minor operations in connection with Siege of Paris
320 Medical and sanitary services. Hospital services
321 Alsace-Lorraine annexation question
323 German occupation and evacuation
(324) War indemnity
See HJ8645
325 Results of the war, etc.
326 Reparation of damages
326.5.A-Z Special topics, A-Z
326.5.P82 Public opinion
Later 19th century
330 General works
331 General special
Third Republic, 1871-1940
334 Periodicals. Sources and documents. Collections
335 General works
337 General special
338 Social life and customs. Civilization
339 Military history
339.5 Naval history
Political and diplomatic history
340 General works
341 Diplomatic history
Biography and memoirs
Collective
342 General works
342.1 Public men
342.3 Women
342.8.A-Z Individual, A-Z
e.g.
Cf. DC280.5.A+, Biography, 1830-1870
342.8.B7 Boulanger, Georges Ernest J.M.

History
By period
19th century
Later 19th century
Third Republic, 1871-1940
Biography and memoirs
Individual, A-Z -- Continued
Brazza, Pierre Savorgnan de, see DT546.267.B72
342.8.C6 Clemenceau, Georges Eugène B.
342.8.F4 Ferry, Jules François C.
342.8.F6 Foch, Ferdinand
342.8.F62 Pamphlets, etc.
342.8.G2 Gallieni, Joseph Simon
342.8.G3 Gambetta, Léon Michel
342.8.J4 Jaurès, Jean Léon
342.8.J6 Joffre, Joseph Jacques C.
342.8.L6 Louis, Georges
342.8.L8 Lyautey, Louis Hubert G.
342.8.P3 Paris, Louis Philippe A. d'Orléans, comte de
342.8.P4 Pétain, Henri Philippe B.O.
Savorgnan de Brazza, Pierre de, see DT546.267.B72
344 Thiers, Adolphe, 1871-1873
Cf. DC280.5.T5, Biography
Cf. DC310, Gouvernement de la défense nationale
346 MacMahon, Marie Edme P.M. de, duc de Magenta
348 Grévy, Jules
350 Carnot, Marie François S., 1887-1894
351 Casimir-Périer, Jean Paul P., 1894-1895
Faure, Félix, 1895-1899
352 General works
353 General special
Dreyfus case
354 General works
354.8 Special aspects
354.9 Illustrative material
20th century
361 General works
363 General special
(365) Social life and customs. Civilization
See DC33.7
365.5 Internal propaganda
367 Military history
368 Naval history
369 Political and diplomatic history
(370) Moroccan question
see DT317
Biography and memoirs
Collective
371.A1-A5 Serials

History
By period
20th century
Biography and memoirs
Collective -- Continued
371.A6-Z General
373.A-Z Individual, A-Z
e.g.
373.B5 Blum, Léon
373.B7 Briand, Aristide
373.C25 Caillaux, Joseph
373.D3 Daladier, Édouard
Gaulle, Charles de, see DC420+
373.H4 Herriot, Édouard
373.L33 Lattre de Tassigny, Jean Joseph M.G. de
373.L35 Laval, Pierre
373.L4 Leclerc de Hautecloque, Philippe
373.M3 Maurras, Charles Marie P.
373.R45 Reynaud, Paul
373.T5 Thomas, Albert
375 Loubet, Émile, 1899-1906
380 Fallières, Clément Armand, 1906-1913
Poincaré, Raymond, 1913-1920
385 General works
387 Period of World War I, 1914-1918
For the war itself, see D501+
Reconstruction, 1919-1940
389 General works
391 Deschanel, Paul Eugène L., 1920
393 Millerand, Alexandre, 1920-1924
394 Doumergue, Gaston, 1924-1931
395 Doumer, Paul, 1931-1932
396 Lebrun, Albert François, 1932-1940
397 1940-1946
Including the period of World War II, 1939-1945, totalitarian state, Pétain, interim regime
Fourth Republic, 1947-1958. Post-war period
398 Periodicals. Sources and documents. Collections
400 General works
401 General special
402 Social life and customs. Civilization
403 Military and naval history
404 Political and diplomatic history
Biography and memoirs
406 Collective
407.A-Z Individual, A-Z
e.g.
407.M4 Mendès-France, Pierre
407.P5 Pinay, Antoine
407.S3 Schuman, Robert
408 Auriol, Vincent, 1947-1953
409 Coty, René, 1954-1958

History
By period
20th century -- Continued
Fifth Republic, 1958-
411 Periodicals. Sources and documents. Collections
412 General works
414 General special
415 Social life and customs. Civilization
416 Military and naval history
417 Political and diplomatic history
Biography and memoirs
418 Collective
419.A-Z Individual, A-Z
Gaulle, Charles de, 1958-1969
420 General works on life and administration
Pompidou, Georges, 1969-1974
421 General works on life and administration
Giscard d'Estaing, Valèry, 1974-1981
422 General works on life and administration
Mitterrand, François, 1981-1995
423 General works on life and administration
Chirac, Jacques, 1995-
424 General works on life and administration
Local history and description
600 Islands of France (General)
For individual islands, see DC611, DC801, DT469, etc.
600.3 Overseas departments (General)
Cf. DT469.R3+, Réunion
Cf. F2066, Guadeloupe
Cf. F2081, Martinique
Cf. F2441+, French Guiana
Larger geographical divisions
North. Northeast
601.1 Periodicals. Societies. Serials
601.23 Gazetteers. Directories. Dictionaries
601.25 Biography (Collective)
601.3 General works. Description and travel. Guidebooks
601.4 Antiquities
601.45 Social life and customs. Civilization
History
601.5 General
By period
601.7 Medieval and early modern
601.8 Modern
601.9 Special topics (not A-Z)
East
603.1 Periodicals. Societies. Serials
603.3 General works. Description and travel. Guidebooks
History

Local history and description
Larger geographical divisions
East
History -- Continued
603.8 Modern
603.9 Special topics (not A-Z)
Central
605.1 Periodicals. Societies. Serials
605.3 General works. Description and travel. Guidebooks
605.4 Antiquities
605.5 History
605.9 Special topics (not A-Z)
South. Gulf of Lyons
607.1 Periodicals. Societies. Serials
607.2 Sources and documents
607.23 Gazetteers. Directories. Dictionaries
607.25 Biogaphy (Collective)
607.3 General works. Description and travel. Guidebooks
607.4 Antiquities
607.45 Social life and customs. Civilization
History
607.5 General works
By period
607.7 Medieval and early modern
Modern
607.8 General works
Biography and memoirs
607.82 Collective
607.83.A-Z Individual, A-Z
607.9 Special topics (not A-Z)
Riviera
Cf. DG975.R6, Italian Riviera
608.3 General works. Description and travel. Guidebooks
608.45 Social life and customs. Civilization
History
608.5 General works
By period
608.8 Modern
608.9 Special topics (not A-Z)
West. Southwest
609.1 Periodicals. Societies. Serials
609.15 Congresses
609.2 Sources and documents
609.3 General works. Description and travel. Guidebooks
609.4 Antiquities
609.45 Social life and customs. Civilization
History
609.5 General works
By period

Local history and description
Larger geographical divisions
West. Southwest
History
By period -- Continued
609.7 Medieval and early modern
Modern
609.8 General works
Biography and memoirs
609.82 Collective
609.83.A-Z Individual, A-Z
Regions, provinces, departments, etc., A-Z
For works limited to local history between 1589 and 1715, see DC121.9.A+
For works limited to local history during the February Revolution of 1848, see DC271.A+
For works limited to local history during the Revolution and Consulate, see DC195.A+
611.A16 Agenais
611.A26-A27 Ain
611.A26 Periodicals. Societies. Serials
611.A261 Sources and documents
611.A2615 Congresses
611.A262 Gazetteers. Directories. Dictionaries, etc.
611.A263 Biography (Collective)
611.A264 General works. Description and travel. Guidebooks
611.A265 Antiquities
611.A266 Social life and customs. Civilization
611.A27 History. Biography. Special topics
611.A298-A299 Aisne
Including old district, Thiérache
611.A298 Periodicals. Sources. Antiquities
611.A299 General works. Description and travel. History
611.A3 Alais
611.A33-A35 Albigeois
611.A33 Periodicals. Sources. Gazetteers
611.A34 General works. Description and travel
Including biography, guidebooks, antiquities, social life and customs, civilization
611.A35 History. Special topics
611.A435-A437 Allier
611.A435 Periodicals. Sources. Gazetteers. Directories
611.A436 General works. Description and travel
Including biography, guidebooks, antiquities, social life and customs, civilization
611.A437 History. Special topics
611.A553-A557 Alpes (Basses-, Hautes-, Maritimes)
Cf. DQ820+, Swiss Alps
611.A553 Periodicals. Societies. Serials
611.A554 Sources and documents
611.A555 Gazetteers. Dictionaries, etc.
611.A556 Description and travel. History

Local history and description
Regions, provinces, departments, etc., A-Z
Alpes (Basses-, Hautes-, Maritimes) -- Continued

611.A557 Other
Alsace, see DC647+
611.A601-A609 Anjou (Table D-DR11)
611.A645-A655 Aquitaine
611.A645 Periodicals. Societies. Serials
611.A646 Sources and documents
611.A647 Collected works
611.A648 Biography
611.A649 Gazetteers. Directories, etc.
611.A65 General works. Description and travel. Guidebooks
611.A652 Antiquities
611.A653 Social life and customs. Civilization
611.A654 Ethnography
611.A655 History
611.A66 Arcachon Basin
611.A67 Ardèche
611.A673-A678 Ardennes
611.A673 Periodicals. Societies. Serials
611.A676 General works. Description and travel. Guidebooks
611.A677 Antiquities. Civilization. Social life and customs
611.A678 History
611.A7 Ariège (Department)
For description and travel before 1790, see DC611.F67
611.A7263 Arles
611.A7265-A7295 Armagnac (Comté and family)
Cf. DC109, Armagnacs in the 15th century
611.A7265 Periodicals. Sources. Biography. General works
611.A727 Social life and customs
611.A7295 History
611.A8 Artois (Province)
Cf. DC611.P281+, Pas-de-Calais
611.A887-A896 Aube
611.A887 Periodicals. Societies. Serials
611.A888 Sources and documents
611.A889 Gazetteers
611.A89 Biography (Collective)
611.A891 General works. Description and travel. Guidebooks
611.A892 Antiquities
611.A8925 Social life and customs. Civilization
611.A893 History (General)
By period
611.A894 Early
611.A895 Medieval
611.A896 Modern
611.A92-A925 Aude

Local history and description
Regions, provinces, departments, etc., A-Z
Aude -- Continued

611.A92 Periodicals. Societies. Sources
611.A922 Dictionaries. Gazetteers
611.A923 General works. Description and travel. Guidebooks
611.A924 History
611.A925 Other
611.A94-A946 Auvergne
611.A94 Periodicals. Societies. Serials
611.A941 Sources and documents
611.A942 General works. Description and travel. Guidebooks
611.A943 Biography (Collective)
611.A945 History
611.A9455 Social life and customs
611.A946 Special topics (not A-Z)
611.A954 Avesnes
611.A961-A963 Aveyron (Table D-DR12)
611.B25 Barrois. Bar (County or Duchy)
611.B31-B319 Basque District

For works treating both French and Spanish Districts, see DP302.B41+

611.B31 Periodicals. Societies. Serials
611.B312 Sources and documents
611.B3123 Gazetteers, directories, dictionaries, etc.
611.B3125 Biography (Collective)
611.B313 General works. Description and travel. Guidebooks
611.B314 Antiquities

History

611.B315 General works
611.B316-B318 By period

Including history and description and travel

611.B316 Early
611.B317 Medieval and early modern
611.B318 Modern
611.B319 Special topics (not A-Z)

Basses-Alpes, see DC611.A553+

Bayonne (Diocese)

611.B34 Periodicals. Societies. Serials
611.B35 Sources and documents
611.B356 Gazetteers. Dictionaries, etc.
611.B36 General works. Description and travel. History
611.B37-B375 Béarn
611.B37 Periodicals. Societies. Sources
611.B372 General works. Description and travel. Guidebooks
611.B373 General history
611.B375 Other
611.B377 Beauce
611.B38 Beaujolais
611.B395 Beauvais

Local history and description
Regions, provinces, departments, etc., A-Z -- Continued

611.B425-B427	Belfort (Table D-DR12)
611.B522	Bernaville
611.B531-B533	Berry
611.B531	Periodicals. Societies. Sources
611.B532	General works. Description and travel. Guidebooks
611.B533	History
611.B574	Béziers
611.B577	Bidasoa River and Valley Cf. DP302.B64, General and Spain
611.B6	Boisbelle (Cher)
611.B751-B752	Bouches-du-Rhône
611.B751	Periodicals. Societies. Sources
611.B752	General works. Description and travel. History
	Bouillon, see DH801.B6
	Boulogne, see DC801.B75+
611.B764-B767	Bourbonnais
611.B764	Periodicals. Societies. Sources
611.B765	General works. Description and travel. Guidebooks
611.B766	Antiquities
611.B7665	Social life and customs
611.B767	History
611.B771-B787	Burgundy (Bourgogne)
611.B771	Periodicals. Societies. Serials
611.B772	Sources and documents
611.B7723	Gazetteers. Directories. Place names, etc.
611.B7725	Biography (Collective)
611.B773	General works. Description and travel
611.B774	Antiquities
611.B7742	Social life and customs
	History
611.B7743	Historiography
	Biography of historians, area studies specialists, archaeologists, etc.
611.B7745	Collective
611.B7747A-Z	Individual, A-Z
611.B775	General works
	By period
611.B776	Early and medieval to 1477
611.B777	Early to 843
611.B778	843-1032 For House of Savoy, see DG611.5
611.B779	1032-1361, Dukes of the Capetian dynasty
611.B78	1361-1477, Dukes of Burgundy
611.B781	1467-1477, Charles le Téméraire For Wars of Burgundy, see DQ101+
611.B782	1477-1789
611.B785	1789-
611.B787	Other special

	Local history and description
	Regions, provinces,
	departments, etc., A-Z -- Continued
611.B841-B9173	Brittany (Bretagne)
611.B841	Periodicals. Societies. Serials
611.B842	Sources and documents
611.B843	Collected works
611.B844	Pamphlets, etc.
611.B845	Biography (Collective)
611.B846	Gazetteers. Directories, etc.
611.B847	General works
611.B848	Description and travel
	Including the picturesque
611.B85	Antiquities
611.B851	Social life and customs. Civilization
611.B852	Ethnography
611.B854	History
611.B855	General special
	By period
611.B856	Early to 877. Armorica
611.B863-B909	877-1492
	General works, see DC611.B854
611.B864	General special
611.B865	Alain III, 877-907
611.B866	Alain IV, 937-952
611.B867	Conan I, 952-992
611.B868	Geoffroy I, 992-1008
611.B869	Alain V, 1008-1040
611.B87	Conan II, 1040-1066
611.B871	Hoël V, 1066-1084
611.B873	Alain VI, 1084-1112
611.B874	Conan III, 1112-1148
611.B876	Conan IV, 1156-1169
611.B877	Geoffroy II, 1169-1186
611.B878	Arthur I, 1196-1203
611.B879	Constance
611.B881	Alix
611.B882	Pierre I de Dreux, 1213-1237
611.B884	Jean I, 1237-1286
611.B885	Jean II, 1286-1305
611.B887	Arthur II, 1305-1312
611.B888	Jean III, 1312-1341
611.B89	Jean de Montfort
611.B891	Charles de Blois
611.B895	Period of Hundred Years' War
611.B897	Interregnum, 1345-1364
611.B898	Jean IV, 1364-1399
611.B899	Jean V, 1399-1442
611.B9	François I, 1442-1450
611.B902	Pierre II, 1450-1457
611.B904	Françoise d'Amboise
611.B905	Arthur III de Richemont, 1457-1458
611.B906	François II, 1458-1488

Local history and description
Regions, provinces, departments, etc., A-Z
Brittany (Bretagne)
History
By period
877-1492 -- Continued
611.B908 Anne, Consort of Louis XII, 1488-1492
611.B909 Period during which union with France was effected, 1458-1492
611.B91 Union with France, 1492-1789
611.B915 1789-1815
611.B916 1815-1945
611.B917 1945-
Biography and memoirs
611.B9172 Collective
611.B9173A-Z Individual, A-Z
611.B92 Brie
Cf. DC611.S45+, Seine-et-Marne
611.B923 Brivadois
611.B931-B933 Bugey (Table D-DR12)
Burgundy, see DC611.B771+
611.C166-C168 Calvados
611.C166 Periodicals. Sources. Gazetteers
611.C167 General works. Description and travel
Including biography, guidebooks, antiquities, social life and customs, civilization
611.C168 History. Special topics
611.C2 Camargue
611.C228-C23 Cantal
611.C228 Sources
611.C229 History
611.C23 Description and travel
Carcassonne, see DC801.C22+
611.C29 Carlat (Comté)
611.C32 Causses
611.C33 Cauterets Valley
611.C34 Caux
Cf. DC611.S44+, Seine-Inférieure
611.C395 Cerdagne
For works treating both the French and Spanish regions, see DP302.C715
611.C423-C425 Cévennes Mountains (Table D-DR12)
611.C44-C4986 Champagne. Champagne-Ardenne
611.C44 Periodicals. Serials
611.C445 Societies
611.C446 Sources and documents
611.C447 Collected works
611.C448 Biography
611.C449 Gazetteers, etc.
611.C45 General works
611.C451 Description and travel
611.C453 Antiquities
611.C455 Ethnography

Local history and description
Regions, provinces, departments, etc., A-Z
Champagne. Champagne-Ardenne -- Continued
History
611.C456 General works
By period
Early and medieval to 1314
611.C457 General works
611.C46 Earliest to 814
611.C462 Counts of Troyes, 814-923
611.C464 Counts of Vermandois, 923-1019
611.C465 Herbert I, 923-943
611.C466 Robert II, 943-968
611.C467 Herbert II, 968-993
611.C468 Étienne I, 993-1019
611.C47 Counts of Blois, 1019-1314
611.C471 Eudes I, 1019-1037
611.C472 Étienne II, 1037-1048
611.C473 Eudes II, 1048-1063
611.C474 Thibaud I, 1063-1089
611.C475 Eudes III, 1090-1093
611.C476 Hugues, 1093-1125
611.C477 Thibaud II, 1125-1152
611.C478 Henri I, 1152-1181
611.C479 Henri II, 1181-1197
611.C48 Thibaud III, 1197-1201
611.C482 Thibaud IV, 1201-1253
611.C484 Blanche de Navarre, 1201-1222
611.C485 Thibaud V, 1253-1270
611.C486 Marguérite de Bourbon, 1253-1256
611.C487 Henri III, 1270-1274
611.C488 Jeanne, 1274-1305
611.C489 Louis, 1305-1314
611.C49 Union with France to Revolution, 1314-1789
611.C492 Period of Hundred Years' War, 1328-1453
611.C494 1461-1610, Louis XI to Henri IV
611.C496 1610-1789, Louis XIII to Louis XVI
611.C498 1789-1815
19th-20th centuries
611.C4983 General works
Biography and memoirs
611.C4985 Collective
611.C4986A-Z Individual, A-Z
611.C51-C52 Charente (and Charente-Inférieure)
For Poitou-Charentes, see DC611.P731+
611.C51 Periodicals. Societies. Serials
611.C52 Description and travel. History
Including biography, guidebooks, antiquities, social life and customs, civilization
611.C56-C563 Cher
611.C56 Periodicals. Societies. Serials
611.C562 General works. Description and travel. Guidebooks

Local history and description
Regions, provinces, departments, etc., A-Z
Cher -- Continued
611.C563 History
611.C65 Clermontois
611.C753 Cornouaille
611.C771-C779 Corrèze (Table D-DR11)
611.C8-C8355 Corsica
611.C8 Periodicals. Societies. Serials
611.C801 Sources and documents
611.C802 Collected works
611.C804 Pamphlets, etc.
611.C806 Biography and memoirs (Collective)
611.C808 Gazetteers. Directories, etc.
611.C81 General works
Description and travel
611.C811 Through 1815
611.C812 1816-
611.C815 Antiquities
611.C816 Social life and customs. Civilization
611.C818 Ethnography
611.C82 History
611.C822 General special
By period
611.C826 Early and medieval
611.C828 16th-17th centuries
611.C83 Modern
611.C831 18th century
Biography and memoirs
611.C8314 Collective
611.C8315A-Z Individual, A-Z
611.C832 Theodor I (baron Neuhof), 1736-1738
611.C833 Annexation to France, 1768
611.C834 Period of the French Revolution
611.C835 19th-20th centuries
Biography and memoirs
611.C8354 Collective
611.C8355A-Z Individual, A-Z
611.C842-C85 Côte d'Or
611.C842 Periodicals. Societies. Serials
611.C843 Sources. Gazetteers. Directories. Biography
611.C844 General works. Description and travel. Guidebooks
611.C845 Antiquities
611.C846 History (General)
611.C847 History (Early)
611.C848 History (Medieval and early modern)
611.C849 History (Modern)
611.C86 Cotentin
611.C87 Côtes-du-Nord. Cotes-d'Amor
611.C9-C909 Creuse
611.C9 Periodicals. Societies. Serials
611.C9023 Gazetteers, directories, dictionaries, etc.

	Local history and description
	Regions, provinces, departments, etc., A-Z
	Creuse -- Continued
611.C903	General works. Description and travel. Guidebooks
611.C904	Antiquities
611.C9045	Social life and customs. Civilization
611.C905	History (General)
	By period
611.C906	Early
611.C907	Medieval and early modern
611.C908	Modern
611.C909	Biography
611.D241-D305	Dauphiné
611.D241	Periodicals. Societies. Serials
611.D242	Sources and documents
611.D243	Collected works
611.D244	Pamphlets, etc.
611.D245	Biography and memoirs
611.D246	Gazetteers. Directories, etc.
611.D247	General works
611.D248	Description and travel
611.D25	Antiquities
611.D251	Social life and customs. Civilization
611.D252	Ethnography
611.D254	History
	By period
611.D26	Early and medieval to 1032
611.D27	Under Germany, 1032-1350
611.D271	First dynasty of Dauphins, 1063-1162
611.D272	Guigue II, 1063-1080
611.D273	Guigue III, 1080-1125
611.D274	Guigue IV, 1125-1143
611.D275	Guigue V, 1143-1162
611.D276	Second dynasty of Dauphins, 1192-1281
611.D277	André, 1192-1237
611.D278	Guigue VI, 1237-1269
611.D279	Jean I, 1269-1281
611.D28	Third dynasty of Dauphins, 1281-1350
611.D281	Humbert I, 1281-1307
611.D282	Jean II, 1307-1319
611.D283	Guigue VII, 1319-1333
611.D284	Humbert II, 1333-1350
611.D29	Union with France, 1350-1789
611.D3	15th-16th centuries
611.D302	17th-18th centuries
611.D305	1789-
	Deux-Sèvres, see DC611.S51+
611.D5	Dinan (District)
611.D663	Dole
611.D69	Dombes
611.D695	Donges (Vicomté)
611.D7	Dordogne (Department, River, and Valley)

Local history and description
Regions, provinces, departments, etc., A-Z -- Continued

611.D75 Doubs
611.D781-D786 Drôme
611.D781 Periodicals. Societies. Serials
611.D782 Gazetteers. Directories. Dictionaries
611.D783 General works. Description and travel. Guidebooks
611.D784 Antiquities. Social life and customs
611.D785 History
611.D786 Special topics (not A-Z)
611.D921-D923 Dunois (Table D-DR12)
Escaut, see DH801.S35
611.E75 Essonne
611.E86-E89 Eure
611.E86 Periodicals. Societies. Collections. Sources. Gazetteers
611.E87 General works. Description and travel. Guidebooks
611.E88 Antiquities
611.E885 Social life and customs
611.E889 History
611.E91-E94 Eure-et-Loir
611.E91 Periodicals. Societies. Serials
611.E93 General works. Description and travel. Guidebooks
611.E94 History
611.F497-F499 Finistère (Table D-DR12)
Flandre-Wallone, see DC611.N821+
611.F67 Foix (Comté)
611.F711-F719 Forez (Table D-DR11)
611.F811-F819 Franche-Comté
611.F811 Periodicals. Societies. Serials
611.F812 Sources and documents
611.F8123 Gazetteers. Directories. Dictionaries
611.F813 General works. Description and travel. Guidebooks
611.F814 Antiquities
611.F815 History (General)
By period
611.F816 Early
611.F817 Medieval and early modern
611.F818 Modern
Biography and memoirs
611.F8182 Collective
611.F8183A-Z Individual, A-Z
611.F819 Special topics (not A-Z)
611.G215-G217 Gard
611.G215 Periodicals. Societies. Serials
611.G216 History
611.G217 Description and travel
611.G23 Garrone, Haute-

	Local history and description
	Regions, provinces, departments, etc., A-Z -- Continued
611.G24-G26	Gascony and Guyenne
611.G24	Periodicals. Societies. Collections
611.G25	History
611.G26	Description and travel
611.G3	Gatinais
611.G35	Gers
611.G4	Gévaudan
611.G5	Gironde
611.G7	Groix, Isle of
	Guyenne, see DC611.G24+
	Haut-Rhin, see DC611.R44
	Haute-Garonne, see DC611.G23
	Haute-Loire, see DC611.L817+
	Haute-Marne, see DC611.M365+
	Haute-Saône, see DC611.S336+
	Haute-Savoie, see DC611.S361+
	Haute-Vienne, see DC611.V6
	Hautes-Alpes, see DC611.A553+
611.H38	Hauts-de-Seine
611.H51-H53	Hérault (Table D-DR12)
611.I26-I27	Ile-de-France
611.I26	Periodicals. Sources and documents
611.I27	General works. Description and travel. History Including biography, guidebooks, antiquities, social life and customs, civilization
611.I29-I3	Ille-et-Vilaine
611.I29	Periodicals. Serials. Sources and documents. Congresses
611.I3	General works. Description and travel. History Including biography, guidebooks, antiquities, social life and customs, civilization
611.I36-I38	Indre (Département)
611.I36	Periodicals. Societies. Serials
611.I363	Collective biography
611.I37	General works. Description and travel. Guidebooks
611.I38	History
611.I41-I43	Indre-et-Loire (Table D-DR12)
611.I7-I75	Isère (Department)
611.I7	Periodicals. Societies. Serials
611.I723	Gazetteers, directories, dictionaries, etc.
611.I73	General works. Description and travel. Guidebooks
611.I74	Antiquities
611.I745	Social life and customs. Civilization
611.I75	History
611.J8-J88	Jura (Department). Jura Mountains
611.J8	Periodicals. Societies. Serials
611.J83	Description
611.J845	Social life and customs. Civilization

Local history and description
Regions, provinces, departments, etc., A-Z
Jura (Department) -- Continued

611.J85 History (General)
611.J88 History (Modern)
611.L255-L257 Landes (Table D-DR12)
611.L27-L271 Langres
611.L27 Periodicals. Societies. Serials
611.L271 General works. Description and travel. History
611.L285-L323 Languedoc
611.L285 Periodicals. Societies. Serials
611.L286 Sources and documents
611.L287 Collected works
611.L288 Pamphlets, etc.
611.L289 Biography (Collective)
611.L29 Gazetteers. Directories, etc.
611.L291 General works
611.L292 Description and travel
611.L294 Antiquities
611.L295 Social life and customs. Civilization
611.L296 Ethnography
611.L298 History
611.L299 General special
By period
611.L3 Early and medieval to 1229
1229-1789, see DC611.L298
611.L313 Period of Hundred Years' War, 1328-1453
611.L317 1453-1610
611.L319 1610-1789
611.L32 1789-
Biography and memoirs
611.L322 Collective
611.L323A-Z Individual, A-Z
611.L4 Laonnais
611.L731-L735 Limousin
611.L731 Periodicals. Societies. Collections
611.L732 General works. Description and travel. Guidebooks
611.L733 Antiquities
611.L7335 Social life and customs. Civilization
611.L734 History (General)
611.L735 Special topics (not A-Z)
611.L801-L809 Loire (Department) (Table D-DR11)
611.L81 Loire River. Loire River Valley
611.L817-L824 Loire, Haute-
611.L817 Periodicals. Sources and documents
611.L819 Dictionaries. Gazetteers
611.L82 General works. Description and travel. Guidebooks
611.L821 Antiquities
611.L8215 Social life and customs
611.L824 History
611.L826-L829 Loire-Inférieure. Loire-Atlantique

Local history and description
Regions, provinces, departments, etc., A-Z
Loire-Inférieure.
Loire-Atlantique -- Continued

611.L826	Periodicals. Societies. Serials
611.L827	General works. Description and travel. Guidebooks
611.L828	Antiquities
611.L829	History
611.L83-L831	Loiret
611.L83	Periodicals. Serials. Sources and documents. Congresses
611.L831	General works. Description and travel. History Including biography, guidebooks, antiquities, social life and customs, civilization
611.L832-L835	Loire-et-Cher
611.L832	Periodicals. Societies. Serials
611.L833	History
611.L835	Description and travel
(611.L84)	Lorraine see DC652-DC655.6
611.L881-L883	Lot (Table D-DR12)
611.L884-L886	Lot-et-Garonne (Table D-DR12)
611.L924-L926	Lozère
611.L924	Periodicals. Societies. Serials
611.L925	History
611.L926	General works. Description and travel. Guidebooks
611.L95-L97	Lyonnais
611.L95	Periodicals. Societies. Serials
611.L96	General works. Description and travel. Guidebooks
611.L97	History
611.M221-M229	Maine
611.M221	Periodicals. Societies. Serials
611.M222	Sources and documents
611.M223	General works. Description and travel. Guidebooks
611.M224	Antiquities
611.M225	History (General)
611.M226	History (Early)
611.M227	History (Medieval and early modern)
611.M228	History (Modern)
611.M229	Biography
611.M241-M249	Maine-et-Loire (Table D-DR11)
611.M267-M275	Manche
611.M267	Periodicals. Societies. Serials
611.M268	Sources and documents
611.M269	General works. Description and travel. Guidebooks
611.M271	History (General)
611.M272	History (Early)
611.M273	History (Medieval and early modern)

	Local history and description
	Regions, provinces, departments, etc., A-Z
	Manche -- Continued
611.M274	History (Modern)
611.M275	Other
611.M31-M319	Marche (Table D-DR11)
	Maritime Alps, see DC611.A553+
611.M352-M36	Marne
611.M352	Periodicals. Societies. Serials
611.M354	General works. Description and travel. Guidebooks
611.M355	Antiquities. Social life and customs. Civilization
611.M356	History (General)
611.M358	History (Medieval and early modern)
611.M359	History (Modern)
611.M36	Other
611.M365-M374	Marne, Haute-
611.M365	Periodicals. Societies. Serials
611.M367	Sources and documents
611.M3673	Gazetteers. Directories. Dictionaries
611.M369	History (General)
611.M3705	Social life and customs. Civilization
611.M373	History (Medieval and early modern)
611.M374	History (Modern)
611.M4	Marne River. Marne River Valley
611.M43-M45	Maurienne
611.M43	Periodicals. Societies. Serials
611.M44	Sources and documents
611.M45	Description and travel
611.M466-M4693	Mayenne
611.M466	Periodicals. Societies. Sources and documents. Collections
611.M467	Gazetteers. Directories. Dictionaries
611.M468	General works. Description and travel. Guidebooks
611.M469	History, etc.
611.M4692	Collective biography
611.M4693A-Z	Individual biography, A-Z
611.M573	Meurthe
611.M591-M593	Meurthe-et-Moselle (Table D-DR12)
611.M597-M6	Meuse
611.M597	Periodicals. Societies. Serials
611.M598	General works. Description and travel. Guidebooks
611.M599	Antiquities
611.M6	History
611.M68	Mont Blanc. Mont Blanc Region
611.M695	Montagnes Noires (Brittany)
611.M831-M833	Morbihan (Table D-DR12)
611.M859	Morinie
611.M891-M893	Morvan (Table D-DR12)
611.M897-M91	Moselle (Department, River, and Valley)

	Local history and description
	Regions, provinces, departments, etc., A-Z
	Moselle (Department, River, and Valley) -- Continued
611.M897	Periodicals. Societies. Serials
611.M898	General works. History and description
611.M9	Biography (Collective)
611.M91	Other
	Cf. DC611.M591+, Meurthe-et-Moselle
	Cf. DD801.M7, Moselle River (Germany)
611.M925	Mouthier-en-Bresse
611.N217-N219	Narbonne (Table D-DR12)
611.N324	Navarre, French
611.N542-N544	Nièvre (Dept.)
611.N542	Periodicals. Sources
611.N543	General works. Description and travel. Guidebooks
611.N544	History
611.N73-N737	Nivernais
611.N73	Periodicals. Societies. Serials
611.N731	Sources and documents
611.N732	Biography (Collective)
611.N733	General works. Description and travel. Guidebooks
611.N734	History (General)
611.N7345	Civilization
611.N736	Gazetteers. Directories. Guidebooks
611.N737	Special topics (not A-Z)
611.N821-N823	Nord (Dept.) Nord-Pas-de-Calais
611.N821	Periodicals. Societies. Serials
611.N8213	Museums. Exhibitions
611.N8215	Congresses
611.N822	General works. Description and travel. Guidebooks
611.N823	History. Antiquities. Civilization
611.N841-N899	Normandy
611.N841	Periodicals. Societies. Serials
611.N842	Sources and documents
611.N843	Collected works
611.N844	Pamphlets, etc.
611.N845	Biography (Collective)
611.N846	Gazetteers. Directories, etc.
611.N847	General works
611.N848	Description and travel
611.N85	Antiquities
611.N851	Social life and customs. Civilization
611.N852	Ethnography
611.N854	History
611.N855	General special
	By period
611.N856	Early and medieval to 1204
611.N86	Earliest to 911
611.N862	Norman princes, 911-1106

Local history and description
Regions, provinces, departments, etc., A-Z
Normandy
History
By period
Norman princes, 911-1106 -- Continued
611.N863 Rollon, 911-931
611.N864 Guillaume I, 927-942
611.N865 Richard I, 942-996
611.N866 Richard II, 996-1026
611.N867 Richard III, 1026-1027
611.N868 Robert I, 1027-1035
611.N869 Guillaume II (William I of England), 1035-1087
611.N87 Robert II, 1087-1106
611.N872 Anglo-Norman kings, 1106-1204
611.N874 Henry I, 1106-1135
611.N8743 Stephen, 1135-1144
611.N8746 Geoffroy, 1144-1151
611.N875 Henry II, 1151-1189
611.N876 Richard IV (I of England), 1189-1199
611.N877 John, 1199-1204
611.N878 Conquest of Normandy by Philippe Auguste, 1200-1204
Capetians, 1204-1329
611.N8795 Sources and documents
611.N88 General works
611.N89 1329-1461
Biography and memoirs
611.N8925 Collective
611.N8926A-Z Individual, A-Z
1461-1790
611.N893 Sources and documents
611.N894 General works
Biography and memoirs
611.N895 Collective
611.N896A-Z Individual, A-Z
611.N897 Napoleonic period
611.N898 19th century
611.N899 20th century
611.O36-O38 Oise (Table D-DR12)
611.O61-O65 Orléanais
611.O61 Periodicals. Societies. Serials
611.O62 Gazetteers. Directories. Dictionaries
611.O63 General works. Description and travel. Guidebooks
611.O64 History
611.O65 Special topics (not A-Z)
611.O74-O76 Orne (Table D-DR12)
611.O795 Ossau Valley
611.P281-P286 Pas-de-Calais
611.P281 Periodicals. Societies. Serials
611.P283 Gazetteers. Directories, etc.

Local history and description
Regions, provinces, departments, etc., A-Z
Pas-de-Calais -- Continued
611.P284 Biography
611.P285 General works. Description and travel. Guidebooks
611.P286 History
Pays Basque, see DC611.B31+
611.P42-P425 Perche
611.P42 Periodicals. Sources. Documents. Gazetteers. Biography
611.P422 General works. Description and travel. Guidebooks
611.P423 Antiquities
611.P424 History
611.P425 Special topics (not A-Z)
611.P441-P449 Périgord (Table D-DR11)
611.P581-P589 Picardy (Table D-DR11)
611.P731-P78 Poitou
Including Poitou-Charentes
611.P731 Periodicals. Societies. Serials
611.P732 Sources and documents
611.P733 Collected works
611.P734 Pamphlets, etc.
Biography
611.P736 Collective
611.P737A-Z Individual, A-Z
611.P738 Gazetteers. Directories, etc.
611.P739 General works
611.P74 Description and travel
611.P742 Antiquities
611.P743 Social life and customs. Civilization
611.P744 Ethnography
611.P745 History
611.P746 General special
By period
611.P747 Early and medieval
611.P748 Celtic and Gallo-Roman period
611.P749 Merovingian period
611.P75 Counts of Poitou, 778-1204
611.P765 Poitou Angevin and English, 1152-1204
611.P772 1203-1339 (Alfonse, 1228-1271)
611.P775 Hundred Years' War to Reformation
611.P777 Annexation to crown of France, 1416-
611.P778 Reformation and religious wars
611.P78 17th-18th centuries
611.P8045-P805 Ponthieu (Comté)
611.P8045 Civilization
611.P805 History
(611.P817-P819) Ponts
611.P9 Privas
611.P951-P979 Provence
611.P951 Periodicals. Societies. Serials

Local history and description
Regions, provinces, departments, etc., A-Z
Provence -- Continued

611.P952 Sources and documents
611.P953 Collected works
611.P954 Pamphlets, etc.
611.P955 Biography (Collective)
611.P956 Gazetteers. Directories, etc.
611.P957 General works
611.P958 Description and travel
611.P96 Antiquities
611.P961 Social life and customs. Civilization
611.P962 Ethnography
History
Study and teaching
611.P9635 General works
611.P9636A-Z By region or country, A-Z
611.P964 General works
611.P965 General special
By period
611.P966 Early and medieval to 1486
611.P967 Early to 933
611.P969 Feudal period: Boson dynasty, 934-1113
611.P97 Bérenger dynasty; Counts of Barcelona, 1113-1246
611.P972 Anjou dynasty, 1246-1481
611.P974 Union with France, 1486-1789
611.P976 1486-1610
611.P977 1610-1789
611.P978 1789-1815
611.P979 1815-
Mainly with modern departments and southern France, e.g. DC611.A553+, DC611.B751+, DC611.V281+
611.P98 Puy-de-Dôme
611.P981-P989 Pyrenees (General, and French). Pyrénées-Atlantiques. Hautes Pyrénées (Table D-DR11)
For Spanish Pyrenees, see DP302.P8
611.Q4 Quercy
611.R237 Rance River (Côtes-du-Nord)
611.R281-R282 Ré Island
611.R281 Periodicals. Serials. Sources and documents. Congresses
611.R282 General works. Description and travel. History
Including biography, guidebooks, antiquities, social life and customs, civilization
611.R43 Rethelois
611.R435 Retz
611.R44 Rhin, Haut-
611.R46-R465 Rhône (Department)
611.R46 Periodicals. Societies. Serials

Local history and description
Regions, provinces, departments, etc., A-Z
Rhône (Department) -- Continued

611.R463 General works. Description and travel. Guidebooks
611.R465 History
611.R478 Rhône River. Rhône River Valley
611.R85-R87 Roussillon
611.R85 Sources and documents
611.R855 Biography (Collective)
611.R86 History
611.R87 Miscellanea
611.S101-S104 Saint A
Subarrange by first letter following A
611.S115-S128 Saint B
Subarrange by first letter following B, e.g.
611.S126 Saint-Brieuc
611.S129-S143 Saint C
Subarrange by first letter following C
611.S144-S148 Saint D
Subarrange by first letter following D
611.S149-S153 Saint E
Subarrange by first letter following E, e.g.
611.S152 Saint-Étienne (Loire)
611.S154-S16 Saint F
Subarrange by first letter following F
611.S161-S169 Saint G
Subarrange by first letter following G
611.S17-S174 Saint H
Subarrange by first letter following H
611.S175-S178 Saint I
Subarrange by first letter following I
611.S179-S183 Saint J
Subarrange by first letter following J
611.S184-S192 Saint K
Subarrange by first letter following K
611.S193-S208 Saint L
Subarrange by first letter following L
611.S209-S224 Saint M
Subarrange by first letter following M
611.S225-S236 Saint N
Subarrange by first letter following N
611.S237-S24 Saint O
Subarrange by first letter following O
611.S241-S25 Saint P
Subarrange by first letter following P
611.S251-S255 Saint Q
Subarrange by first letter following Q
611.S256-S265 Saint R
Subarrange by first letter following R
611.S266-S278 Saint S
Subarrange by first letter following S

Local history and description
Regions, provinces,
departments, etc., A-Z -- Continued

611.S279-S29 Saint T
Subarrange by first letter following T

611.S291-S292 Saint U
Subarrange by first letter following U

611.S293-S299 Saint V
Subarrange by first letter following V

611.S3 Saint W
Subarrange by author

611.S302 Saint X
Subarrange by author

611.S304 Saint Y
Subarrange by author

611.S306 Saint Z
Subarrange by author

611.S31-S318 Sainte A-Sainte Z
e.g.

611.S317 Sainte-Ramée

611.S321-S33 Single words beginning Saint...
e.g.

611.S325-S327 Saintonge

611.S325 Periodicals. Societies. Serials

611.S326 Biography

611.S327 General works. Description and travel. History
Including biography, guidebooks, antiquities, social life and customs, civilization

611.S336-S338 Saône, Haute- (Table D-DR12)

611.S339 Saône River

611.S34-S345 Saône-et-Loire

611.S34 Periodicals. Societies. Serials

611.S3423 Gazetteers, directories, dictionaries, etc.

611.S343 General works. Description and travel. Guidebooks

611.S344 Antiquities

611.S345 History

611.S351-S353 Sarthe (Table D-DR12)

611.S361-S369 Savoie. Haute-Savoie (Table D-DR11)
Cf. DC611.T169+, Tarentaise

611.S38 Sedan

611.S4 Seine (Department)

611.S44-S444 Seine-Inférieure. Seine-Maritime

611.S44 Periodicals. Societies. Serials

611.S441 Gazetteers, directories, dictionaries, etc.

611.S442 General works. Description and travel. Guidebooks

611.S443 Antiquities

611.S444 History

611.S45-S455 Seine-et-Marne

611.S45 Periodicals. Societies. Serials

611.S451 Antiquities

Local history and description
Regions, provinces, departments, etc., A-Z
Seine-et-Marne -- Continued

611.S452 General works. Description and travel. Guidebooks
611.S454 History
611.S455 Other
611.S458-S46 Seine-et-Oise
611.S458 Periodicals. Societies. Serials
611.S459 Biography
611.S46 General works. Description and travel. History
Including guidebooks, antiquities, social life and customs, civilization
611.S461 Seine River
611.S476-S478 Senlis (Table D-DR12)
611.S49 Sennecey-le-Grand
611.S51-S513 Sèvres, Deux-
611.S51 Periodicals. Societies. Serials
611.S512 General works. Description and travel. Guidebooks
611.S513 History
611.S682-S684 Soissons (Table D-DR12)
611.S8 Somme
611.T169-T171 Tarentaise (Table D-DR12)
611.T183-T184 Tarn
611.T183 Periodicals. Serials. Sources and documents. Congresses
611.T184 General works. Description and travel. History
Including biography, guidebooks, antiquities, social life and customs, civilization
611.T187-T189 Tarn-et-Garonne (Table D-DR12)
Thiérache, see DC611.A298+
611.T717-T719 Toulouse (Table D-DR12)
611.T721-T781 Touraine
611.T721 Periodicals. Societies. Serials
611.T722 Sources and documents
611.T723 Collected works
611.T724 Pamphlets, etc.
611.T725 Biography (Collective)
611.T726 Gazetteers. Directories, etc.
611.T727 General works
611.T728 Description and travel
611.T73 Antiquities
611.T731 Social life and customs. Civilization
611.T732 Ethnography
611.T734 History
611.T735 General special
By period
611.T736 Early and medieval
611.T738 Under Gaul
611.T739 Gallo-Roman
611.T74 Merovingian and Carolingian
611.T743 Comté de Tours

Local history and description
Regions, provinces, departments, etc., A-Z
Touraine
History
By period
Early and medieval
Comté de Tours -- Continued
611.T745 Thibaud I, 940-978
611.T746 Eudes I, 978-995
611.T747 Thibaud II, 995-1004
611.T748 Eudes II, 1004-1037
611.T749 Thibaud III, 1037-1044
611.T75 Geoffroy I Martel, 1044-1060
611.T751 Geoffroy II le Barbu (d. 1103?)
611.T752 Foulque IV le Réchin, d. 1109
611.T753 Geoffroy III, Martel, d. 1106
611.T754 Foulque V le Jeune, 1109-1129
611.T755 Geoffroy IV le Bel, Plantagenet, 1129-1151
611.T756 Geoffroy V Plantagenet, 1151-1158
611.T758 1158-1204. English period
611.T76 1204-1360
611.T77 Duchy, 1360-1584
611.T78 Union with France, 1584-1789
611.T781 1789-
611.T92 Trièves
611.V12 Val-de-Marne
611.V13 Val-d'Oise
611.V14 Valence
611.V151 Valenciennes
611.V21 Valois
611.V281-V283 Var (Table D-DR12)
611.V356-V357 Vaucluse
611.V356 Periodicals. Serials. Sources and documents. Congresses
611.V357 General works. Description and travel. History
Including biography, guidebooks, antiquities, social life and customs, civilization
611.V358-V359 Vaudois valleys
611.V358 Periodicals. Serials. Sources and documents. Congresses
611.V359 General works. Description and travel. History
Including biography, guidebooks, antiquities, social life and customs, civilization
611.V433-V435 Velay (Table D-DR12)
611.V44 Venaissin
611.V45-V459 Vendée
611.V45 Periodicals. Societies. Serials
611.V452 Sources and documents
611.V4523 Gazetteers, directories, dictionaries, etc.
611.V4525 Biography (Collective)
611.V453 General works. Description and travel. Guidebooks
611.V454 Antiquities

Local history and description
Regions, provinces, departments, etc., A-Z
Vendée -- Continued
611.V4545 Social life and customs. Civilization
611.V455 History (General)
611.V456 History (Early)
611.V457 History (Medieval and early modern)
611.V458 History (Modern)
611.V4583A-Z Individual biography, A-Z
611.V459 Special topics (not A-Z)
611.V464-V466 Vendôme (Table D-DR12)
611.V5 Vermandois
611.V58 Vienne
611.V6 Vienne, Haute-
611.V8 Vivarais
611.V961-V963 Vosges (Dept.) (Table D-DR12)
Vosges Mountains, see DC645+
611.Y54-Y56 Yonne
611.Y54 Periodicals. Societies. Sources
611.Y55 Gazetteers. Collective biography
611.Y56 General works. Description and travel. History. Antiquities
611.Y9 Yvelines
Alsace-Lorraine
For individual departments composing this region, see DC611.M897+, DC611.R44, etc.
630 Periodicals. Societies. Serials
631 Sources and documents
632 Gazetteers. Directories
633 General works
634 Description and travel
635 Antiquities
636 Social life and customs. Civilization
History
637 Biography (Collective)
By period
639 Early and medieval
640 1500-1789
641 1789-1871
642 1871-1945
643 1945-
Special regions, etc.
645 Vosges Mountains
Other regions, see DC611.A+
Cites, towns, etc , see DC801.A+
Alsace
647 Periodicals. Societies. Serials
647.3 Sources and documents
647.6 Gazetteers. Directories, etc.
648 General works
648.3 Description and travel
648.6 Antiquities
649 Social life and customs. Civilization

Local history and description
Alsace-Lorraine
Alsace -- Continued
History
649.5 Biography (Collective)
650 General works
By period
650.2 Early and medieval
650.3 1500-1789
Biography and memoirs
650.34 Collective
650.36.A-Z Individual, A-Z
650.4 1789-1871
650.5 1871-1945
Biography and memoirs
650.53 Collective
650.54.A-Z Individual, A-Z
650.6 1945-
Lorraine
652 Periodicals. Societies. Serials
652.2 Congresses
652.3 Sources and documents
652.6 Gazetteers. Directories, etc.
653 General works
653.3 Description and travel
653.6 Antiquities
654 Social life and customs. Civilization
History
654.5 Biography (Collective)
655 General works
By period
655.2 Early and medieval
655.3 1500-1789
655.4 1789-1871
655.5 1871-1945
Biography and memoirs
655.53 Collective
655.54.A-Z Individual, A-Z
655.6 1945-
Paris
701 Periodicals. Societies. Serials
702 Sources and documents
703 Collected works
704 Directories. Dictionaries
Biography and memoirs
705.A1 Collective
705.A2-Z Individual, A-Z
707 General works. Description and travel. Pictorial works
708 Guidebooks
709 Pamphlets, etc.
711 Antiquities. Museums
715 Social life and customs. Culture. Civilization

Local history and description
Paris -- Continued
Ethnography
717 General works
718.A-Z Individual elements in the population, A-Z
718.A34 Africans
718.A36 Afro-Americans
718.A4 Algerians
718.A44 Americans (U.S.)
718.A72 Arabs
718.A74 Asians
718.B72 Bretons
718.B74 British
718.C45 Chileans
718.C47 Chinese
718.C67 Corsicans
718.C83 Cubans
718.G47 Germans
718.G7 Greeks
718.H84 Hungarians
718.I24 Icelanders
718.J37 Japanese
718.L37 Latin Americans
718.L43 Lebanese
718.L55 Limousins
718.N67 Norwegians
718.P64 Poles
718.P67 Portuguese
718.R75 Romanians
718.R8 Russians
718.S35 Senegalese
718.S65 Spaniards
718.S95 Swiss
718.T64 Togolese
718.T85 Tunisians
718.V53 Vietnamese
719 Political history
History
General works, see DC707
723 General special
By period
Including description and social life and customs
725 Earliest to 1515
727 16th century
729 17th-18th centuries
731 1789-1815
733 1815-1870
735 1871-1914
Description, see DC707
Social life and customs, see DC715
Siege of Paris, see DC311+
Commune, see DC316+

Local history and description
Paris
History
By period -- Continued
736 1914-1921
737 1922-
Sections, districts, etc.
Arrondissements, faubourgs, etc.
752.A-Z Individual, A-Z
752.A01 1er Arrondissement. Louvre
752.A02 2e Arrondissement. Bourse
752.A03 3e Arrondissement. Temple
752.A04 4e Arrondissement. Hôtel-de-Ville
752.A05 5e Arrondissement. Panthéon
752.A06 6e Arrondissement. Luxembourg. Saint-Sulpice
752.A07 7e Arrondissement. Palais Bourbon
752.A08 8e Arrondissement. Elysée
752.A09 9e Arrondissement. Opéra
752.A10 10e Arrondissement. Enclos-Saint-Laurent
752.A11 11e Arrondissement. Popincourt
752.A12 12e Arrondissement. Reuilly-Bois de Vincennes
752.A13 13e Arrondissement. Gobelins
752.A14 14e Arrondissement. Observatoire
752.A15 15e Arrondissement. Vaugirard
752.A16 16e Arrondissement. Passy
752.A17 17e Arrondissement. Batignolles-Monceau
752.A18 18e Arrondissement. Butte-Montmartre
752.A19 19e Arrondissement. Buttes-Chaumont
752.A20 20e Arrondissement. Ménilmontant
Batignolle-Monceau, see DC752.A17
752.B45 Belleville
Bourse, see DC752.A02
Butte-Montmartre, see DC752.A18
Buttes-Chaumont, see DC752.A19
752.C45 Chaillot
752.D43 Défense
Elysée, see DC752.A08
Enclos-Saint-Laurent, see DC752.A10
752.F68 Faubourg-Saint-Antoine
752.F7 Faubourg-Saint-Germain
Gobelins, see DC752.A13
752.G67 Goutte d'or
752.H34 Les Halles
Hôtel-de-Ville, see DC752.A04
752.I4 Ile de la Cité
752.I45 Ile Saint-Louis
La Défense, see DC752.D43
La Villette, see DC752.V54
752.L38 Latin Quarter. Quartier latin
Left Bank, see DC752.R52
Louvre, see DC752.A01
Luxembourg, see DC752.A06
752.M37 Marais

Local history and description
Paris
Sections, districts, etc.
Arrondissements, faubourgs, etc.
Individual, A-Z -- Continued
Ménilmontant, see DC752.A20
(752.M7) Montmartre
See DC752.A18
752.M8 Montparnasse
Observatoire, see DC752.A14
Opéra, see DC752.A09
Palais Bourbon, see DC752.A07
Panthéon, see DC752.A05
Passy, see DC752.A16
Popincourt, see DC752.A11
752.Q2 Quartier Barbette
Quartier de Chaillot, see DC752.C45
Quartier du Marais, see DC752.M37
Quartier du Val-de-Grâce, see DC752.V3
Quartier La Villette, see DC752.V54
Quartier latin, see DC752.L38
752.Q67 Quartier Saint-Georges
Quartier Saint-Germain-des-Prés, see DC752.S25
752.Q8 Quartier Saint Victor
Reuilly-Bois de Vincennes, see DC752.A12
752.R52 Rive gauche. Left Bank
752.S25 Saint-Germain des-Prés
752.S48 Saint-Merri
Saint-Sulpice, see DC752.A06
Temple, see DC752.A03
752.V3 Val-de-Grâce
Vaugirard, see DC752.A15
752.V54 La Villette
753 Catacombs. The underground city
755 Cemeteries
757 Fountains
Parks (General)
759 General works
760.A-Z Individual, A-Z
e.g.
760.M6 Montsouris
Streets, bridges, waterfront, etc.
761 General works
762.A-Z Individual, A-Z
e.g.
762.P6 Place Vendôme
762.P7 Pont neuf
762.R75 Rue du Bac
Suburbs. Communes suburbaines
768 General works
769.A-Z Individual, A-Z
e.g.
769.A8 Auteuil

Local history and description
Paris
Sections, districts, etc.
Suburbs. Communes suburbaines
Individual, A-Z -- Continued
769.P3 Passy
Buildings
Cf. NA1050, NA4298.P2, NA5550, Architecture
771 General works
Churches, monasteries, etc.
General works
774.A-Z Individual, A-Z
e.g.
774.M2 Madeleine, La
774.N7 Notre-Dame (Cathedral)
774.N8 Notre-Dame des champs
774.S3 Sainte-Chapelle
777 Halls and markets
Public buildings, palaces, etc.
781 General works
782.A-Z Individual, A-Z
e.g.
782.E4 Palais de l'Élysée
782.I5 Hôtel des invalides
Cf. DC212.5, Burial of Napoleon
782.T9 Tuileries
782.V5 Hôtel de ville
Theaters
785 General works
786.A-Z Individual, A-Z
789.A-Z Other buildings, A-Z
e.g.
789.B2 Château de Bagatelle
790.A-Z Other, A-Z
e.g.
790.A6 Arc de triomphe de l'Étoile
790.C6 Colonne Vendôme
Other cities, towns, etc., A-Z
e.g.
801.A325 Aix-en-Provence
801.A51 Amiens
801.A55 Angers
801.A6 Annecy
801.A7-A72 Arles (Table D-DR12)
801.A79 Arras
801.A96 Avignon
801.B45 Beauvais
801.B66 Blois
801.B71-B73 Bordeaux (Table D-DR12)
801.B75-B77 Boulogne-sur-Mer (Table D-DR12)
801.B83-B85 Brest (Table D-DR12)
801.C11 Caen
801.C19 Cannes

Local history and description
Other cities, towns, etc., A-Z -- Continued

801.C22-C24 Carcassonne
801.C22 Periodicals. Societies. Serials
801.C23 Museums. Antiquities
801.C24 General works. Description and travel. History
Including biography, guidebooks, social life and customs, civilization, special topics
801.C28 Carnac
801.C32-C34 Châlons-sur-Marne (Table D-DR12)
801.C42 Chantilly
801.C47-C48 Chartres (City)
801.C47 Serials
801.C48 Monographs
Chartres (Diocese), see DC611.E91+
Château de Fontainebleau, see DC801.F67
Château de Saint Germain-en-Laye, see DC801.S19
Château de Versailles, see DC801.V55+
801.C56-C58 Clermont-Ferrand (Table D-DR12)
801.C657 Colmar
801.C7 Compiègne
801.D4 Deauville
801.D56 Dieppe
801.D59-D61 Dijon
801.D59 Periodicals. Societies. Serials. Sources
801.D6 General works. Description and travel. Guidebooks
801.D61 History
801.D72 Douai
801.E71 Ermenonville
801.F67 Fontainebleau
801.G399-G4 Gien
801.G399 Serials
801.G4 Monographs
801.G81-G83 Grenoble (Table D-DR12)
801.H38 Havre
801.L15-L4339 La A - La Z
e.g.
801.L43 La Rochelle
801.L434-L4624 Laa - Laz
e.g.
801.L4375 Laon
801.L4626-L6469 Le A - Le Z
e.g.
Le Havre, see DC801.H38
801.L48-L49 Le Mans
801.L48 Periodicals. Serials. Sources and documents. Congresses
801.L49 General works. Description and travel. History
Including biography, guidebooks, antiquities, social life and customs, civilization
801.L6462 Le Vésinet
801.L647-L652 Lea - Lerz

	Local history and description
	Other cities, towns, etc., A-Z -- Continued
801.L653-L655	Les A - Les Z
	e.g.
801.L6534	Les Baux-de-Provence
801.L656-L6639	Lesa - Lez
	e.g.
801.L658	Levroux
801.L681-L689	Lille (Table D-DR11)
801.L71-L73	Limoges (Table D-DR12)
801.L78	Lisieux
801.L79	L'Isle-Adam
801.L96-L968	Lyons (Table D-DR11)
	Mans, Le, see DC801.L48+
801.M34-M38	Marseille
801.M34	Periodicals. Societies. Serials
801.M345	Sources and documents
801.M35	Directories, etc.
801.M355	Antiquities
801.M36	History and description
801.M37	By period
801.M38	Special topics (not A-Z)
801.M54	Mentone (Menton)
801.M65	Metz
801.M7515	Mont-Saint-Michel
801.M93	Mulhouse
801.N16	Nancy
801.N2	Nantes
801.N68	Nice
801.N71-N72	Nîmes
801.N71	Periodicals. Sources and documents
801.N72	General works. History. Description and travel
	Including biography, civilization, social life and customs, etc.
801.O6-O64	Orléans
801.O6	Periodicals. Sources and documents
801.O63	General works. Description and travel. Guidebooks
801.O64	History
801.P32	Pau
801.P77	Poitiers
801.R16	Rambouillet
801.R35-R36	Reims
801.R35	Periodicals. Serials. Sources and documents. Congresses
801.R36	General works. Description and travel. History
	Including biography, guidebooks, antiquities, social life and customs, civilization
	Rochelle, La, see DC801.L43
801.R84-R86	Rouen (Table D-DR12)
801.S1003	Sablé-sur-Sarthe
801.S11-S12	Saint A
	e.g.

	Local history and description
	Other cities, towns, etc., A-Z
	Saint A -- Continued
801.S113	Saint-Antoine-de-Viennois (Isère)
801.S121-S14	Saint B
801.S141-S158	Saint C
	e.g.
801.S141	Saint-Calais
801.S15	Saint-Cloud
801.S159-S17	Saint D
	e.g.
801.S16	Saint-Denis
801.S168	Saint-Dizier
801.S171-S175	Saint E
	e.g.
801.S173	Saint-Étienne (Loire)
801.S176-S185	Saint F
	e.g.
801.S18	Saint-Florent-lès-Saumur
801.S186-S195	Saint G
	e.g.
801.S19	Saint-Germain-en-Laye
801.S192	Saint-Gilles
801.S196-S2	Saint H
801.S201-S205	Saint I
801.S206-S21	Saint J
	e.g.
801.S207	Saint-Jean d'Angély
801.S211-S212	Saint K
801.S213-S23	Saint L
801.S231-S25	Saint M
	e.g.
801.S234-S235	Saint-Malo
801.S251-S27	Saint N
801.S271-S275	Saint O
	e.g.
801.S273	Saint-Omer
801.S276-S285	Saint P
801.S286-S29	Saint Q
	e.g.
801.S288	Saint-Quentin (Aisne)
801.S291-S3	Saint R
801.S301-S32	Saint S
	e.g.
801.S304	Saint-Sauveur-en-Rue
801.S321-S335	Saint T
801.S336	Saint U
801.S337-S35	Saint V
801.S351	Saint W
801.S353	Saint X
801.S355	Saint Y
801.S357	Saint Z
801.S365	Sainte-Menehould

Local history and description
Other cities, towns, etc., A-Z -- Continued
801.S3655 Saintes
801.S3664 Saïx
801.S443 Sélestat
801.S5 Sens
801.S65 Soissons
801.S77 Strasbourg
801.T72 Toulon
801.T724-T726 Toulouse (Table D-DR12)
801.T74 Tours
801.T86-T87 Troyes
801.T86 Periodicals. Serials. Sources and documents. Congresses
801.T87 General works. Description and travel. History
Including biography, guidebooks, antiquities, social life and customs, civilization
801.V45 Verdun
801.V55-V57 Versailles. Trianons (Table D-DR12)
Vésinet, Le, see DC801.L6462
(900) French colonies
Collective, see JV1800+
Individual colonies
See subclasses D-F
Andorra
921 Periodicals. Societies. Serials
922 Sources and documents
923 Directories. Dictionaries
924 General works. Description and travel
For 20th century description and travel, see DC928
925 History (General)
By period
926 Early
927 Medieval and early modern
928 Modern
930 Special topics (not A-Z)
Monaco
941 Periodicals. Societies. Serials
942 Sources and documents
Biography
943.A1 Collective
943.A2-Z Individual, A-Z
e.g.
943.G7 Grace, Princess of Monaco, 1929-1982
943.G74 Grimaldi family
943.M6 Monaco, Catherine Charlotte de Gramont, princesse de
943.R3 Rainier III, Prince of Monaco, 1923-
945 General works. History and description
946 Monte Carlo
947 Other special
Nice, see DC801.N68

	History of Germany
1	Periodicals. Serials
	Museums, exhibitions, etc.
1.5	General works
1.6.A-Z	By place, A-Z
2	Societies
3	Sources and documents. Collections
	e.g.
3.M8	Monumenta Germaniae historica. By subtitle, A-Z
3.M8A8	Auctores antiquissimi
3.M8S5	Scriptores rerum Germanicarum
3.M8Z5	Index
3.M825	Criticism of the Monumenta
3.M83	Continuation, by Deutsche Institut für Erforschung der Mittelalters
	Collected works
4	Several authors
5	Individual authors
14	Gazetteers. Dictionaries, etc.
15	Place names (General)
15.5	Directories
16	Guidebooks
17	General works
18	Compends
20	Monumental and picturesque. Pictorial works Including castles, cathedrals, monuments, etc.
21	Historical geography
21.3	Geography
	Description and travel
21.5	History of travel
22	Earliest through 910
23	911-1518
29	1519-1648
31	1649-1744
33	1745-1788
35	1789-1815
37	1816-1829
39	1830-1870
41	1871-1918
42	1919-1945
43	1946-
	Antiquities
51	General works
51.3	Museums. Collections
51.5	General works
51.9	Pamphlet collections
52	Pre-Roman
53	Roman
54	Merovingian and Carlovingian
55	Medieval
	Local see DD701+

Social life and customs. Civilization. Intellectual life
60 Sources and documents
61 General works
61.3 Addresses, essays, lectures
61.8 General special
By period
Earliest
62 General works
62.5 Roman
Medieval
63 General works
64 Special
65 1517-1789. Early modern
66 1789-1871
67 1871-
68 German culture in foreign countries
Including general works on Germans in foreign countries
For Germans in a particular country, see the country
Ethnography
73 Sources and documents
74 General works
75 General special. Early period
76 National characteristics, etc.
78.A-Z Individual elements in the population, A-Z
78.A5 Alemanni
78.A52 Americans
78.B28 Bajuwarii
78.B29 Balts
78.B44 Belarusians
78.B55 Blacks
Franks, see DC64
78.F7 Friesians
78.G5 Gepidae
78.G6 Goths
78.H55 Hindus
78.H83 Huguenots
78.H85 Hungarians
78.I73 Iraqis
78.K67 Koreans
78.K87 Kurds
78.M3 Marcomanni
Cf. DD801.B348, Races of Bavaria
78.O24 Obodrites
78.P64 Poles
78.P67 Portuguese
78.R87 Russians
78.S3 Saxons
78.S5 Slavs
78.S6 Sorbs. Wends
78.S8 Suevi
78.S93 Swedes

Ethnography
Individual elements
in the population, A-Z -- Continued
78.T87 Turks
78.U3 Ubii
78.V54 Vietnamese
Wends, see DD78.S6
78.W5 Westphalians
Germans in foreign countries (General), see DD68
History
84 Dictionaries. Chronological tables, outlines, etc.
Biography (Collective)
For individual biography, see special period, reign, or place
85 General works
85.2 Women
85.4 Public men
85.6 Rulers, emperors, etc.
85.7 Queens, princesses, etc.
85.8.A-Z Houses, noble families, etc., A-Z
e.g.
85.8.L4 Leiningen, House of
Historiography
86 General works
Biography of historians
86.5 Collective
86.7.A-Z Individual, A-Z
e.g.
86.7.A8 Arndt, Ernst Moritza
86.7.G4 Gervinus, Georg Gottfried
86.7.R5 Riehl, Wilhelm Heinrich
86.7.T7 Treitschke, Heinrich Gotthard von
Cf. DD219.T7, Treitschke as statesman
86.8 Study and teaching
General works
87 Through 1600. Chronicles
88 1601-1800
89 1801-
90 Compends
91 History of several states or cities
92 Lost territory
93 Addresses, essays, lectures. Anecdotes, etc.
Special aspects, see DD73+
Pamphlets, etc , see DD93
96 Comic and satiric works
General special
97 Philosophy of German history
Military history
For individual campaigns and engagements, see the special period
99 Sources and documents
Biography (Collective)
100.A2 General

History
General special
Military history
Biography (Collective) -- Continued
100.A3-Z Officers
101 General works
101.5 General special
101.7 Pamphlets, etc.
By period
102 Early to Reformation
102.5 Medieval
102.7 Early modern
103 19th century
104 20th century
106 Naval history
Including sea power
Political and diplomatic history
110 Sources and documents
112 General works
By period
113 Early
114 Medieval. Städtewesen, etc.
Cf. D134, The medieval city
Cf. DD63+, Medieval civilization in Germany
Reformation, see DD184
Modern since the Reformation
115 General works
116 17th-18th centuries
Cf. DD197.5, French Revolutionary and Napoleonic period, 1789-1815
117 19th-20th centuries
Cf. DD221, Political and diplomatic history, 1871-
Cf. DD228.6, Diplomatic history, 1888-1918
Cf. DD240, Political and diplomatic history, 1918-
118 Kulturkampf
Expansionist movements. Imperialism
Cf. D135+, Migrations
118.5 General works
119 Pangermanism
119.2 Drang nach Osten
Cf. DK43, Germans in the Soviet Union
Germans outside of Germany, see DD68
119.5 German propaganda
119.7 Anti-German propaganda
120.A-Z Foreign relations with individual regions or countries, A-Z
By period
Earliest to 481

History
By period
Earliest to 481 -- Continued
121 General works
Cf. DD51+, Antiquities
123 Battle of Teutoburger Wald, 9 A.D.
124 Other special events
Early and medieval to 1519
125 General works
125.5 Biography (Collective)
Medieval Empire, 481-1273
126 General works
126.5 Empire and papacy
Cf. D133, Church and state
481-918
127 General works
128 Merovingians, 481-752
Carolingians, 752-911
129 Sources and documents
130 General works
131 General special
132 Pepin le Bref, 752-768
Cf. DC72+, Biography and reign in France
Charlemagne, 768-814
133 General works on Germany during the period of Charlemagne
Life and reign of Charlemagne, see DC73+
133.9.A-Z Biography of contemporaries, 752-814
133.9.W4 Widukind (Wittekind)
Louis I le Pieux, 814-840
Cf. DC74+, Reign in France
134 General works on life and reign
134.1 Special
134.2 840-843
Ludwig I der Deutsche (First king of Germany), 843-876
134.3 General works on life and reign
134.4 Ludwig II (Emperor), 855-875
134.5 Ludwig III der Jüngere, 876-882
Karl III der Dicke (876), 882-887
Cf. DC77.8+, Reign in France (Karl II)
134.6 General works on life and reign
134.7 Arnulf, 887-899
Ludwig IV das Kind, 899-911
134.8 General works on life and reign
134.9 Ludwig III (Emperor), 901-905
135 Konrad I, 911-918
House of Saxony, 919-1024
136 Sources and documents
137 General works
137.5 General special

History
By period
Early and medieval to 1519
Medieval Empire, 481-1273
House of Saxony, 919-1024 -- Continued
137.9.A-Z Biography, A-Z
137.9.B8 Bruno I, Saint, Abp. of Cologne (Bruno, the Great)
138 Heinrich I, 919-936
139 Otto I, 93-973
140 Otto II, 973-983
140.4 Otto III, 983-1002
140.7 Heinrich II, 1003-1024
House of Franconia, 1024-1125
141.A2 Sources and documents
141.A3-Z General works
141.5 General special
For the Concordat of Worms, see BX1199
For the investiture dispute, see BX1198
Biography and memoirs
141.8 Collective
141.9.A-Z Individual, A-Z
e.g.
141.9.B4 Benno II, Bp. of Osnabrück
142 Konrad II, 1024-1039
142.5 Heinrich III, 1039-1056
Heinrich IV, 1056-1105
143 General works
143.6 Rudolf von Schwaben, 1077-1088
143.7 Hermann von Luxemburg-Salm, 1081-1093
143.8 Konrad (son of Heinrich IV), 1087-1093
144 Heinrich V, 1106-1125
Hohenstaufen period, 1125-1273
145 Sources and documents
146 General works
147 General special
147.5.A-Z Biography, A-Z
e.g.
147.5.A7 Arnold von Selehofen, Abp. of Mainz
147.5.C64 Conradin of Hohenstaufen
147.5.H5 Heinrich der Löwe, Duke of Saxony
147.5.W5 Wibald, Abbot of Corvey
148 Lothar III der Sachse, graf von Supplinburg, 1125-1137
148.5 Konrad III, 1138-1152
Friedrich I Barbarossa, 1152-1190
149 General works on life and reign
149.7 General special
150 Heinrich VI, 1190-1197
150.3 Philipp, 1198-1208
150.5 Otto IV, von Braunschweig, 1198/1208-1215/1218
Friedrich II, 1215-1250
151 General works

History
By period
Early and medieval to 1519
Medieval Empire, 481-1273
Hohenstaufen period, 1125-1273
Friedrich II, 1215-1250 -- Continued
152 Heinrich VII, 1220-1235
152.5 Heinrich Raspe IV, von Thüringen, 1246-1247
153 Wilhelm von Holland
154 Konrad IV, 1250-1254
155 Interregnum, 1254-1273. League of the Rhine cities, 1254
Houses of Habsburg and Luxemburg, 1273-1519
156.A2 Sources and documents
156.A3-Z General works
157 General special
158.A-Z Biography, A-Z
e.g.
158.B3 Berthold VII, Count of Henneberg
159 Rudolf I, 1273-1291
160 Adolf, 1292-1298
161 Albrecht I, 1298-1308
162 Heinrich VII, 1308-1313
Ludwig IV (der Baier), 1314-1347
163 General works on life and reign
163.5 General special
164 Friedrich III der Schöne, 1314-1330
165 Karl IV, 1347-1378
166 Günther, 1349
167 Wenzel, 1378-1400
168 Ruprecht, 1400-1410
169 Jobst, 1410-1411
Sigismund, 1411-1437
170 General works on life and reign
170.3 General special
1438-1519. 15th century
171.A2 Sources and documents
171.A3-Z General works
171.5.A-Z Biography, A-Z
e.g.
171.5.R2 Rechberg, Hans von
172 Albrecht II, 1438-1439
Friedrich III (IV), 1440-1493
173 General works on life and reign
173.5 General special
Maximilian I, 1493-1519
174 General works on life and reign
174.3 General special
174.4 Bundschuh Insurrections, 1493-1517
174.6 German resistance
Modern, 1519-
Including Germany since 1740
175 General works

History
By period
Modern, 1519- -- Continued
1519-1648. Reformation and Counter-reformation
176.A2 Sources and documents
176.A3-Z General works
176.8 General special
Biography and memoirs
177.A1 Collective
177.A2-Z Individual, A-Z
e.g.
177.B4 Berlichingen, Götz von
177.F8 Fürstenberg, Wilhelm Egon, graf von, cardinal
177.M3 Masius, Andreas
177.S2 Sastrow, Bartholomäus
177.S5 Sickingen, Franz von
Karl V, 1519-1558
178 Sources and documents
General works on life and reign
Cf. DH182+, Reign in the Netherlands
Cf. DP172, Reign and life in Spain
178.9 Through 1768
179 1769-
180 General special
180.5 Biography of Karl V
180.6 Correspondence and works
Peasant's War, 1524-1525
181 Sources and documents
182 General works
183 General special
Diet of Spires, 1529, see BR355.S7
184 Schmalkaldic League and War, 1530-1547. Diet of Ratisbon, 1532
Including earlier political history of the Reformation
184.5 Treaty of Passau, 1552
184.7 Sievershausen, Battle of, 1553
185 Ferdinand I, 1558-1564
Maximilian II, 1564-1576
186 General works on life and reign
186.5 General special
187 Rudolf II, 1576-1612
187.8 Matthias, 1612-1637
188 Ferdinand II, 1619-1637
For his reign, see DD189
188.5 Ferdinand III, 1637-1657
Class here biography only
For his reign, see DD189
188.7 Ferdinand IV, 1653-1654
Including election, biography, etc.
189 Period of the Thirty Years' War, 1618-1648
For the war itself, see D251+

History
By period
Modern, 1519- -- Continued
1648-1740
190.A2 Sources and documents
190.A3-Z General works
Biography and memoirs
190.3.A1 Collective
190.3.A2-Z Individual, A-Z
e.g.
190.3.J6 Josef Clemens, Abp. and Elector of Cologne
190.3.K4 Karl Ludwig, Elector Palatine
190.3.M3 Manteuffel, Ernst Christoph, graf von
190.35 1648-1658
190.4 1658-1705
For biography of Leopold I, see DB67+
190.6 1705-1711
For biography of Joseph I, see DB68+
190.8 1711-1740
For biography of Karl VI, see DB69+
1740-1789. 18th century
191 Sources and documents
Biography and memoirs
192.A1 Collective
192.A2-Z Individual, A-Z
e.g.
192.L4 Laukhard, Friedrich Christian
192.M6 Möser, Justus
192.S29 Schönborn, Friedrich Karl, graf von, bp.
193 General works
193.5 Social life and customs. Civilization. Intellectual life
194 Karl VII, 1742-1745
195 Franz I, 1745-1765
196 1765-1790
For biography of Joseph II, see DB74+
1789-1815. French Revolutionary and Napoleonic period
197 General works
Cf. DC139+, France, 1789-1815
197.5 Political and diplomatic history
1789-1806
198 General works
198.4 1790-1792
For biography of Leopold II, see DB74.8
198.7 1792-1806
For biography of Franz II, see DB81
199 1806-1815
Including Confederation of the Rhine, 1806-1813, etc.
19th century
201 Sources and documents
203 General works

History
By period
Modern, 1519-
19th century -- Continued
204 General special
Biography and memoirs
205.A2 Collective
205.A3-Z Individual, A-Z
e.g.
205.B6 Blum, Robert
Dahlberg, Karl Theodor von, see DD205.K3
205.G6 Görres, Johann Joseph von
205.H7 Hohenlohe-Schillingsfürst, Chlodwig Karl V., fürst zu
205.J3 Jahn, Friedrich Ludwig
205.K3 Karl Theodor, Abp. and Elector of Mainz
205.K7 Krupp, Alfred
205.W4 Windthorst, Ludwig Josef F.G.
206 1815-1848
1848-1849
207 General works
207.5 Special aspects
208 Prussia and Berlin
208.5 Other
209.A-Z Local, A-Z
1850-1871
210 General works
211.A-Z Biography and memoirs, A-Z
e.g.
211.J2 Jacoby, Johann
211.R6 Roon, Albrecht Theodor E., graf von
212 Period of war with Denmark, 1864
Cf. DD431, Prussia during the war
For the war itself, see DL236+
214 Period of Austro-Prussian War, 1866
For the war itself, see DD436+
216 Period of Franco-German War, 1870-1871
For the war itself, see DC281+
New Empire, 1871-1918
217 Sources and documents
Biography
217.5 Collective
Individual
Including memoirs
Bismarck
218.A1-A29 Autobiography and family letters
218.A3-Z Biography and recollections
218.2 General special
218.3.A-Z Writings, political correspondence, speeches, table talk, etc. By title, A-Z
218.6 Clippings
218.7 Memorial addresses, funeral orations, etc.
218.8 Other

History
By period
Modern, 1519-
New Empire, 1871-1918
Biography
Individual -- Continued
218.9 Bismarck family
218.91 Johanna
218.93 Herbert
219.A-Z Other, A-Z
e.g.
219.E8 Eulenburg-Hertefeld, Philipp, fürst zu
219.G6 Goltz, Robert Heinrich I., graf von der
219.H6 Holstein, Friedrich von
219.K5 Kiderlen-Waechter, Alfred von
219.M7 Moltke, Helmuth Karl B., graf von
219.S7 Stoecker, Adolf
219.T7 Treitschke, Heinrich Gotthard von
Cf. DD86.7.T7, Treitschke as historian
219.W3 Waldersee, Alfred Heinrich K.L., graf von
220 General works
221 Political and diplomatic history
221.5 Diplomatic history
222 General special
Wilhelm I, 1871-1888
223 General works on life and reign
Cf. DD225, Political history of reign
223.7 Augusta, Consort of William I
223.8 Other members of royal family
223.9 Special topics
Including Drei-kaiser-jahr (1888); Elise Radziwill, Polish princess; war scare of 1875; etc.
Friedrich III, 1888
224 General works on life and reign
224.3 Writings, speeches, diaries, etc.
224.6 Illness
224.8 Pamphlets, etc.
224.9 Victoria, Consort of Frederick III
224.92 Henry, Prince of Prussia
224.95 Victoria, Princess of Prussia
225 Political history, Wilhelm I and Friedrich III
226 Special topics
Including courts and courtiers
Kulturkampf, see DD118
Wilhelm II, 1888-1918
228 General works on reign
228.2 General special
228.3 Social life and customs. Civilization. The court
228.5 Political history
228.6 Diplomatic history

History
By period
Modern, 1519-
New Empire, 1871-1918
Wilhelm II, 1888-1918
General special
Diplomatic history -- Continued
Individual countries, see DD120.A+
228.8 Period of World War I, 1914-1918
For the war itself, see D501+
228.9 Abdication and flight of Wilhelm II
Biography
Wilhelm II
229 General works
229.1 Letters (Collections). By imprint date
229.2 Portraits, caricatures, etc.
229.3 Speeches (Collective and individual), etc.
Alphabetically by title
229.5 Pamphlets, etc.
Imperial family
229.6 General works
229.7 Auguste Viktoria, Consort of Wilhelm II
229.8.A-Z Other members of family, A-Z
229.8.A8 August Wilhelm, Prince of Prussia
229.8.C4 Cecilie, Crown Princess
229.8.W5 William, Crown Prince
Biography and memoirs of contemporaries
231.A2 Collective
231.A3 Portraits
231.A4-Z Individual, A-Z
e.g.
231.B3 Ballin, Albert
231.B5 Bethmann-Hollweg, Theobald von
231.B8 Bülow, Bernhard Heinrich M.K., fürst von
231.C4 Chamberlain, Houston Stewart
231.E25 Eckardstein, Hermann, freiherr von
231.F3 Falkenhayn, Erich Georg A.S. von
231.H5 Hindenburg, Paul von
231.L5 Lichnowsky, Karl Max, fürst
231.L8 Ludendorff, Erich
231.M2 Mackensen, Anton Ludwig F.A. von
231.M3 Maximilian, Prince of Baden
231.P4 Peters, Karl
231.R3 Rathenau, Walther
231.S4 Schlieffen, Alfred, graf von
231.S47 Seeckt, Hans von
231.S8 Stinnes, Hugo
231.S83 Stresemann, Gustav
231.T5 Tirpitz, Alfred Peter F. von
231.W3 Weddigen, Otto
20th century
232 General works
232.5 Sources and documents

History
By period
Modern, 1519-
20th century -- Continued
Revolution and Republic, 1918-
233 Periodicals. Societies
234 Sources and documents
Collected works
235 Several authors
236 Individual authors
237 General works
Including pictorial works
238 General special
239 Social life and customs. Civilization
240 Political and diplomatic history
Biography and memoirs
Collective
243 General
244 Public men
245 Women
247.A-Z Individual, A-Z
e.g.
247.B7 Brüning, Heinrich
247.E2 Ebert, Friedrich
247.G6 Goebbels, Joseph
247.G67 Göring, Hermann
247.G85 Gustloff, Wilhelm
247.H37 Hess, Rudolf
247.H5 Hitler, Adolf
247.P3 Papen, Franz von
247.R47 Ribbentrop, Joachim von
247.R58 Rosenberg, Alfred
247.S335 Schacht, Hjalmar Horace G.
247.S346 Schlageter, Albert Leo
247.S8 Strasser, Otto
247.T45 Thälmann, Ernst
By period
248 Revolution, 1918
249 Ebert, 1919-1925
For biography of Ebert, see DD247.E2
251 Hindenburg, 1925-1935
For biography of Hindenburg, see DD231.H5
Hitler, 1933-1945. National socialism
For biographies of Hitler and other National Socialist leaders, see DD247.A+
Contemporary works
For postwar works on the Hitler period, see DD256.45+
253.A1 Periodicals. Societies. Collections
253.A2-Z General works

History
By period
Modern, 1519-
20th century
Revolution and Republic, 1918-
By period
Hitler, 1933-1945.
National socialism -- Continued
The Nazi Party (Nationalsozialistische Deutsche Arbeiter-Partei)
This scheme was developed for a special collection at the Library of Congress
253.2 Serials. Party documents. By title
Including serials entered under the party name without subheading
253.25 General works
Including party organization
Party meetings (Reichsparteitage)
253.27 General works
253.28 Individual meetings. By date
Meetings were held in 1923, 1926, 1927, 1929, 1933-1938
Administrative offices of the party
253.29 General works
253.3.A-Z Individual offices, A-Z
By subhead descriptive of the Reich, if possible
Offices are variously styled Ämter, Beauftragte, Dienststellungen, Hauptämter, Institute, Kanzleien, Kommissionen, Reichsführungen, Reichsleitungen, etc.
For works where subject matter is not dominated by party interests, see the subject
Territorial divisions of the party, its Hoheitsgebiete
253.39 General works
253.4.A-Z By Gau, A-Z
Under each Gau:
.A1 Serials. Collections
253.4.B3 Gau Baden
Subarrangement:
.A1 Serials. Collections
Auslandsorganisation
Rated as a Gau
253.412 Arbeitsbereich. General government
253.413 Landesgruppen

History
By period
Modern, 1519-
20th century
Revolution and Republic, 1918-
By period
Hitler, 1933-1945. National socialism
The Nazi Party
(Nationalsozialistische Deutsche Arbeiter-Partei)
Territorial divisions of the party, its Hoheitsgebiete -- Continued

253.42.A-Z By Kreis, A-Z
Under each Kreis:
.A1 Serials. Collections

253.43.A-Z By Ortsgruppe, A-Z
Under each Ortsgruppe:
.A1 Serials. Collections

253.44.A-Z By Zelle, A-Z
Under each Zelle:
.A1 Serials. Collections

253.45.A-Z By Block, A-Z
Under each Block:
.A1 Serials. Collections

253.46 Branches of the party, its Gliederungen
Individual formations
Bund der Jungmädel
253.47.A1 Serials. Collections
253.47.A2-Z General works
Bund Deutscher Mädel
253.48.A1 Serials. Collections
253.48.A2-Z General works
Deutsches Jungvolk
253.49.A1 Serials. Collections
253.49.A2-Z General works
Dozentenbuch, see L33
Frauenschaft, see DD253.58.A1+
Hitler-Jugend
Cf. HQ799.A+, Youth of Germany
253.5.A1 Serials. Collections
253.5.A2-Z General works
253.53.A-Z Local, A-Z
Kraftfahrerkorps
253.56.A1 Serials. Collections
253.56.A2-Z General works
Marinesturmabteilung, see DD253.73
Nationalsozialistische Frauenschaft
253.58.A1 Serials. Collections
253.58.A2-Z General works
Dozentenbuch, see L33
Schutzstaffel

History
By period
Modern, 1519-
20th century
Revolution and Republic, 1918-
By period
Hitler, 1933-1945. National socialism
The Nazi Party
(Nationalsozialistische Deutsche Arbeiter-Partei)
Branches of the party, its Gliederungen
Individual formations
Schutzstaffel -- Continued

253.6.A1 Serials. Collections
253.6.A2-Z General works
Local
253.62.A-Z By key word, A-Z
e.g.
253.62.R5 Rhine
253.63 By number, A-Z
e.g.
253.63 39th 39th
Waffenschutzstaffel
Cf. D757.85, World War II
253.65.A1 Serials. Collections
253.65.A2-Z General works
Studentenbund, see LA729.A1+
253.7 Sturmabteilung
253.73 Marinesturmabteilung
253.76 Affiliated organizations not elsewhere provided for
253.8.A-Z Individual organizations. By key word, A-Z
e.g.
253.8.K7 Kriegerbund
253.8.S8 Stahlhelm
Propaganda in other countries
254 General works
255.A-Z Individual regions or countries, A-Z
(256) Period of World War II, 1939-1945
see D731+, for the war itself; DD253, for contemporary works on the Hitler period; DD256.45+, for postwar works on the Hitler period
Resistance movements against National Socialist regime
256.3 General works
256.35 Assassination attempts against Hitler
256.4.A-Z Local, A-Z
Postwar works on the Hitler period
For contemporary works on the Hitler period, see DD253.A1+

History
By period
Modern, 1519-
20th century
Revolution and Republic, 1918-
By period
Hitler, 1933-1945. National socialism
Postwar works
on Hitler period -- Continued

256.45 Periodicals. Societies. Serials
256.46 Congresses
Sources and documents, see DD253.A1+
256.47 Dictionaries
256.48 Historiography
256.49 Study and teaching
256.5 General works
256.6 Social life and customs. Civilization. Intellectual life
256.7 Political history
256.8 Foreign and general relations
Biography and memoirs, see DD243+
Propaganda, see DD254
Resistance movements, see DD256.3+

Period of Allied occupation, 1945-1990
257.A1 Periodicals. Societies
257.A2-Z General works
257.2 General special
257.25 Reunification question
257.4 Political and diplomatic history
Biography and memoirs, see DD243+

West Germany
258 Periodicals. Societies. Serials
258.2 Congresses
258.23 Gazetteers. Dictionaries, etc.
258.24 Directories
258.25 Guidebooks
258.3 General works
258.35 Pictorial works
Description and travel
258.39 History of travel
258.4 Through 1980
258.42 1981-
258.45 Antiquities
For local antiquities, see DD801.A+
Ethnography
258.5 General works
258.55.A-Z Individual elements in the population, A-Z
258.55.E35 Egyptians
258.55.G74 Greeks
258.55.P64 Poles
258.55.P67 Portuguese
258.55.R87 Russian Germans
258.55.T87 Turks

West Germany
Ethnography
Individual elements
in the population, A-Z -- Continued
258.55.V53 Vietnamese
258.55.Y83 Yugoslavs
History
Periodicals. Societies. Serials, see DD258
258.6 Biography (Collective)
258.7 General works
258.75 Political history
Foreign and general relations
For general works on the diplomatic history of a period, see the period
258.8 General works
For works on relations with a specific country regardless of the period, see DD258.85.A+
258.85.A-Z Relations with individual regions or countries, A-Z
By period
258.9 Through 1949
Konrad Adenauer, 1949-1963
For biography of Adenauer, see DD259.7.A+
259 General works on life and administration
259.2 General special
259.25 Social life and customs. Civilization. Intellectual life
259.4 Political history
259.5 Foreign and general relations
Biography and memoirs
259.63 Collective
259.7.A-Z Individual, A-Z
1963-
260 General works
260.2 General special
260.3 Social life and customs. Civilization. Intellectual life
260.4 Political history
260.5 Foreign and general relations
Biography and memoirs
260.6 Collective
260.65.A-Z Individual, A-Z
Ludwig Erhard, 1963-1966
260.7 General works on life and administration
Kurt Kiesinger, 1966-1969
260.75 General works on life and administration
Willy Brandt, 1969-1974
260.8 General works on life and administration
Helmut Schmidt, 1974-1982
260.85 General works on life and administration
Helmut Kohl, 1982-
262 General works on life and administration
Local history and description, see DD701+
East Germany

East Germany -- Continued
280 Periodicals. Societies. Serials
280.3 Congresses
280.35 Sources and documents
280.4 Gazetteers. Dictionaries, etc.
280.5 Guidebooks
280.6 General works
280.7 Pictorial works
280.8 Description and travel
280.9 Antiquities
For local antiquities, see DD801.A+
Ethnography
281 General works
281.2.A-Z Individual elements in the population, A-Z
281.2.E27 East Europeans
281.2.M68 Mozambicans
281.2.S55 Slavs
History
Periodicals. Societies. Serials, see DD280
281.5 Biography (Collective)
281.6 Historiography
282 General works
282.5 Military history
283 Political history
284 Foreign and general relations
For works on relations with a specific country regardless of the period, see DD284.5.A+
For general works on the diplomatic history of a period, see the period
284.5.A-Z Relations with individual regions or countries, A-Z
By period
285 Through 1949
1949-1961
286 General works
286.2 General special
286.3 Social life and customs. Civilization. Intellectual life
286.4 Political history
286.5 Foreign and general relations
Biography and memoirs
286.6 Collective
286.7.A-Z Individual, A-Z
e.g.
286.7.P53 Pieck, Wilhelm
1961-1990
287 General works
287.2 General special
287.3 Social life and customs. Civilization. Intellectual life
287.4 Political history
287.5 Foreign and general relations
Biography and memoirs
287.6 Collective

East Germany
History
By period
1961-1990
Biography and memoirs -- Continued
287.7.A-Z Individual, A-Z
288 1961-1971
289 1971-1990
289.5 1990-
Local history and description, see DD701+
Reunified Germany, 1990-
290 Periodicals. Societies. Serials
290.2 Congresses
290.22 Sources and documents
290.23 Dictionaries
290.24 Historiography
290.25 General works
290.26 Social life and customs. Civilization. Intellectual life
290.27 Military history
290.28 Naval history
290.29 Political history
290.3 Foreign and general relations
Biography and memoirs
290.32 Collective
290.33.A-Z Individual, A-Z
Prussia
301 Periodicals. Serials
302 Societies
303 Sources and documents
Collected works
304 Several authors
305 Individual authors
308 Gazetteers. Dictionaries, etc.
Guidebooks, see DD16
310 General works
312 Monumental and picturesque
Description and travel
314 Earliest to 1648
315 1649-1788
316 1789-1815
319 1816-1870
320 1871-
325 Antiquities
For local, see DD701+
331 Social life and customs. Civilization. Intellectual life
Ethnography
335 General works
Individual
336 Prussians
337 Poles
338 Other Slavic

Prussia
Ethnography
Individual -- Continued
339 Other
History
341 Dictionaries
Biography (Collective)
For individual biography, see the special period, reign, or place
343 General works
343.2 Women
343.4 Public men
343.6 Rulers, kings, etc.
343.7 Queens, princesses, etc.
343.8 Houses, noble families, etc.
e.g.
343.8.E7 Eulenberg family
345 Historiography
General works
346 Through 1800. Chronicles
347 1801-
350 Special aspects (not A-Z)
Including elements in the population, e.g. Danes
351 Pamphlets, etc.
354 Military history
Cf. DD99+, Military history of Germany
Biography (Collective), see DD100.A2+
358 Naval history
Cf. DD106, Naval history of Germany
Political and diplomatic history
For diplomatic history of special periods, reigns, etc., see the period or reign
361 General works
363 Medieval
365 Modern
House of Hohenzollern
369 Periodicals. Societies. Serials
370 History
By period
Early to 1640
Class here general works
For knights of the Teutonic order, see CR4775.A+
For local, see DD801-DD900.76, or DD901
375 Sources and documents
377 General works
378 General special
1415-1640. Hohenzollern dynasty
Class here works on the general period only
380 Sources and documents
Biography and memoirs
381.3 Collective
381.3.A-Z Individual, A-Z
382 General works

Prussia
History
By period
Early to 1640
1415-1640. Hohenzollern dynasty -- Continued
383 General special
385 Period of the Reformation
Cf. DD176+, Germany during the Reformation
387 Period of the Thirty Years' War, 1618-1648
Cf. DD189, Period of the Thirty Years' War in Germany
For the war itself, see D251+
Modern, 1640-
389 General works
17th century
390 Sources and documents
391.A-Z Biography and memoirs, A-Z
392 General works
Friedrich Wilhelm, 1640-1688
394 General works on life and reign
394.3 General special
394.5 Political and diplomatic history
395.A-Z Biography and memoirs of contemporaries, A-Z
395.G4 Georg Friedrich, Prince of Waldeck
395.L8 Luise Henriette, Consort of Frederick William
18th century
396.A1 Sources and documents
Biography and memoirs
396.A2 Collective
396.A3-Z Individual, A-Z
e.g.
396.N5 Nettelbeck, Joachim Christian
396.V9 Voss, Sophie Wilhelmine C.M. (von Pannwitz), gräfin von
397 General works
Friedrich I (III), 1688-1713
398 General works on life and reign
398.3 General special
398.6 Coronation ceremonies, etc.
398.7 Other minor
398.8.A-Z Biography and memoirs of contemporaries, A-Z
e.g.
398.8.S7 Sophie Charlotte, Consort of Frederick I
Friedrich Wilhelm I, 1713-1740
399 General works on life and reign
399.8.A-Z Biography and memoirs of contemporaries, A-Z
e.g.
399.8.S7 Sophie Dorothea, Consort of Frederick William I
Friedrich II der Grosse, 1740-1786

Prussia
History
By period
Modern, 1640-
18th century
Friedrich II der
Grosse, 1740-1786 -- Continued
401 Sources and documents
Biography and memoirs of contemporaries
402.A1 Collective
402.A2-Z Individual, A-Z
402.H4 Heinrich, Prince of Prussia
402.L2 La Motte-Fouqué, Heinrich August, freiherr de
402.W6 Wilhelmine, Consort of Frederick William, margrave of Bayreuth
402.Z5 Zieten, Hans Joachim von
403 General works on reign
403.8 General special
Biography
404 Friedrich II
404.5 Elisabeth Christine
404.7 Friedrich II in literature and art
Works
Complete and posthumous works
405 In French. By editor or date
405.1 In German
By editor or date
405.12 In English
By editor or date
Political correspondence
405.2 In French
By editor or date
405.22 In German
By editor or date
405.23 In English
By editor or date
Selections (not confined to any one subject elsewhere classified)
405.3 In French
By editor or date
405.32 In German
By editor or date
405.33 In English
By editor or date
405.34 In other languages (not A-Z)
By editor or date
Memoirs
405.5 In French
By editor or date
405.52 In German
By editor or date

Prussia
History
By period
Modern, 1640-
18th century
Friedrich II der Grosse, 1740-1786
Works
Memoirs -- Continued
405.53 In English
By editor or date
Correspondence (other than political)
405.6 In French
By editor or date
405.62 In German
By editor or date
405.63 In English
By editor or date
405.8 Doubtful and spurious
By title and date
Silesian wars, 1740-1745
406 General works
406.5 Diplomatic history
407.A-Z Special events, battles, etc., A-Z
407.F8 Füssen, Treaty of, 1745
407.H7 Hohenfriedeberg, Battle of, 1745
407.K4 Kesselsdorf, Battle of, 1745
407.5 Peace of Dresden, 1745
Cf. DD801.S398, Saxony
Austrian succession, 1740-1748
See DB72
408 1745-1756
Seven Years' War, 1756-1763
Cf. DA500, England during Seven Years' War
Cf. DC133+, France under Louis XV, 1715-1774
409 Sources and documents
410.A-Z Memoirs of contemporaries, A-Z
Cf. DD402.A1+, Biography of contemporaries, 1740-1786
411 General works
411.5 General special
412 Pamphlets, etc.
Cf. DA67+, English military history (18th century)
Cf. DA503, English pamphlets, 1714-1760
412.6.A-Z Special events, battles, etc., A-Z
412.6.H7 Hochkirch, Battle of, 1758
412.6.K8 Kunersdorf, Battle of, 1759
412.6.L6 Leuthen, Battle of, 1757
412.6.P7 Prague, Battle of, 1757
412.6.R7 Rossbach, Battle of, 1757

Prussia
History
By period
Modern, 1640-
18th century
Friedrich II der Grosse, 1740-1786
Seven Years' War, 1756-1763
Special events,
battles, etc., A-Z -- Continued
412.6.T6 Torgau, Battle of, 1760
412.8 Peace of Hubertsburg, 1763
For Treaty of Paris, see D297+
413 1763-1778
413.2 1778-1786
Friedrich Wilhelm II, 1786-1797
414 General works on life and reign
414.9.A-Z Biography and memoirs of contemporaries, A-Z
e.g.
414.9.L5 Lichtenau, Wilhelmine (Enke), gräfin von
414.9.L6 Louis Ferdinand, Prince of Prussia
19th century
415 Sources and documents
416.A-Z Biography and memoirs, A-Z
e.g.
Cf. DD205.A2+, German 19th century biography
416.B3 Bernhardi, Theodor von
416.B4 Bernstorff, Albrecht, graf von
416.B8 Bunsen, Christian Karl J., freiherr von
416.R2 Radziwill, Luise, ksiezna
416.S8 Stein, Heinrich Friedrich K., freiherr vom und zum
417 General works
1789-1815. Period of the French Revolution
Cf. DC139+, French Revolutionary and Napoleonic period
418 Sources and documents
Biography and memoirs
418.6.A2 Collective
418.6.A3-Z Individual, A-Z
e.g.
418.6.B6 Blücher, Gebhard Leberecht von
418.6.B7 Boyen, Hermann von
418.6.G6 Gneisenau, August Wilhelm A., graf Neithardt von
418.6.S3 Scharnhorst, Gerhard Johann D. Von
418.6.S33 Schill, Ferdinand Baptista von
418.6.Y7 Yorck von Wartenburg, Hans David L., graf
419 General works
Military history, see DC236+
Friedrich Wilhelm III, 1797-1840
420 General works on life and reign

Prussia
History
By period
Modern, 1640-
19th century
Friedrich Wilhelm
III, 1797-1840 -- Continued
Biography and memoirs
421 Friedrich Wilhelm III
421.3 Luise, Consort of Frederick William III
421.4 Auguste, Princess of Liegnitz, Consort of Frederick William III
422.A-Z Contemporaries, A-Z
e.g.
Cf. DD205.A2+, German 19th century biography
422.C5 Clausewitz, Karl von
422.H2 Hardenberg, Karl August, Fürst von
422.H8 Humboldt, Wilhelm, Freiherr von
422.M35 Marwitz, Friedrich August L. von der
423 Confederation, 1816-1866
Friedrich Wilhelm IV, 1840-1861
424 General works on reign
424.3 Pamphlets, etc.
Biography and memoirs
424.8 Friedrich Wilhelm IV
424.9.A-Z Contemporaries, A-Z
e.g.
Cf. DD205.A2+, German 19th century biography
424.9.F7 Friedrich Karl, Prince of Prussia
424.9.H2 Hansemann, David Justus L.
424.9.M2 Manteuffel, Edwin Karl R., freiherr von
Wilhelm I, 1861-1888
425 General works on reign as king of Prussia
Biography, see DD223+
Biography and memoirs of contemporaries, see DD219.A+
429 General special
431 Prussia during the war with Denmark, 1864
For general works on the war, see DL236+
Austro-Prussian War, 1866
436 Sources and documents
437.A-Z Memoirs and reminiscences, A-Z
438 General works
439.A-Z Special campaigns, battles, etc., A-Z
For campaigns in Italy, see DG558
439.K7 Königgrätz (Hradec Králové), Battle of, 1866
439.P8 Prague, Peace of, 1866
439.T7 Trautenau (Trutnov), Battle of, 1866
440 Other
442 North German Confederation, 1866-1870

Prussia
History
By period
Modern, 1640-
19th century
Wilhelm I, 1861-1888 -- Continued
446 Period of Franco-German War, 1870-1871
Cf. DC281+, Franco-German or Franco-Prussian War, 1870-1871
New Empire, 1871-1918
448 General works
Friedrich III, 1888, see DD224+
William II, 1888-1918
451 General works on reign as king of Prussia
Biography, see DD229+
Biography and memoirs of contemporaries, see DD231.A2+
452 Period between World Wars, 1918-1945
Biography and memoirs, see DD247.A+
453 1918-1933
454 1933-1945
(491.A-Z) Local history and description
See DD701+, DK4600+
Local history and description
Larger geographic divisions
701-709 North and Central
701 Periodicals. Societies. Serials
704 General works. Description and travel. Guidebooks
704.5 Antiquities
704.7 Social life and customs. Civilization. Intellectual life
704.8 Ethnography
History
705 General works
By period
706 Early and medieval
707 16th-18th centuries
708 19th-20th centuries
711-719 Northeast
Including Baltic Sea Region
711 Periodicals. Societies. Serials
714 General works. Description and travel. Guidebooks
714.5 Antiquities
714.7 Social life and customs. Civilization. Intellectual life
History
715 General works
By period
716 Early and medieval
717 16th-18th centuries
718 19th-20th centuries

Local history and description
Larger geographic divisions
Northeast -- Continued
719 Special topics (not A-Z)
721-729 Northwest
Including North Sea Region
721 Periodicals. Societies. Serials
724 General works. Description and travel. Guidebooks
724.5 Antiquities
724.7 Social life and customs. Civilization. Intellectual life
725 General works
History
By period
726 Early and medieval
727 16th-18th centuries
728 19th-20th centuries
729 Special topics (not A-Z)
Eastern, see DD280+
West, see DD258+
781-789 Southern
781 Periodicals. Societies. Serials
784 General works. Description and travel. Guidebooks
784.5 Antiquities
784.7 Social life and customs. Civilization. Intellectual life
784.8 Ethnography
History
785 General works
By period
786 Early and medieval
787 16th-18th centuries
788 19th-20th centuries
801.A-Z States, provinces, regions, etc., A-Z
801.A28 Allgäu Alps
801.A44 Alps, Bavarian
801.A47 Ammersee
801.A48 Amrum
801.A53 Angeln
801.A71-A79 Anhalt (Table D-DR13)
801.A85 Ansbach
801.B11-B19 Baden (Table D-DR13)
801.B23-B239 Baden-Württemberg (Table D-DR13 modified)
Established in 1952 by the reunion of Württemberg and Baden which in 1945 had been divided into three parts named Württemberg-Baden, Württemberg-Hohenzollern, and Baden
801.B23 Periodicals. Societies. Serials
801.B24 Bamburg
801.B25 Bardengau
801.B31-43 Bavaria (Bayern)

Local history and description
States, provinces, regions, etc., A-Z
Bavaria (Bayern) -- Continued

801.B31 Periodicals. Societies. Serials
801.B32 Sources and documents
801.B322 Collections
801.B33 Gazetteers. Dictionaries, etc.
801.B335 Biography (Collective)
Including House of Wittelsbach
801.B34 General works. Description and travel
801.B345 Antiquities
801.B347 Social life and customs. Civilization
801.B348 Ethnography
801.B35 History
By period
801.B36 Earliest to 1180
801.B361 Individual rulers. By date of accession
801.B362 Wittelsbach period, 1180-1508
801.B365 Individual rulers. By date of accession
801.B37 1508-1806
801.B371 Wilhelm IV, 1508-1550
801.B372 Albrecht V, 1550-1579
801.B3725 Wilhelm V, 1579-1597
801.B373 Maximilian I, 1597-1651
801.B3733 Ferdinand Maria, 1651-1679
801.B3735 Maximilian II, 1679-1726
801.B3738 Karl Albrecht, 1726-1745
801.B374 Maximilian III, 1745-1777
801.B375 Karl Theodor, 1777-1799
801.B376 Bavarian succession, 1778-1779
801.B377A-Z Biography and memoirs of contemporaries, 1508-1799, A-Z
1792-1815, see DD801.B381
801.B378 19th century
Maximilian I, 1799/1806-1825
801.B38 General works on life and reign
801.B381 1792/1799-1815
801.B382 Ludwig I, 1825-1848
801.B383A-Z Biography and memoirs of contemporaries, 1806-1848, A-Z
801.B385 Maximilian II, 1848-1864
801.B387 Ludwig II, 1864-1886
801.B39 Luitpold, 1886-1912
801.B395 Biography and memoirs of contemporaries, 1848-1912, A-Z
801.B397 20th century
801.B4 Ludwig III, 1912-1918
801.B41 Period of World War I, 1914-1918
801.B42 1919-1945
801.B422 Period of World War II, 1939-1945
801.B423 Period of Allied occupation, 1945-
801.B43A-Z Biography and memoirs, A-Z
e.g.

Local history and description
States, provinces, regions, etc., A-Z
Bavaria (Bayern)
History
By period
20th century
Biography and memoirs, A-Z -- Continued

801.B43R8 Rupprecht, Crown Prince of Bavaria
801.B441-B449 Bavaria, Lower (Table D-DR13)
801.B451-B459 Bavaria, Upper (Table D-DR13)
Bavarian Alps, see DD801.A44
Bayern, see DD801.B31+
801.B47 Berg (Duchy)
801.B48 Bergisches Land
801.B63-B64 Black Forest (Schwarzwald)
801.B63 Periodicals. Serials. Sources and documents. Congresses
801.B64 General works. Description and travel. History
Including antiquities, social life and customs, civilization, biography
Bodensee, see DD801.C71+
801.B681-B689 Brandenburg (Table D-DR13)
801.B71-B79 Breisgau (Table D-DR13)
801.B793 Bremen
801.B81-B89 Brunswick (Table D-DR13)
801.C48 Chiemgau
801.C71-C79 Constance, Lake of, and adjacent territory (Table D-DR13)
Including Bishopric
801.C83 Cottbus (Bezirk)
801.D56-D562 Dithmarschen
801.D56 Periodicals. Serials. Sources and documents. Congresses
801.D562 General works. Description and travel. History
Including antiquities, social life and customs, civilization, biography
801.D74 Dresden (Bezirk)
801.D85 Düren
801.D86 Düsseldorf (Regierungsbezirk)
801.E23 East Friesland (Ostfriesland)
Including East Frisian Islands
801.E25 Eider River and Valley
801.E26 Eiderstedt (Germany)
801.E272 Eifel
801.E3 Elbe River (General, and Germany)
For Elbe River in Czechoslovakia, see DB2500.L33
801.E462 Ems River and Valley
801.E72 Erfurt (Bezirk)
801.E772 Erzgebirge (Ore Mountains)
801.F45 Fichtelgebirge
801.F5 Finkenwärder
801.F53 Fläming
801.F55 Fohr Island

Local history and description
States, provinces, regions, etc., A-Z -- Continued
801.F561-F569 Franconia (Franken) (Table D-DR13)
801.F57 Franconia, Lower
801.F573 Franconia, Middle
801.F575 Franconia, Upper
Franken, see DD801.F561+
801.F63 Frankenwald
801.F64 Frankfurt an der Oder (Bezirk)
801.F661-F662 Fränkische Schweiz
801.F661 Periodicals. Societies. Museums. Collections
801.F662 General works. Description and travel. History
Including antiquities, social life and customs, civilization, biography
Friesland, East, see DD801.E23
Friesland, North, see DD801.N56
801.G4 Gera (Bezirk)
Glatz (Frafschaft). Klodzko, see DK4600.K53
801.G64 Göppingen (Bezirk)
801.H14 Halle (Bezirk)
801.H15 Hallig Island
Hamburg, see DD901.H21+
801.H16 Hanau-Lichtenberg
801.H1641-H1649 Hanover (Table D-DR13)
801.H17-H25 Hansa towns. Hanseatic League
801.H17 Periodicals. Societies. Serials
801.H175 Congresses
801.H18 Sources and documents
801.H19 Gazetteers, directories, dictionaries, etc.
801.H2 General works. Description and travel. Guidebooks
History
801.H21 General works
By period
801.H22 Early and medieval
801.H23 16th-18th centuries
801.H24 19th-20th centuries
801.H25 Special topics (not A-Z)
801.H31-H39 Harz Mountains (Table D-DR13)
801.H3982 Helgoland
801.H51-H59 Hesse (Table D-DR13)
Including Hesse (Grand Duchy), Hesse-Darmstadt, Hesse-Kassel, Hesse-Nassau, Nassau (Duchy), and Hesse-Homburg
801.H632 Hiddensee
801.H641 Hildesheim
801.H7 Hohenlohe
801.H742 Hohenzollern
Hohes Venn, see DH801.H35
801.H8 Hunsrück
801.J862 Julich
801.K34 Karl-Marx-Stadt (Bezirk)
801.K36 Karwendelgebrige

Local history and description
States, provinces, regions, etc., A-Z -- Continued

801.K38 Kassel (Bezirk)
801.K58 Klötze
801.K6 Könnigssee
801.K9 Kyffhäuser Mountains
801.L29 Landsberg am Lech
801.L36 Lauenberg
Lausitz, see DD801.L851+
801.L43 Lech River and Valley
801.L45 Leipzig (Bezirk)
801.L71-L79 Lippe (Table D-DR13)
Lower Bavaria, see DD801.B441+
Lower Franconia, see DD801.F57
Lower Saxony, see DD801.N4
801.L82 Ludwigsburg
801.L831-L839 Lüneburg (Regierungsbezirk). Lüneburg Heath (Lüneburger Heide) (Table D-DR13)
801.L851-L859 Lusatia (Lausitz) (Table D-DR13)
801.L862 Lusatia, Lower
801.L872 Lusatia, Upper
801.M16 Magdeburg (Bezirk)
801.M2 Main River and Valley
801.M31-M39 Meckleburg-Schwerin (Table D-DR13)
Including Mecklenburg as a whole
801.M5 Mecklenburg-Strelitz
Middle Franconia, see DD801.F573
801.M66 Moers
801.M7 Moselle River and Valley
Cf. DC611.M897+, France
801.M952 Münsterland
801.N3 Nahe River and Valley
Nassau (Duchy), see DD801.H51+
801.N35 Neckar River and Valley
801.N37 Neubrandenburg (Bezirk)
801.N4 Niedersachsen (Lower Saxony)
801.N56 North Friesland (Nordfriesland)
Including North Frisian Islands
801.N6 North Rhine-Westphalia
801.O24 Oberbergischer Kreis
Oberpfalz, see DD801.P5
801.O3 Odenwald
Oder-Neisse area, see DK4600.O33
801.O42-O43 Oldenburg
801.O42 Periodicals. Serials. Congresses. Sources and documents
801.O43 General works. Description and travel. History
Including antiquities, social life and customs, civilization, biography
Ore Mountains, see DD801.E772
801.O84 Osnabrück (District)
801.P41-P49 Palatinate (Pfalz). Rhineland Palatinate (Table D-DR13)

Local history and description
States, provinces, regions, etc., A-Z -- Continued

801.P5 Palatinate, Upper
Pfalz, see DD801.P41+
801.P66 Potsdam (Bezirk)
801.R12 Rappoltstein
801.R15 Ratzeburg
801.R2 Regnitz River and Valley
801.R3 Reuss (Elder line)
801.R4 Reuss (Younger line)
801.R682 Rhine Province. Rhineland
801.R71-R79 Rhine River and Valley (Table D-DR13)
Rhineland Palatinate, see DD801.P41+
801.R78 Rhön
801.R796 Rosenheim
801.R797 Rostock (Bezirk)
801.R7982 Rügen (Island)
801.R8 Ruhr River and Valley
801.S13-S139 Saar River and Valley (Table D-DR13)
801.S14-S149 Saarland (Table D-DR13)
Sächsische Schweiz, see DD801.S281
801.S1672 Sauerland
801.S17 Saxe-Altenburg
801.S2-S21 Saxe-Coburg-Gotha
801.S2 Periodicals. Sources and documents. Collections
801.S21 History
801.S23 Saxe-Meiningen
801.S26 Saxe-Weimar (-Eisenach)
801.S281 Saxon Switzerland (Sächsische Schweiz)
Cf. DB2500.E53, Elbe Sandstone Rocks
801.S31-S45 Saxony
Including Saxony-Anhalt
801.S31 Periodicals. Societies. Serials
801.S32 Sources and documents
801.S322 Collections
801.S33 Gazetteers, dictionaries, etc.
801.S34 General works. Description and travel
801.S345 Antiquities
801.S347 Social life and customs. Civilization
801.S348 Ethnography
801.S35 History
801.S352 General special
801.S354 Military history
801.S357 Reigning houses, etc.
By period
801.S36 Early and medieval
801.S361 Earliest to 806
801.S362 806-1089
801.S364 1089-1288
801.S367 Individual reigns. By date
801.S37 1288-1485
801.S375 Individual reigns. By date
801.S38 1485-1694

	Local history and description
	States, provinces, regions, etc., A-Z
	Saxony
	History
	By period
	Early and medieval
	1485-1694 -- Continued
801.S382	Friedrich III, 1486-1525
801.S383	Johann, 1525-1532
801.S384	Johann Friedrich, 1532-1547
801.S386	Moritz, 1547-1553
801.S387	August, 1553-1586
801.S388	Christian I, 1586-1591
801.S389	Christian II, 1591-1611
801.S39	Johann Georg I, 161-1656
801.S392	Johann Georg II, III, IV, 1656-1694
801.S393	Modern
801.S394	1694-1763
	Friedrich August I, 1694-1733
801.S395	General works on life and reign
	Cf. DK4315, Reign in Poland
801.S396	General special
	Friedrich August II, 1733-1763
801.S397	General works on life and reign
	Cf. DK4325, Reign in Poland
801.S398	General special
801.S399	Friedrich Christian, 1763
801.S4A-Z	Biography and memoirs of contemporaries, A-Z
	e.g.
801.S4B7	Brühl, Heinrich Reichsgraf von
801.S4M3	Maria Antonia Walpurgis, Consort of Friedrich Christian
	Friedrich August I, 1763-1827
801.S401	General works on life and reign
801.S403	1763-1806
801.S405	1789-1806
801.S406	1806-1815/1827
801.S409A-Z	Biography and memoirs of contemporaries, A-Z
	e.g.
801.S409F8	Funck, Karl Wilhelm F. von
801.S409O6	Oppel, Julius Wilhelm von
801.S41	1827-1902. 19th century
801.S412	Anton, 1827-1836
801.S414	Friedrich August II, 1836-1854
801.S416	Johann, 1854-1873
801.S42	Albrecht, 1873-1902
801.S425	1902-
801.S43	Georg, 1902-1904
801.S44	Friedrich August III, 1904-

Local history and description
States, provinces, regions, etc., A-Z
Saxony
History
By period
Modern
1902-
Friedrich August
III, 1904- -- Continued

801.S45 Affair of Louisa of Tuscany, formerly Louise Antoinette Marie, Archduchess of Austria

(801.S58) Saxon Switzerland
see DD801.S281

Saxony, Lower, see DD801.N4

801.S62-S63 Schaumburg-Lippe

801.S62 Periodicals. Serials. Congresses. Sources and documents

801.S63 General works. Description and travel. History
Including antiquities, social life and customs, civilization, biography

801.S6331-S6339 Schleswig-Holstein (Table D-DR13)

Schwaben, see DD801.S942

801.S65 Schwarzburg-Rudolstadt

801.S68 Schwarzburg-Sondershausen

Schwarzwald, see DD801.B63+

801.S69 Schwerin (Bezirk)

801.S7 Siebengebirge

801.S8 Spessart Mountains

801.S82 Spree Forest

801.S83 Stade

801.S833 Staffelstein

801.S835 Starnberger See

801.S838 Steigerwald

801.S86 Suhl (Bezirk)

801.S942 Swabia (Schwaben)

801.S96 Sylt

801.T27 Taunus Mountains

801.T3 Teck

801.T314 Tegernsee

Teutoburger Wald, see DD801.W5

801.T36 Tharandter Wald

801.T41-T49 Thuringia (Thuringian States) (Table D-DR13)

801.T5 Thuringian Forest

801.T8 Tübingen (Grafschaft)

801.U5 Unstrut River and Valley

Upper Bavaria, see DD801.B451+

Upper Franconia, see DD801.F575

Upper Lusatia, see DD801.L872

Upper Palatinate, see DD801.P5

801.V7 Vogtland

Vosges Mountains, see DC645

801.W2-W29 Waldeck (Table D-DR13)

Local history and description
States, provinces, regions, etc., A-Z -- Continued
Warthegau, see DK4600.W55
801.W5 Weser Mountains. Weser River and Valley. Teutoburg Forest
For the Battle of Teutoburger Wald, see DD123
801.W53 Westerwald
801.W541-W549 Westphalia (Table D-DR13)
801.W59 Wursten
801.W6-W82 Württemberg
801.W6 Periodicals. Societies. Serials
801.W61 Sources and documents
Collected works
801.W612 Several authors
801.W614 Individual authors
801.W62 Biography (Collective)
801.W625 Gazetteers. Dictionaries, etc.
801.W627 Guidebooks
801.W63 General works
Description and travel
801.W634 Through 1800
801.W635 1801-1900
801.W636 1901-
801.W64 Monumental and picturesque
Including castles, ruins, etc.
801.W645 Antiquities
801.W647 Social life and customs. Civilization
801.W648 Ethnography
801.W65 History
801.W652 General special
801.W653 Pamphlets, etc.
801.W654 Military history
801.W656 Political history
801.W657 Reigning houses
By period
Early and medieval
801.W66 General works
801.W662 Earliest to 1241
801.W663A-Z Individual counts, A-Z
801.W664-W688 1241-1495
General works, see DD801.W66+
801.W665 Ulrich I, 1241-1265
801.W666 Ulrich II, 1265-1279
801.W669 Eberhard I, 1265/1279-1325
801.W671 Ulrich III, 1325-1344
801.W673 Eberhard II, 1344-1392
801.W675 Ulrich IV, 1344-1366
801.W677 Eberhard III, 1392-1417
801.W678 Eberhard IV, 1417-1419
801.W68 1419-1482, Division and reunion
801.W683 Henriette, Consort of Eberhard IV
801.W684 Ludwig I, 1442-1450
801.W685 Ulrich V, 1442-1480

Local history and description
States, provinces, regions, etc., A-Z
Württemberg
History
By period
Early and medieval
1241-1495
1419-1482, Division and reunion -- Continued

801.W686 Ludwig II der Jüngere, 1450-1457
801.W687 Eberhard II der Jüngere, 1480-1482
801.W688 Eberhard V (I as Duke), 1457-1496
Modern
801.W69 1495-1806
801.W693 Eberhard II, 1496-1498
801.W694 Ulrich, 1498-1550
801.W696 Christoph, 1550-1568
801.W698 Ludwig, 1568-1593
801.W7 Friedrich I, 1593-1608
801.W702 Period of Thirty Years' War, 1618-1648
801.W704 Johann Friedrich, 1608-1628
801.W71 Eberhard III, 1628-1674
801.W713 Ludwig Friedrich, 1628-1633
801.W714 Julius Friedrich, 1628-1633
801.W717 Wilhelm Ludwig, 1674-1677
801.W72 Eberhard Ludwig, 1677-1733
801.W723 Friedrich Karl, 1677-1693
801.W725 Karl Alexander, 1733-1737
801.W73 Karl Eugen, 1737-1793
801.W734 Karl Rudolf, 1737-1738
801.W735 Friedrich Karl, 1738-1744
801.W737 Ludwig Eugen, 1793-1795
801.W738 Friedrich Eugen, 1795-1797
801.W739A-Z Biography and memoirs, A-Z
e.g.
801.W739S7 Süss-Oppenheimer, Joseph
801.W74 19th-20th centuries
801.W745 Biography (Collective)
801.W75 Friedrich I, 1797-1816
Wilhelm I, 1816-1864
801.W76 General works on life and reign
801.W762 Catharine, Consort of William I
Cf. DK190.6.C2, Sister of Alexander I of Russia
801.W763 Pauline, Consort of William I
801.W764A-Z Biography and memoirs, A-Z
801.W765 1871-1917
801.W77 Karl I, 1864-1891
Wilhelm II, 1891-1918
801.W78 General works on life and reign
801.W79 Period of World War I, 1914-1918

Local history and description
States, provinces, regions, etc., A-Z
Württemberg
History
By period
Modern
19th-20th centuries -- Continued
801.W8 1918-
Class here works on the period of German Revolution, Republic, etc.
801.W82A-Z Biography and memoirs, A-Z
e.g.
801.W82B55 Bolz, Eugene Anton
801.W82M3 Maier, Reinhold
Berlin
851 Periodicals. Societies. Serials
852 Sources and documents
853 Collected works
854 Directories. Dictionaries
Biography
857.A2 Collective
857.A3-Z Individual, A-Z
859 Guidebooks
860 General works. Description
862 Views. Monumental, etc.
864 Antiquities
866 Social life and customs. Civilization
866.8 Intellectual life
Ethnography
867 General works
867.5.A-Z Individual elements in the population, A-Z
867.5.A37 Africans
867.5.A42 Americans
867.5.C48 Chinese
867.5.C93 Czechs
867.5.P64 Poles
867.5.R86 Russian Germans
867.5.R87 Russians
867.5.U37 Ukrainians
History and description
870 Through 1600
871 1600-1788
875 1789-1815
876 1816-1870
878 1871-1914
879 1914-1921
880 1922-1945
881 1946-
883.A-Z Sections, districts, etc., A-Z
885 Parks
887 Streets, bridges, etc.
889 Suburbs
Buildings

Local history and description
Berlin
Buildings -- Continued
891 General works
892 Churches
894 Hotels
895 Palaces
896 Public buildings (governmental)
897 Theaters
899 Other
900 Other special
Bonn
900.2 Periodicals. Societies. Serials
Sources and documents
900.25 Several authors
900.26 Individual authors
900.27 Directories. Dictionaries. Gazetteers
900.28 Guidebooks
900.29 General works
900.3 Description
900.33 Pictorial works
900.34 Antiquities
900.35 Social life and customs. Intellectual life. Civilization
History
900.38 Biography (Collective)
For individual biography, see the specific period
900.4 General works
By period
900.42 Early and medieval
900.43 1519-1949
900.45 1949-
Sections, districts, suburbs, etc.
900.6 Collective
900.62.A-Z Individual, A-Z
Streets. Bridges
900.7 Collective
900.72.A-Z Individual, A-Z
Buildings
900.75 Collective
900.76.A-Z Individual, A-Z
Other cities, towns, etc., A-Z
e.g.
901.A1 General
901.A25-A26 Aachen (Aix-la-Chapelle) (Table D-DR14)
901.A283 Aalen
901.A28739 Aldenhoven
901.A35 Altenburg
901.A91-A92 Augsburg (Table D-DR14)
901.B109 Bad Bentheim
901.B11255 Bad Endorf
Bad Kissingen, see DD901.K6

	Local history and description
	Other cities, towns, etc., A-Z -- Continued
	Bad Nauheim, see DD901.N25
901.B119	Bad Windsheim
901.B12-B13	Baden (Table D-DR14)
901.B2	Bamberg
901.B4	Bayreuth
901.B443	Berchtesgaden
901.B4487	Betzenstein
901.B56	Bochum
	Bonn, see DD900.2+
901.B63	Bramstedt
901.B65	Brandenburg
	Braunschweig, see DD901.B95
901.B71-B79	Bremen (Table D-DR13)
901.B82	Bremerhaven
	Breslau, see DK4780
901.B8914	Brückenau
901.B95	Brunswick (Braunschweig)
901.B9675	Buhlenberg
901.B9677	Buldern
901.B9678	Bühlstadt
901.B976	Burghausen
901.B9774	Burhave (Butjadingen)
901.C65	Coburg
	Colmar, see DC801.C657
901.C71-C79	Cologne (Köln) (Table D-DR13 modified)
901.C765	Period of the Reformation
901.C777	1789-1815
	Sections, districts, suburbs, etc.
901.C785	Collective
901.C7852A-Z	Individual, A-Z
901.C85	Constance (Konstanz)
	Danzig, see DK4650+
901.D3	Darmstadt
901.D43	Detmold
901.D6	Dortmund
901.D71-D79	Dresden (Table D-DR13)
901.D95	Duesseldorf (Düsseldorf) (Table D-DR14)
901.D96	Duingen
901.D97	Duisburg
901.E2	Eberbach
901.E23436	Egelsbach
901.E25	Eichstätt
	Elbing (Elblag), see DK4800.E4
901.E5	Emden
901.E6	Erfurt
901.E75	Essen
901.F5	Flensburg
901.F71-F79	Frankfurt am Main (Table D-DR13)
901.F85	Freiberg
901.F87	Freiburg im Breisgau
901.F892	Friedberg (Hesse)

Local history and description
Other cities, towns, etc., A-Z -- Continued

901.F894125	Frielendorf
901.F8942	Fuerstenau (Fürstenau)
901.F8943	Fuerth (Fürth)
901.F9	Fulda
901.G346	Geldern
901.G44	Giessen
901.G55	Goettingen (Göttingen)
901.G68	Goslar
	Gottorf Castle, see DD901.S2
901.G8	Greifswald
901.H17	Halberstadt
901.H19	Halle
901.H21-H29	Hamburg (Table D-DR13)
901.H32	Hameln
901.H325	Hamm
901.H35	Hanau
901.H41-H49	Hanover (Table D-DR13)
901.H522	Hedehusum
901.H523	Heek
901.H55-H56	Heidelberg (Table D-DR14)
901.H612	Heiden über Detmold
901.H62	Heilbronn (Württemberg)
901.H64	Heilsbronn (Bavaria)
901.H657	Hersfeld
901.H66	Hildesheim
901.H68	Hirsau
901.H69	Hirschau
901.H73	Hoechst am Main (Höchst am Main)
901.H755	Hof
901.H784	Hollingstedt
901.H855	Höxter
901.H857	Hüfingen
901.H96	Husum
901.I594	Immendingen
901.I63	Ingelheim am Rhein
901.I8	Iserlohn
901.I823	Isinger
901.J4	Jena
901.J85	Jünkerath
901.J86	Junkersdorf
901.K3	Karlsruhe
901.K33	Kassel
901.K48-K49	Kiel (Table D-DR14)
901.K6	Kissingen, Bad
901.K75-K76	Koblenz (Table D-DR14)
	Köln, see DD901.C71+
(901.K8)	Königsberg See DK651.K1213
	Konstanz, see DD901.C85
901.K9	Krefeld
	Landeshut, see DK4800.K34

Local history and description
Other cities, towns, etc., A-Z -- Continued

901.L2649 Langenhain (Ober-Mörlen)
901.L37 Lauterbach
901.L496 Leipheim
901.L51-L59 Leipzig (Table D-DR13)
Leszno (Lissa), see DK4800.L48
Liegnitz, see DK4800.L44
901.L817 Ludwigsburg
901.L82 Ludwigshafen am Rhein
901.L83-L84 Luebeck (Lübeck) (Table D-DR14)
901.L93 Lueneburg (Lüneburg)
901.L934 Luenen (Lünen)
901.L936 Luetau (Lütau)
901.L95 Luhe
901.L968 Lühen
901.L97 Lustadt
901.M15 Magdeburg
901.M2-M21 Mainz (Table D-DR14)
901.M2618 Malente-Gremsuhlen
901.M27 Mannheim
901.M275 Marburg
Marienburg, Malbork, see DK4800.M35
901.M2837 Markgröningen
Mechtal (Silesia), see DK4800.M35
901.M5 Meissen
(901.M54-M56) Metz
see DC801.M65
901.M585 Mönchengladbach
Formerly München-Gladbach
901.M62513 Moordorf
(901.M63-M66) Muehlhausen (Mülhausen)
see DC801.M93
901.M693 Muehlheim an der Ruhr (Mülheim an der Ruhr)
901.M696 Muenster (Münster)
Munich
901.M71 Periodicals. Societies. Serials
901.M72 Sources and documents
901.M73 Collected works
901.M74 Dictionaries. Directories
901.M76 Guidebooks
901.M77 General works. Description
901.M79 Pictorial works
901.M8 Antiquities
901.M83 Social life, customs, etc. Culture
History and description
General works, see DD901.M77
By period
901.M86 Early
901.M87 16th-18th centuries
901.M88 1789-1815
901.M89 1815-1871
901.M9 1871-1950

	Local history and description
	Other cities, towns, etc., A-Z
	Munich
	History and description
	By period -- Continued
901.M912	1951-
	Sections, districts, etc.
901.M92A1	General works
901.M92A2-M92Z	Individual, A-Z
	Buildings
901.M93	General works
901.M94A-Z	Individual, A-Z
901.M95	Other
901.M98	Mussbach
901.N25	Nauheim. Bad
901.N3	Naumburg
	Neisse, see DK4800.N9
901.N91-N92	Nuremberg (Table D-DR14)
901.O2	Oberammergau
901.O4	Oldenburg
901.O75	Osnabrück
901.P1	Paderborn
901.P5	Pforzheim
	Posen, see DK4750
901.P8	Potsdam
901.R4	Ratisbon. Regensburg
901.R42	Ravensberg
901.R425	Recklinghausen
	Regensburg, see DD901.R4
901.R8	Rostock
901.R85	Rothenburg ob der Tauber
901.S129	Saarbrücken
901.S15	Saverne (Alsace)
901.S2	Schleswig
	Sélestat, see DC801.S443
901.S6	Soest
901.S7	Spires (Speyer)
	Steglitz, see DD883.A+
	Stettin, see DK4800.S93
901.S8	Stralsund
	Strassburg, see DC801.S77
901.S96-S97	Stuttgart (Table D-DR14)
901.T789	Treuchtlingen
901.T8-T81	Trier (Treves) (Table D-DR14)
901.T88	Trifels
901.T9	Tuchel
901.T91-T92	Tuebingen (Tübingen) (Table D-DR14)
901.T975	Tuttlingen
901.U26	Uebach
901.U3	Ueberlingen
901.U4	Ulm
901.U47	Unna
901.W4	Weimar

Local history and description

Other cities, towns, etc., A-Z -- Continued

901.W47	Wernigerode
901.W55	Wetzlar
901.W57	Wiedenbruck
901.W58	Wiesbaden
901.W62	Wismar
901.W71-W763	Worms
901.W77	Worpswede
901.W91-W963	Wuerzburg (Würzburg)
901.X3	Xanten
	Zabern, see DD901.S15
901.Z9	Zwickau
(905)	German colonies
	For collective, see JV2000+
	For individual colonies, see Classes D-F

History of the Greco-Roman world
Including the Mediterranean Region
Class here general classical antiquities and history
Cf. CC1+, Classical archaeology
Cf. JC51+, Ancient state
Cf. PA1+, Classical philology
For Greek antiquities and history, see DF10+
For Roman antiquities and history, see DG11+

1 Periodicals. Serials
2 Societies
Museums, exhibitions, etc., see DE46
2.5 Congresses
Collected works
3 Several authors
3.5 Pamphlets, etc.
4 Individual authors
5 Dictionaries. Encyclopedias
6 Tables, outlines, etc.
7 Biography (Collective)
Cf. D107, Rulers, kings, etc., in works covering ancient and modern history
7.P5 Plutarch's lives (English translation)
For texts and other translations, see PA4369
Historiography
8 General works
Biography of historians and archaeologists
9.A1 Collective
9.A2-Z Individual, A-Z
Study and teaching
15 General works
15.5.A-Z By region or country, A-Z
Subarrange by author
Geography
Cf. D973, Modern geography
Cf. G83+, Ancient geography
Periodicals and societies, see DE1
23 Sources and documents. Collections. Classical authors
24 Collected works (Modern)
25 Dictionaries
Comprehensive works. Orbis antiquus
27 Classical authors
Modern authors
28 Through 1800
29 1801-
31 General special
Description and travel
See D911, D971+, DS45+
Antiquities. Civilization. Culture
Cf. CC1+, Archaeology
Cf. N5320+, Ancient art
For classical antiquity in modern literature, see PN883, PR127

Antiquities. Civilization. Culture -- Continued
Periodicals and societies, see DE1
46 Museums. Exhibitions, etc.
46.5.A-Z Individual. By place, A-Z
Collected works, see DE3+
Dictionaries and encyclopedias, see DE5
57 Works through 1800
58 General special
Works, 1801-
59 General works
59.5 Preservation
59.7 Expertising
60 General special
61.A-Z Special topics, A-Z
61.A4 Agora. Market place
61.A55 Amphoras
61.A77 Art
61.B87 Burial
61.C4 Children
61.D5 Diptychs
61.E25 Ecology
61.E5 Elephants
61.F2 Family
61.F66 Food
61.F67 Forgeries
61.H35 Harbors
61.H38 Heracles
61.H42 Heroes
61.H7 Hotels, taverns, etc.
61.H86 Hunting
61.I48 Implements, utensils, etc.
61.I58 Intellectuals
61.L32 Labor. Working class
61.L34 Lamps
61.M5 Military antiquities, etc.
61.M65 Monuments
61.N3 Naval antiquities, etc.
61.P42 Peace
61.P5 Pirates
61.P66 Pottery
61.P75 Propaganda
61.P8 Public and political antiquities
61.R44 Religious life and customs
61.S43 Seafaring life
61.S48 Sepulchral monuments
Slavery, see HT863
61.S7 Spectacles, circuses, etc.
61.T4 Temples
61.T43 Terra-cotta sculpture
61.U53 Underwater antiquities
Utensils, see DE61.I48
61.W35 War
61.W54 Wine and wine making

Antiquities. Civilization. Culture
Works, 1801-
Special topics, A-Z -- Continued
61.Y68 Youth
71 Social life and customs. Civilization. Culture
Cf. CB311+, History of ancient civilization and culture
72 Greco-Roman world in the time of Christ
Cf. BR170, Relations of Christianity to the Roman Empire and Eastern Empire
Cf. BS2375, Historical criticism of the New Testament
Cf. BS2410, History of Christianity in New Testament times
Ethnography
73 General works
73.2.A-Z Individual elements in the population, A-Z
73.2.B55 Blacks
73.2.C37 Carthaginians
Cf. DT269.C3+, Carthaginian Empire and civilization
73.2.P56 Phoenicians
73.2.S4 Sea peoples
73.2.S9 Swiss
History
80 General works
83 General special
84 Military and naval history
85 Political history
For specific periods, see the period
Foreign and general relations
For works on relations with a specific country regardless of period, see DE85.5.A+
For general works on the diplomatic history of a period, see the period
85.3 General works
85.5.A-Z Relations with individual regions or countries, A-Z
By period
Ancient to 476. Greco-Roman era
Cf. DT269.C3+, Carthage
86 General works
87 Pamphlets, etc.
88 Military and naval history
89 Political and diplomatic history
92 Beginning of Christian era
94 476-1517
96 1517-1789
96.5 1789-1815
97 1815-1914
98 1914-1945
100 1945-

History of Greece
Ancient Greece
Cf. DF750+, General Greek history
10 Periodicals. Serials
11 Societies
Museums, exhibitions, etc.
11.2 General works
11.3.A-Z Individual. By place, A-Z
12 Sources and documents. Collections. Classical authors
e.g.
12.P3 Paros, Chronicle of
Collected works
13 Several authors
14 Individual authors
16 Dictionaries
Geography. Travel
Dictionaries, see DF16
General works
27 Classical authors (Translations)
For Greek and Latin texts, see PA
Modern authors
28 Through 1800
29 1801-1900
30 1901-
35 Historical geography
41 Travel
Local
see DF221, DF251+
Antiquities. Civilization. Culture
Cf. CC1+, Archaeology
Cf. N5630+, Ancient Greek art
Periodicals, see DF10
Societies, see DF11
Dictionaries, see DF16
General works
75 Selections from classical authors
76 Through 1800
77 1801
78 General special
Including social life and customs
Cf. DF91+, Private life
79 Pamphlets, etc.
Public and political antiquities
Cf. JC71+, Political theory of the state
81 General works
82 General special
82.5 Pamphlets, etc.
83 Administration. Finance. Archons
Cf. DF277, History and political antiquities of Athens
Cf. HJ217, Public finance in ancient Greece

Ancient Greece
Antiquities. Civilization. Culture
Public and political antiquities -- Continued
85 Federations. Colonies
Cf. JV93, History of ancient Greek colonization
86 Archives and diplomatics
For treaties, see KL4111+
(87) Legal antiquities
see KL4100-KL4399
Military and naval antiquities
Cf. U33, History of ancient Greek military science
89 General works
89.5 Pamphlets, etc.
90 Naval antiquities alone
Cf. V37, History of ancient Greek naval science
Private antiquities
Including private life
Cf. DF78, Social life and customs
91 General works
93 Family. Woman. Children
Cf. HQ510, Social history
Cf. HQ1134, Women and feminism in ancient Greece
95 Education
Cf. LA75, History of education
Cf. LB85.A+, Educators and writers of ancient Greece
(97) Athletics. Games
See GV21+
99 Dwellings. Baths, etc.
Dress and costume, see GT550
100 Eating. Drinking. Cooking, etc.
Funeral customs. Sepulchral customs
Cf. GT3170, Treatment of the dead in antiquity
101 General works
101.5 Sepulchral monuments
Cf. NA6139, Architecture
Cf. NB143, Bronze sculpture
105 Agriculture
Cf. HD133+, Land in ancient Greece (Economic history)
Cf. S429, Production of plants, animals, etc.
Cf. S490.8+, Production of plants, animals, etc.
107 Commerce. Industries
Cf. HC37, National production (Economics)
Cf. HF375+, Commerce in ancient Greece (Economics)

Ancient Greece
Antiquities. Civilization. Culture -- Continued
109 Other social institutions
Cf. HN9+, Social problems in ancient Greece
Religious antiquities
For Greek mythology, see BL780+
121 General works
122 Cultus
123 Festae
124 Mysteries
125 Divination. Oracles
126 Magic
127 Temples. Altars, etc.
129 Other special (not A-Z)
Art antiquities
130 General works
131 Gargoyles
Numismatics, see CJ301+
Weights and measures, see QC84
Greek art, see N5630+
Ethnography
135 General works
136.A-Z Particular tribes and peoples, A-Z
136.A2 Achaeans
136.A3 Aeolians
136.D6 Dorians
136.I6 Ionians
136.P44 Pelasgi
History
Periodicals, societies, collections, dictionaries, see DF750+
207 Chronological tables, etc.
Biography (Collective)
208 General works
208.5 Prosopography
Source books, see DF12
Historiography
211 General works
Biography of historians and archaeologists
212.A2 Collective
212.A3-Z Individual, A-Z
e.g.
212.B7 Brøndsted, Peter Oluf
212.C8 Curtius, Ernst
212.E82 Evans, Sir Arthur John
212.S4 Schliemann, Heinrich
Study and teaching
212.3 General works
212.4.A-Z By region or country, A-Z
212.5.A-Z Individual schools, A-Z
General works

Ancient Greece
History
General works -- Continued
213 Classical authors (Translations)
For texts of several authors, see DF12
For texts of individual authors, see PA
Modern authors
213.5 Through 1800
214 1801-
215 Compends. Textbooks. Juvenile works
216 Syllabi, etc.
217 General special
218 Pamphlets, etc.
By period
Early to ca. 1100 B.C.
Bronze Age. Aegean civilization
Including islands of the Aegean
220 General works
220.3 Minoan civilization. Minoans
Cf. DF221.C8, Crete
220.5 Mycenaean civilization
Cf. DF221.M9, Mycenae
221.A-Z Special local exploration, etc., A-Z
For antiquities later than Minoan and Mycenean ages, see DF261.A+
For medieval and modern period, see DF901.A+
Achaea, see DF221.A27
221.A27 Achaia
221.A35 Aegina
221.A45 Aigeira
221.A5 Aíyion
221.A78 Argolis (Province)
221.A8 Argos
221.A84 Asine
221.A87 Attica
221.A95 Ayios Stefanos
221.B63 Boeotia. Voiōtia
221.C56 Chorsiai
221.C6 Corinth
221.C8 Crete
Including local sites and adjacent islands, e.g. Pseira Island
221.C93 Cyclades Islands
221.D4 Dendra
221.D56 Dimini Site
221.D58 Dimitra Site
221.E7 Eretria
221.G53 Gla Site
221.H25 Hagion Gala
221.H94 Hymettus Mountain
221.I84 Ithaca Island
221.K33 Kárpathos Island
221.K34 Kastanas Site

Ancient Greece
History
By period
Early to ca. 1100 B.C.
Special local exploration, etc., A-Z -- Continued

221.K36 Kea (Keōs) Island
221.K5 Kíthira Island
221.K7 Korakon
221.L37 Lárisa
221.L47 Lerni
221.L48 Levkás Island
221.L56 Lithares Site
221.M35 Manika
221.M9 Mycenae
221.N39 Naxos Island
221.N52 Nichoria
221.O4 Olympia
221.P47 Peratí Mountains
221.P49 Pevkakia Magoula Mound
221.P56 Phaestus
221.P58 Phthiōtis
221.P6 Phylakopi
221.P63 Pílos
221.P68 Poliochnē
221.P77 Prósimna
Pseira Island, see DF221.C8
221.R56 Rhodes
221.T33 Thasos
221.T35 Thebes. Thēvai
221.T38 Thera Island
221.T4 Thessaly
Thēvai, see DF221.T35
221.T45 Thorikon
221.T5 Tiryns
221.T8 Troy
Including Troas
Voiōtia, see DF221.B63

ca. 1125-500 B.C.
221.2 General works
221.3 Dorian invasions, ca. 1125-1025 B.C.
221.5 Geometric period, ca. 900-700 B.C.
775-500 B.C. Age of Tyrants. Archaic period
222 General works
222.2 General special
223 Addresses, essays, lectures
224.A-Z Biography, A-Z
e.g.
224.P4 Pisistratus
224.S7 Solon

Persian Wars, 499-479 B.C.
225 General works
225.2 General special

Ancient Greece
History
By period
Persian wars, 499-479 B.C. -- Continued

225.25 Pamphlets, etc.
225.3 Ionian revolt, 499-494
225.33 Burning of Sardis, 498
225.35 Capture of Miletus, 494
225.37 Conquest of Thrace, 494-492
225.4 Marathon, 490
225.5 Thermopylae, 480
225.53 Naval battles of Artemisium, 480
225.55 Burning of Athens, 480
225.6 Salamis, 480
225.7 Plataea, 479
225.75 Mycale, 479
225.8 Capture of Sestus, 478
225.9.A-Z Other special events, A-Z
226.A-Z Biography, A-Z
e.g.
226.M5 Miltiades
226.T45 Themistocles

Athenian supremacy. Age of Pericles. 479-431 B.C.

227 General works
227.4 Pamphlets, etc.
227.5 General special
Including the First Delian League, etc.
227.6 Capture of Eion, 476
227.63 Battles of the Eurymedon, 468
227.65 Revolt of Thasos, 465
227.7 Third Messenian War, 464-456
227.75 War with Aegina and Corinth, 459-456
227.77 Athenian expedition to Egypt, 454
227.8 Peace of Cimon/Callias, 449-448 B.C.
227.83 Revolt of Euboa and Megara, 446-445
227.85 Samian War, 440-439
227.9.A-Z Other special events, A-Z
228.A-Z Biography, A-Z
e.g.
228.A7 Aristides, the Just
228.A8 Aspasia
228.P4 Pericles
229 Peloponnesian War, 431-404 B.C.
For Thucydides use:
.T5 English text. By translator, A-Z
.T55 English selections. By translator, A-Z
.T56A-Z Other languages. By language, A-Z, and date
.T6 Biography and criticism
229.1 Pamphlets, etc.
229.2 General special

Ancient Greece
History
By period
Peloponnesian War, 431-404 B.C. -- Continued

229.3 First period, 431-421
229.35 Second period, 421-413
229.37 Third period, 413-404
229.4 Siege and fall of Plataea, 429-427
229.43 Revolt and capitulation of Mytilene, 428-427
229.45 Fortification of Pylus, 425
229.47 Capture of Sphacteria, 425
229.5 Invasion of Boeotia, 424
229.53 Invasion of Thrace, 424
229.55 Truce, 423
229.57 Peace of Nicias, 421
229.6 Mantinea, 418
229.63 Conquest of Melos, 416
229.65 Invasion of Sicily, 415
229.67 Siege of Syracuse, 414-413
229.69 Battle in the Great Harbor, 413
229.7 Revolt of Athenian allies, 412
229.73 Revolution of the Four Hundred, 411
229.75 Cynossema, 411
229.77 Cyzicus, 410
229.8 Notium, 407
229.83 Arginusae, 406
229.85 Aegospotami, 405
229.87 Siege and fall of Athens, 404
229.9.A-Z Other special events, A-Z
230.A-Z Biography, A-Z
e.g.
230.A4 Alcibiades
230.C6 Cleon
230.T6 Theramenes

Spartan and Theban supremacies, 404-362 B.C.

230.9 Sources and documents
231 General works
231.2 General special
231.25 Pamphlets, etc.
231.3 Thirty tyrants, 404
231.32 Expedition of Cyrus, etc., 401-400
231.35 War in Asia Minor against Persians, 399-394
231.4 Corinthian War, 395-387
231.45 Cnidus, 394
231.5 Coronea, 394
231.55 Peace of Antalcidas, 387
231.6 War between Sparta and Thebes, 378-371
231.7 Naxos, 376
231.75 Tegyra, 375
231.8 Leuctra, 371
231.87 Mantinea, 362
231.9.A-Z Biography, A-Z
e.g.

Ancient Greece
History
By period
Spartan and Theban supremacies, 404-362 B.C.
Biography, A-Z -- Continued
231.9.C6 Conon, Athenian general
Macedonian epoch. Age of Philip, 359-336 B.C.
232.5 Sources and documents
233 General works
233.2 General special
Including the Corinthian League
233.25 Pamphlets, etc.
233.3 Operations in Chalcidice and Thrace, 358-357
233.35 Social War, 357-355
233.4 Sacred War, 356-346
233.45 Fall of Olynthus, 348
233.5 Subjugation of Thrace, 342-341
233.55 Amphissian War, 339-338
233.6 Chaeronea, 338
233.7.A-Z Other special events, A-Z
233.8.A-Z Biography, A-Z
e.g.
233.8.P6 Phocion
Alexander the Great, 336-323 B.C.
234.A1 Sources and documents
234.A3-Z General works
234.2 General special
234.25 Pamphlets, etc.
234.3 Iconography. Personality, etc.
234.31 Amphictyonic Council, 336
234.33 Campaigns in Thrace and Illyria, 335
234.34 Destruction of Thebes, 335
234.35 Battle of the Granicus, 334
234.37 Conquest of Asia Minor, 334-333
234.38 Issus, 333
234.4 Siege of Tyre, 332
234.45 Conquest of Egypt, 332
Cf. DT92+, Alexander and Ptolemies, 332-330 B.C.
234.5 Gaugamela (Arbela), 331
234.53 Capture of Babylon and Susa, 331
234.55 Capture of Persepolis, 330
234.57 Conquest of Bactria and Sogdiana, 328
234.6 Invasion of India, 327-325
234.65 Mutiny at Opis, 324
234.7.A-Z Other special events, A-Z
234.9.A-Z Biography of contemporaries, A-Z
Hellenistic period, 323-146 B.C.
Sources and documents
235.A1 General works
235.A2 History and criticism of sources
235.A3-Z General works
235.3 General special

Ancient Greece
History
By period
Hellenistic period, 323-146 B.C. -- Continued
323-281. Macedonian hegemony. Struggles of the Diadochi
Cf. DF261.M2, Macedonia
235.4 General works
235.45 General special
Biography and memoirs
235.47 Collective
235.48.A-Z Individual, A-Z
e.g.
235.48.P9 Pyrrhus, King of Epirus
235.5 Lamian War, 323-322
235.7 Athenian Revolution, 286
280-220. Aetolian and Achaean leagues
236 General works
236.3 General special
236.4 Galatian Invasion, 279-278
236.5 Chremonidean War, 267-262
236.7 Pamphlets, etc.
237.A-Z Biography, A-Z
237.A6 Antigonus Gonatas
237.A7 Aratus of Sicyon
220-146. Macedonian wars and Roman conquest
Cf. DG250+, Ancient Rome, 753-27 B.C.
238 General works
238.3 General special
238.7 Pamphlets, etc.
238.9.A-Z Biography, A-Z
238.9.P4 Perseus, King of Macedonia
238.9.P5 Philip V, King of Macedonia
Roman epoch, 140 B.C.-323/476 A.D.
239 General works
240 General special
241 Pamphlets, etc.
Local history and description
251 Territories, colonies, regions, etc. (in combinations)
For particular tribes and people, see DF136.A+
261.A-Z Separate states, territories, islands, etc., A-Z
Cf. DS156.A+, Ancient states of Asia Minor
261.A17 Achaea. Akhaia
261.A177 Aegean Sea Region
Including islands of the Aegean
Cf. DF895+, General history and description
Cf. DS51.A+, Turkish islands of the Aegean
261.A18 Aegina
261.A2 Aetolia
261.A26 Aineia
Akhaia, see DF261.A17
261.A34 Akanthos

Ancient Greece
Local history and description
Separate states, territories, islands, etc., A-Z -- Continued

261.A39 Aliki
261.A4 Almyros
261.A47 Amphipolis
261.A5 Andros (Island)
261.A65 Argolis Peninsula
261.A7 Asine
Athens, see DF275+
261.A8 Attica. Attikí
261.B5 Boeotia. Voiotia
261.B7 Bosporus (Kingdom)
261.B77 Brauron
261.C28 Caria
261.C4 Chalcis
261.C44 Chios Island
261.C5 Claros
261.C6 Clazomenae
261.C65 Corinth
261.C7 Cos (Island)
261.C8 Crete
261.D3 Delos (Island)
261.D35 Delphi
261.D36 Demetrias
261.D38 Dervéni
261.D53 Dion (Pieria)
261.D6 Dodona
261.E3 Elatea
261.E4 Eleusis
261.E413 Eleutherna
261.E42 Elis
261.E5 Ephesus
261.E6 Epidaurus
261.E65 Epirus
For Northern Epirus (Albania), see DR996.E64
261.E7 Eretria
261.E9 Euboea
261.F5 Flious
261.G6 Gonnoi
261.G62 Gorítsa
261.G64 Gortyna
261.I34 Ialysos
261.I58 Iolkos
261.I6 Ionian Islands
261.I85 Isthmía
261.K377 Kastellorizo (Island). Megisti
261.K38 Kastelos (Chania, Crete)
261.K45 Kekhriai
261.K5 Kleitor
261.K55 Knossos
261.K87 Kymē (Euboea Island)

Ancient Greece
Local history and description
Separate states, territories, islands, etc., A-Z -- Continued

261.K9 Kynouria
261.L2 Lakōnia
261.L3 Larissa
261.L34 Lathouresa
261.L49 Lesbos Island
261.L53 Leukantion
261.L63 Locris
261.M2 Macedonia
Cf. DF232.5+, Greek history
For Macedonia (General, and Yugoslavia), see DR2152+
For modern Bulgarian Macedonia, see DR95.B55
For modern Greek Macedonia, see DF901.M3
261.M3 Mantinea
261.M34 Maronea
261.M4 Megalopolis
Megisti, see DF261.K377
261.M45 Messēnia
261.M46 Metapontum
261.M465 Methana Peninsula
261.M47 Methydrion
261.M49 Midea
261.M5 Miletus
261.M55 Míthimna
Morea, see DF261.P3
261.M9 Myrina
261.N3 Naucratis
261.N45 Nemea
261.N55 Nikopolis
261.O5 Olympia
261.O53 Olynthus
261.O57 Omólion
261.O77 Orthagoria
261.P2 Paros
261.P27 Pella
261.P3 Peloponnesus
261.P48 Phaselis
261.P5 Pherae
261.P53 Philippi
261.P55 Phōkis. Phocis
261.P57 Plataea
261.P6 Potidaea
261.P64 Potidaion
261.P8 Priene
261.P94 Pylos (Ēleia, Greece)
261.R47 Rhodes
261.S16 Salamis (Island)
261.S2 Samos
261.S3 Samothrace

Ancient Greece
Local history and description
Separate states, territories, islands, etc., A-Z -- Continued

261.S45	Serrai (Eparchy)
261.S55	Sími
261.S56	Síndos
261.S8	Sparta
261.T15	Tanagra
261.T2	Thasos
261.T3	Thebes
261.T4	Thera
261.T45	Therme
261.T48	Thesprōtia
261.T5	Thessaly
261.T6	Thrace For Bulgarian Thrace, see DR95.T45 For general works on Thrace, see DR50+ For modern Greek Thrace, see DF901.T75 For Turkish Thrace, see DR701.T5
261.T64	Tinos
261.T8	Troezen
261.V2	Vari
261.V28	Vergina
261.V3	Veroia
261.V56	Vitsa
	Voiotia, see DF261.B5
	Athens Cf. DF624, Medieval Athens Cf. DF915+, Modern Athens
	Antiquities. Culture
275	General works
277	Political antiquities
	History
285	General works
285.5	Historiography
287.A-Z	Localities, buildings, etc., A-Z
287.A2	Acropolis
287.A23	Agora
287.A83	Asklepieion
287.B3	Basilicas
287.C4	Ceramicus. Kerameikos
287.E6	Erechtheum
287.H4	Hephaisteion
287.M65	Monument of Philopappus
287.O3	Odeum of Pericles
287.O48	Olympieion
287.P3	Parthenon
287.P4	Piraeus
287.P6	Pnyx
287.P75	Propylaea
287.S27	Sanctuary of the Nymph
287.S74	Stoa of Attalos

Ancient Greece
Local history and description
Athens
Localities, buildings, etc., A-Z -- Continued
287.S75 Stoa Poecile
287.T5 Tholos
287.T66 Tourkovouni
287.T68 Tower of the Winds
287.W3 Walls
289 Other special
Medieval Greece. Byzantine Empire, 323-1453
Cf. DF750+, General Greek history
501 Periodicals. Societies. Serials
501.5 Congresses. Conferences, etc.
Sources and documents
503 General works
504 Pamphlets, etc.
504.5 General works
Historiography
505 General works
Biography of historians, area studies specialists, archaeologists, etc.
505.5 Collective
505.7.A-Z Individual, A-Z
e.g.
505.7.J6 Joannes Malalas
505.7.P7 Procopius, of Caesarea
Study and teaching
505.8 General works
505.82.A-Z By region or country, A-Z
Subarrange by author
Biography (Collective)
For individual biography, see the specific period, reign, or place
506 General works
506.5 Rulers, kings, etc.
518 Historical geography
520 Antiquities
For local antiquities, see DF895+
Social life and customs. Civilization. Intellectual life
For specific periods, see the period or reign
521 General works
531 General special
(541) Special topics (not A-Z)
For specific periods, see the period or reign
Ethnography
542 General works
542.4.A-Z Individual elements in the population, A-Z
542.4.B84 Bulgarians
542.4.S62 Slavs
542.4.T87 Turkic peoples
543 Military history

Medieval Greece. Byzantine Empire, 323-1453 -- Continued
544 Naval history
545 Political history
Foreign and general relations
For works on relations with a specific country regardless of period, see DF547.A+
For general works on the diplomatic history of a period, see the period
546 General works
547.A-Z Relations with individual regions or countries, A-Z
548 Empire and papacy
Cf. BX1171, Roman Catholic Church and Byzantine Empire
Cf. D133, Church and state (Medieval Europe)
History
General works
Through 1800. Chronicles
550 Byzantine
551 Other
552 1801-
552.5 Compends
552.8 Pamphlets, etc.
Eastern Empire, 323/476-1057
553 General works
553.5 Pamphlets, etc.
323-527
Class here only history specifically Eastern
For general history, see DG315
555 General works
556 General special
557 Constantine the Great, 323-337
558 Constantius II, 337-361
559 Valens, 364-378
560 Theodosius I, 379-395
561 Arcadius, 395-408
Theodosius II, 408-450
562 General works
562.5 Pulcheria, 414-453
Co-empress and sister of Theodosius II
562.6 Eudocia, Consort of Theodosius II
563 Marcian, 450-457
564 Leo I, 457-474
565 Leo II, 474
566 Zeno, 474-475/491
567 Anastasius I, 491-518
568 Justin, 518-527
527-1057
General works, see DF553+
527-720
571 General works
Justinian I, 527-565
572 General works on life and reign

Medieval Greece. Byzantine Empire, 323-1453
History
Eastern Empire, 323/476-1057
527-1057
527-720
Justinian I, 527-565 -- Continued

572.5 Theodora, Consort of Justinian I
572.8.A-Z Biography of contemporaries, A-Z
572.8.B4 Belisarius
573 Justin II, 565-578
573.2 Tiberius II, 578-582
573.5 Maurice, 582-602
573.8 Phocas, 602-610
574 Heraclius, 610-641
575 Constantine III and Heracleonas, 641
575.3 Constans II, 641-668
575.7 Constantine IV Pogonatus, 668-685
576 Justinian II Rhinotmetus, 685-695/711
576.5 Leontius, 695-698
576.8 Tiberius III Apsimar, 698-705
Justinian II (restored), 705-711, see DF576
578 Philippicus Bardanes, 711-713
578.5 Anastasius II, 713-716
579 Theodosius III, 716-717

720-886. Iconoclasts
581 General works
Biography and memoirs
581.3 Collective
581.32.A-Z Individual, A-Z
582 Leo III the Isaurian, 717-741
583 Constantine V Copronymus, 741-775
584 Leo IV Chozar, 775-780
585 Constantine VI, 780-797
586 Irene, 797-802
586.2 Nicephorus I, 802-811
586.4 Stauracius, 811
586.5 Michael I Rhangabe, 811-813
586.7 Leo V the Armenian, 813-820
586.9 Michael II, 820-829
587 Theophilus, 829-842
588 Michael III, 842-867
589 Basil I, 867-886

886-1057
590 Sources and documents
591 General works
Biography and memoirs
591.3 Collective
591.32.A-Z Individual, A-Z
591.35.A-Z Local, A-Z
592 Leo VI the Philosopher, 886-911
593 Constance VII Porphyrogenitus, 912-959.
Alexander, 912-913 (Co-emperor). Romanus I Lecapenus, 920-944 (Co-emperor)

Medieval Greece. Byzantine Empire, 323-1453
History
Eastern Empire, 323/476-1057
527-1057
886-1057 -- Continued
594 Romanus II, 959-963
Basil II Bulgaroctonus, 963-1025
595 General works
595.5 Nicephorus II Phocas, 963-969
595.7 John I Zimisces, 969-976
596 Constantine VIII, 1026-1028
596.5 Romanus III Argyrus, 1028-1041
597 Michael IV the Paphlagonian, 1034-1041
597.5 Michael V Calaphates, 1041-1042
598 Constantine IX Monomachus, 1042-1054
599 Theodora, 1054-1056
599.5 Michael VI Stratioticus, 1056-1057
1057-1453
599.8 Sources and documents
General works
Through 1800. Chronicles
600 Byzantine
600.5 Other
601 1801-
601.3 Pamphlets, etc.
602 Isaac I Comnenus, 1057-1059
602.5 Constantine X Ducas, 1059-1067
602.7 Romanus IV Diogenes, 1067-1071
603 Michael VII Parapinaces, 1071-1078
604 Nicephorus III Botaniates, 1078-1081
Alexius I Comnenus, 1081-1118
605 General works
605.3 Anna Comnena, Princess
606 John II Comnenus, 1118-1143
607 Manuel I Comnenus, 1143-1180
608 Alexius II Comnenus, 1180-1183
608.3 Andronicus I Comnenus, 1183-1185
608.5 Isaac II Angelus, 1185-1195, 1203-1204
608.7 Alexius III Angelus, 1195-1203
608.8 Alexius IV Angelus, 1203-1204
608.9 Alexius V Ducas, 1204
609 Empire of Trebizond, 1204-1461
1204-1261. Latin Empire
610 Sources and documents
General works
610.8 Through 1800. Chronicles
611 1801-
613 Constitution and organization
614 Baldwin I, 1204-1205
615 Henry, 1205-1216
616 Peter, 1217-1219
617 Robert, 1219-1228
618 Baldwin II, 1228-1261

Medieval Greece. Byzantine Empire, 323-1453
History
1057-1453
1204-1261. Latin Empire -- Continued
619 Fall of Empire, 1261
Individual states and empires
622 Thessalonica (Thessalonike)
623 Achaia-Morea
624 Athens
Nicaea
625 General works
626 Theodore I Lascaris, 1204-1222
626.3 John III Ducas, 1222-1254
626.5 Theodore II Lascaris, 1254-1258
626.7 John IV Lascaris, 1258-1259
626.9 Michael VIII Palaeologus, 1259-1261
628.A-Z Other mainland states, A-Z
629.A-Z Island states, A-Z
e.g.
629.A7 Archipelago
1261-1453. Palaeologi
630 Sources and documents
General works
631.A2 Byzantine
631.A3-Z Other
632 General special
633.A-Z Local, A-Z
e.g.
633.A8 Asia Minor
Biography and memoirs
633.3 Collective
633.32.A-Z Individual, A-Z
635 Michael VIII Palaeologus, 1261-1282
Andronicus II Palaeologus, 1282-1328
636 General works
636.5 Catalan Grand Company, 1302-1311
637 Andronicus III Palaeologus, 1328-1341
638 John V Palaeologus, 1341-1391
John VI Cantacuzenus, 1347-1354 (Coregent)
Andronicus IV, 1376-1379 (Rival emperor)
639 Manuel II Palaeologus, 1391-1425
John VII Palaeologus, 1398-1402 (Coregent)
641 John VIII Palaeologus, 1425-1448
642 Constantine XI Dragases, 1448-1453
1453. Fall of Constantinople
Cf. DR502, Turkish accounts
Through 1800
645 Byzantine accounts
647 Other
649 1801-
Modern Greece
701 Periodicals. Societies. Serials
703 Sources and documents

Modern Greece -- Continued
Collected works
705 Several authors
706 Individual authors
714 Gazetteers. Dictionaries, etc.
715 Place names
716 Guidebooks
717 General works. Compends
719 Monumental and picturesque
720 Geography
Description and travel
720.5 History of travel
721 1453-1820
723 1821-1829
725 1830-1900
726 1901-1950
727 1951-1980
728 1981-
Antiquities, see DF75+, DF521+
741 Social life and customs. Civilization. Culture
Ethnography
745 General works
747.A-Z Individual elements in the population, A-Z
747.A3 Albanians
747.A67 Armenians
747.A68 Aromanians
747.B8 Bulgarians
747.G4 Germans
747.M3 Macedonians
747.P65 Pomaks
747.S2 Sarakatsans
747.S8 Suliotes
747.T75 Tsakonians
747.T8 Turk
748 Greeks in foreign countries (General)
For Greeks in a particular country, see the country
History
Including modern Greece, including ancient and medieval
For ancient alone, see DF213+
For medieval alone, see DF550+
Biography (Collective)
750 General works
751 Rulers, kings, etc.
752 Houses, noble families, etc.
753 Public men
754 Women
Historiography
755 General works
Biography of historians, area studies specialists, archaeologists, etc.
755.5 Collective
755.7.A-Z Individual, A-Z

	Modern Greece
	History -- Continued
	Study and teaching
755.8	General works
755.82.A-Z	By region or country, A-Z
	Subarrange by author
757	General works
758	Compends
759	General special
760	Pamphlets, etc.
765	Military history
775	Naval history
	Political and diplomatic history
785	General works
787.A-Z	Foreign relations with individual regions or countries, A-Z
	By period
	Turkish rule, 1453-1821
801	General works
801.9.A-Z	Biography and memoirs, A-Z
	e.g.
801.9.R4	Rhigas, Konstantinos
	1821-
802	General works
	1821-1913. 19th century
803	General works
803.9.A-Z	Biography and memoirs, A-Z
	War of Independence, 1821-1829
804	Sources and documents
	Collected works
804.7	Several authors
804.9	Individual authors
805	General works
805.5	Pictorial works
806	Personal narratives and contemporary accounts
807	Political and diplomatic history
809	Naval history
810.A-Z	Special events, battles, etc., A-Z
810.M4	Mesolóngion, Siege of, 1825-1826
810.N3	Navarino (Pilos, Pylos), Battle of, 1827
811.A-Z	Special topics, A-Z
811.C38	Causes
	Foreign participation
811.F65	General works
811.F652A-Z	By region or country, A-Z
811.I54	Influence
811.P37	Paramilitary forces
811.P48	Philikē Hetaireia
811.P74	Prisoners and prisons
811.R44	Religious aspects
811.S63	Social aspects
811.W64	Women

Modern Greece
History
By period
1821-
1821-1913. 19th century
War of Independence, 1821-1829 -- Continued

814 Pamphlets, etc.
Biography
815.A2 Collective
815.A3-Z Individual, A-Z
e.g.
815.T7 Tompazēs, Iakōbos
Kapodistrias, 1827-1831
816 Sources and documents
817 General works
818 Other
821 1831-1832
Otho I, 1833-1862
823 General works on life and reign
Biography and memoirs
823.2 Collective
823.3.A-Z Individual, A-Z
823.5 Pamphlets, etc.
823.6 Acarnanian Revolt, 1836
823.65 Revolution, 1848
823.68 Arta Revolt, 1854
823.7 Revolution, 1862
George I, 1863-1913
825 General works on life and reign
825.3 Pamphlets, etc.
826 Annexation of Thessaly and Epirus, 1881
827 War with Turkey, 1897
Cf. DR575, Turkey during war with Greece
1897-1913
831 General works
831.5 Military League coup d'état, 1909
Biography and memoirs of contemporaries
832.A2 Olga, Consort of George I
832.A3 Nicolas, Prince of Greece
832.A5-Z Other, A-Z
833 20th century
Biography and memoirs
835 Collective
836.A-Z Individual, A-Z
e.g.
836.C5 Christopher, Prince of Greece
836.V3 Venizelos, Eleutherios
Constantine I, 1913-1917
837 General works on life and reign
For reign, 1920-1922, see DF845

Modern Greece
History
By period
1821-
20th century
Constantine I, 1913-1917 -- Continued
838 Period of World War I, 1914-1918
For the war itself, see D501+
841 Sophia, Consort of Constantine I
843 Alexander, 1917-1920
Constantine I, 1920-1922
For reign, 1913-1917, see DF837+
845 General works on reign, 1920-1922
War with Turkey, 1921-1922
845.5 Sources and documents
845.52 General works
845.53.A-Z Special events, battles, etc., A-Z
e.g.
845.53.I94 Izmir
Biography and memoirs
845.57 Collective
845.58.A-Z Individual, A-Z
847 George II, 1922-1924
For reign, 1935-1947, see DF849+
848 Republic, 1924-1935
George II, 1935-1947
For reign, 1922-1924, see DF847
849 General works on reign, 1935-1947
Civil War, 1944-1949
849.5 Sources and documents
849.52 General works
849.53.A-Z Special events, battles, etc., A-Z
Biography and memoirs
849.57 Collective
849.58.A-Z Individual, A-Z
Paul I, 1947-1964
850 General works on life and reign
851 Phreiderikē, Consort of Paul I
Biography and memoirs of contemporaries
851.3 Collective
851.5.A-Z Individual, A-Z
Constantine II, 1964-1967
852 General works on life and reign
Biography and memoirs of contemporaries
852.3 Collective
852.5.A-Z Individual, A-Z
Period of military rule, 1967-1974
853 General works
Biography and memoirs
853.3 Collective
853.5.A-Z Individual, A-Z
Restoration of democracy, 1974-
854 General works

Modern Greece
History
By period
1821-
20th century
Restoration of
democracy, 1974- -- Continued
Biography and memoirs
854.3 Collective
854.32.A-Z Individual, A-Z
Local history and description
Cf. DF251+, Local history and description of ancient Greece
895 Archipelago (Islands of the Aegean)
Cf. D972, European Orient
Cf. DF901.C9, Cyclades
901.A-Z Regions, provinces, islands, etc., A-Z
e.g.
901.A24 Achaia
901.A25 Achelous River Region
901.A33 Aegina
901.A38 Aigialeia
901.A6 Andros (Island)
Arcadia, see DF901.A73
901.A73 Arkadia. Arcadia
901.A77 Athos, Mount
For Athos (Monasteries), see BX385.A8+
901.A8 Attica. Attikí
901.C4 Cephalonia
Chios, see DF901.K55
901.C7 Corfu
901.C76 Cos. Kos
901.C78-C89 Crete
901.C78 Periodicals. Societies. Serials
901.C786 Place names
901.C79 Biography (Collective)
901.C8 Description and travel
901.C815 Social life and customs. Civilization. Intellectual life
901.C82 History
Antiquities and ancient history
Archaeological explorations, see DF221.C8
General ancient history, see DF261.C8
901.C825 Early and medieval
901.C826 826-961. Arab rule
901.C827 961-1204. Greek rule
901.C83 1204-1669. Venetian rule
Cf. DG678.2, Turkish wars, 1453-1571
Cf. DR534.2+, War of Candia, 1644-1669
901.C835 1669-1898. Turkish rule
19th century
901.C84 General works

Modern Greece
Local history and description
Regions, provinces, islands, etc., A-Z
Crete
History
19th century -- Continued

901.C843 1821-1829
Cf. DF804+, Greek War of Independence, 1821-1829

901.C85 1866-1868

901.C851 Pamphlets, etc.

901.C857 1896-1897
Cf. DF827, War with Turkey, 1897

901.C86 1898-

901.C88A-Z Counties, regions, etc., A-Z
For cities, see DF951.A+

901.C9 Cyclades
Cf. D972, European Orient
Cf. DR701.A2, Aegean Sea

901.D6 Dodecanese

901.D65 Doris

901.E44 Eleia

901.E6 Epirus
For Northern Epirus (Albania), see DR996.E64

901.E8 Euboea

901.G6 Gortynia

901.H9 Hydra

901.I4 Ikaría Island

901.I58-I66 Ionian Islands

901.I58 Periodicals

901.I6 General works. Description and travel

901.I64 History

901.I642 1797-1815

901.I65 1815-1864

901.I66 1864-

901.I695 Ionian Sea

901.I8 Ithaca (Thiaki)

901.K25 Kálimnos Island

901.K27 Kárpathos Island

901.K29 Kastellorizo Island

901.K3 Kastoría (Nomos)

901.K5 Khalkidhikí Peninsula

901.K55 Khíos

901.K57 Kíthira (Island)

Kos, see DF901.C76

901.L28 Lakōnia

901.L35 Lemnos Island

901.L38 Lesbos Island

901.L4 Levkás (Island)

Modern Greece
Local history and description
Regions, provinces,
islands, etc., A-Z -- Continued

901.M3 Macedonia
For ancient Greek Macedonia, see DF261.M2
For Macedonia (General, and Yugoslavia), see DR2152+
For modern Bulgarian Macedonia, see DR95.B55

901.M34 Mani
901.M532 Messēnia (Nomos)
901.M9 Mykonos (Island)
901.N3 Naxos (Island)
901.N57 Nisyro
901.O4 Oinousai Islands
901.O6 Olympus, Mount (Thessaly)
901.P24 Parnassus, Mount
901.P26 Paros
901.P27 Patmos
901.P3 Paxos
901.P4 Peloponnesus
901.P6 Poros
Rhodes
901.R4 Island
901.R42 City
901.R43A-Z Other cities, A-Z
901.S34 Samos
901.S54 Sími Island
901.S6 Skyros
901.S66 Souli
901.S7 Spetsai (Island)
901.S9 Syros
901.T6 Tenos
901.T65 Thasos (Island)
901.T67 Thera Island
901.T68 Thermopylae
901.T7 Thessaly
For archaeological exploration, see DF221.T4
For general ancient history, see DF261.T5

901.T75 Thrace (Western)
For ancient Greek Thrace, see DF261.T6
For Bulgarian Thrace, see DR95.T45
For general works on Thrace, see DR50+
For Turkish Thrace, see DR701.T5

901.T754 Thyreatis
901.Z26 Zagori
901.Z3 Zakinthos Island. Zante
Zante, see DF901.Z3

Athens
915 Periodicals. Societies. Serials
916 Gazetteers
916.4 Guidebooks
917 General works

Modern Greece
Local history and description
Athens -- Continued
Description
918 Early through 1829
919 1830-
Antiquities, see DF275+
920 Social life and customs. Culture
History
Including medieval and modern Athens treated together
921 General works
Ancient, see DF285+
922 Medieval to 1453
Cf. DF624, Athens (Latin Empire)
923 1453-1829
924 1830-1900
925 1901-
930.A-Z Localities. Sections, districts, etc., A-Z
Buildings
935 General works
936.A-Z Individual, A-Z
951.A-Z Other cities, towns, etc., A-Z
e.g.
951.G2 Galaxidi (Galaxeidion)
951.I5 Iōannina (Janina)
951.N4 Néa Erithraía
951.T45 Thessalonike. Salonika

History of Italy
For the general history of Italy, including ancient Rome, see DG466+
Ancient Italy. Rome to 476
11 Periodicals. Serials
12 Societies
Museums, exhibitions, etc.
12.2 General works
12.3.A-Z Individual. By place, A-Z
12.5 Congresses
13 Sources and documents. Collections. Classical authors
Collected works
14 Several authors
15 Individual authors
16 Dictionaries
Geography. Description and travel
Cf. G83+, History of ancient geography
Dictionaries, see DG16
General works
27 Classical authors (Translations)
For texts, see PA
Itineraria. Roman roads
Including bridges
28 General works
28.5 General special
e.g. Roman roads in various regions and countries (not A-Z)
29.A-Z Individual, A-Z
29.A6 Appian Way (Via Appia)
29.A94 Augusta, Via
29.A96 Aurelia, Via
29.C53 Claudia Braccianese, Via. Via Clodia
Clodia, Via, see DG29.C53
29.F47 Ferentina, Via
29.F53 Flaminia, Via
29.L33 Labicana, Via
29.L38 Latina, Via
29.N65 Nomentana, Via
29.P67 Postumia, Via
29.P74 Prenestina, Via
29.R43 Regina, Via
29.S2 Sacra, Via
29.S24 Salaria, Via
29.T53 Tiberina, Via
29.T722 Traiana, Via
29.T87 Tuscalana, Via
29.V35 Valeria, Via
Modern authors
30 General works
31 General special
41 Travel
Local history and description

Ancient Italy. Rome to 476
Local history and description -- Continued
Regions, provinces, etc.
For works on the antiquities of the Roman period, see the history of the specific place

51 North
52 Central. Latium
53 South
Other
55.A-Z Regions in Italy, A-Z
Cf. DG87, Provinces, colonies, municipia (General)
For ancient cities and city regions, see DG61+
55.A27 Abruzzi
55.A32 Accesa Lake
55.A35 Aemilia
Aeoliae Insulae, see DG55.L55
55.A47 Alps
55.A53 Amiata, Monte
55.A63 Apennines
55.A65 Apulia
55.A83 Ascoli Piceno (Province)
55.B34 Bari (Province)
55.B36 Basilicata
55.B4 Belluno
55.B62 Bologna (Province)
55.B63 Bolsena, Lake
55.B64 Bolzano (Province)
(55.B72) Bressanone Region
see DG70.B82
55.B74 Brindisi (Province)
55.C26 Calabria
55.C27 Camonica Valley
55.C28 Campagna di Roma
55.C3 Campania
55.C32 Carpino River Plain
55.C33 Casentino Valley
55.C34 Castellier degli Elleri Mountain
55.C36 Castelporziano, Tenuta di
55.C45 Chiana River and Valley
55.C63 Como (Province)
55.C64 Conca River Valley
55.C65 Cosenza (Province)
55.C87 Curone Valley
55.E45 Elba
55.E48 Elsa Valley
55.E54 Emilia-Romagna
55.E87 Etruria. Tuscany
Cf. DG222.5+, Etruscans
55.E89 Euganean Hills
55.F47 Ferrara Region
55.F57 Forum Julii (Friuli)
Cf. DG975.F85, Friuli (City)

Ancient Italy. Rome to 476
Local history and description
Regions, provinces, etc.
Other
Regions in Italy, A-Z -- Continued

55.F73 Friuli (Region)
55.F74 Friuli-Venezia Giulia
55.G37 Garda, Lake
55.G73 Grado Lagoon
55.G77 Grosseto (Province)
55.I82 Ischia Island
Lavoro, Terra di, see DG55.S9
55.L5 Liguria
55.L55 Lipari Islands. Aeoliae Insulae
Including individual islands, e. g. Vulcano Island
55.L57 Liri River Valley
55.L6 Lombardy
55.M28 Maggiore, Lake, Region
55.M3 Magna Graecia
55.M35 Mantua (Province)
55.M37 Marches
55.M38 Maremma
55.M45 Metauro Valley
55.M63 Modena (Province)
55.M65 Molise
55.N68 Novara
55.O74 Orcia River Valley
55.P44 Peligna Valley
55.P5 Phlegraean Plain
55.P55 Piemonte
55.P6 Po Valley
55.P65 Policastro Gulf region
55.P66 Pontine Marshes
55.P68 Pozzuoli Gulf
Puglia, see DG55.A65
55.R5 Reggio Emilia (Province)
55.R54 Rieti (Province)
55.R65 Romagna
55.S13 Sabbia Valley
55.S16 Salentina Peninsula
55.S2 Sardinia
55.S48 Sibari Plain
55.S5 Sicilia
Including general ancient
55.S5G3 Gelon
55.S54 Siena (Province)
55.S85 Susa Valley
55.S9 Syracuse
55.T47 Terra di Lavoro
55.T73 Trentino-Alto Adige
55.T76 Tronto River Valley
55.T87 Turin (Province)

Ancient Italy. Rome to 476
Local history and description
Regions, provinces, etc.
Other
Regions in Italy, A-Z -- Continued
Tuscany, see DG55.E87
55.T95 Tyrrhenian Sea Region
55.U45 Ufita River Valley
55.U63 Umbria
55.V34 Valle d'Aosta
55.V37 Varese (Province)
55.V45 Veneto
55.V47 Venice (Province)
55.V49 Versilia Plain
55.V57 Viterbo (Province)
Vulcano Island, see DG55.L55
59.A-Z Regions outside of Italy, A-Z
Prefer local history for material relating to the history of individual countries in the Roman period (except for such regions as do not correspond to modern geographical divisions), e.g., DA145+, Roman period in England
Cf. DG87, Provinces, colonies, municipia (General)
59.A2 General works
59.A4 Africa
59.A8 Asia
59.B44 Belgica
59.C9 Cyrene
59.D3 Dacia
Cf. DR239.2, Dacians
59.D4 Dalmatia
59.D43 Danube River Valley
59.G2 Gallia
Hispania, see DP94+
59.I15 Iberia
59.I2 Illyria
Cf. DR39.5, Illyrians
59.M3 Mauretania
59.M7 Moesia
59.M74 Moselle River and Valley
59.N37 Narbonensis
59.N7 Noricum
59.P2 Pannonia
59.R5 Rhaetia
Rhine Valley, see DD801.R71+
Sardinia, see DG55.S2
Sicilia, see DG55.S5
59.S9 Syria

Ancient Italy. Rome to 476
Local history and description -- Continued
Rome (City) to 476
Including description, antiquities, views, etc.
For architectural works with texts, see NA310+
For modern, including medieval, see DG803+

61 Periodicals. Societies. Collections
62 Guidebooks. Outlines, etc.
General works
62.5 Through 1800
63 1801-
63.5 Preservation
64 Minor works. Special (not A-Z)
Including exhibitions, models, photographs, pictures, etc.
65 Archaeological discoveries
Sections, districts, etc.
66 Colles, montes, etc.
Including Capitoline Hill, Palatine Hill, etc.
66.5 Forum Romanum
66.8 Graecostasis
67 Gates (Portae). Walls, aqueducts, bridges, etc.
Buildings
Cf. DG133, Temples, altars, etc.
68 General works
68.1 Individual buildings (not A-Z)
Including Colosseum, Septizonium, Thermae Agrippae, etc.
69 Other special
Including Arch of Titus, Lapis niger in the Comitiu Flaminia, etc.
70.A-Z Other cities, towns, etc., A-Z
For modern history, including ancient and medieval, see DG975.A+
70.A1 General works
70.A24 Acquarossa
70.A25 Acquavina (Siena)
70.A27 Aesernia (Isernia)
70.A3 Agrigentum (Agrigento, Girgenti)
70.A53 Alba Fucens. Alba Funcentia
70.A533 Alba Longa
70.A534 Alba Pompeia (Alba)
70.A535 Albanella
70.A54 Albintimilium
70.A545 Alesa. Halaesa
70.A55 Alife
70.A57 Altino
70.A573 Amelia
70.A576 Amiternum
70.A578 Anagni
70.A58 Ancona
70.A583 Angera
Ansedonia (Cosa), see DG70.C63

Ancient Italy. Rome to 476
Local history and description
Other cities, towns, etc., A-Z -- Continued

	Antemnae, see DG66
70.A6	Aquileia
70.A72	Ardea
70.A73	Arona
70.A74	Arretium (Arezzo)
70.A75	Artena
70.A753	Artimino
70.A76	Ascoli Piceno
70.A77	Ascoli Satriano
70.A774	Asolo
70.A775	Assisi
70.A776	Asti
70.A78	Atella
70.A83	Augustanus Laurentium
70.B27	Balone Site
70.B33	Barcola
70.B34	Barletta
70.B4	Belluno
70.B44	Bergamo
70.B47	Biella
70.B5	Bithia (Sardinia)
70.B54	Blera
70.B7	Bologna
70.B72	Bomarzo
70.B75	Boscoreale
70.B78	Bovino
70.B8	Brescia
70.B82	Bressanone
70.B83	Brindisi
70.B87	Budrio
70.C116	Caelia (Bari Province)
70.C12	Caere (Cerveteri)
70.C125	Cagliari
70.C13	Cairano
70.C15	Cales (Calvi Risorta)
70.C16	Calvatone
70.C17	Camarina
70.C173	Campanella Point
70.C174	Canosa di Puglia
70.C176	Capannori
70.C18	Capena
70.C19	Capiago Intimiano
70.C197	Capracotta
70.C2	Capri
70.C25	Capua
70.C26	Carrara
70.C265	Carsulae
70.C27	Cascia
70.C28	Casignana
70.C29	Cassana

Ancient Italy. Rome to 476
Local history and description
Other cities, towns, etc., A-Z -- Continued

70.C3 Castel di Decima
70.C312 Castel Volturno
70.C313 Castellaneta
70.C315 Castiglion Fiorentino
70.C316 Castiglione del Lago
70.C318 Catania
70.C32 Cattolica
70.C34 Cavallino
Ceccano, see DG70.F33
70.C39 Cerveteri
70.C42 Chianciano Terme
70.C425 Chieri
70.C43 Chieti
70.C44 Chiusi
70.C49 Cittadella
70.C52 Civita di Paterno Site
70.C53 Civitavecchia
70.C56 Codroipo
70.C57 Colle di Val d'Elsa
70.C573 Collemancio (Urbinum Hortense)
70.C574 Comacchio
70.C575 Corchiano
70.C576 Corciano
70.C58 Cornus
70.C6 Cortona
70.C62 Corvaro
70.C63 Cosa (Ansedonia)
70.C65 Cottanello
70.C74 Cremona
70.C77 Crotone
70.C78 Crustumerium
70.C9 Cumae
70.C93 Cupra Marittima
70.D47 Desenzano del Garda
Egnatia, see DG70.G57
70.E68 Entella Site
70.E8 Este
70.F33 Fabrateria Vetus (Ceccano)
70.F34 Falerium Vetus (Civita Castellana)
70.F36 Falerone
70.F47 Ferentinum Hirpinum
70.F49 Fermo
70.F5 Ferrone Site
70.F53 Ficana
70.F535 Fidenae
70.F54 Fiesole
70.F55 Florence
70.F64 Foligno
70.F67 Forlì
70.F68 Fordongianus

Ancient Italy. Rome to 476
Local history and description
Other cities, towns, etc., A-Z -- Continued

70.F69 Formello
Forum Corneli, see DG70.I47
Frascati, see DG70.T8
70.F73 Fregellae
70.G3 Gabii
70.G45 Gela (Sicily)
70.G47 Genoa
70.G5 Ghiaccio Forte
70.G53 Ginosa
70.G55 Gioiosa Ionica
70.G57 Gnathia. Egnatia
70.G65 Golasecca
70.G72 Gravina di Puglia
70.G73 Graviscae
70.G84 Gubbio
Halaesa, see DG70.A545
70.H48 Heraclea
70.H5 Herculaneum
Including Villa of the Papyri
Herdonia, see DG70.O7
70.H9 Hyccara
70.I28 Iato Mountain (Sicily)
70.I35 Idoli Lake
70.I45 Imera (Sicily)
70.I47 Imola (Forum Corneli)
70.I57 Interamna Nahars (Terni)
70.I6 Ipponion
Isernia, see DG70.A27
70.I87 Ittireddu
70.L32 La Giostra Site
70.L36 Laos
70.L37 Laurentum
70.L372 Lavello
70.L373 Lavinium
70.L38 Lecce
70.L4 Leontinoi (Lentini)
70.L47 Leuca
70.L52 Licata (Sicily)
70.L53 Licenza
70.L55 Lipari. Lipari Islands
70.L6 Locri Epizephyrii
70.L83 Lucca
70.L85 Lucera
70.M35 Mantua
70.M36 Marzabotto
70.M37 Matauros
70.M43 Medma
70.M44 Megara Hyblaea
70.M46 Merano
70.M5 Messina

Ancient Italy. Rome to 476
Local history and description
Other cities, towns, etc., A-Z -- Continued

70.M52 Metapontum
70.M56 Milan
70.M6 Minturno
70.M62 Mirandola
70.M623 Misenum (Miseno)
70.M63 Modena
70.M635 Mola di Monte Gelato Site
70.M637 Monte Adranone Site
70.M64 Monte Romano
70.M643 Montecchio Emilia
70.M645 Montemilone
70.M65 Monteroduni
70.M66 Morgantina (Sicily)
70.M67 Motya (Mozia), San Pantaleo Island (Sicily)
70.N35 Naples
70.N37 Narce
70.N39 Nave
70.N42 Neapolis (Sardinia)
70.N45 Nemi
70.N64 Nora (Sardinia)
70.N65 Noto (Sicily)
70.O33 Oderzo
70.O7 Ordona. Herdonia
70.O73 Oria
70.O75 Ornavasso
70.O77 Orune
70.O78 Orvieto
70.O785 Osimo
70.O79 Osteria dell'Osa
70.O8 Ostia
70.O93 Ozieri (Sardinia)
70.P25 Padria
70.P27 Padua
70.P3 Paestum
70.P325 Palermo
70.P33 Palestrina (Praeneste)
70.P35 Pantalica
70.P36 Pantelleria Island
70.P38 Parabiago
70.P39 Parre
70.P393 Passignano sul Trasimeno
70.P396 Pegognaga
70.P4 Perugia
70.P43 Pesaro
70.P45 Petruscio Ravine
70.P52 Piazza Armerina
70.P53 Pietrabbondante (Bovianum Vetus)
70.P55 Pietramelara
70.P57 Pisa
70.P62 Poggio Buco Site

Ancient Italy. Rome to 476
Local history and description
Other cities, towns, etc., A-Z -- Continued

70.P64 Poggio Civitate
70.P65 Poggio Colla Site
70.P66 Poggio Pinci
70.P68 Pomarico Vecchio
70.P7 Pompeii
70.P74 Ponti di Nona
70.P76 Pontecagnano Faiano
70.P765 Ponza Island
70.P77 Populonia
70.P775 Pordenone
70.P777 Porticello
70.P78 Porto Torres
70.P9 Puteoli (Pozzuoli)
70.P95 Pyrgi
70.R34 Ragusa (Sicily)
70.R37 Ravenna
70.R4 Reate (Rieti)
70.R43 Reggio di Calabria
70.R46 Remedello Sotto
Rieti, see DG70.R4
70.R54 Rimini
70.R65 Roccagloriosa
70.R7 Roselle
70.R77 Rubiera
70.R8 Rudiae
70.R87 Russi
70.S213 Sabucina
70.S217 Salapia. Salpi
70.S22 Salento
70.S223 Salerno
70.S23 Salò
Salpi, see DG70.S217
70.S238 San Giovanni di Ruoti Site
70.S24 San Giovenale
70.S242 San Marino
70.S244 San Paolo di Civitate
70.S246 San Piero a Sieve
70.S247 San Severo
70.S248 Sannace Mountain
70.S25 Sant'Antioco Island (Sardinia)
70.S253 Sant'Antonio Abate
70.S255 Sant'Ilario d'Enza
70.S257 Santorso
70.S258 Sanzeno
70.S27 Sarteano
70.S28 Satricum
70.S33 Saturnia
70.S38 Segesta
70.S385 Segni
70.S39 Segusium (Susa)

Ancient Italy. Rome to 476
Local history and description
Other cities, towns, etc., A-Z -- Continued

70.S4	Selinus
70.S43	Sepino
70.S437	Sessa Aurunca
70.S44	Sestino
70.S45	Sesto Fiorentino
70.S52	Sibari
	Siena, see DG70.A25
70.S55	Sipontum
70.S56	Sirai Mountain
70.S58	Siris
70.S62	Solunto
70.S64	Sorgenti della Nova Site
70.S65	Sperlonga
70.S66	Spina
70.S67	Spoleto
70.S77	Stabiae
70.S83	Stróngoli
70.S86	Sulcis
70.S9	Sybaris
	Syracuse, see DG55.S9
70.T3	Tarentum (Taranto)
70.T35	Tarquinia
70.T36	Temesa
70.T37	Tergeste (Trieste)
70.T38	Termini Imerese (Sicily)
	Terni, see DG70.I57
70.T4	Terracina
70.T45	Tessennano
70.T5	Tharros
70.T55	Thiene
70.T6	Tibur (Tivoli)
70.T66	Todi
70.T68	Torre Galli Site
70.T69	Torrita di Siena
70.T74	Trea (Treia)
70.T77	Tridentum (Trento)
70.T78	Turi
70.T79	Tuscania
70.T8	Tusculum (Frascati)
70.U34	Ugento
70.U7	Urbs Salvia
70.V2	Vaglio de Basilicata
70.V24	Valéggio sul Mincio
70.V3	Veii
70.V33	Velia
70.V335	Venosa
70.V34	Verabolo
70.V343	Vercelli
70.V346	Veretum
70.V35	Verona

Ancient Italy. Rome to 476
Local history and description
Other cities, towns, etc., A-Z -- Continued

70.V4 Vetulonia
70.V5 Vicentia (Vicenza)
70.V53 Vico Equense
70.V55 Villa di Settefinestre (Italy)
70.V56 Villadose
70.V58 Viterbo
70.V62 Voghenza
70.V64 Volsinii (Viterbo Province)
70.V65 Volterra (Viterbo Province)
70.V9 Vulci
70.Z8 Zuglio

Antiquities. Civilization. Culture
Cf. CC1+, Archaeology
Cf. N5740+, Ancient art
Periodicals, see DG11
Societies, see DG12
Congresses, see DG12.5
Dictionaries, see DG16

75 Outlines, tables, etc.
General works
76 Through 1800
77 1801-
77.5 Preservation
78 General special
Including social life and customs
Cf. DG90+, Private life
Local, see DG51+
79 Pamphlets, etc.
Public and political antiquities
81 General works
82 General special
For foreign and general relations, see DG214+
Administration
For works on political theory, see JC81+
83 General works
83.A7 Augustales. Severi augustales
83.A8 Honor bisellii
Citizenship
Cf. KJA2930+, Roman law
83.1 General works
83.3 Special classes
Including Patres, Nobiles, Clientes, Plebs, Equestrian order, etc.
83.5.A-Z Magistratus. Dignitaries
Cf. KJA2980+, Roman law
83.5.A1 General works
83.5.A3 Aediles
83.5.C4 Censores
83.5.C7 Consules
Cf. DG202, Fasti consulares

Ancient Italy. Rome to 476
Antiquities. Civilization. Culture
Public and political antiquities
Administration
Magistratus. Dignitaries -- Continued
83.5.C85 Curatores rei publicae
83.5.D2 Decemviri
83.5.D23 Decuriones
83.5.D4 Dictatores
83.5.D8 Ducenarii
83.5.I6 Imperatores
83.5.M2 Magistratus municipales
83.5.M23 Magistri officiorum
83.5.N68 Notarii
83.5.P2 Pontifices
83.5.P3 Praefecti Praetores
83.5.P4 Praefectus urbis
83.5.P5 Praesides provinciarum
83.5.P6 Praetores
83.5.P68 Primipili
83.5.P7 Proconsules
83.5.P8 Procurator Caesaris
83.5.Q2 Quaestores
83.5.Q5 Quinquennales
83.5.R3 Reges
83.5.T3 Tetrarchae
83.5.T7 Tribuni
83.5.V5 Vigiles
85 Finance. Economics. Maintenance
87 Provinces. Colonies. Municipia
Cf. JV98, Roman colonies and colonization
(88) Legal antiquities
see subclass KJA
89 Military and naval antiquities
Including triumphs, trophies, etc.
Cf. U35, Roman military science
Cf. V39, Roman naval science
For legal aspects of prisoners of war, see KJA3328
Private antiquities
Including private life
Cf. DG78, Social life and customs
90 General works
91 Family. Women. Youth
Cf. HQ511, Family, marriage, home (Ancient Rome)
Cf. HQ1136, Women, feminism (Ancient Rome)
93 Education
Cf. LA81, Education in ancient Rome
Cf. LB91.A+, Theories of education by individual educators and writers (Ancient Rome)

Ancient Italy. Rome to 476
Antiquities. Civilization. Culture
Private antiquities -- Continued
(95) Athletics. Games. Circuses. Gladiators
see GV31+
Dwellings. Baths, etc.
Including domestic antiquities in general
Cf. NA324, Roman architecture
97 General works
97.2 Amphoras
97.3 Utilitarian ceramics
Including bricks, tiles, etc.
98 Lamps
(99) Dress. Costume
see GT555
101 Eating, cooking (Convivia)
103 Funeral customs. Sepulchral customs
Cf. GT3170, Treatment of the dead in antiquity
105 Agriculture. Land
Cf. HD137+, Land (Economic history of Rome)
Cf. S431, History of Roman agriculture
Cf. S490.8+, Treatises on agriculture by Roman authors
107 Commerce. Industries
Cf. HC39, Economic history and conditions in ancient Rome
Cf. HF377+, History of commerce (Ancient Rome)
108 Transportation
Cf. DG28+, Roman roads
Cf. HE175, History of transportation and communications in Rome
109 Other social institutions
Cf. HN9+, Social history and conditions (Ancient Rome)
Religious antiquities
For Roman mythology, see BL798+
121 General works
Cultus
123 General works
124 Cult of the emperors
125 Festae
127 Mysteries
129 Divination
131 Magic
133 Temples, altars, etc.
135 Other special
135.5 Amphitheaters
135.6 Aqueducts
Art antiquities
136 General works

Ancient Italy. Rome to 476
  Antiquities. Civilization. Culture
    Art antiquities -- Continued
137 Art metal-work
      Cf. NK6407.3, Decorative arts
139 Sarcophagi
140 Pottery
141 Mosaic pavements
142 Urns
    Chronology, see CE46
    Numismatics, see CJ801+
    Tesserae, see CJ4865
    Weights and measures, see QC84
190 Ethnography
  History
    Periodicals, societies, collections, dictionaries, see DG11
201 Chronological tables, etc.
202 Fasti consulares
      Cf. KJA2992, Roman law
    Biography (Collective)
203 General works
203.5 Prosopography, etc.
204.A-Z Houses, noble families, etc., A-Z
204.S35 Scipio family
204.U47 Ulpii family
    Historiography
205 General works
      Biography of historians and archaeologists
206.A2 Collective
206.A3-Z Individual, A-Z
          e.g.
206.G5 Gibbon, Edward
206.M6 Mommsen, Theodor
206.N5 Niebuhr, Barthold Georg
206.P57 Piso Frugi, Lucius Calpurnis, b. ca. 182 B.C.
206.P7 Pozzo, Cassiano del
206.T32 Tacitus, Cornelius
206.5 Study and teaching
    General works
207 Translations of classical authors
        For texts, see PA
      Modern authors
208 Through 1775
209 1776-
210 Compends. Textbooks
210.5 Syllabi, etc.
211 General special
213 Addresses, essays, lectures

Ancient Italy. Rome to 476
History -- Continued
Foreign and general relations
For works on relations with other countries, regardless of the period, see DG215.A+
For general works on the diplomatic history of a period, see the period
For works on relations with countries which became part of the Roman Empire, see DG55-DG59

214 Sources and documents
214.5 General works
215.A-Z Relations with individual regions or countries, A-Z
By period
Pre-Roman Italy
Including Italic peoples (General)
221 General works
221.5 General special
222 Pamphlets, etc.
Etruria. Etruscans
For Etruscan antiquities in ancient Roman cities, see DG70.A+
For general works on Etruria during the pre-Roman through the Roman periods, see DG55.E87
222.5 Periodicals. Societies. Exhibitions
222.7 Sources and documents
223 General works
223.2 General special
223.3 Social life and customs. Civilization
223.4 Social conditions
223.5 Political and diplomatic history
223.7.A-Z Special topics, A-Z
Art, see N5750
223.7.B75 Bronzes
223.7.C47 Chariots
223.7.C65 Commerce
223.7.F5 Fibulae
223.7.F53 Figurines
223.7.G66 Gold jewelry
223.7.H85 Hunting
Language, see P1078
223.7.M47 Merchant marine
223.7.M54 Mineral industries
223.7.M55 Mirrors
223.7.P35 Palaces
223.7.P67 Pottery
Religion, see BL813.E8
223.7.R62 Roads
223.7.S57 Shrines. Temples
223.7.S68 Sports
Temples, see DG223.7.S57
223.7.T45 Terra-cotta sculpture
223.7.T6 Tombs

Ancient Italy. Rome to 476
History
By period
Pre-Roman Italy
Etruria. Etruscans
Special topics, A-Z -- Continued

223.7.U7 Urns
223.7.V35 Vases
223.7.V67 Votive offerings
Cf. BL760.V6, Etruscan religion
225.A-Z Other, A-Z
225.A8 Aurunci
225.B79 Bruttii
225.C37 Carthaginians
225.C44 Celts
225.D3 Daunii
225.E43 Egyptians
225.F3 Falisci
225.F73 Frentani
225.G38 Gauls
225.G74 Greeks
225.L53 Ligurians
225.L83 Lucani
225.M3 Marsi
225.M4 Messapii
225.O8 Oscans
225.P44 Pelasgi
225.P45 Phenicians
225.S2 Sabines
225.S24 Salassi
225.S26 Samnites
225.V3 Venati
225.V4 Vestini
225.V55 Vittimuli
225.V64 Volsci

Kings and Republic, 753-27 B.C.
Cf. KJA2860, Roman law
Cf. KJA2870, Roman law

231 General works
231.3 General special
231.7 Pamphlets, etc.

Foundations and Kings, 753-510 B.C.

233 General works
233.2 General special
233.25 Pamphlets, etc.
233.3 Romulus, 753-716
233.4 Numa Pompilius, 715-673
233.5 Tullus Hostilius, 673-642
233.6 Ancus Marcius, 642-617
233.7 Tarquinius Priscus, 616-579
233.8 Servius Tullius, 578-535
233.9 Tarquinius Superbus, 535-510

Republic to First Punic War, 509-265 B.C.

	Ancient Italy. Rome to 476
	History
	By period
	Kings and Republic, 753-27 B.C.
	Republic to First Punic War, 509-265 B.C. -- Continued
235	General works
235.2	General special
235.4	Special events to 343. By date
236.A-Z	Biography, 509-343, A-Z
236.B7	Brutus, Lucius Junius
236.V3	Valerius, Publius
	Subjection of Italy, 343-290
237	General works
237.2	General special
237.4	Special events. By date
238.A-Z	Biography, A-Z
238.C5	Claudius Caeus, Appius
	290-265
239	General works
239.2	General special
239.4	Special events. By date
240.A-Z	Biography, A-Z
	Conquest of the Mediterranean world, 264-133 B.C.
241	General works
241.2	General special
242	First and Second Punic wars
	First Punic War, 264-241 B.C.
243	General works
243.2	General special
243.25	Pamphlets, etc.
243.4	Special events. By date
244.A-Z	Biography, 264-219, A-Z
244.R4	Regulus, Marcus Atilius
244.X2	Xanthippus, the Lacedaemonian
245	240-231
246	Illyrian wars, 231-219 B.C.
	Second Punic War, 218-201 B.C.
247	General works
247.1	Causes
247.12	Siege of Saguntum, 219
247.15	Hannibal in Gaul, 218
247.2	Crossing the Alps, 218
247.23	Ticinus, 218
247.24	Trebia, 218
247.26	Trasimenus, 218
247.3	Cannae, 216
247.33	Revolt of Southern Italy
247.36	Winter at Capua, 216
247.4	Nola, 215
247.48	Tarentum, 212
	War in Sicily, 214-210

Ancient Italy. Rome to 476
History
By period
Kings and Republic, 753-27 B.C.
Conquest of the Mediterranean world, 264-133 B.C.
Second Punic War, 218-201 B.C.
War in Sicily, 214-210 -- Continued

247.5 General works
247.55 Syracuse
247.59 War in Spain, 218-211
247.6 Capua
247.7 Metaurus, 207
247.8 Scipio in Carthage, 209
247.82 Scipio in Spain, 206
247.9 Invasion of Africa, 204-201
247.94 Capture of Syphax, 203
247.97 Zama, 202
247.98 Peace with Carthage, 201
248.A-Z Biography, A-Z
248.S3 Scipio Africanus major, Publius Cornelius
Hannibal
249 General works
249.3 General special
249.4 Special events after return to Carthage. By date
For special events during the Second Punic War, see DG247+
200-133 B.C.
250 General works
250.5 General special
War in the East
251 First and Second Macedonian wars, 215-196
251.3 Syrian War, 191-190
251.4 Aetolian War, 189
251.5 Galatian War, 189
251.6 Third Macedonian War, 171-168
251.8 Achaean War, 147-146
Wars in the West
252 Gallic War, 200
252.2 Ligurian War, 200
252.3 Spanish War, 195-179 B.C.
252.4 Istrian War, 178
252.5 Sardinian and Corsican War, 177-175
252.6 Third Punic War, 149-146
252.8 Numantine War, 143-133
252.9 First Servile War, 134-132 (Pergamus)
253.A-Z Biography, A-Z
253.C3 Cato, Marcus Porcius
253.S4 Scipio Aemilianus Africanus minor, Publius Cornelius
253.V5 Viriathus

Ancient Italy. Rome to 476
History
By period
Kings and Republic, 753-27 B.C. -- Continued
Fall of the Republic and establishment of the Empire, 133-27 B.C.

253.5 Sources and documents
254 General works
254.2 General special
254.3 Pamphlets, etc.
254.5 The Gracchi, 133-121
255 Jugurthine War, 111-105
255.5 Cimbri and Teutoni, 113-101
Including Battle of Aquae Sextiae, 102 B.C.
Period of Marius and Sulla, 111-78 B.C.
256 General works
256.2 General special
256.5 Marius (Gaius), life and times
256.7 Sulla (Lucius Cornelius), life and times
257 Second Servile War, 103-99
257.3 Social or Marsic War, 90-88
257.5 First Civil War, 88-86
257.6 First Mithridatic War, 88-84
257.8 Second Civil War, 83-78
Including works covering First and Second Civil Wars
258 Pompey (Gnaeus Pompeius Magnus), life and times
258.3 Third Mithridatic war, 74-61
258.5 Spartacus and the Third Servile War (War of the gladiators), 73-71
259 Conspiracy of Catiline, 65-62
Biography
260.A1 Collective
260.A2-Z Individual, A-Z
e.g.
260.A6 Antonius, Marcus
260.A8 Atticus, Titus Pomponius
260.B3 Balbus, Lucius Cornelius Maior
260.B8 Brutus, Decimus Junius, surnamed Abinus
260.B83 Brutus, Marcus Junius
260.C3 Cato, Marcus Porcius, Uticensis
Cicero, Marcus Tullius
Including as citizen and public man
Cf. PA6278+, Writings
Cf. PA6278+, Writings
260.C5 General works
260.C53 General special
260.C54 Biography before 70 B.C.
260.C55 Events of life, 70-61
260.C56 Banishment, 58-57
260.C57 Events of life, 60-51
260.C58 Events of life, 50-43

Ancient Italy. Rome to 476
History
By period
Kings and Republic, 753-27 B.C.
Fall of the Republic and establishment of the Empire, 133-27 B.C.
Biography
Individual, A-Z
Cicero, Marcus Tullius -- Continued
260.C59 Minor works
260.C7 Crassus, Lucius Licinius
260.C73 Crassus, Marcus Licinius
Triumvir with Caesar and Pompey
260.P6 Pompeius Magnus, Sextus
260.S4 Sertorius, Quintus
260.T7 Trebatius Testa, Gaius (C.)
260.V3 Valerius Messalla, Potitus
260.V4 Verres, Gaius (C.)
Julius Caesar (Gaius Julius Caesar)
261 General works on life and reign
262 General special
262.5 Pamphlets, etc.
263 First Triumvirate, 60 B.C.
264 War in Gaul, 58-56
265 Pompey and Caesar
266 Civil War, 49-45
Including Caesar's Crossing of the Rubicon, 49, the Battle of Dyrrhachium, 48, and the Battle of Pharsalus, 48
267 Dictator, 46. Death, 44
268 Second Triumvirate, 43-31
269 Other
Empire, 27 B.C.-476 A.D.
Cf. KJA2880+, Roman law
269.5 Sources and documents
270 General works
271 General special
272 Civilization. Culture. Antiquities
Including social life and customs
Cf. DG78, Civilization, culture, antiquities (General)
273 Political antiquities
Biography (Collective)
274 General works
274.3 Empresses
Constitutional empire, 27 B.C.-284 A.D.
275 Sources and documents
276 General works
276.5 General special
Twelve Caesars (Julius-Domitian), 27 B.C.-96 A.D.

Ancient Italy. Rome to 476
History
By period
Empire, 27 B.C.-476 A.D.
Constitutional empire, 27 B.C.-284 A.D.
Twelve Caesars (Julius-Domitian), 27 B.C.-96 A.D. -- Continued

277 Classical authors in English translations
For Greek or Latin texts, see subclass PA
277.5 Sources and documents
278 General works
278.3 General special
278.5 Pamphlets, etc.
279 Augustus, 27 B.C.-14 A.D.
Including the life of Livia Drusilla
For Augustus' nonpolitical writings, see PA6220.A85
Julian dynasty, 14-68
281 General works
Tiberius, 14-37
282 General works on life and reign
282.5 Germanicus Caesar
282.6 Agrippina
283 Caligula, 37-41
284 Claudius I, 41-54
Including life of Valeria Messallina
Nero, 54-68
Including the life of Poppaea Sabina
285 General works on life and reign
285.3 General special
285.7 Other
68-96. Flavian emperors
For individual Flavian emperors, see DG286+
286 General works
287 Galba, 68-69
288 Otho-Vitellius, 69
Including Revolt of Civilus
289 Vespasian, 69-79
290 Titus, 79-81
291 Domitian, 81-96
Biography, 27 B.C.-96 A.D.
291.6 Collective
291.7.A-Z Individual, A-Z
e.g.
291.7.A2 Agricola, Gnaeus (Cn.) Julius
291.7.A3 Agrippa, Marcus Vipsanius
291.7.M3 Maecenas, Gaius (C.) Cilnius
291.7.S4 Sejanus, Lucius Aelius
96-180
292 General works
Biography and memoirs
292.5 Collective

Ancient Italy. Rome to 476
History
By period
Empire, 27 B.C.-476 A.D.
Constitutional empire, 27 B.C.-284 A.D.
96-180
Biography and memoirs -- Continued
292.7.A-Z Individual, A-Z
293 Narva, 96-98
294 Trajan, 98-117
295 Hadrian, 117-138
296 Antonius Pius, 138-161
297 Marcus Aurelius, 161-180
180-284
298 General works
Biography and memoirs
298.5 Collective
298.7.A-Z Individual, A-Z
299 Commodus, 180-192
300 Septimius Severus, 193-211
301 Caracalla, 211-217
302 Macrinus, 217-218
303 Elagabalus, 218-222
304 Severus Alexander, 222-235
305 235-284
306 Maximinus, 235-238
306.3 Gordianus III, 238-244
306.5 Philippus, 244-249
306.7 Decius, 249-251
307 Gallus, 251-253
307.3 Valerian, 253-260
307.5 Gallienus, 260-268
307.7 Claudius II, 268-270
308 Aurelian, 270-275
308.3 Tacitus, 275-276
308.5 Florianus, 276
308.7 Probus, 276-282
309 Carus, 282-283
309.3 Carinus and Numerianus, 283-284
284-476. Decline and fall
310 Sources and documents
311 General works
312 Other
312.5.A-Z Biography, A-Z
Prefer individual periods, DG313+
312.5.P7 Praetextatus, Vettius Agorius
312.5.S5 Sidonius, Gaius (C.) Sollius M.A.
Diocletian, 284-305
313 General works
314 Rival Augusti, 306-324
Including life of Gaius Galerius Valerius Maximinus (Maximinus Daia), d. 313

Ancient Italy. Rome to 476
History
By period
Empire, 27 B.C.-476 A.D.
Constitutional empire, 27 B.C.-284 A.D.
284-476. Decline and fall
Diocletian, 284-305 -- Continued
314.8.A-Z Biography of contemporaries, A-Z
315 Constantine the Great, 306-337
Cf. DF557, History specifically Eastern
337-364
316 General works
316.3 Constantine II, 337-340
316.5 Constans, 337-350
316.7 Constantius II, 353-361
317 Julian, 361-363
317.5 Jovian, 363-364
317.7.A-Z Other, A-Z
Valentinian and last emperors. End of the Western Empire, 364-476
319 General works
Biography and memoirs
322 Collective
322.5.A-Z Individual, A-Z
323 Valentinian I, 364-375
Valens, see DF559
375-392
325 General works
326 Gratian, 375-383
329 Valentinian II, 375-392
Theodosius, 392-395
For general works on Theodosius as ruler of the East, 379-395, see DF560
330 General works on life and reign
331 Eugenius, 392-394
332 Honorius, 395-423
335 Joannes, 423-424
338 Valentinian III, 425-455
Including life of Galla Placidia
341 Petronius Maximus, 455
344 Avitus, 455-456
347 Majorianus, 457-461
350 Libius Severus, 461-465
353 Anthemius, 467-472
356 Olybrius, 467-472
359 Glycerius, 473
362 Julius Nepos, 474-475
365 Romulus Augustulus, 475-476
Medieval and modern Italy, 476-
401 Periodicals. Serials
402 Societies
403 Sources and documents
Collected works

Medieval and modern Italy, 476-
Collected works -- Continued
404 Several authors
405 Individual authors
413 Directories
415 Gazetteers, dictionaries, etc.
416 Guidebooks (North. Central. South)
417 General works
418 Compends
420 Monumental and picturesque. Palaces, gardens, etc.
420.5 Preservation of historic monuments, landmarks, scenery, etc.
421 Historical geography
Description and travel
421.5 History of travel
422 476-1500
423 1501-1600
424 1601-1795
425 1796-1815
426 1816-1860
427 1861-1900
428 1901-1918
429 1919-1944
430 1945-1974
430.2 1975-
431 Antiquities
Cf. DG600+, Local history and description
Social life and customs. Civilization
441 General works
442 General special
For brigands, see HV6453.A+
443 Early through 1400
445 1401-1600. Renaissance
447 1601-1789
449 1789-1815
450 1816-1945
451 1945-
453 Italian culture in foreign countries
Class here general works, or those in combinations too broad for any one country
Ethnography
455 General works
457.A-Z Individual elements in the population, A-Z
457.A35 Africans
457.A7 Albanians
457.A75 Americans
457.A77 Arabs
457.A78 Argentines
457.A79 Armenians
457.C47 Chinese
457.C74 Croats
457.E54 English
457.F7 Friulians

Medieval and modern Italy, 476-
Ethnography
Individual elements
in the population, A-Z -- Continued

457.G4 Germans
457.G7 Greeks
457.L3 Ladins
457.M67 Moroccans
457.M87 Muslims
457.N67 North Africans
457.P67 Poles
457.R65 Romanians
457.R78 Russians
457.S45 Senegalese
457.S48 Slavs
457.S5 Slovenes
457.S67 Spaniards
457.U37 Ukrainians
457.W35 Walsers

History

461 Dictionaries. Chronological tables, outlines, etc.

Biography (Collective)
For individual biography, see the special period, reign, or place

463 General works
463.2 Rulers, kings, etc.
463.4 Public men
463.6 Women

Houses, noble families, etc.

463.7 Collective
463.8.A-Z Individual, A-Z
e.g.
463.8.B7 Borgia family
463.8.C27 Caprara family
463.8.C7 Colonna family
463.8.E7 Este family
463.8.M35 Malaspina family
463.8.M37 Malatesta family
463.8.M39 Masino, Counts of
463.8.O33 Odescalchi family
463.8.S4 Sforza family

Historiography

465 General works

Biography of historians

465.5 Collective
465.7.A-Z Individual, A-Z
e.g.
465.7.B7 Botta, Carlo Giuseppe G.
465.7.G5 Giannone, Pietro, 1676-1748
465.7.G56 Giovio, Paolo, 1483-1552
Muratori, Lodovico Antonio, see DG545.8.M8
465.7.R62 Romeo, Rosario
465.7.S72 Spotorno, Giovanni Battista, 1788-1844

Medieval and modern Italy, 476-
History -- Continued
Study and teaching
465.8 General works
465.82.A-Z By region or country, A-Z
General works
Including those beginning with Roman period
466 Through 1800
467 1801-
468 Compends
469 History of two or more provinces, etc.
470 Addresses, essays, lectures (Collectively)
471 Pamphlets, etc.
473 Special aspects
General special
Military history
For individual campaigns and engagements, see the special period
480 Sources and documents
Biography (Collective)
481.A2 General
481.A3-Z Officers
482 General works
By period
483 Early and medieval
483.5 1492-1792
484 1792- . 19th-20th centuries
486 Naval history
For individual campaigns and engagements, see the special period
Political and diplomatic history. Foreign and general relations
Prefer special periods, reigns, etc. in DG500+
491 General works
492 Earliest to 768
493 768-1268
494 1268-1492
495 1492-1789
497 1789-1860
498 1861-1945
(498.2) 1945-
see DG576.8+
499.A-Z Relations with individual regions or countries, A-Z
By period
Medieval, 476-1492
General works
500 Through 1800. Chronicles
501 1801-
502 General special
476-1268
General works
503.A2 Through 1800. Chronicles

Medieval and modern Italy, 476-
History
By period
Medieval, 476-1492
476-1268
General works -- Continued
503.A3-Z 1801-
For Arabs, see DG867.1+
For Normans, see DG867.19+
476-474
504 General works
504.5 Biography (Collective)
505 Odoacer, 476-489
Gothic Kingdom, 489-553
Cf. DG657.2, Goths in Milan
506 General works
507 Theodoric, 489-526
508 Amalasuntha, 526-534
Theodat, 534-536
508.5 General works on life and reign
509 Byzantine War
509.3 Vitiges, 536-539
509.4 Ildibald, 539-541
509.5 Totila, 541-552
509.7 Teja, 552-553
509.9.A-Z Biography, A-Z
509.9.C3 Cassidorus Senator, Flavius Magnus Aurelius
510 Byzantine Exarchate, 553-568
Lombard Kingdom, 568-774
Cf. D145, Lombard migrations
511 General works
511.15 General special
511.2 Pamphlets, etc.
Biography
511.25 Collective
511.27.A-Z Individual, A-Z
Alboin, 568-573
511.4 General works
511.5 Rosamunda, Consort of Alboin
511.6 Cleph, 573-575
511.7 Interregnum, 575-584
511.8 Authari, 584-590
512 Agilulf, 590-615
512.2 Adaloald, 615-625
512.3 Arioald, 625-636
512.4 Rothari, 636-652
512.6 Rodoald, 652-653
512.7 Aribert I, 653-661
512.8 Grimoald, 662-672
513 Berthari, 672-690
513.2 Cunibert, 690-703
513.5 Liutbert, 690-703

Medieval and modern Italy, 476-
History
By period
Medieval, 476-1492
476-1268
476-474
Lombard Kingdom, 568-774 -- Continued
513.6 Raginbert, 704
513.7 Aribert II, 704-712
513.8 Ansprand, 712-713
514 Liutprand, 713-744
514.3 Rachis, 744-749
514.4 Aistulf, 749-756
514.5 Desiderius, 756-774
514.7 Lombard principalities, 9th-11th centuries
Frankish emperors, 774-962
515 General works
517 Bernardo, 810/813-818
517.5 Berengario I, 894-924
517.7 Ugo, 926-947
518 Berengario II, 950-960
519.A-Z Biography, A-Z
German emperors, 962-1268
520 General works
The Commune. Guelfs and Ghibellines
General works
522 Through 1800. Chronicles
523 1801-
527 11th century
529 12th century
1268-1492
530 General works
13th century
General works
531.A2 Through 1800
531.A3-Z 1801-
Biography
531.8.A1 Collective
531.8.A2-Z Individual, A-Z
e.g.
531.8.E8 Ezzelino da Romano
531.8.P5 Pier delle Vigne
531.8.U2 Ubaldini, Ottaviano degli, Cardinal
Renaissance. 14th-16th centuries
General works
532 Through 1800
533 1801-
1300-1492. Signorie
534 General works
14th century
535 General works
536.A-Z Biography, A-Z
e.g.

	Medieval and modern Italy, 476-
	History
	By period
	Medieval, 476-1492
	1268-1492
	Renaissance. 14th-16th centuries
	1300-1492. Signorie
	14th century
	Biography, A-Z -- Continued
536.O66	Orsini, Rinaldo, conte di Tagliacozzo
	15th century
537	General works
	Biography
537.8.A1	Collective
537.8.A2-Z	Individual, A-Z
	e.g.
537.8.B4	Bēssariōn, originally Jōannēs, cardinal
537.8.B8	Bruni, Leonardo Aretino
537.8.G2	Gattamelata, Stefano Giovanni
537.8.P7	Poggio-Bracciolini
537.8.S3	Sforza, Caterina
537.8.S5	Sigismondo, Pandolfo Malatesta, Lord of Rimini
	Modern, 1492-
	Including period of Spanish and Austrian supremacy
538	General works
	16th century. 1492-1618
539.A2	Sources and documents
	General works
539.A3-Z	Through 1800
540	1801-
	Biography and memoirs
540.8.A1	Collective
540.8.A3-Z	Individual, A-Z
	e.g.
540.8.B5	Boccalini, Traiano
540.8.C3	Castiglione, Baldassare, conte
	Cf. BJ601+, Il cortegiano
	For literary works, see PQ4617.C65
540.8.C8	Colonna, Vittoria, marchesa di Pescara
540.8.I7	Isabella d'Este, Consort of Giovanni Francesco II
540.8.M7	Morata, Olympia Fulvia
540.8.S7	Strozzi, Filippo
	1492-1527. Invasions
	General works
541.A2	Through 1800
541.A3-Z	1801-
	Biography and memoirs
541.8.A1	Collective

Medieval and modern Italy, 476-
History
By period
Modern, 1492-
16th century. 1492-1618
1492-1527. Invasions
Biography and memoirs -- Continued

541.8.A2-Z Individual, A-Z
e.g.
541.8.B3 Bayard, Pierre du Terrail, seigneur de
541.8.M4 Medici, Giovanni de' (1498-1526)

17th century
542.5 Historiography
General works
543 Through 1800
544 1801-
Biography and memoirs
544.7 Collective
544.8.A-Z Individual, A-Z
e.g.
544.8.P27 Paleotti, Cristina (Dudley), marchesa

18th century
544.9 Sources and documents
545 General works
545.5 Pamphlets, etc.
Biography and memoirs
545.8.A1 Collective
545.8.A2-Z Individual, A-Z
e.g.
545.8.G3 Galiani, Ferdinando
545.8.M8 Muratori, Lodovico Antonio

1792-1815. Napoleonic period
546 Sources and documents
547 General works
547.2 1792-1796
547.25 1796-1797
547.4 1797-1800
Kingdom of Italy
548 Sources and documents
548.2 Cispadane Republic, 1796
548.4 Transpadane Republic, 1796
548.6 Cisalpine Republic, 1797-1802
548.8 Italian Republic, 1802-1805
549 Kingdom of Italy, 1805-1814

19th century
Including 1789-1848
550.5 Historiography
551 General works
Biography and memoirs
551.7 Collective
551.8.A-Z Individual, A-Z
e.g.
551.8.B24 Balbo, Cesare, conte

Medieval and modern Italy, 476-
History
By period
Modern, 1492-
19th century
Biography and memoirs
Individual, A-Z -- Continued

551.8.G5 Gioberti, Vincenzo
551.8.R5 Ricciardi, Francesco Antonio, conte di
551.8.R65 Rossi, Pellegrino Luigi Edoardo, conte

1848-1871. Risorgimento. Wars of Independence

552.A15 Periodicals. Societies
552.A155 Congresses
552.A2 Sources and documents
552.A3-Z General works
552.5 Political and diplomatic history
552.6 Other special

Biography and memoirs

552.7 Collective
552.8.A-Z Individual, A-Z

e.g.

552.8.A985 Azeglio, Massimo Tapparelli, marchese d'
552.8.B5 Bixio, Nino, 1821-1873
552.8.C2 Capponi, Gino Alessandro G.G., marchese
552.8.C25 Cattaneo, Carlo, 1801-1869
552.8.C3 Cavour, Camillo Benso, conte di
552.8.G2 Garibaldi, Giuseppe
552.8.M3 Mazzini, Giuseppe
552.8.M4 Minghetti, Marco
552.8.O6 Orsini, Felice
552.9 Caricature and satire

1848-1849. Austro-Sardinian War

553 General works
553.2 1848
553.3 1849
553.5.A-Z Special events, battles, etc., A-Z
553.5.C78 Curtatone and Montanara, Battle of, 1848
553.5.C8 Custozza, Battle of, 1848
553.5.M5 Messina, Bombardment, 1848
553.5.N7 Novara, Battle of, 1849
553.5.S5 Sicily, Campaign in, 1849
553.5.V4 Velletri, Battle of, 1849

French expedition, 1849, see DG798.5

1859-1860

554 General works
554.3 Pamphlets, etc.
554.5.A-Z Special events, battles, etc., A-Z
554.5.E96 Expedition of the Thousand, 1860
554.5.G2 Gaeta, Siege of, 1860-1861
554.5.M2 Magenta, Battle of, 1859
554.5.S3 San Martino, Battle of, 1859
554.5.S7 Solferino, Battle of, 1859

Medieval and modern Italy, 476-
History
By period
Modern, 1492-
19th century
1859-1860
Special events,
battles, etc., A-Z -- Continued
554.5.V6 Volturno, Battle of, 1860
1871-1947. United Italy (Monarchy)
555 General works
Biography and memoirs
556.A1 Collective
556.A2-Z Individual, A-Z
e.g.
556.C7 Crispi, Francesco
556.F3 Farini, Domenico
556.M65 Monzani, Cirillo, 1820-1889
556.S6 Spaventa, Silvio
Vittorio Emanuele II, 1861-1878
557 General works on life and reign
557.5 Political and diplomatic history
557.7 Iconography
557.9 Pamphlets, etc.
558 War with Austria, 1866
Includes battles of Custozza, Lissa, etc.
559 Siege and occupation of Rome, 1870
Cf. DG798.7, End of temporal power of Papal States
Umberto I, 1878-1900
561 General works on life and reign
561.5 Personal special
562 Margherita di Savoia, Consort of Humbert I
564 Political and diplomatic history
Vittorio Emanuele III, 1900-1946
For works on his life, see DG575.A4
For works on the regency (1944-1946) and reign (May 9-June 3, 1946) of Umberto II, see DG572
566 General works on life and reign
568 General special
568.5 Political and diplomatic history
Including general and pre-Fascist
569 Pamphlets, etc.
569.5 Period of World War, 1914-1918
For the war itself, see D501+
1919-1945. Fascism
Cf. JN5657.A+, Political parties of Italy
571.A1 Periodicals. Societies. Yearbooks, etc.
571.A2 Sources and documents
571.A3-Z General works
571.16 Historiography

Medieval and modern Italy, 476-
History
By period
Modern, 1492-
1871-1947. United Italy (Monarchy)
Vittorio Emanuele III, 1900-1946
1919-1945. Fascism -- Continued

571.5 Caricature and satire
571.7 Resistance movements against Fascist regime
571.75 March on Rome, 1922
572 Period of World War II, 1939-1945. Interim regimes
Including period of double occupation (Allied and German), regency and reign of Umberto II, and period of Provisional Government, 1943-1947
Cf. D731+, World War II
Biography and memoirs
574 Collective
575.A-Z Individual, A-Z
e.g.
575.A1-A49 Royal family
575.A14 Amedeo, Duke of Aosta
575.A2 Elena, Consort of Victor Emanuel III
Humbert II, see DG575.A4
575.A4 Umberto II
575.A6 Annunzio, Gabriele d'
Cf. PQ4803+, Annunzio as a writer
575.B2 Badoglio, Pietro
575.B3 Balbo, Italo
575.C52 Ciano, Galeazzo, conte
D'Annunzio, Gabriele, see DG575.A6
De Gasperi, Alcide, see DG575.G3
575.G3 Gasperi, Alcide de
575.G5 Giolitti, Giovanni
575.G8 Guiccioli, Alessandro, marchese, 1843-1929
575.M36 Matteotti, Giacomo
575.M8 Mussolini, Benito
575.N5 Nitti, Francesco Saverio
575.R6 Rosselli, Carlo
575.S29 Salvemini, Gaetano, 1873-1957
575.T6 Togliatti, Palmiro
575.T8 Turati, Filippo
1948- . Republic
576 Periodicals. Sources and documents. Collections
576.8 General works
576.9 General special
Social life and customs. Civilization. Intellectual life, see DG451
577 Political history

Medieval and modern Italy, 476-
History
By period
Modern, 1492-
1948- . Republic -- Continued
577.2 Foreign and general relations
By period
1948-1976
577.5 General works
Biography and memoirs
578 Collective
579.A-Z Individual, A-Z
e.g.
579.E4 Einaudi, Luigi
579.N52 Nicola, Enrico de
1976-1994
581 General works
Biography and memoirs
582 Collective
583.A-Z Individual, A-Z
e.g.
583.S45 Segni, Mario
1994-
583.5 General works
Biography and memoirs
583.7 Collective
583.8.A-Z Individual, A-Z
e.g.
583.8.D55 Dini, Lamberto
Northern Italy
600 General works
600.5 Pictorial works
601 Description and travel
Guidebooks, see DG416
603 Antiquities
605 Social life and customs. Civilization
607 History
609 Other
Piedmont. Savoy
610 Periodicals. Societies. Serials
611 Sources and documents
Collected works
611.2 Several authors
611.25 Individual authors
Biography (Collective)
611.3 General works
611.5 House of Savoy
611.7 Public men
611.75 Women
611.8 Gazetteers. Directories. Dictionaries
612 Guidebooks
612.2 General works
612.5 Monumental and picturesque, etc.

Northern Italy
Piedmont. Savoy -- Continued
Description and travel
613 Through 1860
614 1861-1850
614.2 1951-
615 Antiquities
615.6 Social life and customs. Civilization
History
616 General works on Piedmont-Savoy, or Savoy alone
Early and medieval
617 General works on Piedmont-Savoy, or Savoy alone
617.1 Earliest
Savoy
General works on the counts of Savoy, see DG611.5
617.25 Umberto I, 1003-1051
617.27 Adelaide, 1035-1091
617.28 Oddone, d. 1060
617.29 Amedeo I
617.3 Amedeo II, d. 1080
617.32 Umberto II, d. 1103
617.33 Amedeo III, 1103-1148
617.34 Umberto III, 1148-1189
617.37 Tommaso I, 1189-1233
617.38 Amedeo IV, 1233-1253
617.39 Bonifacio, 1253-1263. Tommaso II, regent
617.393 Pietro II, 1263-1268
617.396 Filippo I, 1268-1285
617.4 Amedeo V, 1285-1323
617.43 Edoardo, 1323-1329
617.44 Aimone, 1329-1343
617.45 Amedeo VI, 1343-1383
617.47 Amedeo VII, 1383-1391
617.48 Amedeo VIII, 1391-1439
Piedmont
617.5 General works
617.6 Earliest
617.7 1002-1189
617.8 1189-1311
617.9 1311-1416
Modern
618 General works
15th-17th centuries
618.2 General works
618.3 Lodovico I, 1439-1465
618.31 Amedeo IX, 1465-1472
618.32 Filiberto I, 1472-1482
618.33 Carlo I, 1482-1490
618.34 Carlo II, 1490-1496
618.35 Filippo II of Bresse, 1490/1496-1497
618.36 Filiberto II, 1497-1504
618.38 Carlo III, 1504-1553

Northern Italy
Piedmont. Savoy
History
Modern
15th-17th centuries -- Continued
618.4 Emanuele Filiberto, 1553-1580
618.42 Carlo Emanuele I, 1580-1630
618.44 Vittorio Amedeo I, 1630-1637
618.45 Francesco Giacinto, 1637-1638
618.46 Carlo Emanuele II, 1638-1675
618.48 Christine of France, 1638-1648
1675-1718, see DG618.53+
Kingdom of Sardinia, 1718-1860
618.5 General works
Biography and memoirs
618.52 Collective
618.522.A-Z Individual, A-Z
Vittorio Amedeo I, 1675-1730
618.53 General works on life and reign
618.54.A-Z Biography of contemporaries, A-Z
e.g.
618.54.A7 Anne Marie d'Orléans, Consort of Victor Amadeus I
618.55 Carlo Emanuele I (III), 1730-1773
618.57 Vittorio Amedeo II, 1773-1796
Carlo Emanuele II (IV), 1796-1802
618.58 General works
618.59 Marie Clotilda, Consort of Charles Emanuel IV
618.6 Vittorio Emanuel I, 1802-1821
618.62 Carlo Felice, 1821-1831
618.64 Carlo Alberto, 1831-1849
618.66 1848-1849
Cf. DG553+, Austro-Sardinian War, 1848-1849
618.68 Vittorio Emanuele II, 1849-1860
Piedmont, 1860-
618.7 General works
618.72 1860-1945
1945-
618.75 General works
Biography and memoirs
618.77 Collective
618.78.A-Z Individual, A-Z
Genoa
Class here works on the republic, the city, and the province of Genoa
631 Periodicals. Societies. Serials
631.2 Sources and documents
Collected works
631.4 Several authors
631.5 Individual authors
631.6 Directories. Dictionaries

Northern Italy
Genoa -- Continued
Biography (Collective)
631.7 General works
Houses, noble families, etc.
631.8 Collective
631.82.A-Z Individual, A-Z
e.g.
631.82.D6 Doria family
631.82.G34 Galliera, Dukes of
631.82.G58 Giustiniani family
632 Guidebooks
632.5 Monumental and picturesque, etc.
Description
633 Through 1860
634 1861-1950
634.2 1951-
635 Antiquities
635.6 Social life and customs. Civilization
History
General works
636 Modern
636.3 Early to 1800
Early and medieval
Including Liguria
637 General works
637.15 Earliest to 774
637.2 774-1064
637.3 1064-1167 (Pisa)
637.4 1137-1339. Period of Crusades
637.5 1339-1396. 14th century
For War of Chioggia, 1378-1389, see DG677.7+
Biography and memoirs
637.52 Collective
637.53.A-Z Individual, A-Z
637.55 1392
15th century
637.57 General works
637.6 1396-1421 (France)
637.7 1421-1458 (Milan)
637.8 1458-1464 (France)
637.9 1464-1499 (Milan)
Modern
638 General works
16th century
General works
638.1 Through 1800
638.12 1801-
638.2 Fieschi Conspiracy, 1547
638.25.A-Z Biography, A-Z
e.g.
638.25.D7 Doria, Andrea, principe di Melfi
638.3 17th century

Northern Italy
 Genoa
  History
   Modern -- Continued
638.35 18th century
638.4 1789-1814
 1815-1900
638.5 General works
638.6 1815-1848
638.7 1849-1870
639 1901-
 Sections, districts, suburbs, etc.
643 Collective
643.2.A-Z Individual, A-Z
 Monuments, statues, etc.
643.4 Collective
643.5.A-Z Individual, A-Z
 Parks, squares, cemeteries, etc.
643.7 Collective
643.8.A-Z Individual, A-Z
 Streets. Bridges
644 Collective
644.2.A-Z Individual, A-Z
 Buildings
644.4 Collective
644.5.A-Z Individual, A-Z
645 Other
 Milan. Lombardy
651 Periodicals. Societies. Sources and documents
 Collected works
651.4 Several authors
651.5 Individual authors
651.6 Directories. Dictionaries
651.7 Biography (Collective)
652 Guidebooks
652.2 General works
652.5 Monumental and picturesque, etc.
 Description and travel
 Cf. DG659.52+, Milan (City)
653 Through 1860
654 1861-1950
654.2 1951-
655 Antiquities
655.6 Social life and customs. Civilization
 History
 General works
656 Modern
656.3 Early to 1800
 Early and medieval
657 General works
657.1 Early to 452
657.2 452-774. Huns, Goths, Lombards
657.3 774-1100

Northern Italy
  Milan. Lombardy
    History
      Early and medieval -- Continued
        1101-1237
657.35 General works
657.37 Friedrich I Barbarossa, 1158-1185
657.4 Lombard League, 1167-1183
657.45 Battle of Legnano, 1176
        1237-1535
657.5 General works
657.65 1237-1311. Terriani period
          1311-1447
            Including earlier Visconti period
657.7 General works
            Biography and memoirs
657.72 Collective
657.73.A-Z Individual, A-Z
657.75 1447-1450. Ambrosian Republic
          1447-1535. Sforza (Duchy of Milan)
657.8 General works
657.9.A-Z Biography, A-Z
              e.g.
657.9.B4 Beatrice d'Este, Consort of Lodovico Sforza, il Moro, Duke of Milan
657.9.B5 Bianca Maria Visconti, Duchess of Milan
657.9.G3 Galeazzo Maria Sforza, Duke of Milan
657.9.I7 Isabella d'Argona, Consort of Gian Galeazzo Sforza, Duke of Milan
      Modern
658 General works
658.1 1535-1714. Spanish period
        1714-1796. Austrian period
658.2 General works
          Biography
658.23 Collective
658.25.A-Z Individual, A-Z
        1796-1900
658.3 General works
658.4 1796-1815
658.5 1815-1859. Lombardo-Venetian Kingdom
658.6 1860-1900
658.7.A-Z Biography, 1796-1900, A-Z
            e.g.
658.7.M3 Maffei, Clara (Carrara-Spinelli), contessa
658.8 1901-
    Milan (City)
659.52 Guidebooks
659.54 Description
659.56 Pictorial works
      Ethnography
659.58 General works
659.6.A-Z Individual elements in the population, A-Z

Northern Italy
Milan. Lombardy
Milan (City)
Ethnography
Individual elements in the population, A-Z -- Continued

659.6.F74 French
659.6.S45 Senegalese
History
659.7 General works
By period
660 Through 1860
661 1861-1945
1946-
662 General works
Biography and memoirs
662.2 Collective
662.25.A-Z Individual, A-Z
Sections, districts, suburbs, etc.
663 Collective
663.2.A-Z Individual, A-Z
Monuments, statues, etc.
663.3 Collective
663.5.A-Z Individual, A-Z
Parks, squares, cemeteries, etc.
663.7 Collective
663.8.A-Z Individual, A-Z
Canals
663.9 Collective
663.92.A-Z Individual, A-Z
Streets, bridges, gates, etc.
664 Collective
664.2.A-Z Individual, A-Z
Buildings
664.3 Collective
664.5.A-Z Individual, A-Z

Venice
670 Periodicals. Societies. Serials
671 Sources and documents
Collected works
671.2 Several authors
671.3 Individual authors
Biography (Collective)
671.4 General works
671.43 Women
671.45 Public men
671.5 Rulers, doges, etc.
671.6.A-Z Houses, noble families, etc., A-Z
672 Guidebooks
672.2 General works
Historic monuments, landmarks, etc. (General)
672.4 General works
672.5 Preservation

Northern Italy
Venice -- Continued
Description
673 Through 1860
674 1861-1950
674.2 1951-
674.7 Pictorial works
675 Antiquities
675.6 Social life and customs. Civilization
Ethnography
675.62 General works
675.63.A-Z Individual elements in the population, A-Z
675.63.A84 Asians
675.63.G75 Greeks
History
Historiography
675.7 General works
Biography of historians
675.72 Collective
675.73.A-Z Individual, A-Z
General works
676 Modern
676.3 Early to 1800
676.5 Outlines, syllabi, etc.
676.8 Military history
Political history
For specific periods, see the period
676.88 Sources and documents
676.9 General works
Foreign and general relations
For works on relations with a specific country regardless of period, see DG676.97.A+
For general works on the diplomatic history of a period, see the period
676.93 Sources and documents
676.95 General works
676.97.A-Z Relations with individual regions or countries, A-Z
Early and medieval
General works
677.A2 Through 1800
677.A3-Z 1801-
Early to 811
677.1.A2 Early works through 1800
677.1.A3-Z Works, 1801-
697-810
677.3 General works
677.33 Paolo Lucio Anafesto, 697-717
677.331 Marcello Tegaliano, 717-726
677.332 Orso Ipato, 726-737
677.333 Deodato, 732-755
677.334 Gallo Gaulo, 755-756
677.335 Domenico Monegario, 756-764

Northern Italy
Venice
History
Early and medieval
697-810 -- Continued

677.336 Maurizio Galbajo, 764-787
677.337 Giovanni Galbajo, 787-804
677.338 Obelerio Antenorio, 804-810

811-991

677.35 General works
677.37 Agnello Partecipazio, 811-827
677.371 Giustiniano Partecipazio, 827-829
677.372 Giovanni Partecipazio I, 828-836
677.373 Pietro Tradonico, 836-864
677.374 Orso Partecipazio I, 864-881
677.375 Giovanni Partecipazio II, 881-883
677.376 Pietro Candiano I, 887
677.377 Pietro Tribuno, 888-912
677.378 Orso Partecipazio II, 912-932
677.379 Pietro Candiano II, 932-939
677.38 Pietro Partecipazio, 939-942
677.381 Pietro Candiano III, 942-959
677.382 Pietro Candiana IV, 959-976
677.383 Pietro Orseolo I, 976-978
677.384 Vitale Candiano, 978-979
677.385 Tribuno Memmo, 979-991

991-1096. Relations with Constantinople
Cf. DF553+, Early history of Eastern Empire
Cf. DR481, Early history of Turkey

677.4 General works
677.43 Pietro Orseolo II, 991-1008
677.44 Ottone Orseolo, 1008-1026
677.45 Pietro Centranico, 1026-1031
677.46 Domenico Flabianico, 1032-1043
677.47 Domenico Contrarini, 1043-1070
677.48 Domenico Selvo, 1071-1084
677.49 Vitale Falier, 1085-1096

1096-1172. Crusades. Normans

677.5 General works
677.53 Vitale Michiel I, 1096-1102
677.531 Ordelafo Falier, 1102-1116
677.532 Domenico Michiel, 1117-1130
677.533 Pietro Polani, 1130-1148
677.534 Domenico Morosini, 1148-1156
677.535 Vitale Michiel II, 1156-1172

1172-1311. 13th century

677.6 General works
677.62 Sebastiano Ziani, 1172-1178
677.63 Orio Malipiero, 1178-1192
677.64 Enrico Dandolo, 1192-1205. Fourth crusade
677.65 Pietro Ziani, 1205-1229
677.66 Jacopo Tiepolo, 1229-1249

Northern Italy
Venice
History
Early and medieval
1172-1311. 13th century -- Continued
677.67 Marino Morosini, 1249-1253
677.671 Renier Zeno, 1253-1268
677.672 Lorenzo Tiepolo, 1268-1275
677.673 Jacopo Contarini, 1275-1280
677.674 Giovanni Dandolo, 1280-1289
677.68 Pietro Gradenigo, 1289-1311. Council of ten
1311-1382. 14th century
Including war with Turks and War of Chioggia, 1378-1380
677.7 General works
677.75 Marino Zorzi, 1311-1312
677.76 Giovanni Soranzo, 1312-1328
677.79 Francesco Dandolo, 1329-1339
677.793 Bartolomeo Gradenigo, 1339-1342
677.796 Andrea Dandolo, 1343-1354
677.8 Marino Falier, 1354-1355
677.81 Giovanni Gradenigo, 1355-1356
677.82 Giovanni Dolfin, 1356-1361
677.83 Lorenzo Celsi, 1361-1365
677.84 Marco Cornaro. 1365-1368
677.845 Andrea Contarini, 1368-1382
1381-1501. 15th century
677.85 General works
677.9 Michele Morosini, 1382
677.91 Antonio Venier, 1382-1400
677.92 Michele Steno, 1400-1413
677.93 Tommaso Mocegnigo, 1414-1423
677.94 Francesco Foscari, 1423-1457
677.95 Pasquale Malipiero, 1457-1462
677.96 Cristoforo Moro, 1462-1471
677.97 Nicolò Tron, 1471-1473
677.98 Nicolò Marcello, 1473-1474
677.981 Pietro Mocenigo, 1474-1476
677.982 Andrea Vendramin, 1476-1478
677.983 Giovanni Mocenigo, 1478-1485
677.984 Marco Barbarigo, 1485-1486
677.985 Agostino Barbarigo, 1486-1501
677.99.A-Z Biography of contemporaries, A-Z
e.g.
677.99.B3 Barbaro, Francesco
677.99.C6 Celleoni, Bartolomeo
677.99.D37 Dario, Giovanni, 1414?-1494
677.99.G5 Giuliano, Andrea
677.99.Z4 Zeno, Carlo
Modern
678 General works
678.2 Turkish wars, 1453-1571
Cf. DR501+, History of Turkey, 1451-1571

Northern Italy
Venice
History
Modern
16th century -- Continued
678.22 Sources and documents
General works
678.23 Through 1800
678.235 1801-
Biography and memoirs
678.24.A1 General works
678.24.A2-Z Individual, A-Z
e.g.
678.24.B3 Barbaro, Marco Antonio
678.24.S3 Sanuto, Marino
Leonardo Loredano, 1501-1521
678.25 General works
678.26 League of Cambrai, 1508
678.28 Antonio Grimani, 1521-1523
678.281 Andrea Gritti, 1523-1538
678.282 Pietro Lando, 1539-1545
678.283 Francesco Donato, 1545-1553
678.284 Antonio Marco Trevisan, 1553-1554
678.285 Francesco Venier, 1554-1556
678.286 Lorenzo Priuli, 1556-1559
678.287 Girolamo Priuli, 1559-1567
678.288 Pietro Loredano, 1567-1570
678.289 Alvise Mocenigo I, 1570-1577
678.29 Sebastiano Venier, 1577-1578
678.291 Nicoló da Ponte, 1578-1585
678.292 Pasquale Cicogna, 1585-1595
1595-1718. 17th century
General works
678.3 Through 1800
678.31 1801-
Mariano Grimani, 1595-1605. Papal Conflict
678.315 General works
678.317 Paolo Sarpi
Class here biographical works
For his works, see DG678.315
678.32 Spanish conspiracy, 1618
1644-1718. Period of war with Turkey over Candia
For works on the war itself, see DR534.2+
General works
678.33 Through 1800
678.34 1801-
678.36 Leonardo Donato, 1606-1612
678.361 Marc' Antonio Memmo, 1612-1615
678.362 Giovanni Bembo, 1615-1618
678.363 Nicoló Donato, 1618
678.364 Antonio Priuli, 1618-1623
678.365 Francesco Contarini, 1623-1624

Northern Italy
Venice
History
Modern
1595-1718. 17th century -- Continued
678.366 Giovanni Cornaro, 1625-1629
678.367 Nicoló Contarini, 1630-1631
678.368 Francesco Erizzo, 1631-1646
678.369 Francesco Molin, 1646-1655
678.37 Carlo Contarini, 1655-1656
678.371 Francesco Cornaro, 1656
678.372 Bertucci Valier, 1656-1658
678.373 Giovanni Pesaro, 1658-1659
678.374 Domenico Contarini, 1659-1675
678.375 Nicolò Sagredo, 1675-1676
678.376 Luigi Contarini, 1684-1688
678.377 Marcantonio Giustiniani, 1684-1688
678.378 Francesco Morosini, 1688-1694
678.379 Silvestro Valier, 1694-1700
678.38 Alvise Mocenigo II, 1700-1709
678.381 Giovanni Cornaro II, 1709-1722
678.39 Peace of Passarowitz, 1718
1718-1797. Fall of the Republic
678.4 General works
Biography and memoirs
678.42 Collective
678.43.A-Z Individual, A-Z
678.45 Alvise Sebastiano Mocenigo III, 1722-1732
678.454 Carlo Ruzzini, 1732-1735
678.457 Alvise Pisani, 1735-1741
678.46 Pietro Grimani, 1741-1752
678.47 Francesco Loredano, 1752-1762
678.474 Marco Foscarini, 1752-1763
678.478 Alvise Mocenigo IV, 1763-1778
678.48 Paolo Renier, 1779-1789
678.49 Ludovico Manin, 1789-1797
1797-1900
678.5 General works
1797-1866
678.51 General works
678.53 1797-1814
678.54 1815-1848
For works dealing with the Lombardo-Venetian Kingdom as a whole, see DG658.5
678.55 1848-1866
Including life of Daniele Manin
678.6 1866-1900
678.7.A-Z Biography and memoirs, 1797-1900, A-Z
e.g.
678.7.M3 Maurogonato, Isacco Pesaro
678.8 1901-
679 Other

Northern Italy
Venice -- Continued
Sections, districts, individual islands, etc.
684.15 Collective
684.16.A-Z Individual, A-Z
Monuments, statues, etc.
684.2 Collective
684.22.A-Z Individual, A-Z
Parks, squares, cemeteries, etc.
684.3 Collective
684.32.A-Z Individual, A-Z
Canals
684.4 Collective
684.42.A-Z Individual, A-Z
Streets. Bridges
684.5 Collective
684.52.A-Z Individual, A-Z
684.6 Lagoons (General)
Including dikes, levees, etc.
For threat of destruction, see DG672.5
Buildings
684.7 Collective
684.72.A-Z Individual, A-Z
Other cities of the Republic, see DG975.A+
Central Italy
691 General works
691.5 Biography (Collective)
692 Description and travel
Guidebooks, see DG416
694 Antiquities
Tuscany. Florence
731 Periodicals. Societies. Serials
731.15 Congresses
731.2 Sources and documents
Collected works
731.4 Several authors
731.5 Individual authors
731.6 Directories
Biography (Collective)
For individual biography, see the specific period, reign or place
731.7 General works
Houses, noble families, etc.
731.8 Collective
731.82.A-Z Individual houses, families, etc., A-Z
732 Guidebooks
732.5 General works
732.7 Preservation of historic monuments, landmarks, scenery, etc.
Description and travel
733 Through 1860
734 1861-1950
734.2 1951-1980

Central Italy
Tuscany. Florence
Description and travel -- Continued
734.23 1981-
734.4 Pictorial works
735 Antiquities
735.6 Social life and customs. Civilization
Ethnography
735.7 General works
735.72.A-Z Individual elements in the population, A-Z
735.72.C48 Chinese
History
735.8 Historiography
General works
736 Modern
736.3 Early through 1800
736.5 General special
Medieval
737.A15 Sources and documents
General works
737.A2 Through 1800
737.A3-Z 1801-
Early
General works
737.2 Through 1800
737.22 1801-
Biography
737.24.A1 Collective
737.24.A2-Z Individual, A-Z
e.g.
737.24.H9 Hugo, of Tuscany
737.24.M4 Matilde, Countess of Tuscany
14th century
General works
737.25 Through 1800
737.26 1801-
Biography and memoirs
737.27 Collective
737.28.A-Z Individual, A-Z
Modern
737.3 General works
Early modern. Medicean period
737.4 General works
737.42 Biography of Medici family
15th century
General works
737.5 Through 1800
737.55 1801-
Biography and memoirs
737.58.A1 Collective
737.58.A2-Z Individual, A-Z
e.g.
737.58.S7 Strozzi, Alessandra (Macinghi)

Central Italy
Tuscany. Florence
History
Modern
Early modern. Medicean period
15th century -- Continued

737.6 Giovanni, d. 1429
737.7 Cosimo il Vecchio, 1429-1464
737.8 Pietro I, 1464-1469
737.9 Lorenzo il Magnifico, 1469-1492
737.95 Pietro II, 1492-1494
737.97 Savonarola, Girolamo, 1452-1498

16th century
738 General works
738.13 1494-1530
Biography and memoirs
738.14.A1 Collective
738.14.A2-Z Individual, A-Z
e.g.
738.14.B5 Bianca Cappello, Consort of Francesco Maria de' Medici
738.14.G53 Giannotti, Donato, 1492-1573
738.14.G9 Guicciardini, Francesco
738.14.M2 Machiavelli, Niccolò
For literary works, see PQ4627.M2
738.15 Alessandro, 1532-1537
738.17 Cosimo I, 1537-1574
738.19 Francesco Maria, 1574-1587
738.21 Ferdinando I, 1587-1609

1609-1737
738.22 General works
738.23 Cosimo II, 1609-1621
738.25 Ferdinando II, 1621-1670
738.27 Cosimo III, 1670-1723
738.28 Giovanni Gastone, 1723-1737
Biography and memoirs
738.29.A1 Collective
738.29.A2-Z Individual, A-Z

1737-
738.3 General works
1737-1801. Lorraine dynasty
738.32 General works
738.33 General special
738.34 Francis II, 1737-1765
738.35 Leopold I, 1765-1790
738.37 Ferdinand III, 1790-1801 (1824)
Biography and memoirs
738.39.A1 Collective
738.39.A2-Z Individual, A-Z

19th century
738.4 General works
Napoleonic period
738.42 General works

Central Italy
Tuscany. Florence
History
Modern
1737-
19th century
Napoleonic period -- Continued
1801-1807. Kingdom of Etruria
738.43 General works
738.435 Maria Luigia, Consort of Louis I, King of Etruria
738.44 1808-1814. Under France
1815-1860
738.5 General works
Biography and memoirs
738.6.A1 Collective
738.6.A2-Z Individual, A-Z
e.g.
738.6.R5 Ricasoli, Bettino, barone
1860-1945
738.7 General works
Biography and memoirs
738.79.A1 Collective
738.79.A2-Z Individual, A-Z
1945-
738.792 General works
Biography and memoirs
738.793 Collective
738.794.A-Z Individual, A-Z
739 Other
Local (Florence)
Sections, districts, suburbs, etc.
755 Collective
755.3.A-Z Individual, A-Z
Monuments, statues, etc.
756 Collective
756.3.A-Z Individual, A-Z
Parks, squares, cemeteries, etc.
757.3 Collective
757.3.A-Z Individual, A-Z
e.g.
757.3.C37 Cascine
Streets, bridges, gates, etc.
758 Collective
758.3.A-Z Individual, A-Z
Buildings
759 Collective
759.3.A-Z Individual, A-Z
Other Tuscan cities, see DG975.A+
Papal States (States of the Church). Holy See. Vatican City
Cf. BX800+, Catholic Church
791 Periodicals. Societies. Serials

Central Italy
Papal States (States of the Church). Holy See. Vatican City -- Continued

791.2 Sources and documents

Collected works

791.4 Several authors

791.5 Individual authors

792 Guidebooks

792.5 Monumental and picturesque, etc.

Description and travel

793 Through 1860

794 1861-

795 Antiquities

795.6 Social life and customs. Civilization

History

795.7 Biography (Collective)

Houses, noble families, etc.

795.75 Collective

795.76.A-Z Individual, A-Z

e.g.

795.76.T88 Tuscolo, Counts of

General works

796 Modern

796.3 Early to 1800

796.5 Military and naval history

For the Swiss papal guards, see UA749.5

796.7.A-Z Special aspects, A-Z

Including elements in the population

796.7.B7 British

796.7.F7 French

Early and medieval

797 General works

797.1 Earliest to Pepin, 756

797.2 756-962. Period of Carolingian emperors

797.3 962-1309. Hohenstaufen, etc.

"Babylonian captivity," 1309-1377

797.5 General works

797.55.A-Z Biography, A-Z

e.g.

797.55.A5 Albornoz, Gil Alvarez Carrillo de, Cardinal

797.6 1377-1499

For Alexander VI, pope, see BX1312

1499-1870

797.7 General works

1499-1605

797.8 General works

Cesare Borgia

797.82 General works

797.825 Charlotte d'Albret, duchesse de Valentinois

797.83 Lucrezia Borgia

1605-1700

797.9 General works

Central Italy
Papal States (States of the Church). Holy See. Vatican City
History
1499-1870
1605-1700 -- Continued
Biography and memoirs
797.92 Collective
797.93.A-Z Individual, A-Z
798 1700-1798
798.2 1798-1799. Roman Republic
1799-1870. 19th century
798.3 General works
Biography and memoirs
798.33 Collective
798.34.A-Z Individual, A-Z
798.35 1799-1848
1848-1870
798.4 General works
798.5 1848-1849. Roman Republic
798.6 1859-1870
798.7 1870. End of temporal power
Cf. DG559, Siege and occupation of Rome, 1870
799 Holy See, 1870-
800 Vatican City, 1929-
Rome (Modern city)
803 Periodicals. Societies. Serials
803.5 Biography (Collective)
For individual biography, see the specific period, reign, or place
Houses, noble families, etc.
803.55 Collective
803.6.A-Z Individual houses, families, etc., A-Z
e.g.
803.6.P67 Porcari family
804 Guidebooks. Directories. Dictionaries
804.2 General works
804.5 Preservation of historic monuments, landmarks, scenery, etc.
Description
805 Through 1860
806 1861-1950
806.2 1951-
806.8 Pictorial works
Antiquities (Medieval, etc.)
Including description of the city in Medieval and Renaissance times
807 General works
807.4 Catacombs
807.6 Social life and customs. Civilization
Ethnography
807.7 General works

Central Italy
Rome (Modern city)
Ethnography -- Continued
807.8.A-Z Individual elements in the population, A-Z
807.8.B75 British
807.8.P65 Poles
807.8.S64 Spaniards
History
808 General works
809 General special
Medieval
811 General works
811.6 Rienzo, Cola di
Modern
812 General works
15th century. Renaissance
812.1 General works
812.12 1527. Siege
16th-18th centuries
812.4 General works
812.6.A-Z Biography, A-Z
e.g.
812.6.C4 Cenci, Beatrice
812.7 Napoleonic period, 1809-1814
1815-1870
812.9 General works
Biography and memoirs
812.92 Collective
812.93.A-Z Individual, A-Z
1871-1945
813 General works
Biography and memoirs
813.12 Collective
813.15.A-Z Individual, A-Z
1945-
813.2 General works
Biography and memoirs
813.22 Collective
813.23.A-Z Individual, A-Z
814 Other
Local
For localities, buildings, or objects possessing archaeological interest, see DG61 +
Sections, districts, suburbs, etc.
814.95 Collective
815.A-Z Individual, A-Z
Monuments, statues, etc.
815.19 Collective
815.2.A-Z Individual, A-Z
Cemeteries
815.29 Collective
815.3.A-Z Individual, A-Z
Fountains

Central Italy
Rome (Modern city)
Local
Fountains -- Continued
815.39 Collective
815.4.A-Z Individual, A-Z
Parks, squares, etc.
815.49 Collective
815.5.A-Z Individual, A-Z
815.7 River front (Tiber)
Streets, bridges, gates, etc.
815.89 Collective
815.9.A-Z Individual, A-Z
Buildings
816 General works
Churches and monasteries
816.29 Collective
816.3.A-Z Individual, A-Z
e.g.
816.3.S26 San Giovanni in Laterano
816.3.S33 San Pietro in Vaticano
Palaces and villas
816.49 Collective
816.5.A-Z Individual, A-Z
e.g.
816.5.S3 Castel Sant'Angelo
Public buildings
816.9 General works
817.A-Z Individual, A-Z
e.g.
817.C6 Palazzo della Consulta
817.M3 Palazzo Madama
817.3.A-Z Other buildings, A-Z
Suburbs, see DG814.95+
Southern Italy
819 Periodicals. Societies. Serials
820 General works
820.5 Pictorial works
820.8 Historical geography
821 Description and travel
Guidebooks, see DG416
823 Antiquities
825 Social life and customs. Civilization
Ethnography
825.4 General works
825.5.A-Z Individual elements in the population, A-Z
825.5.A44 Albanians
825.5.G73 Greeks
History
Cf. DG845.8+, Naples. Kingdom of the Two Sicilies
Cf. DG865.9+, Sicily
826 General works

Southern Italy
History -- Continued
By period
Early (Southern Italy), see DG53
Early (Magna Graecia), see DG55.M3
827 Medieval
Cf. DG847.15+, Hohenstaufen period
Cf. DG861+, Byzantine, Saracen, and Norman domination
Modern
828 General works
By period
828.2 1442-1860
Cf. DG848+, Kingdom of Naples
1860-1945
828.3 General works
Biography and memoirs
828.32 General
828.34.A-Z Individual, A-Z
828.5 1945-
829 Other
831 Sicily and Malta
Cf. DG987+, Malta
Naples. Kingdom of the Two Sicilies
840 Periodicals. Societies. Serials
841 Sources and documents
841.2 Collections, by individual authors
Biography (Collective)
841.4 General works
841.5 Rulers, kings, queens, etc.
841.55 Public men
Houses, noble families, etc.
841.6.A1 Collective
841.6.A2-Z Individual, A-Z
e.g.
841.6.B68 Bourbon-Two Sicilies, House of
841.6.C3 Carafa family
841.6.P63 Poerio family
842 Guidebooks. Directories. Dictionaries
842.3 General works
842.5 Monumental and picturesque, etc.
842.6 Preservation of historic monuments, etc.
842.7 Historical geography
Description and travel
Cf. DG821, Southern Italy
843 Through 1860
844 1861-1950
844.2 1951-

Southern Italy
Naples. Kingdom of the Two Sicilies -- Continued
845 Antiquities
For Magna Graecia, see DG55.M3
For other local Roman and pre-Roman antiquities, see DG70.A+
For pre-Roman and Roman antiquities of Naples, see DG70.N35
845.6 Social life and customs. Civilization. Intellectual life
For specific periods, see the period or reign
Ethnography
845.65 General works
845.66.A-Z Individual elements in the population, A-Z
845.66.G47 Germans
History
Cf. DG865.9+, Sicily
Historiography
845.8 General works
Biography of historians, area studies specialists, archaeologists, etc.
845.83 Collective
845.85.A-Z Individual, A-Z
General works
Including Southern Italy
Cf. DG826+, Southern Italy
Cf. DG861+, Sicily
846 Modern
846.3 Early to 1800
846.55 Political history
For specific periods, see the period
846.6 Sources and documents
846.62 General works
Early and medieval
General works
847.A2 Through 1800
847.A3-Z 1801-
Early (Post-Roman) to 1016
Cf. DG70.N35, Pre-Roman and Roman period
847.1 Sources and documents
847.11 General works
1016-1268
847.13 General works
Biography and memoirs
847.135 Collective
847.136.A-Z Individual, A-Z
847.14 1016-1194. Norman period
For individual rulers, see DG867.24+
1194-1268. Hohenstaufen period
847.15 General works
847.16 Heinrich VI, 1194-1197
847.162 Friedrich I (Emperor Friedrich II), 1197-1250

Southern Italy
Naples. Kingdom of the Two Sicilies
History
Early and medieval
1016-1268
1194-1268. Hohenstaufen
period -- Continued
847.164 Konrad IV, 1250-1254
847.166 Konradin, 1254-1268
847.168 Manfredi, 1258-1266
1268-1442. Anjou dynasty
847.17 General works
847.2 Charles I, 1266-1285
847.3 Charles II, 1285-1309
847.4 Robert, 1309-1343
847.5 Jeanne (Giovanna) I, 1343-1382
847.55 Charles III of Durazzo, 1381-1386
847.58 Louis I, 1381-1382
847.6 Wladislaw, 1386-1414
847.65 Louis II, 1386-1390
847.7 Jeanne (Giovanna) II, 1414-1435
847.8 René I, 1435-1442
For biography, see DC102.8.R4
Modern
848 General works
1442-1707. Spanish rule
848.05 Sources and documents
848.1 General works
848.112.A-Z Biography and memoirs, A-Z
e.g.
848.112.A4 Alfonso V, el Magnánimo
Cf. DP133.1, Spain
848.112.F47 Ferdinando II, d'Aragona, King of Naples, 1467-1496
848.112.P47 Pescara, Alfonso d'Avalos, marchese di, ca. 1450-1495
848.115 1442-1504
848.12 1504-1647
848.13 1647-1648. Masaniello
848.15 1648-1707
1707-1735. Austrian rule
848.2 General works
Biography and memoirs
848.23 Collective
848.24.A-Z Individual, A-Z
1735-1861. Bourbon dynasty
848.3 General works
Carlos III, 1735-1759
848.32 Sources and documents
848.33 General works
Biography and memoirs
848.335 Collective
848.34.A-Z Individual, A-Z

Southern Italy
Naples. Kingdom of the Two Sicilies
History
Modern
1735-1861. Bourbon dynasty -- Continued
1759-1815
848.35 General works
848.37.A-Z Biography and memoirs, A-Z
848.37.C3 Carolina Maria, Consort of Ferdinand I, King of the Two Sicilies
848.37.C8 Cuoco, Vincenzo
Maria Carolina, Queen, Consort of Ferdinand I, King of the Two Sicilies, 1752-1814, see DG848.37.C3
848.37.T3 Tanucci, Bernardo, marchese
848.38 Parthenopean Republic, 1799
19th century
848.4 General works
1798-1815
848.42 General works
1806-1815
848.43 General works
848.44 Joseph Bonaparte, 1806-1808
For biography, see DC216.5
848.45 Murat, 1808-1815
For biography, see DC198.M8
1815-1860. Kingdom of the Two Sicilies
848.46 General works
848.48.A-Z Biography and memoirs, A-Z
Ferdinando I, 1815-1825
848.5 General works on life and reign
848.51 1820-1821
848.52 Francesco I, 1825-1830
Ferdinando II, 1830-1859
848.53 General works on life and reign
848.537 María Cristina di Savoia, Consort of Ferdinand II
848.55 1848-1861
848.56 Pamphlets, etc.
848.57 Francesco II, 1859-1860
Expedition of the Thousand, 1860, see DG554.5.E96
1860-1900
848.58 General works
848.6.A-Z Biography and memoirs, A-Z
e.g.
848.6.M2 Maria Sofia Amelia, Consort of Francis II
20th century
849 General works
Biography and memoirs
849.9 Collective
850.A-Z Individual, A-Z
851 1945-

Southern Italy
Naples. Kingdom of the Two Sicilies -- Continued
855 Other
Local
Sections, districts, suburbs, etc.
856 Collective
856.2.A-Z Individual, A-Z
Monuments, statues, etc.
856.3 Collective
856.5.A-Z Individual, A-Z
Parks, squares, cemeteries, etc.
856.7 Collective
856.8.A-Z Individual, A-Z
Streets. Bridges
857 Collective
857.2.A-Z Individual, A-Z
Buildings
857.3 Collective
857.5.A-Z Individual, A-Z
Other cities of the Kingdom of Naples, see DG975.A+
Sicily
861 Periodicals. Societies. Serials
861.2 Sources and documents
Collected works
861.4 Several authors
861.5 Individual authors
861.6 Gazetteers. Dictionaries, etc. Place names
861.7 Biography (Collective)
862 Guidebooks
862.4 General works
862.5 Pictorial works
Historic monuments, landmarks, etc.
862.53 General works
862.55 Preservation
862.57 Historical geography
Description and travel
863 Through 1860
864 1861-1950
864.2 1951-1980
864.3 1981-
865 Antiquities
865.6 Social life and customs. Civilization
Ethnography
865.7 General works
865.8.A-Z Individual elements in the population, A-Z
865.8.A4 Albanians
865.8.B7 British
History
Including history of early southern Italy
For ancient history, see DG55.S5
Historiography
865.9 General works
Biography of historians

Southern Italy
Sicily
History
Historiography
Biography of historians -- Continued
865.915 Collective
865.92.A-Z Individual, A-Z
General works
866 Modern
866.3 Early to 1800
Early and medieval to 1409
General works
867.A2 Through 1800
867.A3-Z 1801-
Saracen period, 827-1016
867.1 Collections
867.11 Arabic authors
European authors
867.12 Through 1800
867.13 1801-
Norman period, 1016-1194
For Norman expeditions before 1016, see D148
867.19 Sources and documents
867.2 General works
867.21 General special
Biography and memoirs
867.214 Collective
867.215.A-Z Individual, A-Z
867.215.R64 Roger Guiscard, Duke of Apulia, Calabria, and Sicily, ca. 1015-1085
867.215.S53 Sichelgaita, di Salerno, d. 1090
867.22 1016-1061
Norman rulers, 1061-1194
867.24 Roger I, 1061-1194
867.245 Simon, 1101-1105
867.25 Roger II, 1105-1154
867.26 William I, 1154-1166
867.27 William II, 1166-1189
867.275 Tancredi, 1190-1194
Sicily under the Hohenstaufen, 1194-1268
867.28 General works
867.29 General special
For individual rulers, see DG847.15+
867.299 1268-1282
867.3 Sicilian Vespers, 1282
1282-1409
867.33 Sources and documents
867.34 General works
Biography and memoirs
867.348 Collective
867.349.A-Z Individual, A-Z
e.g.

Southern Italy
Sicily
History
Early and medieval to 1409
1282-1409
Biography and memoirs
Individual, A-Z -- Continued

867.349.C67 Costanza, di Svevia, Queen of Aragon and Sicily, 1247?-1302
867.35 Pedro de Aragón, 1282-1285
867.4 Jaime, 1285-1295
867.5 Federico II, 1296-1337
867.6 Pedro II, 1337-1342
867.65 Luis, 1342-1355
867.7 Federico III, 1355-1377
867.8 María, etc., 1377-1409

Modern, 1409-
868 General works
868.2 1409-1504
868.3 1504-1648
1648-1806
868.35 General works
Biography and memoirs
868.358 Collective
868.359.A-Z Individual, A-Z
19th century
868.4 General works
868.42 1806-1815
868.44 1815-1871
Expedition of the Thousand, 1860, see DG554.5.E96
868.5 1871-1900
869 20th century
869.2 1900-1945
1945-
869.3 General works
Biography and memoirs
869.34 Collective
869.35.A-Z Individual, A-Z
875 Other
972 Islands of Italy (Collectively)
For individual islands or groups of islands, see DG975.A+
For Sicily, see DG861+
975.A-Z Cities (other than metropolitan), provinces, etc., A-Z
Class here modern and general history, including ancient and medieval
For ancient cities and towns, see DG70.A+
For ancient regions and provinces, see DG55+
975.A2 Abruzzi
975.A224 Alassio
975.A3 Alessandria
Alto Adige, see DG975.B68

Cities (other than metropolitan), provinces, etc., A-Z -- Continued

	Amalfi
975.A415	Serials. Collections
975.A42	Description
975.A43	History
975.A44	Other
	Ancona
975.A48	Serials. Collections
975.A49	General works. Description
975.A5	History
975.A51	Other
975.A598	Aosta
975.A6	Aosta, Valley of
975.A617	Apennines
975.A65	Apulia. Puglia
	Aquilia, see DG975.L24
975.A68	Aquileia
975.A7	Arezzo
975.A75	Arno River and Valley
975.A78	Ascoli Piceno
975.A8	Assisi
	Asti
975.A83	Serials. Collections
975.A84	General works. Description
975.A85	History
975.A86	Other
975.A935	Avesa
975.B25	Bari
975.B27	Barletta
975.B3	Basilicata. Lucania
	Belluno
975.B39	Serials. Collections
975.B4	History and description
975.B41	Other
	Benevento
975.B43	Serials. Collections
975.B44	General works. Description
975.B45	History
975.B46	Other
	Bergamo
975.B48	Serials. Collections
975.B49	General works. Description
975.B5	History
975.B51	Other
975.B54	Biella
	Bologna
975.B57	Serials. Collections
975.B58	Guidebooks
975.B59	Description
	Biography
975.B593A1-B593A3	Collective
975.B593A4-B593Z	Individual, A-Z

	Cities (other than metropolitan), provinces, etc., A-Z
	Bologna -- Continued
975.B595	Antiquities
975.B596	Social life and customs. Civilization. Intellectual life
	History
975.B6	General works
975.B61	Medieval
975.B62	Early modern
975.B63	Napoleonic
975.B64	19th-20th centuries
975.B65	Other
975.B68	Bolzano
975.B73	Borromean Islands
	Brescia
975.B77	Serials
975.B78	Sources and documents
975.B785	Gazetteers
975.B79	Description. Guidebooks
975.B8	Biography
975.B81	Antiquities
975.B82	Social life and customs
975.B825	History
975.B83	Through 1796
975.B84	1797-1849
975.B85	1850-
975.B855	Bressanone
975.B86	Brianza
975.B917	Budrio
975.B93	Busseto
975.C115	Cadore
	Cadore (City), see DG975.P55
	Calabria
975.C13	Serials. Collections
975.C14	Gazetteers. Dictionaries. Place names
975.C145	General works
975.C15	Description
	Biography
975.C155A1-C155A3	Collective
975.C155A4-C155Z	Individual, A-Z
975.C16	History
975.C17	Campagna di Roma. Pontine Marshes
975.C173	Campania
975.C17448	Canale, Val. Kanal Valley
975.C2	Capri
975.C25	Capua
975.C26	Carpi
975.C2664	Cassino
975.C2673	Castel Bolognese
975.C28	Catania
975.C43	Cesena
975.C5	Citta di Castello
975.C54	Civitavecchia

Cities (other than metropolitan), provinces, etc., A-Z -- Continued

975.C6 Comacchio
975.C64 Comasine
Como
975.C7 Serials. Collections
975.C71 General works. Description
975.C72 History
975.C7214 Como (Province)
975.C7215 Como, Lake of
975.C735 Corcumello
975.C7384 Corleone (Sicily)
975.C74 Cortina d'Ampezzo
975.C75 Cortona
Cremona
975.C79 Serials. Documents. Collections
975.C8 History and description
Dolomite Alps
975.D66 Periodicals. Societies. Collections
975.D67 General works. History. Description and travel. Pictorial works
975.D68 Special mountains, peaks, trails, etc. (not A-Z)
975.E3 Elba
975.E5 Emilia
975.E53 Emilia-Romagna
975.E8 Euganean Hills
Ferrara
975.F38 Serials. Collections. Sources and documents
975.F39 Description
975.F395 Biography (Collective)
975.F4 History
975.F42 Medieval
975.F43 16th century
975.F44 19th-20th centuries
Firenze (Florence), see DG731+
Forli
975.F71 Serials. Collections. Sources and documents
975.F72 Biography
975.F73 History and description
975.F74 Other
Frascati. Alban Hills
975.F8 General works. Description
975.F82 History
975.F824 Frassinoro
975.F847 Frignano
975.F85 Friuli
975.F855 Friuli-Venezia Giulia
Class here works on that part of Venezia Giulia remaining in Italy after 1947
For Austrian territories prior to 1919 and the Yugoslav territories after 1947, see DR1350.J84
975.G13 Gaeta

Cities (other than metropolitan), provinces, etc., A-Z -- Continued

975.G18 Gallarate
975.G27 Garda, Lago di
975.G3 Garfagnana
975.G32 Gargano Promontory
975.G35 Genazzano
Genoa, see DG631+
975.G67 Gorizia
For Görz and Gradiska (General and Slovenia), see DR1475.G67
975.I4 Iesi
975.I5 Imola
Ionian Sea, see DF901.I695
975.I6 Ischia (Island)
Jesi, see DG975.I4
Kanal Valley, see DG975.C17448
975.L2 Lake District. Italian lakes
975.L24 L'Aquila
Lazio, see DG975.L245
975.L245 Latium. Lazio
Lecce
Including the city and the province
975.L25 Serials. Sources and documents
Collected works
975.L26 Several authors
975.L27 Individual authors
975.L3 History and description
975.L4 Leghorn (Livorno)
975.L68 Liguria
975.L7 Lipari Islands
Livorno, see DG975.L4
Lucania, see DG975.B3
Lucca
975.L8 Serials. Sources and documents. Collections
975.L81 General works. Description
975.L82 History
975.M16 Maggiore, Lago
975.M22 Maglie
Mantua (Mantova)
975.M27 Serials. Collections
975.M28 Sources and documents
History and description
General works
975.M29 Early through 1800
975.M3 1801-
975.M31 Medieval
975.M32 16th-18th centuries
975.M33 19th-20th centuries
975.M34 Other
975.M4 Marche (Marches)
975.M43 Maremme
975.M52 Merano (Meran)

Cities (other than metropolitan), provinces, etc., A-Z -- Continued

Messina

975.M53 Serials. Collections. Sources and documents

975.M532 Description

975.M533 History

975.M534 Other

Milano (Milan), see DG651+

Modena

975.M6 Serials. Collections. Sources and documents

975.M61 General works. Description

975.M615 Antiquities

975.M62 History

975.M63 Other

975.M65 Molfetta

975.M67354 Montalcino

Monte Bianco (Mont Blanc), see DC611.M68

975.M67375 Montebelluna

975.M67378 Montecarlo

975.M675 Montefeltro

975.M68 Montenero

975.M73 Monza

Napoli (Naples), see DG840+

975.O7 Orvieto

975.O8 Ostia

Padua

975.P12 Serials. Collections. Sources and documents

975.P13 Description

975.P14 Antiquities

975.P15 History

Palermo

975.P19 Serials. Collections. Sources and documents

975.P2 General works. Description

975.P21 History

975.P25 Parma

Including the city, the province, and the duchy of Parma and Piacenza

Pavia

975.P29 Serials. Collections. Sources and documents

975.P3 General works. History. Description and travel

975.P32 Other

975.P37 Pergine Valsugana

975.P375 Pergola (Pesaro e Urbino)

975.P4 Perugia

975.P5 Piacenza

For the duchy of Parma and Piacenza, see DG975.P25

Piemonte (Piedmont), see DG610+

975.P5443 Pietra Ligure

975.P55 Pieve di Cadore

Pisa

975.P59 Serials. Collections. Sources and documents

975.P593 Biography

975.P6 General works. History and description

Cities (other than metropolitan), provinces, etc., A-Z
Pisa
General works. History
and description -- Continued
975.P61 Medieval
975.P615 14th-15th centuries
975.P618 16th-18th centuries
975.P62 19th-20th centuries
975.P63 Other
975.P65 Pistoia
Pontine Marshes, see DG975.C17
Puglia, see DG975.A65
975.R25 Ravenna
975.R3 Reggio di Calabria
975.R5 Rimini
975.R6 Riviera
Romagna
975.R7 Serials. Collections. Sources and documents
975.R71 General works. Description
975.R715 Antiquities
975.R72 History
975.R73 Other
Rome
Ancient city, see DG61+
Medieval and modern city, see DG803+
975.S17 Salò
975.S19 San Gimignano
975.S2 San Marino (Republic)
975.S268 Sant'Andrea (Gorizia). Štandrež
Sardinia
975.S29 Serials. Collections. Sources and documents
975.S3 Description and travel
Biography
975.S304 Collective
975.S306 Individual, A-Z
975.S31 History
Cf. DG618.5+, Kingdom of Sardinia, 1718-1860
975.S33 Other
Savoy, see DG610+
975.S3724 Scrivia Valley
Siena
975.S49 Serials. Collections. Sources and documents
975.S5 History and description
975.S54 Soave
975.S7 Sorrento
975.S795 Sugana Valley
975.S9 Syracuse
975.T2 Taormina
975.T5 Tiber River and Valley
975.T57 Tiepido Valley
975.T6 Tivoli
975.T788 Trent
975.T792 Trentino-Alto Adige

Cities (other than metropolitan), provinces, etc., A-Z -- Continued

975.T8 Treviso

975.T825 Trieste (City and District)

Turin

975.T93 Serials. Collections. Sources and documents

975.T94 Description

975.T95 History

975.T97 Other

975.U3 Udine

975.U5 Umbria

Urbino

975.U7 General works. Description

975.U72 History

975.V2 Vallombrosa

975.V23 Valtellina

975.V267 Varazze

975.V3 Varese

975.V38 Venetia (Veneto)

Venezia (Venice), see DG975.T792

Venezia Giulia, see DG975.F855

Venezia Tridentina, see DG975.T792

975.V43 Ventimiglia

Verona

975.V48 Serials. Collections. Sources and documents

975.V49 Description

975.V495 Antiquities

975.V5 History

975.V51 Medieval

975.V52 Modern

975.V53 Other

975.V6 Vesuvius

In general, prefer QE523.V5

975.V646 Viadana

975.V7 Vicenza

975.V8 Vincigliata, Castello di

975.V85 Viterbo

(980) Italian colonies (Former)

Collective, see JV2200 +

Individual colonies

See DS, DT

History of Malta
987 Periodicals. Societies. Serials
Museums, exhibitions, etc.
987.2 General works
987.3.A-Z Individual. By place, A-Z
987.5 Sources and documents
Collected works (nonserial)
988.2 Several authors
988.3 Individual authors
988.5 Gazetteers. Dictionaries
988.6 Place names (General)
For etymological studies, see PL4731
988.7 Directories
988.8 Guidebooks
989 General works
989.2 General special
989.25 Pictorial works
Historic monuments, landmarks, scenery, etc. (General)
For local, see DG999.A +
989.3 General works
989.35 Preservation
989.4 Description and travel
989.5 Antiquities
For local antiquities, see DG999.A +
989.7 Social life and customs. Civilization. Intellectual life
For specific periods, see the period
Ethnography
989.74 General works
989.75.A-Z Individual elements in the population, A-Z
History
Periodicals. Societies. Serials, see DG987
989.8 Dictionaries. Chronological tables, outlines, etc.
989.83 Biography (Collective)
For individual biography, see the specific period or place
989.85 Historiography
990 General works
990.5 Military history
For individual campaigns and engagements, see the special period
990.7 Naval history
For individual campaigns and engagements, see the special period
991 Political history
For specific periods, see the period
Foreign and general relations
For works on relations with a specific country regardless of period, see DG991.6.A +
For general works on the diplomatic history of a period, see the period
991.5 General works
991.6.A-Z Relations with individual regions or countries, A-Z

History -- Continued
By period
Early to 870. Phoenician, Greek, Roman and Byzantine domination
992 General works
Biography and memoirs
992.12 Collective
992.13.A-Z Individual, A-Z
870-1530. Arabic, Norman, Angevin and Aragonese domination
992.2 General works
Cf. DG867.299. History of Sicily
Biography and memoirs
992.26 Collective
992.27.A-Z Individual, A-Z
992.3 Revolt against Monroy, 1427
1530-1798. Rule of the Knights of Malta
Including wars against the Turks and their North African allies, suppression of the Jesuits (1768), and the conquest by Napoleon (1798)
Cf. DC226.M3, Napoleon's expedition to Egypt and Syria, 1798-1799
992.5 General works
Biography and memoirs
992.56 Collective
992.57.A-Z Individual, A-Z
992.6 Siege of Malta, 1565
992.62 Rebellion of the Turkish slaves, 1722
992.65 Rebellion of the priests, 1775
1798-1964. British colonial rule
992.7 General works
Biography and memoirs
992.76 Collective
992.77.A-Z Individual, A-Z
992.8 1798-1802. Interim between Napoleonic conquest and Treaty of Amiens
993 1802-1947. British administration
Cf. D763.M3, Malta in World War II
993.5 1947-1964. Self-rule under British authority
1964- . Independent
994 General works
Biography and memoirs
994.7 Collective
994.8.A-Z Individual, A-Z
999.A-Z Local history and description, A-Z
e.g.
999.G59 Gozo
999.V3 Valletta

History of Low Countries. Benelux Countries
Including Belgium and the Netherlands treated collectively
1 Periodicals. Societies. Serials
Museums, exhibitions, etc.
2 General works
2.5.A-Z Individual. By place, A-Z
3 Sources and documents
Collected works
4 Several authors
5 Individual authors
14 Gazetteers. Dictionaries, etc.
16 Guidebooks
18 General works. Compends
19 Monumental and picturesque
23 Dikes, canals, sluices, etc.
Description and travel
31 Through 1400
33 1401-1600
36 1601-1700
37 1701-1800
38 1801-1900
39 1901-1950
40 1951-
51 Antiquities
71 Social life and customs. Civilization
Ethnography
91 General works
92.A-Z Individual elements in the population, A-Z
History
Historiography
95 General works
Biography of historians
96 Collective
97.A-Z Individual, A-Z
101 Dictionaries. Chronological tables, outlines, etc.
103 Biography (Collective)
For individual biographies, see the special period, reign, or place
General works
106 Through 1800
107 1801-
109 Pamphlets, etc.
General special
111 History of two or more provinces
113 Military history
121 Naval history
Political and diplomatic history
131 General works
136 The Scheldt question
137 Unification movements
By period
Early and medieval to 1384

History
By period
Early and medieval to 1384 -- Continued
141 General works
146 Roman period
151 Frankish period
156 843-1127
159 1127-1285
162 1285-1384
1384-1555
General works
171 Through 1800
172 1801-
1384-1477. House of Burgundy
175 General works
177.A-Z Biography and memoirs, A-Z
1477-1555
179 General works
180 Marie of Burgundy and Maximilian I, 1477-1482
181 Felipe I, 1483-1506
Karl V, 1506-1555
182 General works on life and reign
183 Margaretha of Austria, 1507-1530
184 Maria of Austria, 1531-1555
Wars of independence, 1555-1648
185 Sources and documents
General works
186 Through 1800
186.5 1801-
Felipe (Philip) II, 1555-1581
General works
187 Through 1800
187.5 1801-
187.9 Pamphlets. By date
188.A-Z Biography and memoirs of contemporaries, A-Z
e.g.
188.E3 Egmont, Lamoral, comte d'
188.G8 Grotius, Hugo
188.M35 Marnix, Philippe de, seigneur de Sainte Aldegonde
188.M4 Maurits, Prince of Orange, stadholder of the Netherlands
188.O4 Oldenbarnevelt, Joan van
188.W7 Willem I, Prince of Orange
189 Margaretha of Parma, 1559-1567
Alba (Alva), 1567-1573
191 General works
191.7 Special
1573-1576
192 General works
192.5 Siege of Leyden, 1573-1574
193 Juan de Austria, 1576-1578
Alessandro Farnese, 1578-1581

History
By period
Wars of independence, 1555-1648
Felipe (Philip) II, 1555-1581
Alessandro Farnese, 1578-1581 -- Continued
194 General works
195 Union of Utrecht, 1579
1581-1609
General works
196 Through 1800
197 1801-
198 Leicester, 1585-1587
199.A-Z Special events, battles, etc., A-Z
199.C4 Deventer, Surrender of, 1587
199.N4 Nieuport, Battle of, 1600
199.O8 Ostend, Siege of, 1601-1604
200 Pamphlets. By date
201 Armistice, 1609-1621
1621-1648
204 General works
206.A-Z Special events, battles, etc., A-Z
206.A55 Antwerp, Siege of, 1584-1585
206.B8 Breda, Siege of, 1624-1625
206.D6 Downs, Battle of, 1639
206.H5 s'Hertogenbosch, Siege of, 1629
207 Pamphlets, 1609-1648. By date

History of Belgium
401 Periodicals. Societies. Serials
403 Sources and documents
Collected works
404 Several authors
405 Individual authors
414 Gazetteers. Dictionaries, etc.
415 Place names (General)
416 Guidebooks
418 General works
421 Compends
424 Monumental and picturesque
425 Preservation of historic monuments, etc.
427 Dikes, canals, sluices, etc.
430 Historical geography
430.5 Geography
Description and travel
431 Through 1830
433 1831-1945
434 1946-1970
435 1971-
451 Antiquities
Cf. DH801+, Local history and description
471 Social life and customs. Civilization. Intellectual life
Including national characteristics
Ethnography
Including nationality, the Flemings, and the Flemish movement
491 General works
492.A-Z Individual elements in the population, A-Z
492.A34 Africans
Flemings, see DH491+
492.G4 Germans
492.G73 Greeks
492.H85 Hungarians
492.I8 Italians
492.M65 Moroccans
492.P64 Poles
492.R87 Russians
492.S65 Spaniards
492.T87 Turks
492.W3 Walloons
492.Z34 Zairians
History
Historiography
503 General works
Biography of historians
505 Collective
506.A-Z Individual, A-Z
e.g.
506.K8 Kurth, Godefroid Joseph F.
506.P5 Pirenne, Henri

History -- Continued
511 Dictionaries. Chronological tables, outlines, etc.
Biography (Collective)
For individual biographies, see the special period, reign, or place
513 General works
514 Rulers, kings, etc.
515 Public men
515.5 Women
516.A-Z Houses, noble families, etc., A-Z
e.g.
516.H8 Howarderie, Seigneurs de la
516.L6 Looz, House of
Study and teaching
516.5 General works
516.6.A-Z Local, A-Z
General works
517 Through 1800. Chronicles
521 1801-
523 Compends
525 Topics (not A-Z)
527 Pamphlets, etc.
General special
531 History of two or more provinces
Military history
For individual campaigns and engagements, see the special period
540 General works
541 Biography (Collective)
542 Early and medieval to 1555
543 1555-1815
545 1815-
551 Naval history
Political and diplomatic history
Cf. DH571+, Special periods, reigns, etc.
566 General works
569.A-Z Foreign relations with individual regions or countries, A-Z
By period
Early and medieval to 1555
Cf. DH801.F4+, Flanders
571 General works
572 General special
574 Roman period
576 Frankish period
578 843-1100
1101-1400
580 General works
581.A-Z Biography and memoirs, A-Z
e.g.
581.A7 Artevelde, Jacob van
581.R6 Robert I, the Friesian, Count of Flanders
1401-1506

History
By period
Early and medieval to 1555
1401-1506 -- Continued
582 General works
583.A-Z Biography and memoirs, A-Z
584 1506-1555
1555-1794. Spanish and Austrian rule
585 General works
1555-1598. 16th century
Cf. DH185+, Wars of independence, 1555-1648
591 General works
598.A-Z Biography and memoirs, A-Z
e.g.
598.C7 Croy, Charles, duc de
598.R6 Roose, Pierre
1598-1714
600 Sources and documents
601 General works
602.A-Z Biography and memoirs, A-Z
602.I8 Isabel, Consort of Albrecht, Archduke of Austria
605 1598-1621
606 1621-1648
607 1648-1700
609 1701-1714
1714-1794. Austrian Netherlands
611 Sources and documents
612 General works
613.A-Z Biography and memoirs, A-Z
614 General special
615 1740-1780
For biography of Maria Theresia, see DB71
1780-1790
For biography of Joseph II, see DB74+
616 General works
Revolution, 1788-1790
Sources and documents
617 Brabant (and Liège)
617.5 Liège
General works
618 Brabant (and Liége)
618.5 Liége
619 1790-1792
For biography of Leopold II, see DB74.8+
1794-1909
620 General works
1794-1830
621 General works
628.A-Z Biography and memoirs, A-Z
e.g.
628.A7 Arenberg, Auguste Marie R., prince d', comte de la Marck

History
By period
1794-1909
1794-1830
Biography and memoirs, A-Z -- Continued
628.M4 Merode, Henri Marie G., comte de
631 French rule, 1794-1813
641 1813-1830
Cf. DJ236, Kingdom of the Netherlands
1830-
645 General works
Revolution of 1830
650 Sources and documents
651 General works
652 General special
Leopold I, 1831-1865
656 General works on life and reign
657 General special
659.A-Z Biography and memoirs of contemporaries, A-Z
e.g.
659.L4 Lebeau, Joseph
659.L7 Louise, Consort of Leopold I
659.P7 Praet, Jules von
659.R7 Rogier, Charles Latour
665 Treaty of London, 1839
Leopold II, 1865-1909
671 General works on life and reign
Biography and memoirs of contemporaries
675 Collective
676.A-Z Individual, A-Z
e.g.
676.B3 Banning, Émile Théodore J.H.
676.F7 Frère-Orban, Hubert Joseph W.
676.L7 Louise, Princess of Belgium
676.M3 Marie, Countess of Flanders
676.M35 Marie Henriette, Consort of Leopold II
20th century
677 General works
Albert, 1909-1934
681 General works on life and reign
681.5 Travels
682 Period of World War I, 1914-1918. Flemish movement
For the war itself, see D501+
683 1920-
Biography and memoirs of contemporaries
685.A1 Collective
685.A2-Z Individual, A-Z
e.g.
685.B6 Borms, August
685.D6 Dorlodot, René de, baron
685.E5 Elizabeth, Consort of Albert I
685.M3 Max, Adolphe

History
By period
20th century
Albert, 1909-1934
Biography and memoirs of contemporaries
Individual -- Continued
685.R64 Rolin, Henri
Leopold III, 1934-1951
687 General works on life and reign
Including his detention in Germany and exile, 1940-1950, and abdication, 1951; regency of Prince Charles, 1944-1950
689.A-Z Biography and memoirs of contemporaries, A-Z
e.g.
689.A8 Astrid, Consort of Leopold III
689.C5 Clercq, Gustaaf de
689.H3 Hagemans, John
689.M3 Man, Henri de
Baudouin I, 1951-1993
690 General works on life and reign
692.A-Z Biography and memoirs of contemporaries, A-Z
Albert II, 1993-
693 General works on life and reign
694.A-Z Biography and memoirs of contemporaries, A-Z
Local history and description
801.A-Z Provinces, regions, etc., A-Z
801.A6-A69 Antwerp (Table D-DR7)
801.A74 Ardennes
801.B6 Bouillon
801.B7-B79 Brabant (Table D-DR7)
801.C3 Campine
801.C5 Ciney (Canton)
801.E8 Eupen and Malmédy
Flanders
801.F4-F49 General
801.F4 Serials. Collections. Sources and documents
801.F41 Minor collections
801.F43 General works. Description and travel
801.F44 Antiquities
801.F443 Social life and customs. Civilization. Culture
801.F45 History
By period
Medieval
801.F46 Early works
801.F462 Modern works
801.F465 General special
801.F468 16th century
801.F47 17th-18th centuries
801.F48 19th-20th centuries
801.F49 Other
801.F5-F59 East Flanders (Table D-DR7)
801.F6-F69 West Flanders (Table D-DR7)
801.H2-H29 Hainaut (Table D-DR7)

Local history and description
Provinces, regions, etc., A-Z -- Continued
801.H35 Hautes Fagnes (Hohes Venn)
801.H4 Hesbaye (Haspengouw)
801.L5-L59 Liége (Table D-DR7)
Cf. DH801.E8, Eupen and Malmédy
801.L7-L79 Limbourg (Table D-DR7)
801.L9-L99 Luxembourg (Belgian province) (Table D-DR7)
Luxembourg (Grand Duchy), see DH901+
801.M6 Moresnet
801.N2-N29 Namur (Table D-DR7)
801.N4 Neufchâteau (Arrondissement)
801.N5 Nivelles (Arrondissement)
801.S35 Scheldt
801.S6 Soignes (Forest)
Brussels
802.A2 Periodicals. Societies. Serials
802.A5-Z Sources and documents
Collected works
802.3 Several authors
802.5 Individual authors
802.7.A-Z Biography, A-Z
803 Directories. Dictionaries
804 Guidebooks
Description
804.3 Through 1800
804.4 1801-1900
804.5 1901-
804.8 Antiquities
804.9 Social life and customs. Culture
History
805 General works
805.5 General special
806 Early and medieval
806.5 16th-17th centuries
806.7 18th century
806.9 Napoleonic period
807 19th century
807.5 20th century
Sections, districts, etc.
809 General works
809.3 Cemeteries
809.4 Churches
809.5 Parks
809.6 Streets. Bridges
Buildings
809.7 General works
809.8.A-Z Individual, A-Z
809.9.A-Z Suburbs, A-Z
809.95 Other special (not A-Z)
e.g. Mannikin Fountain
811.A-Z Other cities, towns, etc., A-Z
Antwerp

Local history and description
Other cities, towns, etc., A-Z
Antwerp -- Continued
811.A55 Periodicals. Societies. Serials
811.A56 Sources and documents
811.A58 General works and description
811.A6 History
811.A63 Early to 1550
811.A64 1550-1600
811.A67 17th-18th centuries
811.A68 19th-20th centuries
Audenarde, see DH811.O8
Bruges
811.B75 Periodicals. Societies. Serials
811.B76 Sources and documents
811.B78 General works and description
811.B79 Antiquities
811.B8 History
811.B82 Early and medieval
811.B83 1550-1660
811.B84 17th-18th centuries
811.B85 19th-20th centuries
Chimay
811.C5 Periodicals. Societies. Serials
811.C52 Sources and documents
811.C53 General works and description
811.C55 History
811.C8 Courtrai (Kortryk)
811.E6 Enghien
Ghent
811.G4 Periodicals. Societies. Collections, etc.
811.G43 General works and description
811.G45 History
811.G46 Early and medieval
811.G47 16th century
811.G48 17th-18th centuries
811.G49 19th-20th centuries
811.L5 Liége
811.L7 Louvain
811.M4 Mechlin (Malines, Mechelen)
811.M75 Mons (Bergen)
811.N2 Namur
811.N7 Nieuport
811.O8 Oudenaarde
811.R6 Roeselare
811.S65 Soiron
811.S7 Spa
811.T3 Tervueren
Tournai (Doornick)
811.T7 Periodicals. Societies. Collections, etc.
811.T73 General works and description
811.T76 History
811.Y8 Ypres

History of Luxembourg
901 Periodicals. Societies. Serials
902 Sources and documents
903 Gazetteers. Dictionaries, etc.
903.2 Guidebooks
904 Biography (Collective)
905 General works
Historic monuments, landmarks, scenery, etc. (General)
For local, see DH925.A+
905.4 General works
905.5 Preservation
Description and travel
906 Through 1945
907 1946-
907.3 Antiquities
907.7 Social life and customs. Civilization
907.9 Ethnography
History
908 General works
Political and diplomatic history
908.5 General works
908.6.A-Z Foreign relations with individual regions or countries, A-Z
By period
909 Early to 1354 (Countship)
1354-1815 (Duchy)
910 General works
911 Union with Burgundy, 1444-1477
912 Austria, 1477-1555
913 Spain, 1555-1713 (France, 1684-1697)
914 Austria, 1714-1795
915 France, 1795-1815
1815- (Grand duchy)
916 General works
Biography and memoirs
918 Collective
918.5.A-Z Individual, A-Z
925.A-Z Local history and description, A-Z
e.g.
925.L8 Luxembourg

History of Netherlands (Holland)

1 Periodicals. Societies. Serials
3 Sources and documents
Collected works
4 Several authors
5 Individual authors
14 Gazetteers. Dictionaries, etc.
15 Place names (General)
16 Guidebooks
18 General works
21 Compends
24 Monumental and picturesque
25 Preservation of historic monuments, etc.
27 Dikes, canals, sluices, etc.
30 Historical geography
30.5 Geography
Description and travel
33 History of travel
34 Through 1500
36 1501-1800
38 1801-1900
39 1901-1945
40 1946-1977
41 1978-
51 Antiquities
Cf. DJ401+, Local history and description
71 Social life and customs. Civilization. Intellectual life
81 Dutch culture in foreign countries
Class here general works, or those works in combinations too broad for any one country
Ethnography
91 General works
91.5 National characteristics
92.A-Z Individual elements in the population, A-Z
92.A7 Armenians
92.B53 Blacks
92.C5 Chinese
92.E3 East Indians
92.F73 French
92.G45 Germans
92.G73 Greeks
92.I53 Indonesians
92.I73 Iranians
92.M64 Moluccans
92.M68 Moroccans
92.M86 Muslims
92.N47 Netherlands Antilleans
92.N67 Norwegians
92.P34 Palestinian Arabs
92.P6 Portuguese
92.S8 Surinamese
92.S95 Swiss

DJ

Ethnography
Individual elements
in the population, A-Z -- Continued
92.T34 Tamil
92.T85 Turks
92.V53 Vietnamese
History
Historiography
95 General works
Biography of historians
97 Collective
98.A-Z Individual, A-Z
e.g.
98.F7 Fruin, Robert Jacobus
101 Dictionaries. Chronological tables, outlines, etc.
Biography (Collective)
For individual biographies, see the special period, reign, or place
103 General works
104 Rulers, kings, etc.
105 Public men
105.5 Women
105.7 Other (not A-Z)
106 Houses, noble families, etc.
Study and teaching
106.5 General works
106.6.A-Z By region or country, A-Z
Subarrange by author
General works
107 Through 1800
109 1801-
111 Compends
114 Special aspects
116 Pamphlets, etc.
General special
121 History of two or more provinces
124 Military history
For individual campaigns and engagements, see the special period
Naval history
For individual campaigns and engagements, see the special period
130 Sources and documents
131 Biography (Collective)
132 General works
133 General special
134 Pamphlets, etc.
135 Early to 1594
136 1594-1700
Including biography
136.R8 Ruyter, Michiel Adriaanszoon de
136.T7 Tromp, Cornelis Maartenszoon
136.T75 Tromp, Maerten Harpertszoon

History
General special
Naval history -- Continued
137 18th century
138 19th-20th centuries
Political and diplomatic history
Cf. DJ151+, Special periods, reigns, etc.
140 Sources and documents
142 General works
143 General special
e.g. the medieval city, etc.
144 Pamphlets, etc.
145 Earliest to 1555
146 1555-1795
147 1795- . 19th-20th centuries
149.A-Z Foreign relations with individual regions or countries, A-Z
Reigning houses
150 House of Orange
Class here general and collective works
By period
Early and medieval to 1555
151 Early works through 1800. Chronicles
152 Works, 1801-
1555-1795. United Provinces
Cf. DH185+, Sources and documents (Wars of independence, 1555-1648)
154 Sources and documents
General works
155 Through 1800
156 1801-
158 General special
170 1609-1621
Cf. DH201, Armistice, 1609-1621 (Wars of independence)
1621-1652
General works
171 Through 1800
172 1801-
173.A-Z Biography and memoirs, 1621-1702
e.g.
Cf. DH188.A+, Biography, 1555-1648 (Low countries)
173.A5 Amalia, Consort of Frederik Hendrik, Prince of Orange
173.F7 Frederik Hendrik, Prince of Orange
173.J6 Johan Maurits, Prince of Nassau-Siegen
Cf. F2532, Period in Brazil
173.R43 Reede van Amerongen, Godard Adriaan
173.W3 Willem II, Prince of Orange
173.W5 Witsen, Nicolaas Corneliszoon
173.W7 Witt, Johan de

History
By period
1555-1795. United Provinces -- Continued
1652-1702
Including Anglo-Dutch wars, 1652-1667
180 Sources and documents
General works
181 Through 1800
182 1801-
Willem III, 1672-1702
For biography, see DA462.A2
General works on life and reign
186 Through 1800
187 1801-
War with France, 1672-1678
For the war itself, see D277+
General works
190 Through 1800
191 1801-
193 Anglo-Dutch War, 1672-1674
Stadtholders, 1702-1747
General works
196 Through 1800
197 1801-
Biography and memoirs
199 Collective
199.2 Individual, A-Z
e.g.
199.2.C65 Corver, Joan, 1628-1716
Willem IV and Willem V, 1747-1795
General works
201 Through 1800
202 1801-
Biography and memoirs, 1702-1795
204.A1 Collective
204.A2-Z Individual, A-Z
e.g.
204.L8 Ludwig Ernst, Duke of Brunswick-Lüneburg
204.R4 Rendorp, Joachim, vrijheer van Marquette
204.S6 Slingelandt, Simon van
Anglo-Dutch War, 1780-1784
General works
205 Through 1800
206 1801-
War with France, 1793-1795
Cf. DC220.6, First and Second coalitions, 1792-1802 (French Revolution)
General works
208 Through 1800
209 1801-
210 Period of French Revolution and Napoleonic Empire, 1792-1815
211 Batavian Republic, 1795-1806

History
By period -- Continued
19th-20th centuries
215 Sources and documents
216 General works
Biography and memoirs
219.A1 Collective
219.A2-Z Individual, A-Z
e.g.
219.B6 Bosch, Joannes, graaf van den
219.C55 Colijn, Henrikus
219.F2 Falck, Anton Reinhard
219.G7 Groen van Prinsterer, Guillaume
219.H7 Hogendorp, Dirk, graaf van
219.H8 Hogendorp, Gijsbert Karel, graaf van
219.S3 Schimmelpenninck, Rutger Jan
219.T5 Thorbecke, Jan Rudolf
226 Kingdom of Holland, 1806-1810
228 Union with France, 1810-1813
236 Kingdom of the Netherlands, 1813-1830
241 Willem I, 1815-1840
251 Willem II, 1840-1849
Willem III, 1849-1890
261 General works on life and reign
Biography and memoirs of contemporaries
263.A1 Collective
263.A3 Emma, Consort of William III
263.A4-Z Other, A-Z
Wilhelmina, 1890-1948
281 General works on life and reign
Biography and memoirs of contemporaries
283.A2 Collective
283.A3-Z Individual, A-Z
e.g.
283.G4 Geer, Dirk Jan de
283.T7 Troelstra, Pieter Jelles
285 Period of World War I, 1914-1918
286 Period between World War I and World War II, 1918-1939
287 World War II and post-war periods, 1939-1948
Juliana, 1948-1980
288 General works on life and reign
Biography and memoirs of contemporaries
289.A1 Collective
Royal family
289.A2 Collective
289.A3 Bernhard, Leopold, Consort of Juliana
289.A4A-Z Other royal, A-Z
(289.A4B4) Beatrix
see DJ290+
289.A5-Z Other contemporaries, A-Z
Beatrix, 1980-
290 General works on life and reign

History
By period
19th-20th centuries
Beatrix, 1980- -- Continued
Biography and memoirs of contemporaries
291.A1 Collective
Royal family
291.A2 General works
291.A3 Claus, Consort of Beatrix
291.A4-Z Other royal, A-Z
292.A-Z Individual, A-Z
Local history and description
401.A-Z Provinces, regions, islands, etc., A-Z
401.A5 Ameland
401.A55 Anna Paulownapolder
401.B7-B79 Brabant, North (Table D-DR8)
401.D7-D79 Drenthe (Table D-DR8)
Flevoland, see DJ401.Z784+
401.F5-F59 Friesland (Table D-DR8)
401.G35 Goeree-en-Overflakee
401.G4-G49 Groningen (Table D-DR8)
401.G7-G79 Guelders. Gelderland (Table D-DR8)
Holland
401.H6-H69 North and South (Holland and Zealand) (Table D-DR8)
401.H7-H79 North (Table D-DR8)
401.H8-H89 South (Table D-DR8)
401.H96 Humsterland
IJssel Lake, see DJ401.Z8
401.L6-L69 Limburg (Table D-DR8)
Including works on the duchy
Early and medieval history
401.L662 General works
Including Battle of Worringen, 1288
401.M3 Marken
Markerwaard, see DJ401.Z784+
North Holland, see DJ401.H7+
401.O8-O89 Overijssel (Table D-DR8)
South Holland, see DJ401.H8+
401.T4 Terschelling (Island)
401.T5 Texel Island
401.T9 Twente
401.U7-U79 Utrecht (Table D-DR8)
401.V4 Veluwe
401.W15 Waddeneilanden. West Frisian Islands
401.W2-W29 Walcheren (Table D-DR8)
West Frisian Islands, see DJ401.W15
401.Z3 Zaanstreek
401.Z5-Z59 Zealand (Table D-DR8)
401.Z784-Z7849 Zuidelijke IJsselmeerpolders (Table D-DR8)
Including Flevoland and the proposed Markerwaard
401.Z8 Zuyder Zee. IJssel Lake

Local history and description -- Continued

411.A-Z Cities, towns, etc., A-Z

e.g.

411.A45 Amersfoort

Amsterdam

411.A5 Periodicals. Societies. Serials

411.A52 Directories. Gazetteers, etc.

411.A53 General works and description

Ethnography

411.A54 General works

411.A545A-Z Individual elements in the population, A-Z

411.A545C55 Chinese

411.A545S95 Surinamese

History

411.A55 General works

411.A56 Early and medieval

411.A57 17th-18th centuries

411.A58 19th-20th centuries

411.A59 Other

e.g. K. Paleis

411.A8 Arnhem

411.B4 Bergen-op-Zoom

411.D46 Delft

411.D5 Deventer

411.D6 Dordrecht

411.G6 Gorinchem

411.G7 Groningen

411.H2 Haarlem

411.H33 Hague ('s Gravenhage) (Table D-DR4)

411.H5 's Hertogenbosch

411.H7 Hoorn

411.K2 Kampen

411.L4 Leeuwarden

411.L5 Leyden

411.M2 Maastricht

411.M3 Mariënweerd, Gelderland (Abbey)

411.M6 Middelburg

411.N6 Nijmegen

411.R8 Rotterdam

411.T4 Tholen (City and island)

411.U9 Utrecht

411.V66 Voorburg

411.Z35 Zandvoort

411.Z95 Zwolle

(500) Dutch colonies

Collective

See JV2500+

Individual

See Classes D-F

History of Eastern Europe (General)
Cf. DR1 +, Balkan Peninsula
1 Periodicals. Societies. Serials
1.5 Congresses
3 Sources and documents
Collected works (nonserial)
4 Several authors
5 Individual authors
6 Gazetteers. Dictionaries, etc.
7 Place names (General)
For etymological studies, see PG303
7.5 Directories
8 Guidebooks
9 General works
10 Pictorial works
Historic monuments, landmarks, scenery, etc. (General)
10.5 General works
10.6 Preservation
11 Historical geography
12 Geography
Description and travel
13 History of travel
14 Early through 1500
15 1501-1800
16 1801-1900
17 1901-1950
18 1951-1980
19 1981-
23 Antiquities
For local antiquities, see individual countries or localities
24 Social life and customs. Civilization. Intellectual life
For specific periods, see the period
Ethnography
26 General works
26.5 National characteristics
27 Slavic peoples (General)
Class here historical studies only
Cf. D147, Slavic migrations
Cf. DR25, Slavs in the Balkan Peninsula
For ethnological studies, see GN549.S6
28.A-Z Other individual elements in the population, A-Z
Cf. DR27.A +, Balkan Peninsula
28.B84 Bulgarians
28.C67 Cossacks
28.F55 Finno-Ugrians (General)
28.G32 Gagauz
28.G4 Germans. Swabians
28.G74 Greeks
Huculs, see DK508.425.H87
28.H86 Hungarians

Ethnography
Other individual elements in the population, A-Z -- Continued

28.L4 Lemky (General)
Cf. DK508.425.L46, Lemky in the Ukraine
28.M32 Macedonians
28.M87 Muslims
28.P64 Poles
28.R85 Russians
28.R87 Ruthenians (General)
For Ruthenians in a particular country, see the country
Scythians, see DJK46.7
28.S9 Swiss
28.T8 Turks

History
Periodicals, societies, serials, see DJK1
30 Dictionaries. Chronological tables, outlines, etc.
31 Biography (Collective)
For individual biography, see the specific period, reign, or place
Historiography
32 General works
Biography of historians, area studies specialists, archaeologists, etc.
33 Collective
34.A-Z Individual, A-Z
Study and teaching. Slavic studies
35 General works
36.A-Z By region or country, A-Z
Subarrange by author
General works
37 Through 1800
38 1801-
39.5 Juvenile works
40 Addresses, essays, lectures. Anecdotes, etc.
Political history
41 Sources and documents
42 General works
By period
See the specific period
Foreign and general relations
43 Sources and documents
44 General works
By period
See the specific period
45.A-Z Relations with individual countries, A-Z
By period
Early and medieval to 1500
46 General works
46.3 Avars

History
By period
Early and medieval to 1500 -- Continued
46.4 Bulgars (General)
For Danubian Bulgars, see DR64+
For the Volgar Bulgars, see DK511.T17
46.45 Cimmerians (General)
For Cimmerians in the former Soviet republics, see DK34.C56
46.5 Pechenegs
46.7 Scythians (General)
For Sycthians in Ukraine, see DK508.425.S39
47 1500-1815
48 1815-1918
Cf. D371+, Eastern question (19th century)
20th century
48.5 General works
49 1918-1945
Cf. D461+, Eastern question (20th century)
50 1945-1989
Cf. D847.2, Warsaw pact, 1955
51 1989-
Local history and description
Black Sea region
For the Black Sea region of individual countries, see the specific country
61 General works
62 General special
63 Description and travel
64 Antiquities
64.5 Social life and customs. Civilization. Intellectual life
65 Ethnography (General)
For individual elements of the Black Sea region, see DJK27
66 History
Carpathian Mountain region
For the Carpathian Mountains of individual countries, see the specific country
71 General works
72 General special
73 Description and travel
74 Antiquities
75 Ethnography (General)
For individual elements of the Carpathian Mountain region, see DJK27
76 History
Danube River Valley
Cf. DR49+, Lower Danube Valley
For the Danube River Valley of individual countries, see the specific country
76.2 General works
76.3 General special

Local history and description
Danube River Valley -- Continued
76.4 Description and travel
76.5 Antiquities
76.6 Social life and customs. Civilization. Intellectual life
76.7 Ethnography (General)
For individual elements in the population of the Danube River Valley, see DJK27
76.8 History
77 Pannonia
Cf. DG59.P2, Roman Pannonia
For regions located in specific countries, see the country

History of Russia. Soviet Union. Former Soviet Republics

1 Periodicals. Societies. Serials
1.5 Commonwealth of Independent States
Museums, exhibitions, etc.
2.A1 General works
2.A2-Z Individual. By place, A-Z
2.5 Congresses
3 Sources and documents
Collected works (nonserial)
4 Several authors
5 Individual authors
14 Gazetteers. Dictionaries, etc.
15 Place names (General)
15.5 Directories
16 Guidebooks
17 General works
18 General special
18.5 Pictorial works
Historic monuments, landmarks, scenery, etc. (General)
For local, see DK500.A+
18.6 General works
18.65 Preservation
18.7 Historical geography
18.8 Geography
Description and travel
19 History of travel
20 Earliest through 861. European Sarmatia
21 862-1612
22 1613-1725
23 1726-1800
25 1801-1855
26 1856-1900
27 1901-1944
28 1945-1969
29 1970-1991
29.2 1992-
30 Antiquities
For local antiquities, see DK500.A+
Social life and customs. Civilization
For specific periods, see the period or reign
32 General works
32.3 Court life. Regal antiquities
32.7 Intellectual life
Ethnography
33 General works
34.A-Z Individual elements in the population, A-Z
Class here works on ethnic groups in the Russian Empire, Soviet Union, or Former Soviet republics collectively
For works on ethnic groups in a specific republic, see the republic
34.A27 Adygei
34.A4 Alani

Ethnography
Individual elements
in the population, A-Z -- Continued

34.A45 Americans
34.A73 Argentinians
34.A75 Armenians
34.A92 Austrians
34.B25 Balts
34.B3 Bashkir
34.B44 Belgians
34.B53 Blacks
34.B7 British
34.B8 Bulgars
34.C54 Chuvash
34.C56 Cimmerians
For Cimmerians (General), see DJK46.45
34.C57 Circassians
Cossacks, see DK35+
34.D65 Dolgans
34.E77 Estonians
34.E97 Europeans, Western
34.F54 Finno-Ugrians
34.F55 Finns
34.G3 Germans
34.G74 Greeks
34.I5 Indo-Aryans
34.I73 Italians
Jews, see DS135.R9
34.K13 Kabardians
34.K14 Kalmyks
34.K26 Karachay (Turkic people)
34.K29 Karaites
34.K45 Khazars
34.K65 Komi
34.K67 Koreans
34.K87 Kurds
34.M37 Mari
34.M39 Mennonites
34.M8 Muslims
34.N64 Nogai
34.O2 Osimo
34.O79 Ossetes
34.P6 Poles
34.S3 Sarmatians
34.S37 Scots
34.S4 Scythians
34.S47 Serbs
34.S88 Swedes
34.S9 Swiss
34.T37 Tatars
34.T8 Turks
34.U35 Ukrainians

Cossacks

DK

Cossacks -- Continued
35 General works
Zaporozhians, see DK508.55
35.5 Russians in foreign countries (General)
For Russians in a particular country, see the country
History
36 Dictionaries. Chronological tables, outlines, etc.
Biography (Collective)
For individual biography, see the special period, reign, or place
37 General works
37.2 Women
37.4 Statesmen
37.6 Rulers, czars, etc.
Houses, noble families, etc.
37.7 General works
37.8.A-Z Special, A-Z
e.g.
37.8.A3 Aksakov family
37.8.B3 Bakunin family
37.8.R3 Razumovskiĭ family
37.8.R6 Romanov, House of
37.8.S5 Sheremetev family
Historiography
38 General works
Biography of historians, area studies specialists, archaeologists, etc.
38.5 Collective
38.7.A-Z Individual, A-Z
e.g.
38.7.K35 Karamzin, Nikolaĭ Mikhaĭlovich
38.7.K6 Kostomarov, Nikolaĭ Ivanovich
Study and teaching
38.8 General works
38.9.A-Z Individual schools, A-Z
General works
39 Through 1800. Chronicles
40 1801-
41 Elementary textbooks
42 Addresses, essays, lectures. Anecdotes, etc.
43 Special aspects
General special
46 Several parts of the union treated together
49 Philosophy of Russian/Soviet history
Military history
For individual campaigns and engagements, see the special period
50 Periodicals. Societies. Serials
Biography (Collective)
50.5 General
50.8 Officers
51 General works
51.7 General special

History
General special
Military history -- Continued
52 Early to 1613
52.5 1613-1801
53 1801-1917
54 1917-
Naval history
For individual campaigns and engagements, see the period
55 Periodicals. Societies. Serials
Biography (Collective)
55.5 General
55.8 Officers
56 General works
56.7 General special
56.9 Addresses, essays, lectures
57 Early to 1689
57.5 1689-1801
58 1801-1917
59 1917-
Political history
Class here general works and works on broad periods of political history
For works on a specific period, see the period
60 Sources and documents
61 General works
62 Early to 1462
62.3 1462-1613
62.6 1613-1762
62.9 1762-1917
1917- , see DK266+
Foreign and general relations
For general works on the diplomatic history of a period, see the period
For works on relations with a specific country regardless of period, see DK67.5, DK68.7, DK69.3, DK69.4
65 Sources and documents
66 General works
Special
Europe
General works, see D34.A+, D1065.A+
Catholic Church, see BX1558+
Balkan Peninsula, see DR38.3.A+
67.5.A-Z Individual countries, A-Z
Asia
Class here works on relations of the former Soviet republics as a group with Asia
For works on relations of Russia and the Soviet Union with Asia, see DS33.4.A+
68 General works
68.5 Middle East

History
General special
Foreign and general relations
Special
Asia -- Continued
68.7.A-Z Individual countries, A-Z
69 United States
Class here works on relations of the former Soviet republics as a group with the United States
For works on the relations of Russia and the Soviet Union with the United States, see E183.8.A+
69.3.A-Z Other American countries
Latin America (General), see F1416.A+
Africa
General works, see DT38.9.S65
69.4.A-Z Individual countries, A-Z
Oceania
69.6 General works
69.7.A-Z Individual countries, A-Z
By period
Early to 1613
Rus' (Eastern Slavs until their trifurcation into Byelorussians, Russians, and Ukrainians)
70.A2 Sources and documents
70.A25 Historiography
General works
70.A3-Z Through 1800. Chronicles
71 1801-
72 Early to 862
862-1054. Kievan Rus', Kievskaia͡ Rus', Kyïvs'ka Rus'
72.8 Sources and documents
72.9 Historiography
73 General works
Biography and memoirs
73.5 Collective
73.6.A-Z Individual, A-Z
75 Vladimir I, Grand Duke of Kiev, 972-1015 (Volodymyr I, Kyïvs'kyĭ kniaz͡', 972-1015)
77 I͡Aroslav I, Grand Duke of Kiev, 1016-1054) (I͡Aroslav Mudryĭ, Kyïvs'kyi kniaz͡', 1016-1054)
1054-1237. Decline of Kievan Rus'
80 General works
81 Kievan succession
82 Vladimir Monomakh, Grand Duke of Kiev, 1093-1125 (Volodymyr Monomakh, Kyïvs'kyĭ kniaz͡', 1093-1125)
83 Andreĭ Bogoli͡ubskiĭ, Grand Duke of Vladimir-Suzdal', 1157-1174

History
By period
Early to 1613
Rus′ (Eastern Slavs until their trifurcation into Byelorussians, Russians, and Ukrainians)
1054-1237. Decline of Kievan Rus′ -- Continued
85 Vsevolod III, 1176-1212
86 I͡Urii II, 1212-1238
89 Daniil Romanovich, Grand Duke of Halychyna, 1201-1264 (Danylo, Halyt͡s′kyĭ kni͡az′, 1201-1264)
1237-1462. Tartar (Mongol) Yoke
90 General works
91 The first invasion, 1224
91.5 Mikhail Vsevolodovich, Grand Duke of Kiev, d. 1245
92 I͡Arislav II, 1238-1246
93 Aleksandr Nevskiĭ, Grand Duke of Vladimir, 1247-1263
94 I͡Urii III, 1303-1325
96 Ivan I Kalita, 1328-1341
97 Semen, Grank Duke of Moscow, 1340-1353
98 Ivan II, 1353-1359
99 Dmitrii Donskoĭ, 1363-1389
99.3 Vasiliĭ I, 1389-1425
99.7 Vasiliĭ II, 1425-1462
Muscovy
1462-1605. Consolidation of Muscovy
99.8 Sources and documents
100 General works
Ivan III, 1462-1505
101 General works on life and reign
102 General special
104 Basil III, 1505-1533
Ivan IV, The Terrible, 1533-1584
106 General works on life and reign
106.5 General special
Biography and memoirs
106.8 Collective
107.A-Z Individual, A-Z
e.g.
107.K8 Kurbskiĭ, Andreĭ Mikhaĭlovich, kni͡az′
108 Theodore I, 1584-1598
109 Boris Godunov, 1598-1605
1605-1613. Time of troubles. Smutnoe vremi͡a
111 General works
112 Demetrius the Imposter (Pseudo-Demetrius)
Biography and memoirs
112.4 Collective
112.42.A-Z Individual, A-Z

History
By period -- Continued
House of Romanov, 1613-1917
112.8 Sources and documents
113 General works
1613-1689. 17th century
113.2 Sources and documents
114 General works
114.12 Social life and customs. Civilization. Intellectual life
114.5.A-Z Biography and memoirs, A-Z
e.g.
114.5.G6 Gordon, Patrick
114.5.M4 Menzies, Paul
115 Michael, Czar of Russia, 1613-1645
Alexis, 1645-1676
116 Sources and documents
117.A-Z Biography and memoirs, A-Z
e.g.
117.M6 Morozov, Boris Ivanovich
118 General works on life and reign
118.5 Rebellion of Stenka Razin, 1667-1671
119 Nikon
120 General special
121 War with Poland
121.5 War with Sweden
122 War with Turkey
122.5 War with Persia
124 Theodore III, 1676-1682
Sophia, 1682-1689
125 General works on life and regency
126 Ivan V, 1682-1696
1689-1801. 18th century
127.A2 Sources and documents
127.A3-Z General works
127.2 Foreign relations
Biography and memoirs
127.4 Collective
127.5.A-Z Individual, A-Z
Peter I the Great, 1689-1725
128 Museums, exhibitions, etc.
Subarrange by author
129 Sources and documents
Biography and memoirs
130.A1 Collective
130.A2-Z Individual, A-Z
e.g.
130.B4 Bergholz, Friedrich Wilhelm von
130.L4 Lefort, François Jacques
Mazepa, Ivan, Hetman of Ukraine, see DK508.752.M3
130.S5 Sheremetev, Boris Petrovich, graf
131 General works on life and reign

History
By period
House of Romanov, 1613-1917
1689-1801. 18th century
Peter I the Great, 1689-1725 -- Continued
131.5 Journal
Personal special
132 General works
132.5 Travels
133 General special. Reforms
e.g. Revolt of the Streltsy, 1698
Military history
134 General works
135 Wars with Turkey
Cf. DR544, Russia in Turkey
136 Wars with Sweden
Cf. DL738, Invasion of Russia by Sweden
137 Wars with Persia
Cf. DS293, Afghan wars, etc.
142 Social life and customs. Civilization. Intellectual life
145 Diplomatic history. Foreign and general relations
146 Alexis
147 Eudoxia Lopukhina
148 Testament of Peter the Great
1725-1762
150 General works
Biography and memoirs
150.5 Collective
150.8.A-Z Individual, A-Z
e.g.
150.8.D6 Dolgorukova, Natalii͡a Borisovna (Sheremeteva), knii͡aginii͡a
150.8.M8 Münnich, Burkhard Christoph, graf von
151 Catherine I, 1725-1727
153 Peter II, 1727-1730
156 Anne, Empress of Russia, 1730-1740
157 Biron, Ernst Johann, Duke of Courland
159 Ivan VI and Anna Leopoldovna, 1740-1741
161 Elizabeth, 1741-1762
166 Peter III, 1762
Catherine II, 1762-1796
168 Sources and documents
Biography and memoirs
168.9 Collective
169.A-Z Individual, A-Z
e. g.
169.B3 Bagration, Petr Ivanovich, kni͡az'
169.D3 Dashkova, Ekaterina Romanovna (Voront͡sova), knii͡aginii͡a

History
By period
House of Romanov, 1613-1917
1689-1801. 18th century
Catherine II, 1762-1796
Biography and memoirs
Indivdual, A-Z -- Continued

169.K8 Kutuzov, Mikhail Illarionovich, svetleĭshiĭ kni͡az′ Smolenskiĭ
169.P8 Potemkin, Grigoriĭ Aleksandrovich, kni͡az′
169.R8 Rumi͡ant͡sev, Petr Aleksandrovich, graf
169.S8 Suvorov, Aleksandr Vasil′evich, kni͡az′ Italiĭskiĭ
169.T3 Tarakanova, Elizaveta kni͡azhna (i.e. the imposter so styled)
169.U8 Ushakov, Fedor Fedorovich
170 General works on life and reign
170.A2 Personal correspondence
171 Reign only
171.5 General special
171.6 Addresses, essays, lectures
171.7 Military history
172 Social life and customs. Civilization. Intellectual life

Foreign and general relations
173 General works
Individual countries, see DK67.5.A+

Political history
180 General works
183 Insurrection of Pugachev, 1773-1775

Paul I, 1796-1801
185 Sources and documents
186 General works on life and reign
186.2 Personal special
186.3 Mary Feodorovna, Consort of Paul I
187 War with France

19th century
188 Sources and documents
188.2 Historiography

Biography and memoirs
188.3 Collective
188.6.A-Z Individual, A-Z
e.g.
188.6.B6 Blaramberg, Ivan Fedorovich
188.6.K6 Konstantin, Grand Duke of Russia
188.6.K65 Koshelev, Aleksandr Ivanovich
188.6.M3 Makarov, Stepan Osipovich
188.6.M5 Mikhail Pavlovich, Grand Duke of Russia
188.6.N4 Nesselrode, Karl Robert, graf von
188.6.V5 Vigel′, Filipp Filippovich

Collected works (nonserial)
188.8 Several authors

History
By period
House of Romanov, 1613-1917
19th century
Collected works (nonserial) -- Continued
188.9 Individual authors
189 General works
189.2 Social life and customs. Civilization. Intellectual life
189.7 Foreign and general relations
Alexander I, 1801-1825
190 Sources and documents
Biography and memoirs
190.3 Collective
190.6.A-Z Individual, A-Z
e.g.
190.6.C2 Catharine, Consort of William I, King of Württemberg
190.6.D3 Davydov, Denis Vasil'evich
Kutuzov, Mikhail Illarionovich, see DK169.K8
190.6.R6 Rostopchin, Fedor Vasil'evich, graf
Speranskiĭ, Mikhail Mikhaĭlovich, graf, see DK201
Collected works (nonserial)
190.8 Several authors
190.9 Individual authors
191 General works on life and reign
192 Personal special
194 General special
195 Addresses, essays, lectures
197 Foreign and general relations
Cf. D383, Holy alliance
Cf. DC235+, Russian campaign, 1812
Cf. DC249, Congress of Vienna
Cf. DR561, Russo-Turkish War
201 Speranskiĭ. Administrative reforms
Nicholas I, 1825-1855
209 Sources and documents
Biography and memoirs
209.3 Collective
209.6.A-Z Individual, A-Z
e.g.
209.6.B4 Bestuzhev, Nikolaĭ Aleksandrovich
209.6.H4 Hertzen, Aleksandr Ivanovich
209.6.N3 Nakhimov, Pavel Stepanovich
Collected works (nonserial)
209.8 Several authors
209.9 Individual authors
210 General works on life and reign
210.4 Coronation
210.7 Alexandra Feodorovna, Consort of Nicholas I
Reign only
211 General works

History
By period
House of Romanov, 1613-1917
19th century
Nicholas I, 1825-1855
Reign only -- Continued
212 Insurrection of December 1825 (Decembrists)
213.5 Russo-Khivan Expedition, 1839
Crimean War, 1853-1856
Cf. DR567, Turkey during the Crimean War
214 General works
215 General special. Diplomatic history
Including the Congress of Paris, 1856; Treaty of Paris, etc.
Special events, battles, etc.
215.1 Alma, September 20, 1854
215.3 Balaklava, October 25, 1854
215.5 Inkerman, November 5, 1854
215.7 Sevastopol, 1854-1855
215.8.A-Z Other, A-Z
215.8.O6 Oltenitza, Battle of, 1853
215.8.P4 Petropavlovsk-Kamchatskiĭ, Battle of, 1854
215.8.S6 Silistria, Siege of, 1854
215.8.S7 Sinope, Battle of 1853
215.9 The war in Asia
215.95 Hospitals, etc.
215.97 Personal narratives
Russo-Turkish War, see DR564
Alexander II, 1855-1881
219 Sources and documents
Biography and memoirs
219.3 Collective
219.6.A-Z Individual, A-Z
e.g.
219.6.A4 Aleksandr Mikhaĭlovich, Grand Duke of Russia
219.6.C43 Chernyshevskiĭ, Nikolaĭ Gavrilovich
219.6.D6 Dobroli͡abov, Nikolai Aleksandrovich
219.6.M5 Mili͡utin, Nikolaĭ Alekseevich
219.6.S35 Samarin, I͡Uriĭ Fedorovich
219.6.S6 Skobelev, Mikhail Dmitrievich
219.6.T54 Ti͡utcheva, Anna Fedorovna
Collected works (nonserial)
219.8 Several authors
219.9 Individual authors
220 General works on life and reign
220.7 Personal special
Reign only. Reforms. Nihilism
221 General works
222 Emancipation of the serfs, 1861
Cf. HT807+, Serfdom

History
By period
House of Romanov, 1613-1917
19th century
Alexander II, 1855-1881 -- Continued
223 Foreign and general relations
Alexander III, 1881-1894
234 Sources and documents
Biography and memoirs
235 Collective
236.A-Z Individual, A-Z
e.g.
236.A2 Mariia Feodorovna, Consort of Alexander III
236.K57 Kon, Feliks IAkovlevich
236.K6 Konstantin Konstantinovich, Grand Duke of Russia
236.P6 Pobedonostsev, Konstantin Petrovich
236.T5 Tikhomirov, Lev Aleksandrovich
Collected works (nonserial)
237 Several authors
238 Individual authors
240 General works on life and reign
240.5 Personal special
241 Reign only
243 Addresses, essays, lectures
20th century
246 General works
247 Social life and customs. Civilization. Intellectual life
Nicholas II, 1894-1917
251 Sources and documents
Biography and memoirs
253 Collective
254.A-Z Individual, A-Z
e.g.
254.A5 Alexandra, Consort of Nicholas II
254.A7 Anastasia, Grand Duchess of Russia
254.A8 Azef, Evno Fishelevich
254.B25 Babushkin, Ivan Vasil'evich
254.F7 Frunze, Mikhail Vasil'evich
254.K3 Kerenskiĭ, Aleksandr Fedorovich
254.L26 Lazo, Sergeĭ Georgievich
254.L3-L46 Lenin, Vladimir Il'ich
Collected works
254.L3A2 By date
254.L3A212-L3A219 Translations. By language and date
Selected works
254.L3A25 By date
254.L3A252-L3A259 Translations. By language and date
Biography
254.L4A1-L4A19 Periodicals. Societies. Serials
254.L4A2-L4A29 Dictionaries. Indexes, etc.

History
By period
House of Romanov, 1613-1917
20th century
Nicholas II, 1894-1917
Biography and memoirs
Individual, A-Z
Lenin, Vladimir Il'ich
Biography -- Continued
Correspondence

254.L4A3-L4A39 General
254.L4A4-L4A49 Individual correspondents
254.L4A5-L4Z General works
254.L42 Memoirs by contemporaries
254.L43 Family
Biographical details
254.L44 Childhood and youth
254.L442 Prison and Siberian exile
254.L443 Emigration. Life abroad
254.L444 Assassination attempt
254.L445 Last years
254.L446 Homes and haunts
254.L447 Anniversaries. Celebrations
254.L45 Iconography. Museums. Exhibitions
254.L455 Juvenile works
254.L46 Special topics (not A-Z)
254.M3 Mariia, Grand Duchess of Russia
254.R3 Rasputin, Grigoriĭ Efimovich
254.S35 Sazonov, Sergeĭ Dmitrievich
254.T6 Trotsky, Leon
254.T8 Tukhachevskiĭ, Mikhail Nikolaevich
254.W5 Witte, Sergeĭ I͡Ul'evich, graf
Collected works (nonserial)
255 Several authors
256 Individual authors
258 General works on life and reign
258.4 Coronation
258.6 Assassination and burial
Personal special
259 Travels, etc.
259.4 Portraits, caricatures, etc.
260 Reign only
262 General works on the state of the empire, 1904-1917
262.8 Foreign and general relations
Russo-Japanese War, 1904-1905, see DS516+
Revolution of 1905
263.A1 Periodicals. Societies. Serials
263.A2 Sources and documents
Biography, see DK254.A+, DK268.A1+
Causes, origins, see DK262
263.A3-Z General works
263.13 Pictorial works. Satire, caricature, etc.

History
By period
House of Romanov, 1613-1917
20th century
Nicholas II, 1894-1917
Revolution of 1905 -- Continued
263.15 Historiography
263.16 Addresses, essays, lectures
264 Special events
Personal narratives
264.12 Collective
264.13 Individual
264.2.A-Z Local revolutionary history. By place, A-Z
Estonia, see DK503.73+
Latvia, see DK504.73+
Lithuania, see DK505.73+
264.3 Prisoners and prisons. Exiles
264.5.A-Z Other topics, A-Z
264.5.I6 Influence
264.5.I67 Intellectuals
264.5.O36 Officers
264.5.P47 Peasantry
264.5.P8 Public opinion
264.5.R45 Religious aspects
264.5.T7 Transportation
Including railroad employees
264.7 Celebrations. Memorials. Monuments
264.8 Period of World War I, 1914-1918
For the war itself, see D501+
Revolution, 1917-1921
265.A1-A19 Periodicals. Societies. Serials
265.A195A-Z Museums, exhibitions, etc. By place, A-Z
Sources and documents
265.A2-A4 Serials
265.A5-A55 Nonserials
265.A553 Historiography
265.A556 Study and teaching
Biography, see DK254.A+, DK268.A1+
Causes, origins, etc , see DK262
265.A56-Z General works
For works by Lenin use:
.L4A1 Collected works. By date
.L4A12-.L4A19 Translations. By language and date
.L4A2 Selected works. By date
.L4A22-.L4A29 Translations. By language and date
.L4A3-.L4Z Individual works. By title, A-Z
265.13 Chronology
265.15 Pictorial works. Satire, caricature, etc.
265.17 Addresses, essays, lectures
265.19 February Revolution, 1917. Provisional government (Kerenskii)
Assassination of Nicholas II, see DK258.6
Military operations

History
By period
Revolution, 1917-1921
Military operations -- Continued
265.2 General works
Individual campaigns, battles, etc , see DK265.8.A+
265.23.A-Z Regimental histories, A-Z
Naval operations
265.3 General works
265.35.A-Z Individual engagements, ships, etc., A-Z
Allied intervention, 1918-1920
265.4 General works
265.42.A-Z By region or country, A-Z
265.5 Prisoners and prisons
265.6 Medical care. Hospitals. Health aspects
Personal narratives
265.69 Collective
265.7.A-Z Individual, A-Z
265.8.A-Z Local revolutionary history. By place, A-Z
For Ukrainian independence movement, as distinct from Bolshevik activities, see DK508.832
265.8.A73 Armenia
265.8.A9 Azerbaijan
265.8.B9 Belarus
265.8.E8 Estonia
265.8.G4 Georgia (Republic). Georgian Sakartvelo
265.8.K39 Kazakhstan
265.8.K57 Kyrgyzstan
265.8.L33 Latvia
265.8.L4 Leningrad
265.8.L58 Lithuania
265.8.M48 Moldova. Bessarabia
265.8.M6 Moscow
265.8.R85 Russia
265.8.S5 Siberia
265.8.S63 Soviet Central Asia
265.8.T27 Tajikistan
265.8.T93 Turkmenistan
265.8.U4 Ukraine
265.8.U9 Uzbekistan
265.9.A-Z Other topics, A-Z
265.9.A35 Akademiia nauk SSSR
265.9.A5 Anarchists. Anarchism
265.9.A6 Armed forces. Army (Political activity)
265.9.A7 Art and the revolution
265.9.A8 Atrocities
265.9.C4 Children
265.9.C5 Civilian relief
265.9.C62 Cossacks
265.9.D45 Democracy and the revolution
265.9.D47 Destruction and pillage
265.9.E2 Economic aspects
265.9.E75 Ethnic relations

History
By period
Revolution, 1917-1921
Other topics, A-Z -- Continued

265.9.F48 Food supply
265.9.F49 Foreign influences
Foreign participation
265.9.F5 General works
265.9.F52A-Z By country, A-Z
265.9.F55 Foreign public opinion
265.9.I5 Influence
265.9.I55 Intellectuals
265.9.J48 Jews
265.9.K73 Krasnaia͡ gvardii͡a. Red Guard
265.9.M42 Medals, badges, decorations of honor
265.9.M45 Mensheviks
265.9.P4 Peasantry
265.9.P6 Press
265.9.P74 Protest movements
265.9.P8 Public opinion
265.9.R25 Rabochai͡a oppozit͡sii͡a (Political party)
Red Guard, see DK265.9.K73
265.9.R3 Refugees
Cf. DK269, Emigrés
265.9.R4 Religious aspects
265.9.S4 Secret service, spies, etc.
265.9.S6 Soviets (Councils)
265.9.T48 Theater and the revolution
265.9.T74 Transportation and the revolution
265.9.W57 Women
265.9.W65 Working class
265.95 Celebrations. Memorials. Monuments

Soviet regime, 1918-1991
266.A2 Periodicals. Societies. Congresses
266.A3 Sources and documents
266.A33 Historiography
266.A4-Z General works
266.3 General special
e.g. Espionage and sabotage
266.4 Social life and customs. Civilization. Intellectual life
266.45 Foreign and general relations
266.5 1918-1924. Lenin
For the biography of Lenin, see DK254.L3+
1925-1953. Stalin
Periodicals, etc , see DK266.A2
267 General works
267.3 Pamphlets, etc. By date
Biography and memoirs
268.A1 Collective
268.A2-Z Individual, A-Z
e.g.
268.D9 Dzerzhinskiĭ, Feliks Ėdmundovich

History
By period
Soviet regime, 1918-1991
1925-1953. Stalin
Biography and memoirs
Individual, A-Z -- Continued
268.K3 Kalinin, Mikhail Ivanovich
268.L5 Litvinov, Maksim Maksimovich
268.M64 Molotov, Vi͡acheslav Mikhaĭlovich
268.S8 Stalin, Joseph
268.3 Social life and customs. Civilization. Intellectual life
268.4 Political history
268.5 Foreign and general relations
269 Emigrés
269.5 Public opinion formation. Internal propaganda
Soviet propaganda in foreign countries
270 General works
272.A-Z In individual countries, A-Z
Anti-Soviet propaganda
272.5 General works
272.7.A-Z In individual countries, A-Z
273 Period of World War II, 1939-1945
Cf. DL1095+, Russo-Finnish War, 1939-1940
For the war itself, see D731+
1953-1985
274.A2 Periodicals. Societies. Serials
274.A3-Z General works
274.3 Addresses, essays, lectures
Biography and memoirs of contemporaries
275.A1 Collective
275.A2-Z Individual, A-Z
e.g.
275.B8 Bulganin, Nikolaĭ Aleksandrovich
275.K5 Khrushchev, Nikita Sergeevich
275.M3 Malenkov, Georgiĭ Maksimilianovich
276 Social life and customs. Civilization. Intellectual life
Soviet propaganda in foreign countries
278 General works
279.A-Z Individual countries, A-Z
Anti-Soviet propaganda
280 General works
281.A-Z Individual countries, A-Z
282 Foreign and general relations
1985-1991
285 Periodicals. Societies. Serials
285.5 Sources and documents
286 General works
286.5 Addresses, essays, lectures
287 Social life and customs. Civilization. Intellectual life
288 Political history

History
By period
Soviet regime, 1918-1991
1985-1991 -- Continued
289 Foreign and general relations
Biography and memoirs
290 Collective
290.3.A-Z Individual, A-Z
e.g.
290.3.A53 Andropov, I͡U. V.
290.3.G67 Gorbachev, Mikhail Sergeevich, 1931-
292 Attempted coup. 1991
293 1991-
Class here works on the former Soviet republics treated collectively
For works on the Commonwealth of Independent States, see DK1.5
(401-444) Poland
see DK4010-DK4800
(445-465) Finland
see DL1002-DL1180
500.A-Z Regions not limited to one Republic, A-Z
e.g.
500.A95 Azov, Sea of, Region
Baltic States, see DK502.3+
500.B55 Black Sea Coast (Soviet Union)
For Black Sea Coast (Ukraine) and other republics and countries, see the republic and country
Caucasus, see DK509
Caucasus, Northern (Russia), see DK511.C2
500.C68 Courland Lagoon and Spit (Lithuania and Russia)
500.D65 Dnieper River
For the Central Dnieper Region (Ukraine), see DK508.9.C46
500.D66 Dniester River (Ukraine and Moldova)
500.D67 Donets Basin (Ukraine and Russia). Donbas
500.F67 Former Polish Eastern Territories
500.K47 Kerch Strait
500.L57 Livonia (Estonia and Latvia)
Northern Soviet Union, see DK501
Palesse, see DK500.P75
Polesie, see DK500.P75
500.P75 Pripet Marshes
Siberia, see DK751+
Southern Soviet Union, see DK509
Soviet Asia, see DK750
Soviet Central Asia, see DK845+
Transcaucasia, see DK509
500.W48 Western Soviet Union. Western Russia
Local history and description
501 Northern Soviet Union (Table D-DR1 modified)
For local, see DK511, DK651, etc.

Local history and description -- Continued
Baltic States
Including Estonia, Latvia, and Lithuania treated collectively
502.3 Periodicals. Societies. Serials
502.35 General works
502.4 Description and travel
502.5 Antiquities
502.6 Social life and customs. Civilization. Intellectual life
Ethnography
502.63 General works
502.64.A-Z Individual elements in the population, A-Z
502.64.G47 Germans
502.64.R87 Russians
502.7 General works
502.715 Foreign and general relations
By period
502.72 Early to 1918
502.73 1918-1940
502.74 1940-1991
502.75 1991-
Estonia
503 Periodicals. Societies. Serials
Museums, exhibitions, etc.
503.12 General works
503.13.A-Z Individual. By place, A-Z
503.14 Congresses
503.15 Sources and documents
Collected works (nonserial)
503.16 Several authors
503.17 Individual authors
503.18 Gazetteers. Dictionaries, etc.
503.19 Place names (General)
503.2 Directories
503.22 Guidebooks
503.23 General works
503.24 General special
503.25 Pictorial works
Historic monuments, landmarks, scenery, etc. (General)
For local, see DK503.9+
503.26 General works
503.27 Preservation
503.28 Historical geography
503.29 Description and travel
503.3 Antiquities
For local antiquities, see DK503.9+
503.32 Social life and customs. Civilization. Intellectual life
For specific periods, see the period
Ethnography
503.33 General works

Local history and description
Estonia
Ethnography -- Continued
503.34 National characteristics
503.35.A-Z Individual elements in the population, A-Z
503.35.G3 Germans
503.35.P6 Poles
503.35.R87 Russians
503.35.S94 Swedes
503.36 Estonians in foreign countries (General)
For Estonians in a particular country, see the country
History
Periodicals. Societies. Serials, see DK503
503.37 Dictionaries. Chronological tables, outlines, etc.
Biography (Collective)
For individual biography, see the specific period or place
503.38 General works
503.39 Rulers, kings, etc.
503.4 Queens. Princes and princesses
Houses, noble families, etc.
503.42 General works
503.43.A-Z Individual houses, families, etc., A-Z
503.44 Statesmen
503.45 Women
Cf. CT3490, Biography of women
Historiography
503.46 General works
Biography of historians, area studies specialists, archaeologists, etc.
503.47 Collective
503.48.A-Z Individual, A-Z
Study and teaching
503.49 General works
503.5.A-Z By region or country, A-Z
Subarrange by author
General works
503.52 Through 1800
503.53 1801-1980
503.54 1981-
503.55 Pictorial works
503.56 Juvenile works
503.57 Addresses, essays, lectures. Anecdotes, etc.
Military history
For individual campaigns and engagements, see the special period
503.6 Sources and documents
503.62 General works
Naval history
For individual campaigns and engagements, see the special period

Local history and description
Estonia
History
Naval history -- Continued
503.63 Sources and documents
503.64 General works
Political history
For specific periods, see the period
503.65 Sources and documents
503.66 General works
Foreign and general relations
For works on relations with a specific country regardless of period, see DK503.69.A+
503.67 Sources and documents
503.68 General works
503.69.A-Z Relations with individual countries, A-Z
By period
503.7 Early to 1200
503.71 1200-1600
503.72 1600-1800
1800-1918
503.73 General works
Biography and memoirs
503.735 Collective
503.736.A-Z Individual, A-Z
1918-1940
For works on the Bolshevik Revolution in Estonia, see DK265.8.E8
503.74 General works
Biography and memoirs
503.745 Collective
503.746.A-Z Individual, A-Z
503.747 War of Independence, 1918-1920
503.748 Communist Coup, 1924
1940-1991
For works on World War II as distinct from the time period 1939-1945, see D731+
503.75 General works
Biography and memoirs
503.76 Collective
503.77.A-Z Individual, A-Z
1991-
503.8 General works
503.82 Social life and customs. Civilization. Intellectual life
503.83 Political history
503.835 Foreign and general relations
Biography and memoirs
503.84 Collective
503.85.A-Z Individual, A-Z
Local history and description
503.9.A-Z Regions, oblasts, etc., A-Z
Cities and towns

Local history and description
Estonia
Local history and description
Cities and towns -- Continued
Tallinn
503.92 Periodicals. Societies. Serials
503.922 Sources and documents
503.923 Directories. Dictionaries. Gazetteers
503.924 Guidebooks
503.925 General works
503.926 Description. Geography
503.927 Pictorial works
503.928 Antiquities
503.929 Social life and customs. Civilization. Intellectual life
Ethnography
503.93 General works
503.932.A-Z Individual elements in the population, A-Z
History
Biography
503.933 Collective
503.934.A-Z Individual, A-Z
503.935 General works
Sections, monuments, parks, streets, buildings, etc.
503.938 Collective
503.939.A-Z Individual, A-Z
503.95.A-Z Other cities, towns, etc., A-Z
e.g.
503.95.T38 Tartu
Latvia
504 Periodicals. Societies. Serials
Museums, exhibitions, etc.
504.12 General works
504.13.A-Z Individual. By place, A-Z
504.14 Congresses
504.15 Sources and documents
Collected works (nonserial)
504.16 Several authors
504.17 Individual authors
504.18 Gazetteers. Dictionaries, etc.
504.19 Place names (General)
504.2 Directories
504.22 Guidebooks
504.23 General works
504.24 General special
504.25 Pictorial works
Historic monuments, landmarks, scenery, etc. (General)
For local, see DK504.9 +
504.26 General works
504.27 Preservation
504.28 Historical geography

Local history and description
Latvia -- Continued
504.29 Description and travel
504.3 Antiquities
For local antiquities, see DK504.9+
504.32 Social life and customs. Civilization. Intellectual life
For specific periods, see the period
Ethnography
504.33 General works
504.34 National characteristics
504.35.A-Z Individual elements in the population, A-Z
504.35.G3 Germans
504.35.P6 Poles
504.35.S53 Slavs
504.36 Latvians in foreign countries (General)
For Latvians in a particular country, see the country
History
Periodicals. Societies. Serials, see DK504
504.37 Dictionaries. Chronological tables, outlines, etc.
Biography (Collective)
For individual biography, see the specific period or place
504.38 General works
504.39 Rulers, kings, etc.
504.4 Queens. Princes and princesses
Houses, noble families, etc.
504.42 General works
504.43.A-Z Individual houses, families, etc., A-Z
504.44 Statesmen
504.45 Women
Cf. CT3490, Biography of women
Historiography
504.46 General works
Biography of historians, area studies specialists, archaeologists, etc.
504.47 Collective
504.48.A-Z Individual, A-Z
Study and teaching
504.49 General works
504.5.A-Z By region or country, A-Z
Subarrange by author
General works
504.52 Through 1800
504.53 1801-1980
504.54 1981-
504.55 Pictorial works
504.56 Juvenile works
504.57 Addresses, essays, lectures. Anecdotes, etc.

Local history and description
Latvia
History -- Continued
Military history
For individual campaigns and engagements, see the special period
504.6 Sources and documents
504.62 General works
Naval history
For individual campaigns and engagements, see the special period
504.63 Sources and documents
504.64 General works
Political history
For specific periods, see the period
504.65 Sources and documents
504.66 General works
Foreign and general relations
For works on relations with a specific country regardless of period, see DK504.69.A+
504.67 Sources and documents
504.68 General works
504.69.A-Z Relations with individual countries, A-Z
By period
504.7 Early to 1200
504.71 1200-1600
504.72 1600-1800
1800-1918
504.73 General works
Biography and memoirs
504.735 Collective
504.736.A-Z Individual, A-Z
504.737 Revolution, 1905-1907
1918-1940
For works on the Bolshevik Revolution in Latvia, see DK265.8.L33
504.74 General works
504.746 Foreign relations
Biography and memoirs
504.75 Collective
504.76.A-Z Individual, A-Z
504.765 War of Independence, 1918-1920
1940-1991
For World War II itself as distinct from the time period 1939-1945, see D731+
504.77 General works
Biography and memoirs
504.78 Collective
504.79.A-Z Individual, A-Z
1991-
504.8 General works
504.815 Social life and customs. Civilization. Intellectual life

Local history and description
Latvia
History
By period
1991- -- Continued
504.82 Political history
504.83 Foreign and general relations
Biography and memoirs
504.84 Collective
504.85.A-Z Individual, A-Z
Local history and description
504.9.A-Z Regions, oblasts, etc., A-Z
Cities and towns
Riga
504.92 Periodicals. Societies. Serials
Museums, exhibitions, etc.
504.9215 General works
504.9217.A-Z Individual. By place, A-Z
504.922 Sources and documents
504.923 Directories. Dictionaries. Gazetteers
504.924 Guidebooks
504.925 General works
504.926 Description. Geography
504.927 Pictorial works
504.928 Antiquities
504.929 Social life and customs. Civilization. Intellectual life
Ethnography
504.93 General works
504.932.A-Z Individual elements in the population, A-Z
History
Biography
504.933 Collective
504.934.A-Z Individual, A-Z
504.935 General works
Sections, monuments, parks, streets, buildings, etc.
504.938 Collective
504.939.A-Z Individual, A-Z
504.95.A-Z Other cities, towns, etc., A-Z
e.g.
504.95.L48 Liepaja
Lithuania
505 Periodicals. Societies. Serials
Museums, exhibitions, etc.
505.12 General works
505.13.A-Z Individual, A-Z
505.14 Congresses
505.15 Sources and documents
Collected works (nonserial)
505.16 Several authors
505.17 Individual authors
505.18 Gazetteers. Dictionaries, etc.

Local history and description
Lithuania -- Continued
505.19 Place names (General)
505.2 Directories
505.22 Guidebooks
505.23 General works
505.24 General special
505.25 Pictorial works
Historic monuments, landmarks, scenery, etc. (General)
For local, see DK505.9+
505.26 General works
505.27 Preservation
505.28 Historical geography
505.285 Geography
505.29 Description and travel
505.3 Antiquities
For local antiquities, see DK505.9+
505.32 Social life and customs. Civilization.
Intellectual life
For specific periods, see the period
Ethnography
505.33 General works
505.34 National characteristics
505.35.A-Z Individual elements in the population, A-Z
505.35.B44 Belarusians
505.35.G3 Germans
505.35.P6 Poles
505.35.R87 Russians
505.35.T38 Tatars
505.36 Lithuanians in foreign countries (General)
For Lithuanians in a particular country, see the country
History
Periodicals. Societies. Serials, see DK505
505.37 Dictionaries. Chronological tables, outlines, etc.
Biography (Collective)
For individual biography, see the specific period or place
505.38 General works
505.39 Rulers, kings, etc.
505.4 Queens. Princes and princesses
Houses, noble families, etc.
505.42 General works
505.43.A-Z Individual houses, families, etc., A-Z
505.44 Statesmen
505.45 Women
Cf. CT3490, Biography of women
Historiography
505.46 General works
Biography of historians, area studies specialists, archaeologists, etc.

Local history and description
Lithuania
History
Historiography
Biography of historians, area studies specialists, archaeologists, etc. -- Continued

505.47 Collective
505.48.A-Z Individual, A-Z
Study and teaching
505.49 General works
505.5.A-Z By region or country, A-Z
Subarrange by author
General works
505.52 Through 1800
505.53 1801-1980
505.54 1981-
505.55 Pictorial works
505.56 Juvenile works
505.57 Addresses, essays, lectures. Anecdotes, etc.
Military history
For individual campaigns and engagements, see the special period
505.6 Sources and documents
505.62 General works
Naval history
For individual campaigns and engagements, see the special period
505.63 Sources and documents
505.64 General works
Political history
For specific periods, see the period
505.65 Sources and documents
505.66 General works
Foreign and general relations
For works on relations with a specific country regardless of period, see DK505.69.A+
505.67 Sources and documents
505.68 General works
505.69.A-Z Relations with individual countries, A-Z
By period
Early to 1569
505.695 General works
Early to 1350
505.7 General works
Biography and memoirs
505.705 Collective
505.706.A-Z Individual, A-Z
1350-1569
505.71 General works
Biography and memoirs
505.713 Collective

Local history and description
Lithuania
History
By period
Early to 1569
1350-1569
Biography and memoirs -- Continued
505.714.A-Z Individual, A-Z
e. g.
505.714.K46 Kęstutis, Grand Duke of Lithuania, ca. 1300-1382
1569-1795
505.72 General works
Biography and memoirs
505.725 Collective
505.726.A-Z Individual, A-Z
1795-1918
505.73 General works
Biography and memoirs
505.734 Collective
505.735.A-Z Individual, A-Z
505.736 Revolution, 1830-1832
505.737 Revolution, 1863-1864
505.738 Revolution, 1905-1907
1918-1940
For works on the Bolshevik Revolution in Lithuania, see DK265.8.L58
505.74 General works
Biography and memoirs
505.75 Collective
505.76.A-Z Individual, A-Z
505.765 War of Independence, 1918-1920
1940-1991
For works on World War II as distinct from the time period 1939-1945, see D731+
505.77 General works
Biography and memoirs
505.78 Collective
505.79.A-Z Individual, A-Z
1991-
505.8 General works
505.82 Political history
Biography and memoirs
505.84 Collective
505.85.A-Z Individual, A-Z
Local history and description
505.9.A-Z Regions, oblasts, etc., A-Z
Cities and towns
Vilnius
505.92 Periodicals. Societies. Serials
505.922 Sources and documents
505.923 Directories. Dictionaries. Gazetteers
505.924 Guidebooks

Local history and description
Lithuania
Local history and description
Cities and towns
Vilnius -- Continued
505.925 General works
505.926 Description. Geography
505.927 Pictorial works
505.928 Antiquities
505.929 Social life and customs. Civilization. Intellectual life
Ethnography
505.93 General works
505.932.A-Z Individual elements in the population, A-Z
505.932.B44 Belarusians
505.932.P64 Poles
History
Biography
505.933 Collective
505.934.A-Z Individual, A-Z
505.935 General works
Sections, monuments, parks, streets, buildings, etc.
505.938 Collective
505.939.A-Z Individual, A-Z
505.95.A-Z Other cities, towns, etc., A-Z
e.g.
505.95.K125 Kaunas
Kovno, see DK505.95.K125
Belarus. Byelorussian S.S.R. White Russia
507.A2 Periodicals. Societies. Serials
Museums, exhibitions, etc.
507.12 General works
507.13.A-Z Individual, A-Z
507.14 Congresses
507.15 Sources and documents
Collected works (nonserial)
507.16 Several authors
507.17 Individual authors
507.18 Gazetteers. Dictionaries, etc.
507.19 Place names (General)
507.2 Directories
507.22 Guidebooks
507.23 General works
507.24 General special
507.25 Pictorial works
Historic monuments, landmarks, scenery, etc. (General)
For local, see DK507.9+
507.26 General works
507.27 Preservation
507.28 Historical geography
507.285 Geography

Local history and description
Belarus. Byelorussian S.S.R. White Russia -- Continued
507.29 Description and travel
507.3 Antiquities
For local antiquities, see DK507.9+
507.32 Social life and customs. Civilization.
Intellectual life
For specific periods, see the period
Ethnography
507.33 General works
507.34 National characteristics
507.35.A-Z Individual elements in the population, A-Z
507.35.D79 Drygavichy
507.35.G3 Germans
507.35.L36 Latvians
507.35.P6 Poles
507.35.T37 Tatars
507.36 Belarusians in foreign countries (General)
For Belarusians in a particular country, see the country
History
Periodicals. Societies. Serials, see DK507.A2
507.37 Dictionaries. Chronological tables, outlines, etc.
Biography (Collective)
For individual biography, see the specific period or place
507.38 General works
507.39 Rulers, kings, etc.
507.44 Statesmen
507.45 Women
Cf. CT3490, Biography of women
Historiography
507.46 General works
Biography of historians, area studies specialists, archaeologists, etc.
507.47 Collective
507.48.A-Z Individual, A-Z
Study and teaching
507.49 General works
507.5.A-Z By region or country, A-Z
Subarrange by author
General works
507.52 Through 1800
507.53 1801-1980
507.54 1981-
507.55 Pictorial works
507.56 Juvenile works
507.57 Addresses, essays, lectures. Anecdotes, etc.
Military history
For individual campaigns and engagements, see the special period

Local history and description
Belarus. Byelorussian S.S.R. White Russia
History
Military history -- Continued
507.6 Sources and documents
507.62 General works
Political history
For specific periods, see the period
507.65 Sources and documents
507.66 General works
Foreign and general relations
For works on relations with a specific country regardless of time period, see DK507.69.A+
507.67 Sources and documents
507.68 General works
507.69.A-Z Relations with individual countries, A-Z
By period
507.7 Early to 1237
For works on the early history of Rus', see DK70+
507.71 1237-1569
1569-1795
507.72 General works
Biography and memoirs
507.725 Collective
507.726.A-Z Individual, A-Z
1795-1917
507.727 General works
Biography and memoirs
507.728 Collective
507.729.A-Z Individual, A-Z
1917-1945
For works on the Bolshevik Revolution in Belorussia, see DK265.8.B9
For works on World War II as distinct from the time period 1939-1945, see D731+
507.73 General works
Biography and memoirs
507.74 Collective
507.75.A-Z Individual, A-Z
1945-1991
507.76 General works
507.762 Social life and customs. Civilization. Intellectual life
507.764 Foreign and general relations
Biography and memoirs
507.77 Collective
507.78.A-Z Individual, A-Z
1991-
507.8 General works
507.815 Social life and customs. Civilization. Intellectual life
507.817 Political history

Local history and description
Belarus. Byelorussian S.S.R. White Russia
History
By period
1991- -- Continued
507.8175 Foreign and general relations
Biography and memoirs
507.82 Collective
507.822.A-Z Individual, A-Z
Local history and description
507.9.A-Z Regions, oblasts, etc., A-Z
Cities and towns
Minsk
507.92 Periodicals. Societies. Serials
507.922 Sources and documents
507.923 Directories. Dictionaries. Gazetteers
507.924 Guidebooks
507.925 General works
507.926 Description. Geography
507.927 Pictorial works
507.928 Antiquities
507.929 Social life and customs. Civilization. Intellectual life
Ethnography
507.93 General works
507.932.A-Z Individual elements in the population, A-Z
507.932.P64 Poles
History
Biography
507.933 Collective
507.934.A-Z Individual, A-Z
507.935 General works
Sections, monuments, parks, streets, buildings, etc.
507.938 Collective
507.939.A-Z Individual, A-Z
Other cities, towns, etc.
507.95.A1 Collective
507.95.A2-Z Individual, A-Z
507.95.B68 Brest
507.95.G7 Grodno. Hrodna
Hrodna, see DK507.95.G7
507.95.M58 Mogilev
507.95.V53 Vitebsk
Ukraine
508.A2 Periodicals. Societies. Serials
Museums, exhibitions, etc.
508.A22 General works
508.A23A-Z Individual, A-Z
508.A25 Congresses
508.A3 Sources and documents
Collected works (nonserial)
508.A32 Several authors

Local history and description
Ukraine
Collected works (nonserial) -- Continued
508.A325 Individual authors
508.A4 Gazetteers. Dictionaries, etc.
508.A45 Place names (General)
508.A46 Directories
508.A5-Z Guidebooks
508.12 General works
508.13 General special
508.15 Pictorial works
Historic monuments, landmarks, scenery, etc. (General)
For local, see DK508.9+
508.154 General works
508.155 Preservation
508.157 Historical geography
508.2 Description and travel
508.3 Antiquities
For local, see DK508.9+
508.4 Social life and customs. Civilization. Intellectual life
For specific periods, see the period
Ethnography
508.42 General works
508.423 National characteristics
508.425.A-Z Individual elements in the population, A-Z
508.425.A74 Armenians
508.425.B35 Balts
508.425.B84 Bulgarians
508.425.C55 Cimmerians
508.425.G47 Germans
508.425.G74 Greeks
508.425.H87 Hutsuls
508.425.I73 Italians
508.425.K37 Karaites
508.425.K53 Khazars
508.425.L46 Lemky
508.425.M32 Macedonians
508.425.P65 Poles
508.425.P67 Poliany
508.425.R87 Russians
508.425.S39 Scythians
508.425.T37 Tatars
508.425.T87 Turks
508.44 Ukrainians in foreign countries (General)
For Ukrainians in a particular country, see the country
History
Periodicals. Societies. Serials, see DK508.A2
508.444 Dictionaries. Chronological tables, outlines, etc.

Local history and description
Ukraine
History -- Continued
Biography (Collective)
For individual biography, see the specific period or place
508.45 General works
508.452 Rulers, kings, etc.
508.454 Queens. Princes and princesses
Houses, noble families, etc.
508.456 General works
508.457.A-Z Individual houses, families, etc., A-Z
508.458 Statesmen
508.459 Women
Cf. CT3490, Biography of women
Historiography
508.46 General works
Biography of historians, area studies specialists, archaeologists, etc.
508.465 Collective
508.47.A-Z Individual, A-Z
508.48 Study and teaching
General works
508.49 Through 1800
508.5 1801-1985
508.51 1986-
508.515 Juvenile works
508.52 Addresses, essays, lectures. Anecdotes, etc.
508.53 Philosophy of Ukrainian history
508.54 Military history
508.55 Zaporozhians. Zaporiz'ka Sich. Cossacks. Nova Sich, etc.
For the period 1648-1775, see also DK508.73+
508.554 Political history
For specific periods, see the period
Foreign and general relations
508.56 General works
508.57.A-Z Relations with individual countries, A-Z
By period
For works on early history of Rus', see DK70+
508.66 Early to 1340
1340-1569. Period of Polish-Lithuanian domination
508.67 General works
Biography and memoirs
508.674 Collective
508.675.A-Z Individual, A-Z
e.g.
508.675.V96 Vyshnevet͡sʹkyĭ, Dymtro, kni͡az', d. 1563
508.68 1569-1648. Period of Polish rule
1648-1775
508.73 Sources and documents

Local history and description
Ukraine
History
By period
1648-1775 -- Continued

508.735 Historiography
508.74 General works
Biography and memoirs
508.75 Collective
508.752.A-Z Individual, A-Z
e.g.
508.752.A6 Apostol, Danylo, Hetman of Ukraine
508.752.K5 Khmel'nyts'kyi, Bohdan, Hetman of Ukraine
508.752.M3 Mazepa, Ivan, Hetman of Ukraine
508.752.P65 Polubotok, Pavlo, Hetman of Ukraine
1648-1657
Including Battle of Berestechko, Treaty of Pereiaslav, etc.
508.753 General works
Biography and memoirs
508.754 Collective
508.755.A-Z Individual, A-Z
1657-1709
Including Battle of Konotop, etc.
508.756 General works
Biography and memoirs
508.757 Collective
508.758.A-Z Individual, A-Z
1709-1775
Including Uprising of 1768
508.759 General works
Biography and memoirs
508.76 Collective
508.761.A-Z Individual, A-Z
1775-1917
508.77 Sources and documents
508.771 Historiography
508.772 General works
508.773 Social life and customs. Civilization. Intellectual life
Biography and memoirs
508.78 Collective
508.782.A-Z Individual, A-Z
e.g.
508.782.D7 Drahomaniv, Mykhailo
508.782.K3 Karmaliuk, Ustym
20th century
508.788 General works
1917-1945
508.79 Sources and documents
508.8 Historiography
508.812 General works

Local history and description
Ukraine
History
By period
20th century
1917-1945 -- Continued
508.813 Social life and customs. Civilization. Intellectual life
Biography and memoirs
508.82 Collective
508.83.A-Z Individual, A-Z
e.g.
508.83.D6 Doroshenko, Dmytro
508.83.K6 Konovalets', I͡Evhen
508.83.P4 Petli͡ura, Symon
508.83.S55 Skoropads'kyĭ, Pavlo, Hetman of Ukraine
508.832 1917-1921. Period of independence
Class here works limited to the Ukrainian independence movement
For Bolshevik Revolution in Ukraine, as distinct from the independence movement, see DK265.8.U4
1921-1944
508.833 General works
Biography and memoirs
508.834 Collective
508.835.A-Z Individual, A-Z
e.g.
508.835.B3 Bandera, Stepan
1945-1991
508.84 General works
Biography and memoirs
508.842 Collective
508.843.A-Z Individual, A-Z
1991-
508.845 Sources and documents
508.846 General works
508.847 Social life and customs. Civilization. Intellectual life
508.848 Political history
508.849 Foreign and general relations
Biography and memoirs
508.850 Collective
508.851.A-Z Individual, A-Z
Local history and description
508.9.A-Z Regions, oblasts, etc., A-Z
e.g.
508.9.B47 Berezhany Region
508.9.B48 Bessarabia
For Bessarabia (General), see DK509.1+
508.9.B56 Black Sea Coast
508.9.B57 Black Sea Lowland
508.9.B65 Boikivshchyna

Local history and description
Ukraine
Local history and description
Regions, oblasts, etc., A-Z -- Continued

508.9.B85 Bukovina (Bukovyna)
For Romanian Bukovina, see DR281.S8
508.9.C37 Carpathian Mountains
508.9.C46 Central Dnieper Region
508.9.C47 Chernihivs'ka oblast'
Crimea, see DK508.9.K78
508.9.D64 Dnepropetrovsk (Dnipropetrovske) Region
508.9.D66 Donets'ka oblast'
508.9.D76 Drogobych (Drohobych) Region
Eastern Galicia, see DK508.9.G35
508.9.G35 Galicia, Eastern
Halychyna Carpathians, see DK508.9.G35
508.9.H87 Hutsulshchyna
508.9.I82 Ivano-Frankovskaia (Ivano-Frankivs'ka) oblast'
Karpaty, see DK508.9.C37
508.9.K53 Khar'kov (Khar'kiv) Region
508.9.K54 Khersonskaia (Khersons'ka) oblast'
508.9.K55 Khmel'nitskia (Khmel'nyts'ka) oblast'
508.9.K56 Khortytsia Island
508.9.K57 Kiev oblast'
508.9.K78 Kryms'ka oblast, Respublika Krym
Lemberg Region, see DK508.9.L85
508.9.L84 Luganskaia (Luhans'ka) oblast'
508.9.L85 L'vivs'ka oblast'
508.9.N55 Nikolaevskaia (Nykolaïvs'ka) oblast'
508.9.O33 Odesskaia oblast'
508.9.P48 Perekop Isthmus
508.9.P64 Podillia
508.9.P65 Poltavskaia (Poltavs'ka) oblast'
508.9.R67 Ros (Ros') River and Region
508.9.R68 Rovenskaia (Rivens'ka) oblast'
508.9.S49 Sevastopol'skaia (Sevastopol's'ka) oblast'
508.9.S59 Sivershchyna
Stanislavskaia oblast, see DK508.9.I82
508.9.S96 Sums'ka oblast'
508.9.T38 Taurida
508.9.T48 Ternopil's'ka oblast'
508.9.U37 Ukraine, Western
Ukrainian Carpathians, see DK508.9.C37
508.9.V47 Verkhovyna Region
508.9.V56 Vinnitskaia (Vynnyts'ka) oblast'
508.9.V65 Volhynian, Volyns'ka oblast'
508.9.V67 Voroshilovgradskaia (Voroshylovhrads'ka) oblast'
Western Ukraine, see DK508.9.U37
508.9.Z35 Zakarpatskaia (Zakarpats'ka) oblast'
508.9.Z36 Zaporozhskaia (Zaporozhs'ka) oblast'
508.9.Z37 Zbruch Valley
508.9.Z49 ZHytomyrs'ka oblast'

Local history and description
Ukraine
Local history and description -- Continued
Cities and towns
Kiev (Kyïv)

508.92 Periodicals. Societies. Serials
508.922 Sources and documents
508.923 Directories. Dictionaries. Gazetteers
508.924 Guidebooks
508.925 General works
508.926 Description. Geography
508.927 Pictorial works
508.928 Antiquities
508.929 Social life and customs. Civilization. Intellectual life

Ethnography
508.93 General works
508.932.A-Z Individual elements in the population, A-Z

History
Biography
508.933 Collective
508.934.A-Z Individual, A-Z
508.935 General works

Sections, monuments, parks, streets, buildings, etc.
508.938 Collective
508.939.A-Z Individual, A-Z

Other cities, towns, etc.
508.95.A1 Collective
508.95.A2-Z Individual, A-Z
e.g.
508.95.B35 Balaklava
508.95.C54 Chernihiv
508.95.C543 Chernivt͡si
508.95.C544 Chersonese (City)
508.95.D64 Dnipropetrovs'k
508.95.D66 Donets'k
508.95.I24 I͡Alta
508.95.I82 Ivano-Frankivs'k
508.95.K47 Kerch
508.95.K53 Kharkiv
Kiev, see DK508.92 +
Lemberg, see DK508.95.L86
508.95.L86 L'viv
508.95.O33 Odesa
508.95.P47 Perei͡aslav-Khmel'nyt͡s'kyĭ
508.95.S49 Sevastopol'
Stanislav, see DK508.95.I82
508.95.T47 Ternopil'
508.95.U83 Uz͡hhorod
508.95.V56 Vinnyt͡sia
Yalta, see DK508.95.I24

Local history and description -- Continued

509 Southern Soviet Union

Including Black Sea, Caucasus, Armenia, Transcaucasia, etc., in various combinations

For Caucasus, Northern, see DK511.C2

Moldova. Moldavian S.S.R. Bessarabia

For Romanian Moldavia, see DR201+

For Ukrainian Bessarabia, see DK508.9.B48

509.1 Periodicals. Societies. Serials

Museums, exhibitions, etc.

509.12 General works

509.13.A-Z Individual, A-Z

509.14 Congresses

509.15 Sources and documents

Collected works (nonserial)

509.16 Several authors

509.17 Individual authors

509.18 Gazetteers. Dictionaries, etc.

509.19 Place names (General)

509.2 Directories

509.22 Guidebooks

509.23 General works

509.24 General special

509.25 Pictorial works

Historic monuments, landmarks, scenery, etc. (General)

For local, see DK509.9+

509.26 General works

509.27 Preservation

509.28 Historical geography

509.29 Description and travel

509.3 Antiquities

For local antiquities, see DK509.9+

509.32 Social life and customs. Civilization. Intellectual life

For specific periods, see the period

Ethnography

509.33 General works

509.34 National characteristics

509.35.A-Z Individual elements in the population, A-Z

509.35.B84 Bulgarians

509.35.G25 Gagauz

509.35.G3 Germans

509.35.P6 Poles

509.35.R88 Russians

509.36 Moldavians in foreign countries (General)

For Moldavians in a particular country, see the country

History

Periodicals. Societies. Serials, see DK509.1

509.37 Dictionaries. Chronological tables, outlines, etc.

Local history and description
Moldova. Moldavian S.S.R. Bessarabia
History -- Continued
Biography (Collective)
For individual biography, see the specific period or place
509.38 General works
509.39 Rulers, kings, etc.
509.44 Statesmen
509.45 Women
Cf. CT3490, Biography of women
Historiography
509.46 General works
Biography of historians, area studies specialists, archaeologists, etc.
509.47 Collective
509.48.A-Z Individual, A-Z
Study and teaching
509.49 General works
509.5.A-Z By region or country, A-Z
General works
509.52 Through 1800
509.53 1801-1980
509.54 1981-
509.55 Pictorial works
509.56 Juvenile works
509.57 Addresses, essays, lectures. Anecdotes, etc.
Military history
For individual campaigns and engagements, see the special period
509.6 Sources and documents
509.62 General works
Political history
For specific periods, see the period
509.65 Sources and documents
509.66 General works
Foreign and general relations
For works on relations with a specific country regardless of period, see DK509.69.A+
509.67 Sources and documents
509.68 General works
509.69.A-Z Relations with individual countries, A-Z
By period
Early to 1812, see DR238+
509.7 1812-1918
1918-1940
For works on the Bolshevik Revolution in Moldavia, see DK265.8.M48
509.71 General works
Biography and memoirs
509.72 Collective
509.73.A-Z Individual, A-Z

Local history and description
Moldova. Moldavian S.S.R. Bessarabia
History
By period -- Continued
1940-1991
For World War II as distinct from the time period 1939-1945, see D731+

509.74 General works
Biography and memoirs
509.75 Collective
509.76.A-Z Individual, A-Z
1991-
509.772 General works
Biography and memoirs
509.773 Collective
509.774.A-Z Individual, A-Z
Local history and description
509.9.A-Z Regions, oblasts, etc., A-Z
Cities and towns
Chisinau. Kishinev
509.92 Periodicals. Societies. Serials
509.922 Sources and documents
509.923 Directories. Dictionaries. Gazetteers
509.924 Guidebooks
509.925 General works
509.926 Description. Geography
509.927 Pictorial works
509.928 Antiquities
509.929 Social life and customs. Civilization. Intellectual life
Ethnography
509.93 General works
509.932.A-Z Individual elements in the population, A-Z
History
Biography
509.933 Collective
509.934.A-Z Individual, A-Z
509.935 General works
Sections, monuments, parks, streets, buildings, etc.
509.938 Collective
509.939.A-Z Individual, A-Z
509.95.A-Z Other cities, towns, etc., A-Z
e.g.
509.95.T57 Tiraspol

Local history and description -- Continued
Russia (Federation). Russian S.F.S.R.
Class here, DK510-DK510.75, only works that discuss the Russian S.F.S.R. since its formation in 1917 by the Soviets
For local history and description for all periods, see DK511+
For local history and description of Siberia for all periods, see DK751+
For works that discuss the same territory for the pre-1917 period, or the pre-1917 and post-1917 periods combined, see DK1+

510 Periodicals. Societies. Serials
Museums, exhibitions, etc.
510.12 General works
510.13.A-Z Individual, A-Z
510.14 Congresses
510.15 Sources and documents
Collected works (nonserial)
510.16 Several authors
510.17 Individual authors
510.18 Gazetteers. Dictionaries, etc.
510.19 Place names (General)
510.2 Directories
510.22 Guidebooks
510.23 General works
510.24 General special
510.25 Pictorial works
Historic monuments, landmarks, scenery, etc. (General)
For local, see DK511+
510.26 General works
510.27 Preservation
510.28 Historical geography
510.29 Description and travel
510.3 Antiquities
For local antiquities, see DK511+
510.32 Social life and customs. Civilization. Intellectual life
For specific periods, see the period
Ethnography
510.33 General works
510.34 National characteristics
510.35.A-Z Individual elements in the population, A-Z
510.35.A23 Abaza
510.35.A75 Armenians
510.35.B38 Bashkir
510.35.C45 Chechens
510.35.C55 Chuvash
510.35.C68 Cossacks
510.35.E76 Estonians
510.35.G3 Germans
510.35.K65 Komi

Local history and description
Russia (Federation). Russian S.F.S.R.
Ethnography
Individual elements
in the population, A-Z -- Continued

510.35.L35 Lakhs
510.35.M35 Mari
510.35.M67 Mordvins
510.35.N63 Nogai
510.35.P6 Poles
510.35.S57 Skolts (Sami people)
510.35.U33 Udmurts
510.35.U35 Ukrainians
510.35.V45 Veps
510.36 Russians in foreign countries (General)
For Russians in a particular country, see the country

History
Periodicals. Societies. Serials, see DK510
510.37 Dictionaries. Chronological tables, outlines, etc.
Biography (Collective)
For individual biography, see the specific period or place
510.38 General works
510.42 Statesmen
510.44 Women
Cf. CT3490, Biography of women
Historiography
510.46 General works
Biography of historians, area studies specialists, archaeologists, etc.
510.47 Collective
510.48.A-Z Individual, A-Z
Study and teaching
510.49 General works
510.5.A-Z By region or country, A-Z
510.52 General works
510.55 Pictorial works
510.555 Philosophy of Russian Federation history
510.56 Juvenile works
510.57 Addresses, essays, lectures. Anecdotes, etc.
Military history, see DK50+
510.6 Political history
For specific periods, see the period
Foreign and general relations, see DK65+
By period
Early to 1917, see DK70+
1917-1945
For works on the Bolshevik Revolution in the Russian S.F.S.R., see DK265.8.R85
For World War II as distinct from the time period 1939-1945, see D731+

Local history and description
Russia (Federation). Russian S.F.S.R.
History
By period
1917-1945 -- Continued
510.7 General works
Biography and memoirs
510.71 Collective
510.72.A-Z Individual, A-Z
1945-1991
510.73 General works
Biography and memoirs
510.74 Collective
510.75.A-Z Individual, A-Z
1991-
510.755 Sources and documents
510.76 General works
510.762 Social life and customs. Civilization. Intellectual life
510.763 Political history
510.764 Foreign and general relations
Biography and memoirs
510.765 Collective
510.766.A-Z Individual, A-Z
Local history and description of European Russian S.F.S.R.
511.A-Z Oblasts, regions, etc., A-Z
e.g.
For regions, etc. of Ukraine, see DK508.9.A+
511.A28 Adygeĭskai͡a avtonomnai͡a oblast'
511.A5 Arkhangel'skai͡a oblast'
A.S.S.R. Nemtsev Povolsh'i͡a, see DK511.V66
511.A7 Astrakhan'skai͡a oblast'
511.B33 Bashkirskai͡a A.S.S.R.
Beloe More, see DK511.W53
511.C07 Caspian Sea
511.C2 Caucasus, Northern
511.C5 Chuvashskai͡a A.S.S.R.
511.D8 Don Cossacks (Province)
East Karelia, see DK511.K18
German Volga A.S.S.R , see DK511.V66
I͡Aroslavskai͡a oblast, see DK511.Y2
511.K12 Kabardia
511.K16 Kalmytskai͡a A.S.S.R.
511.K17 Kama River and Valley
511.K18 Karel'skai͡a A.S.S.R.
Kazan, see DK511.T17
511.K47 Komi A.S.S.R.
511.K475 Komi-Permiatskiĭ natsional'nyĭ okrug
511.K5 Kostromskai͡a oblast'
511.K6 Kubanskai͡a oblast'
511.K8 Kurskai͡a oblast'
Kuĭbyshevskai͡a oblast, see DK511.S233

Local history and description
Russia (Federation). Russian S.F.S.R.
Local history and description of European Russian S.F.S.R.
Oblasts, regions, etc., A-Z -- Continued

511.L13 Ladoga, Lake
511.L195 Leningradskaia oblast'
For city, see DK541+
511.M28 Mariskaia A.S.S.R.
511.M57 Mordovskaia (Mordvinian) A.S.S.R.
511.M6 Moscow oblast'
For city, see DK588+
Nizhni Zemlya, see G800
North Ossetia, see DK511.S44
511.N7 Novgorodskaia oblast'
511.O45 Olonetskaia oblast'
511.O75 Orenburgskaia oblast'
511.P17 Pechora River and Valley
511.P2 Permskaia oblast'
511.P8 Pskovskaia oblast'
511.R9 Riazanskaia oblast'
511.S233 Samarskaia oblast'. Kuibyshevskaia oblast'
511.S3 Saratovskaia oblast'
511.S44 Severo-Ossentiskaia A.S.S.R. North Ossetia
Siberia, see DK751+
Simbirsk, see DK511.U4
511.S7 Smolenskaia oblast'
511.T1 Tambovskaia oblast'
511.T17 Tatarskaia A.S.S.R.
511.T7 Tverskaia oblast'
511.U16 Udmurtskaia A.S.S.R.
511.U2 Ufa Region
511.U4 Ulianovskaia oblast'
511.U7 Ural Mountains
511.V6 Vladimirskaia
511.V65 Volga River and Valley
511.V66 Volga, German (A.S.S.R.)
511.V8 Vologodskaia oblast'
511.V9 Voronezhskaia oblast'
511.W53 White Sea
511.Y2 Yaroslavskaia oblast'

Cities and towns
Saint Petersburg. Leningrad. Petrograd
541 Periodicals. Societies. Serials
543 Biography
545 Directories. Dictionaries. Gazetteers
549 Guidebooks
General works. Description
551 Through 1950
552 1951-
553 Pictorial works
555 Antiquities

Local history and description
Russia (Federation). Russian S.F.S.R.
Local history and description
Cities and towns
Saint Petersburg.
Leningrad. Petrograd -- Continued
557 Social life and customs. Civilization.
Intellectual life
Ethnography
559 General works
559.5.A-Z Individual elements in the population, A-Z
559.5.G45 Germans
559.5.P64 Poles
559.5.S54 Swedes
History
561 General works
By period
565 1703-1800
568 1801-
For works on the Bolshevik Revolution in Leningrad, see DK265.8.L4
Sections, monuments, parks, streets, etc.
571 Collective
572.A-Z Individual, A-Z
Buildings
573 Collective
574.A-Z Individual, A-Z
579 Other
Moscow
588 Periodicals. Societies. Serials
590 Museums, exhibitions, etc.
Subarrange by author
591 Sources and documents
593 Biography
595 Directories. Dictionaries. Gazetteers
597 Guidebooks
599 Antiquities
600 Social life and customs. Civilization.
Intellectual life
Ethnography
600.2 General works
600.3.A-Z Individual elements in the population, A-Z
600.3.A7 Armenians
600.3.G46 Georgians (Transcaucasians)
600.3.G5 Germans
600.3.M64 Moldavians
General works. History and description
601 Through 1950
Cf. DK265.8.M6, Local revolutionary history, 1917-1921
601.2 1951-
601.5 Pictorial works
Sections, districts, suburbs, etc.

Local history and description
Russia (Federation). Russian S.F.S.R.
Local history and description
Cities and towns
Moscow
Sections, districts, suburbs, etc. -- Continued

602 Collective
Individual
602.3 Kreml' (Kremlin)
602.5.A-Z Other, A-Z
Streets, squares, parks, etc.
604 Collective
604.3.A-Z Individual, A-Z
e.g.
Krasnaia ploshchad, see DK604.3.R4
604.3.R4 Red Square. Krasnaia ploshchad'
Buildings
605 Collective
606.A-Z Individual, A-Z
e.g.
606.B64 Bol'shoi Kremlevskii dvorets
609 Other
Other cities, towns, etc.
651.A1 Collective
651.A2-Z Individual, A-Z
651.A65 Arkhangel'sk
651.A7 Astrakhan
Ekaterinburg, see DK651.S85
651.G6 Gorki. Nizhni Novgorod
651.I28 IAroslavl'
651.K1213 Kaliningrad
651.K2 Kazan'
651.K45 Kirov. Vyatka
651.K6 Kostroma
651.K68 Kronstadt
Kuibyshev, see DK651.S36
651.K854 Kuoloiarvi. Salla
Nizhni Novgorod, see DK651.G6
651.P23 Pavlovsk
651.P45 Petrodvorets. Peterhof
651.P8 Pskov
651.P93 Pushkin. TSarskoe Selo
651.R7 Rostov
651.S36 Samara. Kuibyshev
Simbirsk, see DK651.U4
651.S65 Smolensk
651.S7 Stalingrad. Volgograd
651.S85 Sverdlovsk. Ekaterinburg
TSarkoe Selo, see DK651.P93
651.U4 Ulyanovsk. Simbirsk
Ustiug Velikii, see DK651.V3
651.V3 Velikii Ustiug

Local history and description
Russia (Federation). Russian S.F.S.R.
Local history and description
Cities and towns
Other cities, towns, etc.
Individual, A-Z -- Continued

651.V55 Vladimir
Volgograd, see DK651.S7
651.V6 Voronezh
651.V93 Vyborg
Yaroslav, see DK651.I28
Yaroslavl, see DK651.I28

Georgia (Republic). Georgian S.S.R. Georgian Sakartvelo

670 Periodicals. Societies. Serials
Museums, exhibitions, etc.
671.2 General works
671.3.A-Z Individual, A-Z
671.4 Congresses
671.5 Sources and documents
Collected works (nonserial)
671.6 Several authors
671.7 Individual authors
671.8 Gazetteers. Dictionaries, etc.
671.9 Place names (General)
672 Directories
672.2 Guidebooks
672.3 General works
672.4 General special
672.5 Pictorial works
Historic monuments, landmarks, scenery, etc. (General)
For local, see DK679+
672.6 General works
672.7 Preservation
672.8 Historical geography
672.9 Description and travel
673 Antiquities
For local antiquities, see DK679+
673.2 Social life and customs. Civilization. Intellectual life
For specific periods, see the period
Ethnography
673.3 General works
673.4 National characteristics
673.5.A-Z Individual elements in the population, A-Z
673.5.A75 Armenians
673.5.G3 Germans
673.5.G74 Greeks
673.5.K48 Khevzurs
673.5.K55 Kipchak
673.5.O75 Ossetes
673.5.P6 Poles

Local history and description
Georgia (Republic).
Georgian S.S.R. Georgian Sakartvelo
Ethnography -- Continued
673.6 Georgians in foreign countries (General)
For Georgians in a particular country, see the country
History
Periodicals. Societies. Serials, see DK670
673.7 Dictionaries. Chronological tables, outlines, etc.
Biography (Collective)
For individual biography, see the specific period or place
673.8 General works
673.9 Rulers, kings, etc.
674 Queens. Princes and princesses
Houses, noble families, etc.
674.2 General works
674.3.A-Z Individual houses, families, etc., A-Z
674.4 Statesmen
674.5 Women
Cf. CT3490, Biography of women
Historiography
674.6 General works
Biography of historians, area studies specialists, archaeologists, etc.
674.7 Collective
674.8.A-Z Individual, A-Z
Study and teaching
674.9 General works
675.A-Z By region or country, A-Z
Subarrange by author
General works
675.2 Through 1800
675.3 1801-1980
675.4 1981-
675.5 Pictorial works
675.6 Juvenile works
675.7 Addresses, essays, lectures. Anecdotes, etc.
Military history
For individual campaigns and engagements, see the special period
676 Sources and documents
676.2 General works
Political history
For specific periods, see the period
676.5 Sources and documents
676.6 General works
Foreign and general relations
For works on relations with a specific country regardless of period, see DK676.9.A+
676.7 Sources and documents

Local history and description
Georgia (Republic).
Georgian S.S.R. Georgian Sakartvelo
History
Foreign and general relations -- Continued
676.8 General works
676.9.A-Z Relations with individual countries, A-Z
By period
Early to 330
677.1 General works
Biography and memoirs
677.13 Collective
677.14.A-Z Individual, A-Z
677.15 P'arnavaz I, King of the Georgians, fl. 4th - 3rd cent. B.C.
330-1220
677.2 General works
Biography and memoirs
677.23 Collective
677.24.A-Z Individual, A-Z
677.25 Vaxtang I, King of the Georgians, d. 502
677.27 Davit' IV, King of Georgia, 1089-1125
677.275 Demetre I, King of Georgia, 1125-1156
677.28 T'amar, Queen of Georgia, 1184-1213
1220-1801
677.3 General works
Biography and memoirs
677.34 Collective
677.35.A-Z Individual, A-Z
1801-1921
For works on the Bolshevik Revolution in Georgia, see DK265.8.G4
677.4 General works
Biography and memoirs
677.5 Collective
677.6.A-Z Individual, A-Z
1921-1991
For World War II as distinct from the time period 1939-1945, see D731+
677.7 General works
Biography and memoirs
677.8 Collective
677.9.A-Z Individual, A-Z
677.92 Uprising, 1924
1991-
678 General works
678.17 Political history
678.18 Foreign and general relations
Biography and memoirs
678.2 Collective
678.3.A-Z Individual, A-Z
Local history and description
679.A-Z Regions, oblasts, etc., A-Z

Local history and description
Georgia (Republic).
Georgian S.S.R. Georgian Sakartvelo
Local history and description -- Continued
Cities and towns
Tbilisi. Tiflis
679.2 Periodicals. Societies. Serials
679.22 Sources and documents
679.23 Directories. Dictionaries. Gazetteers
679.24 Guidebooks
679.25 General works
679.26 Description. Geography
679.27 Pictorial works
679.28 Antiquities
679.29 Social life and customs. Civilization. Intellectual life
Ethnography
679.3 General works
679.32.A-Z Individual elements in the population, A-Z
History
Biography
679.33 Collective
679.34.A-Z Individual, A-Z
679.35 General works
Sections, monuments, parks, streets, buildings, etc.
679.38 Collective
679.39.A-Z Individual, A-Z
679.5.A-Z Other cities, towns, etc., A-Z
Armenia (Republic). Armenian S.S.R.
For works on the territory of Armenian S.S.R. before 1920, and/or the historic kingdom and region of Armenia as a whole, see DS161+
680 Periodicals. Societies. Serials
Museums, exhibitions, etc.
681.2 General works
681.3.A-Z Individual, A-Z
681.4 Congresses
681.5 Sources and documents
Collected works (nonserial)
681.6 Several authors
681.7 Individual authors
681.8 Gazetteers. Dictionaries, etc.
681.9 Place names (General)
682 Directories
682.2 Guidebooks
682.3 General works
682.4 General special
682.5 Pictorial works
Historic monuments, landmarks, scenery, etc. (General)
For local, see DK689+
682.6 General works

Local history and description
Armenia (Republic). Armenian S.S.R.
Historic monuments, landmarks, scenery, etc. (General) -- Continued
682.7 Preservation
682.8 Historical geography
682.9 Description and travel
683 Antiquities
For local antiquities, see DK689+
683.2 Social life and customs. Civilization. Intellectual life
For specific periods, see the period
Ethnography
683.3 General works
683.4 National characteristics
683.5.A-Z Individual elements in the population, A-Z
683.5.A93 Azerbaijanis
683.5.K87 Kurds
683.5.R9 Russians
683.6 Armenians in foreign countries (General)
For Armenians in a particular country, see the country
History
Periodicals. Societies. Serials, see DK680
683.7 Dictionaries. Chronological tables, outlines, etc.
Biography (Collective)
For individual biography, see the specific period or place
683.8 General works
684 Statesmen
684.2 Women
Cf. CT3490, Biography of women
Historiography
684.6 General works
Biography of historians, area studies specialists, archaeologists, etc.
684.7 Collective
684.8.A-Z Individual, A-Z
Study and teaching
684.9 General works
685.A-Z By region or country, A-Z
General works
685.3 1920-1980
685.4 1981-
685.5 Pictorial works
685.6 Juvenile works
685.7 Addresses, essays, lectures. Anecdotes, etc.
By period
Early to 1920, see DS181+

Local history and description
Armenia (Republic). Armenian S.S.R.
History
By period -- Continued
1920-1991
For works on the Bolshevik Revolution in Armenia, see DK265.8.A73
For World War II as distinct from the time period 1939-1945, see D731+
686.9 Sources and documents
687 General works
Biography and memoirs
687.2 Collective
687.3.A-Z Individual, A-Z
1991-
687.5 General works
687.53 Political history
Biography and memoirs
687.6 Collective
687.62.A-Z Individual, A-Z
Local history and description
689.A-Z Regions, oblasts, etc., A-Z
Cities and towns
Yerevan. Erevan
689.2 Periodicals. Societies. Serials
689.22 Sources and documents
689.23 Directories. Dictionaries. Gazetteers
689.24 Guidebooks
689.25 General works
689.26 Description. Geography
689.27 Pictorial works
689.28 Antiquities
689.29 Social life and customs. Civilization. Intellectual life
Ethnography
689.3 General works
689.32.A-Z Individual elements in the population, A-Z
History
Biography
689.33 Collective
689.34.A-Z Individual, A-Z
689.35 General works
Sections, monuments, parks, streets, buildings, etc.
689.38 Collective
689.39.A-Z Individual, A-Z
689.5.A-Z Other cities, towns, etc., A-Z
e.g.
689.5.A77 Artaxata
689.5.K37 Kirovakan
Azerbaijan. Azerbaijan S.S.R.
690 Periodicals. Societies. Serials
Museums, exhibitions, etc.

Local history and description
Azerbaijan. Azerbaijan S.S.R.
Museums, exhibitions, etc. -- Continued
691.2 General works
691.3.A-Z Individual. By place, A-Z
691.4 Congresses
691.5 Sources and documents
Collected works (nonserial)
691.6 Several authors
691.7 Individual authors
691.8 Gazetteers. Dictionaries, etc.
691.9 Place names (General)
692 Directories
692.2 Guidebooks
692.3 General works
692.4 General special
692.5 Pictorial works
Historic monuments, landmarks, scenery, etc. (General)
For local, see DK699+
692.6 General works
692.7 Preservation
692.8 Historical geography
692.85 Geography
692.9 Description and travel
693 Antiquities
For local antiquities, see DK699+
693.2 Social life and customs. Civilization. Intellectual life
For specific periods, see the period
Ethnography
693.3 General works
693.4 National characteristics
693.5.A-Z Individual elements in the population, A-Z
693.5.A75 Armenians
693.5.M87 Muslims
693.5.P65 Poles
693.5.R9 Russians
693.6 Azerbaijanis in foreign countries (General)
For Azerbaijanis in a particular country, see the country
History
Periodicals. Societies. Serials, see DK690
693.7 Dictionaries. Chronological tables, outlines, etc.
Biography (Collective)
For individual biography, see the specific period or place
693.8 General works
693.9 Rulers, kings, etc.
694 Queens. Princes and princesses
Houses, noble families, etc.
694.2 General works

Local history and description
Azerbaijan. Azerbaijan S.S.R.
History
Biography (Collective)
Houses, noble families, etc. -- Continued
694.3.A-Z Individual houses, families, etc., A-Z
694.4 Statesmen
694.5 Women
Cf. CT3490, Biography of women
Historiography
694.6 General works
Biography of historians, area studies specialists, archaeologists, etc.
694.7 Collective
694.8.A-Z Individual, A-Z
Study and teaching
694.9 General works
695.A-Z By region or country, A-Z
Subarrange by author
General works
695.2 Through 1800
695.3 1801-1980
695.4 1981-
695.5 Pictorial works
695.6 Juvenile works
695.7 Addresses, essays, lectures. Anecdotes, etc.
Military history
For individual campaigns and engagements, see the special period
696 Sources and documents
696.2 General works
Political history
For specific periods, see the period
696.5 Sources and documents
696.6 General works
Foreign and general relations
For works on relations with a specific country regardless of period, see DK696.9.A+
696.7 Sources and documents
696.8 General works
696.9.A-Z Relations with individual countries, A-Z
By period
697.1 Early to 1813
697.2 1813-1917
1917-1991
For works on the Bolshevik Revolution in Azerbaijan, see DK265.8.A9
For works on World War II as distinct from the time period 1939-1945, see D731+
697.3 General works
Biography and memoirs
697.4 Collective
697.5.A-Z Individual, A-Z

Local history and description
Azerbaijan. Azerbaijan S.S.R.
History
By period -- Continued
1991-
697.6 General works
697.68 Political history
Biography and memoirs
697.7 Collective
697.8.A-Z Individual, A-Z
Local history and description
699.A-Z Regions, oblasts, etc., A-Z
Cities and towns
Baku
699.2 Periodicals. Societies. Serials
699.22 Sources and documents
699.23 Directories. Dictionaries. Gazetteers
699.24 Guidebooks
699.25 General works
699.26 Description. Geography
699.27 Pictorial works
699.28 Antiquities
699.29 Social life and customs. Civilization. Intellectual life
Ethnography
699.3 General works
699.32.A-Z Individual elements in the population, A-Z
History
Biography
699.33 Collective
699.34.A-Z Individual, A-Z
699.35 General works
Sections, monuments, parks, streets, buildings, etc.
699.38 Collective
699.39.A-Z Individual, A-Z
699.5.A-Z Other cities, towns, etc., A-Z
e.g.
699.5.G35 Gäncä. Kirovabad
Kirovabad, see DK699.5.G35
699.5.S86 Sumagit
750 Soviet Asia. Soviet Central Asia and Siberia treated together
Cf. DK751+, Siberia
Cf. DK845+, Soviet Central Asia
Siberia
751 Periodicals. Societies. Serials
751.2 Congresses
752 Sources and documents
752.5 Gazetteers. Dictionaries, etc.
752.6 Place names (General)
753 General works
Description and travel

Local history and description
Siberia
Description and travel -- Continued
754 Early through 1800
755 1801-1945
For works on the Bolshevik Revolution in Siberia, see DK265.8.S5
For works on World War II as distinct from the time period 1939-1945, see D731+
756 1946-1980
756.2 1981-
757 Antiquities
757.3 Social life and customs. Civilization. Intellectual life
Ethnography
758 General works
759.A-Z Individual elements in the population, A-Z
759.A77 Assyrians
759.B34 Balts
759.B8 Buriats
759.B94 Byelorussians. Belarusians
759.C45 Chukchi
759.C47 Chulyma Tatars
759.C67 Cossacks
759.E8 Even
759.E83 Evenki. Tungus
759.G4 Germans
759.G5 Gilyaks
(759.G6) Golds
See DK759.N34
759.J37 Japanese
759.K27 Kalmyks
759.K37 Kereks
759.K4 Kets
759.K5 Khakassians
759.K53 Khanty
759.K56 Khirghiz
759.K6 Koryaks
759.L35 Latgals
759.L37 Latvians
759.L58 Lithuanians
759.M33 Mansi
759.M87 Muslims
759.N34 Nanai. Golds
759.N4 Nganasani
759.O4 Olcha
759.O7 Oroches
759.P6 Poles
759.S3 Samoyeds
759.S4 Selkups
759.S56 Shor
(759.S7) Soyotes
See DK759.T93

Local history and description
Siberia
Ethnography
Individual elements in the population, A-Z -- Continued

759.T3 Tatars (General)
Cf. DK759.C47, Chulyma Tatars
759.T4 Teleut
(759.T9) Tungus
See DK759.E83
759.T92 Turkic peoples
759.T93 Tuvinians. Soyotes
759.U9 Uzbeks
759.Y2 Yakuts
759.Y8 Yukaghir

History
761 General works
763 Addresses, essays, lectures. Anecdotes, etc.
By period
764 Early through 1800
766 19th-20th centuries
Historiography
767 General works
Biography of historians, area studies specialists, archaeologists, etc.
768 Collective
768.5.A-Z Individual, A-Z
Biography and memoirs
768.7 Collective
769.A-Z Individual, A-Z
e.g.
Ermak, d. 1585, see DK769.Y4
769.K7 Kropotkin, Petr Alekseevich, kni͡az′
769.Y4 Yermak
770 Exiles. Political prisoners. Political refugees

Local history and description
771.A-Z Regions, oblasts, etc., A-Z
e.g.
771.A25 Altai Mountains
771.A3 Amur River and Valley, Province, etc.
771.B3 Baikal, Lake
Bering Sea, see F951
771.B5 Biro-Bidjan. Evreĭskai͡a avtonomnai͡a oblast′
771.B8 Buriat-Mongolia
771.C4 Chukotski Peninsula
Commander Islands, see DK771.K7
771.D3 Dal′ne-Vostochnyĭ kraĭ. Soviet Far East. Far Eastern Territory, etc.
Cf. DS518.7, Far Eastern question
Eniseĭ River and Valley, see DK771.Y4
Evreĭskai͡a avtonomnai͡a oblast, see DK771.B5

Local history and description
Siberia
Local history and description
Regions, oblasts, etc., A-Z -- Continued
IAkutskaia A.S.S.R , see DK771.Y2
771.K2 Kamchatka
771.K7 Kommander Islands
771.M3 Maritime Province
771.N6 Northeastern Siberia
Primor'e, see DK771.M3
Primorskiĭ kraĭ, see DK771.M3
771.S2 Sakhalin
771.T8 Transbaikalia
771.U9 Ussuri
771.W47 Western Siberia
771.Y2 Yakut A.S.S.R.
771.Y4 Yenisey River and Valley
781.A-Z Cities and towns, etc., A-Z
e.g.
781.I7 Irkutsk
781.M3 Magnitogorsk
Novokuznetsk, see DK781.S9
781.S2 Samarovo
781.S9 Stalinsk. Novokuznetsk
781.T6 Tomsk
781.V5 Vladivostok
781.Y4 Yeniseisk
Soviet Central Asia. West Turkestan
Cf. D378+, Central Asian question
Cf. DS327+, Central Asia (General)
845 Periodicals. Societies. Serials
847 Sources and documents
848 Gazetteers. Dictionaries, etc.
851 General works
853 Geography
854 Description and travel
855 Antiquities
855.2 Social life and customs. Civilization. Intellectual life
Ethnography
855.4 General works
855.5.A-Z Individual elements in the population, A-Z
855.5.D8 Dungans
855.5.I73 Iranians
855.5.K25 Kara-Kalpaks
855.5.K3 Karluks
855.5.K33 Kazakhs
855.5.K48 Kipchak
855.5.K5 Khirghiz
855.5.K67 Koreans
855.5.M6 Mongols
855.5.M8 Muslims
855.5.O4 Oghuz

Local history and description
Soviet Central Asia. West Turkestan
Ethnography
Individual elements in the population, A-Z -- Continued

855.5.P64 Poles
855.5.R87 Russians
855.5.S2 Sarts
855.5.S64 Sogdians
855.5.T3 Tajiks
855.5.T85 Turkmen
855.5.U35 Uighur (Turkic people)
855.5.U42 Ukrainians
855.5.U9 Uzbeks
855.5.Y34 Yaghnobi

History
Historiography
855.8 General works
Biography of historians, area studies specialists, archaeologists, etc.
855.82 Collective
855.83.A-Z Individual, A-Z
856 General works
857 Addresses, essays, lectures. Anecdotes, etc.
857.5 Political history
Foreign and general relations
For general works on the diplomatic history of a period, see the period
For works on relations with a specific country regardless of period, see DK857.75
857.7 General works
857.75.A-Z Relations with individual countries, A-Z
By period
858 Early through 1919
For works on the Bolshevik Revolution in Soviet Central Asia, see DK265.8.S5
859 1920-1991
For works on World War II as distinct from the time period 1939-1945, see D731+
1991-
Class here works on states of former Soviet Central Asia treated collectively
859.5 General works
859.56 Political history
859.57 Foreign and general relations
860 Biography (Collective)

Kazakhstan. Kazakh S.S.R.
901 Periodicals. Societies. Serials
Museums, exhibitions, etc.
901.5 General works
901.52.A-Z Individual, A-Z
901.6 Congresses
902 Sources and documents

Local history and description
Kazakhstan. Kazakh S.S.R. -- Continued
Collected works (nonserial)
902.12 Several authors
902.13 Individual authors
902.14 Gazetteers. Dictionaries, etc.
902.16 Place names (General)
902.17 Directories
902.18 Guidebooks
903 General works
903.12 General special
903.2 Pictorial works
Historic monuments, landmarks, scenery, etc. (General)
For local, see DK909+
903.3 General works
903.4 Preservation
903.5 Historical geography
904 Description and travel
905 Antiquities
For local antiquities, see DK909+
906 Social life and customs. Civilization. Intellectual life
For specific periods, see the period
Ethnography
907 General works
907.15.A-Z Individual elements in the population, A-Z
907.15.C67 Cossacks
907.15.G47 Germans
907.15.K67 Koreans
907.15.P65 Poles
907.15.R87 Russians
907.15.T37 Tatars
907.15.U37 Ukrainians
907.2 Kazakhs in foreign countries (General)
For Kazakhs in a particular country, see the country
History
Periodicals. Societies. Serials, see DK901
908.12 Dictionaries. Chronological tables, outlines, etc.
Biography (Collective)
For individual biography, see the specific period or place
908.13 General works
908.144 Rulers, kings, statesmen, etc.
Historiography
908.5 General works
Biography of historians, area studies specialists, archaeologists, etc.
908.52 Collective
908.53.A-Z Individual, A-Z
908.56 By region or country, A-Z

Local history and description
Kazakhstan. Kazakh S.S.R.
History -- Continued
908.6 General works
Military history
For individual campaigns and engagements, see the special period
908.65 Sources and documents
908.66 General works
Political history
908.67 Sources and documents
908.68 General works
By period
See the specific period
Foreign and general relations
For works on relations with a specific country regardless of period, see DK908.75.A+
For general works on the diplomatic history of a period, see the period
908.69 Sources and documents
908.7 General works
908.75.A-Z Relations with individual countries, A-Z
By period
908.82 Through 500
908.83 500-1400
908.84 1400-1700
1700-1850
908.85 General works
Biography and memoirs
908.855 Collective
908.856.A-Z Individual, A-Z
1850-1917
908.86 General works
Biography and memoirs
908.8613 Collective
908.8614.A-Z Individual, A-Z
908.8617 Revolt, 1916
1917-1945
For works on the Bolshevik Revolution in the Kazakhstan, see DK265.8.K39
For works on World War II as distinct from the time period 1939-1945, see D731+
908.8618 General works
Biography and memoirs
908.862 Collective
908.863.A-Z Individual, A-Z
1945-1991
908.864 General works
Biography and memoirs
908.865 Collective
908.866.A-Z Individual, A-Z
1991-
908.867 General works

Local history and description
Kazakhstan. Kazakh S.S.R.
History
By period
1991- -- Continued

908.8673 Social life and customs. Civilization. Intellectual life
908.8675 Political history
Biography and memoirs
908.868 Collective
908.869.A-Z Individual, A-Z
Local history and description
909.A-Z Regions, oblasts, etc., A-Z
Cities and towns
Alma Ata
909.2 Periodicals. Societies. Serials
909.22 Sources and documents
909.23 Directories. Dictionaries. Gazetteers
909.24 Guidebooks
909.25 General works
909.26 Description. Geography
909.27 Pictorial works
909.28 Antiquities
909.29 Social life and customs. Civilization. Intellectual life
Ethnography
909.3 General works
909.32.A-Z Individual elements in the population, A-Z
History
Biography
909.33 Collective
909.34.A-Z Individual, A-Z
909.35 General works
Sections, monuments, parks, streets, buildings, etc.
909.38 Collective
909.39.A-Z Individual, A-Z
909.5.A-Z Other cities, towns, etc., A-Z
e.g.
909.5.C55 Chimkent
909.5.K37 Karaganda
909.5.S46 Semipalatinsk
Kyrgyzstan. Kirghiz S.S.R. Kirghizia
911 Periodicals. Societies. Serials
Museums, exhibitions, etc.
911.5 General works
911.52.A-Z Individual. By place, A-Z
911.6 Congresses
912 Sources and documents
Collected works (nonserial)
912.12 Several authors
912.13 Individual authors
912.14 Gazetteers. Dictionaries, etc.

Local history and description
Kyrgyzstan. Kirghiz S.S.R. Kirghizia -- Continued
912.16 Place names (General)
912.17 Directories
912.18 Guidebooks
913 General works
913.12 General special
913.2 Pictorial works
Historic monuments, landmarks, scenery, etc. (General)
For local, see DK919+
913.3 General works
913.4 Preservation
913.5 Historical geography
914 Description and travel
915 Antiquities
For local antiquities, see DK919+
916 Social life and customs. Civilization. Intellectual life
Ethnography
917 General works
917.15.A-Z Individual elements in the population, A-Z
917.15.A75 Armenians
917.15.B44 Belarusians
917.15.G47 Germans
917.15.K67 Koreans
917.15.P65 Poles
917.15.R87 Russians
917.2 Kirghiz in foreign countries (General)
For Kirghiz in a particular country, see the country
History
Periodicals. Societies. Serials, see DK911
918.12 Dictionaries. Chronological tables, outlines, etc.
Biography (Collective)
For individual biography, see the specific period or place
918.13 General works
918.144 Rulers, kings, statesmen, etc.
Historiography
918.5 General works
Biography of historians, area studies specialists, archaeologists, etc.
918.52 Collective
918.53.A-Z Individual, A-Z
918.6 General works
By period
918.82 Through 500
918.83 500-1700
1700-1917
918.84 General works
Biography and memoirs

Local history and description
Kyrgyzstan. Kirghiz S.S.R. Kirghizia
History
By period
1700-1917
Biography and memoirs -- Continued
918.845 Collective
918.846.A-Z Individual, A-Z
918.848 Uprising, 1916
1917-1945
For works on the Bolshevik Revolution in the Kirghizistan, see DK265.8.K57
For works on World War II as distinct from the time period 1939-1945, see D731+
918.85 General works
Biography and memoirs
918.86 Collective
918.87.A-Z Individual, A-Z
1945-1991
918.871 General works
Biography and memoirs
918.872 Collective
918.873.A-Z Individual, A-Z
1991-
918.875 General works
918.8757 Political history
Biography and memoirs
918.876 Collective
918.877.A-Z Individual, A-Z
Local history and description
919.A-Z Regions, oblasts, etc., A-Z
Cities and towns
Frunze
919.2 Periodicals. Societies. Serials
919.22 Sources and documents
919.23 Directories. Dictionaries. Gazetteers
919.24 Guidebooks
919.25 General works
919.26 Description. Geography
919.27 Pictorial works
919.28 Antiquities
919.29 Social life and customs. Civilization. Intellectual life
Ethnography
919.3 General works
919.32.A-Z Individual elements in the population, A-Z
History
Biography
919.33 Collective
919.34.A-Z Individual, A-Z
919.35 General works
Sections, monuments, parks, streets, buildings, etc.

Local history and description
Kyrgyzstan. Kirghiz S.S.R. Kirghizia
Local history and description
Cities and towns
Frunze
Sections, monuments, parks, streets, buildings, etc. -- Continued
919.38 Collective
919.39.A-Z Individual, A-Z
919.5.A-Z Other cities, towns, etc., A-Z
e.g.
919.5.D95 Dzhalal-Abad
919.5.O75 Osh
919.5.P79 Przheval'sk
Tajikistan. Tajik S.S.R. Tadzhikistan
921 Periodicals. Societies. Serials
Museums, exhibitions, etc.
921.5 General works
921.52.A-Z Individual, A-Z
921.6 Congresses
922 Sources and documents
Collected works (nonserial)
922.12 Several authors
922.13 Individual authors
922.14 Gazetteers. Dictionaries, etc.
922.16 Place names (General)
922.17 Directories
922.18 Guidebooks
923 General works
923.12 General special
923.2 Pictorial works
Historic monuments, landmarks, scenery, etc. (General)
For local, see DK929+
923.3 General works
923.4 Preservation
923.5 Historical geography
924 Description and travel
925 Antiquities
For local antiquities, see DK929+
926 Social life and customs. Civilization. Intellectual life
Ethnography
For individual elements in the population, see DK855.5.A+
927 General works
927.2 Tajiks in foreign countries (General)
For Tajiks in a particular country, see the country
History
Periodicals. Societies. Serials, see DK921
928.12 Dictionaries. Chronological tables, outlines, etc.

Local history and description
Tajikistan. Tajik S.S.R. Tadzhikistan
History -- Continued
Biography (Collective)
For individual biography, see the specific period or place
928.13 General works
928.144 Rulers, kings, etc.
Historiography
928.5 General works
Biography of historians, area studies specialists, archaeologists, etc.
928.52 Collective
928.53.A-Z Individual, A-Z
928.6 General works
By period
928.82 Through 500
928.83 500-1700
928.84 1850-1917
1917-1945
For works on the Bolshevik Revolution in Tajikistan, see DK265.8.T27
For World War II as distinct from the time period 1939-1945, see D731+
928.85 General works
Biography and memoirs
928.852 Collective
928.853.A-Z Individual, A-Z
1945-1991
928.86 General works
Biography and memoirs
928.862 Collective
928.863.A-Z Individual, A-Z
1991-
928.865 General works
928.8657 Political history
Biography and memoirs
928.866 Collective
928.867.A-Z Individual, A-Z
Local history and description
929.A-Z Regions, oblasts, etc., A-Z
Cities and towns
Dushanbe
929.2 Periodicals. Societies. Serials
929.22 Sources and documents
929.23 Directories. Dictionaries. Gazetteers
929.24 Guidebooks
929.25 General works
929.26 Description. Geography
929.27 Pictorial works
929.28 Antiquities
929.29 Social life and customs. Civilization. Intellectual life

Local history and description
Tajikistan. Tajik S.S.R. Tadzhikistan
Local history and description
Cities and towns
Dushanbe -- Continued
Ethnography
929.3 General works
929.32.A-Z Individual elements in the population, A-Z
History
Biography
929.33 Collective
929.34.A-Z Individual, A-Z
929.35 General works
Sections, monuments, parks, streets, buildings, etc.
929.38 Collective
929.39.A-Z Individual, A-Z
929.5.A-Z Other cities, towns, etc., A-Z
e.g.
929.5.L46 Leninabad
929.5.U73 Ura-Tiube
Turkmenistan. Turkmen S.S.R. Turkmenia
931 Periodicals. Societies. Serials
Museums, exhibitions, etc.
931.5 General works
931.52.A-Z Individual, A-Z
931.6 Congresses
932 Sources and documents
Collected works (nonserial)
932.12 Several authors
932.13 Individual authors
932.14 Gazetteers. Dictionaries, etc.
932.16 Place names (General)
932.17 Directories
932.18 Guidebooks
933 General works
933.12 General special
933.2 Pictorial works
Historic monuments, landmarks, scenery, etc. (General)
For local, see DK939+
933.3 General works
933.4 Preservation
933.5 Historical geography
934 Description and travel
935 Antiquities
For local antiquities, see DK939+
936 Social life and customs. Civilization. Intellectual life
Ethnography
For individual elements in the population, see DK855.5.A+
937 General works

Local history and description
Turkmenistan. Turkmen S.S.R. Turkmenia
Ethnography -- Continued
937.2 Turkmen in foreign countries (General)
For Turkmen in a particular country, see the country
History
Periodicals. Societies. Serials, see DK931
938.12 Dictionaries. Chronological tables, outlines, etc.
Biography (Collective)
For individual biography, see the specific period or place
938.13 General works
938.144 Rulers, kings, statesmen, etc.
Historiography
938.5 General works
Biography of historians, area studies specialists, archaeologists, etc.
938.52 Collective
938.53.A-Z Individual, A-Z
938.6 General works
By period
938.82 Through 500
938.83 500-1800
938.84 1800-1917
1917-1945
For works on the Bolshevik Revolution in the Turkmenistan, see DK265.8.T93
For works on World War II as distinct from the time period 1939-1945, see D731+
938.85 General works
Biography and memoirs
938.852 Collective
938.853.A-Z Individual, A-Z
1945-1991
938.86 General works
Biography and memoirs
938.862 Collective
938.863.A-Z Individual, A-Z
1991-
938.865 General works
938.8657 Political history
938.8658 Foreign and general relations
Biography and memoirs
938.866 Collective
938.867.A-Z Individual, A-Z
Local history and description
939.A-Z Regions, oblasts, etc., A-Z
Cities and towns
Ashkhabad
939.2 Periodicals. Societies. Serials
939.22 Sources and documents

Local history and description
Turkmenistan. Turkmen S.S.R. Turkmenia
Local history and description
Cities and towns
Ashkhabad -- Continued
939.23 Directories. Dictionaries. Gazetteers
939.24 Guidebooks
939.25 General works
939.26 Description. Geography
939.27 Pictorial works
939.28 Antiquities
939.29 Social life and customs. Civilization. Intellectual life
Ethnography
939.3 General works
939.32.A-Z Individual elements in the population, A-Z
History
Biography
939.33 Collective
939.34.A-Z Individual, A-Z
939.35 General works
Sections, monuments, parks, streets, buildings, etc.
939.38 Collective
939.39.A-Z Individual, A-Z
Other cities, towns, etc., A-Z
e.g.
939.5.K73 Krasnovodsk
939.5.N43 Nebit-Dag
Uzbekistan. Uzbek S.S.R.
941 Periodicals. Societies. Serials
Museums, exhibitions, etc.
941.5 General works
941.52.A-Z Individual, A-Z
941.6 Congresses
942 Sources and documents
Collected works (nonserial)
942.12 Several authors
942.13 Individual authors
942.14 Gazetteers. Dictionaries, etc.
942.16 Place names (General)
942.17 Directories
942.18 Guidebooks
943 General works
943.12 General special
943.2 Pictorial works
Historic monuments, landmarks, scenery, etc. (General)
For local, see DK949+
943.3 General works
943.4 Preservation
943.5 Historical geography
944 Description and travel

Local history and description
Uzbekistan. Uzbek S.S.R. -- Continued
945 Antiquities
For local antiquities, see DK949+
946 Social life and customs. Civilization. Intellectual life
Ethnography
For individual elements in the population, see DK855.5.A+
947 General works
947.2 Uzbeks in foreign countries (General)
For Uzbeks in a particular country, see the country
History
Periodicals. Societies. Serials, see DK941
948.12 Dictionaries. Chronological tables, outlines, etc.
Biography (Collective)
For individual biography, see the specific period or place
948.13 General works
948.144 Rulers, kings, statesmen, etc.
Historiography
948.5 General works
Biography of historians, area studies specialists, archaeologists, etc.
948.52 Collective
948.53.A-Z Individual, A-Z
Study and teaching
948.55 General works
948.56.A-Z By region or country, A-Z
General works
948.6 Through 1980
948.62 1981-
948.65 Pictorial works
948.66 Juvenile works
948.67 Addresses, essays, lectures. Anecdotes
Military history
For individual campaigns and engagements, see the specific period
948.7 Sources and documents
948.72 General works
Political history
For specific periods, see the period
948.73 Sources and documents
948.75 General works
Foreign and general relations
948.76 Sources and documents
948.77 General works
948.79.A-Z Relations with individual countries, A-Z
By period
948.82 Through 500
948.83 500-1800

Local history and description
Uzbekistan. Uzbek S.S.R.
History
By period -- Continued
948.84 1800-1917
1917-1945
For works on the Bolshevik Revolution in the Uzbekistan, see DK265.8.U9
For works on World War II as distinct from the time period 1939-1945, see D731+
948.85 General works
Biography and memoirs
948.852 Collective
948.853.A-Z Individual, A-Z
1945-1991
948.86 General works
Biography and memoirs
948.862 Collective
948.863.A-Z Individual, A-Z
1991-
948.865 General works
948.8654 Social life and customs. Civilization. Intellectual life
948.8657 Political history
948.8658 Foreign and general relations
Biography and memoirs
948.866 Collective
948.867.A-Z Individual, A-Z
Local history and description
949.A-Z Regions, oblasts, etc., A-Z
Cities and towns
Tashkent
949.2 Periodicals. Societies. Serials
949.22 Sources and documents
949.23 Directories. Dictionaries. Gazetteers
949.24 Guidebooks
949.25 General works
949.26 Description. Geography
949.27 Pictorial works
949.28 Antiquities
949.29 Social life and customs. Civilization. Intellectual life
Ethnography
949.3 General works
949.32.A-Z Individual elements in the population, A-Z
949.32.G73 Greeks
History
Biography
949.33 Collective
949.34.A-Z Individual, A-Z
949.35 General works
Sections, monuments, parks, streets, buildings, etc.

Local history and description
Uzbekistan. Uzbek S.S.R.
Local history and description
Cities and towns
Tashkent
Sections, monuments, parks, streets, buildings, etc. -- Continued

949.38 Collective
949.39.A-Z Individual, A-Z
949.5.A-Z Other cities, towns, etc., A-Z
e.g.
949.5.K65 Kokand
949.5.N35 Namangan
949.5.S35 Samarkand

History of Poland
4010 Periodicals. Societies. Serials
Museums, exhibitions, etc.
4015 General works
4016.A-Z Individual. By place, A-Z
4018 Congresses
4020 Sources and documents
Collected works
4025 Several authors
4027.A-Z Individual authors, A-Z
4030 Gazetteers. Dictionaries, etc.
4035 Place names (General)
4036 Directories
4037 Guidebooks
4040 General works
4042 General special
4043 Monumental and picturesque. Pictorial works
Historic monuments, landmarks, scenery, etc. (General)
4044 General works
4044.5 Preservation
4045 Historical geography
4046 Geography
Description and travel
4047 History of travel
4050 Early to 1815
4060 1815-1866
4070 1867-1944
4080 1945-1980
4081 1981-
Antiquities
4088 Periodicals. Societies. Serials
4090 General works
4092 General special
Local, see DK4600+
Social life and customs. Civilization. Intellectual life
4110 General works
4112 Foreign influences
Including Latin influence
4115 Intellectual life. Culture
By period
See the specific period or reign
Ethnography
4120 General works
4121 National characteristics. Patriotism. Messianism
4121.5.A-Z Individual elements in the population, A-Z
4121.5.A7 Armenians
4121.5.B44 Belarusians
4121.5.C9 Czechs
4121.5.E88 Estonians
4121.5.G4 Germans
4121.5.G73 Greeks
4121.5.I8 Italians

Ethnography
Individual elements
in the population, A-Z -- Continued
4121.5.J32 Jaćwież
Jews, see DS135.P6+
4121.5.K37 Karaites
4121.5.K87 Kurpie
4121.5.L4 Lemky
4121.5.L56 Lithuanians
4121.5.M33 Macedonians
4121.5.P64 Polanie
4121.5.S35 Scots
4121.5.S55 Slovaks
4121.5.S65 Slovinci
4121.5.T3 Tatars
4121.5.U4 Ukrainians
(4121.5.W5) White Russians
see DK4121.5.B44
4122 Poles in foreign countries (General)
For Poles in a particular country, see that country
History
Periodicals, societies, serials, see DK4010
4123 Dictionaries. Chronological tables, outlines, etc.
Biography
For individual biography, see the specific period, reign, or place
4130 General works
4131 Rulers, kings, etc.
4133 Public men
4135 Women
Houses, noble families, etc.
4137 General works
4138.A-Z Individual, A-Z
e.g.
4138.G6 Górka family
4138.J3 Jagiellons
4138.P5 Piasts
4138.5 Princes and princesses. Queens
Historiography
4139 General works
Biography of historians
4139.2 Collective
4139.25.A-Z Individual, A-Z
e.g.
4139.25.B3 Balzer, Oswald Marian
4139.25.D5 Długosz, Jan
4139.25.L4 Lelewel, Joachim
4139.25.N3 Naruszewicz, Adam Stanisław
Study and teaching
4139.3 General works
4139.4.A-Z By region or country, A-Z
Subarrange by author
General works

History
General works -- Continued
Through 1800, see DK4187, DK4190
4140 1801-
4145 Pictorial works. Albums
4147 Juvenile works
4150 Addresses, essays, lectures
General special
4155 Philosophy of Polish history
4160 Several parts of Poland treated together
Military history
4170 General works
4171 General special
4172 Early to 1795
4173 1795-1918
4174 1918-
Naval history
4177 General works
4178 General special
Political and diplomatic history. Politics and government
4178.5 Sources and documents
4179 General works
4179.2 General special
By period
See the specific period or reign
Diplomatic history. Foreign and general relations
4179.5 Sources and documents
4180 General works
4182 Polish question
By period
See the specific period or reign
4185.A-Z Relations with individual countries, A-Z
By period
To 1795
4186 Sources and documents
General works
4187 Through 1800
4188 1801-
4188.2 Social life and customs. Civilization. Intellectual life
To 1572
4189 Sources and documents
General works
4190 Through 1800
4200 1801-
4205 General special
4210 Through 960
4210.5 Goths
4210.7 Romans
960-1386. Piast period
4211 Sources and documents
4212 General works

History
By period
To 1795
To 1572
960-1386. Piast period -- Continued
4212.5 Social life and customs. Civilization. Intellectual life
960-1138. First monarchy
4213 General works
Biography and memoirs
4214 Collective
4214.5.A-Z Individual, A-Z
4215 Mieszko I, 960-992
4215.5 Battle of Cedynia, 972
4220 Boleslaus I the Brave, 992-1025
4222 Mieszko II, 1025-1034
4222.5 Interregnum, 1034-1040
4223 Casimir I the Restorer, 1040-1058
4224 Boleslaus II the Bold, 1058-1079
4225 Vladislaus I Herman, 1079-1102
4226 Boleslaus III, the Wrymouth, 1102-1138
1138-1305. Feudal duchies
4227 General works
Biography and memoirs
4229 Collective
4230.A-Z Individual, A-Z
e.g.
4230.B6 Bolesław Pobozny, Prince of Wielkopolska
4230.P78 Przemysł II, Prince of Wielkopolska and King of Poland
4230.W5 Władysław III, Laskonogi, Duke of Wielkopolska and Kraków
4241 Vladislaus II the Exile, 1138-1146
4242 Boleslaus IV the Curly, 1146-1173
4243 Mieszko III, the Old, 1173-1177/1202
4244 Casimir II the Just, 1177-1194
4245 Leszek the White, 1194/1202-1227
Boleslaus V the Chaste, 1227-1279
4245.5 General works
4245.7 Mongol invasion, 1241
Including the Battle of Legnica, 1241
4246 Leszek the Black, 1279-1289
4246.5 Bohemian intervention, 1289-1305
1305-1386. Reunification
4246.6 General works
Biography and memoirs
4246.7 Collective
4246.8.A-Z Individual, A-Z
e.g.
4246.8.B6 Bolesław II, Duke of Świdnica
4246.8.W5 Władysław Bialy, Duke of Kujawy
4247 Vladislaus I the Short, 1305-1333
4248 Casimir III the Great, 1333-1370

History
By period
To 1795
To 1572
960-1386. Piast period
1305-1386. Reunification -- Continued
4249 Lajos I d'Anjou of Hungary, 1370-1382
4249.4 Interregnum, 1382-1384
4249.5 Jadwiga, 1384-1386
1386-1572. Jagiellons
4249.7 Sources and documents
4250 General works
4252 General special
Biography
see individual reigns
Vladislaus II Jagiełło, 1386-1434
4260 General works
4261 War with Teutonic Knights, 1409-1411
Including the Battle of Grunwald (Tannenberg), 1410
4262 Treaty of Horodlo, 1413
Biography and memoirs
4263 Collective
4264.A-Z Individual, A-Z
e.g.
4264.P3 Pawel Włodkowic z Brudzewa
4265 Vladislaus III Warneńczyk, 1434-1444
4268 Interregnum, 1444-1447
Casimir IV, 1447-1492
4270 General works
Thirteen Years' War, 1454-1466
4271 General works
4272 Peace of Toruń, 1466
Biography and memoirs
4273 Collective
4274.A-Z Individual, A-Z
4275 John I Albert, 1492-1501
4276 16th century (General)
4277 Alexander, 1501-1506
Sigismund I the Old, 1506-1548
4280 General works
4280.5 Polish-Teutonic Knights' War, 1519-1521
4281 Battle of Obertin, 1531
Biography and memoirs
4283 Collective
4284.A-Z Individual, A-Z
e.g.
4284.C6 Copernicus, Nicolaus
Cf. QB36.C8, Copernicus as an astronomer
4284.F7 Frycz Modrzewski, Andrzej
Sigismund II Augustus, 1548-1572
4285 General works

History
By period
To 1795
To 1572
1386-1572. Jagiellons
Sigismund II Augustus, 1548-1572 -- Continued
4286 General special
Livonian War, 1557-1582, see DK4297
4287 Union of Lublin, 1569
Biography and memoirs
4288 Collective
4289.A-Z Individual, A-Z
e.g.
4289.B3 Barbara, Consort of Sigismund II
1572-1763. Elective monarchy
4289.5 Sources and documents
4290 General works
4291 General special
4292 Interregnum, 1572-1573
4293 Henry III Valois, 1573-1574
Stefan Batory, 1575-1586
4295 General works
4297 Livonian War, 1557-1582
Biography and memoirs
4298 Collective
4299.A-Z Individual, A-Z
e.g.
4299.A5 Anna Jagiellonka, Consort of Stefan Batory
Sigismund III, 1587-1632
4300 General works
4301 General special
4301.3 Battle of Byczyna, 1588
4301.4 Battle of Kirchholm, 1605
4301.5 Rebellion of Zebrzydowski, 1606-1609
Swedish-Polish War, 1617-1629, see DL712+
4301.6 Battle of Cecora, 1620
4301.7 Battle of Chocim (Hotin), 1621
Biography and memoirs
4301.9 Collective
4302.A-Z Individual, A-Z
e.g.
4302.C5 Chodkiewicz, Jan Karol
4302.Z3 Zamojski, Jan
4302.Z6 Żółkiewski, Stanisław
4302.5 17th century (General)
Wladyslaw IV Zygmunt, 1632-1634
4303 General works
4303.4 Russo-Polish War, 1632-1634
John II Casimir, 1648-1668
4305 General works
4306 General special

History
By period
To 1795
1572-1763. Elective monarchy
John II Casimir, 1648-1668 -- Continued
Polish-Cossack War (Chmielnicki Uprising), 1648-1654, see DK508.755.A+
4306.3 Uprising of Kostka Napierski, 1651
Swedish-Polish War, 1655-1660, see DL725.6+
4306.35 Polish-Brandenburg War, 1656-1657
4306.36 Russo-Polish War, 1658-1667
Including the Battle of Chudniv (Cudnów), 1660
4306.4 Rebellion of Lubomirski, 1665-1666
Biography and memoirs
4307 Collective
4307.5.A-Z Individual, A-Z
e.g.
4307.5.C9 Czarniecki, Stefan
4307.5.K6 Kordeki, Augustyn
4307.5.L8 Lubomirski, Jerzy Sebastian
4307.5.M3 Marja Ludwika, Consort of John II Casimir
Michael Wiśniowiecki, 1669-1673
4308 General works
4309 Gołąbska Konfederacja, 1672
4309.5 Battle of Chocim (Hotin), 1673
John III Sobieski, 1674-1696
4310 General works
Turco-Polish Wars, 1683-1699
4311 General works
Siege of Vienna, 1683, see DR536
4311.5 Battle of Podgaytsy, 1698
Biography and memoirs
4311.9 Collective
4312.A-Z Individual, A-Z
e.g.
4312.L3 Lubomirski, Hieronym Augustyn
4312.M3 Maria Kazimiera, Consort of John III Sobieski
4312.P3 Pasek, Jan Chryzostom
4312.Z3 Załuski, Andrzej Chryzostom
4314 Interregnum, 1696-1697
Augustus II (Friedrich August I, Elector of Saxony), 1697-1733
For biography, see DD801.S395+
4315 General works on Polish reign
4317 Political and diplomatic history
Battle of Podgaytsy, 1698, see DK4311.5
Northern War, 1700-1721, see DL733+
Biography and memoirs
4318 Collective
4319.A-Z Individual, A-Z
4320 Stanislaus I Leszczyński, 1704-1709

History
By period
To 1795
1572-1763. Elective monarchy -- Continued
Augustus III (Friedrich August II, Elector of Saxony), 1733-1763
For biography, see DD801.S397
4325 General works on Polish reign
4325.5 Social life and customs. Civilization. Intellectual life
4326 Political and diplomatic history
War of Polish Succession, 1733-1738
4326.5 General works
4327 Treaty of Vienna, 1738
Biography and memoirs
4327.5 Collective
4328.A-Z Individual, A-Z
e.g.
4328.K6 Konarski, Stanisław
1763-1795. Partition period
4328.9 Sources and documents
4329 General works
4329.5 General special
Stanislaus II Augustus, 1764-1795
4330 General works
4330.5 Social life and customs. Civilization. Intellectual life
4331 Barska Konfederacja, 1768-1772
4332 First partition, 1772
Sejm, 1788-1792
4333 General works
4334 Constitution of May, 1791
Targowicka Konfederacja, 1792-1793
4335 General works
4336 Russo-Polish War, 1792
4337 Second partition, 1793
Revolution of 1794
4338 Periodicals. Societies. Serials
4339 Sources and documents
Biography, see DK4347+
4340 General works
4341 Pictorial works. Satire, caricature, etc.
4342 General special
4343 Personal narratives
4344.A-Z Local revolutionary history. By place, A-Z
e.g.
4344.R3 Battle of Raclawice, 1794
4345.A-Z Special topics, A-Z
4345.A7 Arms and armament
4345.C37 Catholic Church
4345.F67 Foreign public opinion
Jews, see DS135.P6+
Biography and memoirs

History
By period
To 1795
1763-1795. Partition period
Stanislaus II Augustus, 1764-1795
Biography and memoirs -- Continued
4347 Collective
4348.A-Z Individual, A-Z
e.g.
4348.K6 Kołłątaj, Hugo
4348.K67 Kościuszko, Tadeusz Andrzej
Cf. E207.K8, American Revolution
4348.P8 Pułaski, Kazimierz
4348.S8 Staszic, Stanisław
1795-1918. 19th century (General)
4348.5 Sources and documents
4349 General works
4349.3 General special
4349.4 Social life and customs. Civilization. Intellectual life
4349.5 Biography (Collective)
For individual biography, see the specific period
1795-1864
4349.6 Sources and documents
4349.7 General works
4349.8 General special
1795-1830
4349.9 Sources and documents
4350 General works
4351 General special
4353 Period of Napoleonic Wars, 1795-1815
Including the Duchy of Warsaw
For the wars themselves, see DC220
Biography and memoirs
4354 Collective
4355.A-Z Individual, A-Z
e.g.
4355.C9 Czartoryski, Adam Jerzy
4355.D3 Dąbrowski, Jan Henryk
4355.P6 Poniatowski, Józef Antoni
4355.W88 Wybicki, Józef
1830-1864
4356 Sources and documents
4357 General works
4358 General special
Revolution of 1830-1832
4359 Periodicals. Societies. Serials
4359.3 Museums, exhibitions, etc.
Subarrange by author
4359.5 Sources and documents
Biography, see DK4379+
4360 General works

History
By period
1795-1918. 19th century (General)
1795-1864
1830-1864
Revolution of 1830-1832 -- Continued
4361 Pictorial works. Satire, caricature, etc.
4361.3 Addresses, essays, lectures
4361.5 General special
Military operations
4362 General works
4362.2 Regimental histories
Subarrange by author
4362.3 Personal narratives
4362.5.A-Z Local revolutionary history. By place, A-Z
4363.A-Z Special topics, A-Z
4363.E3 Economic aspects
Female participation, see DK4363.W66
4363.F6 Foreign public opinion
Health aspects, see DK4363.M43
Hospitals, see DK4363.M43
Jews, see DS135.P6+
4363.M43 Medical care. Hospitals. Health aspects
4363.P7 Press
4363.R4 Refugees
4363.W66 Women. Female participation
4363.2 Partisan Campaign, 1833
4364 Revolution of 1846
Revolution of 1848
4365 General works
4365.5.A-Z Local revolutionary history. By place, A-Z
Revolution of 1863-1864
4366 Periodicals. Societies. Serials
4367 Museums, exhibitions, etc.
Subarrange by author
4368 Sources and documents
Biography, see DK4379+
4370 General works
4372 Pictorial works. Satire, caricature, etc.
4372.2 Addresses, essays, lectures
4372.3 General special
Military operations
4373 General works
4373.5 Regimental histories
Subarrange by author
4374 Personal narratives
4376.A-Z Local revolutionary history. By place, A-Z
4378.A-Z Special topics, A-Z
4378.C3 Catholic Church
4378.C65 Communications
Foreign participation
4378.F6 General works
4378.F62A-Z By country, A-Z

History
By period
1795-1918. 19th century (General)
1795-1864
1830-1864
Revolution of 1863-1864
Special topics, A-Z -- Continued
4378.F65 Foreign public opinion
4378.I5 Influence
Jews, see DS135.P6+
4378.P7 Press
4378.P75 Prisoners and prisons
4378.R4 Refugees
4378.S4 Secret service. Spies
4378.S6 Social aspects
Spies, see DK4378.S4
4378.T7 Transportation
4378.V46 Veterans
4378.W6 Women
Biography and memoirs
4379 Collective
4379.5.A-Z Individual, A-Z
e.g.
4379.5.D3 Dąbrowski, Jaroslaw
4379.5.D4 Dembowski, Edward
4379.5.M5 Mierosławski, Ludwik
4379.5.T7 Traugutt, Romuald
4379.5.W5 Wielopolski, Aleksander Ignacy
1864-1918
4379.9 Sources and documents
4380 General works
4381 General special
4381.5 Social life and customs. Civilization. Intellectual life
4382 20th century (General)
Revolution of 1905
4383 Periodicals. Societies. Serials
4384 Sources and documents
Biography, see DK4394+
4385 General works
4385.2 Pictorial works. Satire, caricature, etc.
4385.3 Addresses, essays, lectures
4386 General special
4387 Personal narratives
4388.A-Z Local revolutionary history. By place, A-Z
4389.A-Z Special topics, A-Z
4389.P74 Press
4389.S77 Student strikes
1914-1918. Period of World War I
Including German occupation, 1914-1918
For the war itself, see D501+
4390 General works
4392 Austrian occupation, 1915-1918

History
By period
1795-1918. 19th century (General)
1864-1918 -- Continued
Biography and memoirs, 1864-1918
4394 Collective
4395.A-Z Individual, A-Z
e.g.
4395.B6 Bobrzyński, Michał
4395.K8 Kunicki, Ryszard
1918-1945
4397 Sources and documents
4400 General works
4401 General special
4401.5 Military history
4401.7 Naval history
4402 Political history
4402.5 Foreign and general relations
4403 Social life and customs. Civilization
1918-1926
4403.5 General works
Wars of 1918-1921
Including Russo-Polish War, 1919-1920
4404 Periodicals. Societies. Serials
4404.5 Sources and documents
Biography, see DK4419+
4405 General works
4405.3 Pictorial works. Satire, caricature, etc.
4405.5 General works
4405.7 Diplomatic history
Military operations
4406 General works
4406.3 Regimental histories
Subarrange by author
4406.4 Aerial operations
4406.45 Naval operations
4406.54 Personal narratives
4407.A-Z Individual campaigns, battles, etc. By place, A-Z
e.g.
4407.G3 Galicia
4407.L9 Siege of Lvov, 1918-1919
4409.A-Z Special topics, A-Z
4409.C37 Catholic Church
4409.F65 Foreign participation
Health aspects, see DK4409.M43
Hospitals, see DK4409.M43
4409.M43 Medical care. Hospitals. Health aspects
4409.M54 Military intelligence
4409.P75 Prisoners and prisons
4409.T45 Territorial questions
4409.3 Treaty of Riga, 1921
4409.4 Coup d'Etat, 1926

History
By period
1918-1945 -- Continued

4409.5 1926-1939

1939-1945. Period of World War II

For for the war itself, see D731+

4410 General works

Including German occupation, 1939-1945

4415 Russian occupation, 1939-1941

Biography and memoirs, 1918-1945

4419 Collective

4420.A-Z Individual, A-Z

e.g.

4420.B4 Beck, Józef

4420.P3 Paderewski, Ignacy Jan

4420.P5 Piłsudski, Józef

4420.S5 Sikorski, Władysław

1945-1989. People's Republic

4429 Sources and documents

4430 General works

4433 General special

Biography and memoirs, 1945-

4434 Collective

4435.A-Z Individual, A-Z

e.g.

4435.B5 Bierut, Bolesław

4435.C88 Cyrankiewicz, Józef

4435.G5 Gierek, Edward

4435.G6 Gomułka, Władysław

4436 Political history

4436.5 Foreign and general relations

4437 Social life and customs. Civilization

1945-1956

4438 General works

4439 Uprising, 1956

4440 1956-1980

4442 1980-1989

1989-

4445 Sources and documents

4446 General works

4448 Social life and customs. Civilization. Intellectual life

4449 Political history

4450 Foreign and general relations

Biography and memoirs

4451 Collective

4452.A-Z Individual, A-Z

e.g.

4452.W34 Wałęsa, Lech

Local history and description

Local history and description -- Continued

4600.A-Z Provinces, counties, historical regions, etc., A-Z

Jurisdictions of varying size which are named for the same city are classed in separate cutter numbers; regions named for the same city many be classed with any jurisdiction, as appropriate

e.g.

4600.B37 Beshchady Mountains (Bieszczady)

4600.B4 Beskid Mountains

For Beskids in Czechoslovakia, see DB3000.B4

4600.B52 Białystok (Voivodeship) (Table D-DR5)

4600.B88 Bydgoszcz (Voivodeship) (Table D-DR5)

4600.C3 Carpathian Mountains

For Carpathian Mountains (General), see DJK71+

4600.C54 Cieszyn (Teschen) Silesia (Table D-DR5)

For Ceský Těšín region in Czechoslovakia, see DB2500.C465

4600.C9 Czestochowa

4600.G34 Galicia (Table D-DR5)

4600.G42 Gdańsk (Danzig) (Voivodeship) (Table D-DR5)

4600.G44 Gdańsk Pomerania. Pomerelia (Table D-DR5)

Including Royal Prussia, West Prussia, Polish Pomerania (1919-1936), and Danzig-Westpreussen

4600.G54 Głubczyce Plateau

4600.G56 Gniezno

Grenzmark Posen-Westpreussen, see DK4600.M35

4600.I9 Izera Mountains (Jizerské Hory, Isergebirge)

For Izera Mountains in Czechoslovakia, see DB2500.J58

4600.K34 Kaszuby region (Table D-DR5)

4600.K37 Katowice (Voivodeship) (Table D-DR5)

Cf. DK4600.S48, Silesia (Voivodeship)

4600.K43 Kielce (Voivodeship) (Table D-DR5)

4600.K53 Kłodzko (Glatz) (Table D-DR5)

4600.K6 Kołobrzeg

4600.K67 Kościan

4600.K68 Koszalin (Voivodeship) (Table D-DR5)

4600.K72 Kraków (Voivodeship) (Table D-DR5)

4600.K75 Kraków-Czestochowa Highland

4600.K77 Krkonose Mountains (Karkonosze, Riesengebirge)

For Krkonose Mountains (General and Czechoslovakia), see DB2500.K75

4600.K8 Kujawy

4600.L63 Łódź (Voivodeship) (Table D-DR5)

4600.L67 Łowicz

4600.L82 Lublin (Voivodeship) (Table D-DR5)

4600.L86 Lubusz region

4600.M33 Małopolska (Table D-DR5)

4600.M35 Marchia Graniczna (Grenzmark Posen-Westpreussen)

4600.M36 Masovia (Mazowsze) (Table D-DR5)

4600.M38 Mazury region (Masurenland) (Table D-DR5)

4600.N3 Narew River and Valley

Local history and description
Provinces, counties, historical regions, etc., A-Z -- Continued

4600.O33 Oder-Neisse Line. Western and Northern Territories (Table D-DR5)
Including Oder River and Valley (General)

4600.O44 Olsztyn (Voivodeship) (Table D-DR5)

4600.O66 Opole (Oppeln) (Voivodeship) (Table D-DR5)

4600.O8 Oświęcim (Auschwitz)

4600.P54 Pieniny Range

4600.P6 Podhale Highlands

4600.P64 Podlasie

4600.P67 Pomerania (Pomorze, Pommern) (Table D-DR5)
For localities of the former province of Pomerania now located in East Germany, see DD801.A+
For Pomerelia (Eastern/Gdansk Pomerania), see DK4600.G44

4600.P69 Poznań (Posen) (Voivodeship) (Table D-DR5)
Including Provinz Posen
Cf. DK4600.W55, Wielkopolska

4600.P77 East Prussia (Prusy Wschodnie, Ostpreussen) (Table D-DR5)
Including the Teutonic Knights and Ducal Prussia
For West Prussia, see DK4600.G44

Royal Prussia (Prusy Królewskie), see DK4600.G44

4600.R94 Rzeszów (Voivodeship) (Table D-DR5)

4600.S42 Silesia (Śląsk, Schlesien) (Table D-DR5)
For Silesia, Czechoslovakia, see DB2500.S54

4600.S44 Lower Silesia (Dolny Śląsk, Niederschlesien) (Table D-DR5)
For localities of the former province of Lower Silesia now located in East Germany, see DD801.A+

4600.S46 Upper Silesia (Górny Śląsk, Oberschlesien) (Table D-DR5)
For Cieszyn Silesia, see DK4600.C54
For Opole Silesia, see DK4600.O66

4600.S48 Silesia (Voivodeship)
Cf. DK4600.K37, Katowice (Voivodeship)

4600.S6 Zagłebie Śląsko-Dąbrowskie

Sneika Mountain (Sniezka, Schneekoppe), see DB2500.S65

4600.S656 Spiš (General and Poland)

4600.S7 Sudetes Mountains
For Sudetes (General and Czechoslovakia), see DB2500.S94

4600.S8 Świętokrzysz Mountains

4600.S93 Szczecin (Stettin) (Voivodeship) (Table D-DR5)

4600.T3 Tatra Mountains
For Tatra Mountains (General and Czechoslovakia, see DB3000.T37

4600.V5 Vistula (Wisła) River and Valley
Including Vistula Marsh (Zuławy Wiślane)

4600.W34 Warmia (Ermland) (Table D-DR5)

Local history and description
Provinces, counties, historical regions, etc., A-Z -- Continued

4600.W37 Warsaw (Voivodeship) (Table D-DR5)
4600.W38 Warta River and Valley
For Wartheland, see DK4600.W55
West Prussia (Prusy Zachodnie, Westpreussen), see DK4600.G44
Western and Northern Territories, see DK4600.O33
4600.W55 Wielkopolska (Table D-DR5)
Including Wartheland
Cf. DK4600.P69, Poznań (Voivodeship)
4600.W75 Wrocław (Breslau) (Voivodeship) (Table D-DR5)
Zagłebie Śląsko-Dąbrowskie, see DK4600.S6
4600.Z55 Zielona Góra (Voivodeship) (Table D-DR5)

Warsaw (Warszawa)
4610 Periodicals. Societies. Serials
4611 Museums, exhibitions, etc.
4612 Sources and documents
4613 Biography (Collective)
For individual biography, see the specific period
4614 Directories. Dictionaries. Gazetteers
4616 Guidebooks
General works. Description
4619 Through 1800
4620 1801-1900
4621 1901-1945
4622 1946-
4624 Monumental and picturesque. Pictorial works
4625 Antiquities
4626 Social life and customs. Civilization. Intellectual life
Ethnography
4628 General works
4629.A-Z Individual elements in the population, A-Z
History
4630 General works
4631 Early to 1795
4632 1795-1918
For the Grand Duchy of Warsaw, see DK4353
4633 1918-
Sections, districts, suburbs, etc.
4636 Collective
4637.A-Z Individual, A-Z
e.g.
4637.S7 Stare Miasto
Monuments. Statues, etc.
4638 Collective
4639.A-Z Individual, A-Z
e.g.
4639.P6 Pomnik Kopernika
Parks, Squares. Cemeteries, etc.
4640 Collective

Local history and description
Warsaw (Warszawa)
Parks, Squares. Cemeteries, etc. -- Continued
4641.A-Z Individual, A-Z
e.g.
4641.R9 Rynek Starego Miasta
Streets. Bridges, etc.
4642 Collective
4643.A-Z Individual, A-Z
Buildings. Palaces, etc.
4644 Collective
4645.A-Z Individual, A-Z
Gdansk (Danzig)
4650 Periodicals. Societies. Serials
4651 Museums, exhibitions, etc.
4652 Sources and documents
4653 Biography (Collective)
For individual biography, see the specific period
4654 Directories. Dictionaries. Gazetteers
4656 Guidebooks
General works. Description
4659 Through 1800
4660 1801-1900
4661 1901-1945
4662 1946-
4664 Monumental and picturesque. Pictorial works
4665 Antiquities
4666 Social life and customs. Civilization.
Intellectual life
Ethnography
4668 General works
4669.A-Z Individual elements in the population, A-Z
History
4670 General works
4671 Early to 1793
4672 1793-1919
4673 1919-1945
Class here the Free City of Danzig
4674 1945-
Sections, districts, suburbs, etc.
4676 Collective
4677.A-Z Individual, A-Z
Monuments. Statues, etc.
4678 Collective
4679.A-Z Individual, A-Z
Parks, Squares. Cemeteries, etc.
4680 Collective
4681.A-Z Individual, A-Z
Streets. Bridges, etc.
4682 Collective
4683.A-Z Individual, A-Z
Buildings. Palaces, etc.
4684 Collective

Local history and description
Gdansk (Danzig)
Buildings. Palaces, etc. -- Continued
4685.A-Z Individual, A-Z
e.g.
4685.U6 Uphagenhaus
Krakow (Cracow)
4700 Periodicals. Societies. Serials
4701 Museums, exhibitions, etc.
4702 Sources and documents
4703 Biography (Collective)
For individual biography, see the specific period
4704 Directories. Dictionaries. Gazetteers
4706 Guidebooks
General works. Description
4709 Through 1800
4710 1801-1900
4711 1901-1945
4712 1946-
4714 Monumental and picturesque. Pictorial works
4715 Antiquities
4716 Social life and customs. Civilization.
Intellectual life
Ethnography
4718 General works
4719.A-Z Individual elements in the population, A-Z
History
4720 General works
4721 Early to 1795
1795-1918
4722 General works
4723 1815-1846 (Republic)
4724 1846-1918 (Grand Duchy)
4725 1918-
Sections, districts, suburbs, etc.
4726 Collective
4727.A-Z Individual, A-Z
e.g.
4727.S7 Podgorze
Monuments. Statues, etc.
4728 Collective
4729.A-Z Individual, A-Z
Parks, Squares. Cemeteries, etc.
4730 Collective
4731.A-Z Individual, A-Z
e.g.
4731.R9 Rynek
Streets. Bridges, etc.
4732 Collective
4733.A-Z Individual, A-Z
Buildings. Palaces, etc.
4734 Collective

Local history and description
Krakow (Cracow)
Buildings. Palaces, etc. -- Continued
4735.A-Z Individual, A-Z
e.g.
4735.W3 Wawel (Castle)
Zamek Królewski na Wawelu, see DK4735.W3
4750 Poznan (Posen) (Table D-DR3)
4780 Wroclaw (Breslau) (Table D-DR3)
Other cities and towns
4800.A1 Collective
4800.A2-Z Individual, A-Z
e.g.
4800.B5 Białystok
4800.B9 Bydgoszcz
4800.C5 Cieszyn (Teschen)
For Cesky Těšín, Czechoslovakia, see DB2650.C467
4800.C9 Częstochowa
4800.D3 Darłowo (Rügenwalde)
4800.E4 Elbląg (Elbing)
4800.F7 Frombork (Frauenburg)
Gdańsk (Danzig), see DK4650+
4800.G4 Gdynia
4800.G5 Głogów (Glogau)
4800.G6 Gniezno
4800.G65 Gołdap
4800.G68 Gorzów Wielkopolski (Landesberg)
4800.H4 Hel
4800.J4 Jelenia Góro (Hirschberg)
4800.K3 Kalisz
4800.K32 Kamień Pomorski (Cammin)
4800.K34 Kamienna Góra (Landeshut)
4800.K38 Katowice
4800.K5 Kielce
4800.K6 Kołobrzeg (Kolberg)
4800.K67 Koszalin (Köslin)
Kraków, see DK4700+
4800.K76 Krosno Odrzańskie
4800.L4 Lębork (Lauenburg)
4800.L44 Legnica (Liegnitz)
4800.L48 Leszno
4800.L5 Lidzbark Warmiński
4800.L63 Łódź (Table D-DR4)
4800.L78 Lublin (Table D-DR4)
4800.M35 Malbork (Marienburg) (Table D-DR4)
4800.M5 Miechowice (Mechtal)
4800.M6 Morąg (Mohrungen)
4800.N6 Nowa Huta
4800.N9 Nysa (Neisse)
4800.O4 Olsztyn (Allenstein)
4800.O62 Opole (Oppeln) (Table D-DR4)
Poznań (Posen), see DK4750

Local history and description
Other cities and towns
Individual, A-Z -- Continued

4800.P7	Przemyśl
4800.R3	Racibórz (Ratibor)
4800.R34	Radom
4800.R9	Rzeszów
4800.S3	Sandomierz
4800.S4	Słupsk (Stolp)
4800.S8	Świnoujście (Swinemünde)
4800.S93	Szczecin (Stettin) (Table D-DR4)
4800.T6	Toruń (Thorn)
4800.W3	Wągrowiec (Wongrowitz)
4800.W34	Wałbrzych (Waldenburg)
	Warsaw, see DK4610+
	Wrocław, see DK4780
4800.Z3	Zagań (Sagan)
4800.Z34	Zakopane
4800.Z5	Zielona Góra (Grünberg)

History of Northern Europe. Scandinavia
1 Periodicals. Societies. Serials
1.5 Congresses
3 Sources and documents
Collected works
3.5 Several authors
3.6 Pamphlet collections
3.7 Individual authors
4 Gazetteers. Dictionaries. Guidebooks
4.5 Place names (General)
5 General works
5.5 Compends, outlines, etc.
6 Monumental and picturesque
6.5 Historic buildings, castles, churches, etc.
6.7 Historical geography
6.8 Geography
Description and travel
For Northern Europe, see D965
7 Early through 1500
8 1501-1800
9 1801-1900
10 1901-1950
11 1951-1980
11.5 1981-
Antiquities
General works
20 Through 1800
21 1801-
23 Roman
Social life and customs. Civilization
30 General works
Old Norse. Earliest Scandinavian
31 General works
33.A-Z Special, A-Z
33.D8 Dwellings
Ethnography
41 General works
42.A-Z Individual elements in the population, A-Z
42.B68 Bosnians
42.L36 Lapps. Sami
42.P64 Poles
Sami, see DL42.L36
42.S34 Scots
42.U4 Ukrainians
42.Y84 Yugoslavs
42.5 Scandinavians in foreign regions or countries (General)
For Scandinavians in a particular region or country, see the region or country
History
43 Dictionaries. Chronological tables, outlines, etc.
Biography (Collective)
44 General works
44.1 Rulers, kings, etc.

History
Biography (Collective) -- Continued
44.2 Princes and princesses
44.3 Houses, noble families, etc.
44.5 Public men
44.7 Women
Historiography
44.8 General works
Biography of historians, area studies specialists, archaeologists, etc.
44.85 Collective
44.9.A-Z Individual, A-Z
e.g.
44.9.M3 Maurer, Konrad von
Study and teaching
44.95 General works
44.96.A-Z Local, A-Z
Subarrange by author
General works
45 Through 1800. Chronicles
46 1800-
47 Pamphlets, etc.
49 Special aspects
52 Military history
53 Naval history
Political and diplomatic history
55 General works
57 Scandinavianism
59.A-Z Relations with individual regions or countries, A-Z
By period
Earliest to 1387. Scandinavian Empire
61 General works
65 Northmen. Vikings
Cf. DL101+, Individual countries
For social life and customs, see DL31+
75 1387-1524
78 1524-1814
81 1814-1900
1900-1945
83 General works
85 Period of World War I, 1914-1918
87 1945-
Denmark
101 Periodicals. Societies. Serials
103 Sources and documents
Collected works
103.5 Several authors
103.6 Pamphlet collections
103.7 Individual authors
105 Gazetteers. Dictionaries, etc.
106 Place names, etc.
107 Guidebooks
109 General works

Denmark -- Continued
111 Compends
113 Monumental and picturesque. Pictorial works
Historic monuments, landmarks, scenery, etc. (General)
For local, see DL271.A+
114 General works
114.5 Preservation
Description and travel
115 Early through 1500
116 1501-1800
117 1801-1900
118 1901-1950
119 1951-1970
120 1971-
121 Antiquities
Cf. DL269+, Local history and description
Social life and customs. Civilization
131 General works
133 Early and medieval
Ethnography
141 General works
141.5 National characteristics
142.A-Z Individual elements in the population, A-Z
142.A43 Americans
142.B65 Bosnians
142.C48 Chileans
142.G4 Germans
142.G7 Greenlanders
142.P34 Pakistanis
142.P6 Poles
142.R87 Russians
142.5 Danes in foreign regions or countries (General)
History
143 Dictionaries. Chronological tables, outlines, etc.
143.5 Albums. Pictorial atlases
Including collections of prints and portraits, etc.
Biography (Collective)
For individual biography, see the special period, reign, or place
144 General works
144.1 Rulers
144.2 Queens. Princes and princesses
Houses, noble families, etc.
144.3 Collective
144.32.A-Z Individual houses, families, etc., A-Z
144.5 Public men
144.7 Women
Historiography
146 General works
Biography of historians, area studies specialists, archaeologists, etc.
146.5 Collective

Denmark
History
Historiography
Biography of historians, area studies specialists, archaeologists, etc. -- Continued
146.7.A-Z Individual, A-Z
e.g.
146.7.J6 Jørgensen, Adolph Ditlev
146.7.P4 Petersen, Henry
General works
147 Through 1800. Chronicles
Including Saxo Grammaticus, etc.
148 1801-
149 Compends
151 Pamphlets, etc.
General special
153 Several parts of the country treated together
154 Military history
Naval history
156.A1 Sources and documents
156.A2 Biography (Collective)
156.A3-Z General works
156.1 Pamphlets, etc.
156.2 Early and medieval
16th-18th centuries
156.5 General works
Biography
156.52 Collective
156.53.A-Z Individual, A-Z
19th-20th centuries
156.7 General works
Biography
156.72 Collective
156.73.A-Z Individual, A-Z
158 Political history
Diplomatic history. Foreign and general relations
159 General works
159.5.A-Z Relations with individual regions or countries, A-Z
By period
Early and medieval to 1523
General works
Early, see DL147+
160 Modern
161 Earliest to 750
750-1042
162 General works
162.5 Harald Klak, 812-840
163 Gorm den Gamle, d. 936?
163.5 Harald Blaatand, 940-985

Denmark
History
By period
Early and medieval to 1523
750-1042 -- Continued
164 Svend Tjugeskaeg (Tvesdaeg), 985-1014
Cf. DA159, Invasion, rule, etc., of England, 1013-1014
165 Knud den Store, 1014-1035
Cf. DA160, Invasion, rule, etc., of England, 1017-1035
166 Hardeknud, 1035-1042
Cf. DA162, Invasion, rule, etc., of England, 1040-1042
166.8.A-Z Biography and memoirs of contemporaries, A-Z
1042-1241
167 General works
168 Norwegian rule, 1042-1047
169 Svend Estridsøn, 1047-1076
169.5 Harald Hén, 1076-1080
170 Knud IV den Hellige, 1080-1086
170.1 Oluf Hunger, 1086-1095
170.3 Erik Ejegod, 1095-1103
170.5 Niels, 1103-1134
170.7 Erik Emune, 1134-1137
170.75 Erik III Lam, 1137-1147
170.8 Svend Grade, 1147-1157
Including Battle of Gradehede, 1157
171 Valdemar I, 1157-1182
172 Knud VI, 1182-1202
173 Valdemar II, 1202-1241
173.8.A-Z Biography and memoirs of contemporaries, A-Z
e.g.
173.8.B3 Berengaria, Consort of Valdemar II
1241-1387
174 General works
174.1 Erik IV, 1241-1250
174.2 Abel, 1250-1252
174.3 Christoffer I, 1250-1259
174.4 Erik V, 1259-1285
174.5 Erik VI, 1285-1320
Christoffer II, 1320-1332
174.6 General works
174.7 Valdemar III, 1326-1330
174.8 Interregnum, 1332-1340
175 Valdemar IV, 1340-1375
176 Oluf Haakonssøn, 1375-1387
Biography and memoirs
176.7 Collective
176.8.A-Z Individual, A-Z
e.g.
176.8A.E2 Ebbesen, Niels
1387-1523

Denmark
History
By period
Early and medieval to 1523
1387-1523 -- Continued
177 General works
Margrete, 1375/1387-1412
178 General works on life and reign
Cf. DL483, Reign in Norway
179 Union of Kalmar, 1397
Cf. DL485, History of Norway
Cf. DL694, History of Sweden
180 Erik VII, 1412-1439
181 Christoffer III, 1439-1448
181.6.A-Z Biography and memoirs of contemporaries, 1387-1448, A-Z
Oldenburg dynasty, 1448-1523
182 General works
183 Christian I, 1448-1481
Hans, 1481-1513
183.5 General works
183.6 Christine, Consort of John, 1461-1521
Christian II, 1513-1523
183.8 General works on life and reign
183.9.A-Z Biography and memoirs of contemporaries, 1448-1523, A-Z
e.g.
183.9.A6 Andersen, Jens, called Beldenak
183.9.E38 Elisabeth, Consort of Christian II
Modern, 1523-
184 General works
1523-1670
185 General works
Biography and memoirs
185.7 Collective
185.8.A-Z Individual, A-Z
e.g.
185.8.S57 Skram, Peder
185.8.U5 Ulfeldt, Leonora Christina, grevinde
186 Frederik I, 1523-1533
186.8 Interregnum, 1533-1534
187 Christian III, 1534-1559
Frederik II, 1559-1588
188 General works on life and reign
188.5 Northern Seven Years' War, 1563-1570 (Three Crowns' War)
188.8.A-Z Biography and memoirs of contemporaries, A-Z
e.g.
188.8.R3 Rantzau, Daniel
188.8.R32 Rantzau, Henrik
188.8.S6 Sophie, Consort of Frederik II
Christian IV, 1588-1648
189 General works on life and reign

Denmark
History
By period
Modern, 1523-
1523-1670
Christian IV, 1588-1648 -- Continued
Thirty Years' War, see D263
190 War with Sweden, 1643-1645
Including Treaty of Brömsebro, 1645, etc.
190.3 General special
Biography and memoirs of contemporaries
190.5.A1 Collective
190.5.A2-Z Individual, A-Z
e.g.
190.5.B7 Brock, Eske
190.5.S4 Sehested, Christen Thomesen, 1590-1657
190.5.U4 Ulfeldt, Corfitz
Frederik III, 1648-1670
191 General works on life and reign
191.5 General special
192 Dano-Swedish wars, 1657-1660
Including Battles of Huen, 1659; the Sound, 1658; Siege of Copenhagen, 1658-1660; etc.
192.3 Coup d'etat, 1660
192.8.A-Z Biography and memoirs of contemporaries, A-Z
e.g.
192.8.R7 Rosenkrantz, Gunde
192.8.U5 Ulfeldt, Bjørn
192.8.U6 Ulfeldt, Christopher
1670-1808
193.A2 Sources and documents
193.A3-Z Biography and memoirs of contemporaries, A-Z
e.g.
193.B5 Bernstorff, Johan Hartvig E. greve
193.G8 Griffenfeld, Peder, greve af
194 General works
Christian V, 1670-1699
195 General works on life and reign
195.3 General special
195.8.A-Z Biography and memoirs of contemporaries, A-Z
195.8.A7 Arenstorff, Frederik von
195.8.G9 Gyldenløve, Ulrik Frederik
Frederik IV, 1699-1730
196 General works on life and reign
196.3 Denmark during Northern War, 1700-1721
Cf. DL733+, Northern War
196.8.A-Z Biography and memoirs, 1699-1746, A-Z
e.g.
196.8.A5 Anna Sophie, Consort of Frederik IV
196.8.H8 Huitefeldt-Kaas, Henrik Jørgen
196.8.S4 Sehested, Christen Thomesen, 1664-1736
197 Christian VI, 1730-1746

Denmark
History
By period
Modern, 1523-
1670-1808 -- Continued
Frederik V, 1746-1766
198 General works on life and reign
198.3 General special
198.8.A-Z Biography and memoirs of contemporaries, A-Z
e.g.
198.8.H6 Holstein, Ulrik Adolf, greve
Christian VII, 1766-1808
199 General works on life and reign
199.3 General special
199.8.A-Z Biography and memoirs of contemporaries, A-Z
e.g.
199.8.B4 Bernstorff, Andreas Peter, greve
199.8.C3 Caroline Mathilde, Consort of Christian VII
199.8.S8 Struensee, Johann Friedrich, greve
1808-1906. 19th century
201 General works
202 General special
203 Social life and customs. Civilization. Intellectual life
Biography and memoirs
204.A1 Collective
204.A2-Z Individual, A-Z
e.g.
204.E8 Estrup, Jacob Brønnum S.
204.M6 Monrad, Ditlev Gothard, Bp.
Frederik VI, 1808-1839
205 General works on life and reign
206 War of 1807-1814
207 Other special
e.g. 1814 (Denmark and Sweden)
208.A-Z Biography and memoirs of contemporaries, A-Z
e.g.
208.R5 Rist, Johann Georg
Christian VIII, 1839-1848
209 General works on life and reign
210 General special
212.A-Z Biography and memoirs of contemporaries, A-Z
e.g.
212.H62 Hørup, Viggo Lauritz B.
Frederik VII, 1848-1863
213 Sources and documents
214 General works on life and reign
215 General special
216 Pamphlets, etc.
Schleswig-Holstein War, 1848-1850

Denmark
History
By period
Modern, 1523-
1808-1906. 19th century
Frederik VII, 1848-1863
Schleswig-Holstein
War, 1848-1850 -- Continued
217 General works
For political history (Schleswig-Holstein question, etc.), see DD801.S6331+
218 General special
219.A-Z Special events, battles, etc., A-Z
219.F8 Frederiksstad, Siege of, 1850
223 Treaty of Berlin, 1850
(225) Constitutional amendments, 1855
See JN7144
228.A-Z Biography and memoirs of contemporaries, A-Z
e.g.
228.A5 Andrae, Carl Christopher G.
228.L4 Lehmann, Orla
Christian IX, 1863-1906
229 General works on life and reign
1863-1866
230 Sources and documents
231 General works
232 General special
232.5.A-Z Pamphlets, A-Z
234 Period of constitutional amendments, 1863
Schleswig-Holstein War, 1864
Cf. DD431, Prussia during the war with Denmark
236 General works
239 Political and diplomatic history.
Special works on Danish relations
For general works on the Schleswig-Holstein question, see DD801.S6331+
Personal narratives
239.5 Collective
239.6.A-Z Individual, A-Z
241 The new constitution, 1866
246 1866-1873
248 1873-1906
249.A-Z Biography and memoirs of contemporaries, A-Z
e.g.
249.B27 Bajer, Fredrik
20th century
250 General works
251 General special
Biography and memoirs of contemporaries
252.A1 Collective

Denmark
History
By period
Modern, 1523-
20th century
Biography and memoirs
of contemporaries -- Continued
252.A2-Z Individual, A-Z
e.g.
252.S8 Steincke, Karl Kristian V.
Frederik VIII, 1906-1912
253 General works on life and reign
254.A-Z Biography and memoirs of contemporaries, A-Z
Christian X, 1912-1947
255 General works on life and reign
256 Period of World War I, 1914-1918
256.5 1919-1947
Including period of World War II, 1939-1945
257.A-Z Biography and memoirs of contemporaries, A-Z
e.g.
257.A6 Alexandrine, Consort of Christian X
257.C45 Christmas Møller, John
257.H3 Hanssen, Hans Peter
257.K75 Kristensen, Knud
257.S3 Scavenius, Erik Julius C.
257.S8 Stauning, Thorvald
Frederik IX, 1947-1972
258 General works on life and reign
Biography and memoirs of contemporaries
260.A1 Collective
260.A2-A5 Royal family
260.A2 General works
260.A27 Frederik, Prince of Denmark
260.A3 Ingrid, Consort of Frederik IX
260.A6-Z Other, A-Z
e.g.
260.P7 Prien, Henri
Margrethe II, 1972-
261 General works on life and reign
Biography and memoirs of contemporaries
263 Collective
263.2 Royal family
263.3.A-Z Other, A-Z
Local history and description
269 Islands of Denmark (General)
For individual islands, see DL271.A+
271.A-Z Counties, regions, islands, etc., A-Z
e.g.
271.A2 Aalborg
271.A3 Aarhus
271.A6 Anholt (Island)
271.B7 Bornholm

Denmark
Local history and description
Counties, regions,
islands, etc., A-Z -- Continued

271.D5 Djursland
271.F15 Falster
271.F2 Faroe (Faeroe) Islands (Table D-DR2)
271.F8 Fyen (Fyn)
Greenland, see G725+
271.H64 Holbaek
271.J8 Jutland (Jylland)
For South Jutland (Sønderjyllnd), see DL271.S6
271.L2 Laaland (Lolland)
271.M7 Møen
271.R2 Randers
271.R4 Ribe
271.S3 Samsø
Seeland, Sjaelland, see DL271.Z5
271.S5 Skagen
271.S6 Sønderjylland (South Jutland)
271.V38 Vejle
271.V4 Vendsyssel
271.Z5 Zealand (Seeland, Sjaelland)
Cities, towns, etc.
276 Copenhagen (Table D-DR3)
291.A-Z Other, A-Z
e.g.
291.A2 Aalborg
291.A3 Aarhus
Elsinore, see DL291.H37
291.E76 Esbjerg
291.E8 Esrom (Lake and monastery)
291.F68 Fredericia
291.F7 Frederiksberg
291.H3 Haderslev
291.H37 Helsingør
291.H5 Hillerød
291.H63 Horsens
291.J28 Jaegersborg
291.K56 Kolding
291.L9 Lyngby
291.O3 Odense
291.R4 Ribe
291.R6 Roskilde
291.V45 Viborg
Iceland
301 Periodicals. Societies. Serials
303 Sources and documents
Collected works
303.5 Several authors
303.7 Individual authors
304 Gazetteers. Guidebooks, etc.
305 General works. Compends

	Iceland -- Continued
	Description and travel
309	Early through 1800
312	1801-1900
313	1901-1950
314	1951-1980
315	1981-
321	Antiquities
	Cf. DL396+, Local history and description
	Social life and customs. Civilization
326	General works
328	Early and medieval
	Ethnography
331	General works
334.A-Z	Individual elements in the population, A-Z
334.C44	Celts
334.D34	Danes
334.N65	Northmen
334.5	Icelanders in foreign countries (General)
	For Icelanders in a particular country, see the country
	History
335	Biography (Collective)
	Historiography
335.5	General works
	Biography of historians, area studies specialists, archaeologists, etc.
335.6	Collective
335.7.A-Z	Individual, A-Z
	General works
336	Through 1800. Chronicles
	For sagas, see PT7181+, PT7281+
338	1801-
339	Pamphlets, etc.
	By period
	Early and medieval to 1540
351	General works
	874-1262
352	General works
353	Ulfljotr, 927-929
355	1262-1540
356.A-Z	Biography and memoirs, A-Z
	1540-1800
357	General works
358	Reformation, 1540-1551
360.A-Z	Biography and memoirs, A-Z
	1801-1918
365	General works
367	Althing re-introduced, 1843
369	Troubles with Denmark, 1848
371	New constitution, 1874
373.A-Z	Biography and memoirs, A-Z

Iceland
History
By period -- Continued
1918-
Class here works on Iceland as a sovereign state under Danish monarch (1918-1944) and as an independent republic (1944-)
375 General works
380.A-Z Biography and memoirs, A-Z
Local history and description
396.A-Z Districts, regions, etc., A-Z
e.g.
396.V35 Vatnajökull
398.A-Z Cities, towns, etc., A-Z
e.g.
398.R5 Reykjavík
Norway
401 Periodicals. Societies. Serials
402 Exhibitions (Historical)
403 Sources and documents
Collected works
403.5 Several authors
403.7 Individual authors
405 Gazetteers. Dictionaries, etc.
406 Place names, etc.
407 Guidebooks
409 General works
411 Compends
413 Monumental and picturesque
414 Historic buildings, castles, churches, etc.
Description and travel
415 Early through 1500
416 1501-1800
417 1801-1900
418 1901-1950
419 1951-1980
419.2 1981-
420 Preservation of historic monuments, landmarks, scenery, etc.
421 Antiquities
Cf. DL576+, Local history and description
Social life and customs. Civilization
431 General works
433 Early and medieval
Ethnography
Including national characteristics
441 General works
442.A-Z Individual elements in the population, A-Z
442.F5 Finns
442.G73 Greeks
442.L3 Lapps. Sami
442.P34 Pakistanis
Sami, see DL442.L3

Norway
Ethnography -- Continued
442.5 Norwegians in foreign regions or countries (General)
For Norwegians in a particular region or country, see the region or country
History
443 Dictionaries. Chronological tables, outlines, etc.
Biography (Collective)
For individual biography, see the special period, reign, or place
444 General works
444.1 Rulers, kings, etc.
444.2 Princes and princesses
444.3 Houses, noble families, etc.
444.5 Public men
444.7 Women
Historiography
445 General works
Biography of historians, area studies specialists, archaeologists, etc.
445.5 Collective
445.7.A-Z Individual, A-Z
e.g.
445.7.F7 Friis, Peder Claussøn
445.7.M8 Munch, Peter Andreas
General works
446 Through 1800. Chronicles
For Heimskringla, see PT7276+
For sagas (collections), see PT7261+
For sagas (history and criticism), see PT7181+
448 1801-
449 Compends
451 Pamphlets, etc.
451.5 Comic and satiric works
453 History of two or more provinces
454 Military history
456 Naval history
Political and diplomatic history. Foreign and general relations
458 General works
459.A-Z Relations with individual regions or countries, A-Z
By period
Early and medieval to 1387
460 General works
461 Early to 872
872-1035
462 General works
Harald I, 860-930
463 General works
464 Havsfjord, 872
465 Eirik Blodøks, 930-935
466 Haakon I den Gode, 935-961
467 Olav I Trygvesson, 995-1000

Norway
History
By period
Early and medieval to 1387
872-1035 -- Continued
468 Olav II and Christianity, 1015-1030
Biography and memoirs
468.49 Collective
468.5.A-Z Individual, A-Z
e.g.
468.5.H34 Hakon Eiriksson, 998-1030
1035-1319
469 General works
471 Magnus I, 1035-1047
471.1 Harald III, d. 1066
471.2 Magnus III, d. 1103
471.3 Sigurd I Magnusson, d. 1103
471.5 Sverre, 1177-1202
472 Haakon den Gamle, 1217-1263
474 Union of Iceland with Norway, 1262
Erik II Magnussøn, 1280-1299
475 General works
476 War with Hansa towns
477 Haakon V Hálegyr, 1299-1319
478 1319-1387
1387-1814
480 General works
482 General special
482.5 Social life and customs. Civilization. Intellectual life
483 Margrete, 1387-1412
Cf. DL178+, Biography and reign as queen of Denmark
485 Union of Kalmar, 1397
490 Special events. By date
Prefer DL182+
Biography and memoirs
495.A2 Collective
495.A3-Z Individual, A-Z
e.g.
495.I5 Inger Ottesdatter
495.L6 Lofthus, Christian Jenssøn
495.L8 Lunge, Vincents Vincentssøn
Napoleonic period
497 Sources and documents
498 General works
499 War of 1807-1814
1814. Union with Sweden
Cf. DL805, History of Sweden
500 Sources and documents
501 General works
502.A-Z Biography and memoirs, A-Z
1814-1905. 19th century

Norway
History
By period
1814-1905. 19th century -- Continued
503 Sources and documents
Biography and memoirs
504.A2 Collective
504.A3-Z Individual, A-Z
e.g.
504.B2 Bachke, Ole Andreas
504.L6 Løvenskiold, Severin
504.S8 Sverdrup, Johan
504.V7 Vogt, Jørgen Herman
504.W4 Wedel-Jarlsberg, Herman, greve
506 General works
507 Social life and customs. Civilization. Intellectual life
509 1814-1818. Karl XIII
Cf. DL792+, Life; reign as king of Sweden
1818-1844. Karl XIV Johan
Cf. DL816+, Life and reign as king of Sweden
General works on life and reign
513.A-Z Biography and memoirs of contemporaries, A-Z
e.g.
513.K6 Knudssøn, Ingelbrecht
515 1844-1859. Oskar I
Cf. DL836, Life and reign as king of Sweden
517 1859-1872. Karl XV
Cf. DL841, Life and reign as king of Sweden
1872-1905. Oskar II
Cf. DL851+, Life and reign as king of Sweden
518 General works on life and reign
519 General special
521 Struggle for foreign representation and consuls, 1844
525 Dissolution of the Swedish-Norwegian union, 1905
526.A-Z Biography and memoirs of contemporaries, A-Z
e.g.
526.S4 Schøning, Jakob Marius
20th century
527 General works
528 General special
528.5 Social life and customs. Civilization. Intellectual life
Biography and memoirs
529.A1 Collective
529.A2-Z Individual, A-Z
e.g.

Norway
History
By period
20th century
Biography and memoirs
Individual, A-Z -- Continued

529.C3 Castberg, Johan
529.H3 Hambro, Carl Joachim
529.N8 Nygaardsvold, Johan
529.Q5 Quisling, Vidkun

Haakon VII, 1905-1957
530 General works on life and reign
530.2 Royal family
(530.3) Olav, crown prince
See DL534+
530.4.A-Z Other royal, A-Z
530.4.A7 Astrid, princess
530.4.M3 Märtha, crown princess
531 Period of World War I, 1914-1918
532 Period of World War II, 1939-1945
533 1945-1957

Olav V, 1957-1991
534 General works on life and reign
Biography and memoirs of contemporaries
535.A1 Collective
535.A2-A5 Royal family
535.A2 General works
(535.A3) Harald, crown prince
See DL536
535.A6-Z Other, A-Z

Harald V, 1991-
536 General works on life and reign
Biography and memoirs of contemporaries
537.A1 Collective
537.A2-A5 Royal family
537.A6-Z Other, A-Z

Local history and description
576.A-Z Counties, regions, etc., A-Z
e.g.
576.B4 Bergen
576.F5 Finmark (Finnmarken)
576.G8 Gudbrandsdal
576.H17 Hålogaland
576.H3 Hardanger
576.H4 Hedmark
576.H5 Helgeland
576.H7 Hordaland
576.J2 Jaederen
576.L7 Lofoten
576.N55 Nord-Trøndelag
576.N6 Nordfjord
576.N8 Nordland
576.N95 Norway, Northern

Norway
Local history and description
Counties, regions, etc., A-Z -- Continued

576.O4 Østfold
576.R65 Rogaland
576.S57 Søndhordland
576.S63 Solør
576.S7 Spydeberg
576.S8 Stavanger
576.S9 Sunnmøre
576.T4 Telemark
576.T8 Troms
576.T9 Trondheim
576.Y8 Ytre Flekkerøy

Cities, towns, etc.

581 Oslo (Christiania) (Table D-DR3)
596.A-Z Other, A-Z

e.g.

596.A5 Aker
596.A6 Akershus Castle
596.B4 Bergen
596.B9 Bygdøy
596.D3 Dalene
596.D8 Drammen
596.E3 Eidsvold
596.F83 Fredrikstad
596.F84 Fredriksten
596.H22 Halden (Fredrikshald)
596.H25 Hamar
596.H28 Haugesund
596.H75 Hurum (Buskerud)
596.H8 Hvitebjørn
596.K68 Kristiansand
596.K7 Kristiansund
596.K8 Kvinesdal
596.M3 Mandal
596.M7 Moss
596.S3 Sandefjord
596.S53 Sem
596.S65 Skiringssal
596.S8 Stavanger
596.T7 Tønsberg
596.T8 Tromsø
596.T9 Trondheim
596.V6 Voss

Sweden

601 Periodicals. Societies. Serials

Museums, exhibitions, etc.

602 General works
602.5.A-Z Individual. By place, A-Z
603 Sources and documents

Collected works

604 Several authors

Sweden
Collected works -- Continued
604.5 Individual authors
605 Gazetteers. Dictionaries, etc.
606 Place names (General)
607 Guidebooks
609 General works
611 Compends
613 Monumental and picturesque
Historic monuments, landmarks, scenery, etc. (General)
For local, see DL971+
614 General works
614.5 Preservation
Description and travel
614.55 History of travel
615 Early through 1500
616 1501-1800
617 1801-1900
618 1901-1950
619 1951-1980
619.5 1981-
621 Antiquities
Cf. DL971+, Local history and description
Social life and customs. Civilization
631 General works
633 Early and medieval
635 Intellectual life
Ethnography
Including national characteristics
639 General works
641.A-Z Individual elements in the population, A-Z
641.A47 Africans
641.A49 Americans
641.A85 Assyrians
641.B34 Balts
641.C45 Chileans
641.C94 Czechs
641.E8 Estonians
641.E86 Ethiopians
641.F55 Finns
641.G47 Germans
641.G68 Goths
641.H85 Hungarians
641.I7 Iranians
641.I8 Italians
641.K87 Kurds
641.L35 Lapps. Sami
641.L38 Latvians
641.N68 Norwegians
641.P64 Poles
Sami, see DL641.L35
641.S34 Scots
641.S67 South Asians

Sweden
Ethnography
Individual elements
in the population, A-Z -- Continued
641.T87 Turks
641.W34 Walloons
641.Y8 Yugoslavs
642 Swedes in foreign regions or countries (General)
History
643 Dictionaries. Chronological tables, outlines, etc.
Biography (Collective)
For individual biography, see the special period, reign, or place
644 General works
644.1 Rulers, kings, etc.
644.2 Queens. Princes and princesses
644.3.A-Z Houses, noble families, etc., A-Z
e.g.
644.3.B34 Bernadotte, House of
644.5 Public men
644.7 Women
Historiography
645 General works
Biography of historians, area studies specialists, archaeologists, etc.
645.5 Collective
645.7.A-Z Individual, A-Z
e.g.
645.7.G4 Geijer, Erik Gustaf
645.7.H35 Hildebrand, Hans Olof H.
Study and teaching
645.9 General works
645.95.A-Z By region or country, A-Z
Subarrange by author
General works
646 Through 1800. Chronicles
For sagas, see PT7181+, PT7261+
648 1801-
649 Compends
650 Pictorial works
651 Pamphlets, etc.
652 Addresses, essays, lectures. Anecdotes, etc.
653 History of two or more provinces
654 Military history
656 Naval history
Political and diplomatic history. Foreign and general relations
658.A2 Sources and documents
658.A3-Z General works
658.2 Early to 1523
1523-
General works, see DL658.A3+
658.4 1523-1654

Sweden
History
Political and diplomatic history. Foreign and general relations
1523- -- Continued
658.5 1654-1720
658.6 1720-1818
658.8 1818- . 19th-20th centuries
659.A-Z Relations with individual regions or countries, A-Z
By period
660 Early and medieval to 1523
660.5 General special
661 Earliest to 750
750-1060
662 General works
Biography and memoirs
663 Collective
663.5.A-Z Individual, A-Z
664 Olof, 993-1022
665 Anund, 1022-1050
666 Emund, 1050-1060
1060-1134
667 General works
669 Stenkil, 1060-1066
1134-1234
672 General works
673 Sverker, 1134-1155
675 Erik IX, 1150-1160. Introduction to Christianity
679.A-Z Biography and memoirs, A-Z
1234-1523
681 General works
685 Valdemar, 1250-1274
687 Magnus I Ladulås, 1275-1290
688 Birger, 1290-1318
689 Magnus II Eriksson (Smek), 1319-1363
691 Albrecht von Mecklenburg, 1363-1388
692 1389-1397, Regency of Margrete
Cf. DL178+, Life and reign as queen of Denmark
694 Union of Kalmar, 1397
Cf. DL179, History of Denmark
695.A-Z Biography and memoirs of contemporaries, A-Z
1397-1523
696 Sources and documents
697 General works
698 Other
1513-1523
699 General works
700 Kristian II, 1520-1521
Cf. DL183.8+, Life and reign as king of Denmark

Sweden
History
By period
Early and medieval to 1523
1234-1523
1397-1523 -- Continued
700.9.A-Z Biography and memoirs of contemporaries, A-Z
e.g.
700.9.G3 Gadh, Hemming, Bp.
700.9.K3 Karl Knutsson, King of Sweden
700.9.S8 Sture, Sten Gustafsson
Modern, 1523-
Vasa dynasty, 1523-1654
701 General works
702.A-Z Biography and memoirs, A-Z
e.g.
702.A2 Adler Salvius, Johan
702.C4 Cecilia Vasa, Princess of Sweden
702.D3 De Geer, Louis
702.K3 Katarina Jagellonica, Consort of John III
702.S7 Stiernsköld, Nils
703 Gustaf I Vasa, 1523-1560
703.8 Erik XIV, 1560-1568
Johan III, 1568-1592
704 General works on life and reign
704.2 General special
704.5 Sigismund, 1592-1599
17th century
704.6 General works
704.7 General special
704.8 Karl IX, 1600/1604-1611
Gustaf II Adolf, 1611-1632
705.A2 Sources and documents
Biography and memoirs of contemporaries
705.A3 Collective
705.A4-Z Individual, A-Z
e.g.
705.O8 Oxenstierna, Axel Gustafsson, greve
706 General works on life and reign
708 Political and diplomatic history
709 Social life and customs. Civilization
Military history
General works, see DL706
710 War with Denmark. Kalmar War, 1611-1613
711 War with Russia
War with Poland, 1617-1629
712 General works
Special events, battles, etc.
712.5 Oliwa, Battle of, 1627
713 Period of Thirty Years' War, 1618-1648
For the war itself, see D251+
715 Personal special
Kristina, 1632-1654

Class	Subject
	Sweden
	History
	By period
	Modern, 1523-
	17th century
	Kristina, 1632-1654 -- Continued
717	Sources and documents
	Biography and memoirs of contemporaries
717.5	Collective
718.A-Z	Individual, A-Z
719	General works on life and reign
	Political and diplomatic history
719.2	General works
719.5	Peace with Denmark, 1645
719.7	Abdication, 1654
	Personal special
719.75	Writings
719.8	Conversion to Catholicism
719.9	Later life
	Zweibrücken dynasty, 1654-1718
721	General works
	Karl X Gustaf, 1654-1660
725	General works on life and reign
725.5	General special
	Swedish-Polish War, 1655-1660
725.6	General works
725.62.A-Z	Special events, battles, etc., A-Z
725.62.O44	Oliwa, Peace of, 1660
725.7	Russo-Swedish War, 1656-1658
	Dano-Swedish War, 1657-1660, see DL192
	Karl XI, 1660-1697
727	General works on life and reign
728	General special
729.A-Z	Biography and memoirs of contemporaries, A-Z
	e.g.
729.K6	Könismarck, Karl Johan von grefve
729.K62	Könismarck, Maria Aurora von, grevinna
	Karl XII, 1697-1718
730	Sources and documents
732	General works on life and reign
732.7.A-Z	Biography and memoirs of contemporaries, A-Z
	e.g.
732.7.G9	Gyldenstolpe, Edvard, greve
732.7.H4	Hermelin, Olof Nilsson S.
	Northern War, 1700-1721
733	General works
735	General special
736	Invasion of Denmark (Holstein)
737	Invasion of Poland
738	Invasion of Russia
739	Invasion of Turkey
740	Invasion of Norway (First and Second)
743.A-Z	Special events, battles, etc., A-Z

Sweden
History
By period
Modern, 1523-
Zweibrucken dynasty, 1654-1718
Karl XII, 1697-1718
Northern War, 1700-1721
Special events,
battles, etc., A-Z -- Continued
743.A5 Altranstädt, Peace of, 1707
743.H25 Hangö, Battle of, 1714
743.H3 Helsingborg (Hälsingborg), Battle of, 1710
743.K54 Kliszów (Poland), Battle of, 1702
743.N47 Narva, Battle of, 1700
743.N8 Nystad, Treaty of, 1721
743.P8 Pultowa, Battle of, 1709
743.V5 Viborg, Battle of, 1710
1718-1818
747 Sources and documents
748 General works
749 General special
Biography and memoirs
750.A1 Collective
750.A2-Z Individual, A-Z
e.g.
750.A8 Armfelt, Gustaf Mauritz, friherre
750.D6 Döbeln, Georg Carl, friherre von
750.F4 Fersen, Hans Axel von, grefve
753 Ulrika Eleonora, 1718-1720
Fredrik I, 1720-1751
755 General works on life and reign
757 General special
Biography and memoirs of contemporaries
758 Collective
759.A-Z Individual, A-Z
e.g.
759.T47 Terstegen, Carl, 1715-1797
761 Adolf Fredrik, 1751-1771
Gustaf III, 1771-1792
Including Russo-Swedish War, 1788-1790
766 General works
770.A-Z Biography and memoirs of contemporaries, A-Z
e.g.
770.M8 Munck, Adolf Fredrik, greve, 1749-1831
772 Napoleonic period
Gustaf IV Adolf, 1792-1809
776 General works on life and reign
780 General special
782 Political and diplomatic history
785 Special events
790 Revolution and loss of Finland, 1809
Including Russo-Swedish War, 1808-1809

Sweden
History
By period
Modern, 1523-
1718-1818 -- Continued
Karl XIII, 1809-1818
792 General works on life and reign
796 General special
801 Special events
Including Treaty of Örebro, 1812, etc.
805 Union with Norway, 1814
Cf. DL500+, History of Norway, 1814
1814-1907. 19th century
807 Sources and documents
808 General works
809 General special
Biography and memoirs of contemporaries
810 Collective
811.A-Z Individual, A-Z
e.g.
811.G7 Gripenstedt, Johan August, friherre
811.H4 Hedin, Adolf
811.K4 Key, Emil
811.L6 Löwenhielm, Gustaf Carl F., greve
Karl XIV Johan (Bernadotte), 1818-1844
816 Sources and documents
Biography and memoirs of contemporaries
818 Collective
819.A-Z Individual, A-Z
e.g.
819.D5 Desideria, Consort of Charles XIV
819.H48 Heurlin, Christoffer Isak
820 General works on life and reign
Cf. DC227+, French Revolution and Napoleonic wars, 1805-1814
822 Coronation
Reign only
824 General works
826 General special
827 Social life and customs. Civilization
828 Political history
829 Diplomatic history
830 Military history
833 Special events. By date
836 Oskar I, 1844-1859
841 Karl XV, 1859-1872
Oskar II, 1872-1907
851 Sources and documents
852 General works on reign
853 General special
854 Biography
855 Personal special
Dissolution of union with Norway, see DL525

Sweden
History
By period
Modern, 1523-
1814-1907. 19th century
Oskar II, 1872-1907 -- Continued
Biography and memoirs of contemporaries
858 Collective
859.A-Z Individual, A-Z
e.g.
859.B4 Bernadotte, Oscar, prins
859.S55 Smith, Lars Olsson
859.T5 Themptander, Oscar Robert
859.W3 Waldenström, Paul Petter
20th century
860 General works
861 General special
862 Social life and customs. Civilization. Intellectual life
Biography and memoirs of contemporaries
865.A2 Collective
865.A3-Z Individual, A-Z
e.g.
865.B7 Branting, Hjalmar
865.H4 Hedin, Sven
865.L48 Lindhagen, Carl Albert
865.L5 Lindham, Arvid
865.S8 Staaff, Karl Albert
Gustaf V, 1907-1950
867 General works on life and reign
867.5 Political and diplomatic history
868 Period of World War I, 1914-1918
868.5 1919-1950
Biography and memoirs of contemporaries
869 Collective
870.A-Z Individual, A-Z
e.g.
870.B47 Bernadotte af Wisborg, Folke, greve
870.H2 Hamilton, Hugo Erik G., greve
870.H3 Hansson, Per Albin
870.N6 Nothin, Torsten
Gustaf VI Adolf, 1950-1973
872 General works on life and reign
Biography and memoirs of contemporaries
875 Collective
875.5 Royal family
876.A-Z Individual, A-Z
e.g.
876.A1 Louise, Consort of Gustaf VI
876.A23 Åsbrink, Eva
876.B47 Bernadotte, Kerstin
876.B48 Bertil, Prince
Carl Gustaf, Crown Prince, see DL877+

Sweden
History
By period
Modern, 1523-
20th century -- Continued
Karl XVI Gustaf, 1973-
877 General works on life and reign
Biography and memoirs of contemporaries
878 Collective
878.5 Royal family
879.A-Z Individual, A-Z
Local history and description
971.A-Z Provinces, regions, etc., A-Z
e.g.
971.A4 Älvsborg
971.B5 Blekinge
Bohuslän, see DL971.G6
971.D2 Dalecarlia (Dalarna)
971.G6 Gothenburg and Bohus
971.G7 Gotland
971.H15 Hälsingland
971.H17 Härjedalen
971.H2 Halland
971.I5 Inlands Torpe
971.J3 Jemtland (Jämtland)
971.J5 Jönköping
971.K8 Kronoberg
971.L2 Lapland (General, and Sweden)
971.M15 Mälar Lake and region
971.M4 Medelpad
971.N3 Närke (Närike, Nerike)
971.N6 Norrbotten
971.N65 Norrland
971.O33 Öland
971.O7 Örebro
971.O8 Östergötland
971.R6 Roslagen
971.S3 Scania (Skåne)
971.S55 Småland
971.S6 Södermanland
971.T5 Tiveden
Uppland
971.U5 General works
971.U6 Special
971.V2 Värmland
971.V3 Västerbotten
971.V4 Västergötland
971.V5 Västernorrland
971.V6 Västmanland
971.V7 Visingsö (Island)
Cities, towns, etc.
976 Stockholm (Table D-DR3)

Sweden
Local history and description
Cities, towns, etc. -- Continued
991.A-Z Other, A-Z
e.g.
991.A538 Alingsäs
991.A7 Arboga
991.B6 Birka
991.B63 Borås
991.F3 Falun
991.G6 Göteborg (Table D-DR4)
991.H4 Helsingborg (Hälsingborg)
991.J6 Jönköping
991.K8 Kristianstad
991.L3 Landskrona
991.L9 Lund
991.M2 Malmö
991.M3 Marstrand
991.N6 Norrköping
991.P5 Piteå
991.S3 Sala
991.S58 Skellefteå
991.S8 Strängnäs
991.U4 Uddevalla
991.U7 Uppsala
991.V5 Visby
Finland
1002 Periodicals. Societies. Serials
Museums, exhibitions, etc.
1003 General works
1003.5.A-Z Individual. By place, A-Z
1004 Congresses
1005 Sources and documents
Collected works (nonserial)
1006 Several authors
1006.5 Individual authors
1007 Gazetteers. Dictionaries, etc.
1008 Place names (General)
For etymological studies, see PH261+
1010 Guidebooks
1012 General works
1013 General special
1014 Pictorial works
1014.5 Historic monuments, landmarks, scenery, etc.
For local, see DL1170+
1014.7 Historical geography
Description and travel
1015 Through 1900
1015.2 1901-1944
1015.3 1945-1980
1015.4 1981-
1016 Antiquities
For local antiquities, see DL1170+

Finland -- Continued
1017 Social life and customs. Civilization. Intellectual life
For specific periods, see the period
Ethnography
1018 General works
1019 National characteristics
1020.A-Z Individual elements in the population, A-Z
1020.K37 Karelians
1020.L34 Lapps. Sami
1020.P64 Poles
Sami, see DL1020.L34
1020.S93 Swedes
1022 Finns in foreign regions or countries (General)
For Finns in a particular region or country, see the region or country
History
Periodicals. Societies. Serials, see DL1002
1024 Biography (Collective)
For individual biography, see the specific period or place
Historiography
1025 General works
Biography of historians, area studies specialists, archaeologists, etc.
1026 Collective
1026.5.A-Z Individual, A-Z
Study and teaching
1027 General works
1027.5.A-Z By region or country, A-Z
Subarrange by author
1032 General works
1033 Addresses, essays, lectures. Anecdotes, etc.
Military history
For individual campaigns and engagements, see the special period
1036 Sources and documents
1037 General works
Naval history
For individual campaigns and engagements, see the special period
1040 Sources and documents
1042 General works
Political history
For specific periods, see the special period
1043 Sources and documents
1044 General works
Foreign and general relations
For works on relations with a specific country, regardless of period, see DL1048.A+
For general works on the diplomatic history of a period, see the period
1045 Sources and documents

Finland
History
Foreign and general relations -- Continued
1046 General works
1048.A-Z Relations with individual regions or countries, A-Z
By period
Early to 1523
1050 Sources and documents
1052 General works
1052.3 Erik's Crusade, 1157
1052.5 1249-1362
1052.7 1362-1397
1052.9 Danish rule, 1397-1523
Modern, 1523-
1055 Sources and documents
1056 General works
1523-1617
1058 Sources and documents
1058.5 General works
1617-1721
1060 Sources and documents
1060.5 General works
1721-1809
1063 Sources and documents
1063.5 General works
Biography
1063.7 Collective
1063.8.A-Z Individual, A-Z
1063.9 Russian conquest, 1808-1809
Russian administration, 1809-1917
1065 Sources and documents
1065.3 General works
Biography
1065.4 Collective
1065.5.A-Z Individual, A-Z
1065.6 1809-1899
1065.8 1899-1917
20th century
1066 Sources and documents
1066.5 General works
1066.7 General special
Biography
1067 Collective
1067.5.A-Z Individual, A-Z
Revolution, 1917-1918. Civil War
1070 Sources and documents
1072 General works
Personal narratives
1073 Collective
1073.5 Individual
1074.A-Z Local history. By place, A-Z
1075 Special topics, A-Z
1075.P75 Propaganda

Finland
History
By period
Modern, 1523-
20th century
Revolution, 1917-1918. Civil War
Special topics, A-Z -- Continued
1075.P86 Punakaarti
1075.S86 Swedish participation
1078 Treaty of Peace, 1918
1080 Treaty of Peace with Russia, 1920
1918-1939
1082 Sources and documents
1084 General works
1086 General special
Biography
1088 Collective
1088.5.A-Z Individual, A-Z
1939-1945
For World War, 1939-1945, in Finland, and the Continuation War, 1941-1945, see D765.3+
1090 Sources and documents
1092 General works
Biography
1093 Collective
1093.5.A-Z Individual, A-Z
Russo-Finnish War, 1939-1940
1095 Periodicals. Societies. Serials
1096 Sources and documents
1097 General works
1098 Diplomatic history
1099 Military operations (General)
For individual battles, campaigns, etc., see DL1103.A+
Personal narratives
1102 Collective
1102.5 Individual
1103.A-Z Local history. By place, A-Z
1105.A-Z Special topics, A-Z
1105.C45 Children
Foreign participation
1105.F67 General works
1105.F672A-Z By region or country, A-Z
1105.J67 Journalists
1105.R44 Religious aspects
1105.V47 Veterans
1945-1981
1122 Periodicals. Societies. Serials
1123 Sources and documents
1125 General works
1127 General special

Finland
History
By period
Modern, 1523-
20th century
1945-1981 -- Continued
1129 Social life and customs. Civilization. Intellectual life
1132 Political history
1133 Foreign and general relations
Biography and memoirs
1135 Collective
1135.5.A-Z Individual, A-Z
1981-
1140 Periodicals. Societies. Serials
1140.2 Congresses
1140.4 Sources and documents
1140.6 General works
1140.8 Social life and customs. Civilization. Intellectual life
1141 Political history
1141.2 Foreign and general relations
Biography and memoirs
1141.5 Collective
1141.6.A-Z Individual, A-Z
Local history and description
1170.A-Z Regions, provinces, historical regions, etc., A-Z
Cities, towns, etc.
Helsinki (Helsingfors)
1175 Periodicals. Societies. Serials
1175.2 Museums, exhibitions, etc.
Subarrange by author
1175.24 Directories. Dictionaries. Gazetteers
1175.25 Guidebooks
1175.26 General works
1175.28 Description
1175.3 Antiquities
1175.32 Social life and customs. Intellectual life
Ethnography
1175.34 General works
1175.36.A-Z Individual elements in the population, A-Z
History
1175.4 Biography (Collective)
For individual biography, see the specific period
1175.42 General works
By period
1175.44 Through 1800
1175.46 1800-1917
1175.48 1917-
Sections, districts, suburbs, etc.
1175.5 Collective
1175.55.A-Z Individual, A-Z

Finland
Local history and description
Cities, towns, etc.
Helsinki (Helsingfors) -- Continued
Streets. Bridges
1175.8 Collective
1175.85.A-Z Individual, A-Z
Buildings
1175.9 Collective
1175.95.A-Z Individual, A-Z
1180.A-Z Other cities, towns, etc., A-Z
Salla, see DK651.K854

	History of Spain
1	Periodicals. Societies. Serials
2	Congresses
3	Sources and documents
	Collected works
4	Several authors
5	Individual authors
11	Directories
12	Gazetteers. Dictionaries, etc.
13	Place names
14	Guidebooks
17	General works
22	Monumental and picturesque
23	Preservation of historic monuments, etc.
26	Compends
27	Historical geography
27.3	Geography
	Description and travel
27.5	History of travel. Old roads, etc.
28	Through 710
32	711-1491
34	1492-1788
38	1789-1813
41	1814-1900
42	1901-1950
43	1951-1980
43.2	1981-
44	Antiquities
	Cf. DP285+, Local history and description
	Social life and customs. Civilization
48	General works
48.9	Spanish culture in foreign countries (General)
	Including general works on Spaniards in foreign countries
	For Spaniards in a particular region or country, see the region or country
	Ethnography
	Including national characteristics
52	General works
53.A-Z	Individual elements in the population, A-Z
53.A35	Africans
53.A43	Americans
53.A9	Autrigones
53.C44	Celts
53.C83	Cubans
53.F54	Finns
53.F74	French
53.I2	Iberians
53.I74	Irish
53.L38	Latin Americans
53.M37	Maragatos
53.M49	Mexicans
	Moriscos, see DP104

Ethnography
Individual elements
in the population, A-Z -- Continued

53.M65 Moroccans
53.N67 North Africans
53.P47 Peruvians
53.P63 Poles
53.P65 Portuguese
53.T85 Turmogos
53.V48 Vettones

Spanish people in foreign countries (General), see DP48.9

History

56 Dictionaries. Chronological tables, outlines, etc.

Biography (Collective)
For individual biography, see the special period, reign, or place

58 General works
59 Rulers, kings, etc.
Including royal houses
59.2 Aragon
59.4 Castile and Leon
59.6 Leon
59.8 Navarre
59.9 Queens, princesses, etc.

Houses, noble families, etc.
60.A2 Collective
60.A3-Z Individual, A-Z
e.g.
60.A4 Acevedo family
60.L3 Lara family
60.M4 Mendoza family
61 Public men
62 Women

Historiography
63 General works

Biography of historians, area studies specialists, archaeologists, etc.
63.5 Collective
63.7.A-Z Individual, A-Z
e.g.
63.7.A7 Argote de Molina, Gonzalo
63.7.C285 Capmany y de Montpalau, Antonio de, 1742-1813
63.7.C52 Chabás y Llorens, Roque, 1844-
63.7.E67 Escandell Bonet, Bartolomé, 1925-
63.7.L3 Lastanosa y Baráiz de Vera, Vincencio Juan de
63.7.M37 Mayans y Siscar, Juan Antonio, 1781-1801
63.7.Q3 Quadrado, José María
63.7.S17 San Felipe, Vicente Bacallar y Sanna, marqués de, 1669-1726
63.7.S2 Sánchez-Albornoz, Claudio, 1893-
63.7.S4 Sepúlveda, Juan Ginés de
63.7.T85 Tuñón de Lara, Manuel

DP

History -- Continued
Study and teaching
63.8 General works
63.82.A-Z By region or country, A-Z
63.83.A-Z Individual schools, A-Z
63.9 Philosophy of Spanish history
General works
64 Through 1550. Chronicles
65 1550-1800
66 1801-
68 Compends
69 Anecdotes, etc.
70 Comic and satiric works
72 Pamphlets, etc.
74 Several parts of the kingdom treated together
75 Special topics (not A-Z)
e.g. Germans in Spain
General special
Military history
For individual campaigns and engagements, see the special period
76.A2 Sources and documents
Biography and memoirs
76.A3 Collective
76.A5 Officers
76.A6-Z General works
76.5 General special
77 Early to 1492
77.5 1492-1700
78 1701-1808
78.5 1808- . 19th-20th centuries
Naval history
For individual campaigns and engagements, see the special period
80 Sources and documents
Biography and memoirs
80.5 Collective
80.7 Officers
Individual biography, see the historical period
81 General works
81.2 General special
81.3 Early to 1492
81.5 1492-1700
81.6 1701-1808
81.7 1808- . 19th-20th centuries
Political and diplomatic history. Foreign and general relations
For special periods, reigns, etc., see the period or reign
83 Sources and documents
84 General works
84.5 Early to 1516
1516- , see DP84

History
General special
Political and diplomatic history. Foreign and general relations
1516- -- Continued
85.3 1516-1700
85.5 1700-1814
85.8 1814-
86.A-Z Relations with individual regions or countries, A-Z
By period
Earliest to 711
91 General works
General early and medieval, see DP98+
92 Pre-Roman period
For cities, see DP402.A+
For provinces, etc., see DP302.A+
Roman period, 218 B.C.-414 A.D.
94 General works
95 Celtiberi. Numantia
Cf. DG59.I15, Iberia (Roman province)
96 Visigoths in Spain, 414-711. Gothic period
Moorish domination and the Reconquest, 711-1516.
Arab period
97.3 Congresses
97.4 Sources and documents
97.6 Historiography
General works
98 Through 1800. Chronicles
99 1801-
Moors in Spain
100 Sources and documents
General works
101 Through 1800
102 1801-
103 General special. Moslem civilization, etc.
103.5 Pamphlets, etc.
103.7 Biography
104 Mudéjares. Moriscos
Including Moriscos after 1516
Córdoba
105 Sources and documents
106 General works
107 Omayyads, 756-1016
108 Hammudites, 1016-1017
109 Omayyads, 1017
110 Hammudites, 1017-1023
111 Omayyads, 1023-1024
112 Hammudites, 1024-1026
113 Omayyads, etc., 1026-1148
Almohades, 1148-1229
114 General works
114.3 Battle of Navas de Tolosa, 1212
114.5 1229-1236

History
By period
Moorish domination and the Reconquest, 711-1516.
Arab period -- Continued
Kingdom of Granada
115 Sources and documents
General works
115.8 Through 1800
116 1801-
118 Individual rulers. By date of accession
Subarrange by author, A-Z
Reconquest, 1476-1492
121 Sources and documents
122 General works
123 General special
Aragon (Catalonia)
For modern province of Aragon, see DP302.A61+
For modern province of Catalonia, see DP302.C57
124 Sources and documents
124.7 Historiography
General works
124.8 Through 1800
125 1801-
126 General special
Dynasty of Navarre
127 General works
127.2 Ramiro I, 1035-1063
127.4 Sancho I (V of Navarre), 1063-1094
127.5 Pedro I, 1094-1104
Alfonso I, 1104-1134
127.6 General works on life and reign
127.7.A-Z Biography and memoirs of contemporaries, A-Z
127.8 Ramiro II, 1134-1137
127.9 Petronilla, 1137-1164
Dynasty of Barcelona
128 General works
128.3 Ramon-Berenguer, 1131-1162
128.4 Alfonso II, 1162-1196
128.7 Pedro II, 1196-1213
Jaime I, 1213-1276
129 General works on life and reign
129.4.A-Z Biography and memoirs of contemporaries, A-Z
130 Pedro III, 1276-1285
130.2 Alfonso III, 1285-1291
Jaime II, 1291-1327
130.3 General works on life and reign
130.4 General special
130.5 Alfonso IV, 1327-1336
Pedro IV, 1336-1387
130.7 General works on life and reign
130.8.A-Z Biography and memoirs of contemporaries, A-Z
131 Juan I, 1387-1395

History
By period
Moorish domination and the Reconquest, 711-1516. Arab period
Aragon (Catalonia)
Dynasty of Barcelona -- Continued
131.3 Martin, 1395-1410
131.6 Interregnum, 1410-1412
Dynasty of Castile
132 General works
133 Fernando I, 1412-1416
133.1 Alfonso V, 1416-1458
Cf. DG848.112.A4, Italy
Juan II
133.4 General works on life and reign
133.5.A-Z Biography and memoirs of contemporaries, A-Z
133.7 Fernando II, 1479-1516
Castile and Leon
For modern provinces of Leon, see DP302.L46
134 Sources and documents
General works
134.8 Through 1800
135 1801-
136 General special
136.2 Fernán González, Conde de Castilla, d. 970
136.4 García Fernández, Conde de Castilla, 938-995
137 Fernando I, 1035-1065
137.3 Sancho II, 1065-1072
137.6 Alfonso I (VI), 1065-1109
138 Urraca, 1109-1126
Alfonso II (VII), 1126-1157
138.3 General works on life and reign
138.4.A-Z Biography and memoirs of contemporaries, A-Z
138.6 Sancho III, 1157-1158
138.7 Fernando II of Leon, 1157-1188
139 Alfonso III (VIII) of Castile, 1158-1214
139.5 Enrique I, 1214-1217
139.7 Alfonso IX of Leon, 1188-1230
140 Fernando III, 1217-1252
140.3 Alfonso X, 1252-1284
140.6 Sancho IV, 1284-1295
141 Fernando IV, 1295-1312
141.3 Alfonso XI, 1312-1350
Pedro I, 1350-1369
141.6 General works on life and reign
141.7.A-Z Biography and memoirs of contemporaries, A-Z
141.8 Enrique II, 1369-1379
142 Juan I, 1379-1390
142.3 Enrique III, 1390-1406
Juan II, 1406-1454
142.5 General works on life and reign
Biography and memoirs of contemporaries
142.58 Collective

History
By period
Moorish domination and the Reconquest, 711-1516. Arab period
Castile and Leon
Juan II, 1406-1454
Biography and memoirs of contemporaries -- Continued
142.6.A-Z Individual, A-Z
Enrique IV, 1454-1474
143 General works on life and reign
Biography and memoirs of contemporaries
143.18 Collective
143.2.A-Z Individual, A-Z
e.g.
143.2.A34 Alfonso, Infante of Castile, 1453-1468
143.4 Isabel I, 1474-1504
143.6 Juana, 1504-1506
143.7 Felipe I, 1504-1506
143.8 Fernando V, 1507-1516
León (Asturias)
Cf. DP302.O8, Oviedo
145 Sources and documents
General works
145.8 Through 1800. Chronicles
146 1801-
147 General special
Dynasty of Pelayo
148 General works
148.2 Pelayo, 718-737
148.3 Favila, 737-739
Dynasty of Alfonso I
148.4 General works
148.5 Alfonso I, 739-757
148.7 Fruela I, 757-768
148.9 Aurelio, 768-774
149 Silo, 774-783
149.2 Mauregato, 783-789
149.4 Bermudo I, 789-792
149.5 Alfonso II, 792-842
150 Ramiro I, 842-850
150.3 Ordoño I, 850-866
150.5 Alfonso III, 866-910
151 Garcia, 910-914
151.2 Ordoño II, 914-923
151.3 Fruela II, 923-925
151.5 Alfonso IV, 925-931
151.7 Ramiro II, 931-950
151.8 Ordoño III, 951-956
151.9 Sancho I, 955-967
152 Ordoño IV, 955-960
152.3 Ramiro III, 967-982
152.5 Bermudo II, 982-999

History
By period
Moorish domination and the Reconquest, 711-1516. Arab period
Leon (Asturias)
Dynasty of Alfonso I -- Continued
152.7 Alfonso V, 999-1027
152.8 Bermudo III, 1027-1037
Navarre
For modern province, see DP302.N21+
153 Sources and documents
General works
153.8 Through 1800
154 1801-
155 General special
Dynasty of García
156 General works
156.15 Iñigo Arista, 800-851
156.2 García Iñíguez, 851-870
156.23 Fortún Garcés, 870-905
Including regency of García Jiménez, 870-882
156.3 Sancho Garcés I, 905-925
156.4 García Sánchez I, 925-970
156.43 Sancho Garcés II, Abarca, 970-994
156.46 García Sánchez II, el Temblon, 994-1000
156.5 Sancho Garcés III, el Mayor, 1000-1035
156.6 García Sánchez III, el de Nájera, 1035-1054
156.7 Sancho Garcés IV, el de Peñalén, 1054-1076
156.8 Sancho V (I of Aragon), 1076-1094
156.9 1094-1104
For biography of Pedro I, see DP127.5
1104-1134
For biography of Alfonso I, see DP127.6+
157 General works
157.2 García V, el Restaurador, 1134-1150
157.3 Sancho VI, el Sabio, 1150-1194
157.5 Sancho VII, el Fuerte, 1194-1234
Dynasty of Champagne
157.6 General works
157.7 Thibaud I, 1234-1253
157.8 Thibaud II, 1253-1270
157.9 Henri I, 1270-1274
Dynasty of Capetians
158 General works
158.2 Jeanne I, 1274-1305
158.4 Philippe I (IV of France), 1284-1305
158.6 Louis I, 1305-1316
158.7 Philippe II (V of France), 1316-1322
158.8 Charles I, 1322-1328
Dynasty of Evreux
159 General works
159.3 Jeanne II, 1328-1349

History
By period
Moorish domination and the Reconquest, 711-1516. Arab period
Navarre
Dynasty of Evreux -- Continued
159.5 Philippe III, 1328-1343
159.7 Charles II, 1349-1387
159.9 Charles III, 1387-1425
Dynasty of Aragon
160 General works
Juan I, 1425-1479
160.2 General works on life and reign
160.25.C25 Carlos, heir apparent of Aragon, Prince of Viana
160.3 Blanche d'Evreux, 1425-1441
160.4 Leonor, 1479
1479-1516
160.5 General works
Dynasty of Foix
160.6 François Phoebus, 1479-1483
Dynasty of Albret
160.7 Catherine de Foix, 1483-1517
160.8 Jean d'Albret, 1484-1516
Modern, 1479/1516-
160.9 Periodicals. Societies. Serials
161 General works
1479-1516. Fernando V and Isabel I
161.5 Sources and documents
General works on reign
161.8 Through 1800
162 1801-
Biography
163 Isabel
163.5 Fernando
164 General special
166.A-Z Biography and memoirs of contemporaries, A-Z
e.g.
166.F4 Fernández de Córdova y Aguilar, Gonzalvo, called el Gran capitán
166.G7 Gómez de Fuensalida, Gutierre
166.X5 Ximénez de Cisneros, Francisco, cardinal
Habsburgs, 1516-1700
170 Sources and documents
General works
170.8 Through 1800
171 1801-
171.5 Social life and customs. Civilization
Karl I (V of Germany), 1516-1556
172 General works on life and reign in Spain
Cf. DD180.5, General biography of Karl V
174 General special

History
By period
Modern, 1479/1516-
Habsburgs, 1516-1700
Karl I (V of Germany), 1516-1556 -- Continued
175.A-Z Biography and memoirs of contemporaries, A-Z
e.g.
175.I8 Isabel de Portugal, Consort of Charles V
Felipe II, 1556-1598
176 Sources and documents
General works on life and reign
177 Through 1776
178 1777-
179 General special
180 Elizabeth of Valois (Isabel de Valois, Consort of Philip II)
181.A-Z Biography and memoirs of contemporaries, A-Z
e.g.
181.A6 Alba, Fernando Alvarez de Toledo, duque de
181.C3 Carlos, Prince of Asturias
181.C37 Catalina Micaela de Austria, Duchess, Consort of Carlo Emmanuele I, called Il Grande, Duke of Savoy, 1567-1597
181.E2 Eboli, Ana de Mendoza y la Cerda, princesa de
181.G65 Gómez de Silva, Ruy, príncipe de Eboli, 1516-1573
Mendoza de la Cerda, Ana, Princesa de Eboli, 1540-1592, see DP181.E2
181.P4 Pérez, Antonio
181.V7 Villahermosa, Martín de Aragón y Gurrea, duque de
Felipe III, 1598-1621
182 General works on life and reign
183 General special
183.9.A-Z Biography and memoirs of contemporaries, A-Z
e.g.
183.9.G6 Gondomar, Diego Sarmiento de Acuña, conde de
183.9.O7 Osuna, Pedro Téllez Girón, 3. duque de
183.9.S6 Spinola, Ambrogio, marchese di
Felipe IV, 1621-1665
184 General works on life and reign
185 General special
185.9.A-Z Biography and memoirs of contemporaries, A-Z
e.g.
185.9.O6 Olivares, Gaspar de Guzmán, conde-duque de
Carlos II, 1665-1700
186 General works on life and reign
186.3 María Louisa de Orleáns, Consort of Charles II
186.4 Maria Anna, Consort of Charles II
187 General special

History
By period
Modern, 1479/1516-
Habsburgs, 1516-1700
Carlos II, 1665-1700 -- Continued
189.A-Z Biography and memoirs of contemporaries, A-Z
e.g.
189.V5 Villars, Marie (Gigault de Bellefonds), marquise de
Bourbons, 1700-1808. 18th century
192 General works
192.5 Social life and customs. Civilization
Biography and memoirs
193.A2 Collective
193.A3-Z Individual, A-Z
e.g.
193.C3 Campomanes, Pedro Rodriquez, conde de
193.F5 Floridablanca, José Moñino y Redondo, conde de
193.J7 Jovellanos, Gaspar Melchor de
193.O5 Olavide y Jáuregui, Pablo Antonio J. de
Felipe V, 1700-1746
194 General works on life and reign
194.3 General special
194.7 Isabel Farnese, consort of Philip V
195 Luis I, 1724
196 Spanish succession
For works on War of Spanish Succession, see D281+
197.A-Z Biography and memoirs of contemporaries, A-Z
e.g.
197.A6 Alberoni, Giulio, cardinal
197.E5 Ensenada, Zenón Somodevilla y Bengoechea, marqués de la
197.M7 Montgon, Charles Alexandre de
197.O8 Orsini, Anne Marie (de la Trémoille Noirmoustier), duchessa di Bracciano
Fernando VI, 1746-1759
198 General works on life and reign
198.7 María Bárbara de Portugal, Consort of Ferdinand VI
Carlos III, 1759-1788
199 General works on life and reign
199.3 General special
Biography and memoirs of contemporaries
199.7 María Amalia, Consort of Charles III
199.9.A-Z Other, A-Z
e.g.
Campomanes, Pedro Rodriquez, conde de, see DP193.C3
199.9.M7 Múzquiz, Miguel de, conde de Gausa
Carlos IV, 1788-1808
200 General works

History
By period
Modern, 1479/1516-
Bourbons, 1700-1808. 18th century
Carlos IV, 1788-1808 -- Continued
Biography and memoirs of contemporaries
200.3 María Luisa, Consort of Charles IV
200.8.A-Z Other, A-Z
e.g.
200.8.G7 Godoy Alvarez de Faria Rios Sánchez y Zarzosa, Manuel de, príncipe de la Paz
1808-1886. 19th century
201 Sources and documents
201.3 Historiography
Biography and memoirs
202.A2 Collective
202.A3-Z Individual, A-Z
e.g.
202.A7 Arenal de García Carrasco, Concepción
202.C2 Cánovas del Castillo, Antonio
202.C3 Castelar y Ripoli, Emilio
202.D6 Donoso Cortés, Juan, marqués de Valdegamas
202.G3 García de Leon y Pizarro, José
202.M5 Merlin, María de las Mercedes Santa Cruz y Montalvo, comtesse de
202.P3 Palafox y Melci, José de Rebolledo, duque de Zaragoza, 1776?-1847
202.P7 Prim y Prats, Juan, marques de los Castillejos
202.S3 Sagasta, Práxedes Mateo, 1825-1903
203 General works
203.5 Social life and customs. Civilization
1808-1814. Napoleonic period
204 Sources and documents
205 General works
Joseph Bonaparte
207 General works
207.5 General special
Biography, see DC216.5
208 Peninsular War period
For works on the war itself, see DC231+
Bourbon restoration, 1814-1868
212 General works
Fernando VII, 1808; 1814-1833
214 General works on life and reign
214.5 General special
215 Revolution, 1820-1823
Other members of the royal family
215.5 Marie Antoinette Thérèse de Bourbon, princesse de Naples
215.6 María Isabel de Braganza, Consort of Ferdinand VII
215.7 Josefa Fernanda Luisa, infanta of Spain

	History
	By period
	Modern, 1479/1516-
	1808-1886. 19th century
	Bourbon restoration, 1814-1868
	Fernando VII, 1808; 1814-1833
	Other members of the royal family -- Continued
215.8	María Cristina, Consort of Ferdinand VII
215.9.A-Z	Biography and memoirs of contemporaries, A-Z
	Isabel II, 1833-1868
216	General works on life and reign
217	General special
217.5.A-Z	Biography and memoirs of contemporaries, A-Z
	e.g.
217.5.N3	Narváez, Ramón María, duque de Valencia
	The Pretenders
218	General works on the Carlist movements
218.3	Don Carlos I, 1788-1855
218.5	Don Carlos II, 1818-1861
	Don Carlos III, 1848-1909, see DP226
	Biography and memoirs of their partisans
218.7.A1	Collective
218.7.A2-Z	Individual, A-Z
	e.g.
218.7.C3	Cabrera y Griñó, Ramón, conde de Morella
	Carlist War, 1833-1840
219	General works
219.2	General special
220	Period of war with Morocco, 1859-1860
	For works on the war itself, see DT324+
	1868-1886
222	General works
	Biography and memoirs
222.3	Collective
222.4.A-Z	Individual, A-Z
	Revolution, 1868-1870
224	General works
226	Don Carlos III
	Cf. DP218+, The Pretenders
228	Amadeo I, 1870-1873
	First Republic, 1873-1875
	Including Carlist War, 1873-1876
230	Sources and documents
231	General works
231.3	General special
231.5.A-Z	Local, A-Z
	e.g.
231.5.C2	Cartagena
231.5.M8	Murcia
	Alfonso XII, 1875-1885
232	General works on life and reign

History
By period
Modern, 1479/1516-
1808-1886. 19th century
1868-1886
Alfonso XII, 1875-1885 -- Continued
232.5 General special
232.55 María de las Mercedes, Consort of Alfonso XII
232.6 María Cristina, Consort of Alfonso XII
20th century. 1886-
233 General works
233.5 Social life and customs. Civilization
233.8 Foreign and general relations
Alfonso XIII, 1886-1931
234 Sources and documents
Biography and memoirs of contemporaries
235 Collective
236.A-Z Individual, A-Z
e.g.
236.A2 Victoria Eugenia, Consort of Alfonso XIII
236.A27 Borbón y Battenburg, Jaime de, 1908-
236.A3 Borbón y Battenburg, Juan de
236.A4 Torlonia, Beatriz de Borbón y Battenberg
236.A5 Eulalia, infanta of Spain
236.B3 Barea, Arturo
236.C6 Costa y Martínez, Joaquín
236.F4 Ferrer Guardia, Francisco
236.G3 Galán, Fermín
236.M35 Maura y Montaner, Antonio
236.M6 Mola, Emilio
236.P7 Primo de Rivera y Orbaneja, Miguel, marqués de Estella
236.V35 Vázquez de Mella y Fanjul, Juan
General works on life and reign
238 General works
238.3 Before coronation
238.4 Coronation
243 General special
245 Period of war with America, 1898
For works on the war itself, see E714+
246 Period of World War I, 1914-1918
247 1918-1931
Second Republic, 1931-1939
250 Periodicals. Societies. Serials
250.5 Congresses
251 Sources and documents
Collected works
252 Several authors
253 Individual authors
254 General works
255 General special

History
By period
Modern, 1479/1516-
20th century. 1886-
Second Republic, 1931-1939 -- Continued
Political and diplomatic history. Foreign relations
257 General works
258.A-Z Relations with individual regions or countries, A-Z
Biography and memoirs of contemporaries
260 Collective
264.A-Z Individual, A-Z
e.g.
264.C3 Calvo Sotelo, José
264.F7 Franco, Francisco, 1892-1975
264.L4 Lerroux, Alejandro
264.P75 Primo de Rivera, José Antonio, marqués de Estella
264.S3 Sanjurjo y Sacanell, José, marqués del Rif
267 Alcalá Zamora y Torres, 1931-1936
268 Azaña, 1936-1939
Civil War, 1936-1939
269.A1-A19 Periodicals. Collections. Conferences, etc.
Sources and documents
269.A2-A4 Serials
269.A5-A55 Nonserials
Biography, see DP260+
Causes, origins, etc , see DP257+
269.A56 Historiography
269.A57-Z General works
269.15 Pictorial works. Satire, caricature, etc.
(269.16) Poetry, drama (Collections)
See PB-PT
269.17 Pamphlets, addresses, sermons, etc.
Political and diplomatic history, see DP257+
Military operations
General works, see DP269.A57+
269.2.A-Z Individual campaigns, battles, etc., A-Z
269.2.A4 Alcazar (Toledo), Siege of, 1936
269.2.G8 Guadalajara, Battle of, 1937
Madrid, see DP269.27.M3
269.2.P68 Pozoblanco (Spain), Battle of, 1937
Regimental histories
269.23 Loyalist
269.25 Insurgent
269.27.A-Z Local history, A-Z
e.g.
269.27.B33 Basque Provinces. País Vasco
Cantabria, see DP269.27.S23
269.27.C3 Catalonia

History
By period
Modern, 1479/1516-
20th century. 1886-
Second Republic, 1931-1939
Civil War, 1936-1939
Military operations
Local history, A-Z -- Continued
269.27.C8 Cuenca
269.27.M3 Madrid
País Vasco, see DP269.27.B33
269.27.S23 Santander. Cantabria
Naval operations
269.3 General works
269.35.A-Z Individual engagements, ships, etc., A-Z
269.4 Aerial operations
269.42 Engineering operations
Foreign participation
269.45 General works
269.47.A-Z By nationality, etc., A-Z
e.g.
269.47.B7 British
269.47.G3 German
269.47.I8 Italian
269.47.R8 Russian
Atrocities
269.5 General works
269.53 Loyalist
269.55 Insurgent
Prisoners and prisons
269.6 General works
269.63 Loyalist
269.65 Insurgent
269.67 Concentration camps outside Spain
269.7 Medical and sanitary services. Hospitals
269.8.A-Z Other topics, A-Z
Anniversaries, see DP269.8.M4
269.8.A7 Art and the war
Celebrations, see DP269.8.M4
Charities, see DP269.8.R3
269.8.C4 Children
Displaced persons, see DP269.8.R3
269.8.E2 Economic aspects
269.8.E38 Education and the war
269.8.E68 Equipment and supplies
269.8.I5 Influence and results
269.8.J68 Journalists
269.8.L5 Literature and the war
For belles-lettres, see Class P
269.8.M4 Memorials. Monuments. Celebrations
269.8.M6 Motion pictures about the war
269.8.M8 Museums, relics, etc.
269.8.P65 Posters

History
By period
Modern, 1479/1516-
20th century. 1886-
Second Republic, 1931-1939
Civil War, 1936-1939
Other topics, A-Z -- Continued

269.8.P75 Psychological aspects
269.8.P8 Public opinion
269.8.R3 Refugees
Cf. DP269.67, Concentration camps outside Spain
269.8.R4 Religious aspects
269.8.S4 Secret service. Spies, etc.
269.8.S65 Social aspects
269.8.W7 Women
269.9 Personal narratives

1939-1975

269.97 Sources and documents
270 General works
Biography and memoirs
271.A2 Collective
271.A3-Z Individual, A-Z

1975-

272 General works
272.29 Foreign and general relations
Biography and memoirs
272.3 Collective
272.4.A-Z Individual, A-Z
e.g.
272.4.J8 Juan Carlos I, King of Spain

Local history and description

285 Northern Spain
291 Northwestern Spain
295 Southern Spain

Local history and description -- Continued

302.A-Z Provinces, regions, etc., A-Z

e.g.

TABLE DP302/1:
Provinces, regions, etc., A-Z (Spain)

1	*Periodicals. Societies. Collections*
2	*Congresses. Conferences, etc.*
	Biography
3.A1-A29	*Collective*
3.A3-Z	*Individual, A-Z*
4	*Dictionaries. Gazetteers. Directories, etc.*
5	*Guidebooks*
6	*General works. Description and travel. Views. Geography*
6.5	*Antiquities*
6.7	*Social life and customs. Civilization*
6.8	*Ethnography*
	History
6.9	*Study and teaching*
7	*General works*
8	*General special*
	By period
9	*Earliest (Roman and Gothic)*
10	*Moorish, 750-1492*
11	*1492-1789*
12	*1789-1815*
13	*19th-20th centuries*
15	*Other*

302.A0197 Alagón River and Valley

302.A02 Alava

302.A05 Albacete

302.A09 Alboran

302.A11-A25 Alicante

Apply Table DP302/1

302.A32 Almanzora River and Valley

302.A33 Almería

302.A38 Alpujarras

302.A383 Alt Camp Region

302.A384 Alt Urgell Region

302.A3844 Alta Ribagorça Region

302.A39 Ampurdán

302.A395 Ancares Mountains

302.A41-A55 Andalusia

Apply Table DP302/1

302.A56 Aneo Valley

	Local history and description
	Provinces, regions, etc., A-Z -- Continued
302.A61-A75	Aragon
	Cf. DP124+, History of Aragon (Catalonia) to 1516
	Apply Table DP302/1
302.A752	Aragon River and Valley
302.A753	Aramayona Valley
302.A77	Aro Valley
	Asturias, see DP302.O8
302.A87	Avila
302.A89	Axarquía Region
302.B05	Badajoz
302.B14	Bages Region
302.B15	Baix Camp Region
302.B152	Baix Ebre Region
302.B155	Baix Llobregat Region
302.B157	Baix Penedès Region
	Balearic Islands
302.B16	Periodicals. Societies. Collections
	Biography
302.B18A1-B18A29	Collective
302.B18A3-B18Z	Individual, A-Z
302.B19	Dictionaries. Gazetteers. Directories
302.B2	Guidebooks
302.B21	General works. Description and travel
302.B215	Antiquities
302.B217	Social life and customs. Civilization. Intellectual life
302.B22	History
302.B23	General special
302.B24	Cabrera
302.B25	Formentera
302.B255	Guardia
302.B26	Iviza
302.B27	Majorca
302.B275	1789-1814
302.B28	Minorca
302.B281	Special
302.B284	Capture by French, 1756
302.B34	Banets Island
302.B36	Barcelona
302.B37	Barcelonès Region
302.B41-B55	Basque Provinces (General, and Spain)
	Including Alava, Guipuzcoa, Vizcaya
	Cf. DC611.B31+, France
	Apply Table DP302/1
302.B616	Benasque Valley
302.B64	Bidasoa River and Valley (General, and Spain)
302.B81	Burgos
302.C106	Cabrera Region
302.C12	Cáceres

Local history and description
Provinces, regions, etc., A-Z -- Continued
Cadiz
For the city, see DP402.C2

302.C16	Periodicals. Societies. Collections
	Biography
302.C18A1-C18A29	Collective
302.C18A3-C18Z	Individual, A-Z
302.C19	Dictionaries. Gazetteers. Directories
302.C2	Guidebooks
302.C21	General works. Description and travel
302.C215	Antiquities
302.C217	Social life and customs. Civilization. Intellectual life
302.C22	History
302.C23	General special
302.C25	Calamocha Region
302.C258	Calatayud Region
302.C297	Camp de Tarragona Region
302.C32	Campo de Gibraltar Region
302.C36-C51	Canary Islands The islands are divided into two provinces: (1) Las Palmas (Fuerteventura, Gran Canaria, and Lanzarote islands) and (2) Santa Cruz de Tenerife (Gomera, Ferro, Palma, and Teneriffe islands)
302.C36	Periodicals. Societies. Collections
302.C365	Congresses
	Biography
302.C37A1-C37A19	Collective
302.C37A3-C37Z	Individual, A-Z
302.C38	Dictionaries. Gazetteers. Directories, etc.
302.C385	Guidebooks
302.C39	General works. Description and travel. Geograph
302.C395	Antiquities
302.C397	Social life and customs. Civilization. Intellectual life
302.C398	Ethnography
	History
302.C4	General works
	By period
302.C41	Early and medieval
302.C42	Modern
302.C43	Fuerteventura
302.C44	Gomera
302.C447	Graciosa
302.C45	Gran Canaria
302.C46	Ferro (Hierro)
302.C47	Lanzarote
302.C48	Palma
302.C49	Teneriffe

	Local history and description
	Provinces, regions, etc., A-Z -- Continued
302.C54	Cantabrian Mountains
	Class here works on the mountainous region which extends across Northern and Northwestern Spain; For works on the Autonomous region, 1978- formerly Santander Province, see DP302.S31-DP302.S36
302.C55	Castellón
302.C553	Castilla-La Mancha
302.C556	Castilla y León
	Class here works on the autonomous region, 1978-
	For works on the Kingdom to 1516, see DP134+
	Catalonia
302.C57	Periodicals. Societies. Collections
302.C575	Congresses
	Biography
302.C58A1-C58A29	Collective
302.C58A3-C58Z	Individual, A-Z
302.C59	Dictionaries. Gazetteers. Directories, etc.
302.C6	Guidebooks
302.C61	General works. Description and travel
302.C615	Antiquities
302.C616	Social life and customs. Civilization. Intellectual life
302.C617	Ethnography
	History
	Historiography
302.C619	General works
	Biography of historians, area studies specialists, archaeologists, etc.
302.C6195	Collective
302.C6197A-Z	Individual, A-Z
302.C62	General works
302.C63	General special
	By period
302.C64	Early to 711
302.C65	Medieval
	Cf. DP124+, History of Aragon (Catalonia) to 1516
302.C66	17th-18th centuries
302.C67	1789-1815
302.C68	19th-20th centuries
302.C69	Other
302.C715	Cerdaña
302.C74	Ciudad Real (La Mancha)
302.C745	Collau Zorru Mountains
302.C747	Collserola Mountains
302.C75	Columbretes
302.C754	Conca de Barbara Region
302.C76	Córdoba
	For the city, see DP402.C7

Local history and description
Provinces, regions, etc., A-Z -- Continued

302.C78 Corunna (Coruña)
302.C95 Cuenca
302.D37 Daroca Region
302.D8 Duero River and Valley
302.E2 Ebro River and Valley
302.E57 Entença
302.E74 Esla River and Valley
302.E83 Estremadura
302.F42 Fenar Valley
302.F56 Finisterre, Cape
302.F72 Francia Mountain Range
Galicia
302.G11 Periodicals. Societies. Collections
Biography
302.G12A1-G12A29 Collective
302.G12A3-G12Z Individual, A-Z
302.G13 Dictionaries. Gazetteers. Directories, etc.
302.G14 Guidebooks
302.G15 General works. Description and travel. Geography
302.G155 Antiquities
302.G157 Social life and customs. Civilization. Intellectual life
302.G158 Ethnography
History
302.G16 General works
By period
302.G17 Early and medieval
302.G18 16th-18th centuries
302.G19 19th-20th centuries
302.G2 Other
302.G205 Garraf Region
302.G206 Garrigues Region
302.G208 Gata, Cape
Gerona
302.G21 Periodicals. Societies. Collections
Biography
302.G23A1-G23A29 Collective
302.G23A3-G23Z Individual, A-Z
302.G24 Dictionaries. Gazetteers. Directories, etc.
302.G25 Guidebooks
302.G26 General works. Description and travel
302.G265 Antiquities
History
By period
302.G27 Early and medieval
302.G28 16th-18th centuries
302.G29 19th-20th centuries
302.G3 Other
Gibraltar
302.G31 Periodicals. Societies. Collections
302.G32 Congresses. Conferences, etc.

Local history and description
Provinces, regions, etc., A-Z
Gibraltar -- Continued
Biography

302.G33A1-G33A29	Collective
302.G33A3-G33Z	Individual, A-Z
302.G34	Dictionaries. Gazetteers. Directories, etc.
302.G35	Guidebooks
302.G36	General works. Description and travel
302.G38	History
	By period
302.G39	Early to 1704
302.G4	18th-20th centuries
302.G41	Other
302.G435	Gironès Region
302.G51-G65	Granada
	Apply Table DP302/1
302.G58	History
302.G67	Gredos Mountains
	Guadalajara
302.G71	Periodicals. Societies. Collections
	Biography
302.G73A1-G73A29	Collective
302.G73A3-G73Z	Individual, A-Z
302.G74	Dictionaries. Gazetteers. Directories, etc.
302.G75	Guidebooks
302.G76	General works. History and description
302.G765	Antiquities
302.G78	Guadalquiver River and Valley
302.G785	Guadiama River and Valley
302.G788	Gūdar Mountains
302.G81-G95	Guipúzcoa
	Apply Table DP302/1
302.H45	Henares River and Valley
302.H7	Huelva
302.H78	Huerna River and Valley
302.H8	Huesca
302.H86	Hurdes Mountains
302.I93	Izaro Island
302.J1	Jaen
302.J355	Jerez de los Caballeros Region
302.J37	Jerte River and Valley
	La Coruña, see DP302.C78
	La Mancha, see DP302.C74
302.L18	La Rioja
	Las Palmas, see DP302.C36
302.L2-L35	León
	Apply Table DP302/1
302.L46	Lérida
302.L48	Levante Coast. Maresme
302.L59	Llobregat River and Valley
302.L595	Lluçanés
	Los Vélez Region, see DP302.V35

Local history and description
Provinces, regions, etc., A-Z -- Continued

302.L75 Luiñas Region
302.M1 Madrid
302.M13 Maestrazgo
Majorca, see DP302.B27
302.M21-M35 Malaga
Apply Table DP302/1
Mancha, see DP302.C74
302.M356 Manzanares River and Valley
Maresme, see DP302.L48
302.M39 Mastia
302.M44 Mena Valley
302.M52 Miño River and Valley
Minorca, see DP302.B28
302.M576 Moncayo Mountains
302.M579 Monfragüe Region
302.M64 Montsià
302.M8 Murcia
302.N21-N35 Navarre
Apply Table DP302/1
302.N58 Noguera Region
302.N6 Noguera Ribagorzana River and Valley
302.O6 Orense
302.O75 Oscos Region
302.O77 Osona Region
302.O78 Oteros Region
302.O8 Oviedo. Asturias
País Vasco, see DP302.B41+
302.P1 Palencia
302.P25 Pallars
Including the regions of Pallars Jussà and Pallars Sobirà
302.P38 Pedroches Region
302.P47 Picos de Europa
302.P58 Pla D'Urgell
302.P6 Pontevedra
302.P62 Pontevedra Estuary
302.P75 Puenteáreas (Partido Judicial)
302.P8 Pyrenees
For works treating both French and Spanish Pyrenees, see DC611.P981+
302.R47 Ribagorza Region
Including the condado of Ribagorza
302.R475 Ribera Baixa Region
302.R477 Ribera D'Ebre Region
302.R48 Ribera de Xúquer Region
302.S11-S25 Salamanca
For the city, see DP402.S1
Apply Table DP302/1
302.S27 Sanabria Region
Santa Cruz de Tenerife, see DP302.C36+
302.S31-S365 Santander. Cantabria (Autonomous region)

Local history and description
Provinces, regions, etc., A-Z
Santarder. Cantabria (Autonomous region) -- Continued

302.S31 Periodicals. Societies. Collections
Biography
302.S33A1-S33A29 Collective
302.S33A3-S33Z Individual, A-Z
302.S34 Dictionaries. Gazetteers. Directories, etc.
302.S35 Guidebooks
302.S36 General works. History and description
302.S365 Antiquities
302.S41-S465 Saragossa
302.S41 Periodicals. Societies. Collections
Biography
302.S43A1-S43A29 Collective
302.S43A3-S43Z Individual, A-Z
302.S44 Dictionaries. Gazetteers. Directories, etc.
302.S45 Guidebooks
302.S46 General works. History and description
302.S465 Antiquities
302.S48 Segovia
302.S52 Segrià Region
302.S56-S6 Seville
For the city, see DP402.S36+
302.S56 Periodicals. Societies. Collections
Biography
302.S563A1-S563A29 Collective
302.S563A3-S563Z Individual, A-Z
302.S57 Dictionaries. Gazetteers. Directories, etc.
302.S58 General works. Description and travel. Guidebooks
302.S585 Antiquities
302.S59 History
302.S6 Other
302.S634 Sierra del Rincón
302.S64 Sierra Morena
302.S65 Sierra Nevada
302.S68 Solsonès Region
Soria
302.S71 Periodicals. Societies. Collections
302.S72 Dictionaries. Gazetteers. Directories, etc.
302.S725 Guidebooks
302.S73 General works. Description and travel
302.S735 Antiquities
302.S74 History
302.S75 Other
302.S89 Sueve Mountains
302.T06 Tagus River and Valley (General, and Spain)
302.T07 Tajuña River and Valley
302.T08 Talarn (Corregimiento)
Tarragona
302.T11 Periodicals. Societies. Collections

	Local history and description
	Provinces, regions, etc., A-Z
	Tarragona -- Continued
302.T13	General works. Description and travel
302.T135	Antiquities
302.T14	History
302.T15	Other
302.T29	Terra Alta Region
302.T295	Terra de Trives Region
	Teruel
302.T31	Periodicals. Societies. Collections
302.T32	Dictionaries. Gazetteers. Directories, etc.
302.T325	Guidebooks
302.T33	General works. Description and travel
302.T335	Antiquities
302.T34	History
302.T35	Other
302.T46	Tiétar River and Valley
302.T51	Toledo
	For the city, see DP402.T7
302.T83	Tudmīr
302.U73	Urgell Region
302.V109	Valdeorras Region
	Valencia
302.V11	Periodicals. Societies. Collections
	Biography
302.V13A1-V13A29	Collective
302.V13A3-V13Z	Individual, A-Z
302.V14	Dictionaries. Gazetteers. Directories, etc.
302.V15	Guidebooks
302.V16	General works. Description and travel. Pictorial works
302.V165	Antiquities
302.V167	Social life and customs. Civilization
302.V17	History
302.V18	General special
	By period
302.V2	Early and medieval to 1516
302.V201	Earliest to 715
302.V203	Moors, 715-1238
302.V205	1238-1516
302.V21	1516-1789
302.V22	16th century
302.V225	Expulsion of Moors, 1609
302.V23	1789-1815
302.V24	19th-20th centuries
302.V25	Other
302.V29	Vall d'Albaida Region
302.V31	Valladolid
302.V33	Vallès Occidental Region
302.V334	Vallès Oriental Region
302.V35	Vélez Region
302.V41-V5	Vizcaya

Local history and description
Provinces, regions, etc., A-Z
Vizcaya -- Continued
302.V41 Periodicals. Societies. Collections
Biography
Collective
Individual, A-Z
302.V43 Dictionaries. Gazetteers. Directories, etc.
302.V44 Guidebooks
302.V45 General works. Description and travel. Geography
302.V455 Antiquities
302.V457 Social life and customs. Civilization. Intellectual life
302.V458 Ethnography
History
302.V46 General works
By period
302.V47 Early and medieval
302.V48 16th-18th centuries
302.V49 19th-20th centuries
302.V5 Other
302.Z1 Zamora
Zaragoza, see DP302.S41+
302.Z65 Zona Centro Region
Madrid
350 Periodicals. Societies. Collections
352 Directories. Dictionaries
353 Biography (Collective)
For individual biography, see the period
354 General works. Description and travel
355 Guidebooks
356 Antiquities
357 Social life and customs. Culture
Ethnography
358 General works
358.3.A-Z Individual elements in the population, A-Z
358.3.A36 Africans
History and description
General works, see DP354
By period
359 Through 1500
360 1501-1800
361 1801-1950
362 1951-
364.A-Z Sections, districts, etc., A-Z
Monuments, statues, etc.
365 Collective
365.5.A-Z Individual, A-Z
Streets, suburbs, etc.
367.A3 Collective
367.A4-Z Individual, A-Z
e.g.
367.A5 Alcalá

Local history and description
Madrid
Streets, suburbs, etc.
Individual, A-Z -- Continued
367.C5 Ciudad Lineal
367.P84 Puerta del Sol
367.T7 Toledo
Buildings
370 General works
371.A-Z Special. Churches, theaters, etc., A-Z
371.P3 Palacio nacional
374 Other special
402.A-Z Other cities, towns, etc., A-Z
e.g.
402.A173 Ajofrín
402.A3 Alcalá de Henares
402.A4 Alhambra
Cf. NA387, Moorish architecture
402.A42 Alicante
402.A47 Ampurias
402.A85 Avila
Barcelona
402.B2 Periodicals. Societies. Collections
402.B22 Directories. Dictionaries
402.B23 Biography (Collective)
402.B24 Guidebooks
402.B25 General works. Description and travel. Geography
402.B26 Antiquities
402.B265 Social life and customs. Civilization. Intellectual life
402.B267 Ethnography
Including individual elements in the population
History
402.B27 General works
402.B28 Early and medieval
402.B29 Modern
Sections, districts, suburbs, etc.
402.B2912 General works
402.B292A-Z Individual, A-Z
Buildings
402.B295 General works
402.B296A-Z Individual, A-Z
402.B3 Other
402.B5 Bilbao
402.B8 Burgos
402.C15 Cáceres
Cadiz
402.C2 Periodicals. Societies. Collections
402.C21 Directories. Dictionaries, etc.
402.C22 Biography (Collective)
402.C23 Guidebooks
402.C24 General works. Description
402.C25 Social life and customs. Culture

Local history and description
Other cities, towns, etc., A-Z
Cadiz -- Continued

402.C26 Antiquities
402.C27 History
402.C28 Early and medieval
402.C29 Modern
402.C3 Other
402.C4 Cartagena
(402.C544) Ceuta (Spain)
see DT329.C5
402.C6 Ciudadela (Minorca)
402.C7 Córdoba
402.C795 Cudillero
402.C8 Cuenca
402.E8 Escorial
402.G4 Gerona
402.G6 Granada
402.G9 Guadalupe
402.J3 Játiva
402.J4 Jerez de la Frontera
402.L3 León
402.L33 Lérida
Madrid, see DP350+
402.M2 Malaga
Melilla (Spain), see DT329.M4
402.M9 Murcia
402.N64 Noja
402.P33 Palma (Majorca)
402.P35 Pamplona
402.P382 Paterna
402.R6 Roncesvalles
402.S1 Salamanca
402.S145 Sanlúcar de Barrameda
402.S17 Social life and customs. Civilization. Intellectual life
402.S2 San Sebastian
402.S214 Santa Eulalia
402.S23 Santiago de Compostela
402.S3-S32 Saragossa
402.S3 Periodicals. Societies. Collections. Documents
402.S302 Directories. Dictionaries, etc.
402.S303 Biography (Collective)
402.S31 General works. Description and travel. Guidebooks
402.S317 Social life and customs. Civilization. Intellectual life
402.S32 History
402.S35 Segovia
402.S36-S48 Seville
402.S36 Periodicals. Societies. Collections. Sources and documents
402.S37 Directories. Dictionaries, etc.

Local history and description
Other cities, towns, etc., A-Z
Seville -- Continued

402.S373 Biography (Collective)
402.S38 Guidebooks
402.S4 General works. Description and travel
402.S41 Antiquities
402.S415 Social life and customs. Intellectual life
402.S42 History
By period
402.S43 Early history
402.S44 Arab period, 711-1492
402.S45 16th-18th centuries
402.S46 19th-20th centuries
Buildings
402.S469 Collective
Individual
402.S47 Alcázar
402.S48A-Z Other, A-Z
402.T25 Tarazona
402.T3 Tarragona
Tarshish (Kingdom), see DP402.T36
402.T36 Tartessos (Kingdom)
402.T7-T746 Toledo
402.T7 General works. Description and travel. Guidebooks
402.T71 Social life and customs. Intellectual life
402.T72 History
By period
402.T73 Early and medieval
402.T74 Modern
Buildings
402.T745 Collective
402.T746A-Z Individual, A-Z
402.T85 Tossa
402.V15-V25 Valencia
402.V15 Periodicals. Societies. Sources and documents
402.V16 Directories. Dictionaries, etc.
Biography
402.V17 Collective
402.V172A-Z Individual, A-Z
402.V18 Guidebooks
402.V19 General works. Description
402.V195 Antiquities
402.V2 History
By period
402.V22 Early and medieval
402.V23 Modern
Buildings
402.V235 Collective
402.V236A-Z Individual, A-Z
402.V25 Pamphlets, etc.
402.V3 Valladolid

Local history and description
Other cities, towns, etc., A-Z -- Continued
402.V5 Vigo
402.V56 Vitoria
Zaragoza, see DP402.S3

History of Portugal
501 Periodicals. Societies. Congresses
503 Sources and documents
Collected works
504 Several authors
505 Individual authors
513 Directories
514 Gazetteers. Dictionaries, etc.
515 Place names
516 Guidebooks
517 General works
518 Compends
519 Monumental and picturesque
520 Historical geography
520.5 Geography
Description and travel
Cf. DP27.5+, Spain
521 Through 1138
522 1139-1788
524 1789-1815
525 1816-1950
526 1951-1980
526.5 1981-
528 Antiquities
Cf. DP702.A+, Local history and description
Social life and customs. Civilization
532 General works
532.3 Through 1500
532.5 1501-1800
532.7 1801- . 19th-20th centuries
Ethnography
Including national characteristics
533 General works
534.A-Z Individual elements in the population, A-Z
534.M67 Moroccans
534.5 Portuguese in foreign regions and countries (General)
For Portuguese in a particular region or country, see the region or country
History
535 Dictionaries. Chronological tables, outlines, etc.
Biography (Collective)
For individual biography, see the special period, reign, or place
536 General works
536.1 Rulers, kings, etc.
536.2 Princes and princesses
Houses, noble families, etc.
536.3.A1 Collective
536.3.A2-Z Individual, A-Z
e.g.
536.3.A6 Albuquerque family
536.5 Public men
536.7 Women

History -- Continued
Historiography
536.8 General works
Biography of historians and antiquarians
536.9.A2 Collective
536.9.A3-Z Individual, A-Z
e.g.
536.9.L6 Lopes, Fernão
536.9.O6 Oliveira Martins, Joaquim Pedro
Study and teaching
536.95 General works
536.96.A-Z By region or country, A-Z
Subarrange by author
General works
537 Through 1800. Chronicles
538 1801-
539 Compends
540 Anecdotes, etc.
542 Pamphlets, etc.
543.A-Z Special topics, A-Z
543.B7 British in Portugal
543.I8 Italians in Portugal
546 Philosophy of Portuguese history
547 Military history
Naval history
Biography and memoirs
550 Collective
550.5 Officers
Individual biography, see the historical period
551 General works
Political and diplomatic history. Foreign and general relations
Cf. DP558+, Special periods, reigns, etc.
555 Sources and documents
556 General works
556.1 General special
556.2 Early to 1580
1580-
556.4 General works
556.6 1580-1816
556.8 1816- . 19th-20th centuries
557.A-Z Relations with individual regions or countries, A-Z
By period
Early and medieval to 1580
General works
558 Through 1800. Chronicles
559 1801-
Earliest to 1095
General works
561 Through 1800
562 1801-
House of Burgundy, 1095-1383
General works

History
By period
Early and medieval to 1580
House of Burgundy, 1095-1383
General works -- Continued
568 Through 1800
569 1801-
569.8 Henrique, 1095-1112
570 Affonso Henriques, 1112-1185
571 Sancho I, 1185-1211
572 Affonso II, 1211-1223
573 Sancho II, 1223-1279
574 Affonso III, 1248-1279
Diniz, 1279-1325
575 General works on life and reign
Biography and memoirs of contemporaries
575.2 Collective
575.3.A-Z Individual, A-Z
576 Affonso IV, 1325-1357
577 Pedro I, 1357-1367
Including biography of Inez de Castro
578 Fernão I, 1367-1383
Including biography of Leonor, Consort of Ferdinand I
580 Interregnum, 1383-1385
House of Aviz, 1385-1580
582 General works
583 Discovery and explorations
Cf. DS411.7, Portuguese in India, 1498-1761
Cf. E123+, Portuguese discoveries in America
Cf. G280+, Portuguese discoveries, explorations, and travel (General)
For Prince Henry the Navigator, see G286.H5
583.5 Social life and customs. Civilization. Intellectual life
João I, 1385-1433
585 General works on life and reign
588 Expedition to Ceuta, 1415
Cf. DT329.C5, Portuguese possession, 1415-1580
590.A-Z Biography and memoirs of contemporaries, A-Z
e.g.
590.A4 Fernando, infante of Portugal
590.A5 Alvares Pereira, Nuno
Duarte, 1433-1438
592 General works on life and reign
593 Expedition to Tangier, 1437
594.A-Z Biography and memoirs of contemporaries, A-Z
Affonso V, 1438-1481
596 General works on life and reign

History
By period
Early and medieval to 1580
House of Aviz, 1385-1580
Affonso V, 1438-1481 -- Continued
598.A-Z Biography and memoirs of contemporaries, A-Z
e.g.
598.A15 Isabel, Consort of Alphonso V
598.J6 Joanna, Princess
598.P4 Pedro, infante of Portugal
João II, 1481-1495
600 General works on life and reign
602.A-Z Biography and memoirs of contemporaries, A-Z
e.g.
602.L4 Leonor de Lencastre, Consort of John II
Manoel I, 1495-1521
604 General works on life and reign
605 General special
606.A-Z Biography and memoirs of contemporaries, A-Z
e.g.
606.A43 Albergaria, Lopo Soares de, ca. 1453-ca. 1532
606.B3 Barbosa, Duarte
João III, 1521-1557
608 General works on life and reign
610.A-Z Biography and memoirs of contemporaries, A-Z
e.g.
610.C3 Catharina de Austria, Consort of John III
610.D8 Duarte, infante of Portugal
610.G6 Goes, Damião de
610.L6 Loureiro, Luiz de
Sebastião, 1557-1578
612 General works on life and reign
614 Expedition to Morocco, 1578
615 Sebastianism. Sebastianists
616.A-Z Biography and memoirs of contemporaries, A-Z
e.g.
616.G6 Gomes, Simão
618 Henrique I, 1578-1580
1580-
General works
620 Through 1800
621 1801-
622 Spanish dynasty (Sixty years' captivity), 1580-1640
624 Felipe I (II of Spain), 1580-1598
625 Felipe II (III of Spain), 1598-1621
627 Felipe III (IV of Spain), 1621-1640
628 Revolution of 1640
629.A-Z Biography and memoirs of contemporaries, A-Z
e.g.
629.A6 Antonio, prior of Crato
629.F7 Freire de Andrade, Ruy

History
By period
1580-
Spanish dynasty (Sixty years' captivity), 1580-1640
Biography and memoirs of contemporaries, A-Z -- Continued

629.M7 Moura, Christovão de, marquez de Castello Rodrigo
632 1640-1816. House of Braganza
João IV, 1640-1656
634 General works on life and reign
634.5 Pamphlets, etc
Biography and memoirs of contemporaries
634.79 Collective
634.8.A-Z Individual, A-Z
e.g.
634.8.D7 Duarte, infante of Portugal
634.8.L8 Lucena, Francisco de
634.8.V5 Villa Franca, Rodrigo da Camara, conde de
635 Affonso VI, 1656-1683
Pedro II, 1683-1706
636 General works on life and reign
636.8.A-Z Biography and memoirs of contemporaries, 1656-1706, A-Z
e.g.
636.8.A2 Maria Sophia Isabel, of Bavaria, Consort of Peter II
636.8.C3 Castel Melhor, Luiz de Vasconcellos e Sousa, conde de
636.8.F67 Francisca, infanta of Portugal
636.8.M3 Manuel, infante of Portugal
638 João V, 1706-1750
José I, 1750-1777
639 General works on life and reign
640 Tavora plot, 1758
641 Marquis de Pombal, 1699-1782
641.7 Pamphlets, etc.
641.9.A-Z Biography and memoirs of contemporaries, A-Z
e.g.
641.9.M3 Marianna Victoria, Consort of Joseph I
642 Maria I and Pedro III, 1777-1816
Including biography of Maria I
642.7 Biography of Pedro III, Consort of Maria I
643 Regency of João, 1792-1816
For works on his life and reign, see DP650+
644 Period of Peninsular War, 1805-1814
For the war itself, see DC231+
644.9.A-Z Biography and memoirs of contemporaries, A-Z
e.g.
644.9.C6 Costa e Almeida, Francisco Bernardo da
644.9.M27 Manique, Diogo Ignacio de Pina
644.9.N5 Nisa, Domingos Zavier de Lima, marques de

History
By period
1580- -- Continued
1816-1853/1908
645.A1 Sources and documents
Biography and memoirs
645.A2 Collective
645.A3-Z Individual, A-Z
e.g.
645.L6 Lobo, Francisco Alexandre, Bp.
645.S2 Saldanha, João Carlos de Saldanha de Oliveira e Daun, 1. duque de
645.S25 Santarem, Manuel Francisco de Barros, 2. visconde de
645.S3 Saraiva, Francisco de São Luiz, cardinal
645.S6 Sousa-Holstein, Pedro de, duque de Palmella
646 General works
647 Social life and customs. Civilization. Intellectual life
João VI, 1816-1826. Revolution of 1820
650 General works on life and reign
651.A-Z Biography and memoirs of contemporaries, A-Z
653 Pedro IV (I of Brazil), 1826
654 Maria II, 1826-1828
Miguel I, 1828-1834
655 General works on life and reign
Biography and memoirs
656 Collective
656.2.A-Z Individual, A-Z
657 Wars of succession, 1826-1840
659 Maria II (restored), 1834-1853
660.A-Z Biography and memoirs of contemporaries, A-Z
e.g.
660.F4 Fernando II, Consort of Maria II
1853-1908
661.A1 Sources and documents
Biography and memoirs
661.A2 Collective
661.A3-Z Individual, A-Z
e.g.
661.M5 Miguel, Duke of Bragança
661.Q8 Quillinan, Luiz de
662 General works
Pedro V, 1853-1861
664 General works on life and reign
664.5 Estephania, Consort of Peter V
666 Luiz I, 1861-1889
667.A-Z Biography and memoirs of contemporaries, A-Z
e.g.
667.A6 Affonso Henriques, Crown Prince
667.Q6 Oliveira Martins, Joaquim Pedro
Carlos I, 1889-1908
668 General works on life and reign

History
By period
1580-
1853-1908
Carlos I, 1889-1908 -- Continued
Biography and memoirs of contemporaries
669.A2 Collective
669.A3-Z Individual, A-Z
e.g.
669.A6 Amelia, Consort of Charles I
20th century
670 Sources and documents
670.5 Social life and customs. Civilization. Intellectual life
Biography and memoirs
671.A2 Collective
671.A3-Z Individual
e.g.
671.B7 Bragança, Duarte Nuno de Bragança, duque de
671.P3 Paiva Couceiro, Henrique de
672 General works
673 Manoel II, 1908-1910
674 Revolution of October 1910
675 Republic, 1910-
Biography and memoirs
676.A2 Collective
676.A3-Z Individual, A-Z
e.g.
676.A6 Almeida, Antonio José de
676.C34 Carmona, Antonio Oscar de Fragoso
676.M3 Machado, Bernardino
676.S25 Salazar, Antonio de Oliveira
677 Period of World War I, 1914-1918
Cf. D501+, World War I
678 Revolution of 1919
1919-1974
680 General works
680.5 Pamphlets, etc.
1974-
681 General works
Biography and memoirs
682 Collective
682.2.A-Z Individual, A-Z
e. g.
682.2.S69 Soares, Mário
Local history and description
702.A-Z Provinces, regions, etc., A-Z
702.A11-A2 Alentejo region, 1936- (Alentejo province, before 1936) (Table D-DR9)
Individual provinces
702.A22 Alto Alentejo
702.A23 Baixo Alentejo

Local history and description
Provinces, regions, etc., A-Z -- Continued

702.A25-A34	Algarve. Faro (District)
702.A25	Periodicals. Societies. Collections
702.A26	Biography
702.A27	Dictionaries. Gazetteers. Directories, etc.
702.A28	Guidebooks
702.A29	General works. Description and travel.
702.A295	Social life and customs. Civilization. Intellectual life
	History
	General works
	By period
702.A31	Early and medieval
702.A32	16th-18th centuries
702.A33	19th-20th centuries
702.A34	Other
702.A42	Arrábida Mountain Range
702.A45	Atlantic Coast
702.A51-A6	Aveiro (Table D-DR9)
702.A81-A99	Azores
702.A81	Periodicals. Societies. Collections
702.A83	Biography (Collective)
702.A84	Dictionaries. Gazetteers. Directories, etc.
702.A85	Guidebooks
702.A86	General works. Description and travel. Pictorial works
702.A865	Social life and customs. Civilization
	History
702.A87	General works
702.A88	Early and medieval
702.A89	16th-18th centuries
702.A9	19th-20th centuries
702.A91-A99	Individual islands
702.A91	Corvo
702.A92	Fayal (Faial)
702.A93	Flores
702.A94	Graciosa
702.A95	Pico
702.A96	Santa Maria
702.A97	São Jorge
702.A98	São Miguel (Saint Michael)
702.A99	Terceira
702.B05	Bairrada (Region)
702.B11-B2	Beira region (Table D-DR9) Including Beira province before 1936
702.B2	Individual provinces, 1936-
702.B22	Beira Alta
702.B23	Beira Baixa
702.B24	Beira Litoral
702.B26-B35	Beja
702.B26	Periodicals. Societies. Collections
702.B3	General works. Description and travel

	Local history and description
	Provinces, regions, etc., A-Z
	Beja -- Continued
702.B31	History
702.B35	Other
702.B46-B55	Braga
702.B46	Periodicals. Societies. Collections
702.B5	Description and travel
702.B51	History
702.B61-B7	Bragança (Table D-DR9)
702.C11-C2	Castello Branco (Table D-DR9)
	Coimbra
702.C41	Periodicals. Societies. Collections
702.C412	Biography (Collective)
702.C413	Dictionaries. Gazetteers. Directories, etc.
702.C414	Guidebooks
702.C42	General works. Description and travel. Pictorial works
	History
702.C43	General works
702.C44	Early and medieval
702.C45	Modern
702.C49	Coura River and Valley
702.D6	Douro-Litoral
702.E21-E3	Entre-Minho-e-Douro (Table D-DR9)
702.E34	Estoril Coast
702.E35	Estrella (Estrêla), Serra da
702.E46-E55	Estremadura
702.E46	Periodicals. Societies. Collections
702.E49	Guidebooks
702.E5	General works
702.E52	History
702.E55	Other
702.E71-E8	Evora (Table D-DR9)
	Faro (District), see DP702.A25+
702.G3	Gafanha
702.G8	Guarda
702.L2	Leiria
702.L25	Lima River and Valley
702.L3	Lisbon (Lisboa)
	Madeira
702.M11	Periodicals. Societies. Collections
702.M12	Biography
702.M13	Dictionaries. Gazetteers. Directories, etc.
702.M15	Guidebooks
702.M16	General works. Description and travel. Pictorial works
702.M165	Social life and customs. Civilization. Intellectual life
702.M17	History
702.M18	General special
	By period
702.M19	Early and medieval

Local history and description
Provinces, regions, etc., A-Z
Madeira
History
By period -- Continued
702.M2 16th-18th centuries
702.M21 19th-20th centuries
702.M23 Other
Minho, see DP702.E21+
702.M67 Mondego River and Valley
702.M7 Montemuro
702.O5 Oporto
702.P8 Portalegre
Porto, see DP702.O5
702.R5 Ribatejo
702.S2 Santarém
702.S47 Setubal
702.T36 Tamega River and Valley
702.T8 Traz-os-Montes (Trás-os-Montes).
Including Tras-os-Montes e Alto Douro (later name)
702.V4 Vianna do Castello (Viana do Castelo)
702.V5 Villa Real (Vila Real)
702.V6 Viseu (Vizeu)
Lisbon
752 Periodicals. Societies. Collections
754 Directories. Dictionaries
755.A-Z Biography, A-Z
756 General works. Description and travel. Pictorial works
757 Guidebooks
758 Antiquities
759 Social life and customs. Culture
History and description
759.6 Historiography
General works, see DP756
By period
761 Through 1580
762 1580-1789
763 1789-1840
764 1840-1950
765 1951-
Sections, districts, etc.
765.95 General works
766.A-Z Individual, A-Z
Parks, squares, cemeteries, etc.
768 Collective
768.5.A-Z Individual, A-Z
Streets, suburbs, etc.
769.A1 Collective
769.A2-Z Individual, A-Z
e.g.
769.B4 Belem
769.C26 Calçada da Ajuda

Local history and description
Lisbon
Streets, suburbs, etc.
Individual, A-Z -- Continued
769.C3 Rua das Canastras
Buildings
772 General works
Special. Churches, theaters, etc.
773.A1 Collective
773.A2-Z Individual, A-Z
e.g.
773.C6 Conceição Velha (Church)
773.P3 Palacio da Ajuda
776 Other special
802.A-Z Other cities, towns, etc., A-Z
e.g.
802.A517 Alcobaça
802.B3 Barcellos
802.B7 Braga
802.B8 Bussaco
802.C45 Chaves
802.C5 Cintra
802.C6 Coimbra
802.C65 Corvilhao
802.E9 Evora
802.F4 Feira
802.F8 Fundâo
802.G8 Guimarães
802.M25 Mafra
802.O6 Oporto
802.P38 Penamacor
Porto, see DP802.O6
802.S2 Santarém
Sintra, see DP802.C5
802.S7 Soure
802.T5 Tomar (Thomar)
802.V5 Vianna do Castello (Viana do Castelo)
802.V7 Villa Nova de Gaia
802.V73 Villa Viçosa
900 Portuguese colonies
Collective, see JV4200+
(900.22) Individual colonies
See Classes D-F

History of Switzerland
1 Periodicals. Societies. Serials
2 Congresses
3 Sources and documents
Collected works
4 Several authors
5 Individual authors
14 Gazetteers. Dictionaries, etc.
15 Place names
16 Guidebooks
17 General works
18 Compends
19 Monumental and picturesque. Pictorial works
20 Historical geography
Description and travel
20.5 History of travel
21 Through 1500
22 1501-1800
23 1801-1900
24 1901-1950
25 1951-1980
26 1981
Antiquities
30 Periodicals. Collections
31 General works
32 General special
34 Earliest. Roman
35 Medieval
Local, see DQ301+
Social life and customs. Civilization. Intellectual life
36 General works
37 Early and medieval
Ethnography
48 General works
49.A-Z Individual elements in the population, A-Z
49.A49 Africans
49.A53 Albanians
49.A87 Austrians
49.C38 Catalans
49.F55 Finns
French, see DQ57
49.G3 Germans
49.H77 Huguenots
49.H8 Hungarians
49.I64 Indochinese
49.P6 Poles
49.R65 Romanians
49.S47 Serbs
49.S56 Slovaks
49.S65 Spaniards
49.S68 Sri Lankans
49.T5 Tibetans

Ethnography
Individual elements
in the population, A-Z -- Continued
49.T87 Turks
49.V54 Vietnamese
49.Z35 Zairians
49.5 Swiss in foreign regions or countries (General)
For Swiss in a particular region or country, see the region or country
History
51 Dictionaries. Chronological tables, outlines, etc.
Biography (Collective)
For individual biography, see the special period, reign, or place
52 General works
52.1 Rulers, presidents, etc.
52.5.A-Z Houses, noble families, etc., A-Z
e.g.
52.5.B4 Benzinger family
52.6 Public men
52.7 Women
Historiography
52.8 General works
Biography of historians, area studies specialists, archaeologists, etc.
52.9.A2 Collective
52.9.A3-Z Individual, A-Z
e.g.
52.9.T7 Tschudi, Aegidius
52.95 Study and teaching
General works
53 Through 1800. Chronicles
54 1801-
55 Compends
55.5 Pictorial works
56 Pamphlets, etc.
57 History of several cantons or cities
Including French-speaking Switzerland, etc.
59 Military history
For individual campaigns and engagements, see the special period
Political and diplomatic history. Foreign and general relations
Cf. DQ78+, Special periods, reigns, etc.
68 Sources and documents
69 General works
70 General special
e.g. Swiss neutrality
71 Pamphlets, etc.
73 Early and medieval to 1516
74 1516-1798
For general modern, see DQ69

History
Political and diplomatic history. Foreign and general relations -- Continued
75 1798- . 19th-20th centuries
Cf. DQ539.4, Neuchâtel question
76.A-Z Relations with individual regions or countries, A-Z
By period
Early and medieval to 1516
78 General works
Earliest to 406. Celts and Romans
79 General works
79.5 Pamphlets, etc.
80 Orgetorix and Divico, 107-58 B.C.
81 Conquest by Rome, 15 B.C.
82 Other special events
Teutonic tribes, 406-687
83 General works
84 General special
Carolingian and German rule, 687-1291
85 General works
87 General special
Federation and Independence, 1291-1516
General works
88 Through 1800. Chronicles
89 1801-
89.5 Pamphlets, etc.
90 First Perpetual League, 1291
91 Commemorative celebrations
92 Tell and Rütli legends
94 Battle of Morgarten, November 15, 1315
95 Renewal of Perpetual League, December 9, 1315
96 Battle of Sempach, 1386. Winkelried
97 Battle of Näfels, 1388
98 Battle of Arbedo, 1422
99 Battle of Sankt Jakob an der Birs, 1444
100 Wars of Mülhausen and of Waldshut, 1468
Wars of Burgundy, 1474-1477
101 General works
103 Battle of Grandson, 1476
104 Battle of Morat, 1476
Wars against Swabian League, 1499
106 General works
107.A-Z By canton, A-Z
e.g.
107.S8 Solothurn
Including Battle of Dornach, 1499
109 Swiss in Italy. Battle of Marignano, 1515
110.A-Z Biography and memoirs, A-Z
e.g.
110.S3 Schinner, Mathaus, cardinal
1516-1798
111 General works

History
By period
1516-1798 -- Continued
1516-1648
113 Sources and documents
114 General works
116 General special
117 Pamphlets, etc.
118.A-Z Biography and memoirs, A-Z
e.g.
118.P6 Platter, Thomas
118.R65 Roll, Walter
Peasants' War, 1641, see DQ421+
1648-1712
121 General works
121.8.A-Z Biography and memoirs, A-Z
e.g.
121.8.T6 Thurn, Fidel von
1712-1798
122 General works
Biography and memoirs
123.A2 Collective
123.A3-Z Individual, A-Z
e.g.
123.L4 Lentulus, Robert Scipio, freiherr von
123.S3 Schinz, Johann Heinrich
123.Z4 Zellweger, Laurenz
19th century
124 General works
Biography
128 Collective
129.A-Z Individual, A-Z
e.g.
129.B7 Bonstetten, Karl victor von
129.D8 Dufour, Guillaume Henri
129.R4 Rengger, Albrecht
129.S8 Stapfer, Philipp Albert
129.W3 Wattenwyl, Niklaus Rudolf von
1789/1798-1815
131 General works
1789-1798
136 Sources and documents
137 General works
139 General special
140.A-Z Individual cantons during the period, A-Z
e.g.
Cf. DC222.S8, French invasion of Switzerland
140.G3 Geneva
140.S25 Saint Gall
1798-1803. Helvetic Republic
141 Sources and documents
143 General works

History
By period
19th century
1789/1798-1815
1798-1803. Helvetic Republic -- Continued
143.7 Pamphlets, etc.
145 Special events. By date
151 1803-1815. Act of Mediation. Federal Pact, 1815
154 1815-1830
1830-1848
156 General works
157 General special
1845-1847. Sonderbund
158 General works
158.9 Special
War of the Sonderbund, 1847
160 Sources and documents
161 General works
1848-1900
171 General works
173 General special
Biography and memoirs
177 Collective
178.A-Z Individual, A-Z
e.g.
178.A46 Ador, Gustave
178.E8 Escher, Johann H. Alfred
178.F87 Furrer, Jonas
178.S35 Schenk, Karl
178.S36 Scherer-Boccard, Theodor
178.S75 Steiger, Edmund von
178.T8 Tschudi, Friedrich von
181 1848-1871
For the Neuchatel question, see DQ539.4
191 1871-1900
20th century
201 General works
203 General special
1900-1945
205 General works
Biography and memoirs
206 Collective
207.A-Z Individual, A-Z
e.g.
207.S35 Schmid, Jacques
1945-
208 General works
Biography and memoirs
209 Collective
210.A-Z Individual, A-Z
Local history and description
Cantons (and cantonal capitals)

Local history and description
Cantons (and cantonal capitals) -- Continued
301-320.35 Aargau (Argovie) (Table D-DR10)
321-340.35 Appenzell (Table D-DR10)
Including Ausserrhoden (Outer Rhodes) and Innerrhoden (Inner Rhodes)
341-360.35 Jura (Table D-DR10)
361-380.35 Basel-Land (Bâle-Campagne) (Table D-DR10)
381-400.35 Basel-Stadt (Bâle-Ville) (Table D-DR10)
Including Basel Canton before 1832
389 Basel (City)
401-420.35 Bern (Berne) (Table D-DR10)
421-440.35 Fribourg (Freiburg) (Table D-DR10)
441-460.35 Geneva (Geneve, Genf) (Table D-DR10)
461-480.35 Glarus (Glaris) (Table D-DR10)
481-500.35 Grisons (Graubünden, Grigioni, Grischun) (Table D-DR10)
Jura, see DQ341+
501-520.35 Lucerne (Luzern) (Table D-DR10)
521-540.35 Neuchatel (Neuenburg) (Table D-DR10 modified)
539.3 19th century
539.4 Neuchatel question
541-560.35 Saint Gall (Saint Gallen, Sankt Gallen) (Table D-DR10)
561-580.35 Schaffhausen (Schaffhouse) (Table D-DR10)
581-600.35 Schwyz (Schwiz) (Table D-DR10)
601-620.35 Solothurn (Soleure) (Table D-DR10)
621-640.35 Thurgau (Thurgovie) (Table D-DR10)
641-660.35 Ticino (Tessin) (Table D-DR10)
661-680.35 Unterwalden (Table D-DR10)
Including Unterwalden nid dem Wald (Lower Walden) and Unterwalden ob dem Wald (Upper Walden)
681-700.35 Uri (Table D-DR10)
701-720.35 Valais (Wallis) (Table D-DR10)
721-740.35 Vaud (Waadt) (Table D-DR10)
741-760.35 Zug (Zoug) (Table D-DR10)
781-800.35 Zurich (Zurich) (Table D-DR10)
Alps
Cf. DB101+, Austrian Alps
Cf. DB761+, Tyrol
Cf. DC611.A553+, French Alps
Cf. DD801.A28, Allgäu Alps
Cf. DG975.D66+, Dolomite Alps
For individual mountains, peaks, etc., see the specific country
820 Periodicals. Collections (General)
821 Societies
Cf. GV199.8+, Mountaineering clubs and societies
822 Congresses
General works
823 Through 1960
823.5 1961-

Local history and description
Alps -- Continued
824 General special
825 Western Alps (Italian and French Alps)
826 Pennine Alps
827 Central Alps (Bernese Oberland)
828 Eastern Alps
829 Ticino Alps
841.A-Z Regions, peaks, etc., A-Z
Including Alps other than in DQ820+
e.g.
841.A35 Aiguille du Dru
841.A4 Aletach Glacier
841.B4 Bernina Alps
841.B6 Biel (Lake). Lac de Bienne
Including Saint-Pierre Island
841.B8 Bregaglia
841.D5 Disentis
841.E47 Eiger
841.E5 Engadine
841.F47 Ferret Valley
841.F7 Freiamt
841.G2 Gaster
841.G4 Geneva (Lake)
841.G6 Gornergrat
841.G77 Grimselpass
841.G8 Grindelwald
841.G9 Gruyère (County)
841.J8 Jungfrau
841.J9 Jura Mountains
841.K6 Klettgau
841.L8 Lucerne (Lake)
841.M4 Matterhorn
Mont Blanc, see DC611.M68
841.M8 Monte Viso
841.O4 Ofenberg. Ofenpass
841.P6 Pilatus, Mount
841.R5 Rigi
841.S12 Saastal
841.S15 Saint Bernard, Great (Pass)
841.S2 Saint Gotthard
Saint-Pierre Island, see DQ841.B6
841.S4 Sense River and Valley
841.S45 Sihl River and Valley
841.S8 Susten Pass
841.T5 Thun (Lake). Thunersee
Cities, towns, etc.
851.A1 Collective
851.A2-Z Individual, A-Z
e.g.
For cantonal capitals, see DQ301+
851.A8 Avenches
851.B13 Baden

Local history and description
Cities, towns, etc.
Individual, A-Z -- Continued

851.B6	Bex
851.B625	Biel
851.C4	Chillon
851.D3	Davos
851.D5	Diessenhofen
851.E3	Einsiedeln
851.E4	Elm
851.H65	Horgen
851.I76	Ittigen
851.K45	Kirchberg
851.L3	Laufen
851.M8	Montreux
851.P6	Pontresina
851.R7	Rorschach Including the castle
851.S24	Saint Moritz
851.T5	Thun
851.V4	Vevey
851.W3	Wallisellen
851.W5	Widen (Castle)
851.W62	Windisch (Vindonissa)
851.W63	Winterthur
851.Y8	Yverdon

History of Balkan Peninsula
Cf. DJK1+, Eastern Europe
Cf. DJK61+, Black Sea region
1 Periodicals. Societies. Serials
1.5 Congresses. Conferences, etc.
1.7 Sources and documents
Collected works
2 Several authors
3 Individual authors
5 Gazetteers. Dictionaries, etc.
6 Place names (General)
7 Guidebooks
General works
9 Through 1800
10 1801-
10.5 Pictorial works
11 Historical geography
Description and travel
11.5 History of travel
12 Early through 1600
13 1601-1800
14 1801-1900
15 1901-1950
16 1951-
20 Antiquities
23 Social life and customs. Civilization. Intellectual life
Ethnography
24 General works
24.5 National characteristics
25 Slavic peoples in the Balkan Peninsula
27.A-Z Other individual elements in the population, A-Z
Cf. DJK28.A+, Eastern Europe
For individual Balkan regions and countries, see DR49+
27.A4 Albanians
27.A8 Aromanians
27.G34 Gagauz
27.G4 Germans. Swabians
27.G8 Greeks
27.K55 Kipchak
27.M87 Muslims
27.P47 Pechenegs
27.R6 Romance-language-speaking peoples. Latins
27.R64 Romanians
27.S58 Slovaks
Swabians, see DR27.G4
27.T8 Turks
27.Y87 Yuruks
History
32 Dictionaries
33 Biography (Collective)
Historiography

History
Historiography -- Continued
34 General works
Biography of historians
34.6 Collective
34.7.A-Z Individual, A-Z
Study and teaching. Balkan studies
34.8 General works
34.9.A-Z By region or country, A-Z
General works
35 Through 1800
36 1801-
37 General special
38 Pamphlets, etc.
38.15 Military history
38.2 Political and diplomatic history
Cf. D371+, Eastern question
Cf. D461+, Eastern question (20th century)
38.3.A-Z Balkan relations with individual regions or countries, A-Z
By period
Early and medieval to 1500
39 General works
39.3 Celts
39.5 Illyrians
Cf. DG59.I2, Roman Illyria (Illyricum)
41 1500-1800
43 1800-1900
20th century (General)
45 General works
1900-1913
45.5 General works
Balkan War, 1912-1913
46.A2 Sources and documents
46.A3 Historiography
46.A4-Z General works
46.05 Pictorial works. Satire, caricature, etc.
46.1 Pamphlets, etc.
46.2 Naval history
46.3 Diplomatic history
Cf. D461+, Eastern question
Special campaigns
46.4 Turkish
46.5 Bulgarian
46.6 Serbian
46.7 Montenegrin
46.8 Greek
46.9.A-Z Local events, battles, etc., A-Z
e.g.
46.9.E3 Edirne (Turkey), Siege of, 1912-1913
46.93.A-Z Special topics, A-Z
46.93.A87 Atrocities
46.93.J68 Journalism, Military

History
By period
20th century (General)
1900-1913
Balkan War, 1912-1913 -- Continued
46.95 Bucharest, Treaty of, 1913
46.97 Personal narratives
47 1913-1919
Cf. D501+, World War I, 1914-1918
48 1919-1945
48.5 1945-1989
Cf. D847.2, Warsaw pact, 1955
48.6 1989-
Local history and description
Lower Danube Valley
For the Danube Valley of individual countries, see the specific country
49 General works
49.2 General special
49.23 Description and travel
49.24 Antiquities
49.25 Ethnography (General)
For individual elements of the Lower Danube Valley, see DR25
49.26 History
49.7 Rumelia. Rumeli (General)
For Eastern Rumelia (Bulgaria), see DR95.R8
Thrace
Class here general works on Thrace and the ancient Thracians.
For ancient Thrace in relation to Greek civilization, see DF261.T6
For modern Bulgarian Thrace, see DR95.T45
For modern Greek Thrace, see DF901.T75
For Turkish Thrace, see DR701.T5
50 Periodicals. Societies. Serials
50.2 Sources and documents
50.3 General works
50.35 Historical geography
50.4 Description and travel
50.43 Antiquities
For local antiquities (Bulgaria), see DR95+
For local antiquities (Greece), see DF901.A+
For local antiquities (Turkey), see DR701+
50.45 Social life and customs. Civilization. Intellectual life
For specific periods, see the period
Ethnography
Including general works on Thracians
50.46 General works
50.47.A-Z Individual elements in the population, A-Z
History
50.5 General works

Local history and description
Thrace
History -- Continued
50.53 General special
By period
50.6 Early to 1362
1362-1913. Turkish rule
For Balkan Wars, 1912-1913, see DR46+
For Eastern Rumelia, 1875-1885, see DR95.R8
50.7 General works
Biography and memoirs
50.73 Collective
50.74.A-Z Individual, A-Z
Preobrazhensko Uprising, 1903
50.76 Sources and documents
50.77 General works
50.78 Personal narratives
50.785.A-Z Local history. By place, A-Z
1913-
50.8 General works
Biography and memoirs
50.83 Collective
50.84.A-Z Individual, A-Z
Bulgaria
51 Periodicals. Societies. Serials
Museums, exhibitions, etc.
51.3 General works
51.4.A-Z Individual. By place, A-Z
51.5 Congresses
52 Sources and documents
Collected works
52.5 Several authors
52.7 Individual authors
53 Gazetteers
53.3 Place names (General)
For etymological studies, see PG961+
53.7 Directories
54 Guidebooks
55 General works
56 Monuments and picturesque. Views
Historic monuments, landmarks, scenery, etc. (General)
For local, see DR95+
56.5 General works
56.7 Preservation
Description and travel
57 Through 1400
58 1401-1800
59 1801-1878
60 1879-1950
60.2 1951-
61 Historical geography
61.5 Geography

Bulgaria -- Continued

62 Antiquities

Cf. DR95+, Local history and description

63 Social life and customs. Civilization

Ethnography

64 General works

64.15 National characteristics

64.2.A-Z Individual elements in the population, A-Z

64.2.A44 Aliani. Kŭzŭlbashi

64.2.A74 Armenians

64.2.A76 Aromanians

64.2.C9 Czechs

64.2.G73 Greeks

64.2.K37 Kapant͡si

64.2.K39 Kariots

Kŭzŭlbashi, see DR64.2.A44

64.2.M33 Macedonians

64.2.M8 Muslims

64.2.P64 Poles

64.2.R84 Russians

64.2.S27 Sarakatsans

64.2.S56 Slovaks

64.2.T87 Turks

64.5 Bulgarians in foreign regions or countries (General)

For Bulgarians in a particular region or country, see the region or country

History

65 Dictionaries. Chronological tables, outlines, etc.

Biography (Collective)

For individual biography, see the special period, reign, or place

66 General works

66.2 Rulers, kings, etc.

66.5 Statesmen

66.6 Women

Historiography

66.7 General works

Biography of historians, area studies specialists, archaeologists, etc.

66.8 Collective

66.9.A-Z Individual, A-Z

Study and teaching

66.95 General works

66.97.A-Z By region or country, A-Z

Subarrange by author

67 General works

67.5 Pictorial works

67.7 Juvenile works

68 Addresses, essays, lectures. Anecdotes, etc.

69 Philosophy of Bulgarian history

69.5 History of several parts of Bulgaria treated together

70 Military history

Bulgaria
History -- Continued
Political and diplomatic history. Foreign and general relations
72 General works
Cf. D371+, Eastern question
Cf. D461+, Eastern question (20th century)
73.A-Z Relations with individual regions or countries, A-Z
By period
Early to 1396
73.7 Sources and documents
74 General works
74.2 Social life and customs. Civilization. Intellectual life
74.25 Military history
74.3 Early to 681
First Bulgarian Empire, 681-1018
74.5 General works
681-893
75 General works
Biography and memoirs
75.2 Collective
75.25.A-Z Individual, A-Z
75.3 Asparukh, 681-701
75.4 Tervel, 701-718
75.5 Kardam, 777-802/3
75.6 Krum, 803-814
75.7 Omurtag, 814-831
75.8 Boris I, 852-889
893-1018
77 General works
Biography and memoirs
77.2 Collective
77.25.A-Z Individual, A-Z
77.3 Simeon, 893-927
77.4 Peter, 927-969
77.6 Samuel, 976-1014
77.8 Ivan Vladislav, 1015-1018
Greek rule, 1018-1185
79 General works
Biography and memoirs
79.2 Collective
79.25.A-Z Individual, A-Z
Second Bulgarian Empire, 1185-1396. Asen dynasty
80 General works
Biography and memoirs
80.2 Collective
80.25.A-Z Individual, A-Z
80.3 Ivan Asen I, 1185-1196
80.35 Petŭr II, 1196-1197
80.4 Kaloian, 1197-1207
80.6 Ivan Asen II, 1218-1241

Bulgaria
History
By period
Early to 1396
Second Bulgarian Empire, 1185-1396. Asen dynasty -- Continued
80.65 Ivailo, 1277-1280
80.7 Ivan Alexander, 1331-1371
80.8 Ivan Shishman, 1371-1393
Turkish rule, 1396-1878
81 Sources and documents
81.5 General works
81.6 Social life and customs. Civilization. Intellectual life
1396-1762
82 General works
82.15 Social life and customs. Civilization. Intellectual life
Biography and memoirs
82.2 Collective
82.25.A-Z Individual, A-Z
82.3 Uprising of 1403
82.5 Uprising of 1598
1762-1878. National revival
82.9 Sources and documents
83 General works
83.15 Social life and customs. Civilization. Intellectual life
Biography and memoirs
83.2.A1 Collective
83.2.A2-Z Individual, A-Z
e.g.
83.2.B6 Botev, Khristo
83.2.L4 Levski, Vasil Ivanov
83.2.R3 Rakovski, Georgi Stoikov
83.2.S8 Stoi͡anov, Zakhari
83.3 Uprising of 1849
83.4 Uprising of 1850
83.5 Uprising of 1857
April Uprising, 1876
83.7 General works
83.72 Pictorial works
83.73 Regimental histories
Subarrange by author
83.74 Personal narratives
83.75.A-Z Local revolutionary history. By place, A-Z
e.g.
83.75.D74 Drianovski manastir
83.76.A-Z Special topics, A-Z
83.76.B85 Bulgarian Orthodox Eastern Church
Health aspects, see DR83.76.M44
Hospitals, see DR83.76.M44
83.76.M44 Medical care. Hospitals. Health aspects

Bulgaria
History
By period
Turkish rule, 1396-1878
1762-1878. National revival
April Uprising, 1876
Special topics, A-Z -- Continued

83.76.P73 Press
83.76.P75 Propaganda
83.76.P83 Public opinion
83.76.W65 Women
83.8 Celebrations. Memorials. Monuments
84 Period of Russo-Turkish War, 1877-1878
For the war itself, see DR573
1878-1944
84.9 Sources and documents
85 General works
85.2 Social life and customs. Civilization. Intellectual life
85.3 Military history
85.4 Foreign and general relations
Biography and memoirs
85.5.A1 Collective
85.5.A2-Z Individual, A-Z
e.g.
Dimitrov, Georgi, see DR88.D5
85.5.G4 Geshov, Ivan Evstratiev
85.5.K5 Kiriakov, Petko, 1844-1900
Petko, voivoda, 1844-1900, see DR85.5.K5
85.5.S7 Stambulov, Stefan
Alexander, 1879-1886
85.9 Sources and documents
86 General works on life and reign
Biography and memoirs of contemporaries
86.2 Collective
86.22.A-Z Individual, A-Z
86.3 Coup, 1881
Serbo-Bulgarian War, see DR2027
86.5 Interregnum, 1886-1887
Ferdinand, 1887-1918
87 General works on life and reign
87.3 General special
87.5 Pamphlets, etc.
87.7 Period of Balkan War, 1912-1913
For the war itself, see DR46+
87.8 Period of World War I, 1914-1918
For the war itself, see D501+
87.9 Vladaya Uprising, 1918
Biography and memoirs of contemporaries
88.A1 Collective
88.A2-Z Individual, A-Z
e.g.
88.B6 Blagoev, Dimitŭr

Bulgaria
History
By period
1878-1944
Ferdinand, 1887-1918
Biography and memoirs of contemporaries
Individual -- Continued
88.D5 Dimitrov, Georgi
88.S77 Stamboliiski, Aleksandŭr S.
88.5 20th century
1918-1944. Boris III, 1918-1943
88.9 Sources and documents
89 General works on life and reign
89.15 Social life and customs. Civilization. Intellectual life
Biography and memoirs of contemporaries
89.2.A1 Collective
89.2.A2-Z Individual, A-Z
89.22 June Uprising, 1923
September Uprising, 1923
89.3 General works
89.32 Pictorial works
89.34 Personal narratives
89.35.A-Z Local revolutionary history. By place, A-Z
89.36.A-Z Special topics, A-Z
89.36.C65 Communications
89.36.I53 Influence
89.36.P73 Press
89.36.W65 Women
89.36.Y68 Youth
89.5 April events, 1925
89.8 1939-1944. Period of World War II
For the war itself, see D731+
1944-1990
Including regency of Simeon II, 1943-1946 and the People's Republic, 1946-
89.9 Sources and documents
90 General works
90.3 Addresses, essays, lectures
91 Social life and customs. Civilization
92 Foreign and general relations
Biography and memoirs
93.A1 Collective
93.A2-Z Individual, A-Z
e.g.
Dimitrov, Georgi, see DR88.D5
93.Z48 Zhivkov, Todor
September Uprising, 1944
93.3 General works
93.32 Pictorial works
93.34 Personal narratives
1990-
93.4 Sources and documents

	Bulgaria
	History
	By period
	1990- -- Continued
93.42	General works
93.43	Social life and customs. Civilization. Intellectual life
93.44	Political history
93.45	Foreign and general relations
	Biography and memoirs
93.46	Collective
93.47.A-Z	Individual, A-Z
	Local history and description
95.A-Z	Provinces, regions, etc., A-Z
	e.g.
95.B54	Black Sea region
95.B55	Blagoevgrad (Okrug). Pirin Macedonia
	Cf. DR95.P46, Pirin Mountains Region
	For ancient Greek Macedonia, see DF261.M2
	For Macedonia (General, and Yugoslavia), see DR2152+
	For modern Greek Macedonia, see DF901.M3
95.D6	Dobruja
	For Dobruja (General, and Romania), see DR281.D5
	Istranca Mountains Region, see DR95.S8
	Pirin Macedonia, see DR95.B55
95.P46	Pirin Mountains Region
95.R8	Rumelia (Eastern)
	For Rumelia (General), see DR49.7
95.S8	Strandzha Mountains Region
95.S87	Struma River and Valley
95.T45	Thrace
	For ancient Greek Thrace, see DF261.T6
	For general works on Thrace, see DR50+
	For modern Greek Thrace, see DF901.T75
	For Turkish Thrace, see DR701.T5
	Cities, towns, etc.
97	Sofia (Table D-DR3)
98.A-Z	Other
98.A1	Collective
98.A2-Z	Individual, A-Z
98.B6	Boboshevo
98.D7	Dragalevtsi
98.T5	Tirnovo, Tŭrnovo (Veliko Tŭrnovo)
98.T7	Troyan (Lovech)
	Tŭrnovo (Veliko Tŭrnovo), see DR98.T5
	Veliko Tŭrnovo, see DR98.T5
(101-196)	Montenegro
	see DR1802+
	Romania
	Including Moldavia and Wallachia
201	Periodicals. Societies. Serials
201.2	Congresses. Conferences, etc.

Romania -- Continued
Museums, exhibitions, etc.
201.3 General works
201.32.A-Z Individual. By place, A-Z
203 Sources and documents
Collected works
203.5 Several authors
203.7 Individual authors
204 Gazetteers. Dictionaries, etc.
204.3 Place names
204.5 Guidebooks
205 General works
206 Monumental and picturesque. Pictorial works
206.5 Historical geography
206.8 Geography
Description and travel
207 Through 1800
208 1801-1865
209 1866-1950
210 1951-
211 Antiquities
Cf. DR279+, Local history and description
212 Social life and customs. Civilization. Intellectual life
Ethnography
213 General works
214.A-Z Individual elements in the population, A-Z
214.A43 Albanians
214.A75 Armenians
214.B8 Bulgarians
Carpi, see DR239.22
214.C69 Croats
214.C73 Csangos
214.C94 Czechs
Dacians, see DR239.2
214.G4 Germans
214.G73 Greeks
214.H9 Hungarians
214.M68 Moti
214.M87 Muslims
214.P64 Poles
214.S47 Serbs
214.S55 Slovaks
214.U47 Ukrainians
214.2 Romanians in foreign regions or countries (General)
For Romanians in a particular region or country, see the region or country
History
215 Dictionaries. Chronological tables, outlines, etc.
216 Biography (Collective)
For individual biography, see the special period, reign, or place
Historiography

Romania
History
Historiography -- Continued
216.7 General works
Biography of historians, area studies specialists, archaeologists, etc.
216.8 Collective
216.9.A-Z Individual, A-Z
e.g.
216.9.B3 Bâlcescu, Nicolae
216.9.I5 Iorga, Nicolae
For literary works, see PC839.I58
216.92 Study and teaching
217 General works
218 Pamphlets, etc.
219 Military history
225 Naval history
Political and diplomatic history. Foreign and general relations
Cf. D371+, Eastern question (19th century)
Cf. D461+, Eastern question (20th century)
For works on relations with a specific region or country, regardless of period, see DR229.A+
For general works on the political and the diplomatic history of a period, see the period
226 General works
229.A-Z Relations with individual regions or countries, A-Z
By period
Early and medieval to 1601
238 General works
Earliest and Roman period
239 General works
239.2 Dacians. Getae
Cf. DG59.D3, Dacia
239.22 Carpi
Medieval period
240 General works
Biography and memoirs
240.5.A2 Collective
240.5.A3-Z Individual, A-Z
e. g.
240.5.M5 Michael, voivode of Wallachia, 1558-1601
240.5.N4 Neagoe Basarab, voivode of Wallachia
240.5.S7 Stephen, Voivode of Moldavia, d. 1504
240.5.V55 Vlad II, Dracul, Prince of Wallachia
240.5.V553 Vlad III, Prince of Wallachia (Vlad Ţepeş)
Phanariote regime, 1601-1822
241 General works
Biography and memoirs
241.5.A2 Collective

Romania
History
By period
Phanariote regime, 1601-1822
Biography and memoirs -- Continued
241.5.A3-Z Individual, A-Z
e.g.
241.5.V55 Vladimirescu, Tudor
1822-1881. 19th century
242 General works
244 1822-1866
246 1866-1876
1876-1881
248 General works
Biography and memoirs
249.A1 Collective
249.A2-Z Individual, A-Z
e.g.
249.S7 Soutsos, Nikolaos, Prince
1866/1881-1944
250 General works
Carol I, 1881-1914
252 Sources and documents
Collected works
252.3 Several authors
252.6 Individual authors
253.A-Z Biography and memoirs of contemporaries, A-Z
254 Elizabeth, Consort of Charles I (Carmen Sylva)
255 General works on life and reign
256 Reign only
257 General special
258 Period of the Balkan War, 1912-1913
For the war itself, see DR46+
Ferdinand, 1914-1927
260 Sources and documents
261 General works on life and reign
Biography and memoirs of contemporaries
262.A1 Collective
Royal family
262.A2 Maria (Marie), Consort of Ferdinand I
262.A3-A4 Other members of the royal family
262.A5-Z Other, A-Z
e.g.
262.A5 Antonescu, Ion
262.C6 Codreanu, Corneliu
263 Period of World War I, 1914-1918
For the war itself, see D501+
1918-1944
264 General works
265 Michael
Class here works on regency of 1927-1930 and as king, 1940-1947
Carol II, 1930-1940

Romania
History
By period
1866/1881-1944
1918-1944
Carol II, 1930-1940 -- Continued
266 General works on life and reign
Biography and memoirs of contemporaries
266.2 Collective
266.3.A-Z Individual, A-Z
266.5 Period of World War II, 1940-1944
For the war itself, see D731+
1944-1989
267 General works
Biography and memoirs
267.5.A1 Collective
267.5.A2-Z Individual, A-Z
e.g.
267.5.C4 Ceauşescu, Nicolae
1989-
268 General works
Biography and memoirs
268.8 Collective
268.82.A-Z Individual, A-Z
Revolution, 1989
269.5 General works
269.6 Personal narratives
Local history and description
Transylvania
279 Periodicals. Societies. Serials
279.2 Sources and documents
279.3 Gazetteers. Dictionaries, etc. Guidebooks
279.5 General works
Description and travel
279.6 Earliest through 1800
279.62 1801-1950
279.64 1951-
279.68 Antiquities
279.7 Social life and customs. Civilization
Ethnography
279.8 General works
279.9 Romanians
279.92.A-Z Other individual elements in the population, A-Z
279.92.B8 Bulgarians
279.92.G4 Germans
Including the so-called "Saxons"
279.92.G74 Greeks
279.92.H8 Hungarians
Saxons, see DR279.92.G4
279.92.S9 Szeklers
279.92.T87 Turks
279.95 Biography (Collective)
For individual biography, see period

Romania
Local history and description
Transylvania -- Continued
History
280 General works
By period
Earliest to 1526
280.2 General works
Biography and memoirs
280.24 Collective
280.26.A-Z Individual, A-Z
1526-1919
280.4 General works
Biography and memoirs
280.42 Collective
280.44.A-Z Individual, A-Z
e.g.
280.44.B4 Bethlen, Gábor, Prince of Transylvania, 1580-1629
1919-
280.7 General works
Biography and memoirs
280.72 Collective
280.74.A-Z Individual, A-Z
Regions, cities, towns, etc , see DR281.A +
281.A-Z Other provinces, regions, etc., A-Z
e.g.
281.B25 Banat
For Hungarian Banat, see DB975.B2
281.C6 Constanţa
281.D5 Dobruja
For Dobruja (Bulgaria), see DR95.D6
281.S8 Suceava. Romanian Bukovina
For Bukovina (General, and Ukraine), see DK508.9.B85
Cities, towns, etc.
286 Bucharest (Table D-DR3)
296.A-Z Other, A-Z
e.g.
296.B74 Braşov. Brasso. Kronstadt. Stalin
296.B784 Buridava
296.C45 Cetatea Şcheia
296.D7 Drăguş
Kronstadt, see DR296.B74
296.R658 Romula
296.S26 Sarmizegetusa (Ancient city)
Şcheia Fortress, see DR296.C45
296.S6 Sinaia
Stalin, see DR296.B74
296.S92 Sucidava
296.T86 Turnu Roşu
296.Z57 Ziridava

(301-396) Yugoslavia
  See DR1202+
Turkey
  For ancient Asia Minor to 1453, see DS155+
401 Periodicals. Societies. Serials
401.2 Congresses
403 Sources and documents
  Collected works
404 Several authors
405 Individual authors
413 Directories
414 Gazetteers. Dictionaries, etc.
415 Place names (General)
416 Guidebooks
417 General works
417.2 Pictorial works
417.4 Juvenile works
418 Compends
419 Geography
  Description and travel
    For guidebooks regardless of the historical period, see DR416
421 To 1453
423 1453-1565
424 1566-1700
425 1701-1829
427 1830-1900
428 1901-1950
429 1951-1980
429.4 1981-
431 Antiquities
  Cf. DR701+, Local history and description
432 Social life and customs. Civilization
  Ethnography
    Cf. DS26+, Turks
434 General works
435.A-Z Individual elements in the population, A-Z
435.A43 Albanians
435.A7 Armenians
435.B35 Balkan Muslims
435.B74 British
435.B84 Bulgarians
435.C57 Circassians
435.G38 Georgians (Transcaucasians)
435.G4 Germans
435.G8 Greeks
435.K87 Kurds
435.L39 Laz
435.L49 Lezgians
435.P6 Poles
435.R65 Romanians
435.Y8 Yuruks

Turkey -- Continued
History
Including Ottoman Empire, 1288-1918
436 Dictionaries. Chronological tables, outlines, etc.
Biography (Collective)
For individual biography, see the special period, reign, or place
438 General works
438.1 Rulers, etc.
438.3 Houses, noble families, etc.
438.5 Public men
438.7 Women
Historiography
438.8 General works
Biography of historians and antiquarians
438.9.A2 Collective
438.9.A3-Z Individual, A-Z
e.g.
438.9.A5 Akçura, Yusuf
Study and teaching
438.94 General works
438.95.A-Z By region or country, A-Z
General works
439 Through 1800
440 1801-
441 Compends
442 Pamphlets, etc.
Several parts of the empire treated together
445 European or European-Asiatic-African
Cf. DR1+, Turkey, Bulgaria, etc.
446 Asiatic-African
Including Egypt and Syria under Turkish dominion
For description and travel, see individual countries
448 Military history
For individual campaigns and engagements, see the special period
451 Naval history
Political and diplomatic history
Cf. DR481+, Special periods, reigns, etc.
470 Sources and documents. Foreign and general relations
471 General works
472 Earliest to 1566
473 1566-1757
474 1757-1812
475 1812-1876
476 1876-1918
Including Panislamism
477 1918-
479.A-Z Relations with individual regions or countries, A-Z
By period
481 Earliest to 1281/1453

Turkey
History
By period -- Continued
1281/1453-1918
General works
485 Through 1800
486 1801-
492 Ertoghrul, 1281-1288
493 Osman I, 1288-1326
494 Orkhan, 1326-1359
495 Murad I, 1359-1389
Including the Battle of Kosovo, 1389; etc.
496 Bajazet I, 1389-1403
Including the Battle of Nikopoli, 1396; etc.
496.5 Süleiman I, 1403-1410
496.7 Musa, 1410-1413
497 Mohammed I, 1413-1421
498 Murad II, 1421-1451
Including the Battles of Varna (1444), Kosovo (1448); etc.
Geōrgios Kastriōtēs, called Scanderbeg, Prince of Epirus, 1443-1468, see DR960+
Mohammed II, 1451-1481
501 General works on life and reign
502 Fall of Constantinople, 1453
Class here mainly Turkish accounts
For general works, see DF645+
502.5 War with Venice, 1470-1474
502.7 Siege of Rhodes, 1480
503 Bajazet II, 1481-1512
504 Selim I, 1512-1520
Solyman I the Magnificent, 1520-1566
505 Sources and documents
506 General works on life and reign
507 General special
Including the Battle of Mohács, 1526; etc.
508 Pamphlets, etc.
509.A-Z Biography and memoirs of contemporaries, A-Z
e.g.
509.S6 Sokolli Mehmet, pasha
1566-1640. Period of decline
511 General works
Selim II, 1566-1574
513 General works on life and reign
Cyprian War, 1570-1571. Holy League, 1571
515 General works
515.5 Pamphlets, etc.
516 Battle of Lepanto, 1571
Murad III, 1574-1595
519 General works on life and reign
521 Border wars with Hungary, 1575-1606
523 Wars with Persia, 1576-1639
525 Mohammed III, 1595-1603

Turkey
History
By period
1281/1453-1918
1566-1640. Period of decline -- Continued
526 Ahmed I, 1603-1617
Mustafa I, 1617-1623
527 General works on life and reign
528 Osman II, 1618-1622
529 Murad IV, 1623-1640
1640-1789
531 General works
533 Ibrahim, 1640-1648
Mohammed IV, 1648-1687
Cf. DG678.33+, Venice
534 General works on life and reign
War of Candia, 1644-1669
534.2 General works
534.25 Pamphlets, etc.
Siege of Candia, 1667-1669
534.3 General works
534.4 Pamphlets, etc.
534.5.A-Z Other special events, A-Z
Chios, Battle of, 1657, see DR534.5.K5
534.5.D3 Dardanelles, Battle of, 1656
534.5.K5 Khíos Island, Greece, Battle of, 1657
536 Siege of Vienna, 1683. Holy League against the Turks, 1684
Cf. DB853, Vienna (17th-18th centuries)
536.5 Siege of Buda, 1686
537 Solyman III, 1687-1691
539 Ahmed II, 1691-1695
Mustafa II, 1695-1703
541 General works on life and reign
541.3 Rebellion of 1703
Ahmed III, 1703-1730
542 General works on life and reign
544 Russia, 1710-1713
Including Battle of Pruth River, 1711, etc.
545 Venice and Austria, 1715-1718
Including Austro-Turkish War, 1714-1718, etc.
Mahmud I, 1730-1754
547 General works on life and reign
548 War with Austria and Russia, 1736-1739. Peace of Belgrad, 1739
549 Osman III, 1754-1757
Mustafa III, 1757-1773
551 General works on life and reign
553 Russia, 1768-1774. Peace of Kuchuk Kainarji
554 Egypt, 1770-1777

	Turkey
	History
	By period
	1281/1453-1918
	1640-1789 -- Continued
	Abdul-Hamid I, 1773-1789
555	General works on life and reign
555.7	Austria and Russia, 1787-1792
	1789-1861. 19th century
556	Sources and documents
557	General works
	Biography and memoirs
557.9	Collective
558.A-Z	Individual, A-Z
	e.g.
558.D8	Dubuc de Rivery, Aimée
	Selim III, 1789-1807
559	General works on life and reign
559.5	1789-1804. War with the Suliotes
	Mustafa IV, 1807-1808
560	General works on life and reign
561	War with Russia, 1806-1812
	Mahmud II, 1808-1839
	Cf. DR301+, Serbia (19th century)
562	General works on life and reign
	Battle of Navarino, 1827, see DF810.N3
564	War with Russia, 1828-1829
	Tanzimat (Reorganization) 1839-1876
565	General works
	Abdul Mejid, 1839-1861
566	General works on life and reign
567	Period of Crimean War
	For the war itself, see DK214+
	1861-1909
568	General works
568.8.A-Z	Biography and memoirs, A-Z
	e.g.
568.8.A46	Ahmet Muhtar Paşa, 1839-1918
568.8.C4	Cevdet, Ahmet, pasha
	Gazi Ahmet Muhtar Paşa, see DR568.8.A46
568.8.I7	Ismail Kemal Bey
568.8.M6	Midhat, pasha
569	Abdul-Aziz, 1861-1876
570	Murad V, 1876
	Abdul-Hamid II, 1876-1909. Constitutional movement
571	General works on life and reign
571.5	Personal special
572	General special

Turkey
History
By period
1281/1453-1918
1861-1909
Abdul-Hamid II, 1876-1909.
Constitutional movement -- Continued
572.5 Committee of Union and Progress (Young Turks) (Ittihat ve Terakki Cemiyeti), 1889-1908
Cf. DR584.5, Committee of Union and Progress (Young Turks), 1908-1918
War with Russia, 1877-1878
572.9 Museums, exhibitions, etc.
Subarrange by author
573 General works
573.3 General special
Military operations
General works, see DR573
573.35 Regimental histories
Subarrange by author
573.4 Personal narratives
573.5.A-Z Special events, battles, etc., A-Z
e.g.
573.5.P6 Pleven, Bulgaria (City), Siege of, 1877
573.5.P76 Prokhod Shipchenski, Battle of, 1877
573.7 Treaty of San Stefano, 1878
Cf. D375.3, Eastern question (19th century)
573.8.A-Z Special topics, A-Z
Hospitals, see DR573.8.M44
573.8.M44 Medical and sanitary affairs. Hospitals
573.8.O78 Orthodox Eastern Church
573.8.R44 Refugees
573.8.T47 Territorial questions
573.8.W6 Women
575 Period of war with Greece, 1897
For the war itself, see DF827
20th century
576 General works
Mohammed V, 1909-1918
583 General works on life and reign
584 General special
584.5 Committee of Union and Progress (Young Turks) (Ittihat ve Terakki Cemiyeti), 1908-1918
Cf. DR572.5, Committee of Union and Progress (Young Turks), 1889-1908
586 Period of Turco-Italian War, 1911-1912
For the war itself, see DT234
587 Period of Balkan War, 1912-1913
For the war itself, see DR46+

Turkey
History
By period
20th century
Mohammed V, 1909-1918 -- Continued
588 Period of World War I, 1914-1918
For the war itself, see D501+
1918-
589 Mohammed VI, 1918-1922
Including Turkish Revolution, 1918-1923
Cf. DF845.5+, War with Greece, 1921-1922
590 First Republic, 1923-1960. Kemalism
Biography and memoirs
592.A1 Collective
592.A2-Z Individual, A-Z
e.g.
592.A4 Adivar, Halide Edib
Atatürk, Kemal, see DR592.K4
592.E55 Enver, pasha
592.I5 Inönü, Ismet
592.K4 Kemal, Mustafa (Kemal Atatürk)
592.N8 Nur, Riza, 1879-1942 or 3
Riza Nur, 1879-1942 or 3, see DR592.N8
Second Republic, 1960-1980
593 General works
600 Coup d'etat, 1971
601 Coup d'etat, 1980
Third Republic, 1980-
603 General works
Biography and memoirs
605.A1 Collective
605.A2-Z Individual, A-Z
605.O35 Öcalan, Abdullah
Local history and description (European Turkey)
701.A-Z Provinces, regions, etc., A-Z
e.g.
701.A2 Aegean Sea
For Aegean Sea region, see DF895
For Turkish islands in the Aegean Sea, see DS51.A+
Albania, see DR901+
701.D2 Dardanelles
701.G3 Gallipoli Peninsula
Janina, see DF951.I5
Kosovo, see DR2075+
Macedonia, see DR2152+
Monastir, see DR2275.B58
Rumelia (Rumeli), see DR49.7
Saloniki (Thessalonike), see DF951.T45

Turkey
Local history and description (European Turkey)
Provinces, regions, etc., A-Z -- Continued
701.T5 Thrace, Eastern (European Turkey)
For ancient Greek Thrace, see DF261.T6
For Bulgarian Thrace, see DR95.T45
For general works on Thrace, see DR50+
For modern Greek Thrace, see DF901.T75
Istanbul (Constantinople)
716 Sources and documents
Cf. DR403, Sources and documents of Turkey
717 Gazetteers
718 Guidebooks
719 General works
Description
720 Early through 1800
For history of Istanbul (early to 1800), see DR729+
721 1801-1900
722 1901-1950
723 1951-
724 Pictorial works
725 Antiquities
726 Social life and customs. Culture
Ethnography
726.5 General works
727.A-Z Individual elements in the population, A-Z
727.A75 Armenians
727.G46 Georgians (Transcaucasians)
727.G74 Greeks
727.I73 Iranians
727.I75 Italians
727.R87 Russians
History
728 General works
By period
729 Early and medieval to 1453
For the Siege of Constantinople, 1203-1204, see D164+
730 1453-1800
731 19th-20th centuries
Sections, districts, etc.
735 Stamboul
736 Seraglio and other palaces, residences of sultans, etc.
Including Yildiz kiosk
737 Galata and Pera (Beyoğlu)
738 Scutari (Uskùdär)
738.5.A-Z Other, A-Z
738.5.B49 Beylerbeyi
738.5.E9 Eyüp Sultan
738.5.F38 Fatih
738.5.H48 Heybeli

Turkey
Local history and description (European Turkey)
Istanbul (Constantinople)
Sections, districts, etc.
Other, A-Z -- Continued
738.5.I4 Ihlamur Mesiresi
738.5.K34 Kadiköy
738.5.P74 Princes' Islands. Adalar İlçesi
738.5.S5 Şişli
738.5.T64 Taksim Meydani (Square)
Buildings, etc.
738.9 Collective
739.A-Z Individual, A-Z
741.A-Z Other cities, towns, etc., A-Z
e.g.
Athos, Mount, see DF901.A77
741.B7 Bosporus (Strait)
741.E4 Edirne (Adrianople)
(741.T5) Tirana, Albania
see DR997
Ancient Asia Minor to 1453, see DS155+
Turkey in Asia after 1453, see DS47+
Albania
901 Periodicals. Societies. Serials
Museums, exhibitions, etc.
902 General works
903.A-Z Individual. By place, A-Z
903.5 Congresses
904 Sources and documents
Collected works
905 Several authors
906 Individual authors
907 Gazetteers. Dictionaries, etc.
908 Place names (General)
909 Guidebooks
910 General works
911 General special
912 Pictorial works
Historic monuments, landmarks, etc. (General)
For local, see DR996+
913 General works
913.5 Preservation
914 Historical geography
914.5 Geography
Description and travel
915 History of travel
916 Through 1900
917 1901-1970
918 1971-
921 Antiquities
For local, see DR996+

Albania -- Continued
922 Social life and customs. Civilization. Intellectual life
For specific periods, see the period or reign
Ethnography
923 General works
924 National characteristics
925.A-Z Individual elements in the population, A-Z
925.G48 Ghegs
925.G7 Greeks
925.M33 Macedonians
925.S53 Slavs, Southern
925.T65 Tosks
925.Y84 Yugoslavs
926 Albanians in foreign regions or countries (General)
For Albanians in a particular region or country, see the region or country
History
Periodicals. Societies. Serials, see DR901+
927 Dictionaries. Chronological tables, outlines, etc
Biography (Collective)
For individual biography, see the specific period, reign, or place
928 General works
929 Rulers, kings, etc.
930 Queens. Princes and princesses
Houses, noble families, etc.
931 Collective
932 Individual houses, families, etc.
933 Statesmen
934 Women
Historiography
935 General works
Biography of historians
936 Collective
937.A-Z Individual, A-Z
Study and teaching
938 General works
939.A-Z By region or country, A-Z
Subarrange by author
General works
939.5 Through 1800
940 1801-1975
941 1976-
942 Pictorial works
943 Juvenile works
944 Addresses, essays, lectures
945 Philosophy of Albanian history
946 History of several parts of Albania treated together
947 Military history
948 Naval history
Political history
For specific periods, see the period or reign

Albania
History
Political history -- Continued
949 Sources and documents
950 General works
Foreign and general relations
For works on relations with a specific region or country regardless of period, see DR953.A+
For general works on the diplomatic history of a period, see the period
951 Sources and documents
952 General works
953.A-Z Relations with individual regions or countries, A-Z
By period
To 1501
954 Sources and documents
955 General works
956 Through 600
Cf. DG59.I2, Illyricum
Cf. DR39.5, Illyrians
957 600-1190
1190-1389. Feudal principalities
958 General works
Biography and memoirs
958.2 Collective
958.25.A-Z Individual, A-Z
1389-1501. Turkish Wars
958.9 Sources and documents
959 General works
Biography and memoirs
959.2 Collective
959.25.A-Z Individual, A-Z
Scanderbeg, 1443-1468
960 General works on life and reign
960.3 Kotodeshi Plain, Battle of, 1444
960.5 Albanian-Venetian War, 1447-1448
Including Battle of the Drin, Battle of Orovnik, etc.
1501-1912. Turkish rule
961 Sources and documents
962 General works
1501-1840
962.9 Sources and documents
963 General works
Biography and memoirs
963.2 Collective
963.25.A-Z Individual, A-Z
e.g.
963.25.V47 Veqilharxhi, Naum, b. 1797
Bushati family. Pashallek of Shkodër, 1757-1831
964 General works
Biography and memoirs

Albania
History
By period
1501-1912. Turkish rule
1501-1840
Bushati family. Pashallek of Shkoder, 1757-1831
Biography and memoirs -- Continued
964.2 Collective
964.25.A-Z Individual, A-Z
965 Ali Paşa, Tepedelinli (Pasha of Janina), 1744?-1822
1840-1912. National renaissance. Independence movement
965.9 Sources and documents
966 General works
966.14 Social life and customs. Civilization. Intellectual life
966.18 Foreign and general relations
Biography and memoirs
966.2 Collective
966.25.A-Z Individual, A-Z
e.g.
966.25.F7 Frashëri, Naum, 1846-1900
966.25.F72 Frashëri, Sami, 1850-1904
966.25.I84 Ismail Kemal Bey, 1844-1919
967 League of Prizren, 1878-1881
968 Congress of Monastir (Bitola), 1908
969 Uprisings, 1910-1912
20th century
969.8 General works
1912-1944
970 Sources and documents
971 General works
971.18 Foreign and general relations
Biography and memoirs
971.2 Collective
971.25.A-Z Individual, A-Z
e. g.
971.25.V45 Vlora, Ekrem, 1885-1964
971.25.W54 William, Prince of Wied, b. 1876
972 1912-1918. Period of Balkan War and World War I
For the Balkan War, 1912-1913, itself, see DR46+
For World War I itself, see D501+
1918-1925
973 General works
973.5 June Revolution, 1924
Zogu I, 1925-1939
974 General works
974.5 Fier Uprising, 1935

Albania
History
By period
20th century
1912-1944 -- Continued
975 1939-1944. Period of World War II
For the war itself, see D731+
1944-1990
976 Sources and documents
977 General works
977.14 Social life and customs. Civilization. Intellectual life
977.18 Foreign and general relations
Biography and memoirs
977.2 Collective
977.25.A-Z Individual, A-Z
e.g.
977.25.H67 Hoxha, Enver, 1908-
1990-
977.9 Sources and documents
978 General works
978.2 Social life and customs. Civilization. Intellectual life
978.3 Political history
978.4 Foreign and general relations
Biography and memoirs
978.5 Collective
978.52.A-Z Individual, A-Z
Local history and description
996.A-Z Provinces, regions, etc., A-Z
996.E64 Epirus, Northern
For ancient Epirus, see DF261.E65
For modern Epirus, see DF901.E6
Cities, towns, etc.
997 Tiranë (Table D-DR3)
998.A-Z Other, A-Z
998.D85 Durrës (Durazzo, Drač)
998.K65 Korçë (Koritsa, Coriza)
998.S48 Shkodër (Scutari, Skadar)
998.V44 Vlorë (Valona, Vlonë)
Yugoslavia
For works limited to specific republics, see the individual republic
1202 Periodicals. Societies. Serials
Museums, exhibitions, etc.
1203 General works
1204.A-Z Individual. By place, A-Z
1205 Congresses
1206 Sources and documents
Collected works
1207 Several authors
1208 Individual authors
1209 Gazetteers. Dictionaries, etc.

Yugoslavia -- Continued
1210 Place names (General)
1212 Directories
1213 Guidebooks
1214 General works
1215 General special
1216 Pictorial works
Historic monuments, landmarks, scenery, etc. (General)
For local, see DR1350+
1217 General works
1217.5 Preservation
1218 Historical geography
Description and travel
1220 Early through 1900
1221 1901-1944
1223 1945-1970
1224 1971-
1227 Antiquities
For local antiquities, see DR1350+
1228 Social life and customs. Civilization. Intellectual life
For specific periods, see the period or reign
Ethnography
1229 General works
1230.A-Z Individual elements in the population, A-Z
For individual elements in specific republics, see the republic
1230.A4 Albanians
1230.A75 Aromanians
1230.C75 Croats
1230.C93 Czechs
1230.G47 Germans
Gypsies, see DX271
1230.H85 Hungarians
1230.I8 Italians
1230.M3 Macedonians
1230.M65 Montenegrins
1230.M87 Muslims
1230.P64 Poles
1230.R65 Romanians
1230.R85 Russians
1230.R87 Ruthenians
1230.S46 Serbs
1230.S55 Slovaks
1230.S56 Slovenes
1230.T87 Turks
1231 Yugoslavs in foreign regions or countries (General)
For Yugoslavs in a particular region or country, see the region or country
History
Periodicals. Societies. Serials, see DR1202
1232 Dictionaries. Chronological tables, outlines, etc.

Yugoslavia
History -- Continued
Biography (Collective)
For individual biography, see the specific period, reign or place
1233 General works
1234 Rulers, kings, etc.
1235 Statesmen
Historiography
1239 General works
Biography of historians, area studies specialists, archaeologists, etc.
1240 Collective
1241.A-Z Individual, A-Z
Study and teaching
1242 General works
1243.A-Z By region or country, A-Z
Subarrange by author
General works
1244 Through 1800
1245 1801-1980
1246 1981-
1246.5 Pictorial works
1246.6 Juvenile works
1247 Addresses, essays, lectures. Anecdotes, etc.
1248 Philosophy of Yugoslav history
1249 History of several parts of Yugoslavia treated together
Military history
For specific periods, including individual campaigns and engagements, see the special period or reign
1250 Sources and documents
1251 General works
Naval history
For specific periods, including individual campaigns and engagements, see the special period or reign
1252 Sources and documents
1253 General works
Political history
For specific periods, see the period or reign
1254 Sources and documents
1255 General works
Foreign and general relations
For works on relations with a specific region or country regardless of period, see DR1258.A+
For general works on the diplomatic history of a period, see the period
1256 Sources and documents
1257 General works
1258.A-Z Relations with individual regions or countries, A-Z
By period

Yugoslavia
History
By period -- Continued
Early and medieval to 1500
1259 Sources and documents
1260 General works
Biography and memoirs
1264 Collective
1265.A-Z Individual, A-Z
1500-1800
1266 Sources and documents
1267 General works
Biography and memoirs
1271 Collective
1272.A-Z Individual, A-Z
1800-1918
1273 Sources and documents
1274 General works
Biography and memoirs
1278 Collective
1279.A-Z Individual, A-Z
1280 1914-1918. Period of World War I
For the war itself, see D501+
1918-
1281 Sources and documents
1282 General works
1283 Biography and memoirs (Collective)
For individual biography, see the specific period
1918-1945. Kingdom of the Serbs, Croats, and Slovenes (1918-1929) and Kingdom of Yugoslavia (1929-1945)
1288 Sources and documents
1289 General works
1290 Social life and customs. Civilization. Intellectual life
1291 Political history
1292 Foreign and general relations
Biography and memoirs
1293 Collective
1294.A-Z Individual, A-Z
e.g.
1294.M54 Mihailović, Draža, 1893-1946
1294.P39 Pavle, Prince of Yugoslavia, 1893-
1294.T78 Trumbić, Ante, 1864-1938
1295 Peter I, 1918-1921
For general works on Peter's life and reign, as well as his reign as King of Serbia, see DR2030
1296 Alexander I, 1921-1934
Peter II, 1934-1945
Including the Regency, 1934-1945
1297 General works on life and reign

Yugoslavia
History
By period
1918-
1918-1945. Kingdom of the Serbs, Croats, and Slovenes (1918-1929) and Kingdom of Yugoslavia
Peter II, 1934-1945 -- Continued
1298 1941-1945. Axis occupation
For World War II, see D731+
1945-1980. Tito regime
1299 Sources and documents
1300 General works on life and administration
1301 Social life and customs. Civilization. Intellectual life
1302 Political history
1303 Foreign and general relations
Biography and memoirs
1304 Collective
1305.A-Z Individual, A-Z
e.g.
1305.D56 Djilas, Milovan, 1911-
1980-1992
1306 Sources and documents
1307 General works
1308 Social life and customs. Civilization. Intellectual life
1309 Political history
1310 Foreign and general relations
Biography and memoirs
1311 Collective
1312.A-Z Individual, A-Z
Yugoslav War, 1991-1995
1313.A2 Sources and documents
1313.A4-Z General works
1313.11 Chronology
1313.12 Pictorial works
1313.15 Juvenile literature
Military operations
1313.2 General works
By region or country
Class here works on military operations occurring in specific places
Bosnia and Hercegovina
1313.3 General works
1313.32.A-Z Local, A-Z
Croatia
1313.4 General works
1313.42.A-Z Local, A-Z
Serbia/Montenegro (Yugoslavia)
1313.5 General works
1313.52.A-Z Local, A-Z
Slovenia

Yugoslavia
History
By period
1918-
1980-
Yugoslav War, 1991-1995
Military operations
By region or country
Slovenia -- Continued

1313.6 General works
1313.62.A-Z Local, A-Z
1313.7.A-Z Special topics, A-Z
1313.7.A47 Aerial operations
1313.7.A85 Atrocities
1313.7.B56 Blockades
1313.7.C56 Children
1313.7.C58 Civilian relief
1313.7.C65 Communications
1313.7.C67 Conscientious objectors. War resisters. Draft resisters
Concentration camps, see DR1313.7.P74
1313.7.D48 Destruction and pillage
1313.7.D58 Diplomatic history
Draft resisters, see DR1313.7.C67
1313.7.E38 Education and the war
1313.7.E58 Environmental aspects
Foreign participation
1313.7.F67 General works
1313.7.F672A-Z By region or country, A-Z
Guerrillas. Guerrilla units, see DR1313.7.U54
1313.7.M43 Medical care
1313.7.P43 Peace
Pillage, see DR1313.7.D48
1313.7.P73 Press coverage
1313.7.P74 Prisoners and prisons
Including concentration camps
Protest movements, see DR1313.7.P83
1313.7.P75 Psychological aspects
1313.7.P83 Public opinion
Including protest movements
1313.7.R42 Reconstruction
1313.7.R43 Refugees
Relief, Civilian, see DR1313.7.C58
1313.7.R45 Religious aspects
1313.7.S64 Social aspects
1313.7.U54 Underground movements. Guerrillas. Guerrilla units
War resisters, see DR1313.7.C67
1313.7.W65 Women
1313.8 Personal narratives
1992-
1315 Sources and documents

Yugoslavia
History
By period
1918-
1992- -- Continued
1316 General works
1317 Social life and customs. Civilization. Intellectual life
1318 Political history
1319 Foreign and general relations
Biography and memoirs
1320 Collective
1321.A-Z Individual, A-Z
Local history and description
For individual regions, geographic features, cities, etc., see the local provisions under specific republics
1350.A-Z Regions not limited to specific republics, A-Z
For areas of the following regions totally within particular republics, see the local provisions under specific republics
1350.A35 Adriatic coastal regions
1350.D35 Danube River and Valley
For the Danube River (General), see DJK76.2+
1350.D55 Dinaric Alps
Including the Karst region
1350.D7 Drava River and Valley
1350.D74 Drina River and Valley
1350.I45 Illyrian Provinces. Illyria (Kingdom)
1350.I78 Istria
1350.J84 Julian March (Venezia Giulia) (General and Yugoslavia)
Including the Littoral (Küstenland)
For Friuli Venezia Giulia (Italy), see DG975.F855
1350.L56 Lim River and Valley
1350.M54 Military Frontier (Vojna Krajina)
1350.M64 Mokra Mountains
1350.N47 Neretva River and Valley
1350.S25 Sandžak
1350.S27 Šar Mountains
1350.S29 Sava River and Valley
1350.S56 Skopska Crna Gora Mountains
Slovenia
Including Carniola
1352 Periodicals. Societies. Serials
1354 Congresses
1355 Sources and documents
Collected works
1356 Several authors
1357 Individual authors
1357.5 Gazetteers. Dictionaries, etc.
1358 Place names (General)

Yugoslavia
Local history and description
Slovenia -- Continued
1358.5 Directories
1359 Guidebooks
1360 General works
1362 Pictorial works
1363 Historic monuments, landmarks, scenery, etc. (General)
For local, see DR1475+
1367 Description and travel
1369 Geography
1371 Antiquities
For local antiquities, see DR1475+
1372 Social life and customs. Civilization. Intellectual life
For specific periods, see the period or reign
Ethnography
1373 General works
1373.5 National characteristics
1374.A-Z Individual elements in the population, A-Z
1374.C76 Croats
1374.G47 Germans
1374.H84 Hungarians
1374.I8 Italians
1375 Slovenes in foreign regions or countries (General)
For Slovenes in a particular region or country, see the region or country
History
Periodicals. Societies. Serials, see DR1352
1375.5 Dictionaries. Chronological tables, outlines, etc.
Biography (Collective)
For individual biography, see the specific period, reign, or place
1376 General works
Houses, noble families, etc.
1378 Collective
1378.5.A-Z Individual houses, families, etc., A-Z
e.g.
1378.5.C44 Celje, Counts of
Historiography
1381 General works
Biography of historians, area studies specialists, archaeologists, etc.
1382 Collective
1382.5.A-Z Individual, A-Z
Study and teaching
1383 General works
1384.A-Z By region or country, A-Z
Subarrange by author
1385 General works

Yugoslavia
Local history and description
Slovenia
History -- Continued
1390 Military history
For specific periods, including individual campaigns and engagements, see the special period or reign
1391 Naval history
For specific periods, including individual campaigns and engagements, see the special period or reign
1392 Political history
For specific periods, see the period or reign
Foreign and general relations
For works on relations with a specific region or country regardless of period, see DR1396.A+
For general works on the diplomatic history of a period, see the period
1395 General works
1396.A-Z Relations with individual regions or countries, A-Z
By period
Early and medieval to 1456
1397 Sources and documents
1398 General works
Biography and memoirs
1402 Collective
1402.5.A-Z Individual, A-Z
1456-1814. Slovenia under Habsburg rule
1405 Sources and documents
1406 General works
1407 Social life and customs. Civilization. Intellectual life
Biography and memoirs
1410 Collective
1410.5.A-Z Individual, A-Z
1411 Peasant Uprising, 1573
Cf. DR1573, Croatian uprising
1411.5 Peasant Uprising, 1635
1809-1814. Slovenia as part of the Illyrian Provinces
1414 Sources and documents
1415 General works
Biography and memoirs
1419 Collective
1419.5.A-Z Individual, A-Z
1814-1918
1422 Sources and documents
1423 General works
1424 Social life and customs. Civilization. Intellectual life

Yugoslavia
Local history and description
Slovenia
History
By period
1814-1918 -- Continued
1425 Political history
Biography and memoirs
1427 Collective
1428.A-Z Individual, A-Z
1430 Revolutionary events, 1848-1849
1849-1918. Awakening of national consciousness
1431 General works
1434 1914-1918. Period of World War I
For World War I, see D501+
1918-1945. Slovenia as part of Yugoslavia
Including the Dravska banovina, 1929-1941
1435 Sources and documents
1436 General works
1437 Social life and customs. Civilization. Intellectual life
1438 Political history
Biography and memoirs
1440 Collective
1441.A-Z Individual, A-Z
1443 1941-1945. Axis occupation
1945-1990. Federal People's Republic
1444 Sources and documents
1445 General works
1446 Social life and customs. Civilization. Intellectual life
1447 Political history
Biography and memoirs
1449 Collective
1450.A-Z Individual, A-Z
1990-
1452 Sources and documents
1453 General works
1454 Social life and customs. Civilization. Intellectual life
1455 Political history
1456 Foreign and general relations
Biography and memoirs
1457 Collective
1457.5.A-Z Individual, A-Z
Local history and description
1475.A-Z Provinces, regions, geographic features, etc., A-Z
e.g.
1475.C37 Carinthia
For Carinthia (General and Austria), see DB281+

Yugoslavia
Local history and description
Slovenia
Local history and description
Provinces, regions, geographic features, etc., A-Z -- Continued
Carniola, see DR1352
1475.G67 Görz and Gradiska (Goriška) (General and Slovenia)
For the Gorizia region (Italy), see DG975.G67
1475.J67 Julian Alps
1475.K37 Karavanke (Karawanken) Mountains
1475.M87 Mur River and Valley
1475.S56 Slovensko Primorje
1475.S89 Styria, Lower
For Styria (General and Austria), see DB681+
Cities and towns
1476 Ljubljana (Table D-DR3)
1485.A-Z Other cities, towns, etc., A-Z
e.g.
1485.C44 Celje
Croatia
1502 Periodicals. Societies. Serials
Museums, exhibitions, etc.
1503 General works
1503.5.A-Z Individual. By place, A-Z
1504 Congresses
1505 Sources and documents
Collected works
1506 Several authors
1507 Individual authors
1507.5 Gazetteers. Dictionaries, etc.
1508 Place names (General)
1508.5 Directories
1509 Guidebooks
1510 General works
1512 Pictorial works
1513 Historic monuments, landmarks, scenery, etc. (General)
For local, see DR1620+
1515 Historical geography
1517 Description and travel
1521 Antiquities
For local antiquities, see DR1620+
1522 Social life and customs. Civilization. Intellectual life
For specific periods, see the period or reign
Ethnography
1523 General works
1523.5 National characteristics
1524.A-Z Individual elements in the population, A-Z
1524.C94 Czechs

Yugoslavia
Local history and description
Croatia
Ethnography
Individual elements in the population, A-Z -- Continued
1524.G47 Germans
1524.H85 Hungarians
1524.S47 Serbs
1524.S49 Slovenes
1525 Croats in foreign regions or countries (General)
For Croats in a particular region or country, see the region or country
History
Periodicals. Societies. Serials, see DR1502+
1525.5 Dictionaries. Chronological tables, outlines, etc.
Biography (Collective)
For individual biography, see the specific period, reign or place
1526 General works
Houses, noble families, etc.
1527 Collective
1528.A-Z Individual houses, families, etc., A-Z
e.g.
1528.F7 Frankopan family
Historiography
1531 General works
Biography of historians, area studies specialists, archaeologists, etc.
1532 Collective
1532.5.A-Z Individual, A-Z
Study and teaching
1533 General works
1534.A-Z By region or country, A-Z
Subarrange by author
1535 General works
1537 Pictorial works
1539 Philosophy of Croatian history
1540 Military history
For specific periods, including individual campaigns and engagements, see the special period or reign
1541 Naval history
For specific periods, including individual campaigns and engagements, see the special period or reign
1542 Political history
For specific periods, see the period or reign

Yugoslavia
Local history and description
Croatia
History -- Continued
Foreign and general relations
For works on relations with a specific region or country, regardless of period, see DR1546.A+
For general works on the diplomatic history of a period, see the period
1545 General works
1546.A-Z Relations with individual regions or countries, A-Z
By period
Early to 1102. Independent kingdom
1547 Sources and documents
1548 General works
Biography and memoirs
1552 Collective
1552.5.A-Z Individual, A-Z
1554 Tomislav, 910-928
1555 Stjepan Drzislav, 969-997
1556 Peter Krešimir, 1058-1074
1557 Dimitrije Zvonimir, 1075-1089
1102-1527. Arpad and Angevin dynasties
1559 Sources and documents
1560 General works
Biography and memoirs
1564 Collective
1564.5.A-Z Individual, A-Z
1566 1463-1526. Turkish invasions
For the Battle of Mohács, see DR507
1527-1918. Croatia under Habsburg rule
1567 Sources and documents
1568 General works
1569 Social life and customs. Civilization. Intellectual life
1570 Political history
Biography and memoirs
1572 Collective
1572.5.A-Z Individual, A-Z
1573 Peasant Uprising, 1573
Cf. DR1411, Slovenian uprising
1574 Zrinski-Frankopan Conspiracy, 1664-1671
1800-1849
1576 General works
Biography and memoirs
1577 Collective
1578.A-Z Individual, A-Z
e.g.
1578.G34 Gaj, Ljudevit, 1809-1872
1578.J44 Jelačić, Josip, 1801-1859
1578.8 Revolutionary events, 1848-1849

Yugoslavia
Local history and description
Croatia
History
By period
1527-1918. Croatia under Habsburg rule -- Continued
1849-1918
1579 General works
Biography and memoirs
1580 Collective
1580.5.A-Z Individual, A-Z
e.g.
1580.5.S8 Starčević, Ante, 1823-1896
1581 Nagodba of 1868
1581.5 Rakovica Rebellion, 1871
1582 1914-1918. Period of World War I
For World War I, see D501+
1918-1945. Croatia as part of Yugoslavia
Including the Savska and Primorska banovinas, 1929-1939, and Banovina Hrvatska, 1939-1941
1583 Sources and documents
1584 General works
1585 Social life and customs. Civilization. Intellectual life
1586 Political history
Biography and memoirs
1588 Collective
1589.A-Z Individual, A-Z
e.g.
1589.P38 Pavelić, Ante, 1889-1959
1589.R33 Radić, Stjepan, 1871-1928
1591 1941-1945. Period of World War II. Independent state
For World War II, see D731+
1945-1990. Federal People's Republic
1592 Sources and documents
1593 General works
1594 Social life and customs. Civilization. Intellectual life
1595 Political history
Biography and memoirs
1597 Collective
1598.A-Z Individual, A-Z
1990-
1600 Sources and documents
1601 General works
1602 Social life and customs. Civilization. Intellectual life
1603 Political history
1604 Foreign and general relations
Biography and memoirs

Yugoslavia
Local history and description
Croatia
History
By period
1990-
Biography and memoirs -- Continued
1605 Collective
1605.2.A-Z Individual, A-Z
e.g.
1605.2.T83 Tuđman, Franjo
Local history and description
Provinces, regions, geographic features, etc.
Dalmatia
1620 Periodicals. Societies. Serials
1620.3 Sources and documents
1620.9 Guidebooks
1621 General works
1621.5 Pictorial works
1622 Description and travel
1623 Antiquities
For local antiquities, see DR1637.A+
1624 Social life and customs. Civilization.
Intellectual life
For specific periods, see the period
Ethnography
1625 General works
1625.5.A-Z Individual elements in the population, A-Z
1625.5.I8 Italians
1625.5.S47 Serbs
History
1625.7 Biography (Collective)
For individual biography, see the specific period
1626 General works
By period
1627 Early to 1420
1628 1420-1797. Venetian rule
1797-1918. Austrian rule
1629 General works
Biography and memoirs
1629.4 Collective
1629.5.A-Z Individual, A-Z
1629.6 French occupation, 1797-1814
1918-
1630 General works
Biography and memoirs
1630.4 Collective
1630.5.A-Z Individual, A-Z
Slavonia
1633 Periodicals. Societies. Serials
1633.3 Sources and documents
1633.9 Guidebooks

Yugoslavia
Local history and description
Croatia
Local history and description
Provinces, regions, geographic features, etc.
Slavonia -- Continued
1634 General works
1634.5 Pictorial works
1635 Description and travel
1635.5 Antiquities
1635.6 Social life and customs. Civilization. Intellectual life
For specific period, see the period
Ethnography
1635.7 General works
1635.75.A-Z Individual elements in the population, A-Z
1635.75.G47 Germans
1635.75.S565 Slovaks
History
1635.8 Biography (Collective)
For individual biography, see the specific period
1636 General works
1636.2 General special
By period
1636.3 Early to 1526
1636.4 1526-1918
1636.5 1918-
1637.A-Z Other regions, etc., A-Z
e.g.
1637.B37 Baranja
For Baranya (General and Hungary), see DB975.B3
1637.H78 Hrvatsko Zagorje
1637.H85 Hvar
1637.M43 Medjimurje
1637.M55 Military Frontier (Militärgrenze)
Cities and towns
1638 Zagreb (Table D-DR3)
1645.A-Z Other cities and towns, etc., A-Z
e.g.
1645.D8 Dubrovnik
Bosnia and Hercegovina
Class here works on Bosnia alone or Bosnia and Hercegovina together
For Hercegovina alone, see DR1775.H47
1652 Periodicals. Societies. Serials
Museums, exhibitions, etc.
1653 General works
1653.5.A-Z Individual. By place, A-Z
1654 Congresses
1655 Sources and documents

Yugoslavia
Local history and description
Bosnia and Hercegovina -- Continued
Collected works
1656 Several authors
1657 Individual authors
1657.5 Gazetteers. Dictionaries, etc.
1658 Place names (General)
1659 Guidebooks
1660 General works
1662 Pictorial works
1663 Historic monuments, landmarks, scenery, etc. (General)
For local, see DR1775+
1665 Historical geography
1667 Description and travel
1671 Antiquities
For local antiquities, see DR1775+
1672 Social life and customs. Civilization. Intellectual life
For specific periods, see the period or reign
Ethnography
1673 General works
1674.A-Z Individual elements in the population, A-Z
1674.C76 Croats
1674.G47 Germans
1674.M87 Muslims
1674.R65 Romanians
1674.S47 Serbs
History
Periodicals. Societies. Serials, see DR1652+
1675.5 Dictionaries. Chronological tables, outlines, etc.
Biography (Collective)
For individual biography, see the specific period, reign, or place
1676 General works
Houses, noble families, etc.
1677 Collective
1678.A-Z Individual houses, families, etc., A-Z
Historiography
1681 General works
Biography of historians, area studies specialists, archaeologists, etc.
1682 Collective
1682.5.A-Z Individual, A-Z
Study and teaching
1683 General works
1684.A-Z By region or country, A-Z
Subarrange by author
1685 General works

Yugoslavia
Local history and description
Bosnia and Hercegovina
History -- Continued
1690 Military history
For specific periods, including individual campaigns and engagements, see the special period or reign
1692 Political history
For specific periods, see the special period or reign
Foreign and general relations
For general works on the diplomatic history of a period, see the period
1695 General works
1696.A-Z Relations with individual regions or countries, A-Z
By period
Early to 1463
1697 Sources and documents
1698 General works
1699 Social life and customs. Civilization. Intellectual life
Biography and memoirs
1702 Collective
1702.5.A-Z Individual, A-Z
Early to 1254
1703 General works
1705 Kulin, 1180-1204
1254-1463. Kotromanić dynasty
1706 General works
1707 Stefan Kotromanić, 1322-1353
1708 Tvrtko I, 1353-1391
1710 Tomaš, 1443-1461
1463-1878. Turkish rule
1711 Sources and documents
1712 General works
1713 Social life and customs. Civilization. Intellectual life
Biography and memoirs
1716 Collective
1717.A-Z Individual, A-Z
Rebellion of 1875
1720 General works
1720.5 Personal narratives
1721.A-Z Local history. By place, A-Z
1878-1918. Austrian administration
1722 Sources and documents
1723 General works
1724 Social life and customs. Civilization. Intellectual life
1725 Political history
Biography and memoirs

Yugoslavia
Local history and description
Bosnia and Hercegovina
History
By period
1878-1918. Austrian administration
Biography and memoirs -- Continued
1727 Collective
1728.A-Z Individual, A-Z
1731 Annexation to Austria, 1908. Bosnian crisis
1732 1914-1918. Period of World War I
For World War I, see D501+
1918-1945. Bosnia and Hercegovina as part of Yugoslavia
Including the Drinska and Vrbaska banovinas, 1929-1944
1733 Sources and documents
1734 General works
1735 Social life and customs. Civilization. Intellectual life
1736 Political history
Biography and memoirs
1738 Collective
1739.5.A-Z Individual, A-Z
1741 1941-1945. Axis occupation
For World War II, see D731+
1945-1992. Federal People's Republic. Socialist Republic
1742 Sources and documents
1743 General works
1744 Social life and customs. Civilization. Intellectual life
1745 Political history
Biography and memoirs
1747 Collective
1748.A-Z Individual, A-Z
1992- . Independent State
1749 Sources and documents
1750 General works
1751 Social life and customs. Civilization. Intellectual life
1752 Political history
1753 Foreign and general relations
Biography and memoirs
1754 Collective
1755.A-Z Individual, A-Z
1756 Partition, 1995
Local history and description
1775.A-Z Provinces, regions, geographic features, etc., A-Z
e.g.
1775.H47 Hercegovina (Hum)
1775.K7 Krajina

Yugoslavia
Local history and description
Bosnia and Hercegovina
Local history and description
Provinces, regions, geographic features, etc., A-Z -- Continued
1775.M34 Majevica Mountains
Cities and towns
1776 Sarajevo (Table D-DR3)
1785.A-Z Other cities and towns, etc., A-Z
e.g.
1785.B35 Banja Luka
Montenegro
1802 Periodicals. Societies. Serials
1804 Congresses
1805 Sources and documents
Collected works
1806 Several authors
1807 Individual authors
1807.5 Gazetteers. Dictionaries, etc.
1808 Place names (General)
1809 Guidebooks
1810 General works
1812 Pictorial works
1813 Historic monuments, landmarks, scenery, etc. (General)
For local, see DR1925+
1817 Description and travel
1821 Antiquities
For local antiquities, see DR1925+
1822 Social life and customs. Civilization. Intellectual life
For specific periods, see the period or reign
Ethnography
1823 General works
1824.A-Z Individual elements in the population, A-Z
1824.A4 Albanians
1825 Montenegrins in foreign regions or countries
History
Periodicals. Societies. Serials, see DR1802+
Biography (Collective)
For individual biography, see the specific period, reign, or place
1827 General works
Houses, noble families, etc.
1828 Collective
1829.A-Z Individual houses, families, etc., A-Z
e.g.
1829.P48 Petrović-Njegosh, House of
Historiography
1832 General works
Biography of historians, area studies specialists, archaeologists, etc.

Yugoslavia
Local history and description
Montenegro
History
Historiography
Biography of historians, area studies specialists, archaeologists, etc. -- Continued

1833 Collective
1833.5.A-Z Individual, A-Z
Study and teaching
1834 General works
1834.5.A-Z By region or country, A-Z
Subarrange by author
1835 General works
1840 Military history
For special periods, including individual campaigns and engagements, see the special period or reign
1841 Naval history
For special periods, including individual campaigns and engagements, see the period or reign
1842 Political history
For special periods, see the period or reign
Foreign and general relations
For works on relations with a specific region or country regardless of period, see DR1846.A+
For general works on the diplomatic history of a period, see the period
1845 General works
1846.A-Z Relations with individual regions or countries, A-Z
By period
Early to 1516
Including the province of Zeta (Duklja)
1847 Sources and documents
1848 General works
Biography and memoirs
1852 Collective
1852.5.A-Z Individual, A-Z
1516-1782. Vladike
1855 Sources and documents
1856 General works
Biography and memoirs
1860 Collective
1860.5.A-Z Individual, A-Z
1863 Danilo I, 1697-1735
Sava, 1735-1782
1864 General works on life and reign
1865 Vasilije, 1740-1766
1866 Stephan Mali, 1768-1774

Yugoslavia
Local history and description
Montenegro
History
By period -- Continued
1782-1918. Expansion and secularization
1867 Sources and documents
1868 General works
1869 Social life and customs. Civilization. Intellectual life
Biography and memoirs
1872 Collective
1873.A-Z Individual, A-Z
1874 Petar I, 1782-1830
1875 Petar II, 1830-1851
Danilo II, 1851-1860
1876 General works on life and reign
Biography and memoirs
1877 Collective
1877.5.A-Z Individual, A-Z
e.g.
1877.5.D37 Darinka, Queen Consort of Danilo, 1836-1892
Nicholas I, 1860-1918
1878 General works on life and reign
Biography and memoirs
1879 Collective
1879.5.A-Z Individual, A-Z
e.g.
1879.5.R33 Radović, Andrija, 1872-
1881 Turco-Montenegrin War, 1876-1878
1883 1912-1918. Period of the Balkan Wars and World War I
For the Balkan Wars, see DR46+
For World War I, see D501+
1918-1945. Montenegro as part of Yugoslavia
Including the Zetska banovina, 1929-1941
1884 Sources and documents
1885 General works
1886 Social life and customs. Civilization. Intellectual life
1887 Political history
Biography and memoirs
1890 Collective
1891.A-Z Individual, A-Z
1892 Christmas Uprising, 1918
1893 1941-1945. Period of World War II
For World War II, see D731+
1945- . Federal People's Republic. Socialist Republic
1894 Sources and documents
1895 General works

Yugoslavia
Local history and description
Montenegro
History
By period
1945- . Federal People's Republic. Socialist Republic -- Continued
1896 Social life and customs. Civilization. Intellectual life
1897 Political history
Biography and memoirs
1899 Collective
1900.A-Z Individual, A-Z
Local history and description
1925.A-Z Provinces, regions, geographic features, etc., A-Z
e.g.
1925.K38 Kotorska Boka
1925.N67 North Albanian Alps
1925.S56 Skadarsko jezero (Scutari Lake)
Cities and towns
1927 Titograd (Podgorica) (Table D-DR3)
1928.A-Z Other cities, towns, etc., A-Z
e.g.
1928.C48 Cetinje
Serbia
1932 Periodicals. Societies. Serials
1934 Congresses
1935 Sources and documents
Collected works
1936 Several authors
1937 Individual authors
1937.5 Gazetteers. Dictionaries, etc.
1938 Place names (General)
1938.5 Directories
1939 Guidebooks
1940 General works
1942 Pictorial works
1943 Historic monuments, landmarks, scenery, etc. (General)
For local, see DR2075+
1945 Historical geography
1947 Description and travel
1951 Antiquities
For local antiquities, see DR2075+
1952 Social life and customs. Civilization. Intellectual life
For specific periods, see the period or reign
Ethnography
1953 General works
1953.5 National characteristics

Yugoslavia
Local history and description
Serbia
Ethnography -- Continued
1954.A-Z Individual elements in the population, A-Z
For individual elements in Kosovo, see DR2080.5.A+
For individual elements in Vojvodina, see DR2095.5.A+
1954.B84 Bulgarians
1954.G74 Greeks
1954.M87 Muslims
1954.P64 Polabian Slavs
1954.R65 Romanians
1954.R87 Russians
1955 Serbs in foreign regions or countries (General)
For Serbs in a particular region or country, see the region or country
History
Periodicals. Societies. Serials, see DR1932+
Biography (Collective)
For individual biography, see the specific period, reign, or place
1956 General works
1956.5 Rulers, kings, etc.
1956.7 Queens. Princes and princesses
Houses, noble families, etc.
1957 Collective
1958.A-Z Individual houses, families, etc., A-Z
e.g.
1958.O26 Obrenović, House of
Historiography
1961 General works
Biography of historians, area studies specialists, archaeologists, etc.
1962 Collective
1962.5.A-Z Individual, A-Z
Study and teaching
1963 General works
1964.A-Z By region or country, A-Z
Subarrange by author
1965 General works
1970 Military history
For specific periods, including individual campaigns and engagements, see the period or reign
1972 Political history
For specific periods, see the period or reign

Yugoslavia
Local history and description
Serbia
History -- Continued
Foreign and general relations
For works on relations with a specific region or country regardless of period, see DR1976.A+
For general works on the diplomatic history of a period, see the period
1975 General works
1976.A-Z Relations with individual regions or countries, A-Z
By period
Early to 1459
1977 Sources and documents
1978 General works
Biography and memoirs
1982 Collective
1982.5.A-Z Individual, A-Z
1983 Early to 1167. House of Višeslav. Rise of Raška
For Zeta, see DR1847+
1985 1167-1389. Nemanja dynasty
1986 Stefan Nemanja, 1167-1196
1987 Stefan Prvovenčani, 1196-1228
1989 Stefan Uros I, 1243-1276
1990 Milutin (Stefan Uroš II), 1282-1321
1991 Stefan Uroš III, Dečanski, 1322-1331
1992 Stefan Dušan, 1331-1355
1993 Uros, 1355-1371
Lazar, 1371-1389
1994 General works on life and reign
Biography and memoirs
1995 Collective
1995.5.A-Z Individual, A-Z
e.g.
1995.5.M37 Marko, Prince of Serbia, 1335-1394
Battle of Kosovo, 1389, see DR495
1389-1459. Despotate
1996 General works
1997 Stefan Lazarevič, 1389-1427
Đurađ Branković, 1427-1456
1998 General works on life and reign
Biography and memoirs
1999 Collective
1999.5 Individual, A-Z
e.g.
1999.5.M5 Micha owicz, Konstanty, b. ca. 1435
Battle of Varna, 1444, see DR498
Battle of Kosovo, 1448, see DR498
1459-1804. Turkish rule
2000 Sources and documents

Yugoslavia
Local history and description
Serbia
History
By period
1459-1804. Turkish rule -- Continued
2001 General works
2002 Social life and customs. Civilization. Intellectual life
2003 Political history
Biography and memoirs
2004 Collective
2004.5.A-Z Individual, A-Z
e.g.
2004.5.B7 Branković, Đorđe, grof, 1645-1711
2004.8 Great Emigration, 1690
2005 Insurrection, 1788
1804-1918. Autonomy and independence
2006 Sources and documents
2007 General works
2008 Social life and customs. Civilization. Intellectual life
2009 Political history
2010 Foreign and general relations
Biography and memoirs
2012 Collective
2012.5.A-Z Individual, A-Z
e.g.
2012.5.G37 Garašanin, Ilija, 1812-1874
2012.5.P37 Pašić, Nikola, 1845-1926
2012.5.R57 Ristić, Jovan, 1831-1899
Insurrections, 1804-1813
2013 Sources and documents
2014 General works
Biography and memoirs
2015 Collective
2015.5.A-Z Individual, A-Z
e.g.
2015.5.K37 Karađorđe, Petrović, 1752-1817
2015.7 Ivankovac, Battle of, 1805
Miloš Obrenović I, 1814-1839
2016 General works on life and reign
Biography and memoirs
2017 Collective
2017.5.A-Z Individual, A-Z
2017.6 Insurrection, 1815-1817
2017.8 Milan II, 1839
2018 Mihail Obrenović III, 1839-1842
Alexander Karađorđević, 1842-1858
2019 General works on life and reign
Biography and memoirs
2020 Collective
2020.5.A-Z Individual, A-Z

Yugoslavia
Local history and description
Serbia
History
By period
1804-1918. Autonomy and independence -- Continued
2021 Miloš I, 1858-1860
Mihail III, 1860-1868
2022 General works on life and reign
Biography and memoirs
2023 Collective
2023.5.A-Z Individual, A-Z
Milan Obrenović IV, 1868-1889
Including the Regency, 1868-1872
2024 General works on life and reign
Biography and memoirs
2025 Collective
2025.5.A-Z Individual, A-Z
2025.8 Serbo-Turkish War, 1876
2026 Serbo-Turkish War, 1877-1878
2026.8 Revolt, 1883
2027 Serbo-Bulgarian War, 1885
Aleksandar Obrenović, 1889-1903
Including the Regency, 1889-1893
2028 General works on life and reign
Biography and memoirs
2029 Collective
2029.5.A-Z Individual, A-Z
e.g.
2029.5.D7 Draga, Queen Consort of Aleksandar, 1867-1903
Peter I Karađorđević, 1903-1918
For Peter's reign as King of the Kingdom of the Serbs, Croats and Slovenes (1918-1921), see DR1295
2029.9 Sources and documents
2030 General works on life and reign
Biography and memoirs
2031 Collective
2031.5.A-Z Individual, A-Z
2032 1912-1918. Period of the Balkan Wars and World War I
For the Balkan Wars, see DR46+
For World War I, see D501+
1918-1945. Serbia as part of Yugoslavia
Including the Dunavska and Moravska banovinas, 1929-1941
2033 Sources and documents
2034 General works
2035 Social life and customs. Civilization. Intellectual life
2036 Political history

Yugoslavia
Local history and description
Serbia
History
By period
1918-1945. Serbia as part of Yugoslavia -- Continued
Biography and memoirs
2038 Collective
2038.5.A-Z Individual, A-Z
2040 1941-1945. Period of World War II
For World War II, see D731+
1945- . Federal People's Republic. Socialist Republic
2041 Sources and documents
2042 General works
2043 Social life and customs. Civilization. Intellectual life
2044 Political history
Biography and memoirs
2046 Collective
2047.A-Z Individual, A-Z
Local history and description
Provinces, regions, geographic features, etc.
Kosovo
For Kosovo Polje, see DR2105.K67
For Metohija alone, see DR2105.M48
2075 Periodicals. Societies. Serials
2075.3 Sources and documents
2075.6 Gazetteers. Dictionaries, etc.
2075.9 Guidebooks
2076 General works
2076.5 Pictorial works
2077 Description and travel
2078 Antiquities
For local antiquities, see DR2105.A+
2079 Social life and customs. Civilization. Intellectual life
For specific periods, see the period or reign
Ethnography
2080 General works
2080.5.A-Z Individual elements in the population, A-Z
2080.5.A4 Albanians
2080.5.S47 Serbs
History
2081 Biography (Collective)
For individual biography, see the specific period, reign, or place
2082 General works
By period
2083 Early to 1389
Battle of Kosovo, 1389, see DR495

Yugoslavia
Local history and description
Serbia
Local history and description
Provinces, regions, geographic features, etc.
Kosovo
History
By period -- Continued
1389-1913. Turkish rule
Including the Kosovo vilayet
2084 General works
Biography and memoirs
2084.4 Collective
2084.5.A-Z Individual, A-Z
1913-1945. Kosovo as part of Serbia and Yugoslavia
2085 General works
Biography and memoirs
2085.4 Collective
2085.5.A-Z Individual, A-Z
e.g.
2085.5.P74 Prishtina, Hasan, 1873-1933
1945- . Autonomous region
2086 General works
Biography and memoirs
2086.4 Collective
2086.5.A-Z Individual, A-Z
Civil War, 1998-
2087 General works
2087.5 Operation Allied Force, 1999
2087.6.A-Z Special topics, A-Z
2087.6.C54 Children
2087.6.D54 Diplomatic history
Foreign participation
2087.6.F65 General works
2087.6.F652.A-Z By region or country, A-Z
2087.6.F67 Foreign public opinion
2087.6.P74 Protest movements
2087.7 Personal narratives
Vojvodina
2090 Periodicals. Societies. Serials
2090.3 Sources and documents
2090.9 Guidebooks
2091 General works
2091.5 Pictorial works
2092 Description and travel
2093 Antiquities
For local antiquities, see DR2105.A+
2094 Social life and customs. Civilization. Intellectual life
For specific periods, see the period or reign

Yugoslavia
Local history and description
Serbia
Local history and description
Provinces, regions, geographic features, etc.
Vojvodina -- Continued
Ethnography
2095 General works
2095.5.A-Z Individual elements in the population, A-Z
2095.5.C75 Croats
2095.5.G47 Germans
2095.5.H85 Hungarians
2095.5.R65 Romanians
2095.5.R87 Ruthenians
2095.5.S47 Serbs
2095.5.S56 Slovaks
History
2096 Biography (Collective)
For individual biography, see the specific period, reign, or place
2097 General works
By period
2098 Early to 1526
1526-1918. Turkish rule and Austro-Hungarian rule
2099 General works
Biography and memoirs
2099.4 Collective
2099.5.A-Z Individual, A-Z
2099.7 Revolutionary events, 1848-1849
1918-1945. Vojvodina as part of Yugoslavia
2100 General works
Biography and memoirs
2100.4 Collective
2100.5.A-Z Individual, A-Z
1945- . Autonomous region
2101 General works
Biography and memoirs
2101.4 Collective
2101.5.A-Z Individual, A-Z
2105.A-Z Other regions, etc., A-Z
e.g.
2105.B32 Bačka (General and Serbia)
Including works on Bács-Bodrog
For Bácska (Hungary), see DB975.B15
2105.B35 Banat
For Banat (General, and Romania), see DR281.B25
2105.I75 Iron Gates region (Đerdap) (General and Serbia)
2105.K67 Kosovo Polje

Yugoslavia
Local history and description
Serbia
Local history and description
Provinces, regions, geographic features, etc.
Other regions, etc., A-Z -- Continued
2105.M48 Metohija
2105.R84 Rui Mountains
For the Rui Mountains (General and Bulgaria), see DR95.R8
2105.T57 Tisa (Tisza) River and Valley
Cities and towns
Belgrade
2106 Periodicals. Societies. Serials
2107 Museums, exhibitions, etc.
Subarrange by author
2108 Sources and documents
Collected works
2108.4 Several authors
2108.5 Individual authors
2108.6 Directories. Dictionaries. Gazetteers
2109 Guidebooks
2110 General works
2111 Description
2113 Pictorial works
2114 Antiquities
2115 Social life and customs. Intellectual life
Ethnography
2116 General works
2116.5.A-Z Individual elements in the population, A-Z
History
2117 Biography (Collective)
For individual biography, see the specific period
2118 General works
By period
2119 Early and medieval
2119.2 1500-1918
2119.3 1918-
Sections, districts, suburbs, etc.
2120 Collective
2120.5.A-Z Individual, A-Z
Monuments, statues, etc.
2121 Collective
2121.5.A-Z Individual, A-Z
Parks, squares, cemeteries, etc.
2122 Collective
2122.5.A-Z Individual, A-Z
Streets. Bridges
2123 Collective
2123.5.A-Z Individual, A-Z
Buildings

Yugoslavia
Local history and description
Serbia
Local history and description
Cities and towns
Belgrade
Buildings -- Continued
2124 Collective
2124.5.A-Z Individual, A-Z
2125.A-Z Other cities, towns, etc., A-Z
e.g.
2125.N57 Niš
Macedonia
Class here works on medieval and modern Macedonia and the Socialist Republic of Macedonia
For Aegean Macedonia (Greece), see DF901.M3
For ancient Greek Macedonia, see DF261.M2
For Macedonian period and King Philip, see DF232.5+
For Pirin Macedonia (Bulgaria), see DR95.B55
2152 Periodicals. Societies. Serials
2154 Congresses
2155 Sources and documents
Collected works
2156 Several authors
2157 Individual authors
2157.5 Gazetteers. Dictionaries, etc.
2158 Place names (General)
2159 Guidebooks
2160 General works
2162 Pictorial works
2163 Historic monuments, landmarks, scenery, etc. (General)
For local, see DR2275+
2165 Historical geography
2167 Description and travel
2171 Antiquities
For local antiquities, see DR2275+
2172 Social life and customs. Civilization. Intellectual life
For specific periods, see the period or reign
Ethnography
2173 General works
2173.5 National characteristics
2174.A-Z Individual elements in the population, A-Z
2174.A52 Albanians
2174.A75 Aromanians
2174.B84 Bulgarians
2174.E36 Egyptians
2174.G73 Greeks
2174.M87 Muslims
2174.S47 Serbs
2174.S55 Slavs

Yugoslavia
Local history and description
Macedonia
Ethnography
Individual elements in the population, A-Z -- Continued
2174.T87 Turks
2175 Macedonians in foreign countries (General)
History
Periodicals. Societies. Serials, see DR2152+
2175.5 Dictionaries. Chronological tables, outlines, etc.
2176 Biography (Collective)
For individual biography, see the specific period, reign, or place
Historiography
2181 General works
Biography of historians, area studies specialists, archaeologists, etc.
2182 Collective
2182.5.A-Z Individual, A-Z
Study and teaching
2183 General works
2184.A-Z By region or country, A-Z
Subarrange by author
2185 General works
2188 History of several parts of Macedonia treated together
2190 Military history
For specific periods, including individual campaigns and engagements, see the special period or reign
2192 Political history
For specific periods, see the period or reign
Foreign and general relations
For works on relations with a specific country regardless of period, see DR2196
For general works on the diplomatic history of a period, see the period
2195 General works
2196 Relations with individual regions or countries, A-Z
By period
Early to 1389
2197 Sources and documents
2198 General works
Biography and memoirs
2202 Collective
2202.5.A-Z Individual, A-Z
Battle of Kosovo, see DR495
1389-1912. Turkish rule
2205 Sources and documents
2206 General works

Yugoslavia
Local history and description
Macedonia
History
By period
1389-1912. Turkish rule -- Continued
2207 Social life and customs. Civilization. Intellectual life
Biography and memoirs
2210 Collective
2210.5.A-Z Individual, A-Z
2211 Karpos Uprising, 1689
1878-1912. Independence movement
2213 Sources and documents
2214 General works
2215 Political history
2216 Foreign and general relations
Biography and memoirs
2217 Collective
2218.A-Z Individual, A-Z
e.g.
2218.D14 Delcev, Goce, 1872-1903
2218.G78 Gruev, Damian Ivanov, 1871-1906
2218.S25 Sandanski, Jane, 1875-1915
2219 Kresna Uprising, 1878
Ilinden Uprising, 1903
2221 Sources and documents
2223 General works
2225 Personal narratives
2226.A-Z Local history. By place, A-Z
2227.A-Z Special topics, A-Z
2227.F67 Foreign public opinion
2227.P73 Press coverage
1912-1945
2229 Sources and documents
2230 General works
2231 Social life and customs. Civilization. Intellectual life
2232 Political history
2233 Foreign and general relations
Biography and memoirs
2234 Collective
2235.A-Z Individual, A-Z
2237 1912-1919. Period of the Balkan Wars and World War I
For the Balkan Wars, see DR46+
For World War I, see D501+
1919-1945. Vardar Macedonia as part of Yugoslavia
Including the Vardarska banovina, 1929-1941
2240 General works

Yugoslavia
Local history and description
Macedonia
History
By period
1912-1945
1919-1945. Vardar Macedonia as part of Yugoslavia -- Continued
2242 1941-1945. Period of World War II
For World War II, see D731+
1945-1992. Federal People's Republic. Socialist Republic
2243 Sources and documents
2244 General works
2245 Social life and customs. Civilization. Intellectual life
2246 Political history
2247 Foreign and general relations
Biography and memoirs
2248 Collective
2249.A-Z Individual, A-Z
1992- . Independent state
2250 Sources and documents
2251 General works
2252 Social life and customs. Civilization. Intellectual life
2253 Political history
2254 Foreign and general relations
Biography and memoirs
2255 Collective
2256.A-Z Individual, A-Z
Local history and description
2275.A-Z Provinces, regions, geographic features, etc., A-Z
e.g.
2275.B58 Bitola
Including the Monastir vilayet
2275.D64 Dojransko ezero
2275.O64 Ohridsko ezero
2275.P44 Pelagonia
2275.P73 Prespansko ezero
2275.V3 Vardar River and Valley
Cities and towns
2276 Skopje (Table D-DR3)
2285.A-Z Other cities and towns, etc., A-Z
e.g.
2285.A1 Collective
2285.P74 Prilep

.A2	Periodicals. Societies
.A3	Sources and documents. Serials
.A5-.Z	General works
.2	Description and travel. Guidebooks. Gazetteers
.3	Antiquities
.4	Social life and customs. Civilization. Intellectual life
.42	Ethnography
	History
.5	General works
.6	Biography (Collective)
	Political history. Foreign and general relations
.62	General works
(.622)	By period See the specific period
.63.A-Z	Relations with individual countries, A-Z
	By period
	Early
.65	General works
	Biography and memoirs
.66.A2	Collective
.66.A3-.66.Z	Individual, A-Z
	Colonial
.7	General works
	Biography and memoirs
.72.A2	Collective
.72.A3-.72.Z	Individual, A-Z
	20th century
.75	General works
	Biography and memoirs
.76.A2	Collective
.76.A3-.76.Z	Individual, A-Z
	Independent
.8	General works
	Biography and memoirs
.82.A2	Collective
.82.A3-.82.Z	Individual, A-Z
.9.A-Z	Local, A-Z

.xA2-.xA29	Periodicals. Societies
.xA3-.xA39	Sources and documents. Serials
.xA5-.xZ	General works
.x2	Description and travel. Guidebooks. Gazetteers
.x3	Antiquities
.x4	Social life and customs. Civilization. Intellectual life
.x42	Ethnography
	History
.x5	General works
.x6	Biography (Collective)
	Political history. Foreign and general relations
.x62	General works
(.x622)	By period See the specific period
.x63A-Z	Relations with individual countries, A-Z
	By period
	Early
.x65	General works
	Biography and memoirs
.x66A2-.x66A29	Collective
.x66A3-.x66Z	Individual, A-Z
	Colonial
.x7	General works
	Biography and memoirs
.x72A2-.x72A29	Collective
.x72A3-.x72Z	Individual, A-Z
	20th century
.x75	General works
	Biography and memoirs
.x76A2-.x76A29	Collective
.x76A3-.x76Z	Individual, A-Z
	Independent
.x8	General works
	Biography and memoirs
.x82A2-.x82A29	Collective
.x82A3-.x82Z	Individual, A-Z
.x9A-Z	Local, A-Z

	To be used only where indicated in schedule
.A2	Periodicals. Societies. Serials
.A3	Museums, exhibitions, etc.
	Subarrange by author
.A4	Guidebooks. Gazetteers. Directories
.A5-.Z	General works. Description
.1	Pictorial works
.13	Addresses, essays, lectures. Anecdotes, etc.
.15	Antiquities
.2	Social life and customs. Civilization. Intellectual life
	History
	Biography
.23.A2	Collective
.23.A3-.23.Z	Individual, A-Z
.25	Historiography. Study and teaching
.3	General works
	Sections, districts, suburbs, etc.
.4.A2	Collective
.4.A3-.4.Z	Individual, A-Z
	Monuments, statues, etc.
.5.A2	Collective
.5.A3-.5.Z	Individual, A-Z
	Parks, squares, cemeteries, etc.
.6.A2	Collective
.6.A3-.6.Z	Individual, A-Z
	Streets, bridges, etc.
.7.A2	Collective
.7.A3-.7.Z	Individual, A-Z
	Buildings
.8.A2	Collective
.8.A3-.8.Z	Individual, A-Z
	Elements in the population
.9.A2	Collective
.9.A3-.9.Z	Individual, A-Z
	Natural features such as mountains, rivers, etc.
.95.A2	Collective
.95.A3-.95.Z	Individual, A-Z

	To be used only where indicated in schedule The x in this table represents the cutter number for the city
.x	Periodicals. Societies. Serials
.x2	Museums, exhibitions, etc. Subarrange by author
.x3	Guidebooks. Gazetteers. Directories
.x4	General works. Description
.x43	Pictorial works
.x45	Addresses, essays, lectures. Anecdotes, etc.
.x47	Antiquities
.x5	Social life and customs. Civilization. Intellectual life
	History
	Biography
.x53A2-.x53A29	Collective
.x53A3-.x53Z	Individual, A-Z
.x55	Historiography. Study and teaching
.x57	General works
	Sections, districts, suburbs, etc.
.x6A2-.x6A29	Collective
.x6A3-.x6Z	Individual, A-Z
	Monuments, statues, etc.
.x65A2-.x65A29	Collective
.x65A3-.x65Z	Individual, A-Z
	Parks, squares, cemeteries, etc.
.x7A2-.x7A29	Collective
.x7A3-.x7Z	Individual, A-Z
	Streets, bridges, etc.
.x75A2-.x75A29	Collective
.x75A3-.x75Z	Individual, A-Z
	Buildings
.x8A2-.x8A29	Collective
.x8A3-.x8Z	Individual, A-Z
	Elements in the population
.x9A2-.x9A29	Collective
.x9A3-.x9Z	Individual, A-Z
	Natural features such as mountains, rivers, etc.
.x95A2-.x95A29	Collective
.x95A3-.x95Z	Individual, A-Z

.xA2-.xA29 Periodicals. Societies
.xA3-.xA39 Sources and documents. Serials
.xA5-.xZ General works
.x2 Description and travel. Guidebooks. Gazetteers
.x3 Antiquities
.x4 Social life and customs. Civilization. Intellectual life
.x42 Ethnography
History
.x5 General works
.x6 Biography (Collective)
Political history. Foreign and general relations
.x62 General works
By period
See the specific period
.x63A-Z Relations with individual countries, A-Z
By period
Early and medieval to 1526
.x65 General works
Biography and memoirs
.x66A2-.x66A29 Collective
.x66A3-.x66Z Individual, A-Z
1526-1815
.x7 General works
Biography and memoirs
.x72A2-.x72A29 Collective
.x72A3-.x72Z Individual, A-Z
1815-1918
.x75 General works
Biography and memoirs
.x76A2-.x76A29 Collective
.x76A3-.x76Z Individual, A-Z
1918-1945
.x8 General works
Biography and memoirs
.x82A2-.x82A29 Collective
.x82A3-.x82Z Individual, A-Z
1945-1989
.x85 General works
Biography and memoirs
.x86A2-.x86A29 Collective
.x86A3-.x86Z Individual, A-Z
1989-
.x88 General works
Biography and memoirs
.x89A2-.x89A29 Collective
.x89A3-.x89Z Individual, A-Z
(.x9) Local, A-Z
See separate cutters in DK4600, DK4800

1	Periodicals. Societies. Serials
2	Congresses
3	Sources and documents. Collections
4	Gazetteers
4.5	Place names
4.7	Directories
5	Guidebooks
6	Description and history (General)
	Description and travel
7	Early and medieval
8	1601-1800
9	1801-1945
9.2	1945-
10	Antiquities
10.5	Social life and customs. Civilization. Intellectual life
10.7	Ethnography
	History
11	Dictionaries, tables, etc.
	Biography
12.A2	Collective
12.A3-Z	Individual, A-Z
12.5	Historiography
	General works
14	Through 1800
15	1801-
15.1	Compends
16	General special
	By period
17	Early and medieval to 1800
18	19th century
19	20th century

.x	Periodicals. Societies. Collections. Sources and documents
.x1	Minor collections
.x3	General works. Description and travel
.x4	Antiquities
.x45	Ethnography
.x47	Social life and customs. Civilization. Culture
.x5	History
	Early and medieval
.x6	Works through 1800
.x62	Works, 1801-
.x7	17th-18th centuries
.x8	19th-20th centuries
.x9	Special topics

.x Periodicals. Societies. Collections
May include "Sources and documents"
.x1 Sources and documents
If preferred, may class with "Periodicals. Societies. Collections"
.x3 General works. Description and travel
.x35 Antiquities
.x4 Biography
In general, class individual biography with the period
.x5 History
By period
Early and medieval
General works
.x6 Through 1800
.x62 1801-
.x64 15th-16th centuries
.x7 17th-18th centuries
.x8 19th-20th centuries
.x9 Other

1 Periodicals. Societies. Collections
2 Biography
3 Dictionaries. Gazetteers. Directories, etc.
4 Guidebooks
5 General works. Description and travel
5.5 Social life and customs. Civilization. Intellectual life
History
By period
7 Early and medieval
8 16th-18th centuries
9 19th-20th centuries
10 Other

1 Periodicals. Societies. Serials
2 Museums, exhibitions, etc.
3 Sources and documents. Collections
4 Gazetteers
4.5 Directories
5 Guidebooks
6 General works
6.5 Monumental and picturesque
Including castles, cathedrals, monuments, etc.
Description and travel
7 Early through 1500
7.2 1501-1800
7.6 1801-1900
8 1901-1950
8.2 1951-
Cantonal capital
Including guidebooks, etc.
9 General works
9.2 Directories
Biography
See 12, 19.3, etc.
9.3 Earliest history and description (Roman and Celtic)
9.4 Middle ages to 1477
9.5 1477-1802
9.6 19th-20th centuries
9.8 Streets. Buildings. Institutions
9.9 Other special
Antiquities
10 General works
10.3 Roman period
10.5 Medieval
10.7 Social life and customs. Civilization. Intellectual life
Ethnography
10.8 General works
10.82.A-Z Individual elements in the population, A-Z
10.82.C46 Chileans
History
11 Dictionaries, tables, etc.
12 Biography and memoirs (Collective)
Historiography
13 General works
Biography of historians and antiquarians
13.3 Collective
13.5.A-Z Individual, A-Z
General works
14 Through 1800
15 1801-
16 General special
By period
17 Early and medieval
15th century
17.5 General works

History
By period
15th century -- Continued
Biography and memoirs
17.53 Collective
17.54.A-Z Individual, A-Z
16th-17th centuries
18 General works
Biography and memoirs
18.53 Collective
18.54.A-Z Individual, A-Z
18th century
19 General works
Biography and memoirs
19.3 Collective
19.35.A-Z Individual, A-Z
19.5 1789-1815
1789-1800
See DQ140
19th century
19.6 General works
Biography and memoirs
19.7 Collective
19.75.A-Z Individual, A-Z
20th century
20 General works
Biography and memoirs
20.3 Collective
20.35.A-Z Individual, A-Z

.x1	Periodicals. Societies. Serials
.x13	Museums, exhibitions, etc.
	Subarrange by author
.x15	Congresses
.x2	Sources and documents
.x23	Gazetteers, directories, dictionaries, etc.
.x25	Biography (Collective)
.x3	General works. Description and travel. Guidebooks
.x4	Antiquities
.x45	Social life and customs. Civilization
.x46	Ethnography
.x5	History (General)
	By period
	Including history and description and travel
.x6	Early
.x7	Medieval and early modern
.x8	Modern
	Biography and memoirs
.x82	Collective
.x83A-Z	Individual, A-Z
.x9	Special topics (not A-Z)

1 Periodicals. Societies. Sources and documents
2 Description and travel. Guidebooks
Including biography, antiquities, social life and customs, civilization
3 History

1	Periodicals. Societies. Serials
1.3	Museums, exhibitions, etc.
	Subarrange by author
1.5	Congresses
2	Sources and documents
3	Gazetteers, directories, dictionaries, etc.
3.5	Biography (Collective)
4	General works. Description and travel. Guidebooks. Geography
4.5	Antiquities
4.7	Social life and customs. Civilization. Intellectual life
4.8	Ethnography
	History
5	General works
	By period
6	Early and medieval
7	16th-18th centuries
8	19th-20th centuries
9	Special topics (not A-Z)

1 Periodicals. Societies. Serials

2 General works. Description and travel. History
Including antiquities, social life and customs, civilization, biography

INDEX

A

INDEX

INDEX

INDEX

INDEX

INDEX

INDEX

C

E

J

INDEX

L

M

INDEX

INDEX

N

INDEX

INDEX

T

V

INDEX

W